ROMFORD
FOOTBALL CL

Volume 3

1945-1959

An exhausted but happy Romford team after beating Clacton Town in the East Anglian Cup final, 5th May 1956   *Authors' collection*

ROMFORD
FOOTBALL CLUB

Volume 3
1945 – 1959

To Wembley and beyond

John Haley and Terry Felton

Heathway Press

First published in Great Britain in 2016 by
Heathway Press
Romford, Essex
www.heathwaypress.co.uk

ISBN 978-0-9566451-3-5

Previous volumes in this series:

Romford Football Club, a comprehensive history 1876-1920
(published 2013, price £15, ISBN 978-0956645111)

Romford Football Club volume 2, 1929-1945: from London to South Essex (published 2015, price £15, ISBN 978-0956645128)

CONTENTS

ROLL OF HONOUR

1945 – 46	FA Challenge Cup	1st Round	Away	Brighton & H.A.	1 – 3
		2nd Leg	Home	Brighton & H.A.	1 – 1
	Essex Senior Cup	Finalist	Neut	Barking	2 – 2
		Replay	Neut	Barking	2 – 3
1946 – 47	Essex Senior Cup	**Winners**	Neut	Tilbury	1 – 0
1947 – 48	Thameside Trophy	Finalist	Neut	Grays Athletic	1 – 5
1948 – 49	FA Challenge Cup	1st Round	Away	Yeovil Town	0 – 4
	FA Amateur Cup	Finalist	Wembley	Bromley	0 – 1**
1949 – 50	FA Challenge Cup	1st Round	Away	Yeovil Town	1 – 4
	Thameside Trophy	Finalist	Away	Ilford	2 – 3
1951 – 52	Essex Senior Cup	Finalist	Neut	Briggs Sports	0 – 1 a.e.t.
	East Anglian Cup	**Winners**	Home	Arsenal "A"	2 – 0
	Thameside Trophy	**Winners**	Away	Leytonstone	1 – 1
		Replay	Away	Leytonstone	4 – 2
1954 – 55	East Anglian Cup	**Winners**	Away	Grays Athletic	2 – 1
1955 – 56	East Anglian Cup	**Winners**	Away	Clacton Town	2 – 1
	Thameside Trophy	**Winners**	Away	Ilford	5 – 4*
1956 – 57	Reg.Sheward Trophy	**Winners**	Home	D.J.Davis All Star XI	5 – 2
1957 – 58	Thameside Trophy	**Winners**	Away	Barking	2 – 1
1958 – 59	Essex Senior Cup	Finalist	Neut	Walthamstow Avenue	0 – 1

* Played in the 1956 – 57 Season
** First ever Amateur Cup Final to be played at Wembley

RESERVES

1950 – 51	Thameside Trophy	**Winners**	Home	Barking Res.	2 – 0*
1957 – 58	E.County Int. Cup	**Winners**	Home	Dagenham Res.	3 – 2
	Thameside Trophy	Finalist	Away	Leyton Res.	0 – 1

* Played in the 1951 – 52 Season

"A" TEAM

1951 -52	Isthmian League "A"	**Champions**			
1957 - 58	S.E.Comb. Div.One	Runners Up to Romford British Legion			
1958 - 59	Eastern "A" Lge.Cup	Finalist	Home	Clapton "A"	1 – 4

MINOR TEAM

1958 – 59	E.C.Andrews Cup	Finalist	Neut	Wilson Marriage Y.C.	2 – 8
	Hch.Minor Lg.Jnr.Cup	**Winners**	Home	Glendale Y.C. "A"	7 – 0

GLOSSARY

FIRST TEAM

IFL	Isthmian Football League
Frdly	Friendly Match
AC	FA Amateur Cup
FAC	FA Challenge Cup
ESC	Essex Senior Cup
RCC	Romford Charity Cup
EAC	East Anglian Cup
ETT	Essex Thameside Trophy
TCC	Thetford Charity Cup
WSTM	Bill Seddon Testimonial Match
RCSC	Romford Charity Senior Cup

RESERVE TEAM

EJC	Essex Junior Cup
RCC	Romford Charity Cup
IFLR	Isthmian Football League Reserve Section
CCC	Carter Charity Cup
EIC	Essex Intermediate Cup
ETR	Essex Thameside Trophy Reserve Section

"A" TEAM

RDLP	Romford & District Football League Premier Division
RLC	Romford & District Football League Cup
EJC	Essex Junior Cup
CCC	Carter Charity Cup
SECD1	South Essex Combination Division One
SEC2	South Essex Combination Division Two
SECC	South Essex Combination Cup
IFLA	Isthmian Football League "A" Section
EAFL	Eastern "A" Football League
ALC	Eastern "A" Football League Cup

MINOR TEAM

HMLD3	Hornchurch Minor League Division 3
L3C	Hornchurch Minor League Division 3 Cup
EAC	Essex County FA "Andrews" Cup

INTRODUCTION

Welcome to this third volume in our history of Romford Football Club. The first in the series, *Romford Football Club, a comprehensive history 1876-1920*, covered the era when most of the players worked for Ind Coope, giving the team the nickname 'The Brewers'. It was followed by *Romford Football Club volume 2, 1929-1945: from London to South Essex*, describing how the club, now at Brooklands, won back-to-back Athenian League titles and lifted the Essex Senior Cup three times.

This volume chronicles the years from 1945 until the end of the 1958–59 season, with the club playing throughout in the powerful Isthmian League. The directors then took the bold decision of turning to semi-professional football for the first time and applying to the Southern Football League. What happened next will be told in *Romford Football Club volume 4, 1959-1978: Brooklands, the final whistle* (currently in preparation).

Sources and acknowledgements

The majority of information in this book has been obtained from official Romford Football Club records, correspondence, minute books, year books, match programmes and the Club Results Book prepared by the long-standing Secretary, Martin Brazier. Additional material has been obtained from local newspapers, particularly the *Romford Times*, *Romford Recorder*, *Essex Weekly News* and *Essex Chronicle*.

Our grateful thanks are due in particular to:

Simon Donoghue and **Jane Finnett** of the London Borough of Havering Local Studies and Family History Centre, at Romford Library. Scanned copies of many of the images in this book have been deposited there. If you wish to view them please contact the staff by e-mailing localstudies@havering.gov.uk

Barbara Tetchner, for photos and information about the Tetchner family

Ron and Ivy Baker, for photographs on pages 182 and 268

Fred Hawthorn, for his help with the Eastern "A" League tables

Linda Rhodes, for contributing additional material and bringing the book to publication

About the authors

John Haley

John's first visit to Brooklands was in 1945 at the age of 13. He immediately began compiling statistics on Romford Football Club. He started contributing statistics to the match programmes in the early 1950s, and worked for the club on a voluntary basis for many years before becoming Football Secretary in 1964 and eventually Company Secretary and Chief Executive Officer.

Terry Felton

Terry was first taken to watch Romford play by his grandfather in the 1960s and has researched its history for over 40 years. He was heavily involved in the re-formation of Romford Football Club in 1992. He was Vice-Chairman during the 1992-3 season.

THE NEW ERA BEGINS

On 7th September 1940, as a depleted Romford team struggled to return from Erith in the early hours of the morning in the midst of an air raid, the club's directors had to make a big decision. Having struggled through the previous season to raise a quality team for their matches, with most young men now in the armed forces, together with dwindling match attendance figures, they reluctantly decided to close for the duration of the war.

At long last, on 8th May 1945, came VE Day, when the nation celebrated the end of the war in Europe. Just over two weeks later, on Wednesday 23rd May, the *Romford Times* featured an interview with the football club's chairman, Mr Tom Macpherson, under the headline DESPITE BIG SNAGS & HOOLIGAN BLITZ, DIRECTORS HOPE THAT ROMFORD FC MAY RE-START THIS YEAR!

Mr Macpherson stressed the enormous difficulties to be overcome if the team were to be ready for the new season in September. On the positive side, the Brooklands pitch was in excellent condition, not having been turned over for "Dig for Victory" allotments or communal air raid shelters as had been the fate of some grounds.

On the other hand, he stated, the club has had no income for five years and is "not in a good financial position". The report goes on to say that "the greatest difficulty is the club's accommodation….stands, dressing rooms, offices – everything has been wrecked by hooligans. Furniture left in offices has vanished, as has lino from the floor. In the dressing rooms lockers have been pulled to pieces. Wash basins, etc., have been smashed, boards have been pulled from the floor and roof. The stands, too, are in an appalling state…"

Romford's grandstand after the war bearing evidence of vandalism and encroachment of weeds
Authors' collection

Another problem was that none of Romford's pre-war players were available except Jim Paviour, not yet demobilized from the armed forces but stationed within reach of Romford. An appeal went out to footballers to come forward and play in trial matches.

A further difficulty was clothes rationing, which was to continue until March 1949. Clothing coupons would be needed to buy the team's shirts, shorts, socks and boots. It wasn't until 11th September, after the playing season had started, that the secretary was able to tell the management committee that he had obtained a grant of 188 coupons and would consult Messrs. Wards of South Street with a view to obtaining the urgently needed kit. Frequent requests were made in match programmes for supporters to donate coupons.

More details of the situation in the aftermath of the war were given in the Directors' Report and Balance Sheet covering the two years ended 31st May 1945. We read that:

> …during the period the Company has sustained a loss of £252 18s 9d, and this figure is arrived at without taking into account contingent liabilities for arrears of Interest on First and Second Mortgages. The Accounts presented to the Shareholders for the year ended 31st May 1940 showed a Net Loss of £416 10s 7d, therefore it will be seen that during the period of the War the figure for loss has increased by £802 2s 2d to £1,218 12s 9d, but this increase is largely accounted for or represented by advances made by certain of your Directors to the Company to enable it to discharge payments on account of Mortgage Interest and Bank Charges…The item shewn [sic] under the heading "Second Mortgages" is monies advanced by your Directors, Messrs T. Macpherson, S.G. Tansley and A.J. Smith. The Bank overdraft continues to be guaranteed by Messrs Macpherson and Tansley.

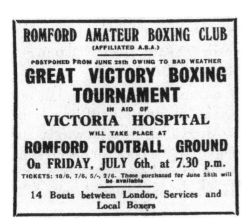

The Victory Boxing Tournament

The following month, June 1945, the club hired out Brooklands to a boxing promoter to hold a 14-bout Victory Boxing Tournament celebrating the end of the war, between teams representing London Services and local boxing clubs. The event was originally scheduled to take place on June 28th, but due to bad weather was postponed until July 6th. Ringside seats cost ten shillings and sixpence, with all profits going to the Victoria Hospital.

Romford FC's chairman becomes an MP

On 5th July 1945 Mr Tom Macpherson (right) was elected MP for Romford in the general election. He represented the Labour party and won 52.8% of the vote. The Labour party gained a landslide victory, and Clement Attlee replaced Winston Churchill as Prime Minister. During the war Mr Macpherson had served as Regional Port Director for Scotland.

Mr Macpherson's fellow Romford FC director Mr Albert J. Smith was appointed MBE for his work as a Major in the Home Guard during the war.

Confirmation of Romford FC's return

On 25th July 1945 the *Romford Times* confirmed that Romford FC would re-start in the coming season in the Isthmian League, in which they had played in 1939-40 and the single match of 1940-41 season. The article stated that "the team will be built round one of Romford's most popular players, Jim R. Paviour, who is expecting his demob from the army shortly. The side will incorporate other famous local players such as W. Bridge, S. Montgomery and George Patterson, as they become available. It is hoped to find remainder of the team from among local lads…The Club has accepted the services of two of its pre-war trainers, Mr "Bill" Seddon, who turned down a fine post with Blackburn Rovers to stay with Romford; and Capt. A. Adlam, who trained one of Romford's most successful sides – that of 1936–37…The Club appeals to supporters to visit the club's ground in Brooklands-road any evening between 7 and 9, and help restore the damage caused by hooligans and get it "ship-shape" for opening of the season…."

Trial matches held

The first two trial matches took place on Saturday August 4th and Tuesday August 7th. A progress report was printed in the *Romford Times* of August 8th headlined ROMFORD STILL SEEK LOCAL SOCCER STARS:

When Romford Football Club's first eleven turn out on Brooklands ground for their first match of the season – against Kingstonian – on September 1st, practically all of them will be young players, and practically all of them local lads. At least, that is the hope and ambition expressed to me by officials of the club at Romford FC's first trial match at Brooklands on Saturday. By starting now with keen youngsters, they feel they may be able to build up a side which will grow progressively more powerful, while, from a "gate" point of view, a team of local lads – provided they are made of the right stuff – are naturally more popular with the crowd than "imported" players…..Any who feel they have a chance of making the grade will be welcomed at the next two trials – on Saturday 11th August at 3pm and Thursday August 16th at 7pm, both at the Brooklands ground.

The paper's account of the first trial match, between Colours and Blues teams, pointed out that the accent was definitely on youth, the youngest player being 15. Some players were singled out for praise:

> From the start, C.J. Adams, the Blues' left winger, took the eye, and his performance was outstanding. Even when hard pressed his passes were accurate an unflurried, and his speed in seizing scoring chances was well shown in the two goals he notched as solo efforts. He had plenty of tricks, too, and trapped the ball very capably from all angles. He is said to have played for Leytonstone, and I should imagine they would be sorry they lost him.
>
> USEFUL DEFENDERS. Both the blues' backs looked useful men, B.G. Moore (Roneo) playing a particularly sound game. D. Webb at left half had some interesting duals with S. Haxwell, another Roneo man on the "Colours" side, and both might have a chance as "possibles." Slater led the blues' forward line well. K.Perry impressed me as the best of the Colours' half back line, and Boom's display at inside left showed he has been getting in some useful practice in the Army.
>
> This was a "free and easy" game, and some positions were switched at half-time to suit the selectors. This is how they lined up at the start.- Blues: K.B. King (Romford Youth team); G. Fleetwood (Havering-rd Youth), B.G.Moore (Roneo); W.Mills, A. Moore, D. Webb; A. Suckling (Barking League), G.Hewitt (Harrow),

J.Slater (Moss United, Glasgow), A.G.Gaynes (ATC and an RAF team), C.J.Adams (Leytonstone and Harrow). Colours: B.Porter (Havering Youth). A.F.Boreham, W.A.Dennis (Brewery and an Army team); K.Perry (B.B.), D.A.Ward (Romford League), E.G.Reynolds (Kent League), V.Bell (Palmers College and Grays), S.Haxwell (Roneo), C.Reynolds (Hornchurch Youth), F.Boom (an Army eleven).

**Note: Only ten players were named for the Colours team in this article.

The following week's issue, published on 15th August, contained a report headed ROMFORD FC SEARCHING FOR SHOOTING STARS:

Still seeking local talent with which to build their Isthmian League team, Romford Football Club held another trial game at the Brooklands ground on Saturday. Some of the youngsters who played in the first trial on Saturday week – reported in last week's Romford Times – were included, but majority were fresh recruits…..

THEY KEPT JIM BUSY. Appearance of Jim Paviour, stalwart of Romford's pre-war team, as the king pin in the Blues' defence system, no doubt contributed largely to that side's win. But he found a lively pair of attackers in the Isaacs brothers (both of Roneo), and it was no surprise when, from a clever movement between the two, D.Isaacs on the right wing, lobbed the ball into the goal, the goalkeeper completely misjudging the flight.

C.J.Adams who gave an outstanding performance the previous week, was again the Blues' left winger, and he dispelled any lingering doubts about his capabilities…. Of the four goalkeepers tried out, Dray (Upminster) impressed most. He picked the ball up cleanly, showed intelligent anticipation and did not indulge in spectacular tactics. McKee made some nice saves, but was inclined to come too far out of goal. This he did once too often, lost the leather in a scramble and one of the Blues' forwards had only to tap it into the empty goal.

In a game which never reached brilliance, and became aimless and scrappy in the second half, best of the play was provided by the defences. Fleetwood (Blues) was always prominent, and sound displays were also given by Goodchild and Webb, who were switched to opposing sides at half time, and Dennis. Lively interest is being taken in these trials, and there was quite a crowd of spectators.

A week later, on 22nd August, the *Romford Times* reflected the growing excitement under the headline FOOTBALL AGAIN! ROMFORD FC CURTAIN RAISER ON SATURDAY:

Football is back again. The Brooklands ground at Romford, for so long desolate and forlorn, will be buzzing with activity this Saturday, when, as a curtain raiser to the opening game of the season, Romford Reserves entertain Grays Reserves in the South Essex Combination. Kick-off is at 3.30. Then on the following Saturday, Romford's first eleven will open their Isthmian League programme with a home match against Kingstonian.

SMALLER ENCLOSURE. Despite the strenuous efforts on behalf of the directors to overcome the deplorable condition of the ground, a lot will still be left to be desired when the season opens. With the enclosure fencing and portable stands in such a dilapidated and dangerous state, it has been decided for time being to shorten the enclosure to that portion immediately in front of the stand at the main gate, the rest of the old enclosure being thrown open to the ordinary admission…..

Because of ticket printing difficulties, the officials have decided against reservation of specific seats in the stand for season ticket holders. Seats to the extent of season tickets sold will be reserved at each match on the "first come – first served" principle. It has yet to be decided how this will affect cup-tie arrangements.

"We hope that season ticket holders and all supporters will realise our difficulties," one of the officials said. "Needless to say, the club are anxious to restore pre-war conditions at the earliest possible moment."

CALLING ALL WORKERS. Help from supporters in improving the ground would be welcomed. For six weeks, Mr Westoby has been toiling at such tasks as grass cutting and repairing fences, and he would be glad of assistance in this work any evening after seven – for there is still plenty to be done.

ROBUST RESERVES. Romford's reserve eleven will be in the capable hands of Mr Jim Parrish, who served the club so well as a goalkeeper in his heyday….

TEAM BUILDING. Most of the players seen in previous trials were again out on Saturday. It would not be fair to anticipate the selection committee in naming probable first team players, but they should not have any great difficulty in picking a very useful side. The club will however still be keenly on the look-out for further players, particularly to strengthen the forward line…..

THURSDAY'S TRIAL. Defences were predominant in Thursday's trial, in which several new players who were given a chance showed much promise that they were promptly earmarked for Saturday's "Probables v possibles" game. Despite the handicap of a strong wind and the long springy grass, it was obvious that there was some useful material on the field…..

Romford's first competitive match of the new era

This was held at Brooklands on 25th August 1945, and was not a first team game but a reserve team match against Grays Athletic Reserves. Grays Athletic had already played the previous season, and their team looked a more solid outfit than the new Romford line-up, who were duly defeated by three goals to one.

Annual General Meeting: future plans for Brooklands revealed

On 4th October 1945 at the Golden Lion the Club held an AGM at which the annual report and accounts for the two years up to 31st May 1945 were presented. The *Essex Times* reported it on Wednesday 10th October under the headline ROMFORD PLANS AGAIN FOR SUPER SPORTS STADIUM:

The scene – curtailed by war – for making Brooklands, Romford Football Club's ground, one of the finest sports grounds around London, catering for a variety of athletic sports in addition to football, is to be pressed forward as soon as financial and other circumstances permit. This was announced at the annual meeting of Romford Football Club Ltd., at Golden Lion, Romford....

Mr T. Macpherson, MP, chairman of directors, presided....The Brooklands ground, he said, was a great asset and a very valuable amenity to Romford...It had long been in the directors' minds that better use should be made of Brooklands in the summer months. To improve the financial position, it was intended to provide facilities for gymkhanas, cycling and other athletic events, and he or the secretary would be happy to enter into negotiations with secretaries of any organizations wishing to arrange such events next year.

It was still the policy of the company to make Brooklands, not only the finest football enclosure round London, but an enclosure where other sports of the highest quality could be staged. Their plan had been to develop the ground bit by bit but this had been interrupted by war. It was the intention of the company that, as and when the situation permitted, they should go ahead with that plan, but it would take a little time, and they had to proceed cautiously and economically to rebuild their financial position.

...The chairman explained that it was hoped to sponsor sporting activities in addition to football, and they wanted to increase the number of directors in order to bring in representatives of other sporting interests in the town.

The annual meeting passed a resolution increasing number of directors from five to seven. Mr A.E. Kittle and Mr W.C. Mann, both of whom have taken the keenest interest in fostering local sport for many years, were elected as additional directors.

Romford FC Board of Directors 1945-50
Back: Albert E. Kittle, Martin Brazier, Bill Mann, Bob Scott, Herbert Muskett (secretary)
Front: Albert J. Smith, Tom Macpherson, Syd Tansley   *Authors' collection*

THE ROMFORD FOOTBALL CLUB LIMITED

Full Members of The Football Association
Full Members of The Isthmian Football League
Affiliated to The Essex County Football Association

Club Colours: Blue and Gold Shirts, White Knickers

Ground: Brooklands Sports Ground, Romford

Chairman: Mr T.Macpherson, MP

Other Directors: Messrs. M.A.Brazier, A.E.Kittle, W.G.Mann
R.Scott, A.J.Smith MBE, S.G.Tansley

Company Secretary: Mr H.W.Muskett

Registered Offices: 110 Hyland Way, Romford

Bankers: Lloyds Bank Limited   **Auditor:** Mr Iion V. Cummings, FCA

Football Club Management Committee:
Chairman: Mr A.J. Smith, MBE
Football Secretary: Mr M.A. Brazier
Press Secretary: Mr A.E. Kittle (acting)   Mr F.Harbott appointed 20th Nov.

Other Committee Members: Messrs.W.G.Mann, R.Scott, S.G.Tansley

First Team Trainer: Mr W.C.(Bill) Seddon

Reserve Team Secretary: Mr J. Gurney (Appointed 20th Nov.)
Reserve Team Trainer: Mr J.W. Parrish

Groundsman: Mr E. Hewitt

LEAGUES & COMPETITIONS ENTERED 1945 – 46

The FA Challenge Cup
The FA Amateur Cup
The Isthmian Football League
The Essex Senior Cup
Essex Thameside Challenge Competition

South Essex Combination
The Essex Junior Cup
The Carter Challenge Cup

Admission Prices

	Adults	OAPs and children
Ground	9d	5d
Enclosure	1/6	10d
Stand	2/6	2/6
Car Park	6d	

Season Tickets

Grandstand	£1.1.0	OAPs & Children	10/6
Ground & Enclosure	15/-	"	7/6
Ground only	12/6	"	6/3

The *Romford Times* cartoonist's view of how Romford FC's best-known personalities reacted to the first match of the season
Authors' collection

First Team Match Details

1 Sept IFL Home Kingstonian   1 – 2 Perry
Attendance: 2,000
Romford: J.F.Dray;J.Brown,W.Dennis;W.F.Mackenzie,J.Paviour(Capt),L.E.Goodchild;
D.Dent,K.Perry,J.H.Bennett,F.W.Le Marechal,C.J.Adams.

8 Sept IFL Away Walthamstow Avenue   2 – 6 Bennett,Mackenzie
Romford: J.F.Dray;J.Brown,W.Dennis;W.F.Mackenzie,J.Paviour(Capt),L.Rowntree;
D.Dent,A.Gaynes,J.H.Bennett,J.Oakes,C.J.Adams.

15 Sept IFL Home Wimbledon   6 – 1 Adams(2)Oakes(pen)Bennett(2)Bridge
Attendance:
Romford: T.Grover;J.Brown,W.Dennis;W.F.Mackenzie,J.Paviour(Capt),P.G.R.Wallace;
D.Dent,W.A.Bridge,J.H.Bennett,J.Oakes,C.J.Adams.

22 Sept FAC1Q Away Eton Manor   1 – 1 Bennett
Romford: T.Grover;P.G.R.Wallace,W.Dennis;W.F.Mackenzie,J.Paviour(Capt),L.Rowntree;
F.L.Chapman,W.A.Bridge,J.H.Bennett,J.Oakes,C.J.Adams.

27 Sept FACRp Home Eton Manor   4 – 3 Oakes(2)Bennett(2)
Romford: T.Grover;P.G.R.WallaceW.Dennis;W.F.Mackenzie,J.Paviour(Capt),L.Rowntree;
F.L.Chapman,H.Clay,J.H.Bennett,J.Oakes,C.J.Adams.

29 Sept IFL Home Walthamstow Avenue   3 – 2 Dent,Benson,Swift(og)
Attendance:
Romford: T.Grover;P.G.R.Wallace,W.Dennis;W.F.Mackenzie,J.Paviour(Capt),L.Rowntree;
D.Dent,W.A.Bridge,W.Benson,J.Oakes,C.J.Adams.

6 Oct   FAC2Q   Home   Crittall Athletic   7 – 1   Rowntree,Clay(3)Brooks,Bennett(2)
Attendance:
Romford: T.Grover;P.G.R.Wallace,W.Dennis;W.F.Mackenzie,J.Paviour(Capt),L.Rowntree;
H.W.Brooks,S.A.Olton,J.H.Bennett,H.Clay,D.A.Langer.

13 Oct   IFL   Home   Tufnell Park   2 – 4   Benson,Langer
Attendance:
Romford: A.Wilsher;P.G.R.Wallace,W.Dennis;W.F.Mackenzie,J.Paviour(Capt),G.H.Howlett;
H.W.Brooks,S.A.Olton,W.Benson,H.Clay,D.A.Langer.

20 Oct   FAC3Q   Home   Leyton   4 – 1   Clay,Langer,Brooks,Denham
Attendance: 7,700   Receipts: £211.18.9
Romford: T.Grover;P.G.R.Wallace,W.Dennis;W.F.Mackenzie,J.Paviour(Capt),G.Fleetwood;
H.W.Brooks,S.A.Olton,H.Clay,J.Denham,D.A.Langer.

27 Oct   IFL   Home   Oxford City   2 – 2   Denham,Clay
Attendance:
Romford: T.Grover;P.G.R.Wallace,W.Dennis;W.F.Mackenzie,J.Paviour(Capt),F.E.Fryatt;
H.W.Brooks,S.A.Olton,H.Clay,J.Denham,D.A.Langer.

3 Nov   FAC4Q   Away   Dulwich Hamlet   2 – 1   Powell(og)Clay
Attendance: 7,149   Receipts: £413
Romford: T.Grover;P.G.R.Wallace,W.Dennis;W.F.Mackenzie,J.Paviour(Capt),F.E.Fryatt;
H.W.Brooks,S.A.Olton,H.Clay,J.Denham,D.A.Langer.

10 Nov   IFL   Away   Corinthian Casuals   5 – 3   Clay(2)Olton,Denham(2)
Romford: W.Sherman;P.G.R.Wallace,W.Dennis;W.F.Mackenzie,J.Paviour(Capt),F.E.Fryatt;
H.W.Brooks,S.A.Olton,H.Clay,J.Denham,D.A.Langer.

17 Nov   FAC1R   Away   Brighton & Hove Albion (1st Leg)   1 – 3   Longdon(og)
Attendance: 7,423   Receipts: £590.6.6   Romford Share: £173.13.11
Romford: T.Grover;P.G.R.Wallace,W.Dennis;W.F.Mackenzie,J.Paviour(Capt),F.E.Fryatt;
H.W.Brooks,S.A.Olton,D.G.Harries,H.Clay,J.Denham.

24 Nov   FAC1R   Home   Brighton & Hove Albion (2nd Leg)   1 – 1   Olton
Attendance: 7,043   Receipts: £546.16.6
Romford: T.Grover;P.G.R.Wallace,W.Dennis;W.F.Mackenzie,J.Paviour(Capt),F.E.Fryatt;
H.W.Brooks,S.A.Olton,D.G.Harries,H.Clay,J.Denham.

1 Dec   IFL   Home   Clapton   1 – 0   Clay
Attendance:
Romford: T.Grover;P.G.R.Wallace,W.Dennis;W.F.Mackenzie,J.Paviour(Capt),F.E.Fryatt;
H.W.Brooks,S.A.Olton,H.Clay,W.A.Bridge,G.W.Patterson.

8 Dec   IFL   Away   Leytonstone   0 – 5
Romford: T.Grover;P.G.R.Wallace,W.Dennis;W.F.Mackenzie,J.Paviour(Capt),F.E.Fryatt;
H.W.Brooks,W.A.Bridge,D.G.Harries,H.Clay,J.Denham.

15 Dec   IFL   Away   Oxford City   0 – 6
Romford: C.Groom;P.G.R.Wallace,W.Dennis;W.F.Mackenzie,J.Paviour(Capt),F.E.Fryatt;
H.W.Brooks,S.A.Olton,R.Gadsden,J.Holt,J.Denham.

22 Dec   IFL   Home   Wycombe Wanderers   3 – 3   Clay(2)Brooks
Attendance:
Romford: J.Letham;P.G.R.Wallace,W.Dennis;F.E.Fryatt,J.Paviour(Capt),J.Ellis;
H.W.Brooks,W.F.Mackenzie,H.Clay,J.Oakes,J.Turner.

25 Dec   IFL   Home   Ilford   6 – 1   Rowntree(2)Brooks,Turner,Holt
Attendance:
Romford: J.Letham;P.G.R.Wallace,W.Dennis;W.F.Mackenzie,J.Paviour(Capt),F.E.Fryatt;
H.W.Brooks,L.Rowntree,J.Holt,J.Oakes,J.Turner.

26 Dec   IFL   Away   Ilford   1 – 1   Brooks
Romford: J.Letham;P.G.R.Wallace,C.Denham;W.F.Mackenzie,J.Paviour(Capt),F.E.Fryatt;
H.W.Brooks,L.Rowntree,J.Holt,C.J.Adams,J.Turner.

29 Dec   IFL   Away   St. Albans City   1 – 3   Brooks
Romford: J.Letham;P.G.R.Wallace,C.Denham;W.F.Mackenzie,J.Paviour(Capt),F.E.Fryatt;
H.W.Brooks,J.Ratiera,J.Holt,C.J.Adams,J.Turner.

5 Jan   IFL   Away   Wycombe Wanderers   6 – 2   Olton,Worthington,Brooks(2)Bennett(2)
Romford: P.I.McCreddie;P.G.R.Wallace,W.Dennis;W.F.Mackenzie,J.Paviour(Capt),F.E.Fryatt;
H.W.Brooks,S.A.Olton,J.H.Bennett,E.Worthington,J.Oakes.

12 Jan ESC1R Home Ford Sports 6 – 2 Olton,Bennett(3)Mackenzie,Brooks
Attendance:
Romford: P.I.McCreddie;P.G.R.Wallace,W.Dennis;W.F.Mackenzie,J.Paviour(Capt),F.E.Fryatt;
H.W.Brooks,S.A.Olton,J.H.Bennett,H.Voisey,J.Oakes.

19 Jan AC1R Home Leytonstone 0 – 0*
Attendance: 5,400   Receipts: £178.14.0   Leytonstone Share: £63.2.6
Romford: P.I.McCreddie;P.G.R.Wallace,W.Dennis;W.F.Mackenzie,J.Paviour(Capt),F.E.Fryatt;
H.W.Brooks,S.A.Olton,J.H.Bennett,W.Benson,G.W.Patterson.

26 Jan ACRp Away Leytonstone 5 – 3 Bennett(2)Brooks(2)Olton
Attendance: 5,000   Receipts: £149.9.6   Romford Share: £58.4.7
Romford: P.I.McCreddie;P.G.R.Wallace,W.Dennis;W.F.Mackenzie,J.Paviour(Capt),F.E.Fryatt;
H.W.Brooks,S.A.Olton,J.H.Bennett,G.W.Patterson,D.A.Langer.

2 Feb AC2R Away Southall 2 – 4 Parker(og)Bennett
Attendance: 4,300   Receipts: £130.6.3   Romford Share: £53.7.0
Romford: P.I.McCreddie;P.G.R.Wallace,W.Dennis;W.F.Mackenzie,J.Paviour(Capt),F.E.Fryatt;
H.W.Brooks,S.A.Olton,J.H.Bennett,H.Voisey,D.A.Langer.

9 Feb ESC2R Away Eton Manor 2 – 1 Oakes(2)
Attendance: 900   Receipts: £28.19.0   Romford Share: £12.3.6
Romford: P.I.McCreddie;P.G.R.Wallace,W.Dennis;W.Bricknell,J.Paviour(Capt),F.E.Fryatt;
H.W.Brooks,S.A.Olton,J.Oakes,H.Voisey,D.A.Langer.

16 Feb IFL Away Clapton 2 – 1 Brooks,Oakes
Romford: R.Mortimer;P.G.R.Wallace,W.Bricknell;W.F.Mackenzie,J.Paviour(Capt),F.E.Fryatt;
H.W.Brooks,S.A.Olton,J.Oakes,E.Worthington,C.Cutmore.

23 Feb IFL Home Dulwich Hamlet 1 – 2 Brooks
Attendance:
Romford: R.Mortimer;P.G.R.Wallace,W.Bricknell;W.F.Mackenzie,J.Paviour(Capt),F.E.Fryatt;
H.W.Brooks,S.A.Olton,J.Oakes,H.Voisey,A.Sargeant.

2 Mar ESCSF Away Crittall Athletic 4 – 0 Langer(3)Brooks
Attendance: 2,500
Romford: R.Mortimer;P.G.R.Wallace,W.Dennis;W.F.Mackenzie,J.Paviour(Capt),F.E.Fryatt;
H.W.Brooks,S.A.Olton,J.Oakes,G.W.Patterson,D.A.Langer.

9 Mar IFL Home Woking 5 – 2 Brooks,Bridge(2)Olton,Rowntree
Attendance:
Romford: J.Letham;P.G.R.Wallace,W.Dennis;W.F.Mackenzie,J.Paviour(Capt),F.E.Fryatt;
H.W.Brooks,S.A.Olton,W.A.Bridge,L.Rowntree,J.Oakes.

16 Mar IFL Away Kingstonian 6 – 3 Bridge(4)Benson(2)
Romford: R.Mortimer;P.G.R.Wallace,W.Dennis;L.Rowntree,F.E.Fryatt,J.Denham;
W.Benson,S.A.Olton,W.A.Bridge,V.Roeder,J.Oakes.

23 Mar IFL Home Corinthian Casuals 8 – 3 Bridge(5)Brooks(2)Rowntree
Attendance:
Romford: R.Mortimer;P.G.R.Wallace,W.Dennis;W.Mackenzie,J.Paviour(Capt),F.E.Fryatt;
H.W.Brooks,S.A.Olton,W.A.Bridge,L.Rowntree,J.Oakes.

30 Mar IFL Home St. Albans City 3 – 2 Brooks,Bridge(2)
Attendance: 6,000
Romford: L.Young;P.G.R.Wallace,W.Dennis;W.F.Mackenzie,J.Paviour(Capt),F.E.Fryatt;
H.W.Brooks,S.A.Olton,W.A.Bridge,E.Worthington,L.Rowntree.

6 Apr IFL Away# Tufnell Park 8 – 0 Rowntree(2)Brooks(2)Denham,Fryatt(2)
Bridge

Attendance: 5,000
Romford: R.Mortimer;P.G.R.Wallace,W.Dennis;W.F.Mackenzie,J.Paviour(Capt),F.E.Fryatt;
H.W.Brooks,L.Rowntree,W.A.Bridge,J.Oakes,J.Denham.

13 Apr IFL Away Wimbledon 0 – 1
Romford: R.Mortimer;P.G.R.Wallace,W.Dennis;G.Fleetwood,F.E.Fryatt,J.Denham;
H.W.Brooks,S.A.Olton,E.Worthington,J.Oakes,C.J.Adams.

20 Apr IFL Away Woking 4 – 2 Bridge(3)Oakes
Romford: R.Mortimer;P.G.R.Wallace,J.Munro;W.F.Mackenzie,J.Paviour(Capt),F.E.Fryatt;
H.W.Brooks,S.A.Olton,W.A.Bridge,J.Oakes,J.Denham.

22 Apr ESCF Ilford Barking 2 – 2 Rowntree,Brooks
Attendance: 12,247 Receipts: £998
Romford: R.Mortimer;P.G.R.Wallace,W.Dennis;W.F.Mackenzie,J.Paviour(Capt),F.E.Fryatt;
H.W.Brooks,L.Rowntree,W.A.Bridge,G.W.Patterson,D.A.Langer.

25 Apr ETT1R Home Barking   4 – 0   Rowntree(2)Brooks,Bridge
Attendance: 3,000
Romford: R.Mortimer;P.G.R.Wallace,W.Dennis;W.F.Mackenzie,J.Paviour(Capt),F.E.Fryatt;
H.W.Brooks,L.Rowntree,W.A.Bridge,J.Oakes,J.Denham.

27 Apr IFL   Away   Dulwich Hamlet   2 – 0   Mackenzie,Worthington
Romford: R.Mortimer;P.G.R.Wallace,W.Dennis;W.F.Mackenzie,J.Paviour(Capt),F.E.Fryatt;
H.W.Brooks,S.A.Olton,W.A.Bridge,E.Worthington,J.Denham.

1 May ETTSF Away   Grays Athletic   1 – 4   Denham
Romford: R.Mortimer;P.G.R.Wallace,W.Dennis;W.F.Mackenzie,J.Paviour(Capt),F.E.Fryatt;
H.W.Brooks,E.Worthington,W.A.Bridge,L.Rowntree,J.Denham.

4 May IFL   Home   Leytonstone   5 – 2   Bridge,Roeder,Mackenzie,Rowntree(2)
Attendance:
Romford: R.Mortimer;P.G.R.Wallace,W.Dennis;W.F.Mackenzie,J.Paviour(Capt),F.E.Fryatt;
H.W.Brooks,L.Rowntree,W.A.Bridge,V.Roeder,J.Denham.

11 May ESCRp Ilford   Barking   2 – 3   Brooks,Patterson
Attendance: 10,264   Receipts: £885
Romford: R.Mortimer;P.G.R.Wallace,W.Dennis;W.F.Mackenzie,J.Paviour(Capt),F.E.Fryatt;
H.W.Brooks,L.Rowntree,W.A.Bridge,G.W.Patterson,J.Denham.

8 June Away   Frdly   Sparta (Rotterdam)   5 – 1   Bridge(3)Langer,Chalmers
Attendance: 16,000
Romford: R.Mortimer;P.G.R.Wallace,W.Dennis;W.F.Mackenzie,J.Paviour(Capt),F.E.Fryatt;
H.W.Brooks,S.A.Olton,L.Chalmers,W.A.Bridge,D.A.Langer.

10 June Away   V.U.C. (The Hague)   1 – 4   Olton
Romford: R.Mortimer;P.G.R.Wallace,W.Dennis;W.F.Mackenzie,J.Paviour(Capt),F.E.Fryatt;
H.W.Brooks,S.A.Olton,L.Chalmers,W.A.Bridge,J.Denham.

*   After Extra Time
\#   Played at Brooklands

ON TOUR TO HOLLAND JUNE 1946

The Romford team photographed in Dutch national costume
Back: Jim Paviour, Bill Seddon, Len Chalmers, Bob Mortimer, Doug Langer, Fred Fryatt, Peter Wallace
Middle: Joe Denham, Harold Brooks, Bill Bridge, Stan Olton, Bill Mackenzie
Front: Bill Dennis   *Authors' collection*

SUMMARY OF RESULTS 1945 – 46

		Home		Goals		Away			Goals		
	P	W	D	L	For	Ag	W	D	L	For	Ag	Pts
Isthmian Football League	26	8	2	3	46	26	7	1	5	37	33	33
FA Challenge Cup	7	3	1	0	16	6	1	1	1	4	5	
FA Amateur Challenge Cup	3	0	1	0	0	0	1	0	1	7	7	
Essex County FA Senior Cup	5	1	0	0	6	2	2	1	1	10	6	
Essex Thameside Chal.Comp.	2	1	0	0	4	0	0	0	1	1	4	
Friendlies (Tour)	2	0	0	0	0	0	1	0	1	6	5	
Total	45	13	4	3	72	34	12	3	10	65	60	

Isthmian Football League
Final Table

					Goals		
	P	W	D	L	For	Ag	Pts
Walthamstow Avenue	26	21	0	5	100	31	42
Oxford City	26	17	6	3	91	40	40
Romford	**26**	**15**	**3**	**8**	**83**	**59**	**33**
Dulwich Hamlet	26	14	2	10	63	59	30
Tufnell Park	26	12	4	10	70	55	28
Woking	26	10	7	9	56	51	27
Ilford	26	12	2	12	56	71	26
Leytonstone	26	11	3	12	61	75	25
Wycombe Wanderers	26	9	3	14	80	88	21
Wimbledon	26	7	6	13	52	72	20
Corinthian Casuals	26	8	4	14	58	83	20
Clapton	26	8	3	15	51	62	19
St. Albans City	26	6	6	14	48	85	18
Kingstonian	26	6	3	17	48	86	15

FIRST TEAM CUP RESULTS

FA Challenge Cup
Final: Derby County 4   Charlton Athletic 1 (a.e.t)

Romford's progress:	1st.Qual	Away	Eton Manor	1 – 1
	Replay	Home	Eton Manor	4 – 3
	2nd Qual	Home	Crittall Athletic	7 – 1
	3rd Qual	Home	Leyton	4 – 1
	4th Qual	Away	Dulwich Hamlet	2 – 1
	1st Round 1st Leg	Away	Brighton & H.A.	1 – 3
	1st Round 2nd Leg	Home	Brighton & H.A.	1 – 1

FA Amateur Challenge Cup
Final: Barnet 3   Bishop Auckland 2

Romford's progress:	1st Round	Home	Leytonstone	0 – 0 **
	Replay	Away	Leytonstone	5 – 3
	2nd Round	Away	Southall	2 – 4

Essex County FA Senior Challenge Cup
Final: Barking 2   Romford 2
Replay: Barking 3   Romford 2

Romford's progress:	1st Round	Home	Ford Sports	6 – 2
	2nd Round	Away	Eton Manor	2 – 1
	Semi-Final	Away	Crittall Athletic	4 – 0
	Final	Ilford	Barking	2 – 2
	Final Replay	Ilford	Barking	2 – 3

16

Essex Thameside Challenge Competition
Final: Leytonstone   6   Grays Athletic   5

Romford's progress: 1st Round   Home   Barking   4 – 0
Semi-Final   Away   Grays Athletic   1 – 4

**   After Extra Time

ESSEX SENIOR CUP FINAL 1945 – 46

BARKING   2   ROMFORD   2
22nd April 1946 at Newbury Park

Back: Bill Seddon, George Patterson, Bill Dennis, Bob Mortimer, Fred Fryatt, Peter Wallace
Front: Harold Brooks, Len Rowntree, Jim Paviour(Capt), Bill Bridge, Doug Langer, Bill Mackenzie   *Authors' collection*

FIRST TEAM DEBUTS 1945 – 46

1945					Previous Club
1st Sept.	v Kingstonian		-	C.J.Adams	Leytonstone
			-	J.H.Bennett	n/k
			-	J.Brown	Brighton & H.A.
			-	W.Dennis	Romford Brewery
			-	D.Dent	Upminster
			-	J.Dray	Upminster
			-	C.Goodchild	Roneo Athletic
			-	W.F.Mackenzie	H.M.Forces
			-	K.Perry	n/k
8th Sept.	v Walthamstow Ave.		-	A.Gaynes	n/k
			-	L.Rowntree	n/k
15th Sept.	v Wimbledon		-	T.Grover	n/k
			-	P.G.R.Wallace	Leytonstone
27th Sept.	v Eton Manor		-	H.Clay	n/k

6th Oct.	v Crittall Athletic	-	**H.W.Brooks**	Clapton
		-	**D.A.Langer**	Clapton
		-	**S.A.Olton**	Clapton
13th Oct.	v Tufnell Park	-	**A.Wilsher**	Chelmsford City
20th Oct.	v Leyton	-	**J.Denham**	Roneo Athletic
		-	**G.Fleetwood**	Havering Road YC
27th Oct.	v Oxford City	-	**F.E.Fryatt**	Dagenham Town
10th Nov.	v Corinthian Casuals	-	**W.Sherman**	n/k
17th Nov.	v Brighton & H.A.	-	**Glyn Harries**	Cambridge Town
15th Dec.	v Oxford City	-	**R.Gadsden**	Ilford
		-	**C.Groom**	Leytonstone
		-	**J.Holt**	R.A.F. & Bradford C.
22nd Dec.	v Wycombe W'drs.	-	**J.Ellis**	South Shields
		-	**J.Letham**	Crystal Palace
		-	**J.Turner**	Briggs Sports
26th Dec.	v Ilford	-	**C.Denham**	Roneo Athletic
29th Dec.	v St.Albans City	-	**J.Ratiera**	Barking

1946

5th Jan.	v Wycombe W'rs.	-	**P.I.McCreddie**	n/k
		-	**E.Worthington**	I.T.C.Warley
12th Jan.	v Ford Sports	-	**H.Voisey**	n/k
9th Feb.	v Eton Manor	-	**W.Bricknell**	n/k
16th Feb.	v Clapton	-	**C.Cutmore**	n/k
		-	**R.Mortimer**	Wimbledon
16th Mar.	v Kingstonian	-	**V.Roeder**	n/k
20th Apr.	v Woking	-	**J.Munro**	n/k
8th June	v Sparta(Rotterdam)	-	**L.Chalmers**	Garashields

FIRST TEAM DEBUTS ON RETURN TO THE CLUB AFTER THE WAR

1945

1st Sept.	v Kingstonian	-	**F.W.Le Marachel**
		-	**J.Paviour**
8th Sept.	v Walthamstow Ave.	-	**J.Oakes**
15th Sept.	v Wimbledon	-	**W.A.Bridge**
22nd Sept.	v Eton Manor	-	**F.J.Chapman**
29th Sept.	v Walthamstow Ave.	-	**W.Benson**
13th Oct.	v Tufnell Park	-	**G.H.Howlett**
1st Dec.	v Clapton	-	**G.W.Patterson**

1946

23rd Feb.	v Dulwich Hamlet	-	**A.Sarjeant**
30th Mar.	v St.Albans City	-	**L.Young**

FIRST TEAM APPEARANCES SEASON 1945 – 46

	A	B	C	D	E	F	Total
Chris Adams	7	2	0	0	0	0	11
Jim Bennett	4	3	3	1	0	0	11
Wally Benson	3	0	1	0	0	0	4
W.Bricknell	2	0	0	1	0	0	3
Bill Bridge	12	1	0	2	2	2	19
Harold Brooks	21	5	3	5	2	2	38
J.Brown	3	0	0	0	0	0	3
L.Chalmers	0	0	0	0	0	2	2
F.J.Chapman,Jnr	0	2	0	0	0	0	2
Tommy Clay	6	6	0	0	0	0	12
Chris Denham	2	0	0	0	0	0	2
Joe Denham	10	4	0	1	2	1	18
Bill Dennis	21	7	3	5	2	2	40

D.Dent	4	0	0	0	0	0	4
J.Dray	2	0	0	0	0	0	2
Gordon Fleetwood	1	1	0	0	0	0	2
Fred Fryatt	21	3	3	5	2	2	36
Tommy Grover	5	7	0	0	0	0	12
Glyn Harries	1	2	0	0	0	0	3
J.Holt	4	0	0	0	0	0	4
Doug Langer	3	3	2	3	0	1	12
Jock Letham	5	0	0	0	0	0	5
Bill Mackenzie	24	7	3	4	2	2	42
Pat McCreddie	1	0	3	2	0	0	6
Bob Mortimer	9	0	0	3	2	2	16
Jimmy Oakes	14	2	0	3	1	0	20
Stan Olton	15	5	3	3	0	2	28
George Patterson	1	0	2	3	0	0	6
Jim Paviour	24	7	3	5	2	2	43
Vic Roeder	2	0	0	0	0	0	2
Pat Rowntree	10	3	0	2	2	0	17
J.Turner	4	0	0	0	0	0	4
Harry Voisey	1	0	1	2	0	0	4
Peter Wallace	24	7	3	5	2	2	43
E.Worthington	5	0	0	0	1	0	6
Others*	15*	0	0	0	0	0	15
Totals	286	77	33	55	22	22	495

Note: *The following 15* players each played in one league game only.
C.Cutmore, J.Ellis, R.Gadsden, A.Gaynes, C.Goodchild, C.Groom, George Howlett, F.W.Le Marachel, J.Munro, K.Perry, J.Ratiera, A.Sarjeant, W.Sherman, A.Wilsher and L.Young.

KEY TO COMPETITIONS

A	Isthmian Football League
B	FA Challenge Cup
C	FA Amateur Challenge Cup
D	Essex County FA Senior Challenge Cup
E	Essex Thameside Challenge Competition
F	Friendly (Tour) Matches

These apply to both the Appearances and Goal Scorers tables.

FIRST TEAM GOALSCORERS SEASON 1945 - 46

	A	B	C	D	E	F	Total
Harold Brooks	14	2	2	4	1	0	23
Bill Bridge	19	0	0	0	1	3	23
Jim Bennett	5	5	3	3	0	0	16
Pat Rowntree	8	1	0	1	2	0	12
Tommy Clay	6	5	0	0	0	0	11
Jimmy Oakes	3	2	0	2	0	0	7
Doug Langer	2	1	0	3	0	1	7
Stan Olton	3	1	1	1	0	1	7
Joe Denham	3	1	0	0	1	0	5
Wally Benson	4	0	0	0	0	0	4
Bill Mackenzie	3	0	0	1	0	0	4
Chris Adams	2	0	0	0	0	0	2
J. Turner	2	0	0	0	0	0	2
Fred Fryatt	2	0	0	0	0	0	2
E.Worthington	2	0	0	0	0	0	2
K.Perry	1	0	0	0	0	0	1

D.Dent	1	0	0	0	0	0	1
J.Holt	1	0	0	0	0	0	1
Vic Roeder	1	0	0	0	0	0	1
George Patterson	0	0	0	1	0	0	1
L. Chalmers	0	0	0	0	0	1	1
Own Goals	1	2	1	0	0	0	4
Total	83	20	7	16	5	6	137

Reserve Team Match Details

25 Aug SEC Home Grays Athletic Res. 1 – 3 Hewitt
Attendance: 300
Romford Res.: T.Grover;K.G.Catton,B.G.Moores;K.Perry,W.Dennis,G.W.Freeman;
D.Dent,T.Parsons,G.Hewitt,F.W.Le Marechal,F.Boom.

1 Sept SEC Away Clapton Res. 2 – 3 Cox,Boom
Romford Res.: T.Grover;K.G.Catton,B.G.Moores;P.G.R.Wallace,D.A.Ward,G.W.Freeman;
S.Cox,-.Clements,K.H.Moores,T.Parsons,F.Boom.

8 Sept SEC Away# Cosser*1 3 – 0 Clay,K.Moores,Hewitt
Romford Res.: T.Grover;C.Blogg,B.G.Moores;P.G.R.Wallace,F.E.Fryatt,G.W.Freeman;
D.A.Ward,G.Hewitt,K.H.Moores,H.Clay,F.Boom.

15 Sept SEC Away Snaresbrook*2 4 – 2 Clay(3)Howlett
Romford Res.: J.F.Dray;G.Fleetwood,-.Morris;A.Newton,F.E.Fryatt,G.Taylor;
G.G.Howlett,-.Davan,H.Clay,C.Goodchild,F.Boom.

22 Sept SEC Home Walthamstow Avenue Res. 6 – 4 Benson(3)Clay(2)Denham
Romford Res.: J.F.Dray;H.Austin,B.G.Moores;G.Fleetwood,F.E.Fryatt,G.W.Freeman;
G.G.Howlett,H.Clay,W.Benson,G.Taylor,J.Denham.

29 Sept SEC Away Walthamstow Avenue Res. 1 – 3 Fleetwood
Romford Res.: W.Sherman;-.Peters,-.Morris;K.Perry,F.E.Fryatt,G.W.Freeman;
H.Clay,G.Hewitt,G.Fleetwood,J.Denham,F.Boom.

6 Oct Frdly Away#2 Barking Res. 5 – 1 Harries(2)Thomas(2)one other.
Romford Res.: A.Willsher;-.Chaney,B.Moores;G.Fleetwood,F.E.Fryatt,G.W.Freeman;
A.Newton,H.Thomas,D.G.Harries,J.Denham,F.Boom.

13 Oct SEC Away Woodford Town Res. 2 – 1 Thomas,Boom
Romford Res.: W.Sherman;-.Chaney,B.G.Moores;G.Fleetwood,F.E.Fryatt,G.W.Freeman;
G.G.Howlett,K.H.Moores,H.Thomas,J.Denham,F.Boom.

27 Oct SEC Away Infantry Training Corps (Warley) 0 – 7
Romford Res.: A.N.Other*;-.Brailey,B.G.Moores;G.W.Freeman,C.Blogg,G.Fleetwood;
A.Newton,A.E.Belsham,J.H.Grinrod,K.H.Moores,F.Boom.

3 Nov SEC Home Cosser*1 5 – 2 Kelly,Chapman,Turnbull(2)Thomas
Romford Res.: A.White;-.Brailey,B.G.Moores;A.Newton,C.Blogg,G.W.Freeman;
F.L.Chapman,H.Thomas,-.Turnbull,K.H.Moores,A.Kelly.

10 Nov SEC Home Metropolitan Police 6 – 3 Harries(4)Kelly(2)
Romford Res.: A.White;G.Fleetwood,B.G.Moores;A.Newton,C.Denham,J.Munro;
W.Benson,H.Thomas,D.G.Harries,F.Wrightson,A.Kelly.

17 Nov SEC Home Roneo Athletic 3 – 2 Benson(2)Thomas
Romford Res.: A.White;J.Munro,B.G.Moores;A.Newton,C.Denham,G.W.Freeman;
W.Benson,H.Thomas,-.Turnbull,F.Wrightson,A.Kelly.

1 Dec EJC3R Away Leytonstone Res. 1 – 3 Kelly
Romford Res.: A.White;J.Munro,B.G.Moores;G.Fleetwood,C.Denham,G.W.Freeman;
W.Benson,H.Thomas,A.Newton,F.Wrightson,A.Kelly.

8 Dec SEC Home Infantry Training Corps (Warley) 4 – 2 Gadsden(2)Roeder,Benson
Romford Res.: A.White;J.Munro,B.G.Moores;A.Newton,C.Denham,G.Fleetwood;
W.Benson,V.Roeder,R.Gadsden,F.Wrightson,-.Finch.

15 Dec SEC Away# Leytonstone Res. 2 – 3 Benson(2)
Romford Res.: **Sel. from** T.Jones;B.G.Moores,J.Munro;A.Newton,C.Denham,G.Fleetwood;
W.Benson,V.Roeder,W.Hussey,F.Wrightson,H.Thomas,A.Kelly.

22 Dec SEC Away Grays Athletic Res. 1 – 5 Scorer unknown
Romford Res.:
Team details unknown.

26 Dec SEC   Home   Snaresbrook*2   4 – 4   Scorers unknown
Romford Res:
Team details unknown.

29 Dec SEC   Home   Clapton Res.   5 – 0   Clay(2)Cook(og)Cutmore,Gadsden
Romford Res.: P.I.McCreddie;J.Munro,B.G.Moores;A.Newton,H.Hall,G.Fleetwood;
G.G.Howlett,V.Roeder,R.Gadsden,H.Clay,C.Cutmore.

5 Jan SEC   Away   Roneo Athletic   5 – 1   Clay,Newton,Spence(og)Benson,Cutmore
Romford Res.: R.Brown;J.Munro,B.G.Moores;A.Newton,H.Hall,C.Denham;
W.Benson,H.Clay,R.Gadsden,J.Denham,C.Cutmore.

19 Jan SEC   Away#3 Downshall Athletic   4 – 3   Scorers unknown
Romford Res.: **Sel from:.** R.Brown;J.Munro,W.Bricknall;G.Fleetwood,C.Denham,A.Newton;
L.Turner,V.Roeder,H.Clay,H.Voisey,C.Cutmore.

26 Jan SEC   Away   Clapton Orient "A"   9 – 3   Clay(3)Turner(2)Gadsden(4)
Romford Res.: **Sel.** R.Brown;J.Munro,W.Bricknall;A.Newton,H.Hall,C.Denham;
L.Turner,H.Clay,R.Gadsden,J.Denham,C.Cutmore.

2 Feb SEC   Home   Frenford*3   8 – 0   Benson(2)Clay(2)Gadsden(2)Roeder,Turner.
Romford Res.: R.Brown;A.Munro,B.G.Moores;W.Freeman,C.Denham,J.Denham;
W.Benson,V.Roeder,R.Gadsden,H.Clay,L.Turner.

9 Feb SEC   Home   Woodford Town Res.   8 – 0   Gadsden(3)Cutmore,Roeder,Clay(2)Benson
Romford Res.: R.Brown;G.Fleetwood,B.G.Moores;A.Newton,H.Hall,C.Denham;
W.Benson,V.Roeder,R.Gadsden,H.Clay,C.Cutmore.

16 Feb Frdly   Home   Tooting & Mitcham Res.   2 – 1   Stocks,Benson
Romford Res.: R.Brown;R.Luchford,B.G.Moores;A.Newton,H.Hall,C.Denham;
W.Benson,V.Roeder,R.Stokes,H.Clay,-.McCaughey.

23 Feb SEC   Away   Ilford Res.   3 – 8   Scorers unknown
Romford Res.: **Sel. From:** R.Brown;J.Munro,B.G.Moores;A.Newton,W.Dennis,J.Denham;
W.Benson,H.Voisey,R.Gadsden,H.Clay,C.Cutmore.

2 Mar SEC   Home   Leytonstone Res.   2 – 2   Worthington,Benson
Romford Res.: L.Young;J.Munro,B.G.Moores;G.Fleetwood,H.Hall,J.Denham;
W.Benson,E.Worthington,H.Clay,H.Voisey,A.Sarjeant.

9 Mar SEC   Away   Metropolitan Police   P – P
Romford had six players sick, the team coach due to take the team to Chingford failed to arrive.

16 Mar SEC   Away#4 R.A.O.C.   2 – 0   Gadsden(2)
Romford Res.: **Sel. From:** L.Young;J.Munro,J.Wright;H.Voisey,H.Hall,A.Newton;
G.G.Howlett,R.Stokes,R.Gadsden,H.Clay,C.Cutmore.

23 Mar Frdly   Away   Woolwich Garrison   P – P**

30 Mar Frdly   Away   Ad Astra   1 – 1   Scorer unknown
Romford Res.: **Sel. From:** R.Mortimer;J.Munro,J.Wright;G.Fleetwood,H.Hall,J.Denham;
W.Benson,V.Roeder,R.Gadsden,H.Clay,W.Cross.

16 Apr CCC1R   Home   Downshall Athletic   3 – 2   Miller(og)Denham,Gadsden
Romford Res.: L.Young; ? , ? ; ? , ? , ? ;
W.Benson, ? ,R.Gadsden, ? ,J.Denham.

19 Apr SEC   Home   Ilford Res.   5 – 2   Scorers unknown
Romford Res.: L.Young;G.Howlett,J.Wright,G.Fleetwood,R.Hall,E.Worthington,
W.Benson,V.Roeder,R.Gadsden,H.Clay,W.Stokes.

23 Apr CCC2R   Home   Ilford Res.   1 – 2   Scorer unknown
Romford Res.:
Team details unknown.

27 Apr SEC   Home   Clapton Orient Res.   9 – 2   Banks,Benson(3)Howlett(3)Gadsden(2)
Romford Res.: **Sel. From:** L.Young;G.Fleetwood,J.Wright;J.Munro,H.Hall,B.Moores;
W.Benson,R.Stokes,R.Gadsden,H.Clay,G.G.Howlett.   (Banks played, on loan from Orient)

4 May SEC   Away   Metropolitan Police   5 – 2   Benson(2)Howlett(2)Loder
Romford Res.: **Sel. From:** L.Young;J.Wright,B.G.Moores;G.Fleetwood,H.Hall,A.Loder;
W.Benson,R.Stokes,R.Gadsden,H.Clay,G.G.Howlett.

N/k   SEC   Home   Downshall Athletic   n/k

N/k   SEC   Home   R.A.O.C.   n/k

* Sherman was taken ill and one of the full backs played in goal.
** Woolwich contacted Romford on Friday evening to say that they could not raise a team.

*1 Cosser withdrew from the league and match declared void.
*2 Snaresbrook either withdrew or were expelled from the league.
*3 Frenford either withdrew or were expelled from the league.

\# Played at Brooklands.
\#1 Woodford Town fielded their first team.
\#2 Played at Barking Park in aid of Merchant Navy Week.
\#3 Played at Ilford.
\#4 Played at Temple Mills.

RESERVE TEAM SUMMARY OF RESULTS SEASON 1945 – 46

		Home		Goals		Away			Goals		
	P	W	D	L	For	Ag	W	D	L	For	Ag	Pts
South Essex Combination*	22	8	1	1	49	20	6	0	6	36	39	29
Essex County Junior Cup	1	0	0	0	0	0	0	0	1	1	3	
Carter Charity Cup	2	1	0	0	3	2	0	0	1	1	2	
Friendlies	3	1	0	0	2	1	1	1	0	6	2	
S.E.Comb/Friendlies**	5	2	1	0	17	6	2	0	0	7	2	
Total	33	12	2	1	71	29	9	1	8	51	48	

* This detail has been compiled from results actually known.
** These were originally South Essex League games but the opponents either withdrew or were expelled from the league.

South Essex Combination
Up to and including 2nd March 1946 (Final Table not found)

	P	W	D	L	Pts
Walthamstow Avenue Res.	13	10	2	1	22
3 Div. Metropolitan Police	15	10	2	3	22
Romford Res.	**18**	**10**	**1**	**7**	**21**
Leytonstone Res.	17	9	2	6	20
I.T.C. (Warley)	13	8	1	4	17
Grays Athletic Res,	15	7	1	7	15
Ilford Res.	16	7	1	8	15
R.A.O.C.	14	7	0	7	14
Downshall Athletic	13	6	2	5	14
Clapton Orient "A"	12	4	1	7	9
Clapton Res.	14	4	1	9	9
Roneo Athletic	15	2	2	11	6
Woodford Town Res.	13	1	2	10	4

Note: Cosser, Snaresbrook and Frenford either withdrew or were expelled from the league, and their records expunged.

RESERVE TEAM CUP RESULTS SEASON 1945 – 46

Essex County FA Junior Challenge Cup
Final: Upminster   3   RAF Earles Colne   2

Romford's progress: 3rd Round   Away   Leytonstone Res.   1 – 3

Carter Charity Cup
Final: n/k

Romford's progress: 1st Round   Home   Downshall Ath.   3 – 2
                     2nd Round   Home   Ilford Res.   1 – 2

RESERVE TEAM APPEARANCES SEASON 1945 – 46

The following players are known to have appeared in the reserve team during the season.

H.Austin	A.E.Belsham	W.Benson	C.Blogg*
F.Boom	-.Brailey	R.Brown	W.Bricknall
K.G.Catton	-.Chaney	F.L.Chapman	H.Clay
-.Clements	S.Cox	W.Cross	C.Cutmore
-.Davan	C.Denham	J.Denham	W.Dennis
D.Dent	J.F.Dray	-.Finch	G.Fleetwood
G.W.Freeman	F.E.Fryatt	R.Gadsden	C.Goodchild(Roneo)
J.H.Grinrod*	T.Grover	H.Hall	D.G.Harries
G.Hewitt	G.G.Howlett	W.Hussey	T.Jones
A.Kelly	F.W.Le Marachel	A.Loder	R.Luchford(Dagenham Town)
-.McCaughey	P.I.McCreddie	B.G.Moores	K.H.Moores
-.Morris	R.Mortimer	J.Munro	A.Newton
T.Parsons	K.Perry	-.Peters	V.Roeder
A.Sarjeant	W.Sherman	R.Stokes(Army)	G.Taylor
H.Thomas	-.Turnbull	L.Turner	H.Voisey
P.G.R.Wallace	D.A.Ward	A.White	A.Willsher
E.Worthington	J.Wright	F.Wrightson	L.Young

* Played for the club pre-war.

DEPARTURES FROM THE CLUB SEASON 1945 – 46

The following appear to have left the club during or by the end of the season. They may have been triallists and only played one or two games and then went elsewhere. New clubs are indicated where known.

C.J.Adams (Tottenham Hotspur), H.Austin, W.Benson (Upminster), C.Blogg, F.Boom, -.Brailey, W.Bricknell (Leyton), J.Brown, R.Brown, K.G.Catton (Old Libertians), -.Chaney, H.Clay (Roneo Athletic), -.Clements, S.Cox, W.Cross, C.Cutmore, -.Davan, C.Denham (Roneo Athletic), D.Dent (Roneo Athletic), J.F.Dray (Clapton), J.Ellis, -.Finch, G.Fleetwood (H.M.Forces), G.W.Freeman, R.Gadsden (Upminster), A.Gaynes, C.Goodchild (Roneo Athletic), J.H.Grinrod (Ilford), C.Groom, T.Grover, H.Hall, D.G.Harries (Dagenham Cables), G.Hewitt, J.Holt, G.H.Howlett (retired), W.Hussey, T.Jones, A.Kelly, F.W.Le Marachel (Leytonstone), A.Loder, R.Luchford (Upminster), -.McCaughey, K.H.Moores, J.Munro (Roneo Athletic), A.Newton, J.Oakes (retired), S.A.Olton (Leytonstone), T.Parsons, K.Perry (Upminster), -.Peters, J.Ratiera (Gidea Park), L.Rowntree (due to work), A.Sarjeant (Ford Sports), W.Sherman, G.Taylor, H.Thomas, -.Turnbull, L.Turner, H.Voisey (Upminster), D.A.Ward, A.White, A.Wilsher (Chelmsford City), E.Worthington (I.T.C.Warley), J.Wright, F.Wrightson, L.Young.

Note: Many of the above named played a game or two for the reserve team on trial, but were not fully signed as Club Members.

Post Season Summary   Season 1945 – 46

Romford's first post-war Isthmian League campaign had a disappointing start. A home defeat from Kingstonian on 1st September was quickly followed by a sound 6-2 thrashing from old rivals Walthamstow Avenue. Happily, Bill Bridge made a welcome return for the next game and Romford handed out a 6-1 defeat to Wimbledon.

Eton Manor were overcome in the FA Cup, although a replay was necessary. The Avenue were then defeated in the return league fixture. 6th October turned out to be a vital day for the club when three players signed from Clapton made their debuts - namely Harold

Brooks, Doug Langer and Stan Olton. They appeared in the side that defeated Crittall Athletic by seven goals to one in the FA Cup. This was followed by a 4-2 defeat from visitors Tufnell Park, who had quite a strong side in those days.

On 20th October nearly 8,000 spectators poured into Brooklands for the next FA Cup encounter to see Leyton defeated by four goals to one. A 2-2 draw at home to Oxford City was followed by a 2-1 win at Dulwich Hamlet and a place in the first round proper of the FA Cup. For this season only matches from then on were played on a two leg basis, and Romford were obliged to travel to Brighton and Hove Albion for the first leg. Although putting up a good performance, Romford had to carry a 3-1 deficit for the return at Brooklands. An entertaining game witnessed by a crowd of over 7,000 ended in a one all draw and Boro were thus beaten 4-2 on aggregate.

Romford gained a 1-0 league victory over lowly Clapton on 1st December before suffering heavy defeats away to Leytonstone and Oxford City by 5-0 and 6-0 respectively. A good measure of success followed, and three times the team scored six goals in a match up to the middle of January.

Then came a 0-0 home draw against Leytonstone in the Amateur Cup on 19th January. The replay the following Saturday drew a huge crowd, and the Stones were two goals up before hundreds of spectators had even got into the ground! Romford's centre forward Bennett was the butt of the Leytonstone fans, one of whom shouted "Big Head!" whenever he was involved in the play. Bennett answered with a magnificent header from near the penalty spot, then turned towards the man taunting him and indicated that his big head had duly obliged! He went on to score a further goal in a fine 5-3 victory, only for Romford to lose 4-2 at Southall in the second round a week later.

Success continued for Boro in the Essex Senior Cup with a hard-fought 2-1 win away to Eton Manor on 9th February. A win over Clapton and defeat at home to Dulwich Hamlet in league matches were followed by a fine 4-0 victory over Crittall Athletic in the Essex Senior Cup semi-final on 2nd March. The following week popular Bill Bridge returned from active service to score two goals in a 5-2 victory over Woking. Then followed a remarkable spell for Bridge, who netted twelve goals in the next four games! He got four against Kingstonian (6-3) on 16th March, an impressive win considering that Harold Brooks, Bill Mackenzie and captain Jim Paviour were all away representing the Isthmian League against the Spartan League at High Wycombe.

Bridge scored five against luckless Corinthian Casuals, who were beaten 8-3. He then recorded two further goals against St Albans City before Romford defeated Tufnell Park 8-0 on 6th April with left half Fryatt scoring two but Bridge only managing one!

The next game on 13th April saw Romford beaten 2-1 at Wimbledon. They were again without Jim Paviour, Bill Bridge and Bill Mackenzie, who had been selected for the Isthmian League against the Athenian League. Available again for the following week, Bridge notched a hat-trick in a 4-2 win over Woking. Next came the thrilling Essex Senior Cup Final on 22nd April before 12,000 spectators at Ilford, when Romford and Barking drew 2-2. Three days later at Brooklands Romford defeated Barking 4-0 in the first round of the Essex Thameside Trophy. They then beat the powerful Dulwich Hamlet 2-0 away in a league game.

Grays Athletic decided to put a stop to Romford's success, defeating them 4-1 in the Thameside Trophy, before Romford rounded off their league programme with a 5-2 home win over Leytonstone on 4th May. Next came the replay of the Essex Senior Cup Final, again at Ilford, before a crowd of 10,000. Boro went into a 2-0 lead through Brooks and Patterson, though Barking managed to draw level before half time. Sadly for Romford, Barking secured victory with a third goal in the second half.

The players, their guests, club officials and committee members enjoyed an end-of-season social at St. John's Hall on 11th May. With the difficulties arising with regard to playing kit, catering and building restrictions described elsewhere, the Directors could take much satisfaction from their year's work. Romford's first season of football after the war was considered a very good one, although the team failed to secure a trophy.

The reward for the players and officials was a short and pleasant tour to Holland in June. Bill Bridge netted a hat-trick in a 5-1 victory over Sparta (Rotterdam) before 16,000 excited spectators, and the team rounded up affairs on a sadder note with a 4-1 loss to old friends V.U.C. (The Hague).

The reserve team was continually changed from week to week with trials given to many players in the search for talent. Around 80 players were used in the reserves during the season and results of matches reflected this, though all results have not been found.

The Romford FC Supporters' Association Committee
Back: W.Cook, T.Peet, E.J.Crook, E.W.Bloss, A.Neeson
Middle: D.H.Clarke, C.E.Montford (chairman), Alderman C.H.Barney, T.F.Collett, H.Chipperton, G.Alexander, C.T.Deverall
Front: W.Turrell, G.Carrick, E.J.Lambert, F.Cope, W.Simpson, F.Montgomery
The secretary, R.Wishart, was not present when the photo was taken   *Authors' collection*

GLEANINGS FROM MANAGEMENT COMMITTEE MINUTE BOOKS
SEASON 1945-46

On **11th September 1945** Mr Brazier reported that Messrs. Gidea Park Coaches, of London Road, Romford, would be supplying a 32-seater conveyance for away matches.

On **18th September** they agreed to give players the use of the Board Room for indoor games and social activities. The chairman offered to donate a table tennis set and dartboard.

On **9th October** the committee decided to appeal for six volunteers to patrol the playing area during matches in an attempt to prevent "encroachment onto the ground", i.e. pitch invasions!

On **30ᵗʰ October** Jim Parrish, the reserve team trainer, complained that they had been given shirts which were not in the club colours.

On **11ᵗʰ December** it was agreed to request affiliation to the London Football Association and entry to the London Senior Cup. (The club had asked for this several times before, but were always turned down for being half a mile outside the boundary). At the same meeting post-war shortages came to the fore when the committee voted to apply "to the Board of Trade, with a view to obtaining permission to purchase additional footballs".

On **15ᵗʰ January 1946** Mr.Tansley reported that a considerable amount of hardcore and soil had been deposited on the ground to improve the banking. The committee agreed to put up chestnut fencing, 4' 6" high with barbed wire on top, adjoining the ground at Medora Road.

On **5ᵗʰ February** they readily agreed to an application by the Isthmian League to use Brooklands for a game versus the Athenian League on 13ᵗʰ April.

ATHENIAN AVENUE/CHESHAM CLOSE DEVELOPMENT

The land that the club sold off prior to the commencement of the war was now being developed into factories and as agreed by the purchaser an access road was being developed leading into the football ground.

Directors' Report 1945-46

In presenting the Seventh Report of the Directors and Balance Sheet to the Shareholders of the Company, the Directors are pleased that this, the first year the Company has renewed activities following the cessation of hostilities and the first time since 1940, the affairs of the Company have shown a profit. A substantial profit of £520 1s 0d on the year's working.

Comparing the Accounts now presented, with those of last year, it will be seen that this year has been a momentous one - the first and second Mortgages, the original bank Overdraft, and the old outstanding Creditors, brought forward since 1940, have all been paid off. Your Directors have had to arrange a new Overdraft with the Company's Bankers however and at Security. Interest at the rate of 4¼ per centum is payable thereunder.

From the Profit that has been made during the year the Directors could recommend the payment of a Dividend, but in view of the previous state of the Balance Sheet, namely, showing a Loss of £1,218 12s 9d, brought about by the War, your Directors recommend that the Profit be treated as shown in the Balance Sheet to reduce the Loss brought forward. Your Directors feel that they should strive to clear the Loss brought forward before paying a Dividend. This course, it is felt, the Shareholders will consider a wise one.

The present satisfactory position has been largely brought about by the excellent performances of the Club teams in Cup ties, at which record crowds have been experienced (it will be seen from the Income and Expenditure Accounts that Revenue from Gates alone amount to over £4,400, Entertainments Duty has cost the Company over £1,000), and the fine response to the Appeal of your Chairman at the last Annual Meeting - and so well published in the Press - for extra Share Capital. As a result of this over £1,700 was received for investment in the Company.

During the year the Directors have been instrumental in the formation of two undertakings closely associated with the Company, The Ball and Broadcasting Fund and The Romford Supporters' Catering Club. Both organisations have operated entirely to the satisfaction of your Directors. A Director or Directors serve on the Committee of each Organisation to represent the interests of the Company and its Shareholders.

Following upon Advertisements in the Press the Ground has been let on a few occasions since the close of the football season, and it is hoped that greater advantage will be taken of the facilities and amenities offered by the Brooklands Sports Ground by more Local and other Organisations in the future.

In conclusion your Directors can say little as to future programme. They have always in mind ground improvements, banking, terracing, stands, and while it is hoped that some improvements to the banking and terracing will be carried out in the near future, the larger schemes must, of necessity, wait until the Company's position is yet more satisfactory than it is today; further, your Directors have no intention of carrying out extensive schemes while costs are at the present high level, unless, of course, they find it imperative to do so to accommodate larger crowds.

Annual General Meeting 1945-46

The above Annual Report was presented to shareholders at the AGM which opened at 8pm on Monday 30th September 1946 at the Golden Lion. This is the report of the meeting in the *Romford Recorder*, Friday 4th October 1946:

No dividend: but shareholders content
Romford FC's great progress

Last season was a momentous one in the history of football in Romford. Heartening facts and figures on post-war recovery were forthcoming at the annual meeting of the Romford Football Club Ltd., which took place at the Golden Lion Hotel, on Monday, when the chairman, Mr T. Macpherson MP, presided. Though no dividend is being paid owing to wartime losses, the company anticipates with maintained support and further share investments to clear its deficit in the coming year.

TEAM BETTER THAN EVER. Moving the adoption of the report Mr Macpherson said that it had been a momentous year in the history of the club and company. It was the first of the post-war activities of the club, and the company made no apology for the fact that during the war years it did nothing, and the club was at a standstill. Some clubs continued, but practically everyone present, including directors and officials, were engaged in the greater game of winning the war. One of the most striking features of the club was the speed with which it had got into its stride. The team and organisation was just as good, if not better, than anything they were able to provide in the pre-war years.

The policy of the board and company, Mr Macpherson continued, was a broad basis of ownership with as many shareholders as possible, and in this aim they were following a democratic principle. They were still open to receive further applications for further shares in the company at 2s 6d, and he hoped sportsmen and supporters would respond.

WONDERFUL PROFIT. They had made, he said, a net profit on this year's working of £520 1s. This was a wonderful achievement with regard to the fact that they had paid off all their old debts, and they had only to find £698 11s 9d to be in a position to resume paying a dividend. Having regard to the way the club was going and the good fortune which attended every activity of the company it was possible they would wipe out the deficit in the coming year.

Their property was increasing in value. They were prevented from embarking on any material or large scale improvements, but everything they were doing was being carried out in accordance with the plans for the ground made years before the war which were well illustrated in their current programmes. The only improvement they had in hand at the moment was to extend the terracing on each side of the 'popular' stand, opposite the grandstand, as it would accommodate a larger number of people [and] prevent crushing and possibly accidents owing to the slippery and uneven nature of the surface. The directors were very conscious of their responsibilities to the public, and they would do all they could within the limitations of licences and permits to make the ground as comfortable as possible for the people who supported them.

TRIBUTES TO OFFICIALS AND PUBLIC. The new directors, Mr W. Mann and Mr A.E. Kittle had, he said, been a tremendous asset to the Board. Mr Kittle had taken on the catering responsibilities, and his activities had enhanced the name and reputation of the club in football and sporting circles generally. Mr Mann was developing into another master of works, and they were indebted to him for what he was doing.

The club, he said, continued to be one of the greatest institutions in the town. Their 'gates' averaged 8,000, evidence that the sporting public of Romford and district appreciated the sport provided and the work of the officials in trying to provide the best amateur fare they could. Their support was something a good many third division clubs would like, and it was a great compliment to the club because 8,000 people could not be wrong.

After paying tribute to other officials, including Mr B.G. Weevers, Mr Westoby and Mr Wright, Mr Macpherson commented on the grand work of the Supporters' Association. 'Without a good supporters' club I doubt whether any football club can function at all', he said.

ASPIRATIONS FOR FUTURE. Two worthy ambitions they had were to see the ground completed and to see Romford win the Amateur Cup. 'I am confident that before many years have passed we shall have achieved both of them', he said. Mr Macpherson concluded by thanking the team manager and trainer, Mr Bill Seddon, and the groundsman, Mr Hewitt.

Seconding the adoption of the report, Mr A.J. Smith, MBE, praised the work of the general secretary, Mr Martin Brazier, and the ground stewards and committee. Speaking on the work of Mr Kittle he said that at every match, including reserve games, he saw that the players had a meal, and this did much to foster the social spirit. He knew of no club where there was a better feeling between players and officials than at Romford.

NORTH STREET ENTRANCE. Continuing, Mr Smith said that recently they had met the directors of the company that had bought the land at North Street. They had reached agreement, and it would not be long before a road was made with a bridge over the Rom and also a ten foot ash path across the allotments leading to the ground.

Concluding, he said that they had had a remarkable year and had patted each other on the back, but it was due to the splendid performances of the players, coupled with the wonderful support they had received from the people of Romford. He thanked Mr J. Gurney for looking after the reserve side.

CLEAR DEBT BEFORE DIVIDEND. The directors' seventh report stated that the first and second mortgages, the original bank overdraft and the old outstanding creditors had been paid off. They had arranged a new overdraft which stood at £3,195 9s on May 31st with the company's ground and property as security. In view of the previous balance sheet which showed a loss of £1,218 12s 9d brought about by the war, they thought they should strive to clear the loss before paying a dividend. Revenue from 'gates' amounted to over £4,400, of which over £1,000 was paid in entertainment duty, and the chairman's appeal at the last annual meeting for extra share capital resulted in over £1,700 being received for investment.

When there appeared to be no questions on the report which was adopted unanimously Mr Macpherson remarked 'Considering we are not paying you a dividend you are all very contented'. (Laughter and applause)…

A refurbished Brooklands dressing room

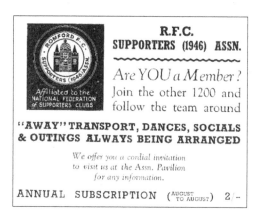

Good value at 2 shillings per annum!

THE ROMFORD FOOTBALL CLUB LIMITED

Full Members of The Football Association
Full Members of Isthmian Football League
Affiliated to Essex County Football Association

Chairman: T.Macpherson MP

Directors: Messrs M.A.Brazier, A.E.Kittle, W.G.Mann, R.Scott,
A.J.Smith MBE, S.G.Tansley

Company Secretary: Mr H.W.Muskett

Registered Offices: 110 Hyland Way, Romford

Ground: Brooklands Sports Ground, Romford

Football Club Management Committee:

President: T.Macpherson MP

Chairman: Mr A.J.Smith MBE   **Vice-Chairman:** Mr A.E.Kittle

Hon.Gen.Secretary: Mr M.A.Brazier   **Hon.Asst.Gen.Secretary:** Mr J.Gurney

Hon.Advt.Secretary: Mr H.Wright   **Hon.Press Secretary:** Mr R.S.Lyons

Chairmen of Sub-Committees:
Ball & Broadcasting Fund: Mr B.G.Weevers   **Car Park:** Mr A.Morris
Catering Section: Mr A.E.Kittle   **Ground Section:** Mr G.H.Westoby
Stand & Membership: Mr R.Scott

Auditor: Mr Iion.V.Cummings,F.C.A.

Representing Supporters' Club: Messrs. C.E.Montford, E.J.Crook, H.Chipperton

First Team Trainer: Mr W.C.Seddon

Reserve Team Trainer: Mr J.W.Parrish (Mr F.H.Adams w.e.f. Feb 1947)

Groundsman: Mr E.Hewitt

LEAGUES AND COMPETITIONS 1946 – 47

The FA Challenge Cup
The FA Amateur Challenge Cup
The Isthmian Football League
The Essex Senior Cup
Essex Thameside Challenge Competition

The Isthmian Football League Reserve Section
Essex Thameside Challenge Competition Reserve Section

Admission Prices Season 1946 – 47

	First Team			Reserve Team		
	Adults	OAP	Child	Adults	OAP	Child
Ground	9d*		5d	5d		3d
Ground & Enclosure	1/6#		10d*	10d		6d
Grandstand	2/6		2/6			

* Includes ½d Entertainment Tax   # Includes 2 ½d Entertainment Tax

Season Ticket Prices Season 1946 – 47

Grandstand	£1.10.0	OAPs & Children	£1.10.0
Ground & Enclosure	£1.1.0	"	12/6
Ground only	12/6	"	7/6

Final Public Trial

Sat.,24ᵗʰ Aug.,1946   Final Trial
BLUES 8   STRIPES 5
Card(4)Bennett(2)Brooks,Dawson   Chalmers(3)Isaacs,Redford
Attendance:
Blues: R.Mortimer;P.G.R.Wallace,H.B.Beaney;W.F.Mackenzie,R.Sheffle,A.E.Belsham;
H.W.Brooks,W.A.Bridge,J.H.Bennett,R.Card,C.Dawson.
Stripes: J.Letham;A.J.Biggs,W.Dennis;W.Isaacs,C.Biggs,B.Moores;
F.Chapman,W.Redford,M.Chalmers,A.Cooper,G.G.Howlett.
Goalkeepers Letham and Mortimer changed sides for the second half.

First Team Match Details

31 Aug IFL   Home   Walthamstow Avenue   0 – 0
Attendance: 6,895   Receipts: £269.15.4
Romford: J.Letham;P.G.R.Wallace,H.B.Beaney;W.F.Mackenzie,J.Paviour(Capt),F.E.Fryatt;
H.W.Brooks,W.A.Bridge,J.H.Bennett,R.Card,C.Dawson.

7 Sept IFL   Away   Oxford City   5 – 3   Brooks(2)Chalmers(2)Dawson
Attendance: 5,000
Romford: J.Letham;P.G.R.Wallace,H.B.Beaney;W.F.Mackenzie,J.Paviour(Capt),F.E.Fryatt;
H.W.Brooks,W.A.Bridge,L.Chalmers,C.C.Pratt,C.Dawson.

12 Sept ETT1R Home   Clapton   3 – 1   Chalmers(2)Dawson
Attendance: 4,915   Receipts: £175.7.5
Romford: J.Letham;P.G.R.Wallace,H.B.Beaney;W.F.Mackenzie,J.Paviour(Capt),F.E.Fryatt;
H.W.Brooks,W.A.Bridge,L.Chalmers,C.C.Pratt,C.Dawson.

14 Sept Frdly   Home   Sparta (Rotterdam)   6 – 3   Paviour(pen)Fryatt(2)Isaacs(2)Bridge
Attendance: 5,774   Receipts: £198.8.6
Romford: R.Mortimer;P.G.R.Wallace,H.B.Beaney;W.F.Mackenzie,J.Paviour(Capt),F.E.Fryatt;
H.W.Brooks,W.A.Bridge,L.Chalmers,W.Isaacs,C.Dawson.

21 Sept FACPR Home   Grays Athletic   2 – 1   Isaacs,Paviour(pen)
Attendance: 9,245   Receipts: £322.16.5
Romford: J.Letham;P.G.R.Wallace,H.B.Beaney;W.F.Mackenzie,J.Paviour(Capt),F.E.Fryatt;
H.W.Brooks,W.A.Bridge,L.Chalmers,W.Isaacs,C.Dawson.

28 Sept IFL   Away   Kingstonian   4 – 2   Brooks,Dawson,Pratt,Isaacs
Romford: J.Letham;P.G.R.Wallace,H.B.Beaney;W.F.Mackenzie,J.Paviour(Capt),F.E.Fryatt;
H.W.Brooks,R.Card,W.Isaacs,C.C.Pratt,C.Dawson.

5 Oct FAC1Q Home   Ekco   3 – 0   Isaacs,Pratt,Paviour(pen)
Attendance: 6,166   Receipts: £257.7.7
Romford: J.Letham;P.G.R.Wallace,H.B.Beaney;W.F.Mackenzie,J.Paviour(Capt),F.E.Fryatt;
H.W.Brooks,W.A.Bridge,W.Isaacs,C.C.Pratt,C.Dawson.

12 Oct IFL   Away   Clapton   4 – 1   Gale,Isaacs(3)
Romford: J.Letham;P.G.R.Wallace,H.B.Beaney;W.F.Mackenzie,J.Paviour(Capt),F.E.Fryatt;
H.W.Brooks,W.A.Bridge,W.Isaacs,F.C.Williams,G.Gale.

19 Oct FAC2Q Away   Tilbury   1 – 2   Isaacs
Romford: J.Letham;P.G.R.Wallace,H.B.Beaney;W.F.Mackenzie,J.Paviour(Capt),F.E.Fryatt;
H.W.Brooks,W.A.Bridge,W.Isaacs,F.C.Williams,G.Gale.

26 Oct IFL   Away   Walthamstow Avenue   3 – 3   Williams(2)Dawson
Romford: J.Letham;P.G.R.Wallace,H.B.Beaney;W.F.Mackenzie,J.Paviour(Capt),F.E.Fryatt;
H.W.Brooks,W.A.Bridge,W.Isaacs,F.C.Williams,C.Dawson.

2 Nov IFL   Home   Wycombe Wanderers   2 – 2   Bridge(2)
Attendance:
Romford: J.Letham;P.G.R.Wallace,H.B.Beaney;W.Isaacs,J.Paviour(Capt),F.E.Fryatt;
H.W.Brooks,A.T.Rodway,W.A.Bridge,W.Allan,C.Dawson.

9 Nov IFL   Home   Woking   5 – 1   Brooks,Bridge,Paviour(2pens)Allan
Attendance:
Romford: J.Letham;P.G.R.Wallace,W.Isaacs;W.F.Mackenzie,J.Paviour(Capt),F.E.Fryatt;
H.W.Brooks,W.Allan,W.A.Bridge,F.C.Williams,C.Dawson.

16 Sept IFL   Away#   Tufnell Park   4 – 1   Bridge,Dawson,Brooks,Allan
Romford: J.Letham;P.G.R.Wallace,W.Isaacs;W.F.Mackenzie,J.Paviour(Capt),A.E.Belsham;
H.W.Brooks,W.Allan,W.A.Bridge,F.C.Williams,C.Dawson.

23 Nov IFL   Home   Oxford City   4 – 3   Williams,Paviour(2)Brooks
Attendance:
Romford: J.Letham;P.G.R.Wallace,W.Isaacs;W.F.Mackenzie,J.Paviour(Capt),A.E.Belsham;
H.W.Brooks,W.Allan,W.A.Bridge,F.C.Williams,C.Dawson.

30 Nov IFL   Away   Wimbledon   0 – 0
Romford: J.Letham;P.G.R.Wallace,W.Isaacs;W.F.Mackenzie,J.Paviour(Capt),F.E.Fryatt;
H.W.Brooks,W.Allan,W.A.Bridge,F.C.Williams,C.Dawson.

7 Dec IFL   Home   Leytonstone   0 – 4
Attendance:
Romford: J.Letham;P.G.R.Wallace,W.Isaacs;W.F.Mackenzie,J.Paviour(Capt),F.E.Fryatt;
G.W.Patterson,G.Butcher,W.A.Bridge,F.C.Williams,C.Dawson.

14 Dec IFL   Away   Dulwich Hamlet   2 – 7   Paviour(pen)Williams
Romford: J.Letham;P.G.R.Wallace,W.Isaacs;W.F.Mackenzie,J.Paviour(Capt),F.E.Fryatt;
G.W.Patterson,F.C.Williams,W.A.Bridge,A.Tidswell,C.Dawson.

25 Dec IFL   Home   Ilford   7 – 3   Paviour(2pens)Langer,Isaacs(2)Patterson,
                                              Bridge
Attendance: 4,000
Romford: J.Letham;P.G.R.Wallace,H.B.Beaney;W.F.Mackenzie,J.Paviour(Capt),F.E.Fryatt;
G.W.Patterson,W.A.Bridge,W.Isaacs,A.Tidswell,D.A.Langer.

26 Dec IFL   Away   Ilford   2 – 2   Langer(2)
Romford: J.Letham;P.G.R.Wallace(Capt),H.B.Beaney;W.F.Mackenzie,F.E.Fryatt,A.E.Belsham;
F.C.Williams,W.A.Bridge,W.Isaacs,A.Tidswell,D.A.Langer.

28 Dec IFL   Away   St. Albans City   2 – 2   Isaacs,Dawson
Romford: J.Letham;P.G.R.Wallace,F.E.Fryatt;F.C.Williams,J.Paviour(Capt),A.E.Belsham;
G.W.Patterson,W.A.Bridge,W.Isaacs,A.Tidswell,C.Dawson.

4 Jan ESC1R   Away   Leytonstone   2 – 1   Bennett,Dawson
Romford: J.Letham;P.G.R.Wallace(Capt),W.Isaacs;W.F.Mackenzie,F.E.Fryatt,A.E.Belsham;
G.W.Patterson,W.A.Bridge,J.H.Bennett,F.C.Williams,C.Dawson.

11 Jan IFL   Away   Wycombe Wanderers   3 – 3   Williams(2)Isaacs
Romford: J.Letham;P.G.R.Wallace,F.E.Fryatt;W.F.Mackenzie,J.Paviour(Capt),A.E.Belsham;
G.W.Patterson,W.A.Bridge,W.Isaacs,F.C.Williams,J.H.Bennett.

18 Jan AC1R   Home   Clapton   0 – 3
Romford: J.Letham;P.G.R.Wallace,H.B.Beaney;W.F.Mackenzie,J.Paviour(Capt),F.E.Fryatt;
G.W.Patterson,W.A.Bridge,J.H.Bennett,W.Isaacs,F.C.Williams.

25 Jan IFL   Home   Corinthian Casuals   3 – 0   Isaacs(2)Dawson
Attendance: 2,000
Romford: J.Letham;P.G.R.Wallace(Capt?),E.O'Sullivan;W.F.Mackenzie,F.E.Fryatt,A.E.Belsham;
G.W.Patterson,W.A.Bridge,W.Isaacs,F.C.Williams,C.Dawson.

1 Feb IFL   Home   St. Albans City   4 – 2   Isaacs(2)Paviour,Patterson
Romford: J.Letham;P.G.R.Wallace,C.W.Guiver;W.F.Mackenzie,F.E.Fryatt,A.E.Belsham;
W.A.Bridge,J.Paviour,W.Isaacs,W.Allan,G.W.Patterson.

8 Feb ESC2R   Home   Eton Manor   1 – 0   Allan
Romford: J.Letham;P.G.R.Wallace(Capt),C.W.Guiver;W.F.Mackenzie,F.E.Fryatt,A.E.Belsham;
W.A.Bridge,F.C.Williams,W.Isaacs,W.Allan,G.W.Patterson.

15 Feb IFL Home Clapton 1 – 2 Bridge
Romford: J.Letham;P.G.R.Wallace,C.W.Guiver;W.F.Mackenzie,J.Paviour(Capt),F.E.Fryatt;
W.A.Bridge,F.C.Williams,W.Isaacs,W.Allan,G.W.Patterson.

1 Mar IFL Away Corinthian Casuals 5 – 3 Cowan(og)Isaacs,Bridge,Paviour(2)
Romford: J.Letham;P.G.R.Wallace,C.W.Guiver;W.F.Mackenzie,F.E.Fryatt,A.E.Belsham;
W.A.Bridge,J.Paviour(Capt),W.Isaacs,W.Allan,G.W.Patterson.

15 Mar IFL Home Tufnell Park 5 – 1 Isaacs,Williams(2)Forber(2)
Romford: J.Letham;P.G.R.Wallace(Capt),C.W.Guiver;W.F.Mackenzie,F.E.Fryatt,A.E.Belsham;
G.W.Patterson,F.C.Williams,W.Isaacs,W.Allan,E.Forber.

22 Mar ESCSF Ilford Grays Athletic 2 – 2 Bridge,Isaacs(pen)
Attendance: 9,069   Receipts: £560
Romford: J.Letham;P.G.R.Wallace,F.E.Fryatt;W.F.Mackenzie,J.Paviour(Capt),A.E.Belsham;
G.W.Patterson,W.A.Bridge,W.Isaacs,F.C.Williams,C.W.Guiver.

29 Mar ESCRp B'king Grays Athletic 6 – 3 Langer(2)Isaacs(3)(2pens)Bridge
Attendance:
Romford: J.Letham;P.G.R.Wallace(Capt),C.W.Guiver;W.F.Mackenzie,F.E.Fryatt,A.E.Belsham;
G.W.Patterson,W.A.Bridge,W.Isaacs,F.C.Williams,D.A.Langer.

4 Apr IFL Home Kingstonian 3 – 3 Isaacs(2)Fryatt
Attendance:
Romford: J.Letham;P.G.R.Wallace,F.E.Fryatt;W.F.Mackenzie,J.Paviour(Capt),A.E.Belsham;
H.W.Brooks,W.A.Bridge,W.Isaacs,W.Allan,G.W.Patterson.

5 Apr Frdly Home V.U.C. (The Hague) 3 – 0 Brooks,Bridge,Isaacs
Attendance:
Romford: J.Letham;P.G.R.Wallace,F.E.Fryatt;W.F.Mackenzie,J.Paviour(Capt),A.E.Belsham;
H.W.Brooks,W.A.Bridge,W.Isaacs,G.W.Patterson,E.Forber.

7 Apr ESCF Ilford Tilbury 1 – 0 Bridge
Attendance: 15,000
Romford: J.Letham;P.G.R.Wallace,F.E.Fryatt;W.F.Mackenzie,J.Paviour(Capt),A.E.Belsham;
H.W.Brooks,W.A.Bridge,W.Isaacs,F.C.Williams,G.W.Patterson.

12 Apr IFL Home Wimbledon 6 – 0 Isaacs(2)Mackenzie,Williams,Brooks(2)
Attendance:
Romford: J.Letham;P.G.R.Wallace,F.E.Fryatt;W.F.Mackenzie,J.Paviour(Capt),C.W.Guiver;
H.W.Brooks,W.A.Bridge,W.Isaacs,F.C.Williams,E.Forber.

19 Apr IFL Away Woking 0 – 1
Romford: J.Letham;P.G.R.Wallace,F.E.Fryatt;W.F.Mackenzie,J.Paviour(Capt),A.E.Belsham;
H.W.Brooks,W.A.Bridge,W.Isaacs,F.C.Williams,E.Forber.

26 Apr IFL Away Leytonstone 0 – 2
Romford: J.Letham;P.G.R.Wallace,F.E.Fryatt;W.F.Mackenzie,J.Paviour(Capt),A.E.Belsham;
G.W.Patterson,W.A.Bridge,W.Isaacs,F.C.Williams,J.Lunn.

8 May ETTSF Away Barking 2 – 4 Isaacs(2)
Romford: J.Letham;P.G.R.Wallace(Capt),C.W.Guiver;W.F.Mackenzie,F.E.Fryatt,A.E.Belsham;
H.W.Brooks,W.A.Bridge,W.Isaacs,F.C.Williams,D.A.Langer.

19 May IFL Home Dulwich Hamlet 2 – 1 Isaacs,Bridge
Romford: P.I.McCreddie;P.G.R.Wallace,F.E.Fryatt;A.E.Belsham,J.Paviour(Capt),C.W.Guiver;
G.W.Patterson,W.A.Bridge,W.Isaacs,F.C.Williams,E.Forber.

\# Played at Cheshunt.

FIRST TEAM SUMMARY OF RESULTS SEASON 1946 – 47

	P	Home			Goals		Away			Goals		Pts
		W	D	L	For	Ag	W	D	L	For	Ag	
Isthmian Football League	26	8	3	2	42	22	5	5	3	34	30	34
FA Challenge Cup	3	2	0	0	5	1	0	0	1	1	2	
FA Amateur Challenge Cup	1	0	0	1	0	3	0	0	0	0	0	
Essex County FA Senior Cup	5	1	0	0	1	0	3	1	0	11	6	
Thameside Chal. Comp.	2	1	0	0	3	1	0	0	1	2	4	
Friendlies	2	2	0	0	9	3	0	0	0	0	0	
Totals	39	14	3	3	60	30	8	6	5	48	42	

Isthmian Football League
Final Table

	P	W	D	L	Goals For	Ag	Pts
Leytonstone	26	19	2	5	92	36	40
Dulwich Hamlet	26	17	3	6	78	46	37
Romford	**26**	**13**	**8**	**5**	**76**	**52**	**34**
Walthamstow Avenue	26	13	4	9	64	37	30
Oxford City	26	12	6	8	70	51	30
Kingstonian	26	12	4	10	52	57	28
Wycombe Wanderers	26	9	8	9	63	61	26
Wimbledon	26	10	5	11	68	64	25
Ilford	26	7	7	12	66	78	21
Tufnell Park	26	8	5	13	45	69	21
Woking	26	7	7	12	34	62	21
Clapton	26	6	8	12	41	59	20
St.Albans City	26	7	5	14	47	79	19
Corinthian Casuals	26	4	4	18	36	80	12

FIRST TEAM CUP RESULTS SEASON 1946 – 47

FA Challenge Cup
Final: Charlton Athletic   1   Burnley   0 **

Romford's progress: Prel.   Home   Grays Athletic   2 – 1
                  1st Qual. Home   Ekco   3 – 0
                  2nd Qual. Away   Tilbury   1 – 2

FA Amateur Challenge Cup
Final: Leytonstone   2   Wimbledon   1
(at Highbury)

Romford's progress: 1st Round   Home   Clapton   0 – 3

Essex County FA Senior Challenge Cup
Final: Romford   1   Tilbury   0
(at Newbury Park, Ilford)

Romford's progress: 3rd Round   Away   Leytonstone   2 – 1
                  4th Round   Home   Eton Manor   1 – 0
                  Semi-Final Ilford   Grays Athletic   2 – 2
                  Replay   Barking   Grays Athletic   6 – 3
                  Final   Ilford   Tilbury   1 – 0

Essex Thameside Challenge Competition
Final: Leytonstone   2   Barking   1 **
(at Brooklands, Romford)

Romford's progress: 1st Round   Home   Clapton   3 – 1
                  Semi-Final Away   Barking   2 – 4

**   After Extra Time

FIRST TEAM DEBUTS SEASON 1946 – 47

1946

31st Aug.	v Walthamstow Ave.	-	**C.Dawson**	Woodford Town
		-	**H.B.Beaney**	Clapton
		-	**R.Card**	Royal Navy
7th Sept.	v Oxford City	-	**C.C.Pratt**	Ilford
14th Sept.	v Sparta(Rotterdam)	-	**W.Isaacs**	n/k
12th Oct.	v Clapton	-	**F.C.Williams**	Walthamstow Avenue

		-	**G.Gale**	n/k
2nd Nov.	v Wycombe W'drs.	-	**W.Allan**	Scottish Football
		-	**A.T.Rodway**	n/k
16th Nov.	v Tufnell Park	-	**A.E.Belsham**	Army
7th Dec.	v Leytonstone	-	**G.Butcher**	HaroldPark
14th Dec.	v Dulwich Hamlet	-	**A.Tidswell**	Tilbury
1947				
25th Jan.	v Corinthian Casuals	-	**E.O'Sullivan**	Ford Sports
1st Feb.	v St.Albans City	-	**C.W.Guiver**	Cranlea
15th Mar.	v Tufnell Park	-	**E.Forber**	Ford Sports
26th Apr.	v Leytonstone	-	**J.Lunn**	Barking

NEWCOMERS

Alf Belsham	**Charlie Guiver**	**Bill Isaacs**	**Fred Williams**
Half Back	Full Back	Centre Forward	Inside Forward

FIRST TEAM APPEARANCES SEASON 1946 – 47

	A	B	C	D	E	F	Total
Bill Allan	10	0	0	1	0	0	11
Horace Beaney	8	3	1	0	1	1	14
Alf Belsham	13	0	0	5	1	1	20
Bill Bennett	2	0	1	1	0	0	4
Bill Bridge	24	3	1	5	2	2	37
Harold Brooks	13	3	0	1	2	2	21
G. Butcher	1	0	0	0	0	0	1
Ron Card	2	0	0	0	0	0	2
L. Chalmers	1	1	0	0	1	1	4
Whippit Dawson	13	2	0	1	1	1	18
E. Forber	4	0	0	0	0	1	5
Fred Fryatt	24	3	1	5	2	2	37
G. Gale	1	1	0	0	0	0	2
Charlie Guiver	6	0	0	3	1	0	10
Bill Isaacs	24	3	1	5	1	2	36
Doug Langer	2	0	0	1	1	0	4
Jock Letham	25	3	1	5	2	1	37
Jackie Lunn	1	0	0	0	0	0	1
Pat McCreddie	1	0	0	0	0	0	1
Bill Mackenzie	23	3	1	5	2	2	36
Bob Mortimer	0	0	0	0	0	1	1
Eddie O'Sullivan	1	0	0	0	0	0	1
George Patterson	13	0	1	5	0	1	20
Jim Paviour	23	3	1	2	1	2	32
Clarrie Pratt	2	1	0	0	1	0	4

A.T. Rodway	1	0	0	0	0	0	1
A. Tidswell	4	0	0	0	0	0	4
Peter Wallace	26	3	1	5	2	2	39
Freddie Williams	18	1	1	5	1	0	26
Totals	286	33	11	55	22	22	429

Key to competitions.

A	Isthmian Football League
B	FA Challenge Cup
C	FA Amateur Cup
D	Essex Senior Cup
E	Essex Thameside Trophy
F	Friendlies

These apply to both the Appearances and Goal Scorers tables.

FIRST TEAM GOALSCORERS SEASON 1946 - 47

	A	B	C	D	E	F	Total
Bill Isaacs	19	3	0	4	2	3	31
Jim Paviour	10	2	0	0	0	1	13
Bill Bridge	8	0	0	3	0	2	13
Freddie Williams	9	0	0	0	0	0	9
Harold Brooks	8	0	0	0	0	1	9
Whippit Dawson	6	0	0	1	1	0	8
Doug Langer	3	0	0	2	0	0	5
M. Chalmers	2	0	0	0	2	0	4
Bill Allan	2	0	0	1	0	0	3
Fred Fryatt	1	0	0	0	0	2	3
Clarrie Pratt	1	1	0	0	0	0	2
George Patterson	2	0	0	0	0	0	2
E. Forber	2	0	0	0	0	0	2
G. Gale	1	0	0	0	0	0	1
Bill Bennett	0	0	0	1	0	0	1
Bill Mackenzie	1	0	0	0	0	0	1
Own Goals	1	0	0	0	0	0	1
Total	76	6	0	12	5	9	108

Reserve Team Match Details

31 Aug IFLR Away Walthamstow Avenue Res. 2 – 5 Chalmers(2)
Romford Res.: R.Mortimer;A.J.Biggs,W.Dennis;W.Isaacs,R.Sheffle,A.E.Belsham;
F.Chapman,W.Ridford,L.Chalmers,A.Cooper,G.G.Howlett.

7 Sept IFLR Home Oxford City Res. 3 – 1 Howlett(2)Chapman
Attendance: 1,000
Romford Res.: R.Mortimer;C.Biggs,W.Dennis;W.Isaacs,A.J.Biggs,A.E.Belsham;
F.Chapman,R.Sheffle,W.Banks,A.Cooper,G.G.Howlett.

14 Sept IFLR Away Woking Res. 4 – 4 Howlett(2)Gale,Chapman(pen)
Romford Res.: J.Letham;C.Biggs,W.Dennis;R.Sheffle,A.J.Biggs,B.G.Moores;
G.G.Howlett,F.Chapman,W.Banks,A.Cooper,G.Gale.

21 Sept IFLR Away Kingstonian Res. 0 – 5
Romford Res.: R.Mortimer;F.W.Dodson,W.Dennis;R.Sheffle,A.J.Biggs,B.G.Moores;
G.G.Howlett,-.Pike,F.Chapman,-.Knott,G.Gale

28 Sept IFLR Home Leytonstone Res. 3 – 1 Gale(2)Banks
Attendance: 1,386   Receipts: £30.8.5
Romford Res.: R.Mortimer;F.W.Dodson,W.Dennis;R.Sheffle,J.Conlon,B.G.Moores;
W.Banks,D.Hayes,J.H.Bennett,V.Roeder,G.Gale.

12 Oct IFLR   Home   Corinthian Casuals Res.   4 – 4   Hayes,Rodway(2)Butcher
Attendance: 650   Receipts: £16.15.6
Romford Res.: R.Mortimer;A.J.Biggs,F.W.Dodson;H.C.Walsh,J.Conlan,A.E.Belsham;
G.G.Howlett,A.T.Rodway,D.Hayes,G.Butcher,J.Denham.

19 Oct IFLR   Home   Tufnell Park Res.   2 – 2   Rodway,Hayes
Attendance: 696   Receipts: £17.10.3
Romford Res.: R.Mortimer;F.W.Dodson,W.Dennis;R.Sheffle,J.Conlon,A.E.Belsham;
F.Chapman,A.T.Rodway,D.Hayes,C.C.Pratt,J.Denham.

26 Oct IFLR   Home   St. Albans City Res.   3 – 2   Howlett,Gale,Banks
Romford Res.: R.Mortimer;F.W.Dodson,W.Dennis;R.Sheffle,J.Conlon,A.E.Belsham;
G.G.Howlett,G.Butcher,W.Banks,W.Allan,G.Gale.

2 Nov IFLR   Away   Clapton Res.   2 – 3   Banks,Chapman
Romford Res.: R.Mortimer;F.W.Dodson,H.C.Mallandine:R.Sheffle,J.Conlon,A.E.Belsham;
G.G.Howlett,G.Butcher,W.Banks,-.Sherlock,F.Chapman.

16 Nov EJC3R Home   Westric   7 – 2   Gale,Chapman,Banks(2)Dukelow
                                                       Butcher(2)
Romford Res.: R.Mortimer;F.W.Dodson,H.C.Mallandine;J.W.Speller,J.Conlon,E.Dukelow;
G.G.Howlett,F.Chapman,W.Banks,G.Butcher,G.Gale.

23 Nov IFLR   Away   Dulwich Hamlet Res.   2 – 3   Campbell,Howlett
Romford Res.: R.Mortimer;F.W.Dodson,H.C.Mallandine;J.W.Speller,J.Conlon,E.Dukelow;
G.G.Howlett,A.T.Rodway,J.Campbell,G.Butcher,G.Gale.

30 Nov IFLR   Home   Ilford Res.   1 – 1   Butcher
Romford Res.: R.Mortimer;F.W.Dodson,H.C.Mallandine;J.W.Speller,J.Conlon,E.Dukelow;
G.G.Howlett,G.Butcher,W.Banks,A.Tidswell,G.Gale.

7 Dec IFLR   Away   Ilford Res.   0 – 7
Romford Res.: J.Coppin;F.W.Dodson,R.Coppin;J.W.Speller,J.Conlon,A.E.Belsham;
C.Hart,W.Allan,W.Banks,A.Tidswell,G.Gale.

14 Dec IFLR   Home   Wimbledon Res.   2 – 6   Howlett,Banks
Romford Res.: J.Coppin;F.W.Dodson,R.Coppin;G.Lumsden,J.Conlon,A.E.Belsham;
-.Bartlett,D.Bailey,W.Banks,W.Allan,G.G.Howlett.

21 Dec EJC4R Away   Ilford Res.   1 – 6   Scorer unknown
Romford Res.:
Team details unknown.

28 Dec IFLR   Home   Dulwich Hamlet Res.   1 – 6   Fisher
Romford Res.:K.McAlpine;F.W.Dodgson,O.Livermore;D.Bailey,J.Conlon,G.Butcher;
G.G.Howlett,V.Roeder,J.H.Bennett,A.Fisher,H.W.Hails.

4 Jan IFLR   Home   Woking Res.   0 – 6
Romford Res.: R.Mortimer;J.Moore,O.Livermore;W.Lindsell,T.C.Horn,G.Butcher;
G.G.Howlett,-.D'Amant,W.Banks,D.Bailey,G.Gale.

11 Jan IFLR   Home   Kingstonian Res.   6 – 3   Butcher(2)Gale(2)Allan(2)
Romford Res.: R.Mortimer;J.Moore,E.O'Sullivan;D.Bailey,O.Livermore,C.W.Guiver;
G.G.Howlett,G.Butcher,W.Banks,W.Allan,G.Gale.

18 Jan IFLR   Away   Wimbledon Res.   0 – 4
Romford Res.: R.Mortimer;F.W.Dodgson,E.O'Sullivan;G.Butcher,J.Moore,C.W.Guiver;
G.G.Howlett,W.Allan,W.Banks,A.Tidswell,E.Forber.

25 Jan IFLR   Away   Tufnell Park Res.   2 – 1   Chapman,Ratiera
Romford Res.: L.Gray;F.W.Dodgson,O.Livermore;D.Bailey,R.Sheffle,C.W.Guiver;
G.G.Howlett,A.Ratiera,E.Chapman,W.Allan,E.Forber.

1 Feb IFLR   Away*   St. Albans City Res.   0 – 3
Romford Res.: L.Gray;F.W.Dodgson,E.O'Sullivan;K.Bailey,R.Sheffle,O.Livermore;
W.Banks,A.Ratiera,G.G.HowlettG.Butcher,,E.Forber.

22 Mar IFLR   Home   Walthamstow Avenue Res. 1 – 9   E.Chapman
Romford Res.: R.Mortimer;J.Moore?,E.Forber;-.Griffin?,R.Sheffle?,   ?   ;
-.Schooling,A.Ratiera,E.Chapman,W.King,J.Lunn.

29 Mar IFLR   Home   Clapton Res.   1 – 1   Lunn
Romford Res.: P.I.McCreddie;-.Morris,E.O'Sullivan;W.Allan,R.Sheffle,E.Forber;
-.Schooling,A.Ratiera,E.Chapman,W.King,J.Lunn.

5 Apr IFLR   Away   Corinthian Casuals Res.   3 – 6   Scorers unknown
Romford Res.: **Sel. From:** P.I.McCreddie;A.Newman,E.O'Sullivan;W.Allan,R.Sheffle,A.Chapman;
G.G.Howlett,A.Ratiera,E.Chapman,A.Green,J.Lunn.

19 Apr Frdly Home Dulwich Hamlet Res. 3 – 1 Savitsky(2)Lunn
Romford Res.: P.I.McCreddie;J.Moore,E.O'Sullivan;W.Allan,K.Lawler,G.Fleetwood;
E.Chapman,A.Ratiera,A.Savitsky,A.Dunn,J.Lunn.

26 Apr IFLR Home Wycombe Wanderers Res. 4 – 1 Savitsky(3)Forber
Romford Res.: P.I.McCreddie;J.Moore,E.O'Sullivan;W.Allan,K.Lawler,G.Fleetwood;
G.G.Howlett,A.Ratiera,A.Savitsky,J.Denham,E.Forber.

3 May IFLR Away Oxford City Res. 1 – 2 Scorer unknown
Romford Res.: **Sel. From:** P.I.McCreddie;J.Moore,E.O'Sullivan;W.F.Mackenzie,K.Lawler,G.Fleetwood;
G.G.Howlett,A.Dunn,A.Savitsky,W.Allan,J.Lunn.

10 May IFLR Away# Leytonstone Res. 0 – 1
Romford Res.: P.I.McCreddie;J.Moore,E.O'Sullivan;W.Allan,K.Lawler,G.Fleetwood;
G.G.Howlett,E.Chapman,A.Savitsky,A.Dunn,J.Lunn.

? May IFLR Away Wycombe Wanderers Res. 2 – 4 Scorers unknown
Romford Res.:
Team details unknown

* Pitch ice-bound.
\# Played at Brooklands.

RESERVE TEAM SUMMARY OF RESULTS 1946 – 47

		Home		Goals		Away			Goals		
	P	W	D	L	For	Ag	W	D	L	For	Ag	Pts
Isthmian League Res.Sect.	26	5	4	4	31	43	1	1	11	18	48	17
Essex County FA Junior Cup	2	1	0	0	7	2	0	0	1	1	6	
Friendly	1	1	0	0	3	1	0	0	0	0	0	
Totals	29	7	4	4	41	46	1	1	12	19	54	

Isthmian Football League Reserve Section
Final Table

	P	W	D	L	Goals For	Ag	Pts
Wycombe Wanderers	26	18	2	6	94	51	38
Dulwich Hamlet	26	18	1	7	95	46	37
Ilford	26	15	5	6	74	42	35
Wimbledon	26	14	5	7	89	51	33
Woking	26	13	6	7	77	59	32
Walthamstow Avenue	26	14	2	10	61	48	30
Leytonstone	26	14	1	11	71	63	29
Clapton	26	11	5	10	50	54	27
St.Albans City	26	10	5	11	67	65	23
Kingstonian	26	9	2	15	51	78	20
Oxford City	26	6	6	14	40	83	18
Romford Reserves	**26**	**6**	**5**	**15**	**49**	**91**	**17**
Tufnell Park	26	6	3	17	44	87	15
Corinthian Casuals	26	3	2	21	42	86	8

RESERVE TEAM CUP RESULTS

Essex County FA Junior Challenge Cup
Final: Halstead Town 6 Eton Manor 3 a.e.t.

Romford's progress: 1st Round Bye
2nd Round Bye
3rd Round Home Westric 7 – 2
4th Round Away Ilford 1 – 6

RESERVE TEAM DEBUTS SEASON 1946 – 47

1946

31st Aug.	v Walthamstow Ave.	-	**A.J.Biggs**	n/k
		-	**W.Isaacs**	n/k
		-	**R.Sheffle**	n/k
		-	**W.Ridford**	n/k
		-	**L.Chalmers**	Garashiels
		-	**A.Cooper**	n/k
7th Sept.	v Oxford City Res.	-	**C.Biggs**	n/k
		-	**W.Banks**	n/k
14th Sept.	v Woking Res.	-	**J.Letham**	Crystal Palace
		-	**G.Gale**	n/k
21st Sept.	v Kingstonian Res.	-	**F.W.Dodson**	n/k
		-	**-.Knott**	n/k
		-	**-.Pike**	n/k
28th Sept.	v Leytonstone Res.	-	**J.Conlon**	n/k
		-	**D.Hayes**	n/k
12th Oct.	v Corinthian Cas.Res.	-	**H.C.Walsh**	n/k
		-	**A.T.Rodway**	n/k
		-	**G.Butcher***	Harold Park
19th Oct.	v Tufnell Park Res.	-	**C.C.Pratt**	Ilford
26th Oct.	v St.Albans City Res.	-	**W.Allan**	Scottish Junior Football

* Played for Romford pre-war.

Note: Due to all team line-ups being not available after 26th October, further debuts are unknown.

RESERVE TEAM APPEARANCES SEASON 1946 – 47

The following players are known to have appeared in the reserve team during the season.

W.Allan	D.Amant	D.Bailey(Ilford)	-.Ball
W.Banks	G.Bartlett	A.E.Belsham	H.(Jim).Bennett
A.Biggs	C.Biggs	-.Borre	G.Butcher
J.Campbell	L.Chalmers	E.Chapman	F.Chapman
J.Conlon	A.Cooper	J.Coppin(Clapton)	R.Coppin(Air Ministry)
J.Denham	W.Dennis	F.Dodson	E.Dukelow
.Dunn	A.Fisher	G.Fleetwood	E.Forber(Ford Sports)
G.Gale	L.Gray	C.W.Guiver	H.W.Hails
C.Hart(Army)	D.Hayes	T.C.Horn	G.G.Howlett
W.Isaacs	W.King	-.Knott	K.Lawler
J.Letham	W.Lindsell	O.Livermore	G.Lumsden
J.Lunn(Barking)	H.C.Mallindine(Army)	K.McAlpine	P.McCreddie
J.Moore(Clapton)	B.G.Moores	-.Morris	R.Mortimer
E.O'Sullivan(Ford Sports)	-.Pike	C.C.Pratt(Ilford)	A.Ratiera
W.Ridford	V.Roeder	A.T.Rodway	A.Savitsky
.Schooling	R.Sheffle	W.Speller	A.Tidswell
H.C.Walsh			

DEPARTURES FROM THE CLUB SEASON 1946 – 47

The following players appear to have left the club during or by the end of the season. They may have been triallists and only played one or two games and then went elsewhere. New clubs are indicated where known.

D.Amant, D.Bailey, -.Ball, G.Bartlett (Leytonstone), H.B.Beaney (HM Forces), J.H.Bennett (retired due to injury), A.Biggs, C.Biggs, -.Borre, G.Butcher (Harold Park), J.Campbell, R.Card (Walthamstow Avenue), L.Chalmers (moved back to Glasgow), J.Conlon (Hornchurch Athletic), A.Cooper, J.Coppin, R.Coppin, C.Dawson (Ilford), J.Denham (Roneo Athletic), W.Dennis (Romford Brewery), F.Dodson, E.Dukelow, -.Dunn, A.Fisher, E.Forber (to South Africa), G.Gale (Harold Park), L.Gray, C.Hart, D.Hayes, T.C.Horn, W.Isaacs (Moved to Canada),

W.King, J.Letham (Crystal Palace), W.Lindsell, O.Livermore, G.Lumsden, H.C.Mallindine, K.McAlpine, P.I.McCreddie (retired), B.G.Moores (Upminster), -.Morris, R.Mortimer, C.C.Pratt, W.Ridford, A.T.Rodway (Erith & Belvedere), V.Roeder, G.R.Schooling, R.Sheffle, W.Speller, A.Tidswell, H.C.Walsh.

Note: Many of the above named played a game or two on trial for the reserves or "A" Team, but were not fully signed on as a Club Member.

Post Season Summary   Season 1946 – 47

Nearly 7,000 fans turned up at Brooklands on 31st August for the opening game of the season, a rather boring goalless draw with Walthamstow Avenue. The crowd noisily voiced their disapproval of the team's performance. A 5-3 away victory over Oxford City and a home Thamesside Trophy win over Clapton were followed by a 6-3 win over Sparta of Rotterdam in a return friendly on 14th September. Home victories over Grays Athletic (attendance over 9,000), Ekco of Southend, and away league wins over Kingstonian and Clapton kept the fans happy. A draw followed by seven consecutive victories and 27 goals – what a start to the season!

Next, on 19th October, came a visit to Tilbury in the second qualifying round of the FA Cup, where a run of the mill victory was expected. A special train was laid on for the Boro fans, but there was confusion when it was found to be starting from Upminster instead of from Romford. The small platform at Romford for the little shuttle to Upminster, via Emerson Park, was crammed full about four deep. When the train arrived people at the far end of the platform jumped onto the track and got into the train from the other side. Hundreds were left stranded, including author John Haley and his brother Eddie. The entrance hall was crammed with people wanting their money back. Thoughts of getting the 370 bus to Grays entered people's minds, but abandoned due to the limited time available. The match itself was a big disappointment and Romford were defeated by two goals to one.

Romford didn't let this setback upset them and went on to play five league games without loss, scoring another 18 goals! Woking (5-1) and Tufnell Park (4-1) were among their victims. On 7th December a long-awaited home clash with Leytonstone resulted in an awful 4-0 defeat. Worse was to follow when Dulwich Hamlet handed out a seven goals to two defeat at Champion Hill. Rumours of discontent among players were starting to surface. A return to form came on Christmas Day, when Ilford were defeated 7-3 at Brooklands. There followed a couple of 2-2 drawn games.

Romford started the new year with a thrilling two one win at Leytonstone in the Essex Senior Cup followed by a three all draw at Wycombe Wanderers. Now for the next Amateur Cup match on 18th January - lowly Clapton would be a pushover, wouldn't it? Alas, supporters were left angry when the result was a 3-0 defeat, and rumours of unhappy players again surfaced.

The boys managed to secure a 4-2 victory over St Albans City, then a 1-0 win over Eton Manor on 8th February in the Essex Senior Cup, giving the faithful hope for the future. The following week, however, Clapton came to Brooklands for an Isthmian League game and went away with both points. A couple of big victories over lowly Corinthian Casuals and Tufnell Park helped to pacify the puzzled Boro supporters.

Grays Athletic were Romford's opponents before 9,000 excited spectators at Ilford's Newbury Park Ground on 22nd March in the semi-final of the Essex Senior Cup. The result was a thrilling 2-2 draw and the need for a replay at Barking the following week. Boro supporters may have been anxious about this because of the absence of captain Jim Paviour, on duty for England against Wales, but there was no need to worry as Romford were easy winners by six goals to three, with Bill Isaacs notching a hat-trick including two calmly-taken penalty kicks.

The busy Easter weekend saw Romford draw 3-3 with Kingstonian on Good Friday followed by a 3-0 win over old friends V.U.C. The Hague the following day. Then came the final of the Essex Senior Cup and a chance to get revenge on Tilbury. A 15,000 crowd crammed into the Newbury Park ground on Easter Monday and saw Romford triumph 1-0, Bill Bridge netting the only goal of the match. Romford celebrated this success with a fine 6-0 victory over Wimbledon at Brooklands the following Saturday.

Supporters were satisfied and it seemed the players were too, until the next three games! Defeats against Woking (0-1) and Leytonstone (0-2) in the league and against Barking (2-4) in the Thameside Trophy dampened supporters' enthusiasm. Only a small crowd turned up at Brooklands on 19th May to witness the last game of the season, an attractive one against League runners-up Dulwich Hamlet. Romford gained revenge for the heavy defeat earlier in the season with a 2-1 victory.

The reserve team met with their usual mixed results as a result of first team calls, suffering some heavy defeats but some good victories in the League. In the Essex Junior Cup it was the same story - a fine 7-2 win over Westric was followed by a 6-1 thrashing at the hands of Ilford Reserves.

The season overall could be regarded as a successful one although many believed it should have been better, especially in the FA and Amateur Cups!

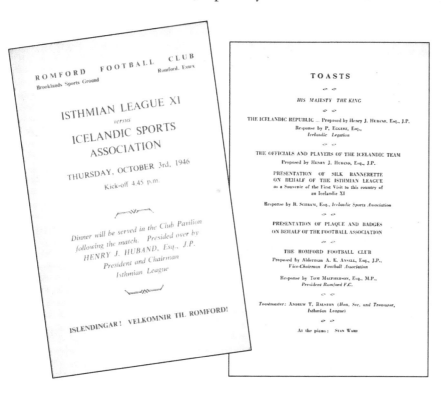

Velkomnir til Romford!
Souvenir of a match at Brooklands between an Isthmian League XI and a team representing the Icelandic Sports Association, October 1947 *Authors' collection*

ESSEX SENIOR CUP WINNERS 1946 – 47

Back: Fred Fryatt, Peter Wallace, Alf Belsham, George Patterson, Bill Mackenzie, Charlie Guiver, Bill Allan
Front: Fred Williams, Bill Isaacs, Jock Letham, Jim Paviour (Captain), Bill Bridge
(Photograph taken at Ilford, March 22nd 1947 versus Grays Athletic in the semi-final. Harold Brooks, not in the picture, played in the final in place of Charlie Guiver). *Authors' collection*

Senior Cup paraded around Romford
As reported in the *Romford Recorder*, Friday 11th April 1947

There were some jubilant scenes at Brooklands on Monday evening when Romford brought home the Essex Senior Cup which they last held in 1937-38 season. When the coach, appropriately named 'Victory Coach', reached the North Street roundabout on the return journey, Jim Paviour (the captain), W. Bridge, P. Wallace and J. Letham clambered through the sliding roof and sat on top with the cup already decorated with Romford's blue and gold ribbons. Accompanied by the cheers of passers-by the coach drove along North Street, South Street, Eastern Road, Junction Road, Market Place and High Street on its way to the ground.

There, the players were welcomed by officials and friends including the president, Mr Tom Macpherson MP, and his wife. A running buffet was provided and the players were the first to drink from the cup. Of the team that last won the cup in 1938, Paviour, Bridge and Patterson remained to share in the present triumph.

The chairman, Mr A.J. Smith MBE, said that the players had put Romford on the map again. They were delighted to have with them Mr and Mrs C.T. Heard with whom he served when the Romford Town club first won the trophy 35 years ago.

Mr Macpherson said that Romford deserved to win the trophy because seldom had they had a team that had played better or created greater enthusiasm in the town than the present one. It was amazing the way things had slipped through their fingers this season. They had always played at their best against strong opposition, and he thanked the players for their loyalty and skill and the pleasure they had given supporters. The trophy they had won was one of the largest in the country, but he hoped that one day they would drink from the Amateur Cup.

Mr Jim Paviour, the captain, suitably replied and said that the team owed a great debt to its manager, Mr Bill Seddon.

Replying, Mr Seddon said that the easiest part of football was playing and he paid tribute to the helpers behind the scenes and the spirit of co-operation that prevailed. He complimented the players and was warm in his praise of Jim Paviour and Bill Bridge, who had both had difficulties with which to contend.

A Romford FC Board of Directors meeting was held at an unusual venue in March 1947 – the House of Commons! The event is reported in the following article from the *Romford Recorder*, Friday 14th March 1947

By invitation of the chairman of Directors (Mr Tom Macpherson MP), the monthly board meeting of the Romford Football Club was held at the House of Commons last week.

The occasion was taken to meet, at dinner, Mr. A.Leitch of Archibald Leitch and Partners, who are responsible for the layout of the Brooklands ground. Short and long-term policy were discussed, considerable thought being given to the ultimate erection of a grandstand to hold 4,000 spectators.

Though it was appreciated that present conditions prevented an early start, instructions were issued to proceed with the final preparatory plans, so that no time would be lost at the word "Go!"….Regret was expressed that the completion of the new terracing, put in hand two months ago, had been held up by the inclement weather.

The winter of 1946-47 was the worst for many years. The same issue of the *Romford Recorder* reported on efforts to keep the Brooklands pitch playable:

The Weather 1, Romford 0.

"Though putting up a great fight, Romford succumbed to our superior forces, but were unlucky to lose. It was the first time we had defeated them on their own ground this season"……Efforts to clear Brooklands on Thursday proved unavailing for when the snow was cleared ridges of ice were exposed which made the ground unfit for play. I felt sorry for the Romford officials as their energetic and enthusiastic efforts had been in marked contrast to the comparative ease with which some professional clubs had given up the struggle against the climate. Still the old adage "It's an ill wind that blows nobody any good" once again proved itself. The 1,000 bread rolls that spectators did not have a chance of eating were presented to Oldchurch Hospital and thankfully accepted.

GLEANINGS FROM MANAGEMENT COMMITTEE MINUTE BOOKS
SEASON 1946-47

On **25th June 1946,** discussing the return friendly with the Sparta club of Rotterdam , the directors agreed to pay for the Sparta party to stay at the Strand Palace Hotel.

On **2nd July** Mr.Tansley reported that he had obtained the services of a woman to work at the ground to launder the playing kit. The committee "Agreed a suitable sink, gas copper and portable wringer be purchased for this purpose".

On **16th July** they decided that "attempts should be made to provide entrance to the ground from Cedar Road and North Street".

On **30th July** we read that "Due to the easing of print regulations, programme to be increased from one to four pages and the price to be increased from 1d to 2d".

On **3rd September** Mr.A.E.Blane agreed to prepare a ten foot pathway from North Street to the river Rom including a footbridge over, and the club to prepare a pathway from the bridge to the ground, subject to Local Authority approval.

On **22nd October** it was reported that player Bill Isaacs had twice been unofficially approached by West Ham United, and a letter of complaint sent to the club.

On **25th March** the directors agreed to allow the BBC to televise part of Romford's home match against Kingstonian on Good Friday.

On **15th April** the Essex County FA gave permission for the club to have the Essex Senior Cup polished and engraved, as it was in poor condition.

PLAYERS' HONOURS

Local newspapers reported that Bill Seddon, Romford's team manager and coach, Jim Paviour, the England and Romford centre half, and Freddie Fryatt, Romford's popular left half, had all been invited to travel the continent with touring teams during the summer.

Jim was named in the FA Eleven which would tour Holland, France and Luxembourg, Freddie would be part of the Isthmian League representative side to visit Denmark, while Bill Seddon, who had played in Denmark on professional tours, was appointed manager of the Isthmian League side.

Romford Football Club Ltd
Annual General Meeting held Tuesday 23rd September 1947

(as reported in the *Romford Recorder*, Friday 26th September 1947)
BIG LOAN OFFER TO ROMFORD FC   MORE SHAREHOLDERS WANTED

An offer to lend the Romford Football Club Ltd £2,707 free of interest, being the balance between the company's authorised share capital of £10,000 and the issued share capital of £7,293 was made by Mr A.E. Blane at the company's meeting at Brooklands on Tuesday. Mr Blane amended an earlier offer to buy up sufficient shares to dispense with the overdraft by offering the loan in order that other people could take up shares if they so desired.

Mr T. Macpherson MP, the chairman of the board, who presided, said that Mr Blane's second proposal was very generous as the company, being a truly democratic one, did not favour an excessive number of shares being held by one individual.

Moving the adoption of the annual report, a summary of which was given in our last issue, Mr Macpherson said that it had been the best year in the company's history and unlike what was happening in other places their consumption was not exceeding production. Having made a profit of £1,675 they were in a position to recommend the payment of a dividend of five per cent, less tax. They were justified in appealing to supporters to take up shares until the authorised share capital was reached.

Speaking of the amenities at Brooklands, Mr Macpherson said he was confident that when the plans were completed they would have the best football ground this side of London. They would like to go ahead with providing more seating accommodation but at present that was out of the question. There was no doubt that when better seating had been secured Romford would receive its fair quota of international and representative games. He estimated that the North Street entrance would be open in two months' time.

Mr Macpherson concluded by thanking the many workers and supporters for their enthusiastic efforts.

There were three nominations for the two vacancies on the board of directors, Mr B.G. Weevers being proposed together with the retiring directors, Messrs A.E. Kittle and R. Scott. Proposing Mr Weevers, Mr T.F. Collett said that he was a founder member of the club who had worked hard in many ways and he suggested that he should be co-opted. Mr Weevers had performed yeoman service in connection with the ball fund though the directors in their wisdom had seen fit to dispense with it and nothing was seen on the balance sheet. He understood, however, that it was not settled until after the close of the year.

Mr Macpherson said that if there was a desire to increase the number of directors it would be necessary to give notice of that fact and call a special meeting. In accordance with the rules they could only fill the two vacancies at that meeting.

Replying, Mr Collett said that he would be loath to lose the services of Mr Scott and Mr Kittle but he had put forward Mr Weevers' name and unless he could be accepted as an additional member he must ask for a ballot. In view of what Mr Weevers had done he was a right and proper person to go on the board. Mr Weevers now felt that he was left on the shelf and if room was found for him they would not regret it.

On a ballot being taken Mr Kittle and Mr Scott were re-elected....

THE ROMFORD FOOTBALL CLUB LIMITED

Full Members of The Football Association
Full Members of Isthmian Football League
Affiliated to Essex County Football Association

Chairman: T.Macpherson MP

Directors: Messrs. M.A.Brazier, A.E.Kittle, W.G.Mann, R.Scott,
A.J.Smith MBE, S.G.Tansley

Company Secretary: Mr H.W.Muskett

Registered Offices: 110 Hyland Way, Romford

Ground: Brooklands Sports Ground, Romford

Football Club Management Committee:

President: T.Macpherson MP

Chairman of Committee: Mr A.J.Smith MBE

Hon.Gen.Secretary: Mr M.A.Brazier   **Hon.Asst.Secretary:** Mr J.Gurney

Hon.Press Secretary: Mr R.S.Lyons   **Hon.Advt.Secretary:** Mr H.A.Wright

Car Park: Mr A.Morris

Hon. Life Vice-Presidents: Mr Glyn Richards and Mr T.F.Collett

Bankers: Lloyds Bank Limited   **Auditor:** Mr I.V.Cummings

First Team Manager & Coach: Mr W.C. (Bill) Seddon

Assistants: Mr E.Hewitt and Mr A.Potter

Reserve Team Manager: Mr F.H.Adams   **Secretary:** Mr G.I.Howlett

Reserve Team Trainer: Mr A.Adlam

"A" Team Manager: Mr Mackenzie,Snr   **Secretary:** Mr E.R.Freeman

"A" Team Trainer: Mr P.Adlam   **Groundsman:** Mr E.Hewitt

LEAGUES & COMPETITIONS 1947 – 48

FA Challenge Cup
FA Amateur Challenge Cup
Isthmian Football League
Essex County FA Senior Challenge Cup
Essex Thameside Challenge Competition

Isthmian Football League Reserve Section
Essex County FA Junior Challenge Cup

Romford & District Football League Premier Division
Essex County FA Junior Challenge Cup**
Carter Charity Cup

** Representing the reserve team.

Admission Prices Season 1947 – 48

	First Team		Reserve Team	
	Adults	OAP & Child	Adults	OAP & Child
Ground	9d	5d	5d	3d
Ground & Enclosure	1/6	10d	10d	6d
Grandstand	2/3			
Programmes	2d			

Season Ticket Prices Season 1947 – 48

Grandstand	£1.10.0	OAPs & Children	£1.10.0
Ground & Enclosure	£1.1.0	"	12/6
Ground only	12/6	"	7/6

Public Trial Match

Sat.,23rd Aug.,1947 3.30 p.m. Final Trial
PROBABLES (2)2 POSSIBLES (0)0
Coleman,Parkinson
Attendance: 2034 Receipts: £67.8.0
Probables: R.Ivey;P.G.R.Wallace,R.Spurgeon;W.F.Mackenzie,J.Paviour,C.W.Guiver;
G.W.Patterson,J.T.Prior,W.A.Bridge,W.Parkinson,R.Coleman.
Possibles: R.S.Lewis;J.Moore,E.O'Sullivan;C.Goodchild,C.D.Tubb,A.E.Belsham;
A.Stevens,W.Allan,L.V.Parminter,N.C.Holloway,J.Lunn.

Alf Belsham (Possibles) and Jim Paviour (Probables) lead their teams out for the Public
Trial Match on 23rd August 1947 *Authors' collection*

First Team Match Details

30 Aug IFL Home Wycombe Wanderers 4 – 2 Bridge(2)Paviour(pen)Parkinson
Attendance: 4,379 Receipts: £159.16.11
Romford: R.C.Ivey;P.G.R.Wallace,F.E.Fryatt;W.F.Mackenzie,J.Paviour(Capt),C.W.Guiver;
G.W.Patterson,F.C.Williams,W.A.Bridge,W.Parkinson,N.C.Holloway.

6 Sept IFL Away Walthamstow Avenue 3 – 1 Bracken(og)Williams,Patterson
Romford: R.C.Ivey;P.G.R.Wallace,F.E.Fryatt;W.F.Mackenzie,J.Paviour(Capt),C.W.Guiver;
G.W.Patterson,F.C.Williams,W.A.Bridge,W.Parkinson,N.C.Holloway.

10 Sept IFL Away Leytonstone 0 – 1
Romford: R.C.Ivey;P.G.R.Wallace,F.E.Fryatt;W.F.Mackenzie,J.Paviour(Capt),C.W.Guiver;
G.W.Patterson,F.C.Williams,W.A.Bridge,W.Parkinson,D.A.Langer.

13 Sept IFL Away Clapton 2 – 0 Bridge,Moran
Romford: R.C.Ivey;P.G.R.Wallace,F.E.Fryatt;W.F.Mackenzie,J.Paviour(Capt),C.W.Guiver;
G.W.Patterson,F.C.Williams,W.A.Bridge,W.Parkinson,J.Moran.

15 Sept ETT1R Away# Leyton 2 – 1 Bridge,Williams
Attendance: 3,397 Receipts: £136.15.8
Romford: R.C.Ivey;P.G.R.Wallace,F.E.Fryatt;W.F.Mackenzie,J.Paviour(Capt),C.W.Guiver;
F.C.Williams,L.V.Parminter,W.A.Bridge,W.Parkinson,G.W.Patterson.

20 Sept FACPR Home Barking 1 – 3 Parkinson
Attendance: 6,181 Receipts: £261.16.5
Romford: R.C.Ivey;P.G.R.Wallace,F.E.Fryatt;W.F.Mackenzie,J.Paviour(Capt),C.W.Guiver;
F.C.Williams,L.V.Parminter,W.A.Bridge,W.Parkinson,G.W.Patterson.

27 Sept IFL Away Kingstonian 1 – 3 Bridge
Romford: R.C.Ivey;P.G.R.Wallace,C.W.Guiver;W.F.Mackenzie,J.Paviour(Capt),F.E.Fryatt;
G.G.Howlett,L.V.Parminter,W.A.Bridge,W.Parkinson,G.W.Patterson.

4 Oct IFL Home Wimbledon 3 – 4 Bridge,Patterson(pen)Williams
Attendance: 4,918 Receipts: £185.16.7
Romford: R.C.Ivey;P.G.R.Wallace,C.W.Guiver;W.F.Mackenzie,J.Paviour(Capt),C.W.Guiver;
G.G.Howlett,W.A.Bridge,R.Gibbs-Kennett,F.C.Williams,G.W.Patterson.

11 Oct IFL Away Oxford City 0 – 1
Romford: R.C.Ivey;C.Tubb,C.W.Guiver;A.E.Belsham,J.Paviour(Capt),F.E.Fryatt;
G.G.Howlett,W.A.Bridge,R.Gibbs-Kennett,N.C.Holloway,L.Mackenzie.

18 Oct IFL Home St. Albans City 1 – 0 Gibbs-Kennett
Attendance: 3,599 Receipts: £134.0.1
Romford: R.C.Ivey;C.Tubb,C.W.Guiver;W.F.Mackenzie,F.E.Fryatt,A.E.Belsham;
G.G.Howlett,W.A.Bridge(Capt),R.Gibbs-Kennett,R.Card,S.Kodish.

25 Oct IFL Home Woking 5 – 1 Bridge(2)Hooker,Patterson(2)
Attendance: 3,899 Receipts: £148.2.7
Romford: R.C.Ivey;P.G.R.Wallace,C.W.Guiver;A.E.Belsham,J.Paviour(Capt),F.E.Fryatt;
G.G.Howlett,T.W.Robertson,W.A.Bridge,R.Hooker,G.W.Patterson.

1 Nov IFL Home Walthamstow Avenue 0 – 1
Attendance: 5,235 Receipts: £204.13.11
Romford: R.C.Ivey;P.G.R.Wallace,C.W.Guiver;A.E.Belsham,F.E.Fryatt,R.Hooker;
G.G.Howlett,T.W.Robertson,W.A.Bridge(Capt),R.Gibbs-Kennett,G.W.Patterson.

8 Nov IFL Away Wycombe Wanderers 0 – 4
Romford: R.C.Ivey;P.G.R.Wallace,C.W.Guiver;W.F.Mackenzie,F.E.Fryatt,R.Hooker;
G.G.Howlett,W.A.Bridge(Capt),R.Gibbs-Kennett,F.C.Williams,G.W.Patterson.

22 Nov IFL Away St. Albans City 3 – 1 Hooker,Bridge,Robertson
Romford: R.C.Ivey;P.G.R.Wallace,J.Moore;A.E.Wilkins,F.E.Fryatt,C.W.Guiver;
G.G.Howlett,T.W.Robertson,W.A.Bridge(Capt),R.Hooker,G.W.Patterson.

29 Nov IFL Home Clapton 3 – 1 Robertson,Howlett,Bridge
Attendance: 2,278 Receipts: £83.11.8
Romford: R.C.Ivey;P.G.R.Wallace,C.D.Tubb;A.E.Wilkins,F.E.Fryatt,C.W.Guiver;
G.G.Howlett,T.W.Robertson,W.A.Bridge(Capt),R.Hooker,G.W.Patterson.

6 Dec IFL Home Dulwich Hamlet 2 – 1 Patterson,Bridge
Attendance: 2,346 Receipts: £89.17.10
Romford: R.C.Ivey;P.G.R.Wallace,C.D.Tubb;A.E.Wilkins,F.E.Fryatt,C.W.Guiver;
G.W.Patterson,T.W.Robertson,W.A.Bridge,R.Hooker,G.G.Howlett.

13 Dec IFL Away Woking 0 – 3
Romford: R.C.Ivey;P.G.R.Wallace,C.D.Tubb;A.E.Wilkins,F.E.Fryatt,C.W.Guiver;
G.G.Howlett,T.W.Robertson,W.A.Bridge(Capt),R.Hooker,V.S.Brown.

20 Dec IFL Home Leytonstone 2 – 3 Bridge,Paviour(pen)
Attendance: 4,570 Receipts: £175.17.11
Romford: R.C.Ivey;P.G.R.Wallace,E.O'Sullivan;W.F.Mackenzie,F.E.Fryatt,C.W.Guiver;
H.W.Brooks,A.E.Wilkins,W.A.Bridge(Capt),D.A.Langer,G.W.Patterson.

25 Dec IFL Home Ilford 1 – 0 Patterson
Attendance: 4,918 Receipts: £199.12.3
Romford: R.C.Ivey;P.G.R.Wallace,E.O'Sullivan;W.F.Mackenzie,F.E.Fryatt,A.E.Wilkins;
H.W.Brooks,W.Allan,W.A.Bridge(Capt),D.A.Langer,G.W.Patterson.

26 Dec IFL Away Ilford 2 – 2 Brooks,Brown
Romford: J.Martin;P.G.R.Wallace,E.O'Sullivan;W.F.Mackenzie,F.E.Fryatt,A.E.Wilkins;
H.W.Brooks,V.S.Brown,W.A.Bridge(Capt),D.A.Langer,G.W.Patterson.

3 Jan ESC1R Home Clapton 0 – 3
Attendance: 4,371 Receipts: £188.14.6
Romford: R.C.Ivey;P.G.R.Wallace,E.O'Sullivan;W.F.Mackenzie,F.E.Fryatt,A.E.Wilkins;
G.W.Patterson,T.W.Robertson,V.S.Brown,W.A.Bridge(Capt),D.A.Langer.

10 Jan IFL Home Oxford City 5 – 2 Robertson(2)Patterson,Williams,Howlett
Attendance: 2,728 Receipts: £104.15.5
Romford: R.C.Ivey;P.G.R.Wallace,E.O'Sullivan;A.E.Wilkins,F.E.Fryatt,C.W.Guiver;
G.W.Patterson,T.W.Robertson,W.A.Bridge(Capt),F.C.Williams,G.G.Howlett.

17 Jan AC1R Away Hastings & St. Leonards 1 – 4 Bridge
Romford: R.C.Ivey;P.G.R.Wallace,E.O'Sullivan;A.E.Wilkins,F.E.Fryatt,C.W.Guiver;
G.W.Patterson,T.W.Robertson,W.A.Bridge,D.A.Langer,H.W.Brooks.

24 Jan IFL Away Dulwich Hamlet 1 – 7 Bridge
Romford: R.C.Ivey;P.G.R.Wallace,E.O'Sullivan;J.Mutter,C.D.Tubb,C.W.Guiver;
G.W.Patterson,S.T.(?J)Robertson,W.A.Bridge(Capt),F.C.Williams,G.G.Howlett.

31 Jan IFL Home Corinthian Casuals 2 – 3 Howlett,Williams
Attendance: 2,310 Receipts: £88.5.7
Romford: R.C.Ivey;P.G.R.Wallace,C.D.Tubb;A.Bamber,F.E.Fryatt,C.W.Guiver;
G.W.Patterson,W.A.Bridge(Capt),R.Marjoram,F.C.Williams,G.G.Howlett.

7 Feb Frdly Home Redhill 6 – 0 Howlett(2)Marjoram(3)Bridge
Attendance: 1,678 Receipts: £71.6.7
Romford: R.C.Ivey;A.Bamber,D.Reinman;D.Kent,F.E.Fryatt,A.E.Collier;
G.W.Patterson,W.A.Bridge(Capt),R.Marjoram,F.C.Williams,G.G.Howlett.

14 Feb IFL Away Wimbledon 1 – 0 Patterson
Romford: R.C.Ivey;A.Bamber,C.W.Guiver;W.F.Mackenzie,J.Hall,F.E.Fryatt;
G.W.Patterson,W.A.Bridge(Capt),R.Marjoram,F.C.Williams,G.G.Howlett.

6 Mar IFL Away Corinthian Casuals 2 – 1 Williams(2)
Romford: R.C.Ivey;G.Foss,C.W.Guiver;D.Kent,A.E.Collier,F.E.Fryatt;
G.W.Patterson,W.A.Bridge(Capt),R.Marjoram,F.C.Williams,D.A.Langer.

13 Mar IFL Home Kingstonian 1 – 3 Marjoram
Attendance: 4,088 Receipts: £154.17.3
Romford: R.C.Ivey;A.E.Collier,G.Foss;D.Kent,W.B.Regan,C.W.Guiver;
J.L.Major,G.W.Patterson,R.Marjoram,F.C.Williams,D.A.Langer.

20 Mar Frdly Home Arsenal "A" 2 – 2 Howlett,Langer
Attendance: 3,680 Receipts: £144.9.5
Romford: R.C.Ivey:G.Foss,A.E.Collier;D.Kent,J.Barton,F.E.Fryatt;
J.L.Major,W.A.Bridge(Capt),G.G.Howlett,G.W.Patterson,D.A.Langer.

28 Mar Frdly Away Sparta(Rotterdam) 2 – 5 Howlett,Williams
Romford: R.C.Ivey;G.Foss,A.E.Collier;J.Barton,W.B.Regan,F.E.Fryatt;
J.L.Major,W.A.Bridge(Capt),G.G.Howlett,F.C.Williams,G.W.Patterson.

29 Mar Frdly   Away   Schiedam   1 – 1   Major
Romford: R.C.Ivey;G.Foss,A.E.Collier;W.B.Regan,D.Kent,F.E.Fryatt;
J.L.Major,W.A.Bridge(Capt),J.Barton,G.W.Patterson,G.G.Howlett.

The above match was then decided on penalties instead of extra time (3 penalties each team)
Barton shot wide, Patterson scored, Opschoor saved from Collier
Ivey saved first shot, second over the bar, Opschoor scored from the third.
Second set of three penalties:
Patterson scored, Opschoor saved from Bridge, Barton scored
Schiedam scored from all three penalties and thus won the match.

10 Apr IFL   Away   Tufnell Park   5 – 1   Patterson,Bridge(2)Barton(2)
Romford: R.C.Ivey;G.Foss,A.E.Collier;D.Kent,W.B.Regan,F.E.Fryatt;
J.L.Major,W.A.Bridge(Capt),J.Barton,G.W.Patterson,D.A.Langer.

15 Apr ETTSF   Away   Barking   2 – 0   Bridge,Brooks
Attendance: 5,000
Romford: J.Martin;G.Foss,A.E.Collier;W.F.Mackenzie,W.B.Regan,F.E.Fryatt;
H.W.Brooks,W.A.Bridge(Capt),J.Barton,G.W.Patterson,D.A.Langer.

17 Apr Frdly   Home   Brentwood & Warley   1 – 2   Langer
Attendance: 3,619   Receipts: £152.19.8
Romford: J.Martin;G.Foss,C.W.Guiver;W.F.Mackenzie,W.B.Regan,F.E.Fryatt;
J.L.Major,W.A.Bridge(Capt),H.W.Brooks,G.W.Patterson,D.A.Langer.

24 Apr Frdly   Home   Tottenham Hotspur XI   5 – 4   Barton(2)Langer,Patterson,Kent
Attendance: 2,218   Receipts: £87.6.8
Romford: R.C.Ivey;G.Foss,C.W.Guiver;D.Kent,W.B.Regan,F.E.Fryatt;
H.W.Brooks,W.A.Bridge(Capt),J.Barton,G.W.Patterson,D.A.Langer.

28 Apr ETTF   B'king   Grays Athletic   1 – 5   Patterson
Attendance: 5,186   Receipts: £219.14.2   Romford Share: £73.4.8
Romford: R.C.Ivey;G.Foss,C.W.Guiver;W.F.Mackenzie,W.B.Regan,F.E.Fryatt;
H.W.Brooks,W.A.Bridge,J.Barton,G.W.Patterson,D.A.Langer.

1 May IFL   Home   Tufnell Park   4 – 1   Bridge,Barrett,Patterson,Langer
Attendance: 2.296   Receipts: £86.0.0
Romford: R.C.Ivey;G.Foss,C.W.Guiver;D.Kent,J.Barton,F.E.Fryatt;
J.L.Major,J.Barrett,W.A.Bridge(Capt),G.W.Patterson,D.A.Langer.

\# Played at Brooklands

The Romford team that beat Clapton 2-0 at the Spotted Dog Ground 13ᵗʰ Sept. 1947
Back: Bill Mackenzie, Peter Wallace, Jim Paviour, Reg Ivey, Fred Fryatt, Charlie Guiver, Norman Holloway,
Front: George Patterson, Fred Williams, Bill Bridge, Bill Parkinson, Jackie Moran   *Authors' collection*

FIRST TEAM SUMMARY OF RESULTS SEASON 1947 – 48

	P	Home W	D	L	Goals For	Ag	Away W	D	L	Goals For	Ag	Pts
Isthmian Football League	26	8	0	5	33	22	6	1	6	20	25	29
FA Challenge Cup	1	0	0	1	1	3	0	0	0	0	0	
FA Amateur Challenge Cup	1	0	0	0	0	0	0	0	1	1	4	
Essex County FA Senior Cup	1	0	0	1	0	3	0	0	0	0	0	
Essex Thameside Chal.Comp.	3	1	0	0	2	1	1	0	1	3	5	
Friendlies	6	2	1	1	14	8	0	1	1	3	6	
Totals	38	11	1	8	50	37	7	2	9	27	40	

Isthmian Football League
Final Table

	P	W	D	L	Goals For	Ag	Pts
Leytonstone	26	19	1	6	88	36	39
Kingstonian	26	16	6	4	74	39	38
Walthamstow Ave.	26	17	3	6	61	37	37
Dulwich Hamlet	26	17	2	7	71	39	36
Wimbledon	26	13	6	7	66	40	32
Romford	**26**	**14**	**1**	**11**	**53**	**47**	**29**
Oxford City	26	10	5	11	50	68	25
Woking	26	10	3	13	63	55	23
Ilford	26	7	8	11	51	59	22
St.Albans City	26	9	2	15	43	56	20
Wycombe Wandrs.	26	7	5	14	51	65	19
Tufnell Park	26	7	4	15	38	83	18
Clapton	26	5	4	17	35	69	14
Corinthian Casuals	26	5	2	19	33	81	12

FIRST TEAM CUP RESULTS 1947 – 48

FA Challenge Cup
Final: Manchester United   4   Blackpool   2

Romford's progress: Prel.Round   Home   Barking   1 – 3

FA Amateur Challenge Cup
Final: Leytonstone   1   Barnet   0
(at Chelsea)

Romford's progress: 1st Round   Away   Hastings & St.Leonards   1 – 4

Essex County FA Senior Challenge Cup
Final: Leytonstone   4   Tilbury   0

Romford's progress: 1st Round   Home   Clapton   0 – 3

Essex Thameside Challenge Competition
Final: Grays Athletic   5   Romford   1

Romford's progress: 1st Round   Home   Leyton   2 – 1
Semi-Final   Away   Barking   2 – 0
Final   Barking   Grays Athletic   1 – 5

FIRST TEAM DEBUTS SEASON 1947 -48

1947					Previous Club
30th Aug.	v Wycombe Wd'rs.	-	**N.C.Holloway**		Supporters team
		-	**R.Ivey**		Tufnell Park
		-	**W.Parkinson**		Army/Dagenham
13th Sept.	v Clapton	-	**J.Moran**		Ford Sports

15th Sept.	v Leyton	-	**L.V.Parminter**	Junior Football
27th Sept.	v Kingstonian	-	**G.G.Howlett**	Old Libertians
4th Oct.	v Wimbledon	-	**R.Gibbs-Kennett**	Tufnell Park
11th Oct.	v Oxford City	-	**L.Mackenzie**	Army
		-	**C.D.Tubb**	Ilford
18th Oct.	v St.Albans City	-	**S.Kodish**	Barking
25th Oct.	v Woking	-	**R.Hooker**	Guildford City
		-	**T.W.Robertson**	R.A.F. Uxbridge
22nd Nov	v St.Albans City	-	**J.Moore**	Clapton
		-	**A.E.Wilkins**	n/k
13th Dec.	v Woking	-	**V.S.Brown***	HM Forces
26th Dec.	v Ilford	-	**J.Martin**	Norton Woodseats

1948

24th Jan.	v Dulwich Hamlet	-	**J.R.Mutter**	n/k
31st Jan.	v Corinthian Casuals	-	**A.Bamber**	n/k
		-	**R.Marjoram**	n/k
7th Feb.	v Redhill	-	**A.E.Collier**	Sheppey United
		-	**D.Kent**	Ilford
		-	**A.Reinman**	n/k
14th Feb.	v Wimbledon	-	**J.T.Hall**	n/k
6th Mar.	v Corinthian Casuals	-	**G.Foss**	Ramsgate
13th Mar.	v Kingstonian	-	**A.J.Major**	Hull City
		-	**W.B.Regan**	R.A.F.
20th Mar.	v Arsenal XI	-	**J.Barton**	Sheffield United
1st May	v Tufnell Park	-	**J.Barrett**	Leyton

Player returned to the Club.
1947

18th Oct.	v St.Albans City	-	**R.Card**	Walthamstow Avenue

* V.Brown played at outside left for Romford in season 1939–40 in the South Essex Combination. It could be that this is the same player.

Ilford and Romford entering the field at Newbury Park on 26th December 1947,
flanked by the Dagenham Girl Pipers   *Authors' collection*

FIRST TEAM APPEARANCES SEASON 1947 – 48

	A	B	C	D	E	F	Total
Bill Allan	1	0	0	0	0	0	1
A.Bamber	2	0	0	0	0	1	3
Jim Barrett	1	0	0	0	0	0	1
Jack Barton	2	0	0	0	2	4	8
Alf Belsham	4	0	0	0	0	0	4
Bill Bridge	25	1	1	1	3	6	37
Harold Brooks	3	0	1	0	2	2	8
Vic Brown	2	0	0	1	0	0	3
Ron Card	1	0	0	0	0	0	1
Albert Collier	3	0	0	0	1	4	8
Gordon Foss	4	0	0	0	2	5	11
Fred Fryatt	24	1	1	1	3	6	36
R.Gibbs-Kennett	5	0	0	0	0	0	5
Charlie Guiver	23	1	1	0	2	2	29
John Hall	1	0	0	0	0	0	1
Norman Holloway	3	0	0	0	0	0	3
R.Hooker	7	0	0	0	0	0	7
Gerry Howlett	15	0	0	0	0	4	19
Reg Ivey	25	1	1	1	2	5	35
Doug Kent	4	0	0	0	0	4	8
Stan. Kodish	1	0	0	0	0	0	1
Doug Langer	8	0	1	1	2	3	15
Bill Mackenzie	12	1	0	1	3	1	18
L.Mackenzie	1	0	0	0	0	0	1
Jackie Major	3	0	0	0	0	4	7
Ray Marjoram	4	0	0	0	0	1	5
Joe Martin	1	0	0	0	1	1	3
J.Moores	1	0	0	0	0	0	1
Jackie Moran	1	0	0	0	0	0	1
J.Mutter	1	0	0	0	0	0	1
Eddie O'Sullivan	5	0	1	1	0	0	7
Bill Parkinson	5	1	0	0	1	0	7
L.Parminter	1	1	0	0	1	0	3
George Patterson	23	1	1	1	3	6	35
Jim Paviour	8	1	0	0	1	0	10
Bill Regan	2	0	0	0	2	4	8
-.Reinman	0	0	0	0	0	1	1
T.W.Robertson	8	0	1	1	0	0	10
Charlie Tubb	7	0	0	0	0	0	7
Peter Wallace	19	1	1	1	1	0	23
A.E.Wilkins	8	0	1	1	0	0	10
Freddie Williams	12	1	0	0	1	2	16
Totals	286	11	11	11	33	66	418

Key to competitions

A   Isthmian Football League
B   Football Association Challenge Cup Competition
C   Football Association Amateur Challenge Cup Competition
D   Essex County Football Association Senior Challenge Cup
E   Thameside Challenge Competition
F   Friendly Matches

These apply to both the Appearances and Goal Scorers tables.

FIRST TEAM GOALSCORERS SEASON 1947 – 48

	A	B	C	D	E	F	Total
Bill Bridge	15	0	1	0	2	1	19
George Patterson	11	0	0	0	1	1	13
Freddie Williams	6	0	0	0	1	1	8
Gerry Howlett	3	0	0	0	0	4	7
T.W. Robertson	4	0	0	0	0	0	4
Ray Marjoram	1	0	0	0	0	3	4
Jack Barton	2	0	0	0	0	2	4
Doug Langer	1	0	0	0	0	3	4
Bill Parkinson	1	1	0	0	0	0	2
R.Hooker	2	0	0	0	0	0	2
Jim Paviour	1	0	0	0	0	0	1
Jackie Moran	1	0	0	0	0	0	1
R.Gibbs-Kennett	1	0	0	0	0	0	1
Vic Brown	1	0	0	0	0	0	1
Jackie Major	0	0	0	0	0	1	1
Harold Brooks	0	0	0	0	1	0	1
Doug Kent	0	0	0	0	0	1	1
Jim Barrett	1	0	0	0	0	0	1
Own Goals	2	0	0	0	0	0	2
Total	53	1	1	0	5	17	77

Reserve Team Match Details

31 Aug Frdly   Away   May & Baker   11 – 0   Scorers unknown
Romford Res.: R.S.Lewis;J.Moore,C.D.Tubb;L.Goodchild,A.E.Wilkins,A.E.Belsham(Capt);
A.Stevens,W.Allan,L.V.Parminter,J.T.Prior,J.Lunn.

6 Sept IFLR   Home   Walthamstow Avenue Res.   3 – 2   Parminter(2)Howlett
Attendance: 795   Receipts: £14.3.3
Romford Res.: R.S.Lewis;J.Moore,C.D.Tubb;L.Goodchild,A.E.Wilkins,A.E.Belsham(Capt);
G.G.Howlett,R.Norris,L.V.Parminter,J.T.Prior,A.Mizen.

13 Sept IFLR   Home   Oxford City Res.   4 – 2   Belsham(pen)Prior,Parminter,Holloway
Attendance: 579   Receipts: £9.11.10
Romford Res.: R.S.Lewis;J.Moore,E.O'Sullivan;L.Goodchild,C.D.Tubb,A.E.Belsham(Capt);
A.Stevens,W.Allan,L.V.Parminter,J.T.Prior,N.C.Holloway.

20 Sept IFLR   Away   Kingstonian Res.   4 – 4   Moore,Howlett,Holloway,Coleman
Romford Res.: Sel. Team: R.S.Lewis;J.Moore,K.Lawler;C.Goodchild,A.E.Wilkins,A.E.Belsham(Capt);
G.G.Howlett,R.Norris,A.Savitsky,N.C.Holloway,J.T.Prior.   R.Coleman played in this match.

27 Sept IFLR   Home   Wimbledon Res.   2 – 4   Holloway,O'Sullivan(pen)
Attendance: 792   Receipts: £14.18.3
Romford Res.: R.S.Lewis;J.Moore,C.D.Tubb;L.Goodchild,A.E.Wilkins,K.Lawler;
C.Goodchild,R.Norris,N.C.Holloway,E.O'Sullivan,R.Coleman.

11 Oct IFLR   Home   Leytonstone Res.   2 – 6   Williams(2)
Attendance: 1,028   Receipts: £19.17.3
Romford Res.: Sel. From: R.S.Lewis;J.Moore,E.O'Sullivan;W.Allan,L.Goodchild,
A.Stevens,R.Norris,L.V.Parminter,W.Parkinson,R.Coleman,F.C.Williams.

18 Oct IFLR   Away   St. Albans City Res.   1 – 3   Scorer unknown
Romford Res.: J.Martin;G.A.Critten,E.O'Sullivan;N.Holloway,J.Moore,K.W.Lawler;
A.Stevens,R.Norris,L.V.Parminter,E.R.Young,-Hall.

25 Oct EJC1R   Away   South Essex A.E.U.   Won   Scorer/s unknown
Romford Res.: J.Martin;G.A.Critten, C.D.Tubb; L.Goodchild, J.Moore,K.W.Lawler;
A.Stevens, A.Muffatt, N.Holloway, E.R.Young,-Hall.

8 Nov IFLR   Home   Woking Res.   0 – 1
Attendance: 857   Receipts: £13.4.5
Romford Res.: J.Martin;J.Moore,C.D.Tubb;W.Allan,A.E.Wilkins,A.E.Belsham(Capt);
A.Stevens,A.Mutter,G.Clark,J.T.Prior,L.Mackenzie.

15 Nov IFLR   Away   Wimbledon Res.   1 – 2   Scorer unknown.
Romford Res.: **Sel.** J.Martin;K.Lawler,C.D.Tubb;R.J.Cornwell,A.E.Wilkins,W.Allan;
A.Stevens,A.Mutter,R.H.See,R.Norris,J.T.Prior.

22 Nov IFLR   Away   Leytonstone Res.   0 – 1
Romford Res.: **Sel.** J.Martin;C.D.Tubb,K.Lawler;W.Allan,J.T.Hall,D.C.Oram;
A.Stevens,J.Mutter,V.S.Brown,R.H.See,J.T.Prior.

29 Nov EJC2R   Away   Staines United   2 – 2**   Goodchild,Brown(pen)
Romford Res.: **Sel.** J.Martin;J.Moore,K.Lawler;C.Goodchild,J.T.Hall,D.C.Oram;
E.Goodchild,R.H.See,R.Norris,J.T.Prior,V.S.Brown.

6 Dec CCCIR   Away   Cranlea   4 – 6   Scorers unknown
Romford Res.: **Sel.** J.Martin;A.Allen,E.O'Sullivan;W.F.Mackenzie,J.T.Hall,D.C.Oram;
E.Goodchild,D.Strickland,R.Norris,J.T.Prior,V.S.Brown.

13 Dec EJCRp   Home   Staines United   3 – 3*   Norris,Lewis(pen)Burton
Attendance: 493   Receipts: £11.10.3
Romford Res.: F.W.Benton;A.Allen,E.O'Sullivan;A.R.Bamber,K.Lawler,D.C.Oram;
E.Goodchild,D.Strickland,R.Norris,C.Bingham,C.Burton.

26 Dec EJCRp   Home   Staines United   0 – 3
Attendance: 365   Receipts: £8.11.6
Romford Res.:
Team details unknown

27 Dec IFLR   Away   Woking Res.   4 – 4   Scorers unknown
Romford Res.:
Team details unknown

3 Jan IFLR   Away   Corinthian Casuals Res.   4 – 1   Scorers unknown
Romford Res.: **Sel.** J.Martin;A.Bamber,J.T.Hall;G.Fleetwood,C.Tubb,A.Belsham(Capt);
E.Goodchild,A.Mutter,D.Strickland,R.Oram,A.Whitehead.

10 Jan IFLR   Away   Dulwich Hamlet Res.   3 – 4   Rumney(2)Brown
Romford Res.: **Sel.** J.Martin;A.R.Bamber,C.D.Tubb;K.Lawler,J.T.Hall,A.E.Belsham(Capt);
E.Goodchild,J.Mutter,A.French,D.C.Oram,W.Rumney.

17 Jan IFLR   Home   Kingstonian Res.   7 – 0   Brown(3)Belsham(2)Rumney,Regan
Attendance: 510   Receipts: £7.10.6
Romford Res.: J.Martin;J.R.Bamber,C.D.Tubb;W.F.Mackenzie,J.T.Hall,W.B.Regan;
E.Goodchild,A.E.Belsham(Capt),W.Rumney,A.French,V.S.Brown.

24 Jan IFLR   Home   Dulwich Hamlet Res.   1 – 3   Cooper
Attendance: 815   Receipts: £13.13.11
Romford Res.: J.Martin;J.R.Bamber,C.D.Tubb;A.E.Belsham(Capt),J.T.Hall,W.B.Regan;
E.Goodchild,W.J.Drake,H.Cooper,A.French,V.S.Brown.

31 Jan IFLR   Away   Clapton Res.   4 – 0   Snegrove,Cooper,E.Goodchild,Brown
Romford Res.: J.Martin; ? ,-.Reinman;A.E.Belsham(Capt),J.T.Hall,W.B.Regan;
E.Goodchild,-.Snelgrove,H.Cooper,V.S.Brown,J.Golder..

7 Feb IFLR   Away   Ilford Res.   1 – 3   Drake
Romford Res.: J.Martin;C.D.Tubb,-.Larson;D.C.Oram,J.T.Hall,A.E.Belsham(Capt);
E.Goodchild,W.J.Drake,H.Cooper,V.S.Brown,J.Golder.

14 Feb IFLR   Home   Ilford Res.   3 – 0   E.Goodchild(2)Kent
Attendance: 1,051   Receipts: £18.18.11
Romford Res.: J.Martin;C.D.Tubb,A.E.Collier;D.Kent,J.Barton,A.E.Belsham(Capt);
E.Goodchild,W.Ward,C.Holderman,J.Barrett,V.S.Brown.

21 Feb IFLR   Away   Walthamstow Avenue Res.   3 – 2   Howlett(2),centre half(og)
Romford Res.: J.Martin; ? ,G.Foss; ? ,J.T.Hall, ? ;
G.G.Howlett, ? , ? , ? ,V.S.Brown.

28 Feb IFLR   Away   Oxford City Res.   2 – 0   Scorers unknown
Romford Res.: **Sel.** J.Martin;G.Foss,C.D.Tubb;W.F.Mackenzie,J.T.Hall,A.E.Belsham(Capt);
J.Barrett,J.Barton,J.Twynham,V.S.Brown,G.G.Howlett.

6 Mar IFLR   Home   St. Albans City Res.   4 – 2   E.Goodchild(2)Barrett,Mackenzie
Attendance: 1,203   Receipts: £23.13.9
Romford Res.: J.Martin;C.D.Tubb,E.O'Sullivan;W.F.Mackenzie,J.Barton,A.E.Belsham(Capt);
E.Goodchild,J.Barrett,G.G.Howlett,V.S.Brown,A.J.Whitehead.

20 Mar IFLR   Away   Wycombe Wanderers Res.   1 – 2   Brown
Romford Res.: J.Martin;C.D.Tubb,R.Sheldon;W.F.Mackenzie,J.Barton,A.E.Belsham(Capt);
C.Goodchild,J.Barrett,R.Marjoram,V.S.Brown,R.Tungate.

27 Mar IFLR Away Tufnell Park Res. 6 – 1 Cooper(3)Belsham(2)Marjoram
Romford Res.:
Team details unknown

10 Apr IFLR Home Wycombe Wanderers Res. 1 – 1 Cooper
Attendance: 839 Receipts: £15.1.7
Romford Res.: **Sel.** J.Martin;H.B.Beaney,R.Sheldon;A.E.Belsham(Capt),J.T.Hall,C.W.Guiver;
H.W.Brooks,J.Barrett,A.Cooper,V.S.Brown,R.Marjoram.

24 Apr IFLR Home Corinthian Casuals Res. 1 – 1 Scorer unknown
Attendance: 394 Receipts: £6.2.6
Romford Res.: **Sel.** J.Martin;G.A.Critten,C.D.Tubb;W.F.Mackenzie,L.G.Wood,A.E.Belsham(Capt);
A.Goodchild,J.Barrett,A.Cooper,V.S.Brown,A.J.Whitehead.

29 Apr IFLR Home Tufnell Park Res. 5 – 0 Scorers unknown
Attendance: 284 Receipts: £2.18.0
Romford Res.:
Team details unknown

1 May IFLR Home Clapton Res. 4 – 1 E.Goodchild(2)L.Mackenzie,Brown
Attendance: ? match followed first team game against Tufnell Park.
Romford Res.: J.Martin;   ?   ,   ?   ;W.F.Mackenzie,   ?   ,A.E.Belsham(Capt);
E.Goodchild,L.Mackenzie,   ?   ,V.S.Brown,V.McDonald.

*   After Extra Time
**   Abandoned in extra time.

RESERVE TEAM SUMMARY OF RESULTS SEASON 1947 – 48

	Home			Goals		Away			Goals		
	P	**W**	**D**	**L**	**For**	**Ag**	**W**	**D**	**L**	**For**	**Ag**	**Pts**
Isthmian League Res.Sect.	26	7	2	4	37	23	5	2	6	34	27	28
Essex County FA Junior Cup	3	0	1	1	3	6	1	0	0	?	?	
Carter Charity Cup	1	0	0	0	0	0	0	0	1	4	6	
Friendly	1	0	0	0	0	0	1	0	0	1	0	
Totals	31	7	3	5	40	29	7	2	7	39	33	

Note: The above summary does not include Essex Junior Cup Tie away to Staines United which was abandoned in extra time with the score two goals each, or the goal(s) scored in the first round tie against South Essex A.E.U.

Isthmian Football League Reserve Section
Final Table

	P	**W**	**D**	**L**	**For**	**Ag**	**Pts**
Wimbledon	26	20	2	4	96	44	42
Dulwich Hamlet	26	16	4	6	88	49	36
Ilford	26	15	6	5	69	55	36
Leytonstone	26	15	2	9	74	41	32
Wycombe Wandrs.	26	13	4	9	81	63	30
Walthamstow Ave.	26	12	5	9	78	50	29
St. Albans City	26	11	7	8	58	42	29
Romford Reserves	**26**	**12**	**4**	**10**	**71**	**50**	**28**
Woking	26	11	3	12	58	63	25
Kingstonian	26	9	4	13	48	73	22
Clapton	26	8	2	16	56	72	18
Oxford City	26	8	2	16	46	88	18
Corinthian Casuals	26	7	2	17	46	96	16
Tufnell Park	26	1	1	24	31	114	3

RESERVE TEAM CUP RESULTS SEASON 1947 – 48

Essex County FA Junior Challenge Cup
Final: Aveley 2 Maldon Town 2
Replay: Aveley 1 Maldon Town 0

Romford's progress: 1st Round Away South Essex A.E.U. n/k
+2nd Round Away Dagenham Naval 3 – 2 *
3rd Round Away Staines United 2 – 2 **
Replay Home Staines United 3 – 3 *
2nd Replay Home Staines United 0 – 3

+ Represented by "A" Team
* After Extra Time
** Abandoned in extra time

Carter Charity Cup
Final: n/k

Romford's progress: 1st Round Away Cranlea 4 – 6

RESERVE TEAM APPEARANCES SEASON 1947 – 48

The following players are known to have appeared in the reserve team during the season.

W.Allan	A.G.Allen	A.R.Bamber	J.Barrett(Leyton)
J.Barton(Sheffield Utd)	H.W.Beaney(H.M.Forces)	A.E.Belsham	F.W.Benton
C.Bingham	H.W.Brooks	V.S.Brown	N.J.Burton
G.Clark(Navy)	A.W.Coleman(Havering)	A.E.Collier(Sheppey United)	H.Cooper
R.J.Cornwell(Barking)	G.A.Critten(Brentwood & W)	W.J.Drake	G.Foss(Ramsgate Ath)
R.A.French	J.Golder	C.Goodchild	L.E.Goodchild
C.W.Guiver	H.W.Hails(Tottenham H.Jnr.)	J.T..Hall -Hall	C.Holderman(Margate)
N.C.Holloway (Junior Football)	G.G.Howlett	D.Kent(Ilford)	-.Larson
K.W.Lawler	R.S.Lewis(Dulwich Hamlet)	J.Lunn	L.Mackenzie(Army)
W.F.Mackenzie	R.Marjoram	J.Martin	V.McDonald
A.Mizen A.Muffatt J.Moore	R.Mutter	R.Norris	
D.C.Oram	E.O'Sullivan	W.Parkinson(Army/Dagenham)	
L.V.Parminter(Junior Football)	J.T.Prior(Ilford)	W.B.Regan(R.A.F)	A.Reinman(Army)
W.Rumney	A.Savitsky	R.H.See	R.G.Sheldon(Ilford)
A.Stevens	D.Strickland(Dartford)	C.D.Tubb(Ilford)	R.Tungate
J.Twynham(Chigwell School)	W.Ward	A.J.Whitehead(Brentwood & Warley)	
A.E.Wilkins	F.C.Williams	L.G.Wood	E.R.Young(Tottenham H.Jnr)

"A" Team Match Details

23 Aug RLPD Away Laindon   1 – 3 Banks
Romford "A": R.G.Creasey;-.Shadbolt,D.Rose;F.B.Terry,A.E.Wilkins,O.Sharman;
J.Moran(Capt),J.R.Thorogood,W.Banks,T.Clarke,R.Parker.

27 Aug RLPD Home Roneo Athletic   1 – 3 Banks
Romford "A": R.G.Creasey;D.Rose,R.Spurgeon; ? ,A.E.Wilkins, ? ;
   ? J.R.Thorogood,W.Banks, ? , ? .

6 Sept RLPD Away Orsett Old Boys United   1 – 3 Savitsky
Romford "A": R.G.Creasey;F.B.Terry,D.Rose;A.Brown,K.Lawler,J.Moran(Capt);
E.Goodchild,G.Wright,A.Savitsky,T.Clarke,H.Archer.

10 Sept RLPD Home Hornchurch Athletic   4 – 2 Archer,Savitsky(3)
Romford "A": F.W.Benton;W.Hammond,D.Rose,F.B.Terry;A.E.Wilkins,J.Moran(Capt),S.Griffin;
E.Goodchild,A.Savitsky,K.Lawler,T.E.Clarke,H.Archer.

13 Sept RLPD Away Heath United   0 – 2
Romford "A": F.W.Benton; ? ?; ? ? S.Griffin;
   ? , ? ,A.Savitsky, ? ,H.Archer.

17 Sept RLPD Home Romford Brewery 2 – 2 E.Goodchild,Savitsky
Romford "A": F.W.Benton;-.Prosser,E.O'Sullivan;F.B.Terry,K.Lawler,J.Moran(Capt);
E.Goodchild,N.C.Holloway,A.Savitsky,T.Clarke,-.Griffin.

20 Sept RLPD Away Wickford 3 – 10 Banks(2)E.Goodchild
Romford "A": ? ; ? , ? ; ? , ? J.Moran(Capt);
E.Goodchild, ? ,W.Banks, ? , ? .

27 Sept RLPD Away Rainham Town "A" 1 – 1 Stevens
Romford "A": ? ; ? , ? ; ? , ? , ? ;
A.Stevens, ? , ? , ? ,H.Archer.

11 Oct RCC1R Away Upminster Res. 2 – 3* Norris,Moran
Romford "A": ? ; ? , ? ; ? , ? J.Moran(Capt);
? ,R.Norris, ? , ? , ? .

18 Oct Frdly Home Old Romfordians Res. 7 – 1 Starr,Stammers,Parfett,Moran(2)
E.Goodchild(2)

Romford "A": ? ; ? , ? J.T.Hall,J.Moran(Capt);
E.Goodchild,E.Starr,D.Summers,Parfett, ? .

25 Oct Frdly Home Park Royal 4 – 0 Summers,E.Goodchild,Starr,McKenzie
Romford "A": F.W.Benton;D.A.Allen,A.Rump;E.D.Hope,J.T.Hall,D.W.Monk;
E.Goodchild,E.Starr,D.Summers,A.McKenzie,H.Archer.

1 Nov RLC2R Away South Essex Waterworks 2 – 3 Norris,Clarke
Romford "A": F.W.Benton;G.A.Critten,D.A.Allen;0.Sharman,J.T.Hall,-.Davis;
E.Goodchild,R.Norris,H.Archer,J.R.Thorogood,,T.Clarke.

8 Nov EJC2R Away Dagenham Naval 3 – 2* Norris,Hall,Purves
Romford "A": F.W.Benton;G.A.Critten,D.A.Allen;D.W.Monk,J.T.Hall,L.S.Spooner;
E.Goodchild,R.Norris,A.J..Purves,R.H.See,H.Archer.
The "A" team represented the reserves in this round of the competition.

22 Nov RLPD Away Billericay Town 0 – 4
Romford "A": A.Brown;G.A.Critten, ? ; ? ,D.A.Allen, ? ;
E.Goodchild, ? , ? , ? , ? .

29 Nov RLPD Home Upminster Old Boys 1 – 2 Clarke
Romford "A": F.W.Benton;D.A.Allen,D.W.Monk;T.Clarke,H.Archer,L.S.Spooner;
P.Thomas,A.J.Purves,G.A.Naughton,G.A.Critten,A.Brown.

13 Dec RLPD Home Wickford Town 1 – 1 Hope
Romford "A": E.A.W.Beasley;G.A.Critten, ? ;E.D.Hope,H.Archer,L.S.Spooner;
? ,A.J.Purves, ? , ? , ? .

20 Dec RLPD Away Hornchurch Athletic 3 – 4 Whitehead,Spooner,Critten(pen)
Romford "A": J.Martin;G.A.Critten,D.A.Allen;O.Sharman,H.Archer,D.W.Monk;
E.Goodchild,E.D.Hope,T.Clarke,L.S.Spooner,A.J.Whitehead.

27 Dec RLPD Home Rainham Town "A" 2 – 6 Clarke,Norris
Romford "A": F.W.Benton; ? , ? ; ? , ? , ? ;
? , ? ,T.Clarke,L.S.Spooner, ? .

10 Jan RLPD Away Clesco 2 – 6 Scorers unknown
Romford "A": F.W.Benton;G.A.Critten,A.Ansell;W.J.Drake,H.Archer,D.W.Monk;
E.D.Hope,R.Norris,W.J.Preston,V.H..Perriman,C.Burton.

17 Jan RLPD Away Beacontree Heath Old Boys 9 – 2 Archer,Norris,Shadbolt(2)Clarke(2)
Marjoram(3)

Romford "A": ? ; ? , ? ; ? , ? ;
-.Shadbolt,R.Norris,R.Marjoram,T.Clarke,H.Archer.

31 Jan RLPD Away Roneo Athletic 5 – 0 Preston,Norris(2)Archer,Whitehead
Romford "A": F.W.Benton; ? ,L.S.Spooner;E.D.Hope,L.G.Wood,H.Archer;
E.Goodchild?,R.Norris,K.Preston,W.Ward,A.J.Whitehead.

7 Feb Frdly Away British Legion 9 – 2 Norris(6)(1pen)Ward(2)Whitlock
Romford "A": F.W.Benton;-.Chapman,L.S.Spooner,-.Walker,L.G.Wood,H.Archer;
G.A.Critten,R.Norris,W.Ward,H.Whitlock,A.J.Whitehead.

14 Feb Frdly Away Rotary Hoes 4 – 1 Littlechild,Critten,Whitehead(2)
Romford "A": F.W.Benton?;-.Chapman?,L.S.Spooner?;-.Walker,H.Whitlock,H.Archer?;
G.A.Critten,R.Norris,D.Littlechild, ? ,A.J.Whitehead.

28 Feb RLPD Home# Laindon 3 – 2 Marjoram,Norris(2)
Romford "A": F.W.Benton?; ? , ? ; ? , ? , ? ;
? ,R.Norris,R.Marjoram, ? ,A.J.Whitehead.

6 Mar Frdly Away Durus Sports 9 – 0 Critten(2)Norris(4)Drake,Hope
Littlechild(pen)
Romford "A": D.Sweetman; ? , ? ;E.D.Hope, ? ,V.H.Perriman;
G.A.Critten,R.Norris,D.Littlechild,W.J.Drake,A.J.Whitehead.

13 Mar RLPD Away Upminster Old Boys 3 – 1 Ward,Littlechild,Norris
Romford "A": D.Sweetman;G.A.Critten,L.S.Spooner;V.H.Perriman,L.G.Wood,H.Archer;
W.J.Drake,R.Norris,D.Littlechild,W.Ward,A.J.Whitehead.

20 Mar Frdly Away Eastells Athletic 2 – 2 Irvine,Critten
Romford "A": E.A.W.Beasley;G.A.Critten,-.Walker;E.D.Hope,L.G.Wood,V.H.Perriman;
-.Francis,D.Littlechild,V.McDonald,W.Ward,-.Irvine.

26 Mar RLPD Home Clesco 2 – 1 Marjoram,Irons(og)
Romford "A": D.Sweetman;G.A.Critten,L.S.Spooner;V.H.Perriman,L.G.Wood,H.Archer;
W.J.Drake,R.Norris,R.Marjoram,W.Ward,K.Lawler.

29 Mar RLPD Away Elm Park 1 – 0 Marjoram
Romford "A": ? ; ? , ? ;V.H.Perriman, ? , ? ;
? , ? ,R.Marjoram, ? , ? .

31 Mar RLPD Home Beacontree Heath Old Boys 6 – 0 Scorers unknown
Romford "A":
Team details unknown

3 Apr RLPD Home Orsett Old Boys 0 – 2
Romford "A": D.Sweetman;G.A.Critten,L.S.Spooner?;V.H.Perriman,L.G.Wood, ? ;
? ,R.Norris,R.Marjoram,W.Ward, ? .

7 Apr RLPD Home Billericay Town 5 – 1 Whitehead(2)Critten,Norris,one other
Romford "A": D.Sweetman;G.A.Critten,L.S.Spooner?; V.H.Perriman?,H.Archer, ? ;
? ,R.Norris, ? ,W.Ward,A.J.Whitehead.

12 Apr RLPD Away Romford Brewery 2 – 2 Preston,Norris
Romford "A": D.Sweetman;G.A.Critten,L.S.Spooner?;V.H.Perriman?L.G.Wood,H.Archer;
P.Thomas,R.Norris,K.Preston,W.Ward,A.J.Whitehead.

21 Apr RLPD Home Elm Park 5 – 4 Drake,Critten(2pens)E.Goodchild,
McDonald
Romford "A": D.Sweetman?;G.A.Critten,L.S.Spooner?;V.H.Perriman?,L.G.Wood?,H.Archer;
E.Goodchild,R.Norris?,V.McDonald,W.J.Drake,A.J.Whitehead.(5th goal was 100th of season)??

28 Apr RLPD Home Heath United 2 – 1 Critten,Drake
Romford "A": D.Sweetman;W.Ward,L.S.Spooner;E.D.Hope,H.Archer,G.A.Critten;
E.Goodchild,R.Norris,V.McDonald,W.J.Drake,A.J.Whitehead.

* After Extra Time
\# Played at Laindon

"A" TEAM SUMMARY OF RESULTS SEASON 1947 – 48

	Home			Goals		Away			Goals		
	P	**W**	**D**	**L**	**For**	**Ag**	**W**	**D**	**L**	**For**	**Ag**	**Pts**
Romford & Dist.League	26	7	2	4	34	27	4	2	7	31	38	26
Essex County FA Junior Cup**	1	0	0	0	0	0	1	0	0	3	2	
Romford & Dist.Lge.Cup	1	0	0	0	0	0	0	0	1	2	3	
Romford Charity Cup	1	0	0	0	0	0	0	0	1	2	3	
Friendlies	6	2	0	0	11	1	3	1	0	24	5	
Totals	35	9	2	4	45	28	8	3	9	62	51	

** Representing the Reserve Team.

Romford & District Football League Premier Division
Final Table

	P	W	D	L	For	Ag	Pts
					Goals		
Orsett OB	26	18	4	4	81	38	40
Hornchurch Ath.	26	19	1	6	102	48	39
Laindon	26	14	3	9	75	60	31
Romford Brewery	26	12	6	8	66	47	30
Billericay	26	12	6	8	56	48	30
Upminster OB	26	11	5	10	59	44	27
Heath United	26	10	6	10	55	62	26
Romford "A"	**26**	**11**	**4**	**11**	**62***	**61***	**26**
Wickford	26	9	7	10	43	57	25
Bec.Heath Old Boys	26	9	5	12	64	87	23
Rainham Town	26	8	5	13	50	76	21
Elm Park	26	7	2	17	38	62	16
Roneo	26	7	2	17	41	73	16
Clesco	26	4	6	16	48	76	14

* The goals for and against in the league table disagrees with the actual results found recorded in the summary.

"A" TEAM CUP RESULTS SEASON 1947 – 48

Essex County FA Junior Challenge Cup
Final: Aveley   1   Maldon Town   0
(After a 2-2 draw)

Romford's progress: 1st Round   See Reserve Team Details
2nd Round   Away   Dagenham Naval   3 – 2*
3rd Round   See Reserve Team Details

Romford & District League Cup
Final: Hornchurch Athletic   3   Billericay   2

Romford's progress: 2nd Round   Away   South Essex Waterworks   2 – 3

Romford Charity Cup
Final: Chadwell Heath   1   Hornchurch Athletic   0

Romford's progress: 1st Round   Away   Upminster Res.   2 – 3*

*   After Extra Time

"A" TEAM APPEARANCES SEASON 1947 – 48

The following players are believed to have appeared in the "A" Team during the season.

H.Archer	D.A.Allen	A.Ansell	W.Banks(Harold Park)
E.A.W.Beasley	F.W.Benton	A.Brown	C.Burton
F.Chapman	T.Clarke	R.G.Creasey	G.A.Critten
-.Davis	W.J.Drake	-.Francis	E.Goodchild
.Griffin	J.T.Hall	N.C.Holloway	E.D.Hope
-.Irvine	K.Lawler	D.Littlechild	R.Marjoram
J.Martin	V.McDonald	A.McKenzie	D.W.Monk
J.Moran	G.A.Naughton	R.Norris	E.O'Sullivan
R.Parker	V.H.Perriman	K.Preston	-.Prosser
A.J.Purves	D.Rose	A.Rump	A.Savitsky
R.H.See	-.Shadbolt	O.Sharman	L.S.Spooner
R.Spurgeon(Ilford)	E.Starr	D.Summers	D.Sweetman
F.B.Terry	P.Thomas	J.R.Thorogood	-.Walker
W.Ward	A.J.Whitehead	H.Whitlock(Collier Row)	A.E.Wilkins
L.G.Wood	G.Wright		

DEPARTURES FROM THE CLUB SEASON 1947 – 48

The following players appear to have left the club during or by the end of the season. They may have been triallists and only played one or two games and then went elsewhere. New clubs are indicated where known.

W.Allan (retired), A.G.Allen, A.R.Bamber, W.Banks (Harold Wood), J.Barrett (West Ham United), H.W.Beaney (H.M.Forces), F.W.Benton (due to work), C.Bingham, N.J.Burton, R.Card (Upminster), G.Clark, A.W.Coleman, R.J.Cornwell (Leytonstone), G.Foss (Kingstonian), R.A.French, J.Golder, C.Goodchild, L.E.Goodchild, C.W.Guiver (Grays Athletic), H.W.Hails (Woodford Town), C.Holderman, N.C.Holloway, D.Kent (Ilford),-.Larson, K.W.Lawler (Hornchurch Wanderers), R.S.Lewis (Carshalton Athletic), J.Lunn (Barking), L.Mackenzie, A.J.Major (Bishop Auckland), A.Mizen, J.Moore (Upminster), J.Moran (Upminster), J.R.Mutter (Woodford Town), D.C.Oram, E.O'Sullivan (Ford Sports), W.Parkinson (Dagenham Cables), L.V.Parminter, J.Paviour (Leytonstone), J.T.Prior, A.Reinman, W.Rumney, A.Savitsky (Upminster), R.H.See, A.Stevens, D.Strickland, R.Tungate, J.Twynham (Brentwood & Warley), P.G.R.Wallace (Barking), H.Whitlock (Collier Row), F.C.Williams (Eastbourne United).

BROOKLANDS CLOSED BY ORDER OF THE FA

Romford were punished as a result of crowd trouble at their ground.
(as reported in the *Romford Times*, Wednesday 12th November 1947)

Romford FC plea to supporters:
Help to end hooliganism that closed our ground

A stern warning that hooligans will be vigorously dealt with and refused admittance to the ground was given on Monday night by Romford Football Club Management Committee who, on Friday, heard that the Football Association had closed their Brooklands ground for two weeks as a result of incidents after a Reserves match on September 27th when missiles were thrown at the referee by a few irresponsible youths.

The Football Club also calls on all Romford's many loyal supporters to act as unofficial stewards when they return to the game after the ban is lifted in a fortnight's time to prevent similar incidents in the future.

The FA's order to close the ground was the biggest blow the Romford Club has received since it re-formed in 1929, and was all the more upsetting since they had been complimented several times recently on the excellent ground arrangements and organisation, when big representative games had been staged.

SCAPEGOATS. There is little doubt that Romford have been made the scapegoats for several unruly incidents which have occurred at other soccer grounds in recent weeks. The FA have been perturbed about them, and warned all clubs on November 5th that serious steps would be taken against clubs which failed to prevent such incidents, and deplored the attitude taken by crowds who threw missiles at referees and other officials. It happened that at about the same time the Romford incident (which occurred some time before) came up for review, and the FA apparently decided to make an example of the club, after reading the referee's report and the reply given by the Romford committee. Nevertheless, the incident was not as serious as two earlier occurrences at other amateur grounds.

Sections of the Romford crowd at the game (between Romford Reserves and Wimbledon Reserves) were angered by the referee's action both before and during the game, when he twice tried to obtain the name of J. Moore, Romford's right back, and when he started to make his way to the dressing rooms he was the target for missiles, which he claimed included stones, laurel branches, and a turnip.

The FA Disciplinary Committee announced their decisions as follows:

That J. Moore (Romford FC) be suspended for seven days from Monday, November 10th.

That the Romford FC ground be closed for 14 days as from Monday, November 10th , and

That FA warning noticed be displayed at the Romford FC ground for one month from November 24th.

In connection with the order that the Romford FC ground should be closed, the FA announces that the club is not permitted to play any club within a six-miles radius during the period of suspension.

EFFECT OF THE BAN. First effect of the ban is that Saturday's game with Oxford City at Brooklands has been called off. The club will probably be away to Wimbledon on Saturday week.

The *Romford Times* report on the Romford Reserves v Wimbledon Reserves game, and the scenes which followed, stated: 'Proceedings prior to the kick-off were strange to Brooklands fans, as the referee assembled both teams in a circle and proceeded to address them.

'The first incident which seemed to rile the crowd was when a Romford player was spoken to by the referee for stopping the ball with his hands. The player seemed to resent this and was again spoken to by the referee. This was a signal for the crowd to bait the referee. As the game proceeded other incidents met with the crowd's disapproval, the climax coming just before the end, when a Romford man was adjudged to have handled and the referee spoke to the player, who was seen walking away with the referee apparently demanding his name.

'Confusion reigned for some moments as the referee, notebook in hand, tried to contact the player, who kept on walking away. Other Romford players seemed to get involved, and it was not clear whether the referee obtained the information he desired'.

The player involved in that incident was J. Moore, right-back, and it was his action during the match which caused the referee to report him, and the FA to suspend him for one week.

SPECTATORS TO BLAME. It was the action of the crowd at the end of the match, as distinct from the action of players on the field during the game, which brought the FA's closure order. Our report on the scenes at the end said: 'The referee was subject to booing and an attempt was made to pelt him with rubbish as he made his way to the dressing rooms. About 200 angry spectators then crowded round the dressing rooms entrance waiting for the referee to re-appear. Not until officials of the club had appealed to the crowd and pointed out that any further trouble might result in the ground being closed, did they disperse'.

CLUB STATEMENT. The statement issued by Romford FC on Monday night stated:

1/ the Romford Club is 100 per cent with the authorities in stamping out bad behaviour of certain sections of the crowds. In this connection, the club has been congratulated many times by officials of the FA, County Associations, Leagues, visiting clubs, etc, and in one case by Mr A. Ralston (secretary of the Isthmian League and member of the FA) has been put up as an example of efficiency in crowd control and general management.

2/ that the moment some irresponsible person or persons foolishly showed their uncontrolled animosity and threw missiles, however small, at the referee the case for the club was damned, and any action, such as reporting the referee thereafter, plus the fact that the game was lost, would have savoured too much of retaliation.

3/ the club look upon this censure as the gravest possible thing that could happen, coming, as it does, at a time when the playing strength is not what it would desire. Its main concern, however, is the feelings of the Isthmian League. Romford has always been proud of their association with their Isthmian friends, and has always gone out of its way to uphold the dignity of the game. It is their earnest hope, and indeed, they have the feeling that this most unfortunate incident will soon be forgotten in the ranks of senior amateur football, and here the Romford Club would like to thank the many clubs and supporters who have so kindly expressed themselves at this time.

The club must warn its following that any such unseemly behaviour will be prosecuted with the utmost vigour. It will insist that the rights of admission will be rigidly upheld, but before this eventuality it trusts that all loyal supporters of the club who have been deprived for 14 days of enjoying their sport will look upon themselves as unofficial stewards, and use every endeavour to ensure that such a happening cannot possibly occur again.

The Romford FC Management Committee minutes of 10th November refer to the incident:

Report following incident in reserve team game versus Wimbledon. Referee stated he was struck by a collection of missiles including stones, laurel branches and a turnip. He further claimed of verbal abuse from three adult spectators and being struck on three occasions. The Club in its defence stated that no evidence of any missile striking the referee was witnessed by players or team officials and in view of the fencing either side of the exit passage it was practically impossible for a person outside to reach the referee. It was agreed that verbal abuse did take place…..

Visitors from Hong Kong

Pages from the souvenir of the match at Brooklands between the Isthmian League XI and Sing Tao Sports Club, September 1947. The event was attended by Stanley Rous (later Sir Stanley), secretary of the Football Association   *Authors' collection*

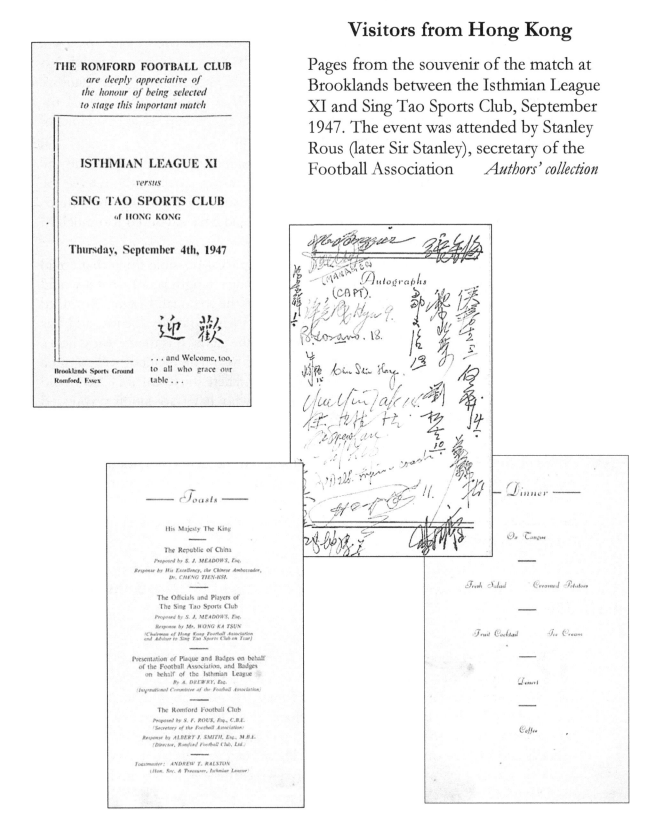

Post Season Summary   Season 1947 – 48

After the high of Romford winning the Essex Senior Cup the previous season, hopes were rising for a successful new campaign. The lads duly obliged and started with a fine 4-2 victory over Wycombe Wanderers at Brooklands on 30th August, followed by a 3-1 away win over old rivals Walthamstow Avenue. A disappointing 1-0 defeat by Leytonstone was a setback, but at last came success against Clapton with a 2-0 win at the Spotted Dog ground. There followed a 2-1 victory over Leyton on 15th September in the Thameside Trophy.

20th September saw the much looked-forward to FA Cup clash against old Athenian League rivals Barking at Brooklands. The friendship ended there, as before a crowd of over 6,000 Romford again disappointed and lost 3-1. Worse was to follow when, despite several team changes, Romford were defeated in three successive league games against Kingstonian, Wimbledon and Oxford City. Victories then followed against St. Albans City (1-0) and Woking (5-1), but the signs were not good as a number of new players made their debuts and the old rumours of discontent were again evident.

A home defeat by Walthamstow Avenue (0-1) on 1st November followed by an away loss at Wycombe Wanderers (0-4) continued to confuse the patient supporters. Two RAF men, Robertson and Hooker, had started to establish themselves in the first team and three successive victories were achieved, against St. Albans City, Clapton and Dulwich Hamlet. League defeats away to Woking (0-3) and at home to Leytonstone (2-3) followed, but nearly 5,000 spectators were at Brooklands on Christmas morning for a 1-0 victory over Ilford . This was followed by a 2-2 draw at Ilford on Boxing Day.

It was now Essex Senior Cup time again, and Romford were drawn at home to their bogey team Clapton in the first round on 3rd January. Nearly four and a half thousand loyal supporters attended. They were dismayed but not really surprised when the Spotted Dog team won 3-0. By this time the fans were expressing their disapproval of the poor performances in critical letters to the local press. The team should be strengthened, they demanded, and they wanted to know why the likes of Walthamstow Avenue, Leytonstone and Dulwich Hamlet could attract the top players while Romford could not. "Shamateurism" was rumoured to be rife in the game. Romford directors Martin Brazier and Bert Kittle, and old stalwarts Glyn Richards and Fred Collett were all really staunch Amateur men and not in favour of the much-mentioned "boot money."

10th January saw a welcome 5-2 victory over Oxford City, but this was followed by three devastating results. The first was in the Amateur Cup, when a trip to Hastings and St. Leonards brought no reward, just a four goals to one defeat. The players took this badly and followed up with a 7-1 reverse at Dulwich Hamlet before losing three two at Brooklands to lowly Corinthian Casuals on 31st January.

A home friendly against old Athenian League rivals Redhill secured a six nil victory and then away league wins at Wimbledon (1-0) and Corinthians Casuals (2-1) raised hopes of a revival. On 13th March over 4,000 were at Brooklands to see their team beaten 3-1 by Kingstonian, Romford missing Bill Bridge who was playing for an Isthmian League XI against the Royal Navy. A good crowd again turned up for the next game, a friendly against a fairly strong Arsenal "A" team which ended in a satisfactory 2-2 draw.

There was then a pleasant trip to Holland over Easter with matches against Sparta (Rotterdam) (2-5) and Schiedam (1-1). In the second game three penalties each were taken to decide the match. Each team scored once and a so second set of three was taken. Bridge and Barton scored for Romford, but Schiedam netted all three penalties to win the match.

A 5-1 victory away to Tufnell Park on 10th April in the Isthmian League followed by a 2-0 win over Barking in the Thameside Trophy promised an improvement. A friendly was then arranged at home to local rivals Brentwood and Warley, but once more Romford crashed, this time by two goals to one. A 5-4 win over a Tottenham Hotspur XI in a friendly on 24th April provided light entertainment for the Brooklands faithful four days prior to Boro taking on Grays Athletic in the Thameside Trophy final at Barking. Grays duly triumphed by five goals to one. A 4-1 victory over luckless Tufnell Park in the final game was little consolation for a very disappointing season. A clue to the reasons can be found in the list of player appearances where 42 names are listed!

This season a third team was formed to compete in the Romford & District League. Both the reserve and "A" teams did well considering the number of times last-minute team changes had to be made, and both finished around halfway in the league tables.

GLEANINGS FROM MANAGEMENT COMMITTEE MINUTE BOOKS
SEASON 1947-48

On **17th June 1947** Bill Seddon reported on the Isthmian League tour to Sweden, in which he was team manager and Boro men Bill Bridge and Fred Fryatt played.

On **10th September** we read that K.Lawler was sent off during an "A" Team match against Hornchurch Athletic, the first time this had occurred to a Romford player since the club's re-formation in 1929. He was "interviewed and informed of the seriousness of this matter".

SOUTHERN COUNTIES AMATEUR CHAMPIONSHIP FINAL
Played at Lynn Road, Ilford FC on 6th May 1950

The winners, Essex, pictured here with their County FA officials, included several Romford players:
Back: 8th left Wally Winsley, 10th left Fred Fryatt.
Front: 1st left Charlie (Pip) Pearson, 4th left Bill Mackenzie, extreme right Doug Langer.   *Authors' collection*

The Essex County FA Honours Badge, for 10 or more appearances for the county ((Cap and Badge previously awarded) was received by the following Romford players: G.W.Andrews, W.A.Bridge, H.W.Brooks, G.S.Burchall, W.F.Mackenzie, C.F.Pearson, G.J.Webb

THE DIRECTORS' ANNUAL REPORT, 1947/48

Comparing the Accounts now presented for the year ended 31st May last, with those of the previous year, it will be seen that financially the year has been a successful one, resulting in a gross profit of £866. While this figure is considerably less than the profit of £1,675 made in the previous year, the difference can largely be attributable to the misfortune and ill-luck attending the first XI in its early dismissal from various Cup competitions in which it was entered, resulting in the loss of important fixtures, and consequently revenue from gate money etc. Having regard to all the circumstances, the team is to be congratulated on finishing sixth in the Isthmian League. Except for the item "Gate income" which is approximately £900 less, all other items in the Accounts compare very favourably with the previous year – some items of expenditure are slightly increased, but this is accounted for by the Company in the year under review running a third team. The ground is rapidly becoming more popular in the Summer Months, and income from lettings is increased by approximately £120.

With regard to the profit shown, your Directors have utilised this in the Appropriation Account (after taking into account the profit balance brought forward from last year of £198) in making provision for Income Tax for 1948-49 of £400, leaving an available surplus of £664.

The Property and Equipment Account has increased to £12,758. This arises from further capital expenditure, in the carrying out of further terracing to the ground, and other improvements, and the purchase of a motor mower.

During the year the Directors were able to pay off the Bank Overdraft shown in the previous year's Accounts of £542, leaving only the Loan Account of £3,000 now owing to the Bank, and at 31st May last on Current No.1 Account, the Company had a credit balance of £540, the first occasion for many years.

Fresh Share Capital from the sale of 11,584 Shares at 2/6d amounting to the sum of £1,448 was received during the year. It will be observed that only 10,070 Shares representing approximately £1,260 remain to be issued, when the Company's Capital will be fully subscribed.

…[The Directors] …feel that they are justified and well able out of the available surplus shown on the Appropriation Account above mentioned to recommend the payment of a dividend on the whole of the Company's paid up share capital for the year ending 31st May 1948 of 5% less tax (which will account for approximately £437) leaving unappropriated sum of £227 to be carried forward to next year's Accounts.

With regard to the ground generally, as forecast in the Report for 1946/47 this year has seen the opening of the North Street entrance and further terracing completed. The Company are still in communication with the parties developing the land on the North side of the ground who are under covenant, among other things, to erect a wall or fence to the Company's property on that side, and a satisfactory conclusion is assured as soon as restrictions allow. Your Directors intend to complete the terracing to the South side immediately. Instructions for the work to be done having recently been given – subject to Licence. The erection of a first class stand is ever in the mind of your Directors, plans for which are ready, and this project will be dealt with as soon as it is considered that circumstances warrant and the materials and finance are available.

Your Directors are continually exploring other ways and means of popularising the ground during the Summer months, and it is the Policy of your Directors to encourage all forms of sport, and they will continue to give their support to any body or organisation who wish to carry on any recognised sport for which the ground is suitable. Some very enjoyable meetings and functions have already been held recently, including Cycling Championship Meeting, Amateur Boxing, Youth Organisation Rally, Fetes and Sports Meetings, and members are requested to publicise the amenities of the ground and its availability.

The Romford Supporters Catering Club is still proving most successful and a necessary amentity to players, officials and spectators at home matches, the tea huts being particularly well supported.....

The above report was presented at the AGM on 24th September, which was reported as follows in the *Essex Times*, Wednesday 29th September 1948:

Romford FC "HAVING A DIFFICULT TIME"

Only about 20 shareholders of Romford Football Club Ltd attended the company's annual meeting at Brooklands on Friday, when another five per cent dividend was declared. Attendance at last year's meeting was over 60. The directors' report (as we have already written) stated that the gross profit last year was £866, compared with £1,675 in 1946-47. The difference was largely due to the first XI's early dismissal from the cup competitions, and the consequent loss of 'gate' money. 'Gate' income was about £900 less, but the ground was used considerably more by other organisations during the summer months, and the increased income amounted to approximately £120.

Moving the adoption of the report, Mr Tom Macpherson MP, chairman, said he thought it provided a very fair resume of events of the past year. On the whole, the finance side of the company had been satisfactory.

MORE CAPITAL WANTED. An additional 11,584 shares had been issued, and only 10,070, representing approximately £1,260, remained before the authorised capital of £10,000 would be fully paid up. 'We can do with some more capital' said Mr Macpherson, and suggested that shareholders at present possessing odd numbers of shares might like to take out some more to 'round off' the totals they hold.

The chairman urged outside organisations to make full use of the ground during the summer months, and looked forward to the time when it would be fully occupied throughout football's close season.

TEAM'S "DIFFICULT PERIOD". About the team, Mr Macpherson said: 'Last season, and again this season, it is passing through a difficult period. It happens to the best of clubs when they lose their best players. It is one of the hardest things in the world to build up a team. You can't go and buy players in a shop. Romford had, however, the makings of a good side, and with patience and understanding would once again have a first class team which would win more laurels'.

.....Though the attendance was small, it was lively and inquisitive. Would the directors reconsider the cost of the car park, it was asked. Present price was 1s.

instead 6d was suggested by a member who thought that spectators stayed away rather than pay 1s parking fee for a matter of two hours.

Mr M. Brazier, replying, said the directors went into the matter thoroughly before fixing the charge. It was costing 30s per week to make the park worthy of the name, and time had to be spent on it in summer, keeping down weeds. Average attendance was 60-70 cars, he said. Mr Brazier promised that the directors would discuss the matter again, and also the question of providing cycle stands.

WHY BLACK? Another questioner wanted to know why Romford had to wear black stockings (he suggested mustard colour), and why players could not be numbered. Mr A.J. Smith said it was impossible to get Romford's blue and gold socks. They had tried everywhere to get something suitable, but had to be content at present with black.

Most members were not content with the directors' reply to the numbering question. It was that the Isthmian League Council had agreed that numbering should not be adopted as a rule by its clubs, and therefore Romford's players would not be numbered. It was pointed out that Leytonstone and Woking were numbering their players, and if Romford did also the other clubs would probably fall in line. Mr Kittle said that Romford had nothing to gain by numbering their players, and had decided not to do so until the League's decision on the matter was unanimous.

WHY "ALL PAY". Mr D.H. Clarke, treasurer of the Supporters' Club, said there was a lot of dissatisfaction over the "all pay at friendly matches" attitude of the club. He thought that members' season tickets should admit them to friendly matches besides all home league games. If the club played badly in cup competitions and had to resort to friendly fixtures they owed it to their supporters to allow them to attend fill-up matches without extra cost.

The directors replied that all friendly games now were arranged on Cup tie terms, which meant a 50-50 division of gate money. The visiting club are also paid half the value of stand seats, and would therefore lose if season ticket holders were admitted free.

It was admitted that season ticket holders were 60 down this season. Mr Clarke said the sole reason for this was the "all pay" question....

Romford's trip to Holland, Easter 1948

This memorable visit was recounted in the *Romford Recorder*, 2nd April 1948

Romford FC stay where Germans plotted
Some aspects of the country and its people

Boys play football on the waste ground that was once the thriving centre of Rotterdam. To the visitor arriving at the roofless station it would appear that the city is one without a heart – but that is only physically accurate.

In the midst of this area, stricken by a German air raid in May 1940 when 35,000 people lost their lives, stands the Hotel Central. When the country was overrun this hotel, deprived of all its glass and half its 100 rooms, became the local headquarters for high-ranking German officers. No-one could enter without a pass. Since, however, the proprietor, a Mr Phillippson, was a true patriot this did not prove too great a handicap to the Dutch underground movement, and .a flow of valuable information came into the hands of the allies. This was not achieved without cost. Outside the hotel still stands one of many white crosses marking the spot where some Dutchmen fell – taken out and shot for espionage activities. Some were stood up against the wall of the hotel. Twice Mrs Phillippson, the proprietor's wife, was threatened with a revolver, but escaped.

Now the scene has changed. Comfortably appointed and with excellent service, the hotel is now the meeting place of men of commerce from all over the world, and the trading firms which used to be its neighbours have now been accommodated in small but attractive single-storey shops elsewhere.

The task of rebuilding Rotterdam is a long and tedious one for though labour is plentiful, materials are not only scarce but expensive.

This then was the destination of the players, officials and friends of the Romford Football Club when they left Romford on Thursday evening.

While we waited at Romford Station a train chugged in on the opposite platform and stopped to disgorge some of Romford's City workers homeward bound. Among them was Harold Brooks, Romford's outside-right, in service kit and replete with cardboard box, the sign of a man just demobilized. A word of greeting, and our train was in and we were on our way.

More meetings followed at Liverpool Street before we boarded the Hook Continental and found our co-travellers to be the Maidenhead Hockey Club. No fewer than 150 sporting organisations, we learned, were spending Easter on the Continent.

At Harwich, we found ourselves at the rear of the queue for the customs, but the advantage of having a policeman in our midst in Reg Ivey, the goalkeeper, soon became apparent. Reg spotted one of his friends in blue, and after a word with him we were shepherded to the front. Once through the dock and at the quayside the diesel ship, Queen Emma, used as a troop carrier in the war, was waiting, a fine vessel luxuriously refitted.

.......A PRACTICAL JOKE. Two officials of our hosts, the Sparta Club, met us at the Hook, and they were augmented by several more at Rotterdam. With the introductions and greetings completed, the party sat down to coffee – a blend of chicory, ground roasted barley and perhaps a little of the real stuff.....Then one of our leading officials (Mr A.J. Smith) had a shock. Called to the telephone, he was informed, in an assumed Dutch accent, that a member of the party had evaded customs duty on some sports equipment. Duty had been paid on two new cricket bats, and our official was worried, until he learned the identity of the caller. It was Mr F.E. Partridge, a well-known Romfordian, who came over on the same boat as ourselves....

...SPARTA'S IMPOSING STADIUM. The players were up early on Sunday for a spell of light training, while the officials visited the local zoo where the chief attraction was a parrot plumed in Romford's colours of blue and gold.

Sightseeing during the trip to Holland, March 1948   *Authors' collection*

Then came the chief purpose of the tour – to participate with three Dutch clubs in Sparta's diamond jubilee festival for which they had put up a cup for competition. Romford did not bring the cup home, but the details of the two games they played will be found elsewhere.

…The climax of the tour came on Monday when at the conclusion of the football tournament at the Sparta Stadium the players, officials and lady friends, altogether numbering over 100, were entertained at a reception. The function was a great social success with the Romford contingent well to the fore with their community singing, which not only earned applause from the Dutch, but encouraged them to join in as well. A five-course dinner, beautifully served, took over three hours to complete with speeches between the courses.

The visitors were welcomed by Mr Salters, president of the Sparta Club, who in the part of his speech that was in English expressed his club's pleasure at being able to entertain Romford again. The Dutch way of life, he said, was very similar to that of the English, but they did not see enough of them. The English usually reserved their visits for when there was a war on!

The chairman of the Romford Football Club committee, Mr A.J. Smith, in reply, said that it was the third time he had had the pleasure of addressing the members of the Sparta club. "We in England have a very great regard for our friends in this country. I have been privileged to visit most countries on the continent, but there is nowhere I know where an Englishman receives such a marvellous welcome as he does in Holland, and we thank you for the grand time you have given us" he said.

……Mr Smith then presented to the Sparta Club a mahogany box with the Romford FC badge superimposed on the lid which bore the inscription "The key of friendship, Easter 1948". The box contained a key, the top of which unscrewed to reveal a scroll which was signed by all the players and officials. Romford also presented Sparta with two footballs.

Mr Salters then led three cheers for the Romford players and the Sparta players lustily "For they are jolly good fellows" in English, which was indeed a fine tribute. Romford returned the compliment.

When the distribution of awards was made, Mr W. Bridge, as captain of the Romford team, received a handsome plaque suitably inscribed, and all the players received medals.

The reception might well have been the end of a busy and exciting day, but the party was then taken to Parksicht a small and select club very similar to those in London, and the evening concluded with dancing.....

ROMFORD SPEEDWAY: AN INTRODUCTION

Back in 1938 Romford had a speedway team carrying its name. It raced not at Romford but at the Dagenham Speedway track in Ripple Road, near Chequers Lane, adjacent to the greyhound stadium. The team were known as the Romford Rommers and competed in the Sunday Amateur Dirt Track League against Dagenham, Eastbourne, Smallford and Rye House. The competition was blighted by withdrawals and late entries. Romford Rommers didn't enjoy much success and were at the bottom of the league. Research has unearthed just one victory, a shock win over Eastbourne, who were eventually declared League champions. There were two fatalities at the track in 1938, causing it to close on 12th August. It reopened on 9th October after a management reshuffle, by which time it seems both Romford and Dagenham had withdrawn from the league.

The Romford Rommers Amateur Dirt Track League results were as follows:

May 1st 1938	Dagenham 44 - 39 Romford
May 8th	Smallford 51 - 30 Romford
May 15th	Romford 40 - 42 Smallford
May 22nd	Dagenham 56 - 26 Romford
June 5th	Romford 46 - 33 Eastbourne
July 24th	Romford 26 - 56 Rye House
July 31st	Romford 40 - 43 Dagenham

The Romford Rommers record

Known matches	Won	Lost	Points for	Points against	League points	League position
7	1	6	247	325	2	5

In the immediate post-war years, the attendances for speedway meetings were competing with football in the popularity stakes and the directors of Romford Football Club saw an opportunity of bringing the masses following the sport through the Brooklands turnstiles. We can track the progress of their ultimately fruitless attempts in the local press.

SPEEDWAY FOR ROMFORD? New move for Brooklands
(as reported in the *Romford Recorder*, Friday 28 November 1947)

Efforts are to be renewed to secure speedway racing at the Romford Football Club ground at Brooklands. The £10 10s licence fee to the Speedway Control Board has already been paid and the promoter, Mrs Arthur Atkinson, wife of the former rider and director of West Ham Speedway, will request the Romford Football Club Ltd to approach the Romford Council on her behalf for the necessary permission. A similar application last March was rejected by the Council as the site is in an area predominantly developed for residential purposes.

Mrs Atkinson who, if she succeeds, will become the first woman speedway promoter in London, told the *Recorder* that now the basic petrol has been stopped people want their amusement nearer at hand, and she is renewing her application because of the considerable demand for speedway. Regularly, she said, 16 coach loads of speedway fans leave Romford for West Ham. Brooklands is ideally suited and will not require a great deal of preparation.

Mrs Atkinson said she understood that her previous application had been refused on the grounds of noise but she did not think it was more noisy than a football match. She was quite prepared to hold afternoon meetings once a week, probably on a Thursday, when noise would not be such a predominant factor.

FOOTBALL CLUB SUPPORT. The secretary of Romford FC, Mr Martin Brazier, said that Mrs Atkinson had not yet communicated with him but he thought the Football Club would welcome the suggestion and be prepared to let the ground to a speedway company for, say, one meeting per week. No-one would be allowed to practice there. It was a clean, healthy and exciting sport for onlookers, and the rent received by the Romford FC Ltd would be spent on improving ground amenities.

'The promoters seem determined to open a track somewhere in Romford, wherever it is. If they are turned down this time, I would not be surprised if they do not call a town's meeting to prove that Romford wants a speedway', he concluded.

R.A. OPPOSE SPEEDWAY BY ONE VOTE
Residents' apathy to meeting
Poor response to circular
(as reported in the *Romford Recorder*, Friday 9th January 1948)

A pamphlet circulated to 500 people residing in the vicinity of the Romford Football Club ground at Brooklands asking whether they were concerned about the proposed speedway racing there, only drew a sparse attendance in a meeting organised by the Town Ward branch of the Romford Ratepayers and Residents Association at the Spiritualist Hall on Tuesday. Of the 13 residents of the Town Ward who voted, seven objected to speedway coming to Romford and six were in favour.....

Mr A.E. Kittle, a director of Romford FC Ltd., who attended with Mr H.W. Muskett, secretary of the Company and the promoters of the proposed speedway, said he felt sorry for Mr Poel if the arguments he was asked to put before the Council were based on the votes of the 13 people. Neither the Football Club's representatives nor the promoters took part in the voting.

Two residents of Brooklands Road, Messrs Gover and H.T. Pardon, raised objections to the scheme on account of the noise that would result, and the fact that the ground was in a residential area. Mr Pardon said there were other disadvantages such as the untidy condition of the roads after the crowds had departed, and he thought the promoters should build a stadium elsewhere. On behalf of local residents, he had written to the Council and had received a courteous reply that first consideration would be given to them.

Other residents, however, spoke in favour. Mrs Tring, mother of a two years-old son, of Medora Road, said she thought Romford should be more go-ahead than to attempt to prevent sports becoming more popular. Romford needed speedway and other forms of entertainment. Another speaker said he would prefer children to attend speedway rather than amusement halls, while Mr Joyce, of Como Street, said it was the cleanest sport in the country.

Mr Muskett said that last April the Council decided that speedway would be detrimental to the neighbourhood, but since then the promoters had approached the Council again. The Football Club had no arrangement, agreement or financial interest in the promotion of speedway at present. It had been advised, however, that the ground, of which it was hoped to make a first-class arena, was eminently suitable for the project.

Mr L.W. Bristo, together interested with Mrs Arthur Atkinson in promoting speedway at Romford, said that 3,000 people went from Romford to West Ham, and they had even travelled as far as Wembley for a meeting. The sport would not attract the crowds it did if it was noisy and dirty. At Romford, he said, it would only be run once a week, probably on a Saturday from seven to nine, and there would be no practice there.

Mr H. ('Tiger') Stevenson said that in two hours, 20 events could be staged, each taking about one minute 20 seconds. The machines had a means of silencing, and were very little noisier than the motor cycles on the road.

The season began at Easter, and had to end by the end of October. No betting was allowed, and it was a sport that attracted all ages and classes.

Cigarette card portraying 'Tiger' Stevenson, issued by John Player & Sons about 1939   *Authors' collection*

The *Romford Times* cartoonist's view of the Residents' Association meeting which rejected speedway at Brooklands by one vote

Mr Kittle said that they saw in speedway, providing everything was in order, a chance to obtain a stadium fit for Romford. At present the stand held only 280 people. When the North Street entrance was completed, he believed that the use of the side roads to the ground would be reduced by half.

SPEEDWAY PLAN REJECTED
199 families voice protest
(as reported in the *Romford Recorder*, Friday 19th March 1948)

Accepting a recommendation of its Town Planning Committee, Romford Council on Wednesday refused the application to allow motorcycle speedway racing at Brooklands football ground.

Main reasons for the refusal were that the football ground was in an area predominantly residential, and the racing would be detrimental to the amenities of the neighbourhood; the noise of the speedway would cause annoyance, particularly to aged persons and invalids in the vicinity; and the site was unsuitable having regard to the large volume of additional traffic using the streets to and from the ground, thus adding to the risk of accidents to children in the neighbourhood.

Most of the points were contained in a petition signed by 393 members of 199 families living in roads around the ground requesting the Council not to grant the application, and the Town Planning Committee reporting on the discussion of the proposal, pointed out that it had met the promoters of the speedway as well as directors of the Football Club, and had considered reports from local authorities which had speedway in their areas.

THE ROMFORD FOOTBALL CLUB LIMITED

Full Members of The Football Association
Full Members of Isthmian Football League
Affiliated to Essex County Football Association

Chairman: T.Macpherson MP
Directors: Messrs M.A.Brazier, A.E.Kittle, W.G.Mann, R.Scott,
A.J.Smith MBE, S.G.Tansley
Company Secretary: Mr.H.W.Muskett

Registered Offices: 110, Hyland Way, Romford

Ground: Brooklands Sports Ground, Romford

Club Officials & Committees:
President: T.Macpherson MP   **Chairman:** Mr.A.J.Smith MBE
Hon.Gen.Secretary: Mr.M.A.Brazier   **Hon.Asst.Secretary:** Mr.J.Gurney
Hon.Press Secretary: Mr.H.A.Hughes (Appointed 6th July)
Hon.Advt.Secretary: Mr.H.A.Wright

Selection Committee: Mr.F.H.Adams, Mr.P.Banks, also Mr.F.Betts (w.e.f. 23rd Nov.)

Trainer/Coach: Mr.W.C.(Bill)Seddon   **Assistant Trainer:** Mr.E.Hewitt
Reserve Team Player Coach: Mr.G.W.Patterson
Reserve Team Trainer: Mr.A.Adlam

"A" Team Trainer: Mr.E.Crooks   **Groundsman:** Mr.W.C.(Bill)Seddon

Bankers: Lloyds Bank Limited   **Auditors:** Mr. Iion V. Cummings

LEAGUES & COMPETITIONS 1948 – 49

FA Challenge Cup
FA Amateur Challenge Cup
Isthmian Football League
Essex County FA Senior Challenge Cup
Essex Thameside Challenge Competition

Isthmian Football League Reserve Section
Essex Thameside Challenge Competition Reserve Section
Carter Charity Cup

Romford & District Football League Premier Division
Romford & District Football League Cup
Essex Junior Cup
Romford Charity Cup
Carter Charity Cup

Admission Prices Season 1948 – 49

	First Team			Reserve Team		
	Adults	OAPs	Child	Adults	OAPs	Child
Ground	9d		5d	5d		3d
Ground & Enclosure	1/6		10d	10d		6d
Grandstand	2/3					

Car Park

All Cars   1/-   Coaches   2/6   Motor Cycles 6d*
* Reduced to 3d w.e.f. 23rd October

Season Tickets

Grandstand	£1.10.0	OAPs & Children	£1.10.0
Ground & Enclosure	£1.1.0	"	12/6
Ground only	12/6	"	7/6

Final Public Trial

Sat.,14th Aug.,1948   **Trial Match**
PROBABLES (2)5   POSSIBLES (1)2
Clarke(2),Abbott(2),Jennings   Barrett,Clarke
Attendance: 1,919   Receipts: £39.0.3
Total Receipts donated to the Essex County Football Association Benevolent Fund.

Teams as follows – second half changes in brackets.
Probables: R.Ivey;G.Foss,C.D.Tubb(R.G.Sheldon);W.F.Mackenzie,D.Kent(V.Roeder),F.E.Fryatt;
E.G.Goodchild,N.W.Abbott(J.Barrett),R.Clarke(N.W.Abbott),V.Roeder(G.W.Jennings),G.W.Patterson.

Possibles: J.Martin;R.G.Sheldon(C.D.Tubb),C.W.Guiver;G.A.Critten,E.Glover,A.E.Belsham;
H.E.Brooks,J.Barrett(W.A.Bridge),W.A.Bridge(R.Clarke),W.B.Regan(V.S.Brown),D.A.Langer.

Trial match: Probables:
? , ? ,Gordon Foss, Reg Ivey, Fred Fryatt, Ron Sheldon
? , ? , George Patterson, George Jennings, Bill Mackenzie   *Authors' collection*

Trial match: Possibles:
Vic Brown, ? , Bill Regan, Joe Martin, ? , Charlie Guiver
Doug. Langer, Harold Brooks, Bill Bridge, ? , Alf Belsham, ? . *Authors' collection*

Note: The eight missing names in the two pictures are from N.W.Abbott, Jim Barrett, R.Clarke, G.A.Critten, E.Glover, E.G.Goodchild, Doug.Kent, V.Roeder and Charlie Tubb

First Team Match Details

28 Aug IFL   Away   Wycombe Wanderers   2 – 1   Jennings,Brooks
Romford: R.Ivey;A.E.Collier,R.G.Sheldon;W.F.Mackenzie,J.T.Hall,F.E.Fryatt(Capt);
H.W.Brooks,W.A.Bridge,R.Clarke,G.W.Jennings,D.A.Langer.

1 Sept ETT1R Away   Leytonstone   0 – 3
Attendance: 4,000
Romford: R.Ivey(Capt);G.A.Critten,R.G.Sheldon;W.F.Mackenzie,J.T.Hall,C.D.Tubb;
H.W.Brooks,W.A.Bridge,V.S.Brown,G.W.Jennings,D.A.Langer.

4 Sept FACEP Home   Ford Sports   5 – 0   Brown(3)Brooks,Langer
Attendance: 3,997   Receipts: £171.16.6   Programmes: £   Car Park: £2.18.0
Romford: R.Ivey;A.E.Collier,R.G.Sheldon;W.F.Mackenzie,J.T.Hall,F.E.Fryatt(Capt);
H.W.Brooks,W.A.Bridge,V.S.Brown,G.W.Jennings,D.A.Langer.

9 Sept Frdly   Home   Sparta (Rotterdam)   1 – 3   Van Gorkon(og)
Attendance: 3,017   Receipts: £126.4.6   Programmes: £   Car Park: £3.11.0
Romford: R.Ivey;A.E.Collier,R.G.Sheldon;W.F.Mackenzie,J.T.Hall,F.E.Fryatt(Capt);
H.W.Brooks,W.A.Bridge,D.H.Billinghurst,V.S.Brown,D.A.Langer.

11 Sept IFL   Home   Woking   4 – 6   Bridge,Brown,Patterson(2)(1pen)
Attendance: 3,753   Receipts: £145.0.0.   Programmes: £   Car Park: £3.0.0
Romford: R.Ivey;A.E.Collier,R.G.Sheldon;W.F.Mackenzie,J.T.Hall,F.E.Fryatt(Capt);
H.W.Brooks,W.A.Bridge,V.S.Brown,G.W.Patterson,D.A.Langer.

18 Sept FACPR Home   Grays Athletic   3 – 0   Bridge,Brooks,Jennings
Attendance: 5,758   Receipts: £251.1.5   Programmes: £   Car Park: £4.8.0
Romford: R.Ivey;A.E.Collier,R.G.Sheldon;W.F.Mackenzie,J.T.Hall,F.E.Fryatt(Capt);
H.W.Brooks,W.A.Bridge,V.S.Brown,G.W.Jennings,G.W.Patterson.

25 Sept IFL   Away   Dulwich Hamlet   2 – 1   Bridge,Patterson(pen)
Romford: R.Ivey;A.E.Collier,R.G.Sheldon;W.F.Mackenzie,J.T.Hall,F.E.Fryatt(Capt);
H.W.Brooks,W.A.Bridge,V.S.Brown,G.W.Patterson,D.A.Langer.

2 Oct   FAC1Q   Away#   Upminster   2 – 1   Brown,Jennings
Attendance: 7,088   Receipts: £301.4.0   Programmes: £   Car Park: £7.11.3
Romford: R.Ivey;A.E.Collier,R.G.Sheldon;W.F.Mackenzie,J.T.Hall,F.E.Fryatt(Capt);
H.W.Brooks,W.A.Bridge,V.S.Brown,G.W.Jennings,G.W.Patterson.

9 Oct   IFL   Home   Wycombe Wanderers   4 – 1   Newman,Brooks,Bridge,Brown
Attendance: 3,752   Receipts: £143.11.6   Programmes: £   Car Park: £4.10.9
Romford: R.Ivey;A.E.Collier,R.G.Sheldon;W.F.Mackenzie,J.T.Hall,F.E.Fryatt(Capt);
H.W.Brooks,G.W.Jennings,C.F.Newman,W.A.Bridge,V.S.Brown.

16 Oct FAC2Q   Home   Brentwood & Warley   3 – 1   Bridge,Newman,Jennings
Attendance: 9,560   Attendance: £397.7.0   Programmes: £   Car Park: £10.2.3
Romford: R.Ivey;A.E.Collier,R.G.Sheldon;W.F.Mackenzie,J.Barton,F.E.Fryatt(Capt);
H.W.Brooks,G.W.Jennings,C.F.Newman,W.A.Bridge,G.W.Patterson.

23 Oct IFL   Away   Clapton   3 – 1   Brooks,Newman(2)
Romford: R.Ivey;A.E.Collier,R.G.Sheldon;W.F.Mackenzie,J.Barton,F.E.Fryatt(Capt);
H.W.Brooks,G.W.Jennings,C.F.Newman,W.A.Bridge,G.W.Patterson.

30 Oct FAC3Q   Home   Barking   3 – 2   Jennings,Brooks,Patterson
Attendance: 9,283   Receipts: £389.12.11 Programmes: £   Car Park: £ ??
Romford: R.Ivey;A.E.Collier,R.G.Sheldon;W.F.Mackenzie,J.T.Hall,F.E.Fryatt(Capt);
H.W.Brooks,G.W.Jennings,C.F.Newman,W.A.Bridge,G.W.Patterson.

6 Nov   IFL   Away   Kingstonian   2 – 1   Mackenzie,Brooks
Romford: R.Ivey;J.Barton,R.G.Sheldon;W.F.Mackenzie,J.T.Hall,F.E.Fryatt(Capt);
H.W.Brooks,G.W.Jennings,C.W.Newman,W.A.Bridge,W.B.Regan.

13 Nov FAC4Q   Home   Gillingham   2 – 1* Newman,Brooks
Attendance: 13,308   Receipts: £726.10.6   Programmes: £   Car Park: £10.12.0
Romford: R.Ivey;A.E.Collier,R.G.Sheldon;W.F.Mackenzie,J.T.Hall,F.E.Fryatt(Capt);
H.W.Brooks,G.W.Jennings,C.W.Newman,W.A.Bridge,G.W.Patterson.

20 Nov AC4Q   Away   Grays Athletic   1 – 0* Jennings
Attendance: 9,000   Receipts: £370.9.0   Romford Share: £175.1.8
Romford: R.Ivey;A.E.Collier,R.G.Sheldon;W.F.Mackenzie,J.T.Hall,F.E.Fryatt(Capt);
H.W.Brooks,G.W.Jennings,C.W.Newman,W.A.Bridge,G.W.Patterson.

27 Nov FAC1R   Away   Yeovil Town   0 – 4
Attendance:
Romford: R.Ivey;A.E.Collier,R.G.Sheldon;W.F.Mackenzie,J.T.Hall,F.E.Fryatt(Capt);
H.W.Brooks,G.W.Jennings,J.Barton,W.A.Bridge,G.W.Patterson.

4 Dec   IFL   Home   Oxford City   2 – 0   Bridge(2)
Attendance: 2,925   Receipts: £108.5.4   Programmes: £   Car Park: £4.12.0
Romford: R.Ivey;A.E.Collier,R.G.Sheldon;W.F.Mackenzie,J.T.Hall,F.E.Fryatt(Capt);
H.W.Brooks,G.W.Jennings,W.A.Bridge,G.W.Patterson,G.G.Howlett.

11 Dec Frdly   Home   Charlton Athletic XI   0 – 2
Attendance: 2,912   Receipts: £122.8.5   Programmes: £   Car Park: £3.11.3
Romford: R.Ivey;A.E.Collier,R.G.Sheldon;W.F.Mackenzie,J.T.Hall,F.E.Fryatt(Capt);
H.W.Brooks,G.W.Jennings,W.A.Bridge,G.W.Patterson,A.Anderson.

18 Dec IFL   Away   Corinthian Casuals   4 – 0   Brooks,Newman,Patterson,Jennings
Romford: R.Ivey;A.E.Collier,R.G.Sheldon;G.Fleetwood,J.T.Hall,F.E.Fryatt(Capt);
H.W.Brooks,W.A.Bridge,C.W.Newman,G.W.Jennings,G.W.Patterson.

25 Dec IFL   Home   Ilford   1 – 1   Bridge
Attendance: 4,382   Receipts: £176.5.5   Programmes: £   Car Park: £8.6.0
Romford: R.Ivey;A.E.Collier,G.Fleetwood;W.F.Mackenzie,J.T.Hall,F.E.Fryatt(Capt);
H.W.Brooks,W.A.Bridge,V.S.Brown,G.W.Jennings,G.W.Patterson.

27 Dec IFL   Away   Ilford   1 – 3   Jennings(pen)
Attendance: 6,000
Romford: R.Ivey;A.E.Collier,G.Fleetwood;W.F.Mackenzie,J.T.Hall,F.E.Fryatt(Capt);
H.W.Brooks,G.W.Jennings,V.S.Brown,W.A.Bridge,G.G.Howlett.

1 Jan   IFL   Away   Oxford City   1 – 4   Bridge
Romford: R.Ivey;A.E.Collier,J.Barton;W.F.Mackenzie,J.T.Hall,F.E.Fryatt(Capt);
H.W.Brooks,G.Fleetwood,C.W.Newman,W.A.Bridge,G.W.Jennings.

8 Jan   ESC1R   Home   Brightlingsea United   4 – 0   Jennings,Patterson,Bridge,Brooks
Attendance: 4,004   Receipts: £173.18.2   Programmes: £   Car Park: £3.7.9
Romford: R.Ivey;A.E.Collier,J.Barton;W.F.Mackenzie,J.T.Hall,F.E.Fryatt(Capt);
H.W.Brooks,W.G.Mann,W.A.Bridge,G.W.Jennings,G.W.Patterson.

15 Jan AC1R Away Hitchin Town 4 – 2 Brooks(2)Bridge(2)
Attendance: 4,260   Receipts: £240.10.3   Romford Share: £115.19.4
Romford: R.Ivey;A.E.Collier,J.Barton;W.F.Mackenzie,J.T.Hall,F.E.Fryatt(Capt);
H.W.Brooks,W.G.Mann,W.A.Bridge,G.W.Jennings,G.W.Patterson.

22 Jan IFL Home Walthamstow Avenue 1 – 2 Brooks
Attendance: 4,388   Receipts: £170.4.8   Programmes: £   Car Park: £5.15.9
Romford: R.Ivey;A.E.Collier,J.Barton;W.F.Mackenzie,J.T.Hall,F.E.Fryatt(Capt);
H.W.Brooks,W.G.Mann,W.A.Bridge,G.W.Jennings,G.W.Patterson.

29 Jan AC2R Home Briggs Sports 1 – 0 Jennings
Attendance: 6,912   Receipts: £304.13.3   Programmes: £   Car Park: £4.14.3
Romford: R.Ivey;A.E.Collier(Capt),J.Barton;W.F.Mackenzie,J.T.Hall,W.B.Regan;
H.W.Brooks,W.G.Mann,W.A.Bridge,G.W.Jennings,G.W.Patterson.

5 Feb IFL Home Kingstonian 2 – 3 Maddick,Patterson(pen)
Attendance: 3,380   Receipts: £127.4.1   Programmes: £   Car Park: £4.15.6
Romford: R.Ivey;A.E.Collier,J.Barton;W.F.Mackenzie,J.T.Hall,F.E.Fryatt(Capt);
H.W.Brooks,A.J.Maddick,W.A.Bridge,G.W.Jennings,G.W.Patterson.

12 Feb AC3R Home Moor Green 5 – 1 Patterson,Maddick(2)Jennings,Brooks
Attendance: 7,649   Receipts: £332.12.0   Programmes: £   Car Park: £7.16.3
Romford: R.Ivey;A.E.Collier,J.Barton;W.F.Mackenzie,J.T.Hall,F.E.Fryatt(Capt);
H.W.Brooks,A.J.Maddick,W.A.Bridge,G.W.Jennings,G.W.Patterson.

19 Feb IFL Away St. Albans City 0 – 4
Romford: R.Ivey;A.E.Collier,J.Barton;W.F.Mackenzie,A.E.Belsham,F.E.Fryatt(Capt);
H.W.Brooks,A.J.Maddick,G.W.Jennings,W.G.Mann,G.W.Patterson.

26 Feb AC4R Away Billingham Synthonia A.F.C. 2 – 1 Brooks,Jennings
Romford: R.Ivey;A.E.Collier,F.E.Fryatt(Capt);W.F.Mackenzie,J.Barton,W.B.Regan;
H.W.Brooks,A.J.Maddick,W.A.Bridge,G.W.Jennings,G.W.Patterson.

5 Mar IFL Home Clapton 3 – 1 Howlett,Brooks,Jennings
Attendance: 3,052   Receipts: £113.8.0   Programmes: £   Car Park: £3.12.6
Romford: R.Ivey;A.E.Collier(Capt),C.D.Tubb;W.F.Mackenzie,J.Barton,A.E.Belsham;
H.W.Brooks,G.Fleetwood,C.W.Newman,G.W.Jennings,G.G.Howlett.

12 Mar ESC2R Home Leytonstone 1 – 2 Patterson
Attendance: 12,322   Receipts: £523.13.1   Programmes: £   Car Park: £11.7.0
Romford: R.Ivey;A.E.Collier,J.Barton;W.F.Mackenzie,J.T.Hall,F.E.Fryatt(Capt);
H.W.Brooks,A.J.Maddick,C.W.Newman,G.W.Jennings,G.W.Patterson.

19 Mar ACSF S'land Crook Colliery Welfare 2 – 2* Patterson(pen)Bridge
Attendance: 24,215   Receipts: £2,443.0.0   Romford Share: £1,351.14.9
Romford: R.Ivey;A.E.Collier,J.Barton;W.F.Mackenzie,J.T.Hall,F.E.Fryatt(Capt);
H.W.Brooks,A.J.Maddick,W.A.Bridge,G.W.Jennings,G.W.Patterson.

26 Mar ACRp W.Ham Crook Colliery Welfare 3 – 0 Bridge,Maddick(2)
Attendance: 25,284   Receipts: £2,810.0.0   Romford Share: £657.3.7
Romford: R.Ivey;A.E.Collier,F.E.Fryatt(Capt);W.F.Mackenzie,J.Barton,W.B.Regan;
H.W.Brooks,A.J.Maddick,W.A.Bridge,G.W.Jennings,G.W.Patterson.

2 Apr IFL Away Woking 1 – 3 Jennings
Romford: R.Ivey;A.E.Collier,F.E.Fryatt(Capt);W.F.Mackenzie,J.Barton,W.B.Regan;
H.W.Brooks,A.J.Maddick,W.A.Bridge,G.W.Jennings,G.W.Patterson.

7 Apr IFL Home Tufnell Park 3 – 2 Jennings(2)Brooks
Attendance: 2,128   Receipts: £74.19.4   Programmes: £   Car Park: £2.7.9
Romford: J.Martin;A.E.Collier,F.E.Fryatt(Capt);W.F.Mackenzie,J.Barton,W.B.Regan;
H.W.Brooks,A.J.Maddick,W.A.Bridge,G.W.Jennings,G.W.Patterson.

9 Apr IFL Home St. Albans City 2 – 1 Maddick,Brooks
Attendance: 3,117   Receipts: £118.0.7   Programmes: £   Car Park: £3.12.6
Romford: R.Ivey;A.E.Collier,A.E.Belsham;W.F.Mackenzie,F.E.Fryatt(Capt),W.B.Regan;
H.W.Brooks,A.J.Maddick,W.A.Bridge,G.W.Jennings,G.W.Patterson.

13 Apr IFL Away Wimbledon 0 – 6
Romford: R.Ivey;W.F.Mackenzie,C.D.Tubb;A.Boreham,F.E.Fryatt(Capt),G.W.Jennings;
H.W.Brooks,W.A.Bridge,C.W.Newman,A.J.Maddick,G.W.Patterson.

15 Apr IFL Away# Tufnell Park 3 – 3 Bridge,Belsham,Maddick
Attendance: 3,542   Receipts: £154.6.10   Programmes: £   Car Park: £3.16.3
Romford: J.Martin;A.E.Collier,F.E.Fryatt(Capt);A.Boreham,J.Barton,W.B.Regan;
H.W.Brooks,A.J.Maddick,W.A.Bridge,A.E.Belsham,V.McDonald.

16 Apr IFL Away Walthamstow Avenue 3 – 2 Brooks,Bridge,Jennings
Romford: R.Ivey;A.E.Collier,F.E.Fryatt(Capt);W.F.Mackenzie,J.Barton,W.B.Regan;
H.W.Brooks,A.J.Maddick,W.A.Bridge,G.Jennings,G.W.Patterson.

23 Apr ACF W'bley Bromley 0 – 1
Attendance: 94,206 Nett Receipts: £17,759.17.11 Romford Share: £4,671.8.11
Romford: R.Ivey;A.E.Collier,F.E.Fryatt(Capt);W.F.Mackenzie,J.Barton,W.B.Regan;
H.W.Brooks,A.J.Maddick,W.A.Bridge,G.W.Jennings,G.W.Patterson.

25 Apr IFL Home Wimbledon 0 – 1
Attendance: 3,534 Receipts: £131.17.2 Programmes: £ Car Park: £3.12.6
Romford: R.Ivey;A.E.Collier,F.E.Fryatt(Capt);W.F.Mackenzie,J.Barton,W.B.Regan;
H.W.Brooks,W.A.Bridge,C.W.Newman,A.J.Maddick,G.W.Patterson.

28 Apr IFL Home Leytonstone 2 – 3 Brooks,Jennings
Attendance: 4,857 Receipts: £180.2.7 Programmes: £ Car Park: £5.15.6
Romford: R.Ivey;A.E.Collier,F.E.Fryatt(Capt);W.F.Mackenzie,J.Barton,A.E.Belsham;
H.W.Brooks,G.Fleetwood,W.A.Bridge,G.W.Jennings,G.W.Patterson.

30 Apr IFL Home Dulwich Hamlet 1 – 1 Fleetwood
Attendance: 3,875 Receipts: £152.19.6 Programmes: £ Car Park: £3.11.9
Romford: R.Ivey;A.E.Collier,F.E.Fryatt(Capt);A.E.Belsham,J.Barton,W.B.Regan;
H.W.Brooks,G.Fleetwood,C.W.Newman,G.W.Jennings,W.A.Bridge.

2 May IFL Away Leytonstone 0 – 2
Romford: R.Ivey;A.E.Belsham,F.E.Fryatt(Capt);A.Boreham,J.Barton,W.B.Regan;
W.A.Bridge,H.W.Brooks,C.W.Newman,A.J.Maddick,G.W.Jennings.

7 May IFL Home Corinthian Casuals 0 – 1
Attendance: 2,376 Receipts: £84.8.11 Programmes: £ Car Park: £2.8.3
Romford: R.Ivey;C.D.Tubb,A.E.Belsham;A.Boreham,J.Barton,W.B.Regan;
G.W.Jennings,G.Fleetwood,S.Frankland,A.J.Maddick,G.W.Patterson(Capt).

* After Extra Time.
\# Played at Brooklands.

FIRST TEAM CUP RESULTS

FA Challenge Cup
Final: Wolverhampton Wanderers 3 Leicester City 1

Romford's progress:	Extra Prel.	Home	Ford Sports	5 – 0
	Prel.	Home	Grays Athletic	3 – 0
	1st Qual.	Home	Upminster	2 – 1
	2nd Qual.	Home	Brentwood & Warley	3 – 1
	3rd Qual.	Home	Barking	3 – 2
	4th Qual.	Home	Gillingham	2 – 1
	1st Round	Away	Yeovil Town	0 – 4

FA Amateur Challenge Cup
Final: Bromley 1 Romford 0
(at Wembley Stadium)

Romford's progress:	Qual.?	Away	Grays Athletic	1 – 0
	1st Round	Away	Hitchin Town	4 – 2
	2nd Round	Home	Briggs Sports	1 – 0
	3rd Round	Home	Moor Green	5 – 1
	4th Round	Away	Billingham Syn. Rec.	2 – 1
	Semi-Final	Sunderland	Crook Col. Welf.	2 – 2*
	Replay	West Ham	Crook Col. Welf.	3 – 0
	Final	Wembley	Bromley	0 – 1

Essex County FA Senior Cup
Final: Leytonstone 3 Leyton 0

Romford's progress:	1st Round	Home	Brightlingsea Utd.	4 – 0
	2nd Round	Home	Leytonstone	1 – 2

Essex ThamesideChallenge Competition
Final:

Romford's progress: 1st Round   Away   Leytonstone   0 – 3

*   After Extra Time

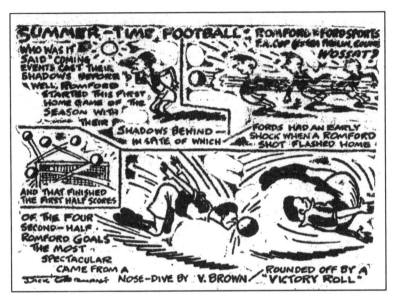

Romford's hat trick hero Vic "Bomber" Brown performs his victory roll during the 5-0 win over Ford Sports in the FA Cup extra-preliminary round   the *Romford Times*

FIRST TEAM SUMMARY OF RESULTS 1948 – 49

	P	Home			Goals		Away			Goals		Pts
		W	D	L	For	Ag	W	D	L	For	Ag	
Isthmian League	26	5	2	6	25	23	6	1	6	22	31	25
FA Challenge Cup	7	6	0	0	18	5	0	0	1	0	4	
FA Amateur Cup	8	2	0	0	6	1	4	1	1	12	6	
Essex Senior Cup	2	1	0	1	5	2	0	0	0	0	0	
Thameside Trophy	1	0	0	0	0	0	0	0	1	0	3	
Friendlies	2	0	0	2	1	5	0	0	0	0	0	
Totals	46	14	2	9	55	36	10	2	9	34	44	

Isthmian Football League
Final Table

	P	W	D	L	Goals		Pts
					For	Ag	
Dulwich Hamlet	26	15	6	5	60	31	36
Walthamstow Ave.	26	16	4	6	65	38	36
Wimbledon	26	15	4	7	64	41	34
Ilford	26	14	3	9	56	36	31
Oxford City	26	13	5	8	48	34	31
Leytonstone	26	12	6	8	49	41	30
Woking	26	14	1	11	64	59	29
Romford	**26**	**11**	**3**	**12**	**47**	**54**	**25**
Kingstonian	26	10	4	12	43	47	24
Corinthian Casuals	26	11	2	13	47	59	24
Wycombe Wanderers	26	11	2	13	49	61	24
St. Albans City	26	6	6	14	40	60	16**
Clapton	26	5	5	16	32	61	15
Tufnell Park	26	1	5	20	28	70	7

**   Two points deducted for breach of rule.

FIRST TEAM DEBUTS 1948 – 49

1948

				Previous Club
28th Aug.	v Wycombe Wand'rs.	-	**E.V.Clarke**	Edgware Town
		-	**G.W.Jennings**	St.Albans City
		-	**R.G.Sheldon**	Ilford
1st Sept.	v Leytonstone	-	**G.A.Critten**	Reserves
9th Sept.	v Sparta	-	**D.H.Billinghurst** Ilford
9th Oct.	v Wycombe Wand'rs.	-	**C.W.Newman**	Barking
11th Dec.	v Charlton Ath. XI	-	**A.Anderson**	n/k

1949

8th Jan.	v Brightlingsea Utd.	-	**W.G.Mann**	Woodford Town
5th Feb.	v Kingstonian	-	**A.J.Maddick**	Aveley
13th Apr.	v Wimbledon	-	**A.Boreham**	Pitsea United
15th Apr.	v Tufnell Park	-	**V.McDonald**	n/k
7th May	v Corinthian Casuals	-	**S.Frankland**	n/k

FIRST TEAM APPEARANCES SEASON 1948 - 49

	A	B	C	D	E	F	Totals
A.Anderson	0	0	0	0	0	1	1
Jack Barton	16	2	7	2	0	0	27
Alf Belsham	8	0	0	0	0	0	8
D.H.Billinghurst	0	0	0	0	0	1	1
Tony Boreham	4	0	0	0	0	0	4
Bill Bridge	23	7	8	1	1	2	42
Harold Brooks	25	7	8	2	1	2	45
Vic Brown	5	3	0	0	1	1	10
E.V.Clarke	1	0	0	0	0	0	1
Albert Collier	22	7	8	2	0	2	41
G.A.Critten	0	0	0	0	1	0	1
Gordon Fleetwood	8	0	0	0	0	0	8
Stan Frankland	1	0	0	0	0	0	1
Fred Fryatt	24	7	7	2	0	2	42
John Hall	12	6	5	2	1	2	28
Gerry Howlett	3	0	0	0	0	0	3
Reg Ivey	24	7	8	2	1	2	44
George Jennings	22	7	8	2	1	1	41
Doug Langer	3	1	0	0	1	1	6
Tony Maddick	11	0	5	1	0	0	17
Bill Mackenzie	21	7	8	2	1	2	41
W.G.Mann	2	0	2	1	0	0	5
Joe Martin	2	0	0	0	0	0	2
V.McDonald	1	0	0	0	0	0	1
Chuck Newman	10	3	1	1	0	0	15
George Patterson	17	6	8	2	0	1	34
Bill Regan	10	0	4	0	0	0	14
Ron Sheldon	8	7	1	0	1	2	19
Charlie Tubb	3	0	0	0	1	0	4
Totals	286	77	88	22	11	22	506

Key to competitions

A	Isthmian Football League
B	F.A. Challenge Cup Competition
C	F.A. Amateur Challenge Cup Competition
D	Essex County F.A. Senior Cup Competition
E	Essex Thameside Challenge Competition
F	Friendlies

These apply to both the Appearances and Goal Scorers tables.

FIRST TEAM GOALSCORERS SEASON 1948 - 49

	A	B	C	D	E	Total
Harold Brooks	11	4	4	1	0	20
George Jennings	9	4	4	1	0	18
Bill Bridge	9	2	4	1	0	16
George Patterson	5	1	2	2	0	10
Tony Maddick	3	0	4	0	0	7
Vic Brown	2	4	0	0	0	6
Charlie (Chuck) Newman	4	2	0	0	0	6
Doug Langer	0	1	0	0	0	1
Bill Mackenzie	1	0	0	0	0	1
Gerry Howlett	1	0	0	0	0	1
Alf Belsham	1	0	0	0	0	1
Gordon Fleetwood	1	0	0	0	0	1
Van Gorkon (own goal)	0	0	0	0	1	1
Totals	47	18	18	5	1	89

Romford versus Leytonstone in the Essex Senior Cup Saturday 12th March 1949

Back: Bill Bridge, Albert Collier, John Hall, Reg Ivey, Jack Barton, George Patterson
Front: Harold Brooks, Tony Maddick, Bill Mackenzie, Fred Fryatt(Capt), George Jennings, Charlie Newman   *Authors' collection*

Reserve Team Match Details

21 Aug Frdly Away Briggs Sports 1 – 1 Clarke
Romford Res.: R.Ivey;A.E.Belsham,R.Sheldon;W.Mackenzie,J.Hall,C.W.Guiver;
E.G.Goodchild,V.Roeder,E.V.Clarke,G.Jennings,G.W.Patterson.

28 Aug IFLR Home Wycombe Wanderers Res. 8 – 4 Brown(3)Goodchild(3)Patterson(2)
Attendance: 1,311 Receipts: £25.9.0 Programmes: £ Car Park: £ None
Romford Res.: J.Martin;C.D.Tubb,C.W.Guiver;G.A.Critten,-.Glover,A.E.Belsham(Capt);
E.G.Goodchild,V.Roeder,V.S.Brown,G.W.Patterson,G.G.Howlett.

6 Sept ETT1R Away Leytonstone Res. 0 – 2
Romford Res.: J.Martin;G.A.Critten,C.D.Tubb;H.Cooper,J.Barton,V.Roeder;
E.G.Goodchild,E.V.Clarke,V.S.Brown,G.W.Patterson,G.G.Howlett.

11 Sept IFLR Away Wycombe Wanderers Res. 2 – 1 Clark(2)
Romford Res.: J.Martin;G.A.Critten,C.D.Tubb;L.G.Wood,J.Barton,N.W.Abbott;
E.G.Goodchild,V.Roeder,R.Clark,H.Cooper,G.G.Howlett.

25 Sept IFLR Home Dulwich Hamlet Res. 3 – 1 Newman(3)
Attendance: 1,287   Receipts: £23.6.2   Programmes: £   Car Park: £0.11.0
Romford "A": J.Martin;C.D.Tubb,A.E.Belsham(Capt);L.G.Wood,J.Barton,W.B.Regan;
E.G.Goodchild,H.Cooper,C.W.Newman,N.W.Abbott,G.G.Howlett.

2 Oct Frdly Away Hoddesden Town 3 – 0 Newman(2)Goodchild
Romford Res.: J.Martin;C.D.Tubb,A.E.Belsham(Capt);   ?   ,J.Barton,W.B.Regan;
E.G.Goodchild,V.Roeder,C.W.Newman,   ?   ,G.G.Howlett.

9 Oct IFLR Away Oxford City Res. 0 – 2
Romford Res.:
Team details unknown

23 Oct IFLR Home Corinthian Casuals Res. 2 – 0 Goodchild,Cooper
Attendance: 1,150   Receipts: £20.14.11   Programmes: £   Car Park: £0.6.6
Romford Res.: J.Martin;E.W.Archer,A.E.Belsham(Capt);W.B.Regan,C.D.Tubb,G.Fleetwood;
E.G.Goodchild,G.Baugh,V.S.Brown,H.Cooper,V.McDonald.

30 Oct IFLR Away Woking Res. 1 – 3 Scorer unknown
Romford Res.:
Team details unknown

6 Nov CCC1R Home J.Smith's Sports Club 5 – 2 Peacock,Cooper,Brown(3)
Attendance: 1,017   Receipts: £24.19.6   Programmes: £   Car Park: £0.18.3
Romford Res.: J.Martin;G.Fleetwood,A.E.Belsham(Capt);L.G.Wood,C.D.Tubb,N.W.Abbott;
E.G.Goodchild,H.Cooper,R.Marjoram,V.S.Brown,-.Peacock.

13 Nov IFLR Away St. Albans City Res. 1 – 3 Roeder
Romford Res.: J.Martin;   ?   ,   ?   ;L.G.Wood,C.D.Tubb,A.E.Belsham(Capt);
V.Roeder ? ? ? ?

20 Nov IFLR Home Tufnell Park Res. 1 – 1 Howlett
Attendance: 529   Receipts: £7.17.6   Programmes: £   Car Park: £0.4.3
Romford Res.: J.Martin;G.Fleetwood,A.E.Belsham(Capt);   ?   ,C.D.Tubb,   ?   ;
   ?   ,   ?   ,   ?   ,   ?   ,G.G.Howlett.

27 Nov IFLR Home St. Albans City Res. 0 – 1##
Attendance: 474   Receipts: £6.5.8   Programmes: £   Car Park: £0.4.9
Romford Res.: J.Martin;G.Fleetwood,E.Archer;G.L.Wood,C.D.Tubb,A.E.Belsham(Capt);
E.Goodchild,W.G.Mann,H.Cooper,N.Abbott,G.G.Howlett.

11 Dec IFLR Away Tufnell Park Res. 2 – 1 Wood(2)
Romford Res.: J.Martin;   ?   ,   ?   ;   ?   ,J.Barton,   ?   ;
   ?   ,L.G.Wood,S.Watkins,   ?   ,G.G.Howlett.

18 Dec IFLR Home Leytonstone Res. 1 – 0 Abbott
Attendance: 563   Receipts: £9.8.0   Programmes: £   Car Park: £0.8.9
Romford Res.: J.Martin;C.D.Tubb,A.E.Belsham(Capt);L.G.Wood,J.Barton,W.B.Regan;
E.G.Goodchild,W.G.Mann,V.S.Brown,N.W.Abbott,G.G.Howlett.

1 Jan IFLR Home Woking Res. 1 – 1 Mann
Attendance: 406   Receipts: £8.5.11   Programmes: £   Car Park: £0.4.6
Romford Res.: J.Martin;E.W.Archer,A.E.Belsham;A.Boreham,C.D.Tubb,W.B.Regan;
E.G.Goodchild,A.Anderson,W.G.Mann,A.Jones,E.V.Clarke.

15 Jan IFLR Home Wimbledon Res. 1 – 5 Maddick
Attendance: 329   Receipts: £5.16.0   Programmes: £   Car Park: £0.5.9
Romford Res.: J.Martin;E.Archer,A.E.Belsham;A.Boreham,C.D.Tubb,   ?   ;
G.G.Howlett,A.J.Maddick,   ?   ,L.Turner,W.B.Regan.

22 Jan IFLR Away Kingstonian Res. 2 – 0 Maddick,McDonald
Romford Res.: J.Martin;G.Fleetwood,A.E.Belsham;   ?   ,C.D.Tubb,   ?   ;
R.Marjoram,A.J.Maddick,A.Jones,V.McDonald,G.G.Howlett.

29 Jan IFLR Away Leytonstone Res. 1 – 3 A.Jones
Romford Res.: J.Martin;G.Fleetwood,A.E.Belsham;A.Boreham,C.D.Tubb,   ?   ;
A.Jones,A.J.Maddick,R.Marjoram,B.Thornton,G.G.Howlett.

12 Feb IFLR Away Dulwich Hamlet Res. 3 – 3 Howlett,Thornton,Regan
Romford Res.: J.Martin;   ?   ,R.G.Sheldon;   ?   ,C.D.Tubb,W.B.Regan;
   ?   ,   ?   ,B.Thornton,   ?   ,G.G.Howlett.

19 Feb IFLR   Home   Ilford Res.   1 – 1   Thornton
Attendance: 1,142   Receipts: £21.10.9   Programmes: £   Car Park: £0.10.0
Romford Res.: J.Martin;E.D.Hope,G.Fleetwood;D.Kent,C.D.Tubb,W.B.Regan;
    ?   ,C.Skinner,B.Thornton,   ?   ,   ?   .

26 Feb IFLR   Home   Walthamstow Avenue Res.   2 – 4   Brown,Skinner
Attendance: 1,385   Receipts: £30.12.2   Programmes: £   Car Park: £1.1.0
Romford Res.: J.Martin;D.Kent,A.E.Belsham;C.D.Tubb,   ?   ,   ?   ;
A.Jones,C.Skinner,B.Thornton,   ?   ,V.S.Brown.

12 Mar IFLR   Away   Clapton Res.   2 – 2   Fleetwood,one other
Romford Res.: **Sel. Team:** J.Martin;D.Kent,A.E.Belsham;A.Boreham,R.Haverson,W.B.Regan;
A.Jones,G.Fleetwood,R.Gadsden,B.Thornton,D.Sammons.

19 Mar IFLR   Home   Kingstonian Res.   3 – 0   Howlett,Brown(2)
Attendance: 1,282   Receipts: £23.6.5   Programmes: £   Car Park: £0.17.9
Romford Res.: J.Martin?;   ?   ,   ?   ;   ?   ,R.Haverson,   ?   ;
G.G.Howlett,   ?   ,   ?   ,   ?   ,V.S.Brown.

26 Mar IFLR   Home   Oxford City Res.   3 – 0   Jones,Thornton,Fleetwood
Attendance: 361   Receipts: £3.13.3   Programmes: £   Car Park: £None
Romford Res.: J.Martin;C.D.Tubb,A.E.Belsham(Capt);A.Boreham,E.W.Archer,V.H.Perriman;
A.Jones,G.Fleetwood,C.W.Newman,B.Thornton,V.McDonald.

2 Apr IFLR   Away   Walthamstow Avenue Res.   1 – 4   Jones
Romford Res.: J.Martin;C.D.Tubb,   ?   ;A.Boreham,   ?   ,   ?   ;
A.Jones,   ?   ,C.W.Newman,   ?   ,   ?   .

9 Apr IFLR   Away   Wimbledon Res.   1 – 1   Howlett
Romford Res.:
Team details unknown

16 Apr IFLR   Away   Ilford Res.   4 – 1   Newman(3)Brown
Romford Res.: D.Sweetman;C.D.Tubb,   ?   ;V.H.Perriman,   ?   ,   ?   ;
A.Jones,   ?   ,C.W.Newman,   ?   ,V.S.Brown.

21 Apr IFLR   Home   Corinthian Casuals Res.   4 – 2   Newman(3)Jones
Attendance: 165   Receipts: £2.8.7   Programmes: £   Car Park: £0.0.6
Romford Res.:   ?   ;G.Fleetwood,   ?   ;   A.Boreham,   ?   ,   ?   ;
A.Jones,   ?   ,C.W.Newman,   ?   ,   ?   .

n/k IFLR   Home   Clapton Res.   n/k
Attendance:
Romford Res.:
Team details unknown

5 May IFLR   Home   St. Albans City Res.   n/k
Attendance: 237   Receipts: £3.5.9
Romford Res.:
Team details unknown

Note: The Reserves last two league games: one was won and one lost, total goals for three, against three.

St. Albans City Reserves arrived late and it was agreed to play thirty minutes each half, but the game was abandoned after forty minutes due to fog.

RESERVE TEAM SUMMARY OF RESULTS SEASON 1948 – 49

		Home			Goals		Away			Goals		
	P	W	D	L	For	Ag	W	D	L	For	Ag	Pts
Isthmian League Res.Sect.	26	8	3	2	33	22	4	3	6	20	24	30
Essex Thameside Ch. C. Res.	1	0	0	0	0	0	0	0	1	0	2	
Carter Charity Cup	1	1	0	0	5	2	0	0	0	0	0	
Friendly	2	0	0	0	0	0	1	1	0	4	1	
Totals	30	9	3	2	38	24	5	4	7	24	27	

Note: The above summary does not include the home game against St. Albans City which was abandoned with the score one nil in St. Albans' favour.

Note: The "A" Team took over the fixtures in the Carter Cup from the second round, going on to lose in the semi-final.

Isthmian Football League Reserve Section
Final Table

	P	W	D	L	Goals For	Ag	Pts
Dulwich Hamlet	26	16	6	4	77	39	38
St.Albans City	26	16	4	6	61	33	36
Leytonstone	26	15	5	6	58	31	35
Wimbledon	26	14	6	6	74	45	34
Walthamstow Avenue	26	14	3	9	79	44	31
Romford Res.	**26**	**12**	**6**	**8**	**53**	**46**	**30**
Woking	26	12	5	9	68	49	25*
Kingstonian	26	10	1	15	51	74	21
Corinthian Casuals	26	9	3	14	43	82	21
Ilford	26	6	7	13	53	65	19
Oxford City	26	8	3	15	52	65	19
Wycombe Wanderers	26	9	1	16	63	90	19
Clapton	26	6	5	15	28	54	17
Tufnell Park	26	5	5	16	29	72	15

* Were four points deducted for breach of rules?

RESERVE TEAM CUP RESULTS SEASON 1948 – 49

Essex Thameside Challenge Competition Reserve Section
Final: n/k

Romford's progress: 1st Round   Away   Leytonstone Res.   0 – 2

Carter Charity Cup
Final: Sun Athletic   2   Fairlop   1

Romford's progress: 1st Round   Home   J.Smith's Sports Club   5 – 2
2nd Round   See "A" Team results

RESERVE TEAM APPEARANCES SEASON 1948 – 49

The following players are known to have appeared in the reserve team during the season.

N.W.Abbott(Redhill)	A.Anderson	E.W.Archer	J.Barton
G.Baugh	A.E.Belsham	A.Boreham(Pitsea Utd)	V.S.Brown
E.V.Clarke(Edgware Town)	H.Cooper	G.A.Critten	G.Fleetwood
R.Gadsden(Ford Sports)	-.Glover(Briggs Sports)	E.G.Goodchild	C.W.Guiver
R.Haverson(Chelsea)	E.D.Hope	G.G.Howlett	A.Jones
D.Kent	A.J.Maddick(Aveley)	W.G.Mann(Woodford Tn)	R.Marjoram
J.Martin	V.McDonald	C.W.Newman	G.W.Patterson
-.Peacock	V.H.Perriman	W.B.Regan	V.Roeder
D.Sammons	R.G.Sheldon(Ilford)	C.Skinner(Upminster)	D.Sweetman
B.Thornton(Upminster)	C.D.Tubb	L.Turner	S.Watkins
L.G.Wood			

"A" Team Match Details

25 Aug RDLP   Home   Heath United#   5 – 0   Norris(3)O.Martin,Drake
Romford "A": J.F.Dray;W.Ward,J.F.Sippitt;E.D.Hope,M.E.L.Braham,E.W.Archer;
V.H.Perriman,R.Norris,W.J.Drake,E.V.Clarke,O.Martin.

28 Aug Frdly   Away   Clapton "A"   0 – 1
Romford "A": J.F.Dray;E.W.Archer,L.S.Spooner;V.H.Perriman,M.E.L.Braham,B.C.Acampora;
E.D.Hope,W.J.Drake,R.Norris,E.V.Clarke,A.J.Whitehead.

1 Sept RDLP Home Beacontree Heath Old Boys 3 – 3 Norris,Drake,Acampora
Romford "A": J.F.Dray;W.Ward,L.S.Spooner;V.H.Perriman,M.E.L.Braham,H.Archer;
D.Rose,E.V.Clarke,R.Norris,W.J.Drake,B.Acampora.

4 Sept Frdly Home Old Romfordians 2 – 2 Whitehead,Marjoram
Romford "A": J.F.Dray;E.D.Hope,L.S.Spooner; G.R.Schooling,M.E.L.Braham,V.H.Perriman;
W.J.Drake,R.Norris,R.Marjoram,B.Acampora,A.J.Whitehead.

6 Sept RDLP Home Romford Brewery 0 – 3
Romford "A": J.F.Dray;W.Ward,L.S.Spooner,E.D.Hope,L.G.Wood,W.Banks;
E.V.Clarke,R.Norris,V.McDonald,B.Acampora,A.J.Whitehead.

18 Sept RDLP Away Orsett United 1 – 1 E.W.Archer(pen)
Romford "A": J.F.Dray;E.W.Archer,L.S.Spooner;V.H.Perriman,H.Archer,B.Acampora;
W.J.Drake,R.Norris,V.McDonald,-.Byatt,O.Martin.

25 Sept Frdly Home Carter Sports 5 – 0 Norris,Acampora,Marjoram(3)
Romford "A": D.Sweetman;E.W.Archer,L.S.Spooner;V.H.Perriman,J.Smith,H.Archer;
-.Collins,R.Norris,R.Marjoram,V.McDonald,B.Acampora.

2 Oct RDLP Away Clesco 4 – 2 McDonald,Perriman,Norris,Marjoram
Romford "A": D.Sweetman;E.W.Archer,L.S.Spooner;E.D.Hope,H.Archer,V.H.Perriman;
W.J.Drake,R.Norris,R.Marjoram,V.McDonald,B.Acampora.

9 Oct EJC1R Away Dagenham Naval 7 – 0 McDonald(2)Acampora(3)Norris(2)
Romford "A": D.Sweetman;E.W.Archer,L.S.Spooner;V.H.Perriman,J.Smith,H.Archer;
O.Martin,R.Norris,R.Marjoram,V.McDonald,B.Acampora.

16 Oct RDLP Away Hornchurch Athletic 2 – 3 Marjoram(2)
Romford "A": D.Sweetman;E.W.Archer,L.S.Spooner;E.D.Hope,V.H.Perriman,H.Archer;
W.J.Drake,R.Norris,R.Marjoram,V.McDonald,B.Acampora.

23 Oct RDLP Away Laindon 1 – 8 Marjoram
Romford "A": D.Sweetman;E.D.Hope,-.Kelly;V.H.Perriman,L.G.Wood,B.Acampora;
R.Marjoram,R.Norris,E.V.Clarke,H.Archer,-.Peacock.

30 Oct RLC1R Away Romford Brewery 1 – 2 Clarke
Romford "A": D.Sweetman;E.D.Hope,L.S.Spooner;V.H.Perriman,H.Archer,B.Acampora;
R.Marjoram,R.Norris,E.V.Clarke,V.McDonald,-.Peacock.

6 Nov EJC2R Home#1Collier Row Athletic 4 – 5* Norris(3)Martin
Romford "A": D.Sweetman;E.W.Archer,L.S.Spooner;E.D.Hope,H.Archer,V.H.Perriman;
O.Martin,R.Norris,E.V.Clarke,V.McDonald,B.Acampora.

13 Nov RDLP Away Billericay Town 3 – 3 Marjoram(2)Acampora
Romford "A": D.Sweetman;E.D.Hope,A.Watts;W.G.Mann,J.Smith,-.Murray;
O.Martin,V.H.Perriman,R.Marjoram,B.Acampora. (ten men due to reserve team calls).

20 Nov RDLP Home#2Orsett United 1 – 1 Perriman
Romford "A": D.Sweetman;E.D.Hope,-.Ashby;W.G.Mann,J.Smith,H.Archer;
E.V.Clarke,V.H.Perriman,R.Marjoram,V.McDonald,-.Murray.

27 Nov CCC2R Away Frenford United 3 – 1** Marjoram(2)Norris
Romford "A": D.Sweetman;E.D.Hope, ? ; ? J.Smith,H.Archer;
R.Marjoram,R.Norris,S.Watkins, ? , ? .

4 Dec RDLP Away Elm Park 3 – 1 Watkins,McDonald,Hope
Romford "A": D.Sweetman;E.D.Hope,L.S.Spooner;V.H.Perriman,J.Smith,E.W.Archer;
R.Marjoram,R.Norris,S.Watkins,V.McDonald,H.Archer.

11 Dec RDLP Away Upminster Old Boys 1 – 1 Marjoram
Romford "A": D.Sweetman;E.D.Hope,L.S.Spooner;V.H.Perriman,J.Smith,H.Archer;
R.Marjoram,R.Norris,V.McDonald,V.Roeder,O.Martin.

18 Dec Frdly Away Havering 2 – 2 Marjoram,Watkins
Romford "A": D.Sweetman;E.D.Hope,L.S.Spooner;-.Watson,V.H.Perriman,J.Deas;
-.Evans,R.Marjoram,S.Watkins,V.McDonald,S.Parker.

25 Dec RDLP Away Romford Brewery 3 – 0 Norris(2)Sweetman
Romford "A": J.Martin;E.D.Hope,L.S.Spooner;V.H.Perriman,E.W.Archer,H.Archer;
R.Marjoram,R.Norris,L.G.Wood,V.McDonald,D.Sweetman.

27 Dec RCC2R Home#3Dagenham Cables 3 – 6* McDonald,Goodchild,Norris
Attendance: 148   Receipts: £4.8.7
Romford "A": D.Sweetman;E.D.Hope,L.S.Spooner;V.H.Perriman,E.W.Archer,H.Archer;
E.G.Goodchild,R.Norris,C.D.Tubb,V.McDonald,A.E.Belsham.

8 Jan RLDP Away South Essex Waterworks## 4 – 2 Marjoram(2)Clarke,Perriman
Romford "A": D.Sweetman;E.D.Hope,L.S.Spooner;V.H.Perriman,E.W.Archer,H.Archer;
R.Marjoram,D.Whitear,A.Lauder,V.McDonald,E.V.Clarke.

15 Jan RLDP Home#4Clesco 1 – 1 Whitear
Romford "A": D.Sweetman;E.D.Hope,L.S.Spooner;V.H.Perriman,R.Haverson,H.Archer;
R.Marjoram,D.Whitear,A.Lauder,V.McDonald,-.Dunham.

22 Jan RDLP Home#6Elm Park 1 – 0 Clarke
Romford "A": D.Sweetman,E.D.Hope,A.J.Whitehead;V.H.Perriman,R.Haverson,H.Archer;
-.Edwards,D.Whitear,E.V.Clarke,-.Walker,S.Parker.

29 Jan RDLP Away Beacontree Heath Old Boys 2 – 3 Parker,Perriman(pen)
Romford "A": D.Sweetman;E.D.Hope,E.W.Archer;-.Walker,V.H.Perriman,H.Archer;
S.Frankland,D.Whitear,E.V.Clarke,V.McDonald,S.Parker.

5 Feb RDLP Away Stifford 1 – 3 Thornton
Romford "A": D.Sweetman;E.D.Hope,E.W.Archer;-.Walker,V.H.Perriman,H.Archer;
S.Frankland,B.Thornton,E.V.Clarke,R.Parker,S.Parker

19 Feb RDLP Away Rainham Town "A" 2 – 2 McDonald,Marjoram
Romford "A": R.Watson;E.W.Archer,L.S.Spooner;V.H.Perriman,R.Haverson,H.Archer;
R.Marjoram,D.Whitear,-.Loman,V.McDonald,B.Futter.

26 Feb CCCRp Away Frenford United 2 – 0 McDonald,Marjoram
Romford "A": D.Sweetman;E.D.Hope,L.S.Spooner;V.H.Perriman,R.Haverson,H.Archer;
R.Marjoram,D.Whitear,E.V.Clarke,V.McDonald,B.Futter.

5 Mar RDLP Home Upminster Old Boys 2 – 5 Whitear,Frankland
Romford "A": R.Watson;E.D.Hope,L.S.Spooner;E.W.Archer,R.Haverson,V.H.Perriman;
S.Frankland,D.Whitear,E.V.Clarke,R.Parker,B.Futter.

12 Mar RDLP Home Billericay Town 2 – 2
Romford "A": D.Sweetman;E.D.Hope,L.S.Spooner;V.H.Perriman,E.W.Archer,H.Archer;
S.Frankland,R.Parker,R.Marjoram,V.McDonald,B.Futter.

19 Mar Frdly Away Chadwell Heath 1 – 0 Marjoram
Romford "A": D.Sweetman;E.D.Hope,H.Rayment;D.Whitear,E.W.Archer,H.Archer;
E.V.Clarke,S.Frankland,R.Marjoram,V.McDonald,B.Futter.

2 Apr CCC3R Away Chigwell 1 – 0 Mann
Romford "A": D.Sweetman;E.D.Hope,H.Rayment;E.W.Archer,R.Haverson,H.Archer;
S.Frankland,W.G.Mann,R.Marjoram,V.McDonald,-.Graham.

9 Apr RDLP Home Hornchurch Athletic 2 – 2 Frankland,Marjoram
Romford "A": D.Sweetman;E.D.Hope,-.Lambert;D.Whitear,E.W.Archer,H.Archer;
-.Walker,S.Frankland,R.Marjoram,V.McDonald,B.Futter.

15 Apr RDLP Home#7Rainham Town "A" 0 – 1
Romford "A": D.Sweetman;E.D.Hope,H.Rayment;E.W.Archer,R.Haverson,V.H.Perriman;
R.Marjoram,S.Frankland,E.V.Clarke,-.Walker,B.Futter.

18 Apr RDLP Away Roneo Athletic 10 – 1 Frankland(2)McDonald(2)Marjoram(2)
Jones(2)H.Archer,Perriman
Romford "A": D.Sweetman;L.S.Spooner,H.Rayment;V.H.Perriman,R.Haverson,H.Archer;
E.F.Jones,S.Frankland,R.Marjoram,V.McDonald,E.V.Clarke.

20 Apr RDLP Home#1Stifford Athletic 2 – 2 Mann,Parker
Attendance: 219 Receipts: £3.5.3
Romford "A": D.Sweetman;E.D.Hope,H.Rayment;D.Whitear,E.W.Archer,H.Archer;
R.Parker,L.S.Spooner,W.G.Mann,V.McDonald,B.Futter.

27 Apr CCCSF Home Fairlop 0 – 0*
Attendance: 212 Receipts: £3.11.2
Romford "A": D.Sweetman;E.D.Hope,H.Rayment;E.W.Archer,R.Haverson,H.Archer;
E.F.Jones,D.Whitear,R.Marjoram,V.H.Perriman,-.Graham.

30 Apr CCCRp Away Fairlop 0 – 2
Romford "A": D.Sweetman;E.D.Hope,H.Rayment;E.W.Archer,R.Haverson,H.Archer;
E.F.Jones,D.Whitear,S.Frankland,V.H.Perriman,E.V.Clarke.

4 May RDLP Home#1Roneo Athletic 5 – 1 Scorers unknown
Attendance: 32 Receipts: £0.8.0
Romford "A":
Team details unknown

7 May RDLP Home#5Laindon 1 – 2 Scorer unknown
Romford "A":
Team details unknown

* After Extra Time
** Abandoned after 78 Minutes due to fog.

#1 Played at Collier Row	#2 Played at Orsett
#3 Played at Brooklands	#4 Played at Clesco, Rainham
#5 Played at Elm Park	#6 Played at Rainham
#7 Played at Laindon	

\# Heath United later withdrew from the league and their record was expunged.
\#\# South Essex Waterworks were voted out of the league and record expunged.

"A" TEAM SUMMARY OF RESULTS SEASON 1948 – 49

	Home			Goals		Away			Goals		
	P	W	D	L	For	Ag	W	D	L	For	Ag	Pts
Romford & Dist.Lge.Prem. Div.	24	2	6	4	20	23	4	4	4	33	28	22
Essex Junior Cup	2	0	0	1	4	5	1	0	0	7	0	
Romford & Dist.Lge.Cup	1	0	0	0	0	0	0	0	1	1	2	
Romford Charity Cup	1	0	0	1	3	6	0	0	0	0	0	
Carter Cup	4	0	1	0	0	0	2	0	1	3	2	
Friendlies	5	1	1	0	7	2	1	1	1	3	3	
League/Friendlies**	2	1	0	0	5	0	1	0	0	4	2	
Totals	39	4	8	6	39	36	9	5	7	51	37	

Note: The above summary does not include match away to Frenford in the Carter Charity Cup which was abandoned with Romford leading by three goals to one.

**   These two games were originally Romford & District League games against Heath United (withdrew from the League) and South Essex Waterworks (voted out of the League).

Romford & District Football League Premier Division
Final Table

					Goals		
	P	W	D	L	For	Ag	Pts
Hornchurch Athletic	24	18	4	2	69	24	40
Laindon	24	18	3	3	87	26	39
Romford Brewery	24	16	4	4	72	33	36
Stifford	24	13	4	7	54	30	30
Billericay	24	13	4	7	66	54	30
Bec.Heath Old Boys	24	11	4	9	58	39	26
Upminster Old Boys	24	11	4	9	70	47	26
Romford "A"	**24**	**6**	**10**	**8**	**53**	**51**	**22**
Clesco	24	9	3	12	39	49	21
Orsett	24	4	6	14	31	63	14
Rainham Town "A"	24	5	4	15	33	82	14
Elm Park	24	2	5	17	29	68	9
Roneo Athletic	24	1	3	20	18	115	5

"A" TEAM CUP RESULTS 1948 - 49

Essex County FA Junior Challenge Cup
Final: Aveley   5   Heybridge Swifts   1

Romford's progress: 1st Round   Away   Dagenham Naval   7 – 0
2nd Round   Away   Collier Row   4 – 5 *

Romford Charity Cup
Final: n/k

Romford's progress: 1st Round   Bye
2nd Round   Home   Dagenham Cables   3 – 6

Carter Charity Cup
Final: n/k

Romford's progress:	1st Round		See Reserve Team Results	
	2nd Round	Away	Frenford	3 – 1 **
	Replay	Fairlop	Frenford	2 – 0
	3rd Round	Away	Chigwell	1 – 0
	Semi-Final	Home	Fairlop	0 – 0 *
	Replay	Away	Fairlop	0 – 2

Romford & District League Cup
Final: Hornchurch Athletic   4   Upminster Old Boys   0
(at Brooklands)

Romford's progress: 1st Round   Away   Romford Brewery   1 – 2

* After Extra Time
** Abandoned after 78 minutes

"A" TEAM APPEARANCES SEASON 1948 – 49

The following players are known to have appeared in the "A" team during the season.

B.C.Acampora	E.W.Archer	H.Archer	-.Ashby
W.Banks	A.E.Belsham	M.E.L.Braham	-.Byatt
E.V.Clarke	-.Collins	J.Deas	W.J.Drake
J.F.Dray(Upminster)	-.Dunham	-.Edwards	-.Evans
S.Frankland	B.Futter	-.Graham	R.Haverson(Chelsea)
E.D.Hope	E.F.Jones	A.Kelly	-.Lambert
A.Lauder	-.Loman	W.G.Mann	R.Marjoram
J.Martin	O.Martin	V.McDonald	-.Murray
R.Norris	R.Parker(Upminster)	S.Parker	-.Peacock
V.H.Perriman	H.Rayment	V.Roeder	D.Rose
G.R.Schooling	J.F.Sippitt	J.E.Smith	L.S.Spooner
D.Sweetman	B.Thornton	C.D.Tubb	-.Walker
W.Ward	S.Watkins(Shoeburyness Town)		-.Watson
R.Watson	A.Watts	D.Whitear(Walthamstow Avenue)	
A.J.Whitehead	L.G.Wood		

DEPARTURES FROM THE CLUB SEASON 1948 - 49

The following players appear to have left the club during or by the end of the season. They may have been triallists and only played one or two games and then went elsewhere. New clubs are indicated where known.

N.W.Abbott, A.Anderson, -.Ashby, W.Banks, G.Baugh, A.Boreham (Walthamstow Avenue), M.E.L.Braham (Briggs Sports), -.Byatt, R.Clark, E.V.Clarke, -.Collins, H.Cooper, G.A.Critten (Rainham Town), J.Deas (Havering), W.J.Drake, J.F.Dray (Ford Sports), -.Dunham (?Denham), -.Edwards, -.Evans, G.Foss (Kingstonian), B.Futter, R.Gadsden (Upminster), -.Glover, -.Graham, C.W.Guiver (Grays Athletic), E.D.Hope, D (C ? A)Jones, A.Kelly, D.Kent, -.Lambert, D.A.Langer (Briggs Sports), A.Lauder, -.Loman, O.Martin, W.G.Mann, V.McDonald, -.Murray, R.Norris, R.Parker, G.W.Patterson (retired), -.Peacock, V.Roeder (Clapton), D.Rose, D.Sammons (Upminster), J.Sippitt, C.Skinner, J.E.Smith(Brighton & H.A), L.S.Spooner, B.Thornton (Upminster), C.D.Tubb (Dagenham), L.Turner, -.Walker, W.Ward, G.Watkins (HM Forces), -.Watson, A.Watts, D.Whitear, A.J.Whitehead, L.G.Wood.

CLUB ATTENDANCE RECORDS FOR SEASON 1948-49

Highest home gates

Isthmian Football League	28th April, 1949	Leytonstone	4,857
FA Challenge Cup	13th Nov., 1948	Gillingham	13,308
FA Amateur Challenge Cup	12th Feb., 1949	Moor Green	7,649
Essex County FA Senior Cup	12th Mar., 1949	Leytonstone	12,322
Friendly matches	9th Sept., 1948	Sparta	3,017

Total attendances

Isthmian Football League	45,469	Average per match	3,497
FA Challenge Cup	49,194	Average per match	8,199
FA Amateur Challenge Cup	14,561	Average per match	7,280
Essex County FA Senior Cup	16,326	Average per match	8,163
Friendly matches	5,929	Average per match	2,964
All matches (25)	131,479	Average per match	5,259

Total Gate Receipts

Isthmian Football League	1,726. 7. 3
FA Challenge Cup	2,237.12. 4
FA Amateur Challenge Cup	637. 5. 3
Essex County FA Senior Cup	697.11. 3
Friendly matches	248.12.11
Total Receipts (25 matches)	5,547. 9. 0

ROMFORD ARE FA CUP GIANT-KILLERS

THE ROMFORD TIMES, WEDNESDAY, NOVEMBER 17, 1948

Romford Shock Gillingham Before A Record Brooklands Crowd

ESSEX VICTORY AT ROMFORD

On Saturday 13th November 1948 Romford caused a big upset in the fourth qualifying round of the FA Cup by beating Southern League professionals Gillingham 2-1 after extra time, in front of a record Brooklands crowd. The match was televised live on the BBC, but sadly no recording was made, so today's fans are unable to re-live that memorable occasion. (None of Romford's televised matches survive on archive film).

The winning goal by Harold Brooks was celebrated with hundreds of coats, hats, scarves and umbrellas hurled into the sky while a couple of spectators did a jig with George Patterson on the halfway line. Needless to say they were quickly removed by the stewards, but it was all taken in good spirit. As Brooklands had no floodlights, extra time was played in a very gloomy atmosphere, and unfortunately the TV cameras shut down before extra time. The BBC sent a cheque for 15 guineas in appreciation! After deducting £3.10s for expenses, the remainder was shared by the two clubs.

The fact of the match being shown on television across the country caused great excitement locally. Here is a report from the *Romford Times*, Wednesday 17th November 1948:

The Cup Tie televised

Cup-tie fever, which year after year attacks ardent supporters of teams on the road to Wembley, often, in the remotest hamlets, has smitten this year some 10,000 jubilant Romford fans, who saw the sensational 2-1 FA Cup defeat of Gillingham, traditional giant-killers, at Brooklands on Saturday.

Almost 5,000 supporters from Kent swelled the gate to 14,500, a new ground record at Brooklands. Official record at the ground previously was 13,800, and certainly a record number saw this game, for another "gate" sat by firesides in scores of homes throughout the district, following the play through the eyes of the television cameras.

POCKET CINEMAS. Lucky owners of television sets invited neighbours to see the game, and for Saturday afternoon many Romford homes became pocket-sized cinemas. With eyes on the small screens, audiences followed the game with as much interest – and certainly in more comfort - as their colleagues at Brooklands. Before the game the cameras spent some time spotlighting the ground with its crowded stands and terraces. Described by a commentator as "this very nice amateur ground", Brooklands certainly looked at its excellent best.

"SHOTS" OF THE CROWD. With the cameras based at the Mawney Road end of the ground, we saw the teams trot onto the ground. A turn of the camera took us into the stand, and we received a vivid impression of the enthusiasm of the enthusiasm of the supporters. Again the camera was swivelled, and we saw the captains' toss. For the first half Romford were playing towards us. Gillingham were easily distinguishable by the large numbers on the shirts, but on changing over, without the aid of this feature, it was often difficult to see which team was in possession of the ball, for we saw only men in dark shirts and white shorts.

During the few Romford attacks in the first half we easily recognized forwards Brooks, Jennings, Newman, Bridge and Patterson. But viewers, as they were constantly referred to by the commentators, saw no goals scored, for half-way through the second half, we were informed that the light was too bad for the continuance of the programme, although at the time I could still follow the game quite clearly. A big disappointment for many.

85 FT MAST. It took a day to erect the stand from which the three cameras (for close-up, long and mid-shots) operated together with the commentators at Brooklands. The transmission mast was 85 feet high.

The television engineers and producers said they received excellent co-operation from club officials. BBC men were enthusiastic about the ground's possibilities and said that the large space available made the match the easiest they have operated. Four large BBC lorries and two GPO vans were needed to bring the equipment. The exhaust from the large van supplying current was so hot that it was used to boil water.

Viewers would probably have seen more of the match if it had been staged in the New Year. That's when the BBC expect to use new cameras (the present are pre-war) which can take pictures in one candle-power light, and are more sensitive than the human eye.

Radio shops in Romford were thronged when the match was being screened. In some places the crowd overflowed onto the pavement.

TELEVISION MAY COME AGAIN. So pleased were the BBC television staff with the reception given to them and the facilities provided at Brooklands on Saturday that they hope to come to the ground again in the spring. The producer, Mr Alan Chivers, told the Recorder sports editor that the decision to stop the broadcast in the second half was made at Alexandra Palace as, in a poor light, the cameras could not cover the far end of the ground very well. Local viewers were disappointed when the broadcast ended, but it must be remembered that viewers in general must be considered and poor quality pictures are not a good advertisement for a wonderful invention still in the development stage.

This anecdote appeared in the *Romford Recorder*, Friday 19ᵗʰ November 1948:

Pinned up in Romford's dressing room was a telegram from the Mayoress, Mrs L.S. Webb, who wrote "All the best of luck. Sorry to miss game, but would not dare come".

The significance of the Mayoress's message will be better understood by pointing out that at Brooklands there is a saying that when she watches Romford the team always loses. In fact, an amusing reference was made to this fact at the reception following the Sparta match which Romford, watched by the Mayoress, lost. The "Jonah" does not apply to the Mayor who told his wife that perhaps it would be better if she stayed away! Few of us admit to being superstitious, but the Mayoress's action is to be admired. I can say that the players very much appreciated her message.

Post Season Summary   Season 1948 – 49

As usual the Brooklands faithful were full of hope for the new campaign. The team duly obliged in the first match on 28th August with a 2-1 victory at Wycombe Wanderers, but Leytonstone then ousted them 3-0 from the Thameside Trophy. Next up was an extra-preliminary FA Cup tie at home on 4th September against works side Ford Sports. This time the lads didn't disappoint and a 5-0 win was achieved. Home defeats by Sparta (Rotterdam) (1-3) and Woking (4-6) followed, before nearly 6,000 spectators were at Brooklands for the next FA Cup tie, against Grays Athletic who were despatched 3-0.

A 2-1 league win over Dulwich Hamlet followed before it was FA Cup time again on 2nd October. Romford were drawn against local rivals Upminster, who played at the Recreation Ground on Corbets Tey Road. Upminster were only allowed to enclose the playing area and charge for admission on a limited number of games, so it was agreed to play the match at Brooklands. Once again the drawing power of Romford when successful was shown as a crowd of 7,000 poured in to show their support. They were not disappointed as Romford won a hard-fought game by the odd goal of three, and the disappointments of previous seasons were temporarily forgotten!

A 4-1 home win over Wycombe Wanderers was preparation for the next FA Cup clash on 16th October. Once again it was to be against a local rival team, on this occasion Brentwood and Warley. Nearly 10,000 people graced the terraces and the Boro boys duly obliged with a 3-1 victory. Even Clapton could not spoil the good run and Romford secured their sixth successive victory with a 3-1 league win. Old foes Barking were next on the FA Cup list and over 9,000 again crammed into Brooklands on 30th October for this third qualifying round tie. Once more the team responded splendidly, a 3-2 victory taking them into the final qualifying round. A run of the mill 2-1 league victory over Kingstonian interrupted the Cup run.

On 13th November, a rather murky day, Romford prepared to meet Southern League professionals Gillingham in the fourth qualifying round of the FA Cup. The BBC were keen to broadcast the match, and a small platform was erected at the Willow Street end of the ground for the cameramen to operate. The match ended goalless but after extra time Romford gained a 2-1 victory.

The following week was Amateur Cup time and a trip to Grays Athletic. A very poor match ended with Boro succeeding 1-0, but in front of a very unhappy band of supporters. Having just seen their team beat professionals Gillingham they expected a better performance, although the players probably had their thoughts on the next FA Cup game! Romford had to travel away this time, and a long trip too. The opponents were Yeovil Town, also a Southern League professional side but higher in the league than Gillingham. It proved to be a step too far, and the Somerset men won 4-0.

Boro defeated Oxford City 2-0 and Corinthian Casuals 4-0 in their next two league encounters and followed this with a one all draw against Ilford on Christmas Day. Ilford won the return game 3-1 two days later, and on New Year's Day Oxford City gained revenge in a 4-1 victory. The Essex Senior Cup was next on the agenda and Brightlingsea United were easily beaten 4-0. A brilliant 4-2 win in the Amateur Cup away to Hitchin Town on 15th January saw Harold Brooks and Bill Bridge bag two goals each, but this was followed by another league defeat, Walthamstow Avenue taking the points.

On 29th January almost 7,000 eager supporters came to Brooklands to see Boro defeat the powerful works side Briggs Sports 1-0 in the Amateur Cup, George Jennings scoring the only goal. Once again cup success was followed by league defeat, Kingstonian winning three two at Brooklands. The 3rd Round of the Amateur Cup beckoned and this time Moor Green, a powerful Midland League side, were the visitors. 7,600 watched at Brooklands on 12th February to see the boys triumph by a resounding five goals to one.

The momentum was being maintained in cup ties, but league games appeared to be of no importance. Romford were well beaten away to St. Albans City (0-4) in the league before the long trip to County Durham on 26th February to meet Billingham Synthonia in the Amateur Cup quarter final. Goals from Brooks and Jennings gave Romford a 2-1 victory to put them through. Boro celebrated with a 3-1 league win over lowly Clapton despite the absence of Fryatt, away representing Essex against the Royal Navy. Next up was the Essex Senior Cup second round, with nearly twelve and a half thousand spectators streaming into Brooklands to see Boro take on the powerful Leytonstone team. It was a thrilling game, but the visitors progressed into the next round by two goals to one.

On 19th March Romford made the long trip up to Roker Park, Sunderland, for the Amateur Cup semi-final tie against Crook Colliery Welfare, a very strong Northern League side. Boro managed to get a two all draw and a replay at Upton Park the following Saturday. The lads didn't disappoint in the replay and secured a 3-0 victory to reach the Amateur Cup final for the first time in the club's history.

Romford were beaten 3-1 away to Woking on 2nd April before wins over Tufnell Park (3-2) and St Albans City (2-1) ensured four much-needed league points were safely in the bag. In their next league fixture, a much-changed defence were no match for the Wimbledon team who triumphed 6-0 at Plough Lane. A 3-3 draw against Tufnell Park and a fine 3-2 victory over old rivals Walthamstow Avenue meant that Boro were in good heart and form for the Amateur Cup Final against Bromley on 23rd April, St George's Day.

It was the first ever Amateur Cup final to be played at Wembley Stadium, and drew a crowd of over 94,000, a record for an Amateur Cup match. Huge numbers of coaches left Romford for Wembley and people unable to go were able to watch the match on TV at the Kings Hall in the Market Place courtesy of a local electrical firm. It was a thrilling encounter with Bromley taking the trophy with a 1-0 victory. Romford did, however, have strong claims for a penalty when Bill Mackenzie was tripped late in the game. To Boro's dismay, the referee placed the ball for the free kick right on the edge of the penalty area.

Dispirited Romford were unable to win any of their final five league games, drawing one and losing four. Just two days after the cup final defeat, Romford met Wimbledon at Brooklands and a bad-tempered game ensued (see overleaf). Leytonstone secured two victories and Boro at last snatched a point in the game against Dulwich Hamlet on 30th April. The season closed on 7th May with an awful 1-0 home defeat by Corinthian Casuals, though it must be admitted that Romford were without four of their best players - Fryatt and Mackenzie were playing for Essex against Cornwall, while Brooks and Bridge had been selected for a Football Association XI against Jersey and Guernsey.

Both the reserve and "A" teams finished in creditable mid-table positions and moderate cup success.

UPMINSTER V ROMFORD
FA Cup Saturday 2ⁿᵈ October 1948
(Played at Brooklands by permission of the Football Association)

Reg Ivey uses his safe hands in an Upminster attack as captain Fred Fryatt stands by
Authors' collection

Angry scenes again at Brooklands!

On Monday 25th April 1949, just two days after Romford's Amateur Cup final at Wembley, there was a near-recurrence of the trouble which had led to the closing of Romford's ground the previous season. Frayed tempers both on the pitch and on the terraces threatened to flare up at the end of the Isthmian League game against Wimbledon. As the match ended, the Wimbledon players were booed off the field. Loudspeaker appeals were made to the crowd, and Romford officials ran on to protect the referee from possible attack.

The cause of the uproar was a series of fouls by both sides, culminating in the sending-off of Romford's right-half Bill Mackenzie, a hero of the Wembley cup final. Previously the referee had stopped the game many times to warn players, and just before Mackenzie was sent off a Wimbledon defender was booked for badly fouling Patterson.

When Mackenzie was sent off many of the 5,000 crowd immediately made for the passage leading from the pitch to the dressing rooms. The referee managed to reach his dressing room safely, but around a thousand continued to wait outside, although further broadcast appeals to disperse were made. Albert Collier, the Romford right back, made a number of appeals and about an hour after the game most of the crowd had gone.

SPARTAN SOUVENIR

Sparta FC of Rotterdam had invited Romford to visit at Easter 1948 to take part in a Tournament to celebrate their Jubilee. In return, Romford welcomed Sparta to England in September that year. The match was followed by a gala dinner

All items from the authors' collection

The teams and officials line up in front of the Brooklands stand

GLEANINGS FROM MANAGEMENT COMMITTEE MINUTE BOOKS
SEASON 1948-49

On **14ᵗʰ December 1948** the following Christmas bonuses were approved: Bill Seddon £10, Ernie Hewitt £5, Arthur Adlam £5 "and each gateman on duty an extra two shillings and sixpence".

On **1ˢᵗ February 1949** the committee heard that owing to fog, the kick-off in the match versus Briggs Sports on 29ᵗʰ January was delayed for 15 minutes. Apparently around 100 people sneaked in (presumably without paying) behind cars before Gate 8 could be closed.

THE DIRECTORS' ANNUAL REPORT 1948/49

The year ended the 31ˢᵗ May 1949 was a most momentous one, not only in the history of this Company but for football in the Borough of Romford whose name this Club has carried with honour, contesting Cup-ties both in the north and south of England.

For the first time an Amateur Cup Final was staged at Wembley Stadium and your Club was one of the finalists. The game was played against Bromley before The Right Hon. The Earl of Athlone, KG, PC, GCB, GCMG, GCVO, DSO, President of the Football Association, and The Princess Alice, Countess of Athlone, GCVO, officials of the Football Association and other dignitaries, and 94,206 other supporters of the Amateur game.

It was perhaps the luck of the game that after such memorable matches in the Amateur Cup Competition against Hitchin Town, Briggs Sports, Moor Green, Billingham Synthonia and Crook Colliery Welfare, all of whom were decisively beaten, that the Club could not just produce the goals in the Final to bring the Cup to Romford, losing to Bromley by the one and only goal. The club also had an exceptional run in the FA Challenge Cup competition, entering the First Preliminary Round and in turn beating Ford Sports, Grays Athletic, Upminster, Brentwood and Warley, Barking, the Southern League Professionals, Gillingham, and in losing in the First Round Proper to the Professionals Yeovil in Somerset (Yeovil going on to defeat in turn Weymouth, Bury, Sunderland and only themselves being beaten in the Fifth Round by Manchester United), altogether a wonderful football season, only made possible by fine team spirit between players and officials alike.

The success of the Football side of the Company's activities has of course reflected itself in the Statement of Accounts and Balance Sheet, resulting in a gross profit for the year of £7,778. The Company's share of the Gate receipts from the Amateur Cup Semi-Final and Final alone, amounting to £6,680 7s 3d.....

...During the year the Directors were able to pay off the Loan Account of £3,000 owing to the Bank, but at the 31ˢᵗ May 1949, the Company owed the Bank on overdraft a sum of £1,832 – this was because at that date the Company's share of the Amateur Cup Semi-Finals and Final had not been received. The sum derived from this source being included in the item Sundry Debtors £6,795 in the Balance Sheet. It is pleasing to observe that the Company's Freehold property and equipment is now free from any mortgage charge or Deposit of Deeds whatsoever.

Fresh Share Capital from the sale of 8,243 shares at 2/6d, amounting to the sum of £1,030 7s 6d, was received during the year with the result that the Capital of the Company is now almost fully subscribed.

In the last report of your Directors it was intimated that the completion of the terracing on the South side was the immediate object. This having been done your Directors feel the time has arrived when every effort should be made to procure a really first-class covered stand with offices and dressing rooms etc. Consequently the plans which had previously been prepared have been revised by the Company's Architects, Messrs Archibald Leitch & Partners, and brought up to date and, your Directors are very pleased to be able to report, approved by the Borough Council, Town and Country Planning and other Authorities.

The proposed Grandstand now becomes a matter of serious consideration for your Directorate upon which more will be verbally reported at the Annual General Meeting, but it is the view of your Directors that the Grandstand should be erected at the earliest possible moment, raising the required finance by charging the Company's property, etc, by way of private mortgage, Bank Loan or Debentures or such other method as is most satisfactory in the opinion of your Directors.

It has always been the policy of your Directors to encourage all kinds of sport, and this year has seen the staging at Brooklands of a series of Grass Cycling Meetings at which a very high standard of sportsmanship was seen and many exciting races and Championships, at which some of the Country's premier riders took part.....

The Romford Supporters Catering Club is still proving highly successful and a welcome amenity to players, Officials and spectators alike, transferring to the Company £150 per annum (included in the item Receipts from Letting of Ground and Property £339) as a rental for the Tea huts....

The Annual Report was presented to the shareholders at the club's Annual General Meeting on Thursday 29th December 1949, which was reported below in the *Romford Times* Wednesday 4th January 1950:

ROMFORD FC PLAN £40,000 GRANDSTAND

Romford FC's new grandstand, planned to make Brooklands the best amateur football ground in the country, will seat 3,000 and cost the company between £25,000 and £40,000. Building will begin as soon as satisfactory estimates have been received and permission given by the Ministry of Works. But just how long that will be is not yet known.

Few professional clubs will have a grandstand equal in the modern design of Romford's stand-to-be, although, of course, many of the larger clubs have proportionately bigger accommodation. Dressing rooms, offices, easy access to seats and exits from them – all will be features in the new building. And – thank goodness! – there will at last be a centrally-situated Press Box, instead of the present 'pigeon loft' on the corner.

LOOKING BACK. All this was announced by Mr Tom Macpherson, MP, when he presided at the annual meeting of shareholders of Romford FC Ltd at the

White Hart, Romford, on Thursday. About 70 of the 448 people who have invested £10,000 in the Company were present. After the meeting members saw a special film of the club, its ground and its personalities; and saw the picture story of last season's historic event – the Amateur Cup Final at Wembley.

As I wrote in the *Romford Times* of December 7th, Romford FC last season made a record profit of £7,778. Gross turnover was £15,940, of which gate receipts amounted to £14,004. The semi-final and final of the Amateur Cup brought a cheque from the FA of £6,795. Long journeys to Yeovil (as a result of the club's wonderful run in the FA Cup) and to Billingham and Sunderland (in the Amateur Cup) helped to swell an expenditure of £8,162 against £5,843 the season before. Part of this extra disbursement included the payment to other clubs of £2,432 as their share of gate receipts, against £1,072 the previous season.

CYCLE RACING PROFIT. Although the item is not shown in the balance sheet because cycling continued after the books closed on May 31st, Mr Macpherson said that the Company's new venture in promoting cycle race meetings in summer had resulted in a profit of about £200.

A dividend of 7½ per cent was declared – highest dividend that can be paid under FA rules. Romford's grand team of last year, who made such a balance sheet possible, were voted the best thanks of the meeting for the splendid games they played and for the prestige they brought to the Borough of Romford.

And as a final "thank you" to George Patterson, veteran Scots international winger who retired last season, the Company presented him with a fine wrist watch.

FINE SPORTSMAN. Said Mr Macpherson: 'I doubt whether the club would be what it is today without the fine services of 'Patt', and his fine example of sportsmanship on and off the field. The Company could not let the occasion pass without some tangible recognition of their regard for him.

Said George Patterson, in reply: 'One thing which he had always enjoyed during his long stay with Romford was the marvellous support the team received. Wherever the club went there were coaches with enthusiasts flying the Romford blue and gold. 'The gift' he said, 'was a surprise, and he thanked the club sincerely for their gesture'.

The optimistic tone of the AGM as depicted in the *Romford Times*

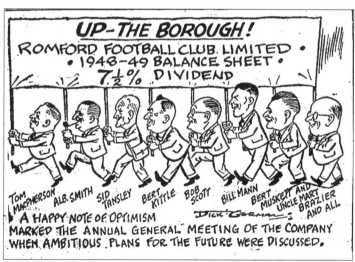

ROMFORD MEET THE STARS!

As the only amateur club invited, six members of the Romford team went to the Empress Hall, Earls Court, on June 4th 1949 to do battle with Brentford, Charlton Athletic, Chelsea, Derby County, Tottenham Hotspur, West Ham United and Wolverhampton Wanderers at an indoor soccer tournament labelled the Festival of Football. Romford did not win the affair, but the occasion provided the six players with what was probably the best instructional afternoon they have ever had. Romford were defeated two one by Chelsea, Bill Mackenzie getting Romford's goal. The teams were:

Romford: Gordon Fleetwood(in goal), W.Mackenzie, W.Bridge, C.Newman and G.Jennings.

Chelsea: J.Harris(in goal), D.Winter, R.Bentley, W.Hughes and R.Campbell.

FORMER ROMFORD FC GROUNDSMAN DIES
(as reported in the *Romford Times,* Nov. 3rd 1948)

Mr Edwin Limehouse, for 17 years groundsman to Romford Football and Cricket Clubs when both occupied Brooklands, died on Monday last, aged 78. Mr. Limehouse, who lived at 62, Pretoria-road, Romford, leaves a widow and three sons and one daughter. Another son and daughter-in-law, together with their three children, were killed in the big blitz incident at Essex-road, in April, 1941, when about 40 lost their lives.

Reckoned one of the best groundsmen the club has had, Mr. Limehouse, held a life long interest in gardening, and had been gardener to several prominent Romfordians.

Funeral took place at Romford Cemetery on Friday, when the principal mourners were Mrs. Limehouse (widow), Mr. and Mrs. Wm. Limehouse, (son and daughter-in-law), Mr. and Mrs. Reg. Limehouse (son and daughter-in-law), Mr. and Mrs. Leslie Limehouse (son and daughter-in-law), Mrs. Finch (daughter), and Mr. Alan Limehouse and Mr. Edward Zarb (grandsons).

Among the floral tributes were wreaths from Romford Football Club and Mr. Arthur Daer (Golden Lion, Romford)....Mr. Tansley was present to represent the Romford Football Club.

BROOKLANDS TO BE A CYCLE RACING CENTRE

When Tom Macpherson MP, Romford's president, announced the summer 1949 programme of cycle racing, he said that the opposition of local residents had killed speedway at Brooklands before it started. But he was now planning to prove "that cycle racing can be just as popular".

ROMFORD FOOTBALL CLUB LTD.

THIS SATURDAY (MAY 21)
(AND EVERY FORTNIGHT)

SPECTACULAR

CYCLE RACING
(N.C.U. RULES)

150 Competitors in a 3-hour Show

Admission 1/-   Children 6d.

At

ROMFORD FOOTBALL GROUND
BROOKLANDS ROAD, ROMFORD
AT 3 p.m.

YOU **MUST** SEE THIS **SPORT**

ROMFORD'S AMATEUR CUP JOURNEY 1948-49

THE FINAL COUNTDOWN

Buses, coaches, motor cars, trains, taxis, perhaps bicycles and even on foot. Grays, Hitchin, Billingham, Sunderland, West Ham and Wembley, BBC Television. What does this all add up to? Read on!

Romford Team Trainer and Coach

Bill Seddon **Ernie Hewitt**

Bill Seddon, the Romford trainer, started his senior football career as an amateur with Aston Villa. After two seasons he turned professional with Arsenal and stayed with the Highbury club from 1924 to 1932. He won an FA Cup winner's medal and a Division One Championship medal before being transferred to Grimsby. A short spell with Luton followed, but, his knees weakened by injury, Bill retired from playing and became head trainer with Notts County. He came to Romford in 1937.

Ernie Hewitt, the assistant trainer, played for Romford until he went on to Leytonstone and then Ilford. At 39 he hung up his boots and offered his services to Romford. He was reserve team trainer until 1936.

MATCH REPORTS OF ROMFORD'S AMATEUR CUP ADVENTURE

> ### 4th Qualifying Round
> Saturday, 20th November 1948
> **Grays Athletic (0)0 Romford (0)1   (After Extra Time)**

Romford's journey to Wembley commenced, and almost ended, at the Recreation Ground, Grays. Having disposed of the strong Gillingham outfit the previous week in the FA Cup, Romford were expected to beat Corinthian League side Grays Athletic, although Grays were having a very successful season. The match was played at a fast pace, though perhaps due to this it was none too skilful.

George Jennings had an excellent game for Romford at inside-right and his teamwork with Bill Bridge and Chuck Newman produced some fast and clever play. Bridge was quite prominent, but he was taking no chances with his ankle injury which had almost prevented him playing in the match. George Patterson on the left wing had a good day, but Harold Brooks, the hero of the previous week, found it hard going against his former Boro colleague Charlie Guiver, who was on top form for Grays.

Romford had to face a strong wind and the sun in the first half, but had their fair share of the game. Newman controlled the ball well and passed with accuracy before unfortunately sustaining an injury. Carmichael, the Grays inside-left, missed a good chance with only Reg Ivey, the Romford custodian, left to beat.

Early in the game Patterson sent a glorious pass to Harold Brooks, who delivered a furious drive only to see the ball come down off the crossbar and be hurriedly cleared by Jack Gatenby. This was followed by another fine effort, by Carmichael, who beat Ivey but again the ball hit the bar and Brand sliced the rebound over it!

Romford's forwards were producing the more skilful moves, whereas Grays were relying on a typical first-time kicking cup tie style. Bill Bridge made a tremendous effort to fasten onto a fast centre from Brooks, but alas he just failed to send it home. At the other end there was a fright for Romford – a scrimmage in the goalmouth after a free kick saw Ivey on the ground, and two successive shots were blocked before John Hall cleared the lines.

Both teams attacked in turn, and Patterson should have given Romford the lead when Watson fumbled a fine shot from Jennings, but the veteran winger shot over the bar. The remainder of the first period saw both sides unable to create a scoring chance, and half time arrived with no score on the board.

In the second half, with the injured Newman now playing at left wing, Romford's defence continued in magnificent form, often thwarting the Grays forwards and if anything did pass them, there was always the reliable Ivey. Romford were expected to assert themselves much more as the game wore on, but Grays were far from a beaten side.

Watson was busy in the Grays goal, tipping over an effort from Jennings and plucking the ball from Hall's head following a corner kick. Ryan came close for Grays when his shot cannoned of keeper Ivey to Mackenzie who blazed over the bar. Jennings and Patterson both struck the crossbar, and Fred Fryatt put in a powerful shot which struck Guiver's foot and rebounded into Watson's arms. The Grays wingers both forced fine saves from Ivey, then in the final minute Ryan blazed the ball across the Boro goalmouth and Ron Sheldon cleared the lines.

In extra time Chuck Newman returned to the centre-forward berth and his leadership gave the Romford forward line the force which had fallen away in the first half. The injured Guiver was also giving Brooks an easier time. Romford could not score and a Patterson shot curled just wide before Albert Collier blocked a Grays effort.

Three minutes into the second period of extra time, the winning goal arrived. An Ivey clearance reached Newman he passed it to Patterson whose centre was fumbled by Watson. In a flash, Jennings had the ball in the net and Romford were a goal to the good. In the remaining minutes Grays had little chance to equalise, as Hall was proving masterly at the centre of the Romford defence and Ivey was well protected in goal. Romford should have had a second goal late in the game, when Harold Brooks produced one of his clever dribbles and passed to Patterson, who could have done better with his effort on goal.

Moments later came the final whistle. Romford had won their tenth successive game and were looking forward to the next round. Grays were perhaps a little unlucky and maybe deserved a draw, but football's oldest adage is "It's goals that count". In this case one goal was enough and Grays Athletic were out of the Amateur Cup.

Grays Athletic: I.Watson; J.Gatenby, C.Guiver; F.Smith, A.Mathews, R.Aldridge; R.Claydon, J.McKenzie, H.Brand, A.Carmichael, J.Ryan.

Romford: R.Ivey; A.Collier, R.Sheldon; W.Mackenzie, J.Hall, F.Fryatt(Capt); H.Brooks, G.Jennings, C.Newman, W.Bridge, G.Patterson.

Thus Romford, after a few scares, had started their Amateur Cup journey. The farthest that they had ever gone in the competition was in the 1930s when they had twice reached the semi-finals only to be denied by the Casuals in 1936 and by Erith & Belvedere in 1938. In the 1930-31 season Romford had set a record by becoming the first team to reach the third round within two years of the club's formation. After seven victories they were defeated by Wycombe Wanderers 6-2, and thus missed out on a place in the last eight.

Following their win at Grays, Romford were drawn to travel to Hertfordshire to meet the highly competent Athenian League side Hitchin Town in the first round proper.

FA Amateur Cup First Round Proper

Saturday, 15th January 1949
Hitchin Town (0)2 Romford (2)4

A special train with 840 seats left Gidea Park Station at 11.40 am on 15th January 1949, filled with enthusiastic Romford supporters. The Hitchin team were very confident, having been unbeaten in league matches for 14 months, although the Bedford Town professional outfit had succeeded there in a cup-tie.

A crowd of 4,260 crowded into the Hitchin ground to witness a thrilling encounter. The football reached a very high standard despite the very muddy state of the pitch. Mann was at inside-right for Boro in place of the injured Chuck Newman and Jack Barton was in the team at the expense of Ron Sheldon who had played at Grays.

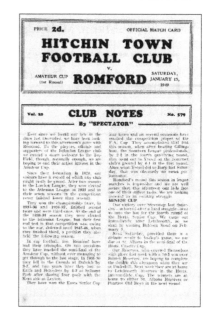

Reg Ivey thrilled the Boro supporters with brilliant saves of what seemed to be certain goals. Bill Bridge, back at his brilliant best, had a foot in all four of Romford's goals and scored two of them. Harold Brooks, too, dazzled with some fine runs and was in brilliant form. George Jennings, as always, attempted to play good football without much luck. Throughout the match Romford were generally on top.

Romford ran Hitchin ragged in the opening minutes but were unable to press their advantage home. They almost paid the penalty when Cole made a splendid run down the wing and centred to leave Rogers a simple tap-in. He hesitated, however, and the brilliant Ivey dived at his feet to save the situation.

After 30 minutes Bridge, facing his own goal, flicked the ball over his head and found the unmarked Brooks. Harold seized the opportunity to fire a low shot which went in off the post. Despite missing two good chances Romford increased their lead a minute from half time when Jennings received a clearance from Barton, then passed to Bridge who drove the ball from the edge of the penalty area well out of goalkeeper Lightfoot's reach.

Kicking down the slope, Hitchin reduced the arrears in the first minute of the second half, Cole heading a Britten centre well clear of Ivey. Hitchin were very much on top at this stage and pressing for an equaliser. They were rewarded when Wingate jabbed the ball through a crowded goalmouth to level the scores in the fourteenth minute.

Things were looking bad for Boro as Hitchin continued raiding their goal. Relieving the pressure, Patterson's corner was kicked out to skipper Fred Fryatt, who promptly returned the ball to Bridge who in turn slipped it through to Brooks. Harold needed no further invitation and drove the ball home from an acute angle with 15 minutes remaining.

Romford were never really in danger after this. The brilliant Bridge, receiving the ball just inside his own half from a Jack Barton clearance, beat Dolan then Leitch before racing through and drawing goalkeeper Lightfoot. Then dribbling round the custodian he slipped the ball into the open goal. It was the most impudent goal seen for a long time and was a fitting climax to a fine exhibition of Cup football. Hitchin Town had fought bravely, but on the day Romford were too good for them.

Hitchin Town: G.Lightfoot; A.Leitch, S.Chapman; L.Dolan, M.Theakstone, W.Westwood; E.Britten, E.Rogers, F.Wingate, A.Ward, A.Cole.

Romford: R.Ivey; A.Collier, J.Barton; W.Mackenzie, J.Hall, F.Fryatt; H.Brooks, W.Mann, W.Bridge, G.Jennings, G.Patterson.

FA Amateur Cup Second Round Proper

Saturday, 29th January, 1949
Romford (0)1 Briggs Sports (0)0

Briggs Sports of Dagenham had been beaten in the first round by Edgware Town who had fielded an ineligible player, so the FA ordered the match to be replayed. Briggs won the replay 2-1 in extra time, earning them the right to meet local rivals Romford.

Saturday 29th January dawned and an excited crowd of 6,912 made their way to Brooklands to witness what would prove to be a great tussle. Kick-off was delayed until 2.45 pm due to the threatening fog which surrounded the ground. The game started with poor visibility, but after half an hour it had improved considerably.

Fred Fryatt, Romford's captain, was taken ill on the morning of the match, so Bill Regan deputised at left-half with Albert Collier taking over the captaincy. Two ex-Romford players, Bill Isaacs and Doug Langer, both had poor games for the Works side. George Bunce, the former Leytonstone player, was the star of the Briggs team but he was well policed by the redoubtable Bill Mackenzie.

Romford's inside forwards Mann and Jennings did not have good games although the latter atoned for this by scoring the winning goal. Harold Brooks started in fine form with a couple of lightning runs, but gradually full-back Jesse Morgan gained the upper hand.

Bill Bridge, not receiving his usual support, found life difficult up against another ex-Boro player in Horace Beaney who was making his debut for Briggs.

Briggs won the toss and Romford attacked their lucky North Street goal. In the early stages a fine ground drive from Mann was saved by Mason who needed to be at his best on this occasion. Romford were well on top for the first 20 minutes but couldn't find the net and Briggs came more into the game. Bill Isaacs beat Hall leaving only goalkeeper Ivey to pass, but delayed his shot and Jack Barton saved the day with a timely tackle.

Most of the play was taking place in the middle of the field and there were few goalmouth incidents. Nonetheless it was proving a thrilling encounter and both sides were in with a chance of victory. Half time arrived with the game scoreless, and the breathless supporters were able to warm themselves up with a hot cuppa before battle resumed.

The second half began with a strong onslaught from Briggs who, as Romford had done in the first half, enjoyed some 20 minutes on top. Both sides let the excitement of the occasion get the better of them and there were frequent stoppages. Bunce had a good chance from ten yards but shot wide, and John Hall saved a couple of efforts with his face! A Langer corner had Boro in trouble and Bunce's overhead kick hit the top of the crossbar. Another fine effort for Briggs saw Stokes shoot just wide after an interchange with Smith.

Romford's attack had been completely subdued for thirty minutes but their defence stood firm. During this spell Collier and Barton were outstanding in the Romford defence. Romford renewed their efforts and took control of the closing ten minutes as Briggs visibly tired. Mason, rushing some fifteen yards out of his goal, saved at Bridge's feet and kept his goal intact. Mason saved his team time and time again as Romford continued the onslaught.

The anxious crowd began to barrack Romford for their failure to score, and were resigning themselves to a replay, which would of course have suited the Briggs team and their supporters. The referee allowed a couple of minutes extra time for stoppages due to injuries to Childs and Jennings, and then Romford pounced.

Regan pushed the ball through to Patterson and the veteran winger proved too good for Childs and centred the ball to Jennings. The inside man took the ball in his stride, swerved past Green and Beaney and drove surely through a crowded goalmouth past an unsighted Mason and into the net. Boro were through!

Romford: R.Ivey; A.Collier, J.Barton; W.Mackenzie, J.Hall, W.Regan; H.Brooks, W.Mann, W.Bridge, G.Jennings, G.Patterson.

Briggs Sports: R.Mason; E.Childs, J.Morgan; J.Donald, H.Beaney, J.Green; A.Smith, W.Stokes, W.Isaacs, G.Bunce, D.Langer.

FA Amateur Cup Third Round Proper

Saturday, 26th February 1949
Romford (3)5 Moor Green (1)1

A crowd of 7,649 were at Brooklands for the next match. The crack Midlands side Moor Green were in town, brimming with confidence. Mann, who had been under the weather in the tie against Briggs, was not selected for this match and Tony Maddick, who had recently joined Romford from neighbours Aveley, was his replacement.

Romford had a brilliant start and scored after only two minutes. Bill Mackenzie sent a fine ball through to Brooks who centred perfectly to Bridge, who stepped over the ball to allow George Patterson to score an easy goal. Romford might have added to their score a few minutes later when a great shot from Brooks hit the angle of crossbar and post.

Garvey, a frequent goalscorer for the visitors, was prominent early in the game, but big John Hall recovered from an uncertain start and began to tackle keenly. In the end Garvey saw little of the ball and had few chances. Moor Green did, however, come more into the game but most of their play was in midfield. After thirty minutes it was suddenly a different story with an opportunist goal from Moor Green's McKenzie who pounced on a back pass from Hall to give Ivey no chance and the scores were now level.

Romford really got going after this setback. A pass down the centre by Fryatt was badly dealt with by centre half Redford and Maddick seized his chance to score with a great drive from nearly thirty yards. Three minutes before the interval Patterson slipped the ball along the wing to Bridge and he centred to Maddick, who cleverly flicked the ball into an open space for George Jennings to run on to and score. Unfortunately in centring the ball Bridge sustained a groin injury and had to leave the field. Half time arrived and Boro were leading by three goals to one.

The second half began with Patterson moving inside to allow Bridge to play on the wing and George Jennings to lead the attack. Inside four minutes Romford had scored again to virtually make the game safe, Harold Brooks scoring from a George Patterson corner kick. Jennings was leading the attack at great speed and the whole forward line looked threatening. Despite their lead Romford did not relax. Shots rained in on the Moor Green keeper who pulled off some remarkable saves from Patterson, Jennings and Patterson again. Finally Maddick beat the goalkeeper again with a fine header from a Brooks cross. Tremelling's problems were not over and he was fortunate to see a Jennings attempt strike the post. Yes, it was certainly Romford's day and they were in the last eight.

"Romford at their greatest" screamed the *Romford Times* headline, whilst the *Recorder* proclaimed "Speed, courage and team spirit lead to success". The Boro supporters were jubilant, in sharp contrast to spells in the previous match with Briggs when the team were frequently barracked. Such is the fickleness of the spectators who of course having paid for admittance are entitled to air their views. Nevertheless when things are not going well in a game it is important that the supporters do just that. Support the boys!

Romford: R.Ivey; A.Collier, J.Barton; W.Mackenzie, J.Hall, F.Fryatt(Capt); H.Brooks, A.Maddick, W.Bridge, G.Jennings, G.Patterson.

Moor Green: K.Tremelling; R.Smith, D.Baker; J.Oldham, J.Redford, J.Binch; G.Hands, L.Wood, G.Garvey, A.McKenzie, N.Love.

Boro were now looking at possible opponents in the next round such as Billingham Synthonia Recreation and Crook Colliery Welfare, all teams from the north of England, or Bromley and Leytonstone from the south.

Who would it be?

FA Amateur Cup Fourth Round Proper
Saturday, 26th February, 1949
Billingham Synthonia Recreation (1)1 Romford (2)2

O ut of the hat came Billingham Synthonia, the pride of the North. Billingham had not lost at home since October and had beaten Penrith 4-1 at home, Clevedon 4-2 away after extra time, and Hendon at home by two goals to one in the previous round.

Romford selected the same team as for Moor Green for this match, although doubts existed regarding the fitness of Bill Bridge. Trainer Bill Seddon had been working on the injury every day.

Some 500 Romford supporters prepared to travel by coach to Billingham as no special train was provided. Ill luck preceded the match, as Boro centre half John Hall went down with flu on the Friday and Jack Barton moved to the pivotal berth. Fryatt then switched to left back and young Bill Regan came in at left half.

This reshuffling seemed to upset the Romford side. In only the third minute of the game.Billingham's centre-forward Buffham put through a fine ball to

VOUCHER No. 1409

Billingham Synthonia Recreation Club
Hon. Gen. Secretary .... Mr. H. S. LODGE
Club Manager .... Mr. J. A. MILLS

BILLINGHAM SYNTHONIA A.F.C.

Colours - - GREEN and WHITE
Ground - - BELASIS LANE

Members of :— The Northern League :
Tees-side League :
Stockton and District League.

President ... ... Mr. L. F. Wharton
Chairman ... ... Mr. J. Ritchie
Hon. Secretary ... ... Mr. R. Piercy
Asst. Hon. Secretary ... Mr. L. Cattermole
Committee : Messrs. Raine, Bullock, Lockerbie, Dent, Dawson, Parke, Hindmarsh, Griffiths, Robson, Dowse, Walton, Trotter and Smith.
Trainers : Messrs. Ridley, Gilbert and Thom.   Coach : Mr. J McFerran

Supporters' Club Official Programme
Price Twopence

To-day, Saturday, 26th February, 1949.   Kick-off 3 p.m.
F.A. AMATEUR CUP, 4th Round.

BILLINGHAM SYNTHONIA
v.
ROMFORD

John W. Baker Ltd., Printers, 7 Finkle Street, Stockton-on-Tees.

Rhodes, who, eluding Collier, lobbed the ball over Ivey's head. The shaken Boro side went into action and five minutes later they were level. Patterson put Bridge away on the left wing and he squared the ball perfectly but Tony Maddick missed the ball and it ran out to Brooks who cut in on goal and drove home from a narrow angle.

Romford went all out after this success, although they had to watch the home team's speedy wingers who were always a threat. After half an hour Patterson had to leave the field with a cut eye and supporters' nerves were jangling. From the dropped ball by the referee to restart the game the ball went along the wing, hotly pursued by the rejuvenated Bridge. He stopped the ball just short of the goal line and sent it into the centre, where keeper Armstrong was able to gather but under pressure dropped it again. Jennings then ran up and cleverly hooked it over Stark's head and into the net from a seemingly impossible angle. Boro were ahead! Just before half time Patterson returned to the field with one eye closed, then Bill Bridge jumped for a high ball, over-reached and tore his groin muscle again. To Romford's relief half time arrived.

For the first ten minutes of the second half the home side showed they meant business and swung the ball about in a determined manner. The Romford defence were in great form however, and the unusual line-up held firm. After fifteen minutes Billingham were beginning to look bewildered, but then came another setback for Romford. Patterson had to go off again, this time with a shoulder injury. He returned after only two minutes and a fit Bridge would surely have scored a goal or two. Brooks thrilled the crowd with his runs and trickery and looked dangerous every time he had the ball, but bad luck dogged both him and the industrious Jennings.

Once again the wonderful stamina of the Romford team, despite the injuries, told its tale. Billingham fell to pieces in the closing minutes, although a centre from Rhodes gave Ivey some trouble. Romford hearts beat again, and with only a matter of minutes to go, supporters felt enough had been done to secure a semi-final place. Indeed it proved to be so. The large crowd back at Brooklands watching the reserve game against Walthamstow Avenue were kept informed of events at Billingham every fifteen minutes, as club official Harold Hughes telephoned with the news updates.

Billingham Synthonia Recreation: Armstrong; Plumer, Chesser; Jeffs, Stark, Bambrough; Wilson, Hand, Buffham, Smith, Rhodes.

Romford: R.Ivey; A.Collier, F.Fryatt(Capt); W.Mackenzie, J.Barton, W.Regan; H.Brooks, A.Maddick, W.Bridge, G.Jennings, G.Patterson.

FA Amateur Cup Semi-Final

Saturday, 19th March, 1949
Crook Colliery Welfare (1)2 Romford (0)2

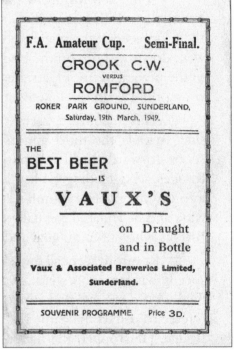

When the draw was made for the semi-final ties, Romford were out of luck again as far as travelling was concerned. They drew Crook Colliery Welfare, the only northern team left in the competition, and would have to travel to Sunderland to meet them.

All the talk in Romford the week before the semi-final centred round the preparations for the tie. Special trains were laid on by British Rail and the club gave a guarantee of 600 passengers at fares of 35 shillings each. The first of the trains would leave Gidea Park Station at 5.10 am. On the team front, the big question was would Bridge be fit enough to play?

The big day arrived and 24,215 spectators were in Roker Park, Sunderland to witness this epic encounter. Romford's John Hall, Durham-born, was playing his first game in the county (since the war) in what was surely the biggest match in his short career.

Ten minutes before the start Marshall, a Crook reserve, was summoned to the dressing room as Nairn, who had got married that morning, was nowhere in sight, but he turned up just in time!

Romford quickly settled down and were on top in all the early play, but they were unlucky in the first ten minutes with Patterson's lob dropping just over the bar and Tony Maddick missing a cross by Bridge and failing to score when he only had the keeper to beat. Romford were made to pay for their misses in the thirteenth minute when a corner kick was awarded to Crook. Both Mackenzie and Fryatt were unable to clear their lines and Weeks, an opportunist striker, sent home a low shot just inside the post.

Barton was up against a dangerous winger in Scott, but the way he eventually shut out the danger was great to watch. On the opposite flank Albert Collier was up against Lockey, who was an equally fine winger, and he too stuck to his task.

Crook held on to their lead with some desperate clearances – at times the ball was sent soaring into the crowd. They were lucky not to concede a penalty when Bridge was brought down just before half time. Nevertheless Boro were still a goal behind at the break.

Romford began the second half in very determined fashion, and were rewarded in the 4th minute when Brooks was brought down as he cut into the penalty box. George Patterson kept his cool, fooling keeper Jarrie with a deceptive run and calm placement of the ball. Boro were level. Wing half Mackenzie was an inspiration for Romford. He played quietly and constructively and never looked worried. Ivey in goal was playing his usual game with many fine saves, but stood no chance with the shots that beat him.

Romford were now well on top, and only a fine effort by the Crook custodian saved the day as Bill Bridge burst through. The Crook team were rattled and another goal had to come. In the tenth minute Maddick created a fine opening, centred the ball where the waiting Bridge headed home, and Romford were leading 2-1. Romford were now on top and the opposing defenders were glad to kick the ball anywhere. Patterson suffered an injury but after treatment he returned and immediately burst through only to shoot just over the bar. Jarrie was proving to be a very adventurous goalkeeper and several times he ventured far out to relieve the situation, but at times he was lucky to get the ball away.

Crook, however, kept their goal intact and then from another corner kick the ball was kept in the Romford goal area for Swan to fire home through a crowded goalmouth and the scores were level again. Crook, encouraged by this goal, then forced several corners but the Boro defence stood firm. In the final minute Crook had their luckiest escape. Brooks slipped a pass through to Maddick who shot from a narrow angle. The ball eased past the keeper and was heading for the goal when Copeland dashed across to save the day. After 90 thrilling minutes the teams were still locked together and extra time loomed.

Captain Fred Fryatt won the toss and Boro's opponents were called upon to face both the sun and the wind. First one team and then the other attacked in turn, with Romford generally the more polished side. Patterson centred, Jennings went up for the ball and Jarrie advanced from his goal only to miss the ball completely – but it rolled slowly past the goalpost. Patterson was prominent at this stage. Dribbling through he lofted the ball over Copeland, raced round him and fired in a shot, only to see Jarrie make a fine save.

At the start of the second half it seemed that Crook would score when a sliced clearance from Hall left Weeks with a good chance, but he hesitated and Jack Barton raced in to save the day. In the minutes that followed Reg Ivey was called upon to make saves from Owens and Lockey. Romford were playing much the better football in the closing minutes and should have capitalised on this. The nearest they came to scoring was when Bill Bridge beat Jarrie with a drive that rattled the crossbar, then the ball rebounded to Brooks whose shot was just off target.

Both teams concentrated on avoiding giving away a goal after this. Thus the game ended as a 2-2 draw and the teams were to meet at West Ham's Upton Park ground a week later. After the game players and supporters learned that the other semi-final between Bromley and Leytonstone was also a draw and they would fight again at Stamford Bridge.

Crook Colliery Welfare: F.Jarrie; W.Copeland, A.Nairn; H.Owens(Capt), A.Swan, J.Dodds; J.Scott, A.Weeks, D.Chicken, W.Gibbons, A.Lockey.

Romford: R.Ivey; A.Collier, J.Barton; W.Mackenzie,J.Hall, F.Fryatt(Capt); H.Brooks, A.Maddick, W.Bridge, G.Jennings, G.Patterson.

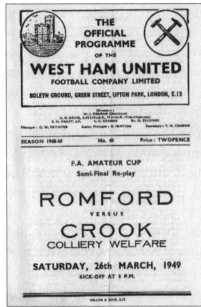

FA Amateur Cup Semi-Final Replay
Saturday, 26th March, 1949
Crook Colliery Welfare   (0)0   Romford   (1)3

Romford was buzzing with excitement during the week as supporters discussed the next episode. Bill Mackenzie was getting married on the morning of the replay, like Crook full back Nairn on the day of the first game. There was a strange feeling of deja vu about all this. Romford's previous Amateur Cup semi-final appearance in 1938 had resulted in a two all draw. Hours before the replay at Crystal Palace, Dave Thomas had been married and Romford were then beaten 4-2 by Erith & Belvedere who went on to lose to Bromley by one goal to nil in the final.

The big day arrived and 25,284 spectators inside West Ham's Boleyn ground were excitedly waiting for the start of the match. A Boro supporter dressed like a Zulu warrior was entertaining the crowd. He carried a long staff bedecked with the club's colours of blue and gold, plus whistles and bells, which he repeatedly brandished towards the Romford supporters.

Fred Fryatt leads the Romford team onto the pitch, amid a massive roar from the crowd at Upton Park, and the stage is set for a fine game. Note the Arsenal-style kit worn by Romford, thanks to Bill Seddon's Arsenal connections! *Authors' collection*

John Hall, still suffering from the effects of flu, was missing from the Boro line-up, Barton moving to centre half, Fryatt to left back and young Bill Regan earning a place at left half. In truth it was not really a great contest, but Romford's greater skill kept them in charge for nearly all the match, though the final clinching two goals only came in the closing minutes of the game.

Bill Bridge, still suffering from injury, burst through three minutes into the game but the awkward bounce on the bone-hard pitch thwarted him. Romford continued to attack and Maddick had a fine shot blocked by the crowded defence. Reg Ivey was virtually a spectator as Romford launched attack after attack, often started by the lively Brooks who was having a great game. He was badly fouled when clean through and the resultant free kick was just turned round the post by Jarrie.

It was obvious that a goal was imminent. In the 14th minute, on receiving from a throw-in, Bill Bridge raced through the defence, beat two men and the referee allowed him to continue after he was tripped. He regained his balance and scored with a grand drive.

Romford were full of confidence. Maddick drove just over the bar and Bridge's shot glanced off the post. Jennings then shot narrowly wide and Crook just managed to keep their goal intact. They managed a breakaway, however, and Ivey lost the ball to the energetic Weeks before Regan and Mackenzie somehow got the ball away.

Jarrie rushed from goal but missed a Brooks cross, the ball fell to Jennings who shot over the bar. Tony Maddick broke through and placed his shot into the net only for the goal to be ruled out for offside. Despite their obvious superiority Romford reached the interval with just the one goal lead.

The second half opened and Brooks was soon up to his old tricks. Collecting a fine pass from Bridge, he cut in and fired a tremendous shot which beat the custodian but rattled the crossbar. Romford remained on top in the early stages of the second period.

Crook controlled the next fifteen minutes, but they relied on the long kicking game and hoped for defensive errors. Chicken did manage a shot from close in, but the reliable Fryatt cleared from the goal line, and the Boro defence remained firm.

Romford came back into the game. Regan sent a great ball through to Bridge but Jarrie raced from goal before the Romford leader and the chance disappeared. Bridge was then unlucky after a great solo run from the halfway line, when Jarrie again left his goal and smothered the shot. Crook kept relying on the offside trap in their efforts to keep the Romford attackers at bay. From a pass by Patterson, Maddick beat the trap but yet again the onrushing Jarrie saved the day, smothering the final shot. Romford were now well on top and Crook looked a tired and beaten side. Their attacks were few and far between and Romford were never really troubled again.

Ten minutes from the end a fierce shot from Harold Brooks was turned behind for a corner. The skilful Brooks placed his ball well and found the veteran George Patterson who shot was blocked. The alert Maddick collected the half clearance and coolly placed his shot in the corner of the net. The brilliant Jarrie had no chance this time, and Romford were two goals ahead. Four minutes later Brooks forced another corner and from the resultant scramble Tony Maddick was again on hand to beat Jarrie. In the closing minutes Jennings, Patterson and Bridge all went close to adding to the score and the final whistle went with Romford very deserving of their three goal victory.

As pre-arranged both teams returned to Brooklands after the match, where they enjoyed some Romford hospitality with a fine meal. It was then learned that Romford were not to meet their Essex rivals in the final, as Leytonstone had been beaten two goals to nil by Bromley at Highbury.

A further co-incidence now reared its head, as Bromley's centre half was a man who had thwarted them 21 years previously. It was Charlie Fuller, the centre half in the Erith & Belvedere side all those years ago, when George Patterson had been in the Romford side! George Brown was centre forward for the Bromley team that had lifted the cup that year and he too would face Romford at Wembley. The young Bill Bridge had made his debut in the Romford first team later that same year.

Crook Colliery Welfare: F.Jarrie; W.Copeland, A.Nairn; A.Owens(Capt), A.Swan, J.Dodds; J.Scott, A.Weeks, D.Chicken, W.Gibbons, A.Lockey.

Romford: R.Ivey; A.Collier, F.Fryatt(Capt); W.Mackenzie, J.Barton, W.Regan; H.Brooks, A.Maddick, W.Bridge, G.Jennings, G.Patterson.

CROOK WERE "HAMMERED" AT UPTON PARK

Tony Maddick scores the third and decisive goal for Romford at Upton Park
Authors' collection

Romford now had to make preparations for their first-ever Amateur Cup Final. At Brooklands the telephone rang non-stop. In the 1940s there was no automated answering system, just poor Bill Seddon, who was the only member of staff at the ground during the day in his other role as groundsman. Bill forwarded all enquiries for Cup Final tickets to Knights Travel in the High Street who were issuing them on behalf of the club. Ticket sales exceeded all expectations and the reception at Knights Travel had never been so busy!

The players were presented to a packed audience at the Havana Cinema in South Street ahead of their Wembley appearance. The Mayor of Romford, Alderman L.S.Webb, announced that a civic reception would be held for the team at the Town Hall, whether they won or lost the final, to celebrate their fantastic achievement.

A WEMBLEY SPECIAL

THE ROMFORD CUP FINAL TEAM

Back: Albert Collier, Bill Regan, Reg Ivey, Jack Barton, Tony Maddick, George Jennings
Front: Harold Brooks, Bill Bridge, Fred Fryatt(Capt), Bill Mackenzie, George Patterson   *Authors' collection*

Team captains Eric Fright (Bromley) (left) and Fred Fryatt (Romford) shake hands in front of club secretaries Charles King (Bromley) and Martin Brazier (Romford)

THE BIG DAY ARRIVES

Romfordians flocked into town to wait for their transport to Wembley. The main pick up point was Como Street, where 80 motorbuses bedecked in blue and gold were lined up ready and raring to go. At Roneo Corner another 31 buses waited to depart. There was a shortage of transport and some buses carrying Romford supporters actually came from the Bromley area! A total of 200 buses headed from Romford to the twin towers carrying 6,000 supporters (this figure doesn't include the many fans travelling by train).

Back at Brooklands, Bill Seddon relaxed with a game of snooker before giving his team briefing. Then it was all aboard the bus and off towards the North Circular. The team stopped off en route at the Cock public house where they enjoyed a swift half of Mann's Brown, by kind permission of Bill Seddon. Could you imagine that happening today? Then they were ready for the last lap of the journey (under police escort) and the twin towers of Wembley were in sight.

The late Jack Henningham, brother-in-law of club secretary Martin Brazier, made a "home movie" silent cine film of the big day which includes scenes of excited fans waiting at Roneo Corner, the team travelling in their bus to Wembley, plus some footage of the match itself.

The players were excited by what awaited them but nerves were not a problem. On arriving at the National Stadium the players were shown to the South (away team) dressing room. After taking light refreshments they made their way out to walk on the hallowed turf. By now the stadium was about half-full; but even then the twenty two players who were to grace Wembley that day could not have imagined a crowd of almost 95,000 coming to watch them play.

WEMBLEY AWAITS THE TWO COMBATANTS

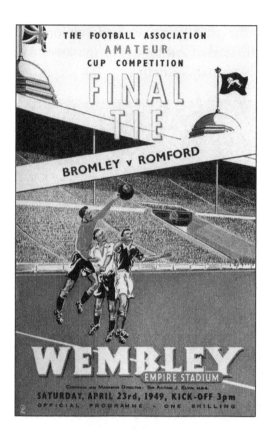

LIVE TV AND WEMBLEY!

Not everybody in the town was able to make it to the final, of course, and in 1949 few homes had television sets.

The *Romford Times* came to the rescue, in conjunction with TV and radio experts Sidney Grey Stores (London) Ltd of the Quadrant Arcade. They offered 500 free tickets, on a first-come first-served basis, to a live screening at the Kings Hall in the Market Place where a bank of nineteen TV sets would show every kick of the match.

A number of local shops issued notice that they would be closed on the afternoon of the game.

Still from the match day film made by Jack Henningham, giving a good impression of the huge Wembley crowd

At 2.45pm on Saturday April 23rd 1949, the two teams walked out onto the Wembley pitch to be presented by their captains to the Earl of Athlone. The massive crowd then joined a rendition of Abide with Me, then the National Anthem.

Club secretaries Charles King and Martin Brazier lead out their teams
Authors' collection

> **We now present the full match report by Arthur Salter,**
> **Amateur Football expert from that era:**

BROMLEY MUST HAVE MY VOTE –
IT'S A CONFIDENT ONE
(As ARTHUR SALTER sees it)

The Preliminaries

For years the Amateur Cup Final had always been played on a Football League Club's ground, but this time the brave step had been taken by the Football Association to play the final tie at Wembley.

This decision proved to be a wise one as there was a tremendous demand for tickets by both clubs, but also by supporters of other Clubs and thousands of local residents who had probably never seen the teams play!

The brilliant organising arrangements by the Football Association ensured that events progressed smoothly before the game started. The Romford team was led onto the field by their likeable football secretary Martin Brazier and Charlie King, his counterpart was at the head of the Bromley team.

Romford line up to be introduced to the Earl of Athlone

The captains wish each other the best of luck

The Earl of Athlone and Bill Seddon

Both teams were introduced to the Earl of Athlone, all dignitaries returned to their seats in the stand and the stage was set for Mr. Stevens the referee to set the game in motion.

WHO'S WHO OF THE CUP FINAL TEAMS

BROMLEY

Cornthwaite Tom. Goalkeeper. Born Bury, played in England trial this season. Served in the RAF during the war and played in representative sides.

Cameron Douglas. Right-back. Born Harlesden. Joined Bromley from Hayes this season. From 1941-46 was a pilot with a bomber squadron, awarded DFM and DFC.

Yenson Ken. Left-back. Joined Bromley this season from Grays Athletic, with whom he gained Corinthian League representative honours. Son of West Ham professional.

Fuller Tom. Right-half. Born Grimsby. England trial cap, and Kent County Cap. Joined Bromley 1946; formerly with Leyton, Erith and Belvedere, and West Ham "A". Another airman, played in All-India matches.

Fuller Charles. Centre-half. Brother of Tom. Born Grimsby. England's present centre-half, also honoured by London FA, Kent and Army. While with the Royal Artillery, played for Southend, Crystal Palace and Wrexham.

Fright Eric. Left-half, Captain. Honours included 11 England amateur and Olympic games caps. Product of Arsenal nursery, had two seasons with Arbroath when in Fleet Air Arm.

Martin Cyril. Outside-right. England and County honours. Joined Bromley 1939. With Olympique de Marseille last year, won French First Division medal.

Hopper Tommy. Inside-right. Born Sittingbourne. Caps include: England, Olympic Games, Kent, and London FA Played for Lloyds, Gillingham, Army, and during the war for Reading.

Brown George. Centre-forward. Born Yarmouth. Most prolific goal-getter in amateur football. Was in Bromley's cup winning team in 1938. First England cap this season. Played in Olympic games, FA and County matches.

Dunmall Reg. Inside-left. Born Keston. Joined Bromley after Tottenham and Chelmsford. Played for Kent and Royal Navy.

Ruddy Martin. Outside-left. 30 County Caps. Has played in every position on the field – including goal.

The Bromley team
Back: Martin, Brown, C.Fuller, Cornthwaite, Cameron, Dunmall
Front: T.Fuller, Hopper, Fright, Yensen, Ruddy

ROMFORD

Ivey Reg. Goalkeeper. 6ft. 1in. Metropolitan Policeman. Has few equals in goal but has been overlooked for international honours.

Collier Albert. Right-back. A printer. Graduated from West Ham and London Schoolboys.

Fryatt Fred. Left-back and Captain. Has captained Isthmian League side in all matches this season. An Essex County player, he is in the building trade. Reached Romford via Brentwood and Warley and Grays Athletic.

Mackenzie William. Right-half. Born Glasgow. Joined Romford after the war. Fearless tackler and 90 minute player. Engineer.

Barton Jack. Centre-half. Engineer. Played for Sheffield United Reserves and "A" team. Moved from left back to take over centre-half position from John Hall for semi-final.

Regan William. Left-half. Played for West Ham Reserves in war time combination matches. His advance this season won his place in re-shuffle for semi-final.

Brooks Harold. Outside-right. Only 5ft. 4in., known as "The Mighty Atom". Has an amazing turn of speed and a powerful shot with either foot.

Maddick Tony. Inside-right. Played regularly for Essex Junior XI before joining Romford from Aveley. Has earned his place in the Cup Final team.

Bridge William. Centre-forward. A local boy who joined Romford in 1937 having captained Romford Boys for three seasons. Normally inside-right, but at home in any forward position.

Jennings George. Inside-left. Joined Romford this season from St. Albans City. A printer. Played for London Schoolboys and Millwall "A" teams. Won DSM in the Navy.

Patterson George. Outside-left. Aged 40, the veteran of the side. Came to Romford in 1931 from Queen's Park. Has five Scottish International medals.

HOW THEY REACHED THE FINAL

BROMLEY			ROMFORD	
		A	Grays Athletic	1-0
H Maidenhead	3-0	A	Hitchin Town	4-2
H Wimbledon	6-1	A	Briggs Sports	1-0
A Barking	5-1	H	Moor Green	5-1
A Pegasus	4-3	A	Billingham S.R.	2-1
Leytonstone	0-0		Crook Col.Wel.	2-2
Leytonstone	2-0		Crook Col.Wel.	3-0

FA Amateur Cup Final
Saturday, 23rd April, 1949
Bromley (1)1   Romford (0)0
Attendance: 94,000

Fred Fryatt won the toss for his team, Bromley were asked to face the sun, the referee's whistle was blown and centre forward George Brown set the game in motion.

Bromley moved smoothly into the classy play with which they were renowned for, Fryatt cleared his lines with a crisp pass to George Patterson who sped past Cameron and crossed to Jennings whose shot went over the bar. The Kent side were pressing hard but

Romford's keen approach saw Patterson chase back some sixty yards to rob Martin. The Boro defence at this stage were inclined to clear too hurriedly and thus create more pressure on their team mates. A threat from Dunmall was snuffed out by Ivey, who dashed out of goal to relieve the situation. In quick succession the alert Ivey who was having a great game made saves from Brown and Hopper.

A rare move saw Maddick thread a shrewd pass through the defence to Brooks whereupon he eluded Fright and Yenson only to shoot narrowly over the crossbar. Play was now going from end to end and Hopper shot just wide before a long lob from Harold Brooks had Cornthwaite in trouble with Cameron nearby to complete the clearance. Patterson and Jennings combined in the best move of the match which ended with Jennings shooting just wide of the mark. Bromley were unsettled by Romford's first time and enthusiastic tackling, but after 19 minutes a fine clearance by Fuller was collected by Ruddy who just kept the ball in play before crossing to the edge of the penalty area. Reg. Dunmall and Brown eased the ball through to Tommy Hopper who carefully placed his shot to Ivey's left and the first goal was scored off the post giving the Boro custodian no chance.

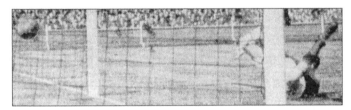

Tommy Hopper inflicts misery on the Boro supporters

Cornthwaite, Bromley's goalkeeper, tips Harold Brooks' fine effort over the bar

Following the kick off Patterson forced a corner kick and from the cross Brooks shot first time but a defender deflected the ball for another corner. Gaining confidence the Romford half backs began to dominate the mid field and Bridge came close to scoring.

Romford were now controlling the game and the forwards were being well supplied with passes but the finishing gave no problems to Cornthwaite in the Bromley goal. A high Bridge cross caused some problems but from the resulting goalmouth melee Brooks, only a few yards out, shot wide of the mark. Jennings was working very hard and created openings but Patterson and Bridge could make no headway against Cameron and Charlie Fuller.

An interchange of passes between Jennings and Maddick looked promising but Cornthwaite just beat Jennings to the ball. Minutes later Jennings was through again and Eric Fright appeared to handle the ball on the edge of the penalty area but this went unnoticed by the officials.

The closing minutes of the first half saw Bridge beat Charlie Fuller and shoot inches wide of the post, but the referee's whistle was blown before the ball crossed the goal line anyway. Half time arrived with the score still one goal to nil in Bromley's favour.

Ruddy and Dunmall changed places at the start of the second half as the former was suffering from a slight injury. Bill Regan made a long run and passed to Maddick, there did not appear to be much danger from his centre but Cameron played the ball out for a corner kick. The resultant corner was fruitless.

Bromley's goal under pressure from a Romford attack

A fine free kick by Yenson gave Brown a chance but his header was turned round the post by Ivey. Romford launched several more dangerous attacks and Patterson put Jennings through but he shot tamely into Cornthwaites hands.

Brooks and Jennings tried long range shots but the Bromley custodian had no difficulty with these efforts, as both went narrowly wide. Patterson slipped a great ball through to Bridge and the centre forward shot into the side netting.

With Romford now on top Albert Collier raced up field beating four men but was unfortunately penalised for hand ball. In a rare moment Charlie Fuller looked dangerous but Ivey punched the ball clear but in a hectic period Brown, Hopper and Ruddy all had shots charged down, resulting in an injury to Jack Barton.

Tony Maddick forced a corner but from the Brooks corner Bill Mackenzie headed over the bar. A great free kick from Collier created an opportunity for Bridge who headed into the goalie's hands.

The main source of danger to Bromley was coming from the hardworking Mackenzie and he shot over the bar on two occasions after bursting through the defence.

Fifteen minutes from the end came the big talking point when Mackenzie from well in his own half went on a run beating three men, only to be brought down on the edge of the penalty area. To many spectators he appeared to be inside the penalty area and referee Mr. Stevens gave a free kick just outside the box.

Mackenzie is flattened!
Is the referee pointing to the spot?
Bill Mackenzie, when interviewed by
the authors, was adamant that it
should have been a penalty

Romford continued to have all the play but Bromley broke away and Ivey saved from point blank range an effort from Brown after Martin had juggled his way past Fryatt.

In the closing minutes the entire Boro team except Ivey and Barton, crowded in the opposing goalmouth for a Patterson corner kick but the Bromley defence stood firm. It was a case now of Romford pressure being rewarded with the equaliser or Bromley making the game safe from a breakaway.

Tony Maddick had a late effort but only half hit the ball and the final chance was gone. The final whistle was blown and so were Romford's hopes. The cup was destined to go to Bromley once more and Romford's time was yet to come.

Bromley: T.Cornthwaite; D.Cameron, K.Yenson; T.Fuller, C.Fuller, E.Fright(Capt); C.Martin, A.Hopper, G.Brown, R.Dunmall, M.Ruddy.

Romford: R.Ivey; A.Collier, F.Fryatt(Capt); W.Mackenzie, J.Barton, W.Regan; H.Brooks, A.Maddick, W.Bridge, G.Jennings, G.Patterson.

The Statistics

Only two of Romford's eight games in the FA Amateur Cup were played at Brooklands (against Briggs Sports and Moor Green), and both fixtures attracted around 7,000 spectators. The following players took part in Romford's Amateur Cup ties:

Barton(7), Bridge(8), Brooks(8), Collier(8), Fryatt(7), Hall(5), Ivey(8), Jennings(8), Maddick(5), Mackenzie(8),Mann(2), Newman(1), Patterson(8), Regan(4) and Sheldon(1). Romford's eighteen goals were scored by Bill Bridge, Harold Brooks, George Jennings and Tony Maddick (four goals each) and George Patterson (two).

The attendance at Wembley Stadium was 94,206 and total receipts were £17,759.17.11 of which Romford's share was £4,671.8.11. The receipts from the two semi-finals and two replays were pooled together and divided between the Football Association and four competing Clubs. Romford's share amounted to £2,008.18.4.

Romford used the majority of this money for ground improvements including the building of the perimeter wall and turnstile blocks. Delays in obtaining the necessary licence from the Ministry meant this work was not started until 1952.

Attendance details of Romford's games

4th. Qual.	Grays Athletic (A)	9,000	£370.9.0
1st Round	Hitchin Town (A)	4,260	£240.10.3
2nd Round	Briggs Sports (H)	6,912	£304.13.3
3rd Round	Moor Green (H)	7,649	£332.12.0
4th Round	Billingham S. R. (A)	n/k	n/k
Semi-Final	Crook C.W.(Roker P)	24,215	£2,443.0.0
Replay	Crook C.W.(W. Ham)	25,284	£2,810.0.0

It's a Fact!

In 1949 Bromley Football Club's President was the Prime Minister, Harold Macmillan.

BIG WELCOME HOME FOR THE ROMFORD TEAM
(as reported in the local press)

From the clamour outside Romford Town Hall at 9.30 pm on the Saturday night, you would have thought Romford had won the cup! Hundreds of fans had gathered in the forecourt calling repeatedly for the Romford team.

But the team wasn't there. Plans were for the players to appear on the balcony if they won, but as they lost, all wanted to make their way home quietly. The crowd grew and with it an insistent cry for the players. For win or lose, Romford supporters wanted to welcome a gallant Romford team.

When the team coaches arrived at Brooklands; the Mayor, Alderman L.S.Webb, went on to the Town Hall, but on seeing the crowd he made haste back to the ground and persuaded the team to journey to the Town Hall (though it was too late for Reg Ivey, Tony Maddick and Harold Brooks who had already gone home). As the clamour increased, players and officials at last made their appearance on the balcony. The Mayor welcomed them back, and said how proud the town was of them. Tom Macpherson on behalf of the club thanked supporters for their enthusiasm and told them the best team lost.

One by one the players were called and loudly cheered. Skipper Fred Fryatt, now a veteran speaker, thanked supporters for a grand reception. Amid more cheers, other players, including Jack Barton, Bill Bridge and George Patterson, added their thank-yous. Lastly there was trainer Bill Seddon, who too had a particular thank you for the loyal Romford fans. The team were naturally disappointed that they didn't bring back the cup, he said, though he thought they had deserved to win it. Then came a rendition of the team's theme song *Babbling Brook*, sung in tribute to player Harold Brooks (see page 243).

WEDNESDAY, MAY 4, 1949

Mayor Honours Romford Team

On 30th April, exactly a week after the match, Alderman and Mrs. L.S.Webb, Mayor and Mayoress of Romford, entertained the team and management committee in the Town Hall in recognition of the club's feat. Pages from the souvenir programme are shown below.

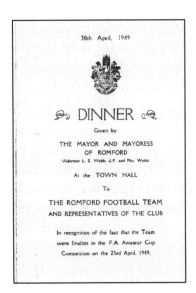

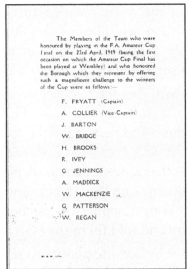

It was the first time in their twenty year history that such a reception had been given to the club, and the event capped what Mrs. Webb described as "The most wonderful and happiest eighteen months of my life". For in three weeks time her term of office and the mayor's would be over.

Dear reader, we have come to the end of this unforgettable Amateur Cup saga, and we hope that you have enjoyed the journey. It will no doubt have brought back memories for those who were there at the time and enlightened the many who were too young to be there.

THE ROMFORD FOOTBALL CLUB LIMITED

Full Members of The Football Association
Full Members of the Isthmian Football League
Affiliated to the Essex County Football Association

Chairman: T.Macpherson MP
Directors: Messrs. M.A.Brazier, A.E.Kittle, W.G.Mann, R.Scott,
A.J.Smith MBE, S.G.Tansley
Company Secretary: Mr H.W.Muskett

Registered Offices: 110,Hyland Way,Romford

Club Officials & Committees:
President: T.Macpherson MP

Chairman: Mr A.J.Smith MBE

Hon.Gen.Secretary: Mr M.A.Brazier   **Hon.Asst.Secretary:** Mr J.Gurney

Hon.Press Secretary: Mr H.A.Hughes   **Hon.Advt.Secretary:** Mr H.A.Wright

First Team Hon. Secretary: Mr Betts.

Trainer/Coach: Mr W.C.Seddon

Reserve Team Coach: Mr W.Benson   **Third Team Coach:** Mr E.Crooks

First Team Selection Committee: Messrs. F.A.Adams, F.Betts and G.W.Patterson
(Assisted by Mr W.C.Seddon)

Second & Third Team Selection Committee: Messrs. G.I.Howlett and R.Freeman

Welfare Officer: Mr T.F.Collett

Groundsman: Mr W.C.(Bill)Seddon (Assisted by Ernie Hewett)

Auditor: Mr I.V.Cummings

LEAGUES & COMPETITIONS 1949-50

FA Challenge Cup
FA Amateur Challenge Cup
Isthmian Football League
Essex County FA Senior Challenge Cup
Essex Thameside Challenge Competition

Isthmian Football League Reserve Section
Essex Thameside Challenge Competition Reserve Section

Romford & District League Premier Division
Essex County FA Junior Challenge Cup

Romford & District League Cup
Romford Charity Cup
Carter Charity Cup

Admission Prices Season 1949 – 50

	First Team	
	Adults	OAPs and Boys
Ground	1/-	6d
Enclosure	1/9	1/-
Grandstand	2/6	

Season Ticket Prices Season 1949 – 50

	Adults	OAPs and Boys
Grandstand (All one price)	£1.10.0	
Ground & Enclosure	£1.1.0	12/6
Ground only	12/6	7/6

PUBLIC TRIAL MATCH

Sat.,13th Aug.,1949				Final Trial
PROBABLES 3				POSSIBLES 5
Bridge(2)Jennings				Bridge(4)O'Reilly
Attendance: 2,117	Receipts: £52.2.9	Programmes: £		Car Park: £1.11.0

Probables: A.Boreham;E.Rayment,P.Phillips;S.A.Tuckey,R.Haverson,R.Phillips;
E.Mocock,S.Frankland,F.James,G.Jennings(Capt),E.Quinlan.
Possibles: C.Bingham;A.E.Belsham,F.Fryatt(Capt);W.Mackenzie,J.Sharod,W.Regan;
H.Brooks,W.A.Bridge,T.Albert,A.O'Reilly,P.King.
Note: Goalkeepers and centre forwards swopped sides at half time.

First Team Match Details

20 Aug Frdly   Home   Schaffhausen   2 – 0 James,Brooks
Attendance: 5,587   Receipts: £280.3.9   Programmes: £24.17.4 Car Park: £4.14.0
Romford: R.Ivey;S.A.Tuckey,F.E.Fryatt(Capt);A.E.Belsham,J.Barton,W.B.Regan;
H.W.Brooks,W.A.Bridge,F.C.James,S.Frankland,P.King.

27 Aug IFL   Home   St. Albans City   1 – 5 Bridge
Attendance: 5,086   Receipts: £238.0.6   Programmes: £25.0.6 Car Park: £5.14.2
Romford: R.Ivey;S.A.Tuckey,F.E.Fryatt(Capt);W.F.Mackenzie,J.Barton,W.B.Regan;
H.W.Brooks,W.A.Bridge,C.W.Newman,J.O'Reilly,P.King.

3 Sept IFL   Away   Corinthian Casuals   1 – 2 Frankland
Attendance:
Romford: C.Bingham;A.E.Collier,F.E.Fryatt(Capt);W.F.Mackenzie,J.Barton,W.B.Regan;
H.W.Brooks,G.Fleetwood,C.W.Newman,S.Frankland,P.King.

8 Sept ETT1R   Home   Barking   0 – 0**
Attendance: 3,940   Receipts: £208.9.9   Programmes: £8.2.11 Car Park: £5.17.6
Romford: C.Bingham;A.E.Collier,F.E.Fryatt(Capt);W.F.Mackenzie,A.Wilson,J.Barton;
H.W.Brooks,E.Mocock,D.Yorston,S.Frankland,E.Berkeimeir.

10 Sept IFL   Home   Woking   1 – 3 Berkeimeir
Attendance: 3,732   Receipts: £176.1.3   Programmes: £19.9.2 Car Park: £3.17.3
Romford: C.Bingham;A.E.Collier,F.E.Fryatt(Capt);W.F.Mackenzie,A.Wilson,W.B.Regan;
H.W.Brooks,E.Mocock,T.Albert,S.Frankland,E.Berkeimeir.

17 Sept IFL   Away   Walthamstow Avenue   1 – 5 Bridge
Attendance:
Romford: R.Ivey;A.E.Collier,F.E.Fryatt(Capt);W.F.Mackenzie,J.Barton,W.B.Regan;
H.W.Brooks,S.Frankland,W.A.Bridge,G.W.Jennings,T.Chamberlain.

24 Sept IFL　　Home　Oxford City　　　　　　　　2 – 0　Albert(2)
Attendance: 4,306　　　Receipts: £204.15.9　Programmes: £20.4.8　Car Park: £4.18.0
Romford: R.Ivey;A.E.Belsham,F.E.Fryatt(Capt);W.F.Mackenzie,J.Barton,W.B.Regan;
W.A.Bridge,G.Askey,T.Albert,G.W.Jennings,H.W.Brooks.

1 Oct IFL　　Away　Leytonstone　　　　　　　　0 – 1
Attendance:
Romford: R.Ivey;R.G.Sheldon,F.E.Fryatt(Capt),W.F.Mackenzie,J.Barton,W.B.Regan;
P.King,G.Askey,J.R.Kurn,W.A.Bridge,H.W.Brooks.

8 Oct IFL　　Home　Wycombe Wanderers　　　　3 – 2　Albert(2)Bridge
Attendance: 4,311　　　Receipts: £210.2.0　Programmes: £21.0.2　Car Park: £5.14.3
Romford: R.Ivey;R.G.Sheldon,P.Phillips;W.F.Mackenzie,J.Barton(Capt),W.B.Regan;
P.King,J.R.Kurn,T.Albert,W.A.Bridge,H.W.Brooks.

15 Oct IFL　　Away　Dulwich Hamlet　　　　　　0 – 4
Attendance:
Romford: R.Ivey;R.G.Sheldon,F.E.Fryatt(Capt);W.F.Mackenzie,J.Barton,W.B.Regan;
P.King,G.Askey,J.R.Kurn,W.A.Bridge,H.W.Brooks.

22 Oct IFL　　Home　Kingstonian　　　　　　　2 – 1　Brooks(2)
Attendance: 4,397　　　Receipts: £209,17.3　Programmes: £22.14.4　Car Park: £6.5.0
Romford: R.Ivey;R.G.Sheldon,F.E.Fryatt(Capt);G.Fleetwood,W.B.Regan,W.F.Mackenzie;
H.W.Brooks,W.A.Bridge,T.Albert,K.Morton,P.King.

29 Oct IFL　　Away　Wimbledon　　　　　　　　2 – 2　Kurn,Bridge
Attendance:
Romford: R.Ivey;R.G.Sheldon,F.E.Fryatt(Capt);G.Fleetwood,W.B.Regan,W.F.Mackenzie;
H.W.Brooks,W.A.Bridge,J.R.Kurn,K.Morton,P.King.

5 Nov IFL　　Home　Clapton　　　　　　　　　1 – 2　King
Attendance: 1,736　　　Receipts: £91.15.6　Programmes: £9.3.6　Car Park: £3.7.3
Romford: R.Ivey;R.G.Sheldon,F.E.Fryatt(Capt);G.Fleetwood,W.B.Regan,W.F.Mackenzie;
H.W.Brooks,W.A.Bridge,J.R.Kurn,K.Morton,P.King.

12 Nov FAC4Q Home　Kingstonian　　　　　　　3 – 0　Bridge,Jennings,Mackenzie
Attendance: 7,099　　　Receipts: £385.4.0　Programmes: £28.1.6　Car Park: £11.4.3
Romford: R.Ivey;R.G.Sheldon,F.E.Fryatt(Capt);G.Fleetwood,J.Barton,W.B.Regan;
H.W.Brooks,W.F.Mackenzie,W.A.Bridge,G.W.Jennings,P.King.

19 Nov Frdly　Home　Cambridge University　　　2 – 1　Mackenzie(2)
Attendance: 2,941　　　Receipts: £150.8.9　Programmes: £16.14.10　Car Park: £4.0.3
Romford: R.Ivey;R.G.Sheldon,F.E.Fryatt(Capt);G.Fleetwood,J.Barton,W.B.Regan;
K.Morton,W.F.Mackenzie,W.A.Bridge,G.W.Jennings,P.King.

26 Nov FAC1R　Away　Yeovil Town　　　　　　　1 – 4　Jennings
Attendance: 12,000
Romford: R.Ivey;R.G.Sheldon,F.E.Fryatt(Capt);G.Fleetwood,J.Barton,W.B.Regan;
H.W.Brooks,W.F.Mackenzie,W.A.Bridge,G.W.Jennings,P.King.

3 Dec IFL　　Away　Clapton　　　　　　　　　3 – 3　Mackenzie,Brooks(2)
Attendance:
Romford: R.Ivey;R.G.Sheldon,F.E.Fryatt(Capt);G.Fleetwood,R.Haverson,W.B.Regan;
H.W.Brooks,W.F.Mackenzie,W.A.Bridge,K.Morton,P.King.

10 Dec IFL　　Home　Tufnell Park　　　　　　6 – 0　Mackenzie(2)Jennings,Sheldon(2pens),
　　　　　　　　　　　　　　　　　　　　　　　　　　　Brooks
Attendance: 2,357　　　Receipts: £103.6.3　Programmes: £12.14.8　Car Park: £1.15.0
Romford: R.Ivey;R.G.Sheldon,F.E.Fryatt(Capt);G.Fleetwood,W.B.Regan,K.Morton;
H.W.Brooks,W.F.Mackenzie,W.A.Bridge,G.W.Jennings,P.King.

17 Dec IFL　　Away　Woking　　　　　　　　　2 – 2　Jennings,Brooks
Attendance:
Romford: R.Ivey;R.G.Sheldon,F.E.Fryatt(Capt);G.Fleetwood,W.B.Regan,K.Morton;
H.W.Brooks,W.F.Mackenzie,W.A.Bridge,G.W.Jennings,P.King.

24 Dec IFL　　Home　Ilford　　　　　　　　　0 – 3
Attendance: 3,195　　　Receipts: £152.19.3　Programmes: £20.2.2　Car Park: £7.14.3
Romford: R.Ivey;R.Cave,F.E.Fryatt(Capt);G.Fleetwood,W.B.Regan,K.Morton;
H.W.Brooks,W.F.Mackenzie,T.Albert,W.A.Bridge,J.Bartholomew.

26 Dec IFL　　Away　Ilford　　　　　　　　　4 – 1　Brooks,Jennings(2)Fleetwood
Attendance: 6,000
Romford: R.Ivey;R.G.Sheldon,F.E.Fryatt(Capt);G.Fleetwood,W.B.Regan,K.Morton;
H.W.Brooks,W.F.Mackenzie,T.Albert,G.W.Jennings,J.Bartholomew.

31 Dec IFL   Away   Wycombe Wanderers   1 – 1   Albert
Attendance:
Romford: R.Ivey;R.G.Sheldon,F.E.Fryatt(Capt);G.Fleetwood,W.B.Regan,W.F.Mackenzie;
H.W.Brooks,G.W.Jennings,T.Albert,C.F.Pearson,K.Morton.

7 Jan   IFL   Away   St. Albans City   3 – 2   King,Sheldon(pen),Bartholomew
Attendance:
Romford: R.Ivey;R.G.Sheldon,F.E.Fryatt(Capt);W.F.Mackenzie,J.Barton,W.B.Regan;
H.W.Brooks,G.Fleetwood,J.Bartholomew,C.F.Pearson,P.King.

14 Jan   AC1R   Home   Windsor & Eton   3 – 2   Jennings,Cooper(og),Pearson
Attendance: 6,989   Receipts: £375.5.0   Programmes: £29.1.10   Car Park: £8.7.3
Romford: R.Ivey;R.G.Sheldon,F.E.Fryatt(Capt);W.F.Mackenzie,J.Barton,W.B.Regan;
H.W.Brooks,G.W.Jennings,T.Albert,C.F.Pearson,P.King.

21 Jan   ESC1R Away   Brentwood & Warley   0 – 1
Attendance: 3,500
Romford: R.Ivey;R.G.Sheldon,F.E.Fryatt(Capt);W.F.Mackenzie,J.Barton,W.B.Regan;
H.W.Brooks,G.W.Jennings,J.Bartholomew,C.F.Pearson,P.King.

28 Jan   AC2R   Home   Clapton   0 – 1
Attendance: 5,053   Receipts: £281.0.3   Programmes: £   Car Park: £5.6.6
Romford: R.Ivey;R.G.Sheldon,F.E.Fryatt(Capt);G.Fleetwood,J.Barton,W.B.Regan;
H.W.Brooks,G.W.Jennings,W.A.Bridge,C.F.Pearson,P.King.

4 Feb   IFL   Home   Corinthian Casuals   1 – 0   Regan
Attendance: 2,588   Receipts: £116.10.0   Programmes: £   Car Park: £3.15.0
Romford: R.Ivey;E.R.Cave,F.E.Fryatt(Capt);G.Fleetwood,J.Barton,W.B.Regan;
H.W.Hails,G.W.Jennings,W.A.Bridge,C.F.Pearson,H.W.Brooks.

11 Feb   Frdly   Home   Gillingham Res.   1 – 4   Bridge
Attendance: 1,937   Receipts: £104.12.6   Programmes: £   Car Park: £1.9.0
Romford: R.Ivey;E.R.Cave,F.E.Fryatt(Capt);W.F.Mackenzie,J.Barton,W.B.Regan;
H.W.Brooks,G.Fleetwood,W.A.Bridge,C.F.Pearson,H.W.Hails.

18 Feb   IFL   Away   Oxford City   2 – 3   Kurn,Pearson
Attendance:
Romford: R.Ivey;E.R.Cave,F.E.Fryatt(Capt);W.F.Mackenzie,J.Barton,K.Morton;
H.W.Brooks,G.Fleetwood,G.W.Jennings,J.R.Kurn,C.F.Pearson.

25 Feb   IFL   Home   Dulwich Hamlet   2 – 0   Jennings(2)
Attendance: 3,878   Receipts: £189.6.3   Programmes: £20.8.8   Car Park: £6.8.9
Romford: R.Ivey;E.R.Cave,F.E.Fryatt(Capt);W.F.Mackenzie,J.Barton,W.B.Regan;
H.W.Brooks,W.A.Bridge,G.W.Jennings,C.F.Pearson,H.W.Hails.

4 Mar   IFL   Away#   Tufnell Park   2 – 3   Bridge,Brooks
Attendance: 2,924   Receipts: £153.2.8   Programmes: £15.4.0   Car Park: £4.2.6
Romford: R.Ivey;R.G.Sheldon,F.E.Fryatt(Capt);G.Fleetwood,J.Barton,C.F.Pearson;
H.W.Brooks,W.A.Bridge,G.W.Jennings,K.Morton,H.W.Hails.

11 Mar   IFL   Away   Kingstonian   0 – 1
Attendance:
Romford: R.Ivey;E.R.Cave,F.E.Fryatt(Capt);W.F.Mackenzie,W.Solley,W.B.Regan;
J.Sharod,H.W.Brooks,T.Albert,C.F.Pearson,H.W.Hails.

18 Mar   IFL   Home   Wimbledon   1 – 2   Pearson
Attendance: 2,545   Receipts: £118.6.6   Programmes: £14.12.10 Car Park: £4.5.9
Romford: R.Ivey;E.R.Cave,F.E.Fryatt(Capt);G.Fleetwood,W.Solley,K.Morton;
P.King,H.W.Brooks,G.W.Jennings,W.A.Bridge,C.F.Pearson.

8 Apr   Frdly   Home   Billingham Synthonia Recreation   3 – 3   Brooks(2)Regan
Attendance: 2,992   Receipts: £160.11.9   Programmes: £15.4.6   Car Park: £3.4.3
Romford: R.Ivey;E.R.Cave,F.E.Fryatt(Capt);W.F.Mackenzie,J.Barton,C.F.Pearson;
H.W.Brooks,R.A.Lamb,T.Horn,W.A.Bridge,W.B.Regan.

10 Apr   ETTRp Away   Barking   5 – 1   Lamb,Horn(2),Bridge,Brooks
Attendance:
Romford: R.Ivey;E.R.Cave,F.E.Fryatt(Capt);W.F.Mackenzie,J.Barton,K.Morton;
H.W.Brooks,W.A.Bridge,T.Horn,R.A.Lamb,W.B.Regan.

15 Apr   IFL   Home   Walthamstow Avenue   2 – 1   Horn(2)
Attendance: 3,645   Receipts: £179.7.6   Programmes: £18.19.6   Car Park: £3.9.0
Romford: R.Ivey;E.R.Cave,F.E.Fryatt(Capt);W.F.Mackenzie,J.Barton,C.F.Pearson;
H.W.Brooks,W.A.Bridge,T.Horn,R.A.Lamb,W.B.Regan.

19 Apr ETTSF Away Grays Athletic 2 – 0 Bridge,Horn
Attendance:
Romford: R.Ivey;E.R.Cave,F.E.Fryatt(Capt);W.F.Mackenzie,J.Barton,K.Morton;
H.W.Brooks,W.A.Bridge,T.Horn,R.A.Lamb,W.B.Regan.

22 Apr Frdly Home Clacton Town 2 – 1 Bridge,Brooks
Attendance: 2,125   Receipts: £109.8.3   Programmes: £10.14.0   Car Park: £2.9.6
Romford: R.Ivey;E.R.Cave,F.E.Fryatt(Capt);W.F.Mackenzie,J.Barton,C.F.Pearson;
H.W.Brooks,W.A.Bridge,T.Horn,R.A.Lamb,W.B.Regan.

29 Apr Frdly Home Brentwood & Warley 5 – 0 Brooks(3)Bridge,Lamb
Attendance: 785   Receipts: £46.9.9   Programmes: £3.11.0   Car Park: £0.17.9
Romford: R.Ivey;E.R.Cave,F.E.Fryatt(Capt);W.F.Mackenzie,J.Barton,W.J.Solley;
H.W.Brooks,W.A.Bridge,T.Horn,R.A.Lamb,G.W.Jennings.

3 May ETTF Away Ilford 2 – 3* Bridge,Brooks
Attendance:
Romford: R.Ivey;E.R.Cave,F.E.Fryatt(Capt);W.F.Mackenzie,J.Barton,K.Morton;
H.W.Brooks,W.A.Bridge,T.C.Horn,R.A.Lamb,W.B.Regan.

6 May IFL Home Leytonstone 2 – 0 Horn(2)
Attendance: 2,402   Receipts: £110.0.0   Programmes: £17.3.2   Car Park: £2.3.3
Romford: R.Ivey;E.R.Cave,R.G.Sheldon;W.J.Solley,J.Barton(Capt),K.Morton;
H.W.Brooks,W.A.Bridge,T.C.Horn,R.A.Lamb,W.B.Regan.

*   After extra time.
**   Abandoned in extra time after 121 minutes
#   Played at Brooklands

SUMMARY OF RESULTS SEASON 1949-50

	P	Home			Goals		Away			Goals		Pts
		W	D	L	For	Ag	W	D	L	For	Ag	
Isthmian League	26	8	0	5	23	14	2	4	7	22	35	24
FA Challenge Cup	2	1	0	0	3	0	0	0	1	1	4	
FA Amateur Cup	2	1	0	1	3	3	0	0	0	0	0	
Essex Senior Cup	1	0	0	0	0	0	0	0	1	0	1	
Thameside Trophy	4	0	1	0	0	0	2	0	1	9	4	
Friendlies	6	4	1	1	15	9	0	0	0	0	0	
Total	41	14	2	7	44	26	4	4	10	32	44	

ISTHMIAN FOOTBALL LEAGUE
Final Table

	P	W	D	L	Goals		Pts
					For	Ag	
Leytonstone	26	17	5	4	77	31	39
Wimbledon	26	18	2	6	72	51	38
Kingstonian	26	16	3	7	59	39	35
Walthamstow Avenue	26	14	6	6	73	42	34
Dulwich Hamlet	26	14	3	9	60	47	31
St. Albans City	26	12	3	11	59	45	27
Woking	26	10	6	10	60	71	26
Wycombe Wanderers	26	9	7	10	51	52	25
Romford	**26**	**10**	**4**	**12**	**45**	**49**	**24**
Ilford	26	10	4	12	46	53	24
Clapton	26	8	6	12	51	59	22
Oxford City	26	6	6	14	35	54	18
Corinthian Casuals	26	4	5	17	41	69	13
Tufnell Park	26	3	2	21	24	91	8

FIRST TEAM CUP RESULTS SEASON 1949-50

FA Challenge Cup
Final:　　Arsenal　2　Liverpool　0

Romford's progress: 4th Qual　　Home　　Kingstonian　3 - 0
1st Round　　Away　　Yeovil Town 1 - 4

FA Amateur Challenge Cup
Final:　　Willington　4　Bishop Auckland　0

Romford's progress: 1st Round　Home　　Windsor & Eton　　3 - 2
2nd Round　Home　Clapton　　　　　0 - 1

Essex County FA Senior Challenge Cup
Final:　　Briggs Sports　4　Leyton　0

Romford's progress: 1st Round　Away　　Brentwood & Warley　0 - 1

Essex Thameside Challenge Competition
Final:　　Ilford　3　Romford　2

Romford's progress: 1st Round　Home　　Barking　　　　0 - 0
Replay　　Away　　Barking　　5 - 1
Semi-Final　Away　　Grays Athletic　2 - 0
Final:　　Away　　Ilford　　2 - 3

FIRST TEAM DEBUTS SEASON 1949 – 50

1949				Previous Club
20th Aug.	v Schaffhausen	-	F.James	Walthamstow Ave.
		-	P.King	Oxford City
		-	S.A.Tuckey	Clapton
27th Aug.	v St.Albans City	-	J.O'Reilly	n/k
3rd Sept.	v Corinthian Cas.	-	C.Bingham	Romford Police
8th Sept.	v Barking	-	E.Berkeimeir	n/k
		-	E.Mocock	n/k
		-	A.Wilson	Southampton
		-	D.J.Yorston	n/k
10th Sept.	v Woking	-	T.Albert	n/k
17th Sept.	v Walthamstow Ave.	-	T.Chamberlain	Fulham
24th Sept.	v Oxford City	-	G.Askey	Fulham
1st Oct.	v Leytonstone	-	J.R.Kurn	Royal Air Force
8th Oct.	v Wycombe W'drs.	-	P.H.Phillips	n/k
22nd Oct.	v Kingstonian	-	K.Morton	Clacton Town
3rd Dec.	v Clapton	-	R.Haverson	n/k
24th Dec.	v Ilford	-	J.Bartholomew	Grays Athletic
		-	E.R.Cave	Mansfield House(Plaistow)
31st Dec.	v Wycombe W'drs.	-	C.F.Pearson	Barking
1950				
4th Feb.	v Corinthian Cas.	-	H.W.Hails	n/k
11th Mar.	v Kingstonian	-	J.W.Sharod	n/k
		-	W.J.Solley	Beckton Gas Works
8th Apr.	v Billingham S.Rec.	-	T.C.Horn	Rainham Town
		-	R.A.Lamb	Barking

FIRST TEAM APPEARANCES SEASON 1949 - 50

	A	B	C	D	E	F	Total
Terry Albert	8	0	1	0	0	0	9
George Askey	3	0	0	0	0	0	3
Jack Bartholomew**	3	0	0	1	0	0	4
Jack Barton	14	2	2	1	4	6	29
Alf Belsham	1	0	0	0	0	1	2
Ernst Berkeimeir	1	0	0	0	1	0	2
Cyril Bingham	2	0	0	0	1	0	3
Bill Bridge	19	2	1	0	3	6	31
Harold Brooks	26	2	2	1	4	5	40
Roy Cave	8	0	0	0	3	4	15
Tosh Chamberlain	1	0	0	0	0	0	1
Albert Collier	3	0	0	0	1	0	4
Gordon Fleetwood	15	2	1	0	0	2	20
Stan Frankland	3	0	0	0	1	1	5
Fred Fryatt	24	2	2	1	4	6	39
Harry Hails	4	0	0	0	0	1	5
Roy Haverson	1	0	0	0	0	0	1
Tommy Horn	2	0	0	0	3	3	8
Reg Ivey	24	2	2	1	3	6	38
Fred James	0	0	0	0	0	1	1
George Jennings	11	2	2	1	0	2	18
Peter King	13	2	2	1	0	2	20
John Kurn	6	0	0	0	0	0	6
Ron Lamb	2	0	0	0	3	3	8
Bill Mackenzie	22	2	1	1	4	5	35
Eddie Mocock	1	0	0	0	1	0	2
Ken Morton	13	0	0	0	3	1	17
Chuck Newman	2	0	0	0	0	0	2
J.O'Reilly	1	0	0	0	0	0	1
Pip Pearson	9	0	2	1	0	3	15
P. Phillips	1	0	0	0	0	0	1
Bill Regan	23	2	2	1	3	5	36
Jim Sharod	1	0	0	0	0	0	1
Ron Sheldon	14	2	2	1	0	1	20
Bill Solley	3	0	0	0	0	1	4
Stan Tuckey	1	0	0	0	0	1	2
A.Wilson	1	0	0	0	1	0	2
Derek Yorston	0	0	0	0	1	0	1
Total	286	22	22	11	44	66	451

Note** Jack Bartholomew was suspended by the Football Association following a commission into the affairs of Grays Athletic Football Club. Many of the club's officials and more than a hundred current and former players were suspended as a result of illegal payments to players. Bartholomew returned to Romford at the conclusion of his suspension in 1951.

Key to competitions

A   Isthmian Football League
B   FA Challenge Cup
C   FA Amateur Challenge Cup
D   Essex County FA Senior Challenge Cup
E   Thameside Challenge Trophy
F   Friendlies

These apply to both the Appearances and Goal Scorers tables.

FIRST TEAM GOALSCORERS SEASON 1949 - 50

	A	B	C	D	E	F	Total
Harold Brooks	8	0	0	0	2	7	17
Bill Bridge	5	1	0	0	3	3	12
George Jennings	6	2	1	0	0	0	9
Tommy Horn	4	0	0	0	3	0	7
Bill Mackenzie	3	1	0	0	0	2	6
Terry Albert	5	0	0	0	0	0	5
Ron Sheldon	3	0	0	0	0	0	3
Pip Pearson	2	0	1	0	0	0	3
Peter King	2	0	0	0	0	0	2
John Kurn	2	0	0	0	0	0	2
Bill Regan	1	0	0	0	0	1	2
Ron Lamb	0	0	0	0	1	1	2
Fred James	0	0	0	0	0	1	1
Stan Frankland	1	0	0	0	0	0	1
Ernst Berkeimeir	1	0	0	0	0	0	1
Gordon Fleetwood	1	0	0	0	0	0	1
Jack Bartholomew	1	0	0	0	0	0	1
Own Goal	0	0	1	0	0	0	1
Total	45	4	3	0	9	15	76

Reserve Team Match Details

27 Aug IFLR Away St. Albans City Res. 3 – 1 Mocock,Belsham,Acampora
Romford Res.: C.Bingham;H.Rayment,P.H.Phillips;J.C.Spelling,R.Haverson,V.H.Perriman;
E.H.Jones,E.Mocock,G.Fleetwood,A.E.Belsham(Capt),B.A.Acampora.

3 Sept IFLR Home Corinthian Casuals Res. 2 – 1 Mocock,Belsham(pen)
Attendance: 989   Receipts: £19.9.9   Programmes: £1.17.9   Car Park: £0.11.6
Romford Res.: T.Koszulinski;G.Fleetwood,P.H.Phillips;A.J.Maddick,R.Haverson,
A.E.Belsham(Capt);E.H.Jones,E.Mocock,H.W.Hails,V.S.Brown,E.Berkeimeir.

10 Sept IFLR Away Woking Res. 4 – 2 Kurn,Howlett(2)Watkins
Romford Res.: T.Koszulinski;E.R.Cave,P.H.Phillips;J.C.Spelling,R.Haverson,A.E.Belsham(Capt);
G.G.Howlett,J.R.Kurn,G.Fleetwood,R.R.Watkins,E.H.Jones.

17 Sept IFLR Home Walthamstow Avenue Res. 2 – 2 Yorston,Kurn
Attendance: 1,291   Receipts: £24.12.3   Programmes: £2.15.0   Car Park: £0.11.6
Romford Res.: J.Martin;E.R.Cave,R.G.Sheldon;G.Fleetwood,R.Haverson,A.E.Belsham(Capt);
E.H.Jones,A.J.Maddick,J.R.Kurn,D.J.Yorston,G.G.Howlett.

24 Sept IFLR Away Oxford City Res. 1 – 1 Wheeler
Romford Res.: C.Bingham;G.Fleetwood,R.G.Sheldon;J.C.Spelling,R.Haverson,P.H.Phillips;
G.G.Howlett,J.D.Wheeler,J.R.Kurn,S.Frankland,V.H.Perriman.

1 Oct IFLR Home Wimbledon Res. 0 – 2
Attendance: 1,123   Receipts: £22.6.0   Programmes: £2.13.3   Car Park: £0.10.0
Romford Res.: C.Bingham;E.R.Cave,P.H.Phillips;J.C.Spelling,R.Haverson,M.Martin;
E.G.Goodchild,G.Fleetwood,T.Morris,S.Frankland,H.Rayment.

8 Oct IFLR Away Tufnell Park Res. 4 – 2 Porley,Perriman(2)Goodchild(pen)
Romford Res.: C.Bingham;E.R.Cave,-.Savage;G.Fleetwood,W.J.Solley,K.Morton;
E.G.Goodchild,J.Bartholomew,V.H.Perriman,W.P.Spelling,J.Porley.

15 Oct IFLR Home Ilford Res. 0 – 3
Attendance: 1,397   Receipts: £29.19.3   Programmes: £3.0.0   Car Park: £0.19.0
Romford Res.: C.Bingham;E.R.Cave,W.J.Solley;G.Fleetwood,R.Haverson,G.Hewitt;
S.Frankland,J.Bartholomew,D.J.Yorston,G.W.Jennings,J.Hutchins.

29 Oct IFLR Home Kingstonian Res. 0 – 3
Attendance: 1,026   Receipts: £19.14.3   Programmes: £2.13.10   Car Park: £0.11.3
Romford Res.: D.Sweetman;J.C.Spelling,P.H.Phillips;P.D.Hall,R.Haverson,V.H.Perriman;
B.W.Palmer,A.S.Warwick,W.Smith,G.Askey,J.Hutchins.

5 Nov   IFLR   Away   Clapton Res.   5 – 3   Bartholomew(4)Frankland
Romford Res.: C.Bingham;E.R.Cave,P.H.Phillips;W.J.Solley,R.Haverson,V.H.Perriman;
-.Connelly,G.W.Jennings,J.Bartholomew,S.Frankland,J.Hutchins.

12 Nov   IFLR   Away   Dulwich Hamlet Res.   2 – 3   Bartholomew,Colwell
Romford Res.: D.Sweetman;E.R.Cave,P.H.Phillips;W.J.Solley,R.Haverson,V.H.Perriman;
A.Colwell,G.Askey,J.Bartholomew,S.Frankland,J.Hutchins.

26 Nov   IFLR   Home   Leytonstone Res.   2 – 2   Bartholomew(2)
Attendance: 1,378   Receipts: £25.0.0   Programmes: £1.18.3   Car Park: £0.11.9
Romford Res.: C.Bingham;W.J.Solley,P.H.Phillips;W.P.Spelling,R.Haverson,V.H.Perriman;
A.Colwell,G.Askey,J.Bartholomew,K.Morton,H.W.Hails.

3 Dec   IFLR   Home   Oxford City Res.   1 – 4   Bartholomew
Attendance: 728   Receipts: £8.16.0   Programmes: £1.0.3   Car Park: £0.4.6
Romford Res.: D.Sweetman;E.R.Cave,P.H.Phillips;W.P.Spelling,W.J.Solley,V.H.Perriman;
J.R.Kurn,G.Askey,J.Bartholomew,S.Frankland,H.W.Hails.

10 Dec   IFLR   Away   Ilford Res.   2 – 2   C.H.(og),Bartholomew
Romford Res.: F.L.Sykes;E.R.Cave,P.H.Phillips;W.P.Spelling,R.Haverson,J.Andrews;
J.W.Sharod,J.R.Kurn,J.Bartholomew,E.Mocock,H.W.Hails.

17 Dec   IFLR   Home   St. Albans City Res.   5 – 1   Kurn(2)Bartholomew,Askey(2)
Attendance: 545   Receipts: £7.5.0   Programmes: £0.15.0   Car Park: £0.7.9
Romford Res.: C.Bingham;E.R.Cave,P.H.Phillips;J.C.Spelling,W.J.Solley,V.H.Perriman;
H.W.Hails,J.Bottomley,J.R.Kurn,G.Askey,J.Bartholomew.

24 Dec   IFLR   Away   Leytonstone Res.   0 – 8
Romford Res.: C.Bingham;J.Sharod,P.Phillips;R.Haverson,W.J.Solley,W.Markham;
H.Hails,J.R.Kurn,C.F.Pearson,V.Perriman,S.Frankland.

31 Dec   IFLR   Home   Clapton Res.   1 – 1   Hails
Attendance: 843   Receipts: £15.4.3   Programmes: £1.15.5   Car Park: £0.11.6
Romford Res.: C.Bingham;R.Mason,P.H.Phillips;R.Haverson,W.J.Solley,J.C.Spelling;
H.W.Hails,J.R.Kurn,J.Bartholomew,V.H.Perriman,P.King.

7 Jan   IFLR   Home   Wycombe Wanderers Res.   3 – 0   Perriman,Hails,Gray
Attendance: 923   Receipts: £16.3.6   Programmes: £1.12.5   Car Park: £0.11.9
Romford Res.: C.Bingham;E.R.Cave,P.H.Phillips;R.Harrison,W.J.Solley,W.P.Spelling;
H.W.Hails,G.W.Jennings,V.H.Perriman,K.Morton,J.Gray.

21 Jan   IFLR   Home   Tufnell Park Res.   3 – 2   Fleetwood(2)Spelling
Attendance: 449   Receipts: £7.12.0   Programmes: £0.15.0   Car Park: £0.6.0
Romford Res.: C.Bingham;E.R.Cave,R.Mason;R.Haverson,W.J.Solley,W.P.Spelling;
H.W.Hails,G.Fleetwood,J.R.Kurn,K.Morton,J.Gray.

28 Jan   IFLR   Away   Kingstonian Res.   3 – 3   Hails,Kurn,R.Smith
Romford Res.: J.Martin;E.R.Cave,W.P.Spelling;P.Stevenson,J.J.Hewitson,V.H.Perriman;
H.W.Hails,J.Bartholomew,R.Smith,J.R.Kurn,J.Gray.

4 Feb   IFLR   Away   Wimbledon Res.   0 – 5
Romford Res.: C.Bingham;R.Mason,W.P.Spelling;R.Haverson,W.J.Solley,K.Morton;
J.W.Sharod,J.R.Kurn,A.S.Warwick,R.Smith,J.Gray.

11 Feb   Frdly   Away   Rainham Working Men's Club   2 – 2   Kurn(2)
Romford Res.: C.Bingham;J.Lawrence,W.P.Spelling;R.Haverson,W.J.Solley,V.H.Perriman;
J.W.Sharod,J.R.Kurn,T.Albert,K.Morton,J.Gray.

18 Feb   IFLR   Home   Dulwich Hamlet Res.   2 – 0   W.Smith,J.Spelling
Attendance: 988   Receipts: £19.9.0   Programmes: £1.17.6   Car Park: £0.13.3
Romford Res.: J.Martin;J.Lawrence,W.P.Spelling;R.Haverson,W.J.Solley,-.Wilcox;
J.W.Sharod,E.Mocock,W.Smith,W.A.Bridge,J.C.Spelling.

25 Feb   IFLR   Away   Corinthian Casuals Res.   0 – 2
Romford Res.: J.Martin;J.Lawrence,W.P.Spelling;G.Fleetwood,R.Haverson,J.Andrews;
J.W.Sharod,E.Mocock,W.Smith,M.Martin,R.G.Sheldon.

4 Mar   ETR1R   Away   Grays Athletic Res.   3 – 3*   W.Smith(2)Kurn
Romford Res.: J.Martin;J.Lawrence,W.P.Spelling;R.Haverson,W.J.Solley,V.H.Perriman;
J.W.Sharod,G.Butcher,W.Smith,J.R.Kurn,-.Wilcox.

11 Mar   IFLR   Home   Woking Res.   7 – 1   Fleetwood,Horn(5)Sheldon
Attendance: 857   Receipts: £16.9.3   Programmes: £1.15.0   Car Park: £1.1.0
Romford Res.: J.Martin;J.Lawrence,R.G.Sheldon;G.Fleetwood,J.J.Hewitson,V.H.Perriman;
J.C.Spelling,S.Macauley,T.Horn,K.Morton,W.P.Spelling.

18 Mar   Frdly   Away   Stanstead Res.   3 – 0   Horn(2)Lamb
Romford Res.: J.Martin;J.Lawrence,R.G.Sheldon;W.P.Spelling,J.Barton,V.H.Perriman;
J.W.Sharod,R.A.Lamb,T.Horn,W.Smith,S.Macauley.

25 Mar IFLR Away Walthamstow Avenue Res. 0 – 5
Romford Res.: J.Martin;J.Lawrence,R.G.Sheldon;G.Fleetwood,J.Barton,W.P.Spelling;
H.W.Hails,R.A.Lamb,T.Horn,J.R.Kurn,S.Macauley.

7 Apr ETRRp Home Grays Athletic Res. 3 – 1 Scorers unknown
Attendance: 1,048 Receipts: £26.18.6 Programmes: £2.12.10 Car Park: £1.10.0
Romford Res.:
Team details unknown

22 Apr IFLR Away Wycombe Wanderers Res. 1 – 1 Frankland
Romford Res.: C.Bingham;J.Lawrence,R.G.Sheldon;G.Fleetwood,W.J.Solley,W.P.Spelling;
H.W.Hails,J.Mepsted,J.R.Kurn,S.Frankland,S.Macauley.

27 Apr ETRSF Away Walthamstow Avenue Res. 0 – 4
Romford Res.:
Team details unknown

5 May Frdly Home Romford League XI 0 – 3
Attendance: 329 Receipts: £6.12.3
Romford Res.:
Team details unknown

RESERVE TEAM SUMMARY OF RESULTS SEASON 1949 – 50

	Home			Goals		Away			Goals		
	P	W	D	L	For	Ag	W	D	L	For	Ag	Pts
Isthmian League Res. Sect.	26	6	3	4	28	22	4	4	5	25	38	27
Thameside Trophy Res.Sect	3	1	0	0	3	1	0	1	1	3	7	
Friendlies	3	0	0	1	0	3	1	1	0	5	2	
Totals	32	7	3	5	31	26	5	6	6	33	47	

Isthmian Football League Reserve Section
Final Table

	P	W	D	L	Goals For	Ag	Pts
Leytonstone	26	19	2	5	89	45	40
Kingstonian	26	17	3	6	81	47	37
Wimbledon	26	16	3	7	71	43	35
Walthamstow Avenue	26	15	3	8	73	45	33
Dulwich Hamlet	26	14	3	9	76	47	31
Romford Res.	**26**	**10**	**7**	**9**	**53**	**60**	**27**
Wycombe Wanderers	26	11	3	12	58	57	25
Clapton	26	10	3	13	62	70	23
Ilford	26	9	4	13	52	54	22
Corinthian Casuals	26	10	2	14	50	61	22
Woking	26	8	5	13	41	63	21
Oxford City	26	6	7	13	47	73	19
St. Albans City	26	7	2	17	43	79	16
Tufnell Park	26	6	1	19	34	86	13

RESERVE TEAM CUP RESULTS SEASON 1949 – 50

Essex Thameside Trophy Reserve Section
Final: n/k

Romford's progress: 1st Round Away Grays Athletic 3 – 3 *
Replay Home Grays Athletic 3 – 1
Semi-Final Away Walthamstow Avenue 0 – 4

* After Extra Time

RESERVE TEAM DEBUTS SEASON 1949 – 50

The following players are believed to have made their reserve team debut in the match indicated. Their previous Club is shown where known.

1949

Date	Match		Player	Previous Club
27th Aug.	v St.Albans C.Res.	-	**B.A.Acampora**	
		-	**E.H.Jones**	
		-	**E.Mocock**	
		-	**P.H.Phillips**	
		-	**H.Rayment**	
		-	**J.C.Spelling**	
3rd Sept.	v Corinthian C.Res.	-	**E.Berkeimeir**	
		-	**T.Koszulinski**	
		-	**H.W.Hails**	
10th Sept.	v Woking Res.	-	**J.R.Kurn**	Royal Air Force
		-	**R.R.Watkins**	
24th Sept.	v Oxford City Res.	-	**C.Bingham**	Romford Police
		-	**S.Frankland**	
		-	**J.D.Wheeler**	
1st Oct.	v Wimbledon Res.	-	**M.Martin**	
		-	**T.Morris**	
8th Oct.	v Tufnell Park Res.	-	**J.Bartholomew**	Grays Athletic
		-	**K.Morton**	Clacton Town
		-	**J.Porley**	
		-	**-.Savage**	
		-	**W.J.Solley**	Beckton Gas Works
15th Oct.	v Ilford Res.	-	**J.Hutchins**	Laindon
		-	**D.J.Yorston**	
29th Oct.	v Kingstonian Res.	-	**G.Askey**	Fulham
		-	**P.D.Hall**	
		-	**B.W.Palmer**	Marley Y.C.
		-	**W.Smith**	
		-	**A.S.Warwick**	
5th Nov.	v Clapton Res.	-	**E.R.Cave**	Royal Air Force
		-	**-.Connolly**	
12th Nov.	v Dulwich Hamlet Res.	-	**A.Colwell**	
26th Nov.	v Leytonstone Res.	-	**W.P.Spelling**	
10th Dec.	v Ilford Res.	-	**J.Andrews**	
		-	**J.W.Sharod**	
		-	**F.L.Sykes**	
17th Dec.	v St.Albans C.Res.	-	**J.Bottomley**	
24th Dec.	v Leytonstone Res.	-	**C.F.Pearson**	Barking
31st Dec.	v Clapton Res.	-	**P.King**	Oxford City
		-	**R.Mason**	

1950

Date	Match		Player	Previous Club
7th Jan.	v Wycombe Wand.Res.	-	**R.Harrison**	
28th Jan.	v Kingstonian Res.	-	**J.J.Hewitson**	
		-	**R.Smith**	
		-	**P.Stevenson**	
11th Feb.	v Rainham Working M.Club	-	**T.Albert**	
		-	**J.Lawrence**	
18th Feb.	v Dulwich Hamlet Res.	-	**-.Wilcox**	
11th Mar.	v Woking Res.	-	**S.Macauley**	
22nd Apr.	v Wycombe Wand.Res.	-	**J.Mepstead**	

PLAYERS RETURNED TO THE CLUB SEASON 1949-50

1949
15th Oct.	v Ilford Res.	-	**G.Hewitt**

1950
7th Jan.	v Wycombe Wand.Res.	-	**J.Gray**	
4th Mar.	v Grays Athletic	-	**G.Butcher**	Harold Park
11th Mar.	v Woking Res.	-	**T.C.Horn**	Rainham Town

RESERVE TEAM APPEARANCES SEASON 1949-50

The following players are known to have appeared in the reserve team during the season.

B.A.Acampora	T.Albert	J.Andrews	G.Askey(Fulham)
J.Bartholomew	J.Barton	A.E.Belsham	E.Berkeimeir
C.Bingham(Romford Police)	J.Bottomley	W.A.Bridge	V.S.Brown
G.Butcher	E.R.Cave	A.Colwell	-.Connelly
G.Fleetwood	S.Frankland	E.G.Goodchild	J.Gray
H.W.Hails	P.D.Hall	R.Harrison	R.Haverson
J.J.Hewitson	G.Hewitt	T.C.Horn	G.G.Howlett
J.Hutchins(Laindon)	G.W.Jennings	E.H.Jones	P.King(Oxford City)
T.Koszulinski	J.R.Kurn(Royal Air Force)	R.A.Lamb	J.Lawrence
S.Macauley	A.J.Maddick	J.Martin	M.Martin
W.Markham,	R.Mason	J.Mepstead	E.Mocock
T.Morris	K.Morton(Clacton Tn)	B.W.Palmer(Marley Y.C.)	C.F.Pearson(Barking)
V.H.Perriman	P.H.Phillips	J.Porley	H.Rayment
.Savage	J.W.Sharod	R.G.Sheldon	R.Smith
W.Smith	W.J.Solley(Beckton Gas Works)	J.C.Spelling	W.P.Spelling
P.Stevenson	D.Sweetman	F.L.Sykes	A.S.Warwick
R.R.Watkins(Cranham)	J.D.Wheeler	-.Wilcox	D.J.Yorston

"A" Team Match Details

24 Aug RDLP Away Rainham Town "A" 0 – 1
Romford "A": C.Bingham;W.P.Spelling,E.W.Archer;G.R.Schooling,R.Haverson,V.H.Perriman;
J.C.Spelling,J.D.Wheeler,R.Parker,D.Coughlin,B.A.Acampora.

3 Sept Frdly Away Clapton "A" 2 – 3 Yorston,E.Archer(pen)
Romford "A": D.Sweetman;E.R.Cave,E.W.Archer;G.McKinnell,H.Archer,J.Andrews;
F.G.Sargeant,J.D.Wheeler,D.J.Yorston,D.Coughlin,B.A.Acampora.

10 Sept RCC1R Away Romford British Legion 4 – 1 H.Archer,E.Archer,Goodchild,Marjoram
Romford "A": D.Sweetman;G.McInnell,H.Sutcliffe;P.D.Hall,E.W.Archer,J.Andrews;
E.G.Goodchild,D.J.Yorston,R.Marjoram,D.Coughlin,H.Archer.

14 Sept RDLP Away Romford Brewery 2 – 2 Acampora,Mocock
Romford "A" : D.Sweetman,E.R.Cave,H.Sutcliffe;P.D.Hall,W.P.Spelling,V.H.Perriman;
E.G.Goodchild,E.Mocock,D.J.Yorston,D.Coughlin,B.A.Acampora.

17 Sept CCC1R Away Chigwell 1 – 2 Palmer
Romford "A": D.Sweetman,V.H.Perriman,H.Sutcliffe;P.D.Hall,E.W.Archer,J.Andrews;
B.W.Palmer,E.Mocock,-.Thompson,D.Coughlin,R.R.Watkins.

24 Sept RDLP Away Elm Park 1 – 1 Cole
Romford "A": D.Sweetman;H.Rayment,E.R.Cave;G.McKinnell,E.W.Archer,H.Sutcliffe;
T.Morris,-.Jackson,-.Cole,D.J.Yorston,B.A.Acampora.

1 Oct RPLC1R Home Laindon 1 – 4 Coughlin
Romford "A": D.Sweetman;E.W.Archer,H.Sutcliffe;J.Andrews,V.H.Perriman,B.A.Acampora;
R.Marjoram,E.Mocock,D.J.Yorston,D.Coughlin,-.Judd.

8 Oct RDLP Away Upminster Old Boys 1 – 1 Mocock
Romford "A": F.L.Sykes;E.W.Archer,H.Sutcliffe;P.D.Hall,G.Hewitt,J.J.Hewitson;
R.Marjoram,E.Mocock,D.J.Yorston,J.Andrews,B.A.Acampora.

15 Oct Frdly Away Collier Row Athletic 5 – 3 Warwick(2)Mocock(2)Palmer
Romford "A": D.Sweetman;H.Sutcliffe,H.Archer,P.D.Hall,J.J.Hewitson,J.Andrews;
B.W.Palmer,E.Mocock,A.S.Warwick,D.Coughlin,B.A.Acampora.

22 Oct RDLP Home Bentley 2 – 0 Yorston,Palmer
Romford "A": D.Sweetman,W.Markham,H.Sutcliffe;P.Hall,J.J.Hewitson,J.Andrews;
B.W.Palmer,E.Mocock,A.S.Warwick,D.J.Yorston,B.A.Acampora.

29 Oct Frdly Away Cranham 3 – 6 Sutcliffe(2)Sharod
Romford "A": F.L.Sykes;J.Lawrence,J.Marshall;G.McKinnell,J.J.Hewitson,H.Archer;
J.W.Sharod,H.Wilson,H.Sutcliffe,L.Dowsett,L.McInnes.

5 Nov EJC2R Away Mayfield Old Boys 4 – 2 Acampora(2)Warwick,Sutcliffe
Romford "A": D.Sweetman;W.Markham,H.Sutcliffe;P.D.Hall,J.J.Hewitson,J.Andrews;
B.W.Palmer,E.Mocock,A.S.Warwick,D.Coughlin,B.A.Acampora.

12 Nov RDLP Away Hornchurch Athletic 1 – 5 Acampora
Romford "A": R.Marjoram;W.Markham,H.Sutcliffe;P.D.Hall,J.J.Hewitson,J.Andrews;
J.W.Sharod,E.Mocock,A.S.Warwick,D.Coughlin,B.A.Acampora.

19 Nov RDLP Home Beacontree Heath Old Boys 6 – 0 Acampora(3)Mocock,Sharod,Warwick
Romford "A": D.Sweetman;W.Markham,H.Sutcliffe;P.D.Hall,J.J.Hewitson,J.Andrews;
J.W.Sharod,E.Mocock,A.S.Warwick,D.Coughlin,B.A.Acampora.

26 Nov EJC3R Home Ship Carbon 3 – 1 Mocock(2)Warwick
Romford "A": D.Sweetman,W.Markham,H.Sutcliffe;P.D.Hall,J.J.Hewitson,J.Andrews;
J.W.Sharod,E.Mocock,A.S.Warwick,D.Coughlin,B.A.Acampora.

3 Dec RDLP Away South Essex Waterworks 1 – 3 Warwick
Romford "A": F.L.Sykes;W.Markham,H.Sutcliffe;P.D.Hall,J.J.Hewitson,J.Andrews;
J.W.Sharod,E.Mocock,A.S.Warwick,D.Coughlin,B.A.Acampora.

17 Dec EJC4R Away Ford Sports 3 – 0 Warwick,Frankland(2)
Romford "A": D.Sweetman;W.Markham,H.Sutcliffe;P.D.Hall,J.J.Hewitson,J.Andrews;
J.W.Sharod,E.Mocock,A.S.Warwick,S.Frankland,B.A.Acampora.

24 Dec RDLP Away Billericay 1 – 1 Mocock
Romford "A": J.Martin;J.Lawrence,J.Andrews;P.D.Hall,J.J.Hewitson,B.A.Acampora;
B.W.Palmer,E.Mocock,A.S.Warwick,-.McInnes,J.Gray.

27 Dec RDLP Home Romford Brewery 5 – 1 Mocock(3)Warwick(2)
Romford "A": D.Sweetman;J.Lawrence,H.Sutcliffe;P.D.Hall,J.J.Hewitson,J.Andrews;
J.W.Sharod,E.Mocock,A.S.Warwick,C.F.Pearson,B.A.Acampora.

31 Dec RDLP Home Billericay 0 – 0
Romford "A": D.Sweetman;J.Lawrence,H.Sutcliffe;P.D.Hall,J.J.Hewitson,J.Andrews;
N.G.Patient,E.Mocock,B.A.Acampora,D.Coughlin,-.Connelly.

7 Jan EJC5R Home Collier Row Athletic 1 – 5 Coughlin
Romford "A": D.Sweetman;W.Markham,H.Sutcliffe;P.D.Hall,J.J.Hewitson,J.Andrews;
J.W.Sharod,E.Mocock,A.S.Warwick,D.Coughlin,B.A.Acampora.

14 Jan RDLP Home Dagenham Dock 8 – 1 Mocock(2)Gray(2)Warwick(3)Sutcliffe(pen)
Romford "A": D.Sweetman;J.Lawrence,H.Sutcliffe;P.D.Hall,J.J.Hewitson,J.Andrews;
J.W.Sharod,E.Mocock,A.S.Warwick,B.A.Acampora,J.Gray.

21 Jan RDLP Away Dagenham Dock 0 – 0
Romford "A": D.Sweetman;J.Lawrence,H.Sutcliffe;P.D.Hall,J.J.Hewitson,J.Andrews;
J.W.Sharod,E.Mocock,A.S.Warwick,D.J.Yorston,-.Willcocks.

28 Jan RDLP Home Orsett United 6 – 1 Mocock(4)Sharod,Sutcliffe
Romford "A": D.Sweetman;J.Markham,H.Sutcliffe;P.D.Hall,J.Lawrence,J.Andrews;
J.W.Sharod,E.Mocock,A.S.Warwick,D.J.Yorston,-.Willcocks.

11 Feb RCCSF Away Clesco 2 – 4* Warwick,Yorston
Romford "A": D.Sweetman;W.Markham,H.Sutcliffe;P.D.Hall,J.J.Hewitson,B.A.Acampora;
-.Day,E.Mocock,A.S.Warwick,D.J.Yorston,-.Willcocks.

18 Feb RDLP Away Laindon 3 – 7 Hall,Sutcliffe,Warwick
Romford "A": D.Sweetman;-.Westlake,H.Sutcliffe;-.Payne,-.Milson,J.Andrews;
P.D.Hall,-.Connelly,A.S.Warwick,J.Marshall,McInnes.
Joe Ling scored from a penalty for Laindon.

4 Mar RDLP Home Rainham Town "A" 2 – 3 Hall,Ayling
Romford "A": -.Triggs;W.Markham,H.Sutcliffe;P.D.Hall,J.J.Hewitson,D.J.Yorston;
P.H..Phillips,-.Ayling,A.S.Warwick,-.McInnes,-.Connelly.

11 Mar RDLP Home South Essex Waterworks 1 – 2 Warwick
Romford "A": D.Sweetman;W.Markham,J.Andrews;-.Crooks,-.Milson,B.A.Acampora;
-.Ayling,D.J.Yorston,A.S.Warwick,-.Thomas,W.J.Markham.

18 Mar RDLP Home Upminster Old Boys 0 – 1
Romford "A": D.Sweetman;W.Markham,-.McInnes;P.D.Hall,J.J.Hewitson,D.J.Yorston;
J.C.Spelling,-.Ayling,-.Thomas,B.A.Acampora,-.Green.

25 Mar RDLP Away Roneo Athletic 2 – 0# Mocock,Spelling
Romford "A": D.Sweetman;W.Markham,J.Andrews;P.D.Hall,J.J.Hewitson,D.J.Yorston;
J.C.Spelling,J.W.Sharod,A.S.Warwick,E.Mocock,H.Sutcliffe.

1 Apr RDLP Away Bentley United 0 – 3
Romford "A": D.Sweetman;J.Lawrence,J.Andrews;W.Markham,J.J.Hewitson,W.P.Spelling;
J.C.Spelling,D.J.Yorston,-.Ayling,E.Mocock,J.W.Sharod.

10 Apr RDLP Home#1 Elm Park 1 – 2 Own goal
Romford "A": J.Martin;J.Lawrence,J.Andrews;-.Mepsted,J.J.Hewitson,D.J.Yorston;
J.C.Spelling,P.D.Hall,A.S.Warwick,-.Ayling,D.Sweetman.

19 Apr RDLP Home Sun Athletic 0 – 0#
Attendance: 244   Receipts: £5.9.0
Romford "A": D.Sweetman;W.Markham,J.Andrews;P.D.Hall,J.Lawrence,D.J.Yorston;
J.C.Spelling,E.Mocock,A.S.Warwick,J.W.Sharod,A.G.Mackenzie.

22 Apr RDLP Away Orsett United 1 – 1 J.Spelling
Romford "A": D.Sweetman;W.Markham,J.Andrews;P.D.Hall,J.J.Hewitson,D.J.Yorston;
J.W.Sharod,E.Mocock,A.S.Warwick,-.Ayling,J.C.Spelling.

24 Apr RDLP Home Laindon 1 – 0 Warwick
Attendance: 75   Receipts: £1.13.9
Romford "A": D.Sweetman;W.Markham,J.Andrews;P.Hall,J.Lawrence,D.J.Yorston;
J.W.Sharod,-.Ayling,A.S.Warwick,A.G.Mackenzie,J.C.Spelling.

26 Apr RDLP Home Hornchurch Athletic 0 – 0
Attendance: 105   Receipts: £2.8.0
Romford "A": D.Sweetman;J.Lawrence,H.Sutcliffe;J.W.Sharod,J.J.Hewitson,J.Andrews;
P.D.Hall,E.Mocock,A.S.Warwick,D.J.Yorston,B.A.Acampora.

29 Apr RDLP Away Clesco 0 – 4
Romford "A":

3 May RDLP Home Clesco 2 – 3 Lawrence,Warwick
Romford "A"

5 May RDLP Away Beacontree Heath Old Boys 0 – 0
Romford "A":

* After Extra Time
\# Match played for four points.
\#1 Played at Elm Park.

"A" TEAM SUMMARY OF RESULTS SEASON 1949-50

		Home		Goals		Away			Goals		
	P	W	D	L	For	Ag	W	D	L	For	Ag	Pts
Romford & Dist.League Prem. Div.	30	7	3	5	34	14	1	8	6	13	29	27
Essex Junior Cup	4	1	0	1	4	6	2	0	0	7	2	
Romford Premier League Cup	1	0	0	1	1	4	0	0	0	0	0	
Carter Charity Cup	1	0	0	0	0	0	0	0	1	1	2	
Friendly Matches	3	0	0	0	0	0	1	0	2	10	12	
Total	39	8	3	7	39	24	4	8	9	31	45	

Romford & District Football League Premier Division
Final Table

					Goals		
	P	W	D	L	For	Ag	Pts
Hornchurch Athletic	30	19	10	1	75	36	48
Clesco United	30	20	4	6	81	39	44
Laindon	30	20	2	8	77	41	42

Elm Park	30	16	8	6	69	44	40
Bentley United	30	16	6	8	87	68	38
Sun Athletic	30	14	5	11	61	50	33
South Essex Waterworks	30	14	5	11	75	63	33
Upminster Old Boys	30	12	5	13	59	71	29
Romford "A"	**30**	**8**	**11**	**11**	**47**	**43**	**27**
Beacontree Heath O.B.	30	11	5	14	68	77	27
Billericay	30	9	7	14	69	69	25
Dagenham Dock	30	9	4	17	52	90	22
Rainham	30	8	4	18	38	75	20
Romford Brewery	30	6	5	19	35	77	17
Roneo Athletic	30	4	8	18	36	51	16

"A" TEAM CUP RESULTS 1949-50

Essex County FA Junior Challenge Cup
Final: Lexden   3   Shoebury Town   1

Romford's progress:	1st Round	Away	Mayfield	4 – 2
	2nd Round	Home	Ship Carbon	3 – 1
	3rd Round	Away	Ford Sports	3 – 0
	4th Round	Home	Collier Row Athletic	1 – 5

Romford & District Football League Cup
Final: Laindon   1   Harold Wood Athletic   1 (a.e.t)
Replay: Harold Wood Athletic   4   Laindon   1

Romford's progress: 1st Round   Home   Laindon Spartans   1 – 4

Romford Charity Cup Premier Section
Final: Clesco United   2   Roneo Athletic   0

Romford's progress:	1st Round	Away	Romford British Legion	4 – 1
	2nd Round	Rainham	Clesco United	2 – 4 *

Carter Charity Cup
Final: n/k

Romford's progress: 1st Round   Away   Chigwell   1 – 2

* After Extra Time

"A" TEAM APPEARANCES SEASON 1949-50

The following players are believed to have appeared in the "A" team during the season.

B.A.Acampora	J.Andrews	E.W.Archer	H.Archer
-.Ayling	C.Bingham	E.R.Cave	-.Cole
-.Connolly	D.Coughlin	-.Crooks	-.Day
L.Dowsett	S.Frankland	E.G.Goodchild	J.Gray
-.Green	P.D.Hall	R.Haverson	J.J.Hewitson
G.Hewitt	-.Jackson	-.Judd	J.Lawrence
A.G.Mackenzie	R.Marjoram	W.J.Markham	J.Marshall
J.Martin	G.McInnell	L.McInnes	J.Mepstead
-.Millson	E.Mocock	T.Morris	B.W.Palmer(Marley Y.C.)
R.Parker	N.G.Patient	-.Payne	C.F.Pearson
V.H.Perriman	P.H.Phillips	H.Rayment	F.G.Sargeant
G.Schooling	J.W.Sharod	J.C.Spelling	W.P.Spelling
H.Sutcliffe	D.Sweetman	Frank L.Sykes	-.Thomas
-.Thompson	-.Triggs	A.S.Warwick	R.R.Watkins(Cranham)
-.Westlake	J.D.Wheeler	-.Wilcocks	H.Wilson
D.J.Yorston			

Arsenal against Spurs? No, it's not the North London derby, but Romford v. Schaffhausen!

Romford President Tom Macpherson meets the Schaffhausen players

Fred Fryatt introduces his team to Schaffhausen President Max Branner.

Goalkeeper Guiseppe Bordoli safely gathers the ball to thwart Bill Bridge (left) and Percy James (below)

All items from the Authors' collection

Players, mascots, club officials and match officials in place for a pre-match photograph

DEPARTURES FROM THE CLUB SEASON 1949 - 50

The following players appear to have left the club during or by the end of the season. They may have been triallists and only played one or two games and then went elsewhere. New clubs are indicated where known.

B.A.Acampora, T.Albert (Royal Air Force, then Barnet), H.Archer (Campbell Athletic), G.Askey (Finchley), A.E.Belsham (Dagenham), E.Berkeimeir (Enfield Town), J.Bottomly, V.S.Brown (Bishops Stortford), G.Butcher (Harold Park), T.Chamberlain (Fulham), A.E.Collier (Redhill), A.Colwell, -.Connelly, E.G.Goodchild, J.Gray, R.Harrison, R.Haverson, J.J.Hewitson (Rainham Town), G.Hewitt, G.G.Howlett (Tufnell Park), J.Hutchins (Laindon Spartans), Reg.Ivey (Hendon), F.C.James (Laindon Spartans), E.H.Jones, P.King (Royal Navy), T.Koszulinski, J.Lawrence (Grays Athletic), S.Macauley, A.J.Maddick (Aveley), R.Mason, J.Mepstead, E.Mocock (Rainham Town), T.Morris, C.W.Newman (Dagenham), J.O'Reilly, Brian W.Palmer(Royal Navy), C.F.Pearson (Dartford), P.H.Phillips, J.Porley, H.Rayment, -.Savage, J.W.Sharod, R.G.Sheldon, R.Smith, W.Smith, J.C.Spelling, P.Stevenson, D.Sweetman, F.L.Sykes, S.A.Tuckey (Ilford), A.S.Warwick (Rainham Town), R.R.Watkins (Cranham), J.D.Wheeler, -.Wilcox, A.Wilson, D.J.Yorston.

Note: Many of the above were probably triallists who played the odd game for the Reserves or "A" Teams and then moved on or back to their previous Club. Due to the lack of information of the composition of "A" sides in the 1950-51 season, it is possible that some of the above players were in those teams, but no definite information is available.

Post Season Summary   Season 1949 – 50

The season began with a friendly at Brooklands against Swiss team Schaffhausen, Romford securing a 2-0 win. With George Patterson now retired, Tony Maddick returned to Aveley and Albert Collier and George Jennings unavailable, Romford prepared to meet St Albans City on 27th August at Brooklands for their first league game. 5,000 spectators saw the boys humbled with a 5-1 defeat. A week later Romford visited Corinthian Casuals, another team from the lower regions of the table, but lost 2-1.

On 8th September a disgruntled crowd witnessed a very poor Thameside Trophy game against Barking ending in a goalless draw. The league campaign was not going well and two further defeats were inflicted by Woking (1-3) and Walthamstow Avenue (1-5). Following unfair criticism from supporters, Albert Collier decided to leave and throw in his lot with Redhill. Bridge was showing a loss of form and had a go at outside right, while Brooks agreed to operate from the left wing for the next game, at home to Oxford City on 24th September. Happily Boro got their first league points, with Terry Albert bagging a couple of goals. A 1-0 reverse at Leytonstone then a home 3-2 victory over Wycombe Wanderers showed up the inconsistency of the team, and much the same was to follow.

Dulwich Hamlet 0-4), Kingstonian (2-1), Wimbledon (2-2) and a humiliating 2-1 home defeat by Clapton did nothing to appease supporters. Next up was a home FA Cup tie on 22nd October against Isthmian League rivals Kingstonian, and this time Bridge, Jennings and Mackenzie goals gave Boro a fine 3-0 win. The 7,000 crowd went home convinced that all was well again. A win over Cambridge University in a friendly filled the gap between FA Cup ties, but Romford's next Cup opponents turned out to be Yeovil Town away. The lads managed a goal, but the West Country team got another four.

Another poor game against bogey side Clapton on 3rd December resulted in a three all draw. Next, lowly Tufnell Park visited Brooklands and received a 6-0 thrashing, and then came a two all draw with Woking. On Christmas Eve Romford entertained Ilford and gave them both points in a three nil defeat. Ilford felt it only fair to return the points in the return game on Boxing Day, when Romford won 4-1 at Newbury Park. Three more league points were picked up against Wycombe Wanderers (1-1) and St. Albans City (3-2).

Three successive cup-ties were next on the menu. On 14th January Romford managed to struggle to a 3-2 victory over Windsor & Eton in the Amateur Cup. The game against Brentwood & Warley the following week in the Essex Senior Cup was a bitter disappointment, Boro losing 1-0 at the Hive. 5,000 supporters turned up at Brooklands for the next Amateur Cup tie, thinking lowly old rivals Clapton were there for the slaughter. Alas, angry Boro fans had to watch Clapton triumph against the odds by a lone goal to nil.

A Bill Regan goal gave Romford the points at home to Corinthian Casuals on 4th February, but further defeat by Gillingham Reserves in a friendly (1-4) and against Oxford City (2-3) did nothing to encourage supporters. A brace of goals from George Jennings against Dulwich Hamlet promised better things, but the return game on 4th March against Tufnell Park (who only managed three league wins all season) was devastating. Romford agreed to play the game at Brooklands and 3,000 turned up, not expecting that Romford would give Park the points as well (2-3). Romford were without Bill Mackenzie who was winning his first Scotland cap in a drawn game against England at Hull.

Kingstonian (0-1) and Wimbledon (1-2) continued to take the points away before some light relief in a three all draw against old friends Billingham Synthonia on 8th April in a friendly. Romford's regularly changed team then had a rush of goals to their head! Five against Barking in the Thameside Trophy replay, two against old rivals Walthamstow Avenue and two against Grays Athletic in the Thameside Trophy semi-final on 19th April. Two more wins in friendly matches against Clacton Town (2-1) and Brentwood & Warley (5-0) meant an unprecedented five successive victories! Then came the Thameside Trophy final on 3rd May, away to Ilford, when Romford were beaten 3-2 after extra time.

Only two and a half thousand turned up on 6th May to see them meet league champions Leytonstone. Tommy Horn netted twice to give Romford the points. In this disappointing season Romford finished below half way in the final table. Nearly 40 played in the first team during the season, whilst around 70 appeared for the reserve team!

The reserves did a little better than the first team, finishing just above half way, a good performance considering demands made by the first team throughout the season. The "A" team had a rather mixed season, probably due to the calls of the reserve team!

GLEANINGS FROM MANAGEMENT COMMITTEE MINUTE BOOKS
SEASON 1949-50

On **9th July 1949** we read that the players were treated to a London outing – a matinee at the Coliseum Theatre followed by dinner at the Frascati Restaurant at 7 pm.

On **17th January 1950** more social players' social events were announced: supper in the Club Pavilion on 24th January, a visit to Brentwood Conservative Club on 2nd February "for games", and a Club Dinner at King's Hall on 20th February.

On **25th March** the committee were concerned that no police officers reported for duty at an Essex Senior Cup match between Briggs Sports and Leytonstone Tie at Brooklands which drew a crowd of 12,000.

On **25th April** the Secretary stated it was advisable to install turnstiles at all entrances to ensure quicker entry. The Club's proposed tour to Switzerland was confirmed and a quotation from BEA (British European Airways) to charter a 28-seater aeroplane was accepted. The cost of this flight would be £525 (nearly £13,000 in today's money!)

ROMFORD'S PRESIDENT NOW LORD MACPHERSON OF DRUMOCHTER

Tom Macpherson, Labour MP for Romford since 1945, was defeated by the Conservative candidate John Lockwood at the General Election on 23rd February 1950. There was consolation in the 1951 New Year Honours List of 1951 when he was awarded a peerage as Lord Macpherson of Drumochter. The local press were slightly disappointed that he hadn't chosen the title Baron Macpherson of Bedfords, as he was credited with ensuring that this beautiful area of countryside was purchased at a low price as a civic amenity, Bedfords Park, for the people of Romford now and in the future.

Lord and Lady Macpherson pose in the ceremonial robes and coronets that they wore for the Queen's Coronation at Westminster Abbey in June 1953.
The Romford Times

DIRECTORS' ANNUAL REPORT 1949/50

Before proceeding to deal with the events during the year ending 31st May, 1950, your Directors feel that they must first refer to the high honour bestowed upon the Chairman of the Board, Mr T. Macpherson, in the New Year's Honours List. Mr Macpherson has been associated with the Romford Football Club since it was founded in 1929, and was one of the few that took vigorous steps to preserve for sport the ground members now know as Brooklands. Since this Company was formed in 1937, Mr Macpherson has been its Chairman, and it truly can be said that the Company has benefited from his sound guidance, and even when his time was most fully occupied as a Member of Parliament for Romford he was always available in the interests of the Company. It is felt that all members will join with your Directors in wishing our Chairman long life, health and happiness to enjoy his elevation to the Peerage....

Turning to the Accounts now presented, it will be seen that the year ended 31st May, 1950, has been a successful one resulting in a gross profit of £1,491....

....The additions to the Property and Equipment Account amounted to the sum of £790, arising from further capital expenditure in the carrying out of Ground Improvements. Uncovered terracing now surrounds the ground on three sides, and your Directors do not propose to extend the existing terracing any higher until progress has been made in connection with the proposed Grandstand which is so urgently needed.

The proposed Grandstand has been under almost continuous consideration by your Directors. The plans that had previously been prepared by the Company's Architects were submitted to and approved by the Local and Town Planning Authorities, Bills of Quantities were prepared, Estimates and Tenders were obtained, and an Application for a Building Licence submitted to the appropriate Ministry; but your Directors are sorry to say that this was not forthcoming. Following further discussions between the Board and its advisors a revised application for a Building Licence was made (this application provided for the erection of a portion of the stand only) but this application was also unsuccessful – no doubt because of the international situation....

Grass Cycling Meetings were again promoted during the summer months on Brooklands, and many exciting races and championships were seen by spectators. As will be seen from the Statement of Accounts, these meetings had a satisfactory financial result, but these promotions give Directors and Officials little respite between one soccer season and another, and in the future Cycling Meetings may have to be organised on a different basis.

While the Company's Sports Arena and property is, in the opinion of the Directors, of a value in excess of the figure shown in the Accounts, in accordance with their policy commenced last year your Directors recommend that a sum of £1,000 be written off for depreciation....Your Directors also recommend (considering that they are justified and well able to do so, having regard for the Company's successful year financially) out of the available surplus shown in the Appropriation Account above mentioned, the payment of a dividend on the whole of the Company's Paid Up Share Capital for the year ending 31st May 1950, of 7½%, less Tax (for which provision of £733 has been made in the Appropriation Account).

Your Directors can say little as to future programme as this must necessarily depend upon national and international developments, but it is felt that members will wish them to pursue the Grandstand project and use every endeavour to obtain the grant of a Building Licence for the whole or some part of the proposed development at the earliest moment to provide the "all weather" accommodation so urgently needed. Your Directors consider that a suitable Grandstand is essential. Football is the national sport. Workers in industry and others, in their well-earned leisure, deserve proper facilities.

With recent and increasing additions to the local population the provision of a Grandstand becomes most urgent, and in the respectful opinion of your Directors the erection should be considered by the appropriate authorities as work in the nature of national importance for the reasons stated, and they hope that in the future the Ground will be at long last graced by a Grandstand worthy of the Borough of Romford, and suitable for the staging of international and other games in which sportsmen can be accommodated in all weathers....

The report was presented to shareholders at the Annual General Meeting on Monday 26th February 1951 and reported as follows in the *Essex Times* on Wednesday 28th February 1951:

ROMFORD FC SHAREHOLDERS CALL FOR NEW BLOOD

The liveliest annual meeting of Romford FC since before the war produced at the White Hart, Romford, on Monday sustained criticism of the management of the club and of the Board's inability to provide the town with a team it deserves, and ended with the election of 38 year-old Mr Jim Parrish as the first ex-Romford player ever to become a director. Seventy year-old Mr S. Tansley, whom Mr Parrish defeated, was later re-elected as a director in a second ballot after he had tied with another new nominee, Mr Cis Mayor. Mr R. Scott, a director since before the war, was defeated.

So great was the shareholders' obvious anxiety about the team and its welfare that Mr Albert Kittle, acting chairman of the management committee, said the Board intended this year bringing young and 'new blood' into the management of the club's affairs.

In moving the adoption of the directors' report and statement of accounts, Lord Macpherson, president, said Romford was one of the soundest and strongest clubs in the country. Their ground was the envy of many, and was being developed to a pre-decided plan, every detail of which had been decided. But the inability of the club to obtain a building permit delayed the next development, which was to increase the seating accommodation with a new grandstand......

"NO-ONE WOULD SEE THEM". It was not until Lord Macpherson had said that he had heard and seen criticism of the club that shareholders began to make themselves heard. Especially when the President said that if the team won every week no-one would go and see them. "Who wants to see a team which always win?" he said. "We do" said the members. But Mr Harold Hughes, in seconding the adoption of the report and accounts, said: Players will come and go, but if the company is conducted as it has been in the past it will continue to progress.

Then members had their say. Said one: The majority of shareholders are not worried about a 7½ per cent dividend. They want to see a good game of football. But too often games have been lost when they should have been easily won. The team has had much more of the play – but seemed completely lacking in a tactical plan. It was obvious that no strategy existed. What are the Board's plans in this direction? What prospects are there that a situation which has existed since the Amateur Cup final was lost at Wembley two years ago will be rectified?

SAME STRATEGY. Replied Mr Kittle: The same strategy which took the team to Wembley exists now. If only members could be in the dressing rooms on training evenings they would say, after listening to the tactical talks, that the team could not lose. But on the field all seemed to be forgotten. The desire to learn was there, but it brought no results. The team just did not "click".

Mr C.E. Montford, chairman of the Supporters' Association, suggested the club appoint a professional coach to show the lads how things should be done.

"They might take notice" he said. It was not suggested to dispense with the excellent services of Bill Seddon, the trainer.

"YOU'VE GOT 'PAT'". Cried another member, "Why get a professional when you've got George Patterson?" Others spoke up for Patterson too. The ex-Romford favourite, one-time Scottish international, was in the limelight.

Several others spoke up for the appointment of a coach. "It would be beneficial" said one. "New ideas are wanted" said another. "We can well afford it" said a third. "Year after year goes on without a plan" said a fourth. And again and again. The shareholders want to see good football – not the 7½ per cent dividend.

One member asked: Are the directors satisfied with the present employee of the company? Lord Macpherson replied: We have every confidence in Bill Seddon. Nobody is more disappointed than he is that the team does not do well. And remember there was a time when all were applauding him for getting the team to Wembley. Criticism at the moment is unfair.

Another query: Why do so many good players leave the club? Said Lord Macpherson: That could be said of any club – Arsenal or Sunderland or the like. The directors were doing their best. They were in the process of trying to build up a team now. And another query: What are relations like between the selection committee, trainer and players? Answer: 100 per cent.

ELECTIONEERING. There were some keen exchanges in the campaign leading to the election of directors. Two of the Board – Mr S.G. Tansley and Mr R. Scott – retired by rotation. Mr Tansley, who is 70, had to resign in any case, in accordance with the Companies Act of 1948.

Both retiring directors were nominated for re-election, and opposed to them were Mr Jim Parrish, a former Romford goalkeeper, and Mr Cis Mayor, a well-known Romford sportsman. It was said of Mr Tansley, who has been on the board since the company was formed 21 years ago, that the club would not be what it was without him. Yet in the ballot for the first vacancy, Mr Tansley was defeated by Mr Parrish by 39 votes to 30. Mr Scott and Mr Mayor were nominated for the second vacancy and Mr Tansley stood again. Result of the voting: Mr Mayor 30, Mr Tansley 30, Mr Scott 14. Lord Macpherson declined to give a casting vote, and there was a second ballot between Mr Mayor and Mr Tansley. Mr Tansley won this with 41 votes against 32. Said Mr Tansley: "It's been a bit of sport".

The same issue also had this snippet of debate from this meeting:

IT'S SABOTAGE!

Why haven't Romford FC been doing so well lately? One follower of the local team's fortunes seems to think he may have the answer. 'Can't something be done about the pitch?' he asked the directors at the company's annual meeting on Monday. 'The ball bounces the wrong way!'

Lord Macpherson, presiding, replied that he did not think there were many amateur grounds better than Romford's, but 'If there is anything we can do to get the ball going the right way, we will!'

THE ROMFORD FOOTBALL CLUB LIMITED

Full Members of The Football Association
Full Members of Isthmian Football League
Affiliated to Essex County Football Association

Club Colours: Blue & Gold Shirts, White Shorts

Ground: Brooklands Sports Ground, Romford

Chairman: Mr T.Macpherson
Directors: Messrs. M.A.Brazier, A.E.Kittle, W.G.Mann,
R.Scott, A.J.Smith MBE, S.G.Tansley
Mr.J.W.Parrish elected to the Board of Directors in February in place of Mr.R.Scott

Company Secretary: Mr H.W.Muskett

Registered Offices: 110,Hyland Way, Romford

Football Club Management Committee: Comprise all Directors

Hon.Gen.Secretary: Mr M.A.Brazier   **Hon.Asst.Secretary:** Mr J.Gurney

Hon.Press Secretary: Mr H.A.Hughes   **Hon.Advt.Secretary:** Mr H.Wright

Selection Committee: Messrs. W.G.Mann(Chairman), F.H.Adams and G.W.Patterson

Trainer & Coach: Mr W.C.(Bill) Seddon

Reserve Team Manager: Mr G.Howlett   **Reserve Team Trainer:** Mr Joe Martin

Groundsman: Mr W.C.(Bill)Seddon

Bankers: Lloyds Bank Limited   **Auditors:** Mr Iion V. Cummings

LEAGUES & COMPETITIONS 1950-51

FA Challenge Cup
FA Amateur Challenge Cup
Isthmian Football League
Essex County FA Senior Challenge Cup
Essex Thameside Challenge Competition

Isthmian Football League Reserve Section
Essex County FA Intermediate Challenge Cup
Essex Thameside Challenge Competition Reserve Section

Southern Essex Combination Division Two
Essex County FA Junior Challenge Cup
Southern Essex Combination Cup
Romford Charity Cup

Admission Prices

	First Team			Reserve Team		
	Adults	OAPs	Child	Adults	OAPs	Child
Ground	1/-	6d		6d		3d
Ground & Enclosure	1/9	1/-		1/-		6d
Grandstand	2/6	2/6		1/-		6d

Season Tickets

	Adults	OAPs & Children
Grandstand (All one price)	£1.10.0	
Ground & Enclosure	£1.1.0	12/6
Ground only	12/6	7/6

First Team Match Details

13 Aug Frdly Away Schaffhauson 5 – 3 Brooks,Jennings,Horn(2)Bridge
Attendance:
Romford: C.Bingham;E.R.Cave,F.E.Fryatt(Capt);W.F.Mackenzie,J.Barton,W.J.Solley;
H.W.Brooks,W.A.Bridge,T.Horn,G.W.Jennings,E.Quinlan.

16 Aug Frdly Away Winterthur 0 – 2
Romford: C.Bingham;E.R.Cave,F.E.Fryatt(Capt);W.F.Mackenzie,J.Barton,W.J.Solley;
H.W.Brooks,W.A.Bridge,W.R.Winsley,K.Morton,E.Quinlan.

20 Aug Frdly Away Baden 1 – 0 Quinlan
Romford: C.Bingham;E.R.Cave,F.E.Fryatt(Capt);W.F.Mackenzie,J.Barton,G.Fleetwood;
H.W.Brooks,W.A.Bridge,T.Horn,G.W.Jennings,E.Quinlan.

26 Aug IFL Away Tufnell Park Edmonton 2 – 1 Brooks,Bridge
Attendance:
Romford: C.Bingham;E.R.Cave,F.E.Fryatt(Capt);G.Fleetwood,W.J.Solley,W.B.Regan;
H.W.Brooks,W.A.Bridge,T.Horn,J.A.Kurn,E.Quinlan.

2 Sept IFL Home Walthamstow Avenue 1 – 4 Quinlan
Attendance: 4,526   Receipts: £231.1.3   Car Park: £6.15.3
Romford: C.Bingham;E.R.Cave,F.E.Fryatt(Capt);W.F.Mackenzie,W.J.Solley,W.B.Regan;
H.W.Brooks,W.A.Bridge,T.C.Horn,J.A.Kurn,E.Quinlan.

9 Sept IFL Away Kingstonian 3 – 1 Bridge,Brooks,Quinlan
Romford: C.Bingham;E.R.Cave,F.E.Fryatt(Capt);W.F.Mackenzie,J.Barton,W.B.Regan;
H.W.Brooks,W.A.Bridge,W.R.Winsley,K.Morton,E.Quinlan.

16 Sept FACPR Home Grays Athletic 7 – 1 Bridge(2)Winsley(3)Quinlan,Brooks
Attendance: 5,540   Receipts: £298.18.0   Car Park: £6.19.0
Romford: C.Bingham;E.R.Cave,F.E.Fryatt(Capt);W.F.Mackenzie,J.Barton,T.Stewart;
H.W.Brooks,W.A.Bridge,W.R.Winsley,K.Morton,E.Quinlan.

23 Sept IFL Away DulwichHamlet 3 – 2 Quinlan,Bridge,Winsley
Romford: C.Bingham;E.R.Cave,W.J.Solley;W.F.Mackenzie,J.Barton(Capt),T.Stewart;
H.W.Brooks,W.A.Bridge,W.R.Winsley,K.Morton,E.Quinlan.

30 Sept FAC1Q Home Tilbury 5 – 1 Winsley(4)Quinlan
Attendance: 6,775   Receipts: £375.8.3   Car Park: £9.17.3
Romford: C.Bingham;E.R.Cave,W.J.Solley;W.F.Mackenzie,J.Barton(Capt),T.Stewart;
H.W.Brooks,W.A.Bridge,W.R.Winsley,K.Morton,E.Quinlan.

7 Oct IFL Home Wycombe Wanderers 7 – 1 Morton,Brooks(2)Winsley(2)Bridge
                                                            Mackenzie(pen)
Attendance: 3,834   Receipts: £193.6.3   Car Park: £7.3.0
Romford: C.Bingham;E.R.Cave,W.J.Solley;W.F.Mackenzie,J.Barton(Capt),T.Stewart;
H.W.Brooks,W.A.Bridge,W.R.Winsley,K.Morton,E.Quinlan.

14 Oct IFL Away Woking 4 – 2 Brooks(2)Winsley(2)
Romford: C.Bingham;E.R.Cave,W.J.Solley;W.F.Mackenzie,J.Barton,V.H.Perriman;
H.W.Brooks,R.A.Lamb,W.R.Winsley,K.Morton,E.Quinlan.

21 Oct FAC2Q Home Briggs Sports 2 – 2 Bridge(2)
Attendance: 10,148 Receipts: £545.4.6 Car Park: £12.8.9
Romford: C.Bingham;E.R.Cave,W.J.Solley;W.F.Mackenzie,J.Barton(Capt),T.Stewart;
H.W.Brooks,W.A.Bridge,W.R.Winsley,K.Morton,E.Quinlan.

26 Oct FACRp Away Briggs Sports 2 – 1 Winsley,Brooks
Romford: C.Bingham;E.R.Cave,W.J.Solley;G.Fleetwood,J.Barton(Capt),W.F.Mackenzie;
H.W.Brooks,W.A.Bridge,W.R.Winsley,K.Morton,E.Quinlan.

28 Oct FAC3Q Away Woodford Town 2 – 2 Brooks,Mackenzie
Attendance:
Romford: C.Bingham;G.Fleetwood,W.J.Solley;W.F.Mackenzie,J.Barton(Capt),T.Stewart;
H.W.Brooks,W.A.Bridge,W.R.Winsley,K.Morton,E.Quinlan.

2 Nov FACRp Home Woodford Town 1 – 1* Solley
Attendance: 4,681 Receipts: £257.16.6 Car Park: £5.17.0
Romford: C.Bingham;G.Fleetwood,W.J.Solley;W.F.Mackenzie,J.Barton(Capt),J.R.Smailes;
H.W.Brooks,W.A.Bridge,W.R.Winsley,K.Morton,E.Quinlan.

4 Nov FACRp Home Woodford Town 1 – 2 Stewart
Attendance: 7,343 Receipts: £399.14.0 Car Park: £8.10.3
Romford: C.Bingham;E.R.Cave,W.J.Solley;W.F.Mackenzie,J.Barton(Capt),T.Stewart;
H.W.Brooks,W.A.Bridge,W.R.Winsley,K.Morton,E.Quinlan.

11 Nov Frdly Home Oxford University 5 – 4 Butler(2)Brooks,Bridge,Winsley
Attendance: 2,550 Receipts: £133.15.0 Car Park: £2.18.3
Romford: C.Bingham;E.R.Cave,W.J.Solley;G.Fleetwood,J.Barton(Capt),T.Stewart;
H.W.Brooks,W.A.Bridge,W.R.Winsley,H.W.Butler,G.W.Andrews.

18 Nov IFL Away Wycombe Wanderers 2 – 0 Andrews,Winsley
Romford: P.Gamman;E.R.Cave,W.J.Solley;G.Fleetwood,J.Barton(Capt),T.Stewart;
H.W.Brooks,W.A.Bridge,W.R.Winsley,H.W.Butler,G.W.Andrews.

25 Nov IFL Home St. Albans City 0 – 1#
Attendance: 1,181 Receipts: £56.4.0 Car Park: £2.14.3
Romford: C.Bingham;W.J.Solley,F.E.Fryatt(Capt);W.F.Mackenzie,J.Barton,T.Stewart;
H.W.Brooks,W.A.Bridge,W.R.Winsley,H.W.Butler,E.Quinlan.

2 Dec IFL Away Clapton 1 – 2 Winsley
Romford: C.Bingham;E.R.Cave,W.J.Solley;W.F.Mackenzie,J.Barton,F.E.Fryatt(Capt);
H.W.Brooks,W.A.Bridge,W.R.Winsley,H.W.Butler,E.Quinlan.

9 Dec IFL Home Clapton 1 – 0 Brooks
Attendance: 2,479 Receipts: £111.17.6 Car Park: £4.16.3
Romford: C.L.Moore;W.J.Solley,F.E.Fryatt(Capt);W.F.Mackenzie,J.Barton,T.Stewart;
H.W.Brooks,W.A.Bridge,H.W.Butler,R.A.Lamb,G.W.Andrews.

16 Dec IFL Away Wimbledon 3 – 2 Butler,Bridge,Quinlan
Romford: C.L.Moore;E.R.Cave,W.J.Solley;J.R.Smailes,J.Barton(Capt),T.Stewart;
H.W.Brooks,W.A.Bridge,H.W.Butler,R.A.Lamb,E.Quinlan.

25 Dec IFL Home Ilford 1 – 2 Bridge
Attendance: 5,231 Receipts: £260.5.9 Car Park: £5.12.3
Romford: C.L.Moore;E.R.Cave,W.J.Solley;G.Fleetwood,J.Barton(Capt),J.R.Smailes;
H.W.Brooks,W.A.Bridge,H.W.Butler,R.A.Lamb,G.W.Andrews.

26 Dec IFL Away Ilford 2 – 2 Brooks,Winsley
Romford: C.L.Moore;C.Perryman,W.J.Solley;G.Fleetwood,J.Barton(Capt),J.R.Smailes;
H.W.Brooks,W.A.Bridge,W.R.Winsley,H.W.Butler,E.Quinlan.

30 Dec IFL Home Woking 2 – 2 Winsley,Bridge
Attendance: 2,296 Receipts: £108.19.6 Car Park: £3.19.6
Romford: C.L.Moore;C.Perryman,W.J.Solley;G.Fleetwood,J.Barton(Capt),J.R.Smailes;
W.F.Mackenzie,W.A.Bridge,W.R.Winsley,H.W.Butler,E.Quinlan.

6 Jan ESC1R Away Harlow Town 3 – 1 Brooks,Winsley,Barton(pen)
Romford: C.L.Moore;G.Fleetwood,W.J.Solley;W.F.Mackenzie,J.Barton(Capt),J.R.Smailes;
H.W.Brooks,W.A.Bridge,W.R.Winsley,H.W.Butler,E.Quinlan.

13 Jan AC1R Away Moor Green 2 – 2 Brooks,Butler
Romford: C.L.Moore;G.Fleetwood,W.J.Solley;W.F.Mackenzie,J.Barton(Capt),T.Stewart;
H.W.Brooks,W.A.Bridge,W.R.Winsley,H.W.Butler,E.Quinlan.

20 Jan ACRp Home Moor Green 0 – 2
Attendance: 8,531 Receipts: £459.4.0 Car Park: £8.14.9
Romford: C.L.Moore;G.Fleetwood,W.J.Solley;W.F.Mackenzie,J.Barton(Capt),T.Stewart;
H.W.Brooks,W.A.Bridge,W.R.Winsley,H.W.Butler,E.Quinlan.

27 Jan ESC2R Away Tilbury 1 – 2 Butler
Romford: C.L.Moore;G.Fleetwood,J.Barton(Capt);W.F.Mackenzie,J.R.Smailes,T.Stewart;
H.W.Brooks,W.A.Bridge,H.W.Butler,K.Morton,G.W.Andrews.

3 Feb IFL Home St. Albans City 3 – 1 Andrews,Butler,Bridge
Attendance: 1,502 Receipts: £75.11.3 Car Park: £2.10.6
Romford: C.L.Moore;W.J.Solley,T.Stewart;W.F.Mackenzie,J.Barton(Capt),J.G.Welch;
H.W.Brooks,G.Fleetwood,H.W.Butler,W.A.Bridge,G.W.Andrews.

10 Feb IFL Home Dulwich Hamlet 1 – 3 Brooks
Attendance: 2,821 Receipts: £137.18.9 Car Park: £6.1.0
Romford: C.L.Moore;W.J.Solley,T.Stewart;W.F.Mackenzie,J.Barton(Capt),J.G.Welch;
H.W.Brooks,G.Fleetwood,H.W.Butler,W.A.Bridge,G.W.Andrews.

24 Feb IFL Away#1 Corinthian Casuals 1 – 7 Barton
Romford: C.L.Moore;W.J.Solley,T.Stewart(Capt);W.F.Mackenzie,J.Barton,J.G.Welch;
H.W.Brooks,G.Fleetwood,H.W.Butler,W.A.Bridge,G.W.Andrews.

3 Mar IFL Home Leytonstone 1 – 1 Barton
Attendance: 3,378 Receipts: £176.8.3 Car Park: £7.17.9
Romford: C.L.Moore;W.J.Solley,J.W.Conner;W.F.Mackenzie,D.R.Lowman,J.G.Welch;
H.W.Brooks,J.Barton(Capt),W.A.Bridge,K.Morton,G.W.Andrews.

10 Mar IFL Away Walthamstow Avenue 1 – 2 Barton(pen)
Romford: C.L.Moore;W.J.Solley,J.W.Conner;W.F.Mackenzie,D.R.Lowman,J.G.Welch;
H.W.Brooks,J.Barton(Capt),W.A.Bridge,K.Morton,G.W.Andrews.

17 Mar IFL Home Corinthian Casuals 0 – 3
Attendance: 2,032 Receipts: £92.2.6 Car Park: £4.5.0
Romford: C.L.Moore;W.J.Solley,J.W.Conner;G.Fleetwood,D.R.Lowman,J.R.Smailes;
H.W.Brooks,H.W.Butler,W.A.Bridge(Capt),E.Quinlan,G.W.Andrews.

24 Mar IFL Away St. Albans City 0 – 2
Romford: C.L.Moore;W.J.Solley,J.G.Welch;G.Fleetwood,D.R.Lowman,J.Barton(Capt);
H.W.Brooks,W.F.Mackenzie,H.W.Butler,W.A.Bridge,G.W.Andrews.

31 Mar IFL Home Tufnell Park Edmonton 2 – 0 Brooks,Butler
Attendance: 1,778 Receipts: £86.9.6 Car Park: £3.12.0
Romford: C.L.Moore;E.R.Cave,W.J.Solley;J.R.Smailes,D.R.Lowman,J.G.Welch;
H.W.Brooks,W.A.Bridge(Capt),H.W.Butler,E.Quinlan,G.W.Andrews.

7 Apr IFL Away Leytonstone 2 – 1 Bridge,Brooks
Romford: C.L.Moore;E.R.Cave,W.J.Solley;J.R.Smailes,D.R.Lowman,J.G.Welch;
H.W.Brooks,W.A.Bridge(Capt),H.W.Butler,E.Quinlan,G.W.Andrews.

14 Apr IFL Away Oxford City 4 – 2 Cunningham,Kenlay(2)Smailes
Romford: C.L.Moore;E.R.Cave,W.J.Solley;J.R.Smailes,D.R.Lowman,J.G.Welch;
H.W.Brooks,W.A.Bridge(Capt),G.J.Kenlay,G.Cunningham,E.Quinlan.

21 Apr IFL Home Oxford City 3 – 0 Brooks,Kenlay(2)
Attendance: 2,097 Receipts: £99.15.9 Car Park: £7.4.0
Romford: C.L.Moore;E.R.Cave,W.J.Solley;J.R.Smailes,D.R.Lowman,J.G.Welch;
H.W.Brooks,W.A.Bridge(Capt),G.J.Kenlay,E.Quinlan,G.W.Andrews.

28 Apr IFL Home Kingstonian 5 – 2 Cunningham(3)Kenlay(2)
Attendance: 1,691 Receipts: £71.8.9 Car Park: £4.4.3
Romford: C.L.Moore;D.R.Lowman,W.J.Solley;J.R.Smailes,R.A.Lamb,J.G.Welch;
H.W.Brooks,W.A.Bridge(Capt),G.J.Kenlay,G.Cunningham,E.Quinlan.

1 May ETT1R Away Leyton 2 – 1 Bridge,Kenlay
Romford: C.L.Moore;W.J.Solley,J.Barton;W.F.Mackenzie,G.Fleetwood,J.G.Welch;
H.W.Brooks,W.A.Bridge(Capt),G.J.Kenlay,G.Cunningham,G.W.Andrews.

5 May IFL Home Wimbledon 3 – 0 Kenlay(2)Cunningham
Attendance: 3,080 Receipts: £154.16.0 Car Park: £5.6.0
Romford: C.L.Moore;D.R.Lowman,W.J.Solley;J.R.Smailes,G.Fleetwood,J.G.Welch;
H.W.Brooks,W.A.Bridge(Capt),G.J.Kenlay,G.Cunningham,G.W.Andrews.

10 May ETTSF Home Leytonstone 3 – 4* Bridge,Cunningham(2)
Attendance: 3,798 Receipts: £203.10.0 Car Park: £6.18.3
Romford: C.L.Moore;W.J.Solley,J.Barton;J.R.Smailes,G.Fleetwood,J.G.Welch;
H.W.Brooks,W.A.Bridge(Capt),G.J.Kenlay,G.Cunningham,G.W.Andrews.

14 May Frdly Home Wageningen(Holland) 1 – 5 Kenlay
Attendance: 4,455 Receipts: £238.10.6 Car Park: £5.0.6
Romford: C.L.Moore;E.R.Cave,W.J.Solley;J.R.Smailes,G.Fleetwood,J.G.Welch;
H.W.Brooks(Capt),E.Quinlan,G.J.Kenlay,G.Cunningham,G.W.Andrews.

* After Extra Time
\# Abandoned after 37 minutes due to fog.
\#1 Played at the Oval Cricket Ground.

FIRST TEAM SUMMARY OF RESULTS 1950 – 51

	P	Home W	D	L	Goals For	Ag	Away W	D	L	Goals For	Ag	Pts
Isthmian League	26	7	2	4	35	25	8	1	4	23	22	33
FA Challenge Cup	7	2	2	1	16	7	1	1	0	4	3	
FA Amateur Cup	2	0	0	1	0	2	0	1	0	2	2	
Essex Senior Cup	2	0	0	0	0	0	1	0	1	4	3	
Thameside Trophy	2	0	0	1	3	4	1	0	0	2	1	
Friendlies	5	1	0	1	6	9	2	0	1	6	5	
Totals	44	10	4	8	60	47	13	3	6	41	36	

Isthmian Football League
Final Table

	P	W	D	L	Goals For	Ag	Pts
Leytonstone	26	20	3	3	72	26	43
Walthamstow Ave.	26	15	4	7	57	37	34
Romford	**26**	**15**	**3**	**8**	**58**	**47**	**33**
Wimbledon	26	13	5	8	58	39	31
Dulwich Hamlet	26	14	2	10	54	43	30
Woking	26	11	6	9	65	55	28
Ilford	26	12	4	10	44	45	28
Corinthian Casuals	26	13	0	13	62	60	26
St. Albans City	26	11	4	11	32	36	26
Kingstonian	26	9	4	13	46	53	22
Wycombe Wandrs.	26	8	3	15	46	66	19
Oxford City	26	7	4	15	47	63	18
Clapton	26	6	5	15	29	50	17
Tufnell Park (Edtn)	26	4	1	21	24	73	9

Romford travelled to the Oval Cricket Ground (left) where they played Corinthian Casuals at their temporary home prior to their move to Cheshunt. Romford were defeated 7-1, and after such an off day they were lucky it wasn't a cricket score!

FIRST TEAM CUP RESULTS

FA Challenge Cup

Final: Newcastle United 2   Blackpool   0

Romford's progress: 1st Qual.   Home   Grays Athletic   7 – 1
2nd Qual.   Home   Tilbury   5 – 1
3rd Qual.   Home   Briggs Sports   2 – 2
Replay   Away   Briggs Sports   2 – 1
4th Qual.   Away   Woodford Town   2 – 2
Replay   Home   Woodford Town   1 – 1*
2nd Replay   Home   Woodford Town   1 – 2

FA Amateur Challenge Cup
Final: Pegasus 2   Bishop Auckland   1

Romford's progress: 1st Round   Away   Moor Green   2 – 2
Replay   Home   Moor Green   0 – 2

Essex County FA Senior Challenge Cup
Final: Briggs Sports 3   Barking   1

Romford's progress: 1st Round   Away   Harlow Town   3 – 1
2nd Round   Away   Tilbury   1 – 2

Essex Thameside Challenge Competition
Final:

Romford's progress: 1st Round   Away   Leyton   2 – 1
Semi-Final   Home   Leytonstone   3 – 4*

*   After Extra Time

Pre-season horse show at Brooklands draws Bank Holiday crowds!

As reported in the *Romford Times,* 9th August 1950
First horse show for 25 years thrills 4,000

The horse show came to town on Monday. And what a day it was! August Bank Holiday, 4,000 people imbued with the festive spirit, not an agricultural show in Romford for 25 years – and the Mid-Essex Agricultural Society decided to hold its annual show in Romford for the first time. The 4,000 found their holiday entertainment at Brooklands, where horses which paraded, pranced and jumped, were the centre of attraction for 11 hours.

In keeping with the spirit of the occasion, the Mayor, Councillor J.R. Poel, and the Mayoress visited the show ground in a coach and four driven by Mr Dave Jacobs, of Chase Cross Road, Romford. The Mayoress presented the prizes and the Mayor thanked the Society for bringing the first agricultural show to Romford for 25 years....

WENT ON TILL DUSK. Although it started late and it was dusk before the final event was completed, the show, with its 150 entries, provided an enthralling entertainment. Besides the fine jumping events and exhibition classes, there was a sheep-dog display organised by Mr W. McClure. As a treat for children the show concluded with a cowboy display by Buster Syd and his Men. Mr Syd Wight, who led the cowboys, recently headed the "Horses through the Ages" procession before the King and Queen at the White City International Horse Show.

"MAC" LOVES HORSES. Among the competitors was Mr Tom Macpherson, Romford's ex-MP, who rode his own hunter, Wally. Wally took third place in his class. When Mr Macpherson started out in life his first job was as a van boy. He often drove the van. "I've loved horses ever since" he said.

THE ROMFORD TIMES, WEDNESDAY, AUGUST 16, 1950

A man of many parts is Mr. Tom Macpherson—businessman, farmer, sportsman, politician. Now he is seen (above) in another role—horseman—as he rides his own hunter "Wally" in the Bank Holiday Mid-Essex Agricultural Show.

The major cups were awarded as follows: Mid-Essex Challenge Cup (jumping), Mr K.E. Chapman; Sir Patrick Hennessey Cup (juvenile jumping), Master H. Cowell; George Wright Memorial Cup (best farmer's turn-out), Land Settlement Ltd., Mid-Essex Society Cup (best rider under 17), Miss A. Conoley; Blackmore Challenge Cup (agricultural horses), Messrs Mann, Crossman and Paulin Ltd.

Official opening of the ground and grandstand at Schaffhausen
Sunday 13th October 1950

The teams line up before the match
Authors' collection

Cheer up lads, you won! Or was this half-time and a goal down? Mackenzie, Bridge and Brooks wearily leave the field
Authors' collection

PRESENTATION TO GEORGE PATTERSON
Saturday 2nd September, 1950

George Patterson, veteran Scottish International winger, stopped playing for Romford after seventeen years with the club – easily a record. George was a great Brooklands favourite and during the interval of the home game against Walthamstow Avenue he was presented with the supporters testimonial from Association president C.H.Barney – a barometer and a voucher for a refrigerator. There was a heartwarming reception for George, who continued to help the club as a team selector. In Scotland "Patt" played for the famous Queens Park Football Club. In England he ended his career playing in the Amateur Cup final at Wembley.

2nd September 1950
Romford   1   Walthamstow Avenue   4   (Isthmian League)
(Attendance 4,526)

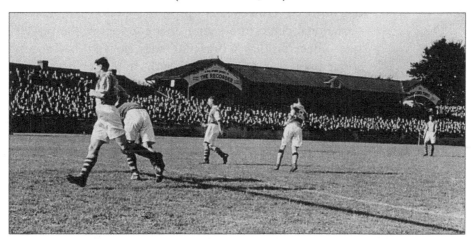

Above: Boro defenders relax for once, as Cyril Bingham has got the ball safely in his hands!

Below: Romford's Fred Fryatt wonders where the ball is while Walthamstow's Jim Lewis tries some sleight of hand!   *Authors' collection*

From a *Romford Times* special feature on Romford Football Club

THE TEAM MEMBERS

Chris Moore (Goalkeeper)

Born in Edmonton on August 13th 1924. Height 5ft 9½ in. Weight 12 stone 10 pounds. Works as a silk manufacturers' clerk. Chris began his soccer career with Hornchurch Athletic FC when he was 18 and after the war he went to Clapton FC for whom he played regularly last season. Joining Romford FC about five weeks ago, he made his first eleven debut on Saturday against his old club Clapton. He holds the position for tomorrow's (Saturday) game. During the war Chris was in the Navy, and was involved in the D Day landings. For a short while he served on HMS Vanguard. He is married and he and his wife live with his parents in Lyndhurst drive, Hornchurch. His football honours include an Essex Junior Cap and one for the Isthmian League reserves against the Middlesex Senior League.

W.J. (Bill) Solley (Right Back)

Aged 25. Height 5ft 11in. Weight 12stone. Occupation turbine driver. A defender of considerable promise, Solley has made a somewhat sensational climb into senior amateur soccer. He played for only one side – Beckton Gas Works Thursday eleven – before joining Romford about a year ago. After three months in the reserves, he made his debut in the first team late last season. He resumed in the side this season when skipper Freddie Fryatt was injured. A versatile defensive player, Solley has in his short career played in all the full and half-back positions. What is his biggest soccer moment so far? In Romford's first FA Cup replay with Woodford Town, a month ago, he scored an equalising goal in the 90th minute!

Fred Fryatt (Captain and Left Back)

In his second season as first eleven skipper. Born 1916. Height 5ft 8½in. Weight 12st 3lb. Occupation bricklayer. Fred has lived in Brentwood all his life, and began his football career there with the C of E school. He recently became football coach to the Brentwood Youth Club. Brentwood and Warley was Fred's first senior club. He has also played for Grays Athletic and Dagenham Town, and he signed amateur forms for West Ham, for whom his brother was a professional, when he was 19. He joined Romford immediately after the last war. Fred's football honours are numerous, and include an Essex County Cap. When in the Forces, he represented Southern Command against Northern Command. He has played for the Isthmian League on many occasions, and took part in the League's tour of Denmark in 1947-48. He captained the Isthmian League eleven against an Indian Olympic side in 1948-49. He has an Essex Senior Cup winner's medal and a runners-up medal. In his long and successful career, Fred has no doubts as to what was his proudest moment in football. It was when he led the Romford team onto the Wembley turf for the first ever Amateur Cup final there in April 1949, against Bromley.

Bill Mackenzie (Right Half)

William Fraser Mackenzie Romford FC and Scotland right half, born in Glasgow in March 9th 1923. Height 5ft 6ins. Weight 10st 9lbs. Occupation toolmaker. Married and living in Princes Road, Romford. "Mac" was capped for Scotland last season and played in two amateur internationals. He began his football career with Bush Elms School and has two junior soccer medals. He played later for Briggs Sports and joined Romford FC immediately after the war. "Mac's" soccer trophies include Essex Senior Cup winners and runners-up medals, and Isthmian League, Athenian League, Spartan League and Essex caps.

Jack Barton (Centre Half and Vice-Captain)

29 years of age. Height 6ft. Weight 11st 6lbs. Occupation assistant chemical engineer. Son of a former Indian Army welter-weight boxing champion. Jack, though, born in Yorkshire, spent his early years in India. On his return to England he was educated at Rotherham Grammar School and took part in most sports. Before he was 20 he had trials with Grimsby, Wolves, West Ham and Doncaster Football Clubs, and had several games with Sheffield United reserves. During the war, Jack served with the Fleet Air Arm, and captained a Navy eleven against the American Army, the New Zealand Army and an Australian side. He was temporarily blinded and paralysed by a shell explosion while with the American Army in the Pacific. Jack's sporting interests extend to cricket. A useful all-rounder, he is captain of Heath Park CC, a local club. He is a King's Scout and holds a scoutmaster's warrant.

Gordon Fleetwood (Left Half)

Romford FC utility player, born in the West Riding of Yorkshire August 15th 1928. Height 5ft 10 ½ in. Weight 11st ?lbs. Works in the plastics department of Messrs. May and Bakers. Unmarried, Gordon lives with his parents – from whom he inherits his love of sport – in Ash Close, Romford. He is something of a "Jack of all sports" and plays cricket for Romford CC. At running he has clocked 220 yards in 24 to 25 seconds. The only sport in which he has shown no skill is swimming – for he cannot swim! Gordon began his football career with Havering Road YC when he was 15, and joined Romford from them after the war. He has been played in all but three positions – goal, centre half and outside left. He has appeared in six different positions in Romford's first eleven. Though he has played twice for Essex Juniors, Gordon feels that soccer is perhaps his "bogey" game. But he plays it because he enjoys it.

Harold Brooks (Outside Right)

Born – November 2nd 1921 at West Ham. Height 5ft 4in. Weight 10st 4lbs. Occupation painter. Harold lives in Princes Road, Romford and has been with Romford FC for about seven years. A West Ham schoolboy representative player, he has also played for Enfield and Clapton. A speedy hard shooting winger, his honours include having represented the Isthmian League, Essex and the Football Association. One of Harold's proudest possessions however, is the Amateur Cup final medal he earned with Romford. Harold's sporting activities are not confined to football. He is also a keen swimmer, and has qualified as a life-saver.

Bill Bridge (Inside Right)

William Albert Bridge, Romford FC inside forward. Born 1920. Height 5ft 8in. Weight 11st 7lbs. Occupation timber merchant. Billy is a Romford man and lives in Rush Green Road. Football is his consuming recreational interest. His first games were for London Road School and he captained Romford schoolboys for three seasons. Before joining Romford FC in 1937-38, he played for Beacontree Heath Old Boys, and was on West Ham's books as an amateur. Last season Billy represented the Football Association. He has also played for the Athenian and Isthmian Leagues and he has an Essex County badge. His trophies include two Essex Senior Cup winners medals and two South Essex Charity Cup medals. Highlights of Billy's career are his appearance at Wembley with the Romford Amateur Cup final team, and his selection to play for the BOAR during the war. He was then the only amateur among many famous professional players. Signalman W.A.Bridge completed six and a half years war service in the Army.

Walter Winsley (Centre Forward)

Walter Raymond Winsley Romford FC centre forward, born at Plaistow on June 15th 1925. Height 5ft 11in. Weight 12st. A painter by occupation. Wally, who lives with his parents at Beam-Way, Dagenham, joined Romford from Briggs Sports at the beginning of the present season. He has also played for Leyton, and was at that time an amateur on West Ham United's books. During he war, while serving in the Army, he played a number of times for Suez Canal Area Combined Services Eleven. He has played twice for Essex, and, while with Briggs, gained a Spartan League Championship plaque and an Essex Senior Cup winner's medal. Last season Wally scored about 60 goals for Briggs and in his earlier games for Romford he showed similar scoring potentialities. Loss of form, however, has resulted in him seeking fresh confidence with the reserves over the past couple of weeks.

Bill Butler (Inside Forward)

Harold William Butler, Romford FC inside forward, born at Ilford April 25th 1925. Height 5ft 11in. weight 12st. Is a shipping office clerk and lives with his parents at Hampton Road, Ilford. Bill joined Romford this season from Ad Astra, and has already played for Romford's first team nine times at inside left or centre forward. He has had a surprisingly rapid rise from junior football, and has an Isthmian League reserve section cap among his trophies. As well as football Bill plays cricket for Ad Astra and enjoys swimming and playing tennis. During the war he served in the Navy on the cruiser HMS Kenya as a torpedo man and visited, among other places, Ceylon.

Roy Cave (Reserve Full Back)

Romford FC right back, 21 years of age. Height 5ft 11ins. Weight 12st. Occupation plumber. Roy, who lives in Marlborough Road, Forest Gate, began his football career in 1941 with East Ham Schoolboys. Playing at centre half or right half, he was also captain of the side. Until he was 18 he played for Fairburn House Boys' Club. Then to the adult section of the Club – the Mansfield House Club (Plaistow) in the Barking League. His next step, taken last season, was to join Romford. After showing considerable ability with the reserves, Roy was introduced to the first eleven about half way through the season. He has since been Romford's regular right back, and is improving well with experience.

FIRST TEAM DEBUTS SEASON 1950 – 51

1950   **Previous Club**

1950					Previous Club
13th Aug.	v Schaffhauson	-	**E.Quinlan**		Royal Air Force
16th Aug.	v Winterthur	-	**W.R.Winsley**		Briggs Sports
16th Sept.	v Grays Athletic	-	**T.Stewart**		Queens Park
14th Oct.	v Woking	-	**V.H.Perriman**		Army
2nd Nov.	v Woodford Town	-	**W.J.Smailes**		Marley Y.C.
11th Nov.	v Oxford Univ.	-	**G.W.Andrews**		Hainault Forest
		-	**H.W.Butler**		Ad Astra
18th Nov.	v Wycombe Wand.	-	**P.Gamman**		Glendale Y.C.
9th Dec.	v Clapton	-	**C.L.Moore**		Clapton
26th Dec.	v Ilford	-	**C.Perryman**		Barkingside
1951					
3rd Feb.	v St.Albans City	-	**J.G.Welch**		Leyton
3rd Mar.	v Leytonstone	-	**J.W.Conner**		Glendale Y.C.
		-	**D.R.Lowman**		Clapton
14th Apr.	v Oxford City	-	**G.Cunningham**		Queens Park
		-	**G.J.Kenlay**		Glendale Y.C.

FIRST TEAM APPEARANCES SEASON 1950 – 51

	A	B	C	D	E	F	Total
George Andrews	14	0	0	1	2	2	19
Jack Barton	17	7	2	2	2	4	34
Cyril Bingham	7	7	0	0	0	4	18
Bill Bridge	25	7	2	2	2	4	42

Harold Brooks	25	7	2	2	2	5	43
Bill Butler	14	0	2	2	0	1	19
Roy Cave	14	5	0	0	0	5	24
Jack Connor	3	0	0	0	0	0	3
Graeme Cunningham	3	0	0	0	2	1	6
Gordon Fleetwood	11	3	2	2	2	3	23
Fred Fryatt	5	1	0	0	0	3	9
Peter Gamman	1	0	0	0	0	0	1
Tommy Horn	2	0	0	0	0	2	4
George Jennings	0	0	0	0	0	2	2
Gerry Kenlay	4	0	0	0	2	1	7
John Kurn	2	0	0	0	0	0	2
Ron Lamb	5	0	0	0	0	0	5
Des Lowman	10	0	0	0	0	0	10
Bill Mackenzie	14	7	2	2	1	3	29
Chris Moore	18	0	2	2	2	1	25
Ken Morton	6	7	0	1	0	1	15
Colin Perryman	2	0	0	0	0	0	2
Vic Perriman	1	0	0	0	0	0	1
Eddie Quinlan	16	7	2	1	0	4	30
Bill Regan	3	0	0	0	0	0	3
Bill Solley	25	6	2	1	2	4	40
Jimmy Smailes	11	1	0	2	1	1	16
Tommy Stewart	8	5	2	1	0	1	17
Johnny Welch	12	0	0	0	2	1	15
Wally Winsley	8	7	2	1	0	2	20
Total	286	77	22	22	22	55	484

FIRST TEAM GOALSCORERS SEASON 1950 – 51

	A	B	C	D	E	F	Total
Wally Winsley	9	8	0	1	0	1	19
Harold Brooks	12	3	1	1	0	2	19
Bill Bridge	9	4	0	0	2	2	17
Gerry Kenlay	8	0	0	0	1	1	10
Eddie Quinlan	4	2	0	0	0	1	7
Bill Butler	3	0	1	1	0	2	7
Graeme Cunningham	5	0	0	0	2	0	7
Jack Barton	3	0	0	1	0	0	4
Tommy Horn	0	0	0	0	0	2	2
Bill Mackenzie	1	1	0	0	0	0	2
George Andrews	2	0	0	0	0	0	2
George Jennings	0	0	0	0	0	1	1
Ken Morton	1	0	0	0	0	0	1
Bill Solley	0	1	0	0	0	0	1
Tommy Stewert	0	1	0	0	0	0	1
Jimmy Smailes	1	0	0	0	0	0	1
Total	58	20	2	4	5	12	101

KEY TO COMPETITIONS

A	Isthmian Football League
B	FA Challenge Cup
C	FA Amateur Challenge Cup
D	Essex County FA Senior Cup
E	Thameside Challenge Trophy
F	Friendlies

This *Romford Times* cartoon tells the story of Boro's 3-2 away win at
Plough Lane in wintry weather on 16th December 1950

Reserve Team Match Details

19 Aug Frdly   Away   Pitsea United   4 – 1   Butler(2)Kurn(2)
Romford Res.: S.Poskett;D.I.Desborough,E.Webb;W.J.Digby,R.Bumpstead,V.H.Perriman;
D.W.Joyce,H.W.Hails,H.W.Butler,J.R.Kurn,G.W.Andrews.

26 Aug IFLR   Home   Tufnell Park Edmonton Res.   4 – 0   Kenlay,Winsley(2)(1pen)Hails
Attendance: 869   Receipts: £16.5.3   Car Park; £0.6.9
Romford Res.: S.Poskett,D.I.Desborough,E.Webb;V.H.Perriman,R.Bumpstead,K.Morton;
G.J.Kenlay,H.W.Hails,W.R.Winsley,H.W.Butler,G.W.Andrews.

2 Sept IFLR   Away   Walthamstow Avenue Res.   1 – 7   Winsley
Romford Res.: S.Poskett;D.I.Desborough,E.Webb;V.H.Perriman,R.Bumpstead,K.Morton;
G.J.Kenlay,H.W.Hails,W.R.Winsley,R.A.Lamb,G.W.Andrews.

9 Sept IFLR   Home   Kingstonian Res.   1 – 3   Butler
Attendance: 746   Receipts: £14.4.9   Car Park: £0.15.9
Romford Res.: F.Curtis;G.Fleetwood,W.P.Spelling;H.W.Butler,W.J.Solley,V.H.Perriman;
G.J.Kenlay,S.Frankland,T.Horn,E.W.Scott,G.W.Andrews.

16 Sept IFLR   Away   Ilford Res.   2 – 0   Kurn,Kenlay
Romford Res.: F.Curtis;F.W.Dale,J.W.Conner;J.Rees,W.J.Solley,V.H.Perriman;
G.J.Kenlay,W.J.Digby,H.W.Butler,J.R.Kurn,G.W.Andrews.

23 Sept IFLR   Home   Clapton Res.   2 – 2   Andrews(2)
Attendance: 984   Receipts: £21.0.3   Car Park: £0.14.6
Romford Res.: F.Curtis,F.W..Dale,J.W.Conner;G.Fleetwood,J.Rees,V.H.Perriman;
G.J.Kenlay,H.W.Hails,H.W.Butler,R.A.Lamb,G.W.Andrews.

30 Sept IFLR   Away   Oxford City Res.   1 – 2   Scorer unknown
Romford Res.:

7 Oct IFLR   Away   Wycombe Wanderers Res.   2 – 2   Butler,Fleetwood
Romford Res.: P.Gamman,A.W.Gilkes,J.W.Conner;G.Fleetwood,J.M.Rees,V.H.Perryman;
G.J.Kenlay,R.B.Payne,H.W.Butler,A.F.Herbert,G.W.Andrews.

14 Oct EIC1R   Away   Sun Athletic   7 – 2   Butler(4)Andrews(2)Hails
Romford Res.: P.Gamman;
   ?   ,   ?   ,H.W.Butler,H.W.Hails,G.W.Andrews.

28 Oct EIC2R   Home   Chadwell Heath   1 – 0   Andrews
Attendance: 305   Receipts: £7.2.9   Car Park: £0.3.9
Romford Res.: P.Gamman;A.W.Gilkes,J.W.Conner;K.Morton,J.R.Smailes,J.M.Rees;
G.J.Kenlay,A.Schneider,H.W.Butler,H.W.Hails,G.W.Andrews.

4 Nov IFLR   Away   Corinthian Casuals Res.   3 – 2   Kenlay, ? others
Romford Res.:
G.J.Kenlay. Remainder of team unknown.

11 Nov IFLR   Away   Leytonstone Res.   0 – 4
Romford Res.:

18 Nov IFLR   Home   Dulwich Hamlet Res.   4 – 3   Kenlay(3)Lamb
Attendance: 917   Receipts: £18.16.3   Car Park: £0.11.6
Romford Res.: C.L.Moore;   ?   ,   ?   ,K.Morton,
G.J.Kenlay, R.A.Lamb, Frank Morton (Ken's brother played first game

25 Nov IFLR   Away   Tufnell Park Edmonton Res.   2 – 1#   Scorers unknown
Romford Res.:

2 Dec EIC3R   Home   Staines United   2 – 3   Scorers unknown
Attendance: 511   Receipts: £9.12.0   Car Park: £0.3.6
Romford Res.: **(Sel)** P.Gamman;D.Evans,J.W.Conner;G.Fleetwood,J.R.Smailes,V.H.Perriman;
C.T.Coleman,W.H.Dowsett,G.J.Kenlay,R.A.Lamb,G.W.Andrews.

9 Dec IFLR   Away   Clapton Res.   1 – 3   Winsley
Attendance;
Romford Res.: P.Gamman;E.R.Cave,
W.Winsley,

16 Dec IFLR   Home   Wimbledon Res.   4 – 1   Winsley(2)Andrews(2)
Attendance: 410   Receipts: £5.19.3   Car Park: £0.4.6
Romford Res.: C.Bingham;V.H.Perriman,J.W.Conner;   ?   ,G.Fleetwood,   ?   ;
G.J.Kenlay,C.T.Coleman,W.R.Winsley,K.Morton,G.W.Andrews.

23 Dec IFLR   Away   Dulwich Hamlet Res.   4 – 2   Scorers unknown
Romford Res.: **Sel.** C.Bingham;C.Perryman,J.W.Conner;W.P.Spelling,L.Manley,V.H.Perriman;
G.J.Kenlay,C.T.Coleman,W.R.Winsley,K.Morton,E.Quinlan.

30 Dec IFLR   Away   Tufnell Park Edmonton Res.   4 – 1   Scorers unknown
Romford Res.:

6 Jan   IFLR   Home   Leytonstone Res.   2 – 4   Dowsett,Nunn
Attendance: 510   Receipts: £9.10.6   Car Park: £0.4.3
Romford Res.: C.Bingham;L.Pink,J.W.Conner;L.Manley,D.Newman.K.Morton;
G.J.Kenlay,W.H.Dowsett,W.Nunn,R.A.Lamb,G.W.Andrews.

13 Jan   IFLR   Home   Ilford Res.   3 – 0   ? (og),Dowsett(2)
Attendance: 583   Receipts: £10.16.9   Car Park: £0.5.9
Romford Res.: M.Croft;L.Penk,J.W.Conner;V.H.Perriman,R.A.Lamb(Capt),J.G.Welch;
W.H.Dowsett,C.T.Coleman,D.J.Sewell,K.Morton,G.W.Andrews.

27 Jan   IFLR   Home   Oxford City Res.   1 – 0   Quinlan
Attendance: 428   Receipts: £7.2.6   Car Park: £-.1.9
Romford Res.: M.Croft;L.Penk,C.Perryman;V.H.Perryman,R.A.Lamb(Capt),J.G.Welch;
C.T.Coleman,D.J.Sewell,W.H.Dowsett,E.Quinlan,G.J.Kenlay.

3 Feb   IFLR   Away   St. Albans City Res.   1 – 3   Kenlay
Romford Res.: C.Bingham;L.Penk,J.W.Conner;V.H.Perriman,R.A.Lamb(Capt),K.Morton;
W.H.Dowsett,D.J.Sewell,J.Bartholomew,E.Quinlan,G.J.Kenlay.

10 Feb   IFLR   Away   Wimbledon Res.   2 – 1   Bartholomew(2)
Romford Res.: J.Martin;L.Penk,J.W.Connor;D.R.Lowman,R.A.Lamb(Capt),J.R.Smailes;
C.T.Coleman,G.J.Kenlay,J.Bartholomew,K.Morton,E.Quinlan.

17 Feb   IFLR   Away   Kingstonian Res.   4 – 3   Quinlan,Dobinson(2)Bartholomew
Romford Res.: C.Bingham; ? , ? ; ? ,R.A.Lamb(Capt), ? ;
C.T.Coleman,H.R.Dobinson,J.Bartholomew,K.Morton,E.Quinlan.

3 Mar   Frdly   Away   Kingstonian Res.   7 – 0   Perriman,Sewell,Quinlan,Butler(2),
                                                     Lamb(pen),Coleman
Romford Res.: C.Bingham; ? , ? ; V.H.Perriman,R.A.Lamb(Capt),J.R.Smailes;
C.T.Coleman,D.J.Sewell,H.W.Butler,R.A.Lamb,E.Quinlan.

10 Mar   IFLR   Home   Walthamstow Avenue Res.   1 – 1   Butler
Attendance: 561   Receipts: £9.8.9   Car Park: £0.3.9
Romford Res.: **Sel**. C.Bingham;L.Penk,S.Poskett;G.Fleetwood,R.A.Lamb(Capt),J.R.Smailes;
C.T.Coleman,J.Bartholomew,H.W.Butler,D.J.Sewell,E.Quinlan.

23 Mar   ETRSF   Home   Leyton Res.   6 – 0   Bartholomew(2)Sewell(3)Newman
Attendance: 632   Receipts: £18.7.3   Car Park: £0.5.0
Romford Res.: M.Croft;L.Penk,S.Poskett;J.R.Smailes,R.A.Lamb(Capt),J.W.Conner;
C.T.Coleman,H.M.Newman,J.Bartholomew,D.J.Sewell,G.W.Andrews.

31 Mar   Frdly   Away   Clapton Res.   5 – 4   Kenlay(2)Cunningham(2)Coleman
Romford Res.:
C.T.Coleman, ? ,G.J.Kenlay,G.Cunningham, ? ,

7 Apr   IFLR   Home   Wycombe Wanderers Res.   5 – 0   Cunningham,Kenlay(2)Fleetwood,Sewell
Attendance: 592   Receipts: £12.8.9   Car Park: £0.7.3
Romford Res.: C.Bingham;L.Penk,J.W.Connor;G.Fleetwood,R.A.Lamb(Capt),W.F.Mackenzie;
C.T.Coleman,D.J.Sewell,G.J.Kenlay,G.Cunningham,K.Morton.

14 Apr   IFLR   Home   Woking Res.   2 – 2   Scorers unknown
Attendance: 811   Receipts: £16.14.9   Car Park: £0.16.9
Romford Res.: M.Croft;L.Penk,J.W.Conner;W.F.Mackenzie,R.A.Lamb(Capt),K.Morton;
C.T.Coleman,H.M.Newman,V.H.Perriman,D.J.Sewell,M.Lawson.

21 Apr   Frdly   Away   Upminster   1 – 1   Coleman
Romford Res.: M.Croft;L.Penk,S.Poskitt;G.Fleetwood,R.A.Lamb(Capt),H.Russell;
C.T.Coleman,H.M.Newman,V.H.Perriman,M.Lawson,J.W.Conner.

28 Apr   Frdly   Away   Walton & Hersham Res.   3 – 2   Wadham,Sewell,Newman
Romford Res.: **Sel**. S.Poskett;L.Penk,W.P.Spelling;G.Fleetwood,H.Russell,W.F.Mackenzie;
C.T.Coleman,H.M.Newman,M.Lawson,K.Morton,J.W.Conner.
(L.Wadham on loan from Upminster and D.J.Sewell both played in the side, replacing who?)

3 May   IFLR   Home   St. Albans City Res.   Won**
Attendance: 390   Receipts: £6.9.0   Car Park: £0.2.0
Romford Res.:

5 May   IFLR   Away   Woking Res.   2 – 1   Spelling(2)
Attendance:
Romford Res.: ? ; ? , ? ; ? ,R.A.Lamb(Capt), ? ;
   ? , ? ,W.P.Spelling, ? , ? .

7 May   IFLR   Home   Corinthian Casuals Res.   Drew**
Attendance: 286   Receipts: £5.0.6   Programmes: Car Park: £ None
Romford Res.:

**   In these two games Romford scored three goals and conceded one. Actual results unknown.
\#   Abandoned after 83 minutes due to fog.

RESERVE TEAM SUMMARY OF RESULTS SEASON 1950 – 51

	P	W	D	L	For	Ag	Pts
Isthmian League Reserve Sect.	26	14	5	7	59	48	33
Essex Intermediate Cup	3	2	0	1	10	5	
Essex Thameside Trophy Res.Sect.	1	1	0	0	6	0	
Friendly Matches	5	4	1	0	20	8	
Total	35	21	6	8	95	61	

Isthmian Football League Reserve Section
Final Table

	P	W	D	L	Goals For	Ag	Pts
Leytonstone	26	19	5	2	70	33	43
Wimbledon	26	18	2	6	69	33	38
St.Albans City	26	14	6	6	61	48	34
Romford Reserves	**26**	**14**	**5**	**7**	**59**	**48**	**33**
Corinthian Casuals	26	14	4	8	61	43	32
Kingstonian	26	12	5	9	55	52	29
Walthamstow Ave.	26	10	7	9	57	36	27
Wycombe Wands.	26	12	2	12	64	57	26
Woking	26	9	6	11	52	57	24
Oxford City	26	7	6	13	45	68	20
Dulwich Hamlet	26	8	2	16	48	64	18
Clapton	26	6	3	17	37	73	15
Ilford	26	6	1	19	39	62	13
Tufnell Park (Edtn)	26	5	2	19	29	72	12

RESERVE TEAM CUP RESULTS 1950 – 51

Essex County FA Intermediate Challenge Cup
Final: Lathol Athletic   1   Leytonstone Res.   0

Romford's progress: 1ˢᵗ Round   Away   Sun Athletic   7 – 2
               2ⁿᵈ Round   Home   Chadwell Heath   1 – 0
               3ʳᵈ Round   Home   Staines United   2 – 3

Essex Thameside Challenge Competition Reserve Section
Final: n/k

Romford's progress: 1ˢᵗ Round   Home   Leyton Res.   6 – 0   ?Semi-Final

RESERVE TEAM APPEARANCES SEASON 1950 – 51

The following players are known to have appeared in the reserve team during the season.

G.W.Andrews	J.Bartholomew**	C.Bingham	R.Bumpstead(Rainham Town)
H.W.Butler(Ad Astra)	E.R.Cave	C.T.Coleman	J.W.Connor
M.Croft	F.Curtis	G.Dale	D.I.Desborough
W.J.Digby	H.Dobinson	W.H.Dowsett	D.Evans(Glendale Y.C.)
R.Fleetwood	S.Frankland	P.Gamman	A.W.Gilkes
H.W.Hails	A.F.Herbert	T.C.Horn	G.J.Kenlay(Glendale Y.C.)
J.R.Kurn	R.A.Lamb	M.Lawson	D.R.Lowman
L.Manley	Joe Martin	C.L.Moore	K.Morton

H.M.Newman	W.Nunn	R.B.Payne	V.H.Perriman
C.Perryman	L.Penk(G.E.Stores)	S.Poskitt	E.Quinlan
J.M.Rees	H.Russell(Royal Navy)	A.Schneider(Glendale Y.C)	E.W.Scott
D.Sewell	J.R.Smailes(Marley Y.C.)	W.J.Solley	W.P.Spelling
Colin Webb(Glendale Y.C)	J.G.Welch	W.R.Winsley	

Note** Jack Bartholomew renewed his association with the club at the end of his suspension by the FA

"A" Team Match Details

19 Aug SEC2   Home   Havering   1 – 3   Scorer unknown
Attendance: 444   Receipts: £11.6.3
Romford "A":

26 Aug SEC2   Home   Upminster Old Boys   7 – 1   Johnson(3)Hall(3)one other
Attendance:
Romford "A": D.Evans, .
     ? , ? ,P.D.Hall,A.Johnson, ? .

6 Sept SEC2   Home   Rainham Town "A"   1 – 0   Scorer unknown
Attendance: 106   Receipts: £2.2.3
Romford "A":

9 Sept SEC2   Away   Rainham Town "A"   1 – 0   Herbert
Romford "A":
A.F.Herbert,

13 Sept RCC1R Home   Harold Park   Won   Scorers unknown
Attendance: 204   Receipts: £4.3.0
Romford "A":

23 Sept SEC2   Away   Dagenham Dock   4 – 1   Paulding(2)Johnson,Joyce
Romford "A":
K.V.Paulding,A.Johnson,D.W.Joyce,

30 Sept SEC2   Home   Ockendon United   1 – 3   Scorer unknown
Romford "A":

7 Oct   SEC2   Away   Cranham   3 – 3   Scorers unknown
Romford "A":

14 Oct Frdly Away   Navestock   1 – 4   Scorer unknown
Romford "A":

21 Oct SEC2   Home   452 O.C.A.   2 – 2   Scorers unknown
Romford "A":

28 Oct RCC2R Away   Barkingside   1 – 3   Scorer unknown
Romford "A":

18 Nov SECC2R Away   Harold Park   3 – 8   Scorers unknown
Romford "A":

25 Nov SEC2   Home   Cranham   2 – 2# Scorers unknown
Romford "A":

9 Dec   SEC2   Home   Hornchurch Athletic "A"   1 – 0   Scorer unknown
Romford "A":

23 Dec SEC2   Away   Collier Row   1 – 4   Scorer unknown
Romford "A":

6 Jan   SEC2   Away   Ockendon United   3 – 2   Scorers unknown
Romford "A":

27 Jan SEC2   Away   452 O.C.A.   0 – 3
Romford "A":

3 Feb   SEC2   Home#1 Collier Row   2 – 6   Scorers unknown
Romford "A":

24 Feb SEC2   Away   Becontree British Legion   3 – 1   Scorers unknown
Romford "A":

3 Mar   SEC2   Away   Beacontree Heath Old Boys   3 – 3   Scorers unknown
Romford "A":

10 Mar SEC2 Away Hornchurch Athletic "A" 3 – 2 Scorers unknown
Romford "A":

17 Mar SEC2 Home#2 Dagenham Dock 3 – 1 Scorers unknown
Romford "A":

31 Mar SEC2 Away Havering 1 – 4 Scorer unknown
Romford "A":

7 Apr SEC2 Away Upminster Old Boys 1 – 5 Scorer unknown
Romford "A":

14 Apr SEC2 Home Beacontree Heath Old Boys 1 – 3 Scorer unknown
Romford "A":

21 Apr SEC2 Home Becontree British Legion 3 – 3 Scorers unknown
Romford "A":

25 Apr SEC2 Home Cranham 1 – 1 Scorer unknown
Romford "A"

\# Match abandoned due to fog.
\#1 Played at Collier Row.
\#2 Played at Dagenham Dock.

"A" TEAM CUP RESULTS 1950 – 51

South Essex Combination Cup
Final: Hornchurch Athletic 3 Upminster Reserves 1
(at Brooklands)

Romford's progress: 1st Round Bye
2nd Round Away Harold Park 3 – 8

Romford Charity Cup
Final: Estric(Romford) 1 Fairlop 2 (a.e.t)

Romford's progress: 1st Round Home Harold Park won
2nd Round Away Barkingside 1 – 3

"A" TEAM SUMMARY OF RESULTS 1950 – 51

	Home			**Goals**		**Away**			**Goals**		
	P	**W**	**D**	**L**	**For**	**Ag**	**W**	**D**	**L**	**For**	**Ag**	**Pts**
South Essex Comb. Division 2	22	4	3	4	23	23	5	2	4	23	28	23
South Essex Combination Cup	1	0	0	0	0	0	0	0	1	3	8	
Romford Charity Cup	2	1	0	0	? *	?	0	0	1	1	3*	
Friendly	1	0	0	0	0	0	0	0	1	1	4	
Total	26	5	3	4	23	23	5	2	7	28	43	

* The score in this victory is unknown.

Southern Essex Combination Premier Division
Final Table

	P	W	D	L	Goals For	Ag	Pts
Collier Row	22	17	3	2	78	28	37
Havering	22	13	4	5	66	41	30
Upminster O.B.	22	13	2	7	61	45	28
Becontree B.L.	22	13	2	7	58	45	28
Rainham Town "A"	22	9	5	8	49	42	23
Romford "A"	**22**	**9**	**5**	**8**	**46**	**51**	**23**
452 O.C.A.	22	8	4	10	47	47	20

Ockendon Utd.	22	6	7	9	40	45	19
Cranham	22	6	5	11	50	63	17
Beacontree Hth.OB	22	5	6	11	36	63	16
Hornchurch Athletic "A"	22	5	4	13	43	78	14
Dagenham Dock	22	3	3	16	36	82	9

"A" TEAM APPEARANCES 1950 – 51

Due to the limited detail in press reports, the following players only are known to have appeared in the "A" Team during the season.

D.Evans(Glendale)   P.D.Hall   A.F.Herbert
A.Johnson   D.W.Joyce   K.V.Paulding(Glendale)

DEPARTURES FROM THE CLUB SEASON 1950 – 51

The following players appear to have left the club during or by the end of the season. They may have been triallists and only played one or two games and then went elsewhere. New clubs are indicated where known.

T.Albert (Barnet), J.Bartholomew (suspended by F.A.), J.Barton (Brentwood & Warley), C.Bingham (Rainham Town), R.Bumpstead (Rainham Town), H.W.Butler (Brentwood & Warley), E.R.Cave (Royal Air Force), C.T.Coleman, M.Croft, F.Curtis (West Thurrock), G.Dale, D.I.Desborough, W.J.Digby, H.Dobinson, R.Fleetwood, S.Frankland (Rainham Town), F.E.Fryatt (Brentwood & Warley), P.Gamman (HM Forces), A.W.Gilkes, H.W.Hails (Woodford Town), T.Horn (Brentwood & Warley), G.W.Jennings (Dagenham), D.W.Joyce, J.A.Kurn (Upminster), M.Lawson, W.F.Mackenzie (Dagenham), J.Martin (retired), L.Manley, K.Morton (Ilford), W.Nunn, R.B.Payne, C.Perryman (Barkingside), S.Poskitt, E.Quinlan (Royal Air Force), J.M.Rees, W.B.Regan (Ford Sports), E.W.Scott (St.Albans City), D.Sewell, T.Stewart (Willington), C.Webb, W.R.Winsley (Grays Athletic).

Post Season Summary   Season 1950 – 51

Romford prepared for the season with a pleasant trip to Switzerland where they beat Schaffhausen 5-3 but suffered a 2-0 defeat against Winterthur. A third game was played against Baden which Romford won 1-0. The league campaign opened with a narrow victory (2-1) away to lowly Tufnell Park followed on 2nd September by a heavy defeat from Walthamstow Avenue (1-4) at Brooklands. Once more the fans voiced their disapproval.

This was followed by a remarkable turn of events with the boys recording six successive victories, including 7-1 beatings of Grays Athletic and Wycombe Wanderers. Tilbury were thrashed 5-1 in the FA Cup on 30th September. Ten thousand spectators crowded into Brooklands for the next FA Cup tie, versus powerful Briggs Sports who went away happy with a 2-2 draw. Romford won the replay 2-1. Alas, bitter disappointment awaited in the next round. After a 2-2 draw at Woodford Town and a 1-1 draw in the replay at Brooklands, a third game, again at Brooklands, drew over 7,000 spectators. Actually there was a much larger audience as the tie was televised by the BBC who paid the club 25 guineas to cover expenses! This inspired Woodford Town who duly recorded a 2-1 victory.

Two league points were obtained away at Wycombe Wanderers on 18th November, but the next game against St Albans City ended early due to the onset of foggy conditions!

Two successive games against lowly Clapton ended with a win apiece, each winning on their own ground by an odd goal. Wimbledon were beaten 3-2 on 16th December, but there followed an unsettled period with defeat by Ilford and draws against Ilford and Woking.

In the New Year hopes were revived with a good 3-1 victory over Harlow Town in the Essex Senior Cup and a fine 2-2 draw away to Moor Green in the Amateur Cup, but disaster was to follow. The replay against the strong Midlanders saw them defeat Romford 2-0 on 20th January before a large and enthusiastic crowd at Brooklands, and Amateur Cup dreams were over for another season. This was followed by exit from the Essex Senior Cup too, with a 2-1 reverse at Tilbury. Only 1,500 witnessed a 3-1 win over St. Albans City which was followed by a disastrous run of results. All was not well in the Romford dressing room. Romford failed to win any of their next six league games, including a 7-1 thrashing away to Corinthian Casuals and a 3-0 defeat in the return at Brooklands. Walthamstow Avenue and St. Albans City in the replayed league game both recorded victories.

After this bad patch the team had an amazing run, recording seven successive victories! Six of the matches were Isthmian League encounters including a fine victory over eventual champions Leytonstone on 7th April and further success against highly placed Wimbledon and Oxford City twice. Leyton were defeated in the Thameside Trophy. The run came to an end on 10th May when Leytonstone gained revenge in the Thameside Trophy semi-final at Brooklands. The Stones won a thrilling clash 4-3 after extra time.

The final game of the season drew nearly 4,500 to Brooklands to witness a fine performance from touring side Wageningen who soundly trounced our heroes 5-1. Thus ended a disappointing season that started well and promised much but achieved little. Third place in the league was the high, but the cup competitions led to great disappointment.

In an effort to find a successful combination many players were given chances but although the team played 44 first team games, only three players appeared in more than twenty of them. The reserve team despite the calls on players for the first team, achieved a creditable fourth place in the reserve section league table. Likewise the "A" team had a below average season – no doubt calls from the reserve team helped contribute to this.

Romford had the honour of staging this Football Association Representative match at Brooklands in October 1950
Authors' collection

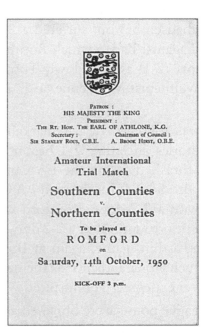

PATRON :
HIS MAJESTY THE KING
PRESIDENT :
THE RT. HON. THE EARL OF ATHLONE, K.G.
Secretary :   Chairman of Council :
SIR STANLEY ROUS, C.B.E.   A. BROOK HIRST, O.B.E.

Amateur International
Trial Match

Southern Counties
v.
Northern Counties

To be played at
ROMFORD
on
Saturday, 14th October, 1950

KICK-OFF 3 p.m.

The story of Romford's 2-2 away draw with Moor Green in the Amateur Cup
first round on 13th January 1951 is told in strip cartoon form in the *Romford Times*

GLEANINGS FROM MANAGEMENT COMMITTEE MINUTE BOOKS
SEASON 1950-51

On **16th May 1950** officials and fifteen senior players attended a dinner at the White Hart at the invitation of the Chairman, Mr A.J. Smith. They were "invited to offer any criticism of Club Management in general or offer any suggestions or recommendations in the interests of the Club".

On **30th May** the Club's "A" team was placed in Division Two of the New Southern Essex Combination which was formed out of a reorganisation of the Romford & District League. The Secretary was asked to communicate with Glendale FC enquiring whether they would be interested in being closely associated with Romford Football Club.

On **13th June** Mr Anderton and Mr Pond, representing Glendale FC, were welcomed to the meeting and they "expressed a very keen desire to assist in any way possible".

On **11th July** the club was notified by the Football Association that the Official Amateur International Trial between Northern Counties and Southern Counties will be played at Brooklands on 14th October. "The Chairman commented on the compliment paid to the Club by the allocation of this important fixture".

On **14th October** the above match took place at Brooklands and was televised by the BBC, who in return paid Romford FC £26.5.0.

On **7th November** 26 players of Glendale FC (a youth club) were approved as playing members of Romford FC.

The teams mingle for an official photo ahead of Romford's friendly against
Dutch side Wageningen at Brooklands on 14th May 1951   *Authors' collection*

DIRECTORS' REPORT FOR THE TWELVE MONTHS ENDED 31ST MAY, 1951

From the Accounts now presented, it will be seen that the year ended 31st May, 1951, has been a successful one resulting in a gross profit of £597. This figure is less than the profit for the previous year, but can be considered satisfactory having regard to the far from successful football season. Fortune did not smile on the efforts of the 1st team – no trophies being won and finishing third in the Isthmian League.

…..The proposed Grandstand has been under almost continuous consideration by your Directors but little progress has been made. Your Directors are sorry to say that a Building Licence has still not been obtained. Your Directors will, however, continue to give this matter attention. Your Directors are, however, pleased to report that they have been successful in obtaining the necessary Licences to proceed with the erection of a pre-cast concrete wall with appropriate gates and pay-boxes to separate the Playing Arena from the Car Park, and instructions have been given to the Company's Architect to proceed with the work forthwith.

Grass Cycling Meetings were again promoted during the summer months on Brooklands, and many exciting races and championships were seen by spectators, but this year these were not promoted by the Company. The Ground was let for the purpose to a Local Cycling Club…..As to future Programme and Policy your Directors are ever mindful that members' first desire is to enjoy at Brooklands good clean sport and with this in mind have permitted during the year under review an Agricultural Show, Wresting and Cycling as well as Football.

It had been hoped to stage the Pageant of Romford in connexion with the Boro' Council's Festival of Britain activities and in this connexion your Director, Mr A.E. Kittle, was co-opted a member of the appropriate Committee of the Boro' Council but as members well know the Pageant was not proceeded with. It is the intention of the Board to continue to encourage every form of sport at Brooklands. Football being the main concern of your Directors it is their continuing endeavour to produce through team spirit and coaching a team of such prowess as will bring the Amateur Cup to Romford.

The report was presented to shareholders at the Annual General Meeting on Monday 24th March 1952. The meeting was reported as follows in the *Romford Times*, Wednesday 26th March 1952:

ROMFORD FC MEMBERS LEARNED LITTLE

Inquiring members of Romford Football Club Ltd, who went along to the annual meeting at the White Hart Hotel on Monday were in for a big disappointment. For the directors refused to be drawn on any controversial point – from the "one amateur league" plan to floodlit football.

Lord Macpherson, chairman of the board, said the question of floodlit football was being considered. The board was following the experiments of other clubs with interest. A detailed scheme for installing the equipment had been submitted, but other grounds would have to be visited before they could make up their minds whether to instal it – or not.

AMALGAMATION. Mr Martin Brazier, the club's secretary, said that the amalgamation of the Athenian and Isthmian leagues might be a good plan. But he could see little progress being made for some time. Maybe next year, maybe the year after. He said the better clubs in the two leagues had no desire to be "dragged down" and therefore saw no chance of Dagenham's Isthmian – Athenian – Corinthian – Delphian amalgamation plan succeeding.

He thought the solution lay in the determination of the two top leagues to strengthen themselves. He thought a club which had been at the bottom of the Isthmian League for some years was on the way out.

WHY NO TRAIN? When members asked why the club did not back the plan to run a special train to Crook (as Walton and Hersham did to Bishop Auckland), Mr A.E. Kittle, chairman of the management committee, said that it was out of their province.

One note was stressed by Lord Macpherson throughout the meeting: the board was determined to maintain the dividend. The reason, he said, was that a good "dividend record" was essential if the company had to seek more capital for their major building schemes with a public share issue.

And so although some said that they would rather see the £736 being paid out retained to offset the cost of building the new wall, members duly voted themselves a dividend of 7½ per cent….

THE BECONTREE WHEELERS CYCLING CLUB TAKE OVER BROOKLANDS DURING THE SUMMER

Visitors take the prizes in 'Bec's' grass track meet
(as reported in the *Romford Times*, May 23rd 1951)

BECONTREE WHEELERS CYCLING CLUB
present
ESSEX
1,000 YDS. SPRINT CHAMPIONSHIP
AT THE SECOND OF FIVE
Cycle Race Meetings
AT ROMFORD FOOTBALL GROUND
BROOKLANDS ROAD, ROMFORD
ON SATURDAY, 2ND JUNE 1951 3 P.M.
ADMISSION 1/-   CHILDREN 6d.

Visitors went away with most of the important prizes at the first of the five grass track meetings. Becontree Wheelers have taken over this year from the Romford Football Club at Brooklands on Saturday.

Bill Hopkins, Becontree Wheelers, retained the Robert Cook Memorial Trophy for the Essex County Cycling and Athletic Association's half-mile championship, winning strongly from the front.

Essex sprint champion Len Watson, Romford Wheelers, and Pete Laxton, of the promoting club, were the only two local riders to be placed in the open events, with the exception of the two courses des primes in which Pete Watson, Romford Wheelers, kept the locals among the prizes.

….a welcome re-appearance was Bill Seddon Jnr, son of Romford Football Club's popular trainer. On leave from the RAF, he missed winning his handicap heat by inches after an exciting tussle with champion Len Watson.

Overall the attendances for cycling were not so good but the enthusiasm was as keen as ever. One of the Becontree Wheelers meetings turned to disaster when the sun baked track developed deep ruts on the notorious North Street bend, which resulted in a number of spills and many of the competitors being removed to Oldchurch Hospital.

The *Romford Times* cartoonist's amusing observations at the first in the series of cycle race meetings held at Brooklands over the summer of 1951

WRESTLING DROPS IN AT BROOKLANDS

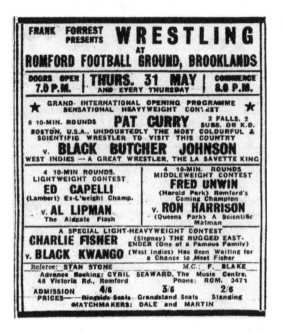

Wrestling arrived at Brooklands in 1951. The first event took place on Thursday 31st May, and topping the bill was Fred Unwin of Romford who beat Ron Harrison of Queens Park. Another two evenings of these wrestling extravaganzas took place at Brooklands and they both had an international appeal with Pat Curry (USA) defeating the famous Mike Marino (Italy) who was removed to Oldchurch Hospital with a leg injury.

Butch Johnson (West Indies) fought out a draw with Charles Fisher (Eltham) and top of the bill on the final night saw the European champion George Kidd defeat the Southern Area champion Jack Quesick by two falls to one.

After the third of these wrestling events it was announced that the series would be suspended until further notice. No reason was given for this. Some of these wrestlers went on to become household names with ITV World of Sport's Saturday afternoon bouts.

Fred Unwin (Romford) v.
Ron Harrison (Queens Park)

THE ROMFORD FOOTBALL CLUB LIMITED

Full Members of The Football Association
Full Members of Isthmian Football League
Affiliated to Essex County Football Association

Club Colours: Blue & Gold Shirts, White Shorts

Ground: Brooklands Sports Ground, Romford

Chairman: The Rt.Hon. Lord Macpherson

Directors: Messrs. M.A.Brazier, A.E.Kittle, W.G.Mann,
J.W.Parrish, A.J.Smith MBE, S.G.Tansley

Company Secretary: Mr H.W.Muskett

Bankers: Lloyds Bank Limited   **Auditors:** Iion V. Cummings & Co.

Registered Offices: 110,Hyland Way, Romford

Football Club Management Committee:
Chairman: Mr A.E.Kittle
Hon.Gen.Secretary: Mr M.A.Brazier   **Hon.Press Secretary:** Mr H.A.Hughes

Other Committee Members: Messrs. A.J.Smith MBE,
W.G.Mann, J.W.Parrish, S.G.Tansley

Hon.Asst.Secretary: Mr J.Gurney   **Hon.Advt.Secretary:** Mr R.S.Lyons

Reserve XI Secretary: Mr G.I.Howlett   **Third XI Secretary:** Mr E.Crooks

Trainer: Mr W.C.(Bill) Seddon   **Hon.Medical Advisor:** Dr I.H.Bourne

Groundsman: Mr W.C.(Bill)Seddon
"A" Team Ground: Cottons Recreation Ground

COMPETITIONS ENTERED SEASON 1951 – 52

FA Challenge Cup
FA Amateur Challenge Cup
Isthmian Football League
Essex County FA Senior Challenge Cup
East Anglian Cup
Essex Thameside Challenge Competition

Isthmian Football League Reserve Section
Essex County FA Intermediate Challenge Cup
Essex Thameside Challenge Competition Reserve Section

Isthmian Football League "A" Section
Romford Charity Cup

Admission Prices Season 1951 – 52

	First Team			Reserve Team		
	Adults	OAPs	Child	Adults	OAPs	Child
Ground	1/-	6d		6d	3d	
Ground & Enclosure	1/9	1/-		1/-	6d	
Grandstand	2/6	2/6		1/-	6d	

Programmes: 1ˢᵗ XI   2d   2ⁿᵈ XI   Single Sheet   1½d

Season Tickets

	Adults	OAPs & Children
Grandstand (All one price)	£1.10.0	
Ground & Enclosure	£1.1.0	12/6
Ground only	12/6	7/6

PUBLIC TRIAL MATCH

Sat.,18ᵗʰ Aug.,1951   3.30 p.m.   Final Trial
POSSIBLES   1   PROBABLES   4
Newman   Andrews,Bridge,Brooks,Kenlay

Attendance: 1,155   Receipts: £56.15.9   Programmes: £   Car Park: £1.13.9
Possibles: C.Bingham;L.Penk;J.Barton;D.Kent,H.Russell,K.Morton;
P.Boreham,H.M.Neweman,J.Casey,J.Hornsby,A.Herbert.

Probables: C.L.Moore;J.Richards,W.J.Solley,J.Smailes,G.Fleetwood,J.G.Welch;
H.W.Brooks,W.A.Bridge,G.J.Kenlay,G.Cunningham,G.W.Andrews.

First Team Match Details

25 Aug   IFL   Home   Oxford City   1 – 5   Cunningham
Attendance: 3,849   Receipts: £186.18.9   Programmes: £21.13.1   Car Park: £5.11.3
Romford: C.L.Moore;W.J.Solley,D.Kent;G.Fleetwood,H.Russell,J.G.Welch;
H.W.Brooks,W.A.Bridge,G.J.Kenlay,G.Cunningham(Capt),G.W.Andrews.

29 Aug   Frdly   Home   Gold Coast XI   2 – 1   Isaacs,Brooks
Attendance: 5,258   Receipts: £263.19.6   Programmes: £23.13.3   Car Park: £6.3.6
Romford: C.L.Moore;W.J.Solley,J.Barton;G.Fleetwood,D.Kent,J.G.Welch;
H.W.Brooks,W.A.Bridge,W.Isaacs,G.Cunningham(Capt),G.W.Andrews.

1 Sept   IFL   Away   Walthamstow Avenue   4 – 0   Cunningham(2)Isaacs,Andrews
Romford: C.L.Moore;W.J.Solley,R.A.Lamb;W.J.Smailes,G.Fleetwood,J.G.Welch;
W.A.Bridge,H.M.Newman,W.Isaacs,G.Cunningham(Capt),G.W.Andrews.

5 Sept   ETT1R   Home   Ilford   6 – 4   Kenlay(2)Cunningham(2)Herbert,
                                                   Newman
Attendance: 3,866   Receipts: £198.13.3   Programmes: £10.7.8   Car Park: £4.12.0
Romford: C.L.Moore;W.J.Solley,R.A.Lamb;W.J.Smailes,G.Fleetwood,J.G.Welch;
G.W.Andrews,H.M.Newman,G.J.Kenlay,G.Cunningham(Capt),A.F.Herbert.

8 Sept   IFL   Home   Wimbledon   3 – 1   Kenlay(3)
Attendance: 3,379   Receipts: £161.18.3   Programmes: £23.1.10   Car Park: £5.5.0
Romford: C.L.Moore;W.J.Solley,R.A.Lamb;W.J.Smailes,G.Fleetwood,J.G.Welch;
H.W.Brooks,H.M.Newman,G.J.Kenlay,W.A.Bridge(Capt),G.W.Andrews.

12 Sept   EAC1R   Home   Chelsea "A"   3 – 0   Newman,Bell(og)Bridge
Attendance: 3,361   Receipts: £170.5.6   Programmes: £7.11.4   Car Park: £5.1.6
Romford: C.L.Moore;W.J.Solley,R.A.Lamb;W.J.Smailes,G.Fleetwood,J.G.Welch;
W.A.Bridge,H.M.Newman,G.J.Kenlay,G.Cunningham(Capt),G.W.Andrews.

15 Sept   IFL   Away   Wycombe Wanderers   0 – 2
Romford: C.L.Moore;W.J.Solley,R.A.Lamb;W.J.Smailes,G.Fleetwood,J.G.Welch;
W.A.Bridge,H.M.Newman,G.J.Kenlay,G.Cunningham(Capt),G.W.Andrews.

22 Sept   IFL   Home   Kingstonian   2 – 0   Bridge,Cunningham
Attendance: 4,195   Receipts: £208.12.0   Programmes: £23.13.9   Car Park: £5.18.9
Romford: C.L.Moore;W.J.Solley,R.A.Lamb;W.J.Smailes,G.Fleetwood,J.G.Welch;
H.W.Brooks,H.M.Newman,W.A.Bridge,G.Cunningham(Capt),G.W.Andrews.

29 Sept FAC1Q Home Barking   1 – 0   Smailes
Attendance: 6,710   Receipts: £365.7.6   Programmes: £28.4.0   Car Park: £15.8.3
Romford: C.L.Moore;W.J.Solley,R.A.Lamb;W.J.Smailes,G.Fleetwood,J.G.Welch;
H.W.Brooks,H.M.Newman,W.A.Bridge,G.Cunningham(Capt),A.F.Herbert.

6 Oct IFL Away Woking   2 – 2   Bridge,Newman
Romford: C.L.Moore;W.J.Solley,R.A.Lamb;W.J.Smailes,G.Fleetwood,J.G.Welch;
H.W.Brooks,H.M.Newman,W.A.Bridge,G.Cunningham(Capt),G.W.Andrews.

13 Oct FAC2Q Away Briggs Sports   1 – 1   Brooks
Attendance: 4,800
Romford: C.L.Moore;W.J.Solley,R.A.Lamb;W.J.Smailes,G.Fleetwood,J.G.Welch;
H.W.Brooks,G.Cunningham(Capt),G.J.Kenlay,W.A.Bridge,G.W.Andrews.

18 Oct FACRp Home Briggs Sports   6 – 2   Bridge,Kenlay(2)Andrews,Cunningham(2)
Attendance: 4,089   Receipts: £215.14.3   Programmes: £13.11.6   Car Park: £7.2.0
Romford: C.L.Moore;W.J.Solley,R.A.Lamb;W.J.Smailes,G.Fleetwood,J.G.Welch;
H.W.Brooks,G.Cunningham(Capt),G.J.Kenlay,W.A.Bridge,G.W.Andrews.

20 Oct IFL Home Leytonstone   2 – 4   Lamb(pen)Andrews
Attendance: 5,058   Receipts: £251.0.9   Programmes: £34.14.7   Car Park: £9.10.3
Romford: C.L.Moore;W.J.Solley,R.A.Lamb;W.J.Smailes,G.Fleetwood,J.G.Welch(Capt);
H.W.Brooks,A.F.Herbert,G.J.Kenlay,W.A.Bridge,G.W.Andrews.

27 Oct FAC3Q Home Brentwood & Warley   3 – 1   Bridge,Kenlay,Brooks
Attendance: 7,482   Receipts: £406.15.0   Programmes: £28.2.4   Car Park: £8.11.3
Romford: C.L.Moore;W.J.Solley,R.A.Lamb;W.J.Smailes,G.Fleetwood,J.G.Welch(Capt);
H.W.Brooks,H.M.Newman,G.J.Kenlay,W.A.Bridge,G.W.Andrews.

3 Nov IFL Away Tufnell Park Edmonton   2 – 2   Andrews,Brooks
Romford: C.L.Moore,W.J.Solley,R.A.Lamb;W.J.Smailes,G.Fleetwood,J.G.Welch(Capt);
H.W.Brooks,H.M.Newman,G.J.Kenlay,W.A.Bridge,G.W.Andrews.

10 Nov FAC4Q Away Gorleston   0 – 1
Attendance: 5,500
Romford: C.L.Moore;W.J.Solley,R.A.Lamb;W.J.Smailes,G.Fleetwood,J.G.Welch;
H.W.Brooks,G.Cunningham(Capt),G.J.Kenlay,W.A.Bridge,G.W.Andrews.

17 Nov IFL Home Wycombe Wanderers   2 – 0   Cunningham,Brooks
Attendance: 2,307   Receipts: £108.5.0   Programmes: £15.17.9   Car Park: £6.10.6
Romford: C.L.Moore;W.J.Solley,R.A.Lamb;W.J.Smailes,G.Fleetwood,J.G.Welch;
H.W.Brooks,W.A.Bridge,G.J.Kenlay,G.Cunningham(Capt),G.W.Andrews.

24 Nov IFL Home St. Albans City   3 – 2   Cunningham,Bee,Brooks
Attendance: 3,133   Receipts: £152.16.0   Programmes: £16.11.6   Car Park: £5.9.9
Romford: C.L.Moore;W.J.Solley,R.A.Lamb;W.J.Smailes,G.Fleetwood,J.G.Welch;
H.W.Brooks,W.A.Bridge,J.Bee,G.Cunningham(Capt),G.W.Andrews.

1 Dec IFL Away Clapton   2 – 1   Bee,Welch
Romford: C.L.Moore;W.J.Solley,R.A.Lamb;W.J.Smailes,G.Fleetwood,J.G.Welch;
H.W.Brooks,W.A.Bridge,J.Bee,G.Cunningham(Capt),G.W.Andrews.

8 Dec IFL Home Woking   5 – 1   Cunningham(2)Bridge(2)Brooks
Attendance: 2,484   Receipts: £127.16.0   Programmes: £15.8.6   Car Park: £4.10.6
Romford: C.L.Moore;W.J.Solley,R.A.Lamb;W.J.Smailes,G.Fleetwood,J.G.Welch;
H.W.Brooks,W.A.Bridge,J.Bee,G.Cunningham(Capt),G.W.Andrews.

15 Dec AC1R Away Stowmarket   2 – 0   Cunningham,Bee
Attendance: 3,800
Romford: C.L.Moore;W.J.Solley,R.A.Lamb;W.J.Smailes,G.Fleetwood,J.G.Welch;
H.W.Brooks,W.A.Bridge,J.Bee,G.Cunningham(Capt),G.W.Andrews.

22 Dec IFL Away Kingstonian   1 – 2   Bridge
Romford: C.L.Moore;D.Evans,R.A.Lamb;W.J.Smailes,W.J.Solley,J.G.Welch;
H.W.Brooks,W.A.Bridge,J.Bee,G.Cunningham(Capt),G.W.Andrews.

25 Dec IFL Home Ilford   1 – 2   Smailes
Attendance: 4,494   Receipts: £226.5.9   Programmes: £21.7.3   Car Park: £6.7.3
Romford: C.L.Moore;D.Evans,R.A.Lamb;W.J.Smailes,W.J.Solley,J.G.Welch;
H.W.Brooks,W.A.Bridge,J.Bee,G.Cunningham(Capt),G.W.Andrews.

26 Dec IFL Away Ilford   6 – 0   Cunningham,Casson(2)Andrews(2)Bee
Romford: W.Dawber;W.J.Solley,R.A.Lamb;J.G.Welch,W.J.Smailes,P.J.Boreham;
A.F.Herbert,L.G.Casson,J.Bee,G.Cunningham(Capt),G.W.Andrews.

29 Dec IFL Away St. Albans City   2 – 2   Herbert,Andrews
Romford: C.L.Moore;W.J.Solley,R.A.Lamb;W.A.Bridge,W.J.Smailes,J.G.Welch;
A.F.Herbert,L.G.Casson,J.Bee,G.Cunningham(Capt),G.W.Andrews.

5 Jan   IFL   Home   Tufnell Park Edmonton   4 – 0   Lamb(2pens)Casson,Kenlay
Attendance: 3,279   Receipts: £156.9.3   Progs: £27.18.0   Car Park: £6.5.6
Romford: C.L.Moore;W.J.Solley,R.A.Lamb;W.J.Smailes,G.Fleetwood,W.A.Bridge;
A.F.Herbert,L.G.Casson,G.J.Kenlay,G.Cunningham(Capt),G.W.Andrews.

12 Jan   AC2R   Away   Boldmere St. Michael's   3 – 3   Bridge(2)Andrews
Attendance: 3,250
Romford: C.L.Moore;W.J.Solley,R.A.Lamb;W.J.Smailes,G.Fleetwood,J.G.Welch;
A.F.Herbert,W.A.Bridge,J.Bee,G.Cunningham(Capt),G.W.Andrews.

19 Jan   ACRP   Home   Boldmere St. Michael's   4 – 0   Cunningham,Andrews,Lamb(pen)Casson
Attendance: 7,847   Receipts: £423.6.3   Programmes: £49.16.6   Car Park: £7.10.0
Romford: C.L.Moore;W.J.Solley,R.A.Lamb;W.J.Smailes,G.Fleetwood,P.J.Boreham;
A.F.Herbert,L.G.Casson,J.Bee,G.Cunningham(Capt),G.W.Andrews.

26 Jan   ESC1R   Away   Leyton   4 – 2   Cunningham,Bee,Coleman,
                                             Ellis-Williams

Romford: C.L.Moore;W.J.Solley,R.A.Lamb;W.J.Smailes,G.Fleetwood,P.J.Boreham;
N.J.Coleman,J.Ellis-Williams,J.Bee,G.Cunningham(Capt),G.W.Andrews.

2 Feb   EAC2R   Away   King's Lynn   3 – 3   Cunningham(2)Bee
Attendance: 5,248
Romford: C.L.Moore;W.J.Solley,R.A.Lamb;W.J.Smailes,G.Fleetwood,P.J.Boreham;
N.J.Coleman,J.Ellis-Williams,J.Bee,G.Cunningham(Capt),G.W.Andrews.

9 Feb   AC3R   Away   Crook Town   4 – 4   Bee,Bridge,Lamb(pen)Andrews
Attendance: 6,000
Romford: C.L.Moore;W.J.Solley,R.A.Lamb;W.J.Smailes,G.Fleetwood,P.J.Boreham;
W.A.Bridge,J.Ellis-Williams,J.Bee,G.Cunningham(Capt),G.W.Andrews.

16 Feb   ACRp   Home   Crook Town   1 – 3   Bee
Attendance: 11,886   Receipts: £631.19.9   Programmes: £50.18.2   Car Park: £8.10.0
Romford: C.L.Moore;W.J.Solley,R.A.Lamb;W.J.Smailes,G.Fleetwood,P.J.Boreham;
N.J.Coleman,W.A.Bridge,J.Bee,G.Cunningham(Capt),G.W.Andrews.

23 Feb   IFL   Away   Dulwich Hamlet   4 – 3   Bee(2)Ellis-Williams,Andrews
Romford: C.L.Moore;W.J.Solley,R.A.Lamb;W.J.Smailes,D.R.Lowman,J.G.Welch;
G.Cunningham(Capt),N.J.Coleman,J.Bee,J.Ellis-Williams,G.W.Andrews.

1 Mar   IFL   Home   Clapton   3 – 0   Ellis-Williams(2)Coleman
Attendance: 2,309   Receipts: £115.14.6   Programmes: £30.16.3   Car Park: £5.9.3
Romford: C.L.Moore;D.R.Lowman,R.A.Lamb;J.G.Welch,G.Fleetwood,P.J.Boreham;
G.Cunningham(Capt),N.J.Coleman,J.Bee,J.Ellis-Williams,G.W.Andrews.

8 Mar   IFL   Away#   Corinthian Casuals   1 – 2   Andrews
Romford: C.L.Moore;D.Evans,R.A.Lamb(Capt);W.J.Smailes,D.R.Lowman,J.G.Welch;
H.W.Brooks,N.J.Coleman,J.Bee,A.F.Herbert,G.W.Andrews.

15 Mar   ESC3R   Home   Walthamstow Avenue   2 – 1   Ellis-Williams,Braham(og)
Attendance: 6,865   Receipts: £367.7.9   Programmes: £39.8.0   Car Park: £8.2.6
Romford: C.L.Moore;D.Evans,R.A.Lamb(Capt);W.J.Smailes,G.Fleetwood,J.G.Welch;
H.W.Brooks,J.Ellis-Williams,N.J.Coleman,A.F.Herbert,G.W.Andrews.

20 Mar   EACRp   Home   King's Lynn   5 – 3   Coleman(2)Bee(2)Lamb
Attendance: 2,857   Receipts: £155.7.3   Programmes: £9.10.1   Car Park: £4.16.9
Romford: C.L.Moore;J.G.Welch,R.A.Lamb;W.J.Smailes,G.Fleetwood,P.J.Boreham;
H.W.Brooks,N.J.Coleman,J.Bee,G.Cunningham(Capt),A.F.Herbert.

22 Mar   IFL   Away   Leytonstone   1 – 1   Coleman
Romford: C.L.Moore;J.G.Welch,R.A.Lamb;W.J.Smailes,G.Fleetwood,P.J.Boreham;
H.W.Brooks,N.J.Coleman,J.Bee,G.Cunningham(Capt),A.F.Herbert.

5 Apr   ESCSF   Ilford   Grays Athletic   3 – 1   Bee(3)
Romford: C.L.Moore;J.G.Welch,R.A.Lamb;W.J.Smailes,G.Fleetwood,P.J.Boreham;
H.W.Brooks,N.J.Coleman,J.Bee,G.Cunningham(Capt),G.W.Andrews.

11 Apr   EACSF   Home   Tottenham Hotspur "A"   3 – 1   Brooks,Cunningham,Bee
Attendance: 9,632   Receipts: £485.9.9   Programmes: £53.15.4   Car Park: £22.16.0
Romford: C.L.Moore;R.A.Lamb,J.G.Welch;W.J.Smailes,G.Fleetwood,P.J.Boreham;
H.W.Brooks,A.F.Herbert,J.Bee,G.Cunningham(Capt),G.W.Andrews.

14 Apr   ESCF   Ilford   Briggs Sports   0 – 1*
Attendance: 13,280
Romford: C.L.Moore;J.G.Welch,R.A.Lamb;W.J.Smailes,G.Fleetwood,P.J.Boreham;
H.W.Brooks,N.J.Coleman,J.Bee,G.Cunningham(Capt),G.W.Andrews.

19 Apr IFL Away Oxford City 3 – 2 Coleman,Lamb,Andrews
Romford: C.L.Moore;J.G.Welch,R.A.Lamb(Capt);W.J.Smailes,G.Fleetwood,P.J.Boreham;
H.W.Brooks,A.F.Herbert,N.J.Coleman,W.A.Bridge,G.W.Andrews.

21 Apr ETTSF Away Barking 3 – 3* Andrews,Cunningham,Kenlay
Romford: C.L.Moore;J.G.Welch,R.A.Lamb;W.J.Smailes,G.Fleetwood,P.J.Boreham;
H.W.Brooks,G.Cunningham(Capt),G.J.Kenlay,A.F.Herbert,G.W.Andrews.

23 Apr IFL Away Wimbledon 2 – 1 Bee(2)
Romford: C.L.Moore;J.G.Welch,R.A.Lamb(Capt);W.J.Smailes,G.Fleetwood,V.H.Perriman;
G.J.Kenlay,P.J.Boreham,J.Bee,G.W.Andrews,A.F.Herbert.

25 Apr ETTRp Home Barking 3 – 0 Cunningham(2)Bee
Attendance: 4,323   Receipts: £218.18.6   Programmes: £None   Car Park: £4.4.3
Romford: C.L.Moore;J.G.Welch,R.A.Lamb;W.J.Smailes,G.Fleetwood,P.J.Boreham;
H.W.Brooks,N.J.Coleman,J.Bee,G.Cunningham(Capt),G.W.Andrews.

26 Apr IFL Home Dulwich Hamlet 1 – 4 Cunningham(pen)
Attendance: 2,212   Receipts: £105.7.0   Programmes: £13.10.9   Car Park: £4.6.9
Romford: C.L.Moore;J.G.Welch,R.A.Lamb;G.Cunningham(Capt),G.Fleetwood,P.J.Boreham;
H.W.Brooks,N.J.Coleman,J.Bee,G.W.Andrews,A.Herbert.

28 Apr IFL Home Corinthian Casuals 3 – 1 Cowan(og)Coleman(2)
Attendance: 1,428   Receipts: £73.9.0   Programmes: £None   Car Park: £2.3.3
Romford: C.Moore;D.Evans,V.Jones;W.J.Smailes(Capt),D.R.Lowman,V.H.Perriman;
H.W.Brooks,P.J.Boreham,N.J.Coleman,G.W.Andrews,A.F.Herbert.

30 Apr EACF Home Arsenal "A" 2 – 0 Bee,Cunningham
Attendance: 7,688   Receipts: £419.5.3   Programmes: £51.14.6   Car Park: £8.0.3
Romford: C.L.Moore;J.G.Welch,R.A,Lamb;W.J.Smailes,G.Fleetwood,P.J.Boreham;
H.W.Brooks,G.Cunningham(Capt),J.Bee,G.W.Andrews,A.F.Herbert.

2 May ETTF Ilford Leytonstone 1 – 1 Bee
Romford: C.L.Moore;J.G.Welch,R.A.Lamb;W.J.Smailes,G.Fleetwood,P.J.Boreham;
H.W.Brooks,G.Cunningham(Capt),J.Bee,A.F.Herbert,G.W.Andrews.

3 May IFL Home Walthamstow Avenue 1 – 2 Brooks
Attendance: 2,328   Receipts: £120.17.9   Programmes: £24.6.1   Car Park: £4.3.6
Romford: W.Dawber;D.Evans,V.Jones;V.H.Perryman,D.R.Lowman,P.Spelling;
H.W.Brooks,P.J.Boreham,J.Bee(Capt),G.W.Andrews,A.F.Herbert.

* After Extra Time
\# Played at Cheshunt.

Romford's Board of Directors, 1951
Back: Herbert Muskett (Secretary), Bill Mann, Jim Parrish, Martin Brazier
Front: Syd Tansley, Albert J. Smith, Lord Macpherson, Albert E. Kittle   *Authors' collection*

PRE-SEASON ENTERTAINMENT AT BROOKLANDS:
Stratford Market Sports Day, 1951

Despite what surely must have been one of the wettest and most miserable bank holidays on record, 1,500 spectators paid to see Stratford Market hold its festival sports meeting on Bank Holiday Monday. Visitors came from Covent Garden, Spitalfields, Brentford and Borough Markets.

The most entertaining races of the day were provided by the half bushel and bushel basket carriers. At the crack of the starting gun they piled their baskets ten or twelve high and with an expert lift balanced the swaying towers upon their heads. Then some of them stripped to the waist and carried their 98lb loads round the track for a 440 yards lap!

The one lap half bushel (12) carrying championship for the Syder Cup was won by "small but tough" Tommy Summers in beautiful style. He also won the open one lap bushel carrying championship outshining the other market competitors.

The tug of war final rounded off the day and was won by the Brentford Market boys. Note the press box top left, nicknamed the Pigeon Loft by reporters who were accommodated there!

All photos on this page are courtesy of Ron and Ivy Baker

The visit of the Gold Coast touring XI, August 1951

A national team from the Gold Coast (now Ghana) played Romford during its tour of the UK in 1951.
Here Romford's Mayor Albert Blaine greets the team at the Town Hall. Romford FC directors Bert
Kittle (extreme left), Martin Brazier and Albert Smith are among the welcoming party.   *Authors' collection*

On the evening of Wednesday 29th August over 5,000 spectators were at Brooklands for the
match. They were amazed to see that the visitors played with only a small strapping around
their feet and no football boots! Here, Captain Graeme Cunningham challenges his bare
footed opponents. Romford won an exciting game by two goals to one.   *Authors' collection*

FIRST TEAM SUMMARY OF RESULTS 1951 – 52

		Home		Goals		Away			Goals		
	P	W	D	L	For	Ag	W	D	L	For	Ag	Pts
Isthmian League	26	8	0	5	31	22	6	4	3	30	20	32
FA Challenge Cup	5	3	0	0	10	3	0	1	1	1	2	
FA Amateur Cup	5	1	0	1	5	3	1	2	0	9	7	
Essex Senior Cup	4	1	0	0	2	1	2	0	1	7	4	
East Anglian Cup	5	4	0	0	13	4	0	1	0	3	3	
Thameside Trophy	4	2	0	0	9	4	0	2	0	4	4	
Friendlies	1	1	0	0	2	1	0	0	0	0	0	
Totals	50	20	0	6	72	38	9	10	5	54	40	

Isthmian Football League
Final Table

					Goals		
	P	W	D	L	For	Ag	Pts
Leytonstone	26	13	9	4	63	36	35
Wimbledon	26	16	3	7	65	44	35
Walthamstow Avenue	26	15	4	7	71	43	34
Romford	**26**	**14**	**4**	**8**	**61**	**42**	**32**
Kingstonian	26	11	7	8	62	48	29
Wycombe Wanderers	26	12	5	9	64	59	29
Woking	26	11	5	10	60	71	27
Dulwich Hamlet	26	11	4	11	60	53	26
Corinthian Casuals	26	11	4	11	55	66	26
St.Albans City	26	9	7	10	48	53	25
Ilford	26	8	5	13	32	47	21
Clapton	26	9	2	15	50	59	20
Oxford City	26	6	3	17	50	72	15
Tufnell Park Edmonton	26	2	6	18	25	73	10

FIRST TEAM CUP RESULTS SEASON 1951 – 52

FA Challenge Cup
Final: Newcastle United   1   Arsenal   0

Romford's progress: 1st Qual.   Home   Barking   1 – 0
           2nd Qual.   Away   Briggs Sports   1 – 1
           Replay   Home   Briggs Sports   6 – 2
           3rd Qual.   Home   Brentwood & Warley   3 – 1
           4th Qual.   Away   Gorleston   0 – 1

FA Amateur Cup
Final: Walthamstow Avenue   2   Leyton   1 *

Romford's progress: 1st Round   Away   Stowmarket Town   2 – 0
           2nd Round   Away   Boldmere St. Michael's   3 – 3
           Replay   Home   Boldmere St. Michael's   4 – 0
           3rd Round   Away   Crook Town   4 – 4
           Replay   Home   Crook Town   1 – 3

Essex County FA Senior Challenge Cup
Final: Briggs Sports   1   Romford   0 *

Romford's progress: 1st Round   Away   Leyton   4 – 2
           2nd Round   Home   Walthamstow Avenue   2 – 1
           Semi-Final   Ilford   Grays Athletic   3 – 1
           Final   Ilford   Briggs Sports   0 – 1 *

East Anglian Cup
Final: Romford   2   Arsenal "A"   0

Romford's progress: 1st Round   Home   Chelsea "A"   3 – 0
           2nd Round   Away   King's Lynn   3 – 3

184

Replay	Home	King's Lynn	5 – 3
Semi-Final	Home	Tottenham Hotspur "A"	3 – 1
Final	Home	Arsenal "A"	2 – 0

Essex Thameside Challenge Competition
Final: Romford 4 Leytonstone 2 **
(After a 1-1 Draw)

Romford's progress:	1st Round	Home	Ilford	6 – 4
	Semi-Final	Away	Barking	3 – 3*
	Replay	Home	Barking	3 – 0
	Final:	Ilford	Leytonstone	1 – 1*
	Replay	Ilford	Leytonstone	4 – 2 **

*   After Extra Time
**   Played in 1952 – 53 Season

Chris Moore's efforts are all in vain as Briggs Sports score the only goal of the match to defeat Romford in the Essex Senior Cup final
Photo from Briggs Monthly Bulletin, April 1952

FIRST TEAM DEBUTS SEASON 1951 – 52

1951   **Previous Club**

Date	Match		Player	Previous Club
25th Aug.	v Oxford City	-	**H.Russell**	Royal Navy
1st Sept.	v Walthamstow Avenue	-	**H.M.Newman**	Dagenham
5th Sept.	v Ilford	-	**A.F.Herbert**	Glendale Y.C.
24th Nov.	v St.Albans City	-	**J.Bee**	Briggs Sports
22nd Dec.	v Kingstonian	-	**D.Evans**	Glendale Y.C.
26th Dec.	v Ilford	-	**W.Dawber**	Leytonstone
		-	**P.J.Boreham**	Marley Y.C.
		-	**L.G.Casson**	Leyton

1952

Date	Match		Player	Previous Club
26th Jan.	v Leyton	-	**N.J.Coleman**	Gorleston
		-	**J.Ellis-Williams**	Aberystwyth
28th Apr.	v Corinthian Casuals	-	**V.Jones**	Eton Manor
3rd May	v Walthamstow Avenue	-	**W.P.Spelling**	n/k

Players returned to the Club
1951

Date	Match		Player	Previous Club
25th Aug.	v Oxford City	-	**D.Kent**	Woodford Town
29th Aug.	v Gold Coast XI	-	**W.Isaacs**	Briggs Sports

FIRST TEAM APPEARANCES SEASON 1951 – 52

	A	B	C	D	E	F	G	Total
George Andrews	25	4	5	4	4	4	1	47
Jack Barton	0	0	0	0	0	0	1	1
Johnny Bee	14	0	5	3	4	2	0	29

Peter Boreham	8	0	3	3	4	3	0	23
Bill Bridge	17	5	4	0	1	0	1	28
Harold Brooks	18	5	1	3	3	3	1	34
Len Casson	3	0	1	0	0	0	0	4
Jim Coleman	7	0	1	4	2	1	0	15
Graeme Cunningham	18	4	5	3	5	4	1	40
Bill Dawber	2	0	0	0	0	0	0	2
Dennis Evans	5	0	0	1	0	0	0	6
Gordon Fleetwood	18	5	5	4	5	4	1	42
Tony Herbert	11	1	2	1	3	3	0	21
Bill Isaacs	1	0	0	0	0	0	1	2
Vic Jones	2	0	0	0	0	0	0	2
Gerry Kenlay	8	4	0	0	1	2	0	15
Doug Kent	1	0	0	0	0	0	1	2
Ron Lamb	23	5	5	4	5	4	0	46
Des Lowman	5	0	0	0	0	0	0	5
Chris Moore	24	5	5	4	5	4	1	48
Mick Newman	6	2	0	0	1	1	0	10
Vic Perriman	3	0	0	0	0	0	0	3
Hugh Russell	1	0	0	0	0	0	0	1
Jimmy Smailes	22	5	5	4	5	4	0	45
Bill Solley	18	5	5	1	2	1	1	33
Paddy Spelling	1	0	0	0	0	0	0	1
Johnny Welch	23	5	2	3	4	4	1	42
John Ellis-Williams	2	0	1	2	1	0	0	6

FIRST TEAM GOALSCORERS SEASON 1951 – 52

	A	B	C	D	E	F	G	Total
Graeme Cunningham	10	2	2	1	4	5	0	24
Johnny Bee	7	0	3	4	5	2	0	21
George Andrews	9	1	3	0	0	1	0	14
Bill Bridge	5	2	3	0	1	0	0	11
Gerry Kenlay	4	3	0	0	0	3	0	10
Harold Brooks	5	2	0	0	1	0	1	9
Tim Coleman	5	0	0	1	2	0	0	8
Ron Lamb	4	0	2	0	1	0	0	7
John Ellis Williams	3	0	0	2	0	0	0	5
Len Casson	3	0	1	0	0	0	0	4
Mick Newman	1	0	0	0	1	1	0	3
Bill Isaacs	1	0	0	0	0	0	1	2
Jimmy Smailes	1	1	0	0	0	0	0	2
Tony Herbert	1	0	0	0	0	1	0	2
Johnny Welch	1	0	0	0	0	0	0	1
Bell (Chelsea "A")	0	0	0	0	1	0	0	1
Braham (Walthamstow A)	0	0	0	1	0	0	0	1
Cowan (Corinthian C)	1	0	0	0	0	0	0	1
Totals	61	11	14	9	16	13	2	126

KEY TO COMPETITIONS

A	Isthmian Football League
B	FA Challenge Cup Competition
C	FA Amateur Challenge Cup Competition
D	Essex County F.A. Senior Cup Competition
E	East Anglian Cup
F	Thameside Challenge Trophy
G	Friendly Match

Reserve Team Match Details

20 Aug ETTF+ Home Barking Res. 2 – 0 Conner,Herbert
Attendance: 844 Receipts: £22.7.0 Programmes: £3.4.9 Car Park: £1.11.9
Romford Res.: J.Head;L.Penk,D.Evans;J.T.Prior,R.Lamb,V.H.Perriman;
C.T.Coleman,H.M.Newman,W,Dowsett,A.F.Herbert, J.W.Conner.

25 Aug IFLR Away Wimbledon Res. 1 – 4 Scorer unknown
Romford Res.: C.Bingham;L.Penk,J.W.Conner;J.T.Prior,J.Barton,R.J.Innes;
C.T.Coleman,H.M.Newman,W.Isaacs,J.A.Hornsby,A.F.Herbert.

1 Sept IFLR Home Clapton Res. 5 – 2 Kenlay(3)Hornsby,Perriman
Attendance: 767 Receipts: £14.9.3 Programmes: £2.13.8 Car Park: £0.3.6
Romford Res.: C.Bingham;L.Penk,J.W.Conner;L.R.Mackenzie,W.P.Spelling,V.H.Perriman;
C.T.Coleman,J.A.Hornsby,G.J.Kenlay,A.F.Herbert,R.J.Leaver.

8 Sept IFLR Away Corinthian Casuals Res. 1 – 5 Scorer unknown
Romford Res.:

15 Sept IFLR Home Wycombe Wanderers Res. 2 – 1 Herbert,Brooks
Attendance: 1,053 Receipts: £23.2.9 Programmes: £3.12.0 Car Park: £0.9.0
Romford Res.: C.Bingham;D.Evans,J.W.Conner;V.H.Perriman,W.P.Spelling,R.J.Innes;
H.W.Brooks,R.Stanton,P.J.Casey,A.F.Herbert,P.J.Boreham.

22 Sept IFLR Away Walthamstow Avenue Res. 1 – 1 Scorer unknown
RomfordRes.:

29 Sept IFLR Away Clapton Res. 1 – 1 Scorer unknown
Romford Res.:

6 Oct IFLR Home Wimbledon Res. 3 – 1 Kenlay(2),One other
Attendance: 1,173 Receipts: £23.4.6 Programmes: £2.16.6 Car Park: £0.10.6
Romford Res.:

13 Oct IFLR Home Tufnell Park Edmonton Res. 1 – 2 Scorer unknown
Attendance: 557 Receipts: £11.1.0 Programmes: £1.15.2 Car Park: £0.4.0
Romford Res.: W.Dawber;G.W.Berry,J.W.Conner;V.H.Perriman,D.R.Lowman,S.Cardew;
P.J.Boreham,L.G.Casson,H.M.Newman,A.F.Herbert,J.A.Hornsby.

27 Oct IFLR Away Kingstonian Res. 1 – 0 Scorer unknown
Romford Res.:

3 Nov EIC2R Home Lathol Athletic 9 – 0 Casson(4)Herbert(2)Innes,Dowsett,
Schneider
Attendance: 778 Receipts: £17.10.3 Programmes: £2.12.6 Car Park: £0.8.9
Romford Res.: W.Dawber;D.Evans,J.W.Conner;V.H.Perriman,D.Lowman,R.J.Innes;
W.Dowsett,L.G.Casson,A.Schneider,A.F.Herbert,P.J.Boreham.

10 Nov IFLR Home St. Albans City Res. 2 – 1 Schneider,Perriman(pen)
Attendance: 1,230 Receipts: £28.0.3 Programmes: £3.10.1 Car Park: £0.11.0
Romford Res.: ? ; ? , ? ;V.H.Perriman, ? , ? ;
G.G.Howlett,A.Schneider,J.Bee, ? , ? .

17 Nov IFLR Away Leytonstone Res. 1 – 0 Boreham
Romford Res.: W.Dawber;D.Evans,J.W.Connor;V.Jones,D.R.Lowman,R.J.Innes;
G.G.Howlett,L.G.Casson,J.Bee,A.Herbert,P.J.Boreham.

24 Nov EIC3R Away Chelmsford Swifts 2 – 2 Perriman,Casson
Romford Res.: W.Dawber;D.Evans,J.W.Connor;V.Jones,R.Innes,V.H.Perriman;
G.G.Howlett,L.G.Casson,A.Sneider,A.Herbert,P.J.Boreham.

1 Dec Frdly Home Bromley Res. 2 – 0 Casson,one other
Attendance: 742 Receipts: £16.11.0 Programmes: £2.16.9 Car Park: £0.6.9
Romford Res.: **Sel.** W.Dawber;D.Evans,J.W.Connor;V.H.Perriman,D.R.Lowman,R.J.Innes;
G.G.Howlett,L.G.Casson,G.J.Kenlay,A.F.Herbert,P.J.Boreham.

8 Dec IFLR Away Woking Res. 5 – 3 Kenlay(3)Casson,Herbert or Howlett
Romford Res.: W.Dawber;D.Evans,J.W.Connor;V.H.Perriman,D.R.Lowman,R.J.Innes;
G.G.Howlett,L.G.Casson,G.J.Kenlay,J.Ellis-Williams,A.F.Herbert.

15 Dec IFLR Home Walthamstow Avenue Res. 5 – 1 Kenlay,Ellis-Williams,Howlett,Perriman,
Boreham
Attendance: 1,091 Receipts: £22.8.3 Programmes: £3.14.5 Car Park: £0.13.3
Romford Res.: W.Dawber;D.Evans,J.W.Connor;V.H.Perriman,D.R.Lowman,R.J.Innes;
G.G.Howlett,J.Ellis-Williams,G.J.Kenlay,A.F.Herbert,P.J.Boreham.

29 Dec IFLR Home Kingstonian Res. 3 – 0 Fleetwood(2)Kenlay
Attendance: 1,259 Receipts: £25.2.9 Programmes: £4.1.5 Car Park: £0.12.3
Romford Res.:
Fleetwood,G.J.Kenlay,

5 Jan EIC4R Away Maldon Town 0 – 1
Attendance: 1,000
Romford Res.: W.Dawber;D.Evans,J.W.Connor;R.J.Innes,D.R.Lowman,V.H.Perriman;
G.G.Howlett, ? , ? , ? , ? .

12 Jan IFLR Home Woking Res. 6 – 2 Coleman(2)Kenlay(2)Ellis-Williams(2)
Attendance: 1,411 Receipts: £29.17.6 Programmes: £4.0.3 Car Park: £0.12.0
Romford Res.: W.Dawber;D.Evans,J.W.Conner;R.J.Innes,S.Cardew,V.H.Perriman;
H.W.Brooks,N.J.Coleman,G.J.Kenlay,J.Ellis-Williams,G.G.Howlett.

19 Jan IFLR Away Dulwich Hamlet Res. 2 – 0 Moir,Kenlay
Romford Res.: W.Dawber;D.Evans,J.W.Conner;V.H.Perriman,D.R.Lowman,R.J.Innes;
W.Dowsett,N.J.Coleman,G.J.Kenlay,J.Moir,G.G.Howlett.

26 Jan Frdly Home Southall Res. 3 – 5 Herbert(2)Casson
Attendance: 387 Receipts: £7.19.6 Programmes: £1.3.5 Car Park: £0.1.6
Romford Res.:W.Dawber;D.Evans,J.W.Connor;J.G.Welch,S.Cardew,R.J.Innes;
H.W.Brooks,L.G.Casson,G.J.Kenlay,A.F.Herbert,G.G.Howlett.

2 Feb IFLR Home Ilford Res. 2 – 2 Brooks,Kenlay
Attendance: 1,617 Receipts: £34.16.3 Programmes: £3.10.3 Car Park: £0.18.9
Romford Res.: W.Dawber;D.Evans,J.W.Conner;V.H.Perriman,W.P.Spelling,R.J.Innes;
H.W.Brooks,L.G.Casson,G.J.Kenlay,W.A.Bridge,G.G.Howlett.

23 Feb IFLR Home Dulwich Hamler Res. 3 – 0 Kenlay,Dowsett(2)
Attendance: 1,070 Receipts: £21.2.9 Programmes: £3.8.8 Car Park: £0.9.9
Romford Res.: W.Dawber;D.Evans,V.Jones;P.J.Boreham, ? , ? ;
H.W.Brooks,L.G.Casson,G.J.Kenlay, ? ,W.Dowsett.

1 Mar IFLR Away Wycombe Wanderers Res. 6 – 1 Dowsett,Perriman(2pns),Herbert(2),Brooks
Romford Res.: W.Dawber;D.Evans,J.W.Conner;P.J.Boreham,W.P.Spelling,V.H.Perriman;
H.W.Brooks,L.G.Casson,W.Dowsett,A.F.Herbert,G.G.Howlett.

8 Mar IFLR Home Corinthian Casuals Res. 5 – 0 Howlett,Boreham(2)Schneider,Kelly
Attendance: 1,111 Receipts: £21.14.9 Programmes: £3.10.10 Car Park: £0.10.0
Romford Res.: W.Dawber;R.Jones,V.Jones;T.R.KellyG.Fleetwood,V.H.Perriman;
G.G.Howlett,L.G.Casson,G.J.Kenlay,P.J.Boreham,A.Schneider.

15 Mar IFLR Away St. Albans City Res. 2 – 1 Kenlay,Dowsett
Romford Res.: **Sel.** W.Dawber;R.Jones,V.Jones;T.R.Kelly,D.R.Lowman,V.H.Perriman;
G.G.Howlett,L.G.Casson,G.J.Kenlay,D.Pryor,W.Dowsett.

22 Mar IFLR Home Oxford City Res. 2 – 1 Kenlay(2)
Attendance: 1,063 Receipts: £21.0.0 Programmes: £4.19.4 Car Park: £0.10.9
Romford Res.: W.Dawber;R.Jones,V.Jones;T.R.Kelly,D.R.Lowman,V.H.Perriman?;
G.G.Howlett?,W.A.Bridge,G.J.Kenlay,J.Ellis-Williams,W.Dowsett?.

5 Apr IFLR Away Oxford City Res. 1 – 5 Dowsett
Romford Res.: W.Dawber;R.Jones?,V.Jones?;T.R.Kelly?,D.R.Lowman?,V.H.Perriman;
G.G.Howlett,W.A.Bridge,G.J.Kenlay,J.Ellis-Williams,W.Dowsett.

12 Apr IFLR Away Tufnell Park Edmonton Res. 2 – 0 Scorers unknown
Romford Res.:

19 Apr IFLR Away Ilford Res. 1 – 1 Cutmore
Romford Res.:

21 Apr ETR1R Home Barking Res. 2 – 1 ? (og),Moir

Attendance: 564 Receipts: £12.10.6 Programmes: £ None Car Park: £0.4.0
Romford Res.: R.Brown;D.Evans,J.W.Conner;R.Jones,W.P.Spelling,V.Jones;
G.G.Howlett,V.H.Perriman,H.Cutmore,J.Moir,W.Dowsett.

29 Apr ETRSF Home Grays Athletic Res. 2 – 4 Dowsett,Brown
Attendance: 591 Receipts: £12.13.0 Programmes: £ None Car Park: £ None
Romford Res.: Mostly "A" Team Players

1 May IFLR Home Leytonstone Res. 0 – 3
Attendance: 942 Receipts: £18.5.9 Programmes: £ None Car Park: £0.10.3
Romford Res.:

+ Final tie for 1950 – 51 season.

RESERVE TEAM SUMMARY OF RESULTS SEASON 1951 – 52

		Home			Away			Goals		
	P	W	D	L	W	D	L	For	Ag	Pts
Isthmian League Res. Section	26	10	1	2	7	3	3	64	38	38
Essex Intermediate Cup	3	1	0	0	1	0	1	11	2	
Essex Thameside Trophy (50/1)	1	1	0	0	0	0	0	2	0	
Essex Thameside Trophy	2	1	0	1	0	0	0	4	5	
Friendlies	2	1	0	1	0	0	0	5	5	
Totals	34	14	1	4	8	3	4	86	50	

Isthmian League Reserve Section
Final Table

	P	W	D	L	For	Ag	Pts
Leytonstone	26	18	3	5	73	34	39
Romford Reserves	26	17	4	5	64	38	38
Oxford City	26	17	4	5	79	48	38
Wimbledon	26	16	3	7	79	42	35
Walthamstow Avenue	26	12	4	10	58	46	28
Dulwich Hamlet	26	11	4	11	65	55	26
Corinthian Casuals	26	11	4	11	50	53	26
Clapton	26	9	7	10	42	54	25
Ilford	26	8	5	13	44	61	21
Woking	26	8	5	13	45	70	21
Wycombe Wanderers	26	8	4	14	63	78	20
St.Albans City	26	8	3	15	42	73	19
Kingstonian	26	6	3	17	56	72	15
Tufnell Park Edmonton	26	5	3	18	36	72	13

Romford reserves lose by three goals to nil at home to Leytonstone in their last game of the season to hand the League Championship to their visitors.

RESERVE TEAM APPEARANCES SEASON 1951 – 52

The following players are known to have appeared in the reserve team during the season.

J.Barton	J.Bee	G.W.Berry	C.Bingham
P.J.Boreham	W.A.Bridge	H.W.Brooks	R.Brown
S.Cardew	P.J.Casey	L.G.Casson	C.T.Coleman
N.J.Coleman	J.W.Conner	H.Cutmore	W.Dawber
W.Dowsett	J.Ellis-Williams	D.Evans	G.Fleetwood
A.F.Herbert	J.A.Hornsby	G.G.Howlett	R.J.Innes
W.Isaacs	R.Jones	V.Jones	T.R.Kelly(Ilford)
G.J.Kenlay	R.J.Leaver	D.R.Lowman	L.R.Mackenzie(Old Libertians)
J.Moir	H.M.Newman	V.H.Perriman	L.Penk(G.E.Stores)
J.T.Prior	D.Pryor	A.Schneider	W.P.Spelling
R.Stanton	J.G.Welch		

RESERVE TEAM CUP RESULTS SEASON 1951 – 52

Essex Thameside Challenge Competition Reserve Section - 1950 – 51 Final
Romford Reserves   2   Barking Reserves   0

Essex County FA Intermediate Challenge Cup
Final: Maldon Town   2   Leytonstone Res.   1

Romford's progress: 1st Round   Bye
2nd Round   Home   Lathol Athletic   9 – 0
3rd Round   Away   Chelmsford Swifts   2 – 1
4th Round   Away   Maldon Town   0 – 1

Essex Thameside Challenge Competition Reserve Section
Final: n/k

Romford's progress: 1st Round   Home   Barking Res.   2 – 1
Semi-Final   Home   Grays Athletic Res.   2 – 4

"A" Team Match Details

25 Aug IFLA   Away   Wimbledon "A"   3 – 3   Scorers unknown
Romford "A": E.Davis;D.Evans,G.W.Berry;H.Cutmore,R.Bull,P.J.Boreham;
D.Callaghan,W.P.Spelling,P.J.Casey,J.Moir,D.Pond.

1 Sept IFLA   Home   Clapton "A"   1 – 2   Scorer unknown
Romford "A":

15 Sept IFLA   Home   Wycombe Wanderers "A"   4 – 2   Dowsett(2)King,Cutmore
Romford "A": E.Davis;L.Penk,D.Callaghan;G.Berry,R.Bull,D.Pryor;
W.Dowsett,T.J.King,H.Cutmore,R.Harman,K.Paulding.

22 Sept IFLA   Away   Walthamstow Avenue "A"   1 – 1   Scorer unknown
Romford "A":

29 Sept IFLA   Away   Ilford "A"   2 – 0   Scorers unknown
Romford "A": D.Brown;G.W.Berry,D.Callaghan;J.Heaphy,L.Penk,J.T.Prior;
W.Dowsett,T.J.King,H.Cutmore,L.G.Casson,R.R..Harman.

6 Oct Frdly   Away   Glendale Youth Club   2 – 0   Dowsett(2)
Romford "A":

13 Oct IFLA   Home   Walthamstow Avenue "A"   1 – 4   Scorer unknown
Romford "A":

20 Oct RCC1R   Home   Green & Silley Weir   0 – 2
Romford "A": D.Brown;R.Jones,V.Jones;J.Heaphy,R.J.Innes,D.Callaghan;
G.G.Howlett,W.P.Spelling,G.W.Berry,J.Moir,P.J.Boreham.

27 Oct IFLA   Home   Tufnell Park Edmonton "A"   4 – 1   Scorers unknown
Romford "A":   **(The next League table indicated only one goal was conceded over these two matches)**

10 Nov IFLA   Home   St. Albans City "A"   5 – 1   Scorers unknown
Romford "A":

24 Nov IFLA   Home   Wimbledon "A"   2 – 0   Scorers unknown
Romford "A":

1 Dec IFLA   Away   Leytonstone "A"   1 – 1   Scorer unknown
Romford "A":

15 Dec IFLA   Away   Clapton "A"   3 – 1   Scorer unknown
Romford "A":

5 Jan IFLA   Home   Ilford "A"   2 – 1   Coleman(2)
Romford "A":

19 Jan IFLA   Home   Woking "A"   1 – 1   Scorer unknown
Romford "A":

26 Jan IFLA   Away   Kingstonian "A"   3 – 2   Scorers unknown
Romford "A":

2 Feb IFLA   Home   Kingstonian "A"   2 – 2   Scorers unknown
Romford "A":

9 Feb IFLA   Home   Leytonstone "A"   2 – 0   Dowsett(2)
Romford "A": (Sel) R.Brown;R.Jones,V.Jones;S.Cardew,W.P.Spelling(Capt),D.Pryor;
H.Cutmore,T.J..King,G.W.Berry,J.Moir,W.Dowsett.

23 Feb Frdly   Away   Glendale Youth Club   2 – 3   Scorers unknown
Romford "A":

1 Mar IFLA   Away   Wycombe Wanderers "A"   4 – 1   Scorers unknown
Romford "A":

8 Mar IFLA   Away   Woking "A"   1 – 1   Scorer unknown
Romford "A":

15 Mar IFLA   Away   St.Albans City "A"   3 – 2   Scorers unknown
Romford "A":

5 Apr IFLA Home Dulwich Hamlet "A" 3 – 0 Scorers unknown
Romford "A":

12 Apr IFLA Away Tufnell Park Edmonton "A" 4 – 1 Scorers unknown
Romford "A":

? Apr IFLA Away Dulwich Hamlet "A" 0 – 4
Romford "A":

"A" TEAM SUMMARY OF RESULTS 1951 – 52

		Home			Goals		Away			Goals		
	P	W	D	L	For	Ag	W	D	L	For	Ag	Pts
Isthmian League "A" Section	22	7	2	2	27	13	6	4	1	25	17	32
Romford Charity Cup	1	0	0	1	0	2	0	0	0	0	0	
Friendlies	2	0	0	0	0	0	1	0	1	4	3	
Total	25	7	2	3	27	15	7	4	2	29	20	

Isthmian Football League "A" Section
Final Table

	P	W	D	L	Goals For	Ag	Pts
Romford "A"	22	13	6	3	52	30	32
Kingstonian	22	13	5	4	86	53	31
Ilford	22	13	3	6	65	50	29
Wimbledon	22	11	5	6	79	59	27
Dulwich Hamlet	22	11	3	8	71	55	25
Walthamstow Avenue	22	9	6	7	56	42	24
Wycombe Wanderers	22	10	4	8	66	58	24
Tufnell Park Edmonton	22	7	5	10	47	54	19
Woking	22	6	6	10	52	77	18
Clapton	22	6	3	13	48	74	15
Leytonstone	22	5	2	15	32	65	12
St.Albans City	22	2	4	16	43	80	8

"A" TEAM CUP RESULTS SEASON 1951 – 52

Romford Charity Cup

Final: Green & Silley Weir 0 Rainham Town Reserves 3

Romford's progress: 1st Round Home Green & Silley Weir 0 – 2

"A" TEAM APPEARANCES SEASON 1951 – 52

The following are known to have played in the "A" team during the season.

G.W.Berry	P.J.Boreham	R.Brown	R.Bull
D.Callaghan	S.Cardew	P.J.Casey	L.G.Casson
N.J.Coleman	H.Cutmore	E.Davis	W.Dowsett
D.Evans	R.R.Harman	J.Heaphy(Glendale)	G.G.Howlett
R.J.Innes	R.Jones	V.Jones	T.J.King
J.Moir	L.Penk(G.E.Stores)	D.Pond(Glendale)	J.T.Prior
D.Pryor	W.P.Spelling		

DEPARTURES FROM CLUB SEASON 1951 – 52

The following appear to have left during or by the end of the season. They may have been triallists and played one or two games. New clubs are indicated where known.

J.Barton (Brentwood & Warley), C.Bingham, R.Bull (Rainham Town), D.Callaghan, C.T.Coleman, N.J.Coleman (Gorleston), H.Cutmore, E.Davis, J.Ellis-Williams (Hayes), R.R.Harman (Collier Row Athletic), J.Heaphy (Upminster Old Boys), J.Hornsby, W.Isaacs (Leytonstone), D.Kent (Briggs Sports), R.J.Leaver, H.M.Newman (Dagenham), L.Penk, D.Pond, J.T.Prior, H.Russell (Royal Navy), A.Schneider, W.J.Smailes (Arsenal), W.J.Solley (retired due to work reasons), R.Stanton (Rainham Town).

PICTURE SPECIAL
Romford win the East
Anglian Cup 1951-52

The semi-final, 11th April 1952
Romford 3, Tottenham Hotspur "A" 1

Johnny Bee scores Romford's third goal to the
delight of the Brooklands crowd.

The final, 30th April
Romford 2, Arsenal "A" 0

Arsenal asked for the kick-off to be
delayed because their centre forward,
England cricketer Brian Close, had
been held up on his way from Lords
Cricket Ground. When the referee
insisted the game kick off, they decided
to start with 10 men and only brought
on a replacement when it became
obvious that Brian wasn't going to
arrive! Cunningham and Bee scored
Romford's goals.

The proud team with the East Anglian Cup

Back: G.Fleetwood, W.Solley, J.Smailes, C.Moore, R.Lamb, P.Boreham
Front: H.Brooks, J.Bee, G.Cunningham(Captain), A.Herbert, G.Andrews
(Although W.Solley is in this photo he did not actually play in the final.
J.G.Welch played in the final). *Authors' collection*

THE ROMFORD TIMES, WED., MAY 7, 1952   11

Romford win a cup—and the crowd goes mad

Romford 2, Arsenal "A" 0

The whistle had hardly left the referee's lips when it happened. Hundreds of cheering, wildly excited supporters forgot Romford F.C. instructions, swarmed across Brooklands and chaired skipper Graeme Cunningham forward to receive the East Anglian Cup on Wednesday. They had seen an inspired Romford side beat Arsenal "A" to win the trophy at their first post-war attempt.

Putting on a display that belied their tough cup and league programme of recent weeks, the Isthmian side treated a crowd of over 10,000 to football taken verbatim from the "copy-book".

An enterprising forward line, backed by a resolute defence, was the recipe for this Romford win, with Cunningham, Bee, Smailes and Fleetwood providing the all-important flavouring with master touches.

To Welch and Brooks, too, honours, please, for pulling Romford out of trouble when the pace began to tell. Welch for his clearance off the goal line when Romford were only one goal ahead, and Brooks for his brilliance on the wing during the same period.

To an Arsenal side, whose only failure was in their inability to finish off good approach work

Close delayed

Young Yorkshire cricketer Brian Close was due to lead the Arsenal attack, but he was delayed on the way to Brooklands. The visitors played with ten men for ten minutes, hoping he would arrive, and then brought in Wood on the right wing. Davis led the attack, and winger Barley moved to inside-right.

Barley was prominent for Arsenal in the opening minutes and his two shots on the run were headed clear by Fleetwood. Bee earned the first cheer from the massed Romford supporters with a fast run into the Arsenal penalty area, but his back-heel to Brooks was intercepted.

Powerful clearances of the visitors' keeper quickly turned defence into attack, but Romford still provided the thrills. Especially Bee, who had several shots just off the

TWO SAVES.—Both by Arsenal 'A' goalkeeper Dunkley. Johnnie Bee watches him field a high ball, above, and in the picture below, the 'keeper turns a Cunningham shot round the post. But two shots eluded him, and Romford won the East Anglian Cup.

Enthusiastic local press coverage of Romford's East Anglian Cup win   *the Romford Times*

Post Season Summary   Season 1951 – 52

Nearly four thousand spectators turned up at Brooklands on 25th August for the opening game of the season against Oxford City and went away thoroughly dumbfounded following a resounding 5-1 defeat.

Boro Captain Graeme Cunningham notched a couple of goals in a 4-0 victory over old rivals Walthamstow Avenue on 1st September at Green Pond Road. He scored another two in the Thameside Trophy fixture against Ilford four days later, which was won by six goals to four. Gerry Kenlay got a hat-trick in the 3-1 victory over Wimbledon before another fine mid-week win against Chelsea "A" in the East Anglian Cup.

This fine run was brought to an end on 15th September at High Wycombe when the Wanderers defeated Boro 2-0 in an Isthmian League match. Kingstonian were beaten 2-0 the following week, and then came an exciting FA Cup tie at Brooklands when Barking were the visitors. Nearly 7,000 spectators witnessed a thrilling battle which ended with a single goal (by Smailes) victory for Romford. A 2-2 draw at Woking was followed by a thrilling 1-1 draw against the strong Briggs Sports team at Dagenham on 13th October. The replay at Brooklands the following Thursday afternoon drew 4,000 people who saw two goals each from Kenlay and Cunningham help Romford to a 6-2 victory!

Leytonstone scored a great 4-2 win at Brooklands in Boro's next game, before Brentwood and Warley came to town on 27th October in the FA Cup. Seven and a half thousand spectators watched Romford secure a fine 3-1 victory. A 2-2 draw away to Tufnell Park preceded Romford's next FA Cup tie. This time they were drawn against powerful professional opposition – away to Gorleston of the Eastern Counties League. Romford held their illustrious opponents (led by player-manager Sailor Brown of Charlton Athletic fame) to a 0-0 scoreline until the 86th minute. With Boro supporters looking forward to a possible replay at Brooklands, Gorleston's right-winger, amateur Jim Coleman, prepared to take a corner kick. He placed it perfectly for a colleague to head the winning goal.

Four fine league victories followed this, before it was Amateur Cup time on 15th December. Romford's opponents, Suffolk team Stowmarket, prepared for a record attendance. Two or three farm trailers were placed on the opposite side of the pitch to the stand, and nearly four thousand people crammed into the ground. Most of the shops in town were closed until after the match as they would do no business and their staff could see the match! Romford partially ruined Stowmarket's day by winning 2-0. It took some time for the departing spectators to exit the ground through the rather narrow gateway!

Romford then suffered a couple of 2-1 defeats from Kingstonian (away) and Ilford at home on Christmas morning. Romford took ample revenge with a 6-0 win at Ilford the following day. They achieved three points in their next two league games, before attracting a three and a half thousand crowd to their Amateur Cup tie away to the strong Birmingham team Boldmere St Michael's. This thrilling match ended in a draw. The following Saturday nearly 8,000 spectators streamed into Brooklands for the replay, which Romford won 4-0.

Further cup ties followed: Leyton were defeated 4-2 away in the Essex Senior Cup and then another Eastern Counties League side, King's Lynn, provided the opposition on 2nd February for an East Anglian Cup tie. 1,600 Romford fans unable to make the journey up to Norfolk turned up at Brooklands for the reserve team's game against Ilford Reserves. News came through from King's Lynn every 15 minutes or so, and their were glum faces as the Linnets scored goal after goal. With fifteen minutes to go Boro were 3-0 down. Then came the amazing news that our local heroes had secured a three all draw!

The following week several coaches took Boro supporters to County Durham for an Amateur Cup tie against Crook Town. It was an amazing clash, with the lead changing several times. Romford were 3-2 down with about five minutes to go, then Ron Lamb from the penalty spot and a goal by George Andrews put them in the lead, only for Crook to equalise right at the end. This gave Romford the opportunity to repay the wonderful hospitality given to their supporters by the friendly Northerners.

The BBC were keen to televise the replay on 16th February, so the turnstiles were opened nearly two hours before kick-off! Almost 12,000 packed into Brooklands in fine weather, creating a passionate cup tie atmosphere and waving to the TV cameras. It was an exciting match but sadly for Romford, Crook saw to it that this time there were no let-ups. Once in command they stayed there, winning by three goals to one. The *Romford Times* cartoonist gives his humorous view of the match on page 201.

Victories against Dulwich Hamlet and Clapton were followed by a 2-1 loss against lowly Corinthian Casuals in league matches, before further adventures in cup ties. Almost 7,000 were at Brooklands on 15th March to see Romford overcome old rivals Walthamstow Avenue 2-1 to reach the semi-final of the Essex Senior Cup, and King's Lynn were beaten in the East Anglian Cup replay at Brooklands. The Lynn game was another thrilling encounter, with Boro winning 5-3. Then came a 1-1 draw away to Leytonstone before the Essex Senior Cup semi-final on 5th April at Ilford. Grays Athletic were their opponents, and a hat-trick from Johnny Bee helped Romford to a 3-1 victory.

Romford had mixed fortunes over the Easter period. It started with a home semi-final East Anglian Cup tie at Brooklands on Good Friday, 11th April. Tottenham Hotspur "A" were the visitors and a crowd of nearly 10,000 saw the game drawing to a close with the Spurs leading 1-0. Incredibly, Boro then scored three goals in four minutes, through Brooks, Cunningham and Bee, to take a 3-1 victory.

On Easter Monday over 13,000 were at Newbury Park to see Romford meet Briggs Sports in the Essex Senior Cup final. After ninety minutes there was no score, but the motormen gained revenge for their earlier defeat in the FA Cup with an extra time winner.

Three away games followed, with two league victories over Oxford City and Wimbledon and another thrilling clash with Barking in the Thameside Trophy semi-final. The match ended three all after extra time. In the replay at Brooklands Romford triumphed 3-0 to reach another cup final. Home league games against Dulwich Hamlet (1-4) and Corinthian Casuals (3-1) were played before the much-anticipated East Anglian Cup final against Arsenal "A" on 30th April. Nearly 8,000 people saw Cunningham and Bee score for Boro in a two nil victory.

Then on 2nd May came the Thameside Trophy Final against Leytonstone at Ilford ending in a 1-1 draw after extra time, with the replay to take place the following season.

These last eleven games had been played over a four week period and it was no surprise that only just over two thousand spectators turned up at Brooklands for the final match of the season, against Walthamstow Avenue. Both teams fielded virtually reserve line-ups and after a rather boring game Romford lost 2-1.

In this magnificent season Romford played 24 cup ties and reached three cup finals! They also managed to secure fourth place in the Isthmian League table, finishing only three points behind champions Leytonstone.

The reserve team won the carried-over final of the Thameside Trophy from the previous season, with a 2-0 victory over Barking reserves. They also secured the runners-up spot in the Isthmian League reserve section table, finishing one point behind Leytonstone reserves. The "A" team ended a fine year by taking the "A" Section league title finishing one point ahead of champions Kingstonian.

Romford players pictured in the dressing room after playing Leytonstone in the Thameside Trophy final
Back: Ron Lamb, Jimmy Smailes, Chris Moore, Gordon Fleetwood, Peter Boreham, Johnny Welch
Front: Harold Brooks, Graeme Cunningham, Johnny Bee, Tony Herbert, George Andrews   *the Romford Recorder*

GLEANINGS FROM MANAGEMENT COMMITTEE MINUTE BOOKS
SEASON 1951-52

On **4th September 1951** the Secretary reported that a sum of £50 17s 0d, raised by a ground collection during the Gold Coast team visit on 29th August, would be donated to the Old Folks War Memorial Fund.

On **18th September** the committee heard that members of the Rainbow Club for the Blind would be entertained at the match versus Kingstonian on 22nd September. Messrs. H.Hughes, G.Richards and Webb would provide the commentary.

On **4th December** the directors agreed to hold a collection at the ground on Christmas morning, the proceeds to be equally divided between the Old Contemptibles, British Legion, Red Cross Society and the Social Services.

On **18th December** they decided that due to increased printing costs the price of the match programme for first team games would go up to 3d in the New Year.

On **1st January 1952** Mr A.J.Smith reported that £55 1s 6d was raised by the Christmas morning ground collection. They discussed the possibility of installing floodlights at Brooklands, and approached the Eastern Electricity Board to review the matter.

On **8th January** 16 track suits were ordered for use on training nights, price £2 17s 4d each.

On **12th February** the committee made arrangements to receive Crook Town for the Amateur Cup replay at Brooklands. They would hire a coach to bring the party from London to Romford, and include a visit to an ice show at Wembley's Empire Pool.

On **19th February** the Secretary reported an injury to a Red Cross man on duty at the match with Crook Town, caused by "an excited spectator!"

On **26th February** they noted that the BBC had sent a cheque for £26 5s 0d for expenses in connection with the televising of the cup replay, but as the cheque was unsigned it had to be sent back!

On **18th March** Mr A.J.Smith, on behalf of the club, presented player Bill Bridge with a clock as a wedding present. An estimate of £5,134 was received from the Eastern Electricity Board for the installation of floodlights. The amount did not include "certain foundation costs" and it was decided to pass the matter to the Board of Directors.

On **25th March** it was agreed to purchase four turnstiles from Woking Football Club, at a cost of £70.

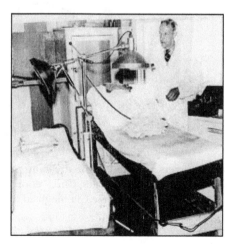

BILL SEDDON AT WORK
Following the appointment of Graeme Cunningham as Player-Coach, Bill Seddon relinquished his position as trainer and became Club Physio/Groundsman

PICTURE SPECIAL
Dipping into the archives

All items from the Authors' collection

Committee meeting minutes from
September 1949 (below) and February
1952 (right).
(The handwriting is Martin Brazier's)

Left: some items of expenditure in the
year 1950-51
Above: breakdown of part of the club's
income in the same year
(The handwriting is Herbert Muskett's)

DIRECTORS' REPORT FOR THE YEAR ENDED 31ST MAY, 1952

The Directors have pleasure in presenting this their Thirteenth Annual Report and Balance Sheet to the Shareholders of the Company, for the year ending 31st May, 1952.

It will be observed that the year under review has been a successful one resulting in a gross profit of £1,209 (more than double that of the previous year) and so far as trophies and honours are concerned the first XI carried off "The East Anglian Cup" and the "Thameside Trophy", were finalists in "The Essex Senior Cup", and finished fourth in the Isthmian League, the 2nd XI were runners up in their Division while the "A" team were Champions of their Division; a very commendable performance.

Income and Expenditure for the year is regarded as favourable having regard to increased costs and the fact that there are now three teams to maintain and equip. Increased expenditure is particularly noticeable and expected in items concerning Wages, Transport, Meals and Entertainment. Players' Sundries, £227, includes such items as Shirts, Boots and similar equipment which in previous years has been included with Players' Expenses A/c.

As to the gross profit of £1,209 already mentioned, your Directors have utilised this sum in the Appropriation A/c (after taking into account the profit balance brought forward from last year of £446) in making provision for depreciation on Ground and Property of £1,000 (a similar amount to last year) and for the payment of a Dividend of 7½% (Net) £387 and providing for Income Tax in the sum of £223 leaving a sum of £45 unappropriated carried forward in the Balance Sheet to 1953/54.

Turning to the Balance Sheet it will be seen that the Property and Equipment A/c has had additions during the year of £1,267 arising from Capital Expenditure on the improvement of the ground and purchase of equipment while there is a deduction of £1,900 in respect of sale of property. The sale referred to is one of the Company's houses. It will be remembered that the Company purchased three houses adjoining the ground a few years ago and this represents the sale price of one of them. It may be said that the others have been sold but the sales not yet completed.

The new wall and payboxes adjoining the Car Park referred to in the last Report (as being about to be constructed) has been completed and your Directors are pleased to report that a Licence for the erection of a similar pre-cast concrete wall along the Cedar Road and Willow Street sides of the Ground (including the construction of a new entrance from Willow Street) has been granted and instructions have been given to the Company's Architect to proceed with the work forthwith....

As to future Programme and Policy your Directors adhere to their policy of long term planning and have no intention of carrying out makeshift schemes any more than can be helped. Ever in the mind of the Board is the erection of a first-class stand with proper accommodation for Players, Officials and Members alike and it is thought that this project can be accomplished in the not too distant future.

Your Directors have under consideration Floodlighting of football such as now indulged in by Arsenal FC and other first-class Clubs and have made it their business to see it in actual operation. Your Directors have had schemes before them as to this and it may well be that such an amenity may yet be possible at not too great an expense to the Company, but it will be appreciated many aspects have to be considered.

The Coronation offers opportunity for the Company to stage some attraction or functions on the Ground, and your Directors are giving consideration to some proposals for this great occasion. The existence of this fine ground should not be overlooked by other Clubs and organisations during the summer months. In football needless to say your Directors have but one ambition, for the Club to win the Amateur Cup; they will continue always to do everything that can be done by encouragement of team spirit, coaching, and good sportsmanship, to bring this about.

The above report was presented to the shareholders at the Annual General Meeting held on Wednesday 21ˢᵗ January 1953 As reported in the *Romford Recorder*, Friday 23ʳᵈ January 1953

FLOODLIT AND TV FOOTBALL APPROVED BY ROMFORD FC

One of the features of football is its uncertainty, said Lord Macpherson at the annual meeting of Romford Football Club Ltd on Wednesday. "If a team always won", he said, "what a dull thing it would be. It is the uncertainty of the game which enables us to follow the team with such interest".

Lord Macpherson added, "A football team is like a woman – a woman knows with equal ease, how to vex and how to please". He continued, "We want to entertain our supporters in comfort and we cannot do that until we obtain adequate seating accommodation in keeping with the enormous population we now serve in the district. We hope to begin work on a stand in the near future. Work on the new concrete wall along the Cedar Road and Willow Street sides of the ground has already begun".

FLOODLIT FOOTBALL? Lord Macpherson mentioned the possibility of football being played under floodlighting in the future and said that directors who had attended floodlit matches in London were greatly impressed.

In conclusion, Lord Macpherson expressed good wishes on behalf of the club to Mr A.E. Kittle, who is sailing to South Africa next week with his wife for a health visit.

TV GAMES. Mr J. Graham hoped that the Club would welcome matches being televised to give the thousands of people who were unable to attend the ground for various reasons, a chance to see the games. Lord Macpherson said that televised matches would benefit the public and the Club, and he assured Mr Graham that the Management Committee and the Board were of the same opinion.

The report and accounts were adopted and the two retiring directors, Lord Macpherson (chairman) and Mr Martin Brazier were re-elected.

A gross profit of £1,209 was reported for the year ended May 31ˢᵗ, a profit of more than double that of the previous year. A recommendation for the payment of a 7½ per cent dividend was approved.

PICTURE SPECIAL
Romford's Amateur Cup third round battle with Crook Town

Saturday 9th February 1952:

Romford's team and supporters have travelled 269 miles to the far north of England for this match. The FA rule was that for Amateur Cup semi-finals, when the clubs were distant from each other, the venue would be the nearest suitable ground available to the club first out of the hat. Crook were first out.

Before the match the teams line up in silent tribute to King George VI, who had died three days before.

Jarrie (Crook Town goalkeeper) thwarts Romford's Johnnie Bee

Romford goalkeeper Chris Moore manages to tip the ball over the bar

Photos from *the Sports Despatch & Northern Despatch*

The long journey was worth it, though. The "thrill-a-minute" match at Crook would be long remembered by all who saw it, as this *Romford Times* report shows

Saturday 16th February 1952

The atmosphere at Brooklands for the replay was electric. Thousands more watched it broadcast live on TV.

The Romford team take to the pitch. To the right is captain, Graeme Cunningham, with a little mascot dressed in Romford's colours.   *The Romford Recorder*

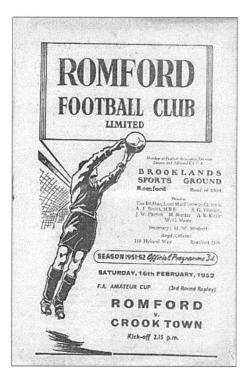

The *Romford Times* cartoonist's verdict on the match, in the shape of the small TV screens of the day!

ROMFORD versus CROOK TOWN: ONE FAN'S STORY
"His hobby is Romford FC"

Jim (first left), Eddie (third), Alf (fourth) and John Haley (sixth left)
with other supporters, photographed in Crook High Street.

At 11pm on Friday 8th February 1952 Romford supporters boarded three coaches at Como Street for the 269-mile journey to Crook in County Durham. After the match they travelled back overnight, returning to Romford at 9am Sunday morning. Among them were John Haley and three of his brothers, Jim, Eddie and Alf. Another brother would have come, but was unable to get the time off work!

Ron Lyons, Romford's Advertising Secretary, interviewed John and discovered he had been compiling statistics on the club since its re-formation in 1945. Mr Lyons then loaned John the official club records to check against the statistics that he had. As a result of this Mr H. Hughes, Romford's Press Secretary, asked John to record his statistics on the club's behalf. So from 1952-53 onwards you will notice John Haley's name on the list of club officials at the beginning of each season.

John's story appeared on the Club Chatter page in this programme for Romford's match against Kingstonian on 9th October 1954 (right and below) when he was interviewed by Ron Lyons using the alias Ronnie Romford   *Authors' collection*

Romford Club Chatter

INTERESTING ITEMS — by Ronnie Romford

His Hobby is Romford F.C.

John Haley, of Gobions, has probably as many records of the Club in recent years as our Hon. Secretary! This is because his hobby is collecting and recording factual information about "The Borough." He is 23 and by profession a coal office manager. He has practically every fact—teams; scorers; most successful partnerships; appearances, and so forth. He follows Romford at home and away—and, because of his job, often has to make his own last-minute arrangements to reach an "away" ground.

John has a record of his very own, which we do not think can be beaten. In that year when we drew with Crook Town in Durham, he went the 250 miles with his three brothers to watch the game. It would have been FOUR BROTHERS, but the fourth had to work and couldn't get away.

Thanks, John, for your interest—it is appreciated by the Club.

THE ROMFORD FOOTBALL CLUB LIMITED

Full Members of The Football Association
Full Members of Isthmian Football League
Affiliated to Essex County Football Association

Club Colours: Blue and Gold Shirts, White Shorts

Ground   Brooklands Sports Ground, Romford

Chairman: The Rt.Hon.Lord Macpherson
Directors: Messrs. M.A.Brazier, A.E.Kittle, W.G.Mann,
J.W.Parrish, A.J.Smith MBE, S.G.Tansley
Company Secretary: Mr H.W.Muskett

Registered Offices: 110,Hyland Way, Romford

Football Club Management Committee:
Chairman: Mr A.E.Kittle
Hon.Gen.Secretary: Mr M.A.Brazier   **Hon.Press Secretary:** Mr H.A.Hughes
Other Committee Members: Messrs. H.F.Knights, W.G.Mann,
J.W.Parrish, A.J.Smith MBE, S.G.Tansley

Hon.Medical Advisor: Dr I.H.Bourne (Resigned June 1953)
Hon.Advt.Secretary: Mr R.S.Lyons
Reserve XI Secretary: Mr G.I.Howlett   **Third XI Secretary:** Mr E.Crook
Programmes: Mr H.Wright
Player Coach: Mr G.Cunningham
Reserve Team Coach: Mr D.Hamilton   **"A" Team Coach:** Mr G.W.Patterson
Selection Committee: W.G.Mann(Chairman) Mr A.Adlam(Secretary), Mr F.H.Adams
plus the three team coaches(Ex. Officio)
Trainer: Mr W.C.Seddon   **Assistant Trainer:** Mr E.Hewitt
Team Assistants (Trainers): Mr Fred Griffiths(Reserves)Mr H.Archer("A" Team)

Groundsman: Mr W.C.(Bill)Seddon
Assistant Groundsman: Mr Arnold (Resigned July 28th)

Bankers: Lloyds Bank Limited   **Auditor:** Messrs Iion V. Cummings and Co.

Statistics: Mr John Haley (ex-Officio)

COMPETITIONS ENTERED SEASON 1952 – 53

The FA Challenge Cup
The FA Amateur Challenge Cup
The Isthmian Football League
The Essex Senior Cup
The East Anglian Cup
The Essex Thameside Trophy

The Isthmian Football League Reserve Section
The Essex Intermediate Cup
The Isthmian Football League "A" Section
The Essex Junior Cup

Admission Prices Season 1952 – 53

	First Team			Reserve Team		
	Adults	OAPs	Child	Adults	OAPs	Child
Ground	1/-		6d	6d		3d
Ground & Enclosure	1/9		1/-	1/-		6d
Grandstand	2/6		2/6	1/-		6d
Grandstand	2/6		2/6	1/-		6d

Season Tickets

	Adults	OAPs & Children
Grandstand (All one price)	£1.10.0	
Ground & Enclosure	£1.1.0	12/6
Ground only	12/6	7/6

ROMFORD PLAYERS FOR SEASON 1952 – 53

The 28 players are a mixture of first team and reserves. Graeme Cunningham holds the East Anglian Cup. Bridge and Welch are missing from this line-up. We presume that the photo of the East Anglian Cup winning team in the previous season was also taken at this session, explaining the absence of Welch from that photo. *Authors' collection*

First Team Match Details

23 Aug IFL Away Bromley 3 – 1 Bee(3)
Romford: C.L.Moore;J.G.Welch,R.A.Lamb;P.J.Boreham,G.Fleetwood,J.V.Eyett;
H.W.Brooks,G.Cunningham(Capt),J.Bee,W.A.Bridge,A.F.Herbert.

27 Aug ETT1R Home Grays Athletic 2 – 1 Cunningham,Brooks
Attendance: 5,335   Receipts: £269.6.6   Programmes: £10.9.9 Car Park: £6.13.3
Romford: C.L.Moore;J.G.Welch,R.A.Lamb;P.J.Boreham,G.Fleetwood,J.V.Eyett;
H.W.Brooks,G.Cunningham(Capt),J.Bee,W.A.Bridge,A.F.Herbert.

30 Aug IFL Home Wycombe Wanderers 8 – 0 Brooks(2)Cunningham(3)(1pen)Bee(2)
Herbert(pen)
Attendance: 4,287   Receipts: £211.6.9   Programmes: £   Car Park: £7.12.3
Romford: C.L.Moore;J.G.Welch,R.A.Lamb;P.J.Boreham,G.Fleetwood,J.V.Eyett;
H.W.Brooks,G.Cunningham(Capt),J.Bee,W.A.Bridge,A.F.Herbert.

3 Sept IFL Home Walthamstow Avenue 1 – 0 Bee
Attendance: 3,947   Receipts: £194.3.0   Programmes: £   Car Park: £8.14.6
Romford: C.L.Moore;J.G.Welch,R.A.Lamb;P.J.Boreham,G.Fleetwood,J.V.Eyett;
H.W.Brooks,G.Cunningham(Capt),J.Bee,W.A.Bridge,A.F.Herbert.

6 Sept IFL Away Wimbledon 1 – 3 Bee
Romford: C.L.Moore;J.G.Welch,R.A.Lamb;P.J.Boreham,G.Fleetwood,J.V.Eyett;
H.W.Brooks,G.Cunningham(Capt),J.Bee,W.A.Bridge,G.W.Andrews.

10 Sept ETTFRpIlford Leytonstone 4 – 2 Bee(3)Brooks
Romford: C.L.Moore;J.G.Welch,R.A.Lamb;P.J.Boreham,G.Fleetwood,V.H.Perriman;
H.W.Brooks,G.Cunningham(Capt),J.Bee,W.A.Bridge,G.W.Andrews.

13 Sept IFL Home St. Albans City 1 – 1 Bee
Attendance: 3,973   Receipts: £197.13.6   Programmes: £31.3.9 Car Park: £7.11.6
Romford: C.L.Moore;J.G.Welch,R.A.Lamb;P.J.Boreham,G.Fleetwood,J.V.Eyett;
G.W.Andrews,G.Cunningham(Capt),J.Bee,S.Shaef,A.F.Herbert.

20 Sept IFL Home Corinthian Casuals 2 – 2 Herbert,Cunningham(pen)
Attendance: 5,018   Receipts: £246.6.9   Programmes: £32.14.5 Car Park: £6.15.0
Romford: C.L.Moore;J.G.Welch,R.A.Lamb;P.J.Boreham,G.Fleetwood,J.V.Eyett;
H.W.Brooks,G.Cunningham(Capt),J.Bee,A.F.Herbert,G.W.Andrews.

27 Sept FAC1Q Away Clacton Town 1 – 1 Andrews
Attendance: 3,505
Romford: C.L.Moore;J.G.Welch,R.A.Lamb;P.J.Boreham,G.Fleetwood,J.V.Eyett;
H.W.Brooks,G.Cunningham(Capt),J.Bee,A.F.Herbert,G.W.Andrews.

2 Oct FACRp Home Clacton Town 1 – 3 Bee
Attendance: 4,012   Receipts: £224.14.0   Programmes: £10.1.2 Car Park: £7.14.6
Romford: C.L.Moore;J.G.Welch,R.A.Lamb;P.J.Boreham,G.Fleetwood,J.V.Eyett;
H.W.Brooks,G.Cunningham(Capt),J.Bee,A.F.Herbert,G.W.Andrews.

4 Oct IFL Away#1 Corinthian Casuals 1 – 0 Bridge
Romford: C.L.Moore;J.G.Welch,V.Jones;P.J.Boreham,G.Fleetwood(Capt),J.V.Eyett;
H.W.Brooks,W.A.Bridge,J.Bee,S.Shaef,G.W.Andrews.

11 Oct IFL Away Kingstonian 2 – 2 Cunningham,Bee
Romford: C.L.Moore;R.A.Lamb,V.Jones;P.J.Boreham,G.Fleetwood,J.V.Eyett;
H.W.Brooks,G.Cunningham(Capt),J.Bee,A.F.Herbert,G.W.Andrews.

18 Oct IFL Home Oxford City 2 – 0 Cunningham,Bee
Attendance: 4,092   Receipts: £195.3.3   Programmes: £28.16.9 Car Park: £6.11.6
Romford: C.L.Moore;J.G.Welch,R.A.Lamb;P.J.Boreham,G.Fleetwood,J.V.Eyett;
H.W.Brooks,G.Cunningham(Capt),J.Bee,W.A.Bridge,G.W.Andrews.

25 Oct EAC1R Home Brentwood & Warley 1 – 0 Cunningham
Attendance: 6,868   Receipts: £375.15.3   Programmes: £40.12.10 Car Park: £8.17.9
Romford: C.L.Moore;J.G.Welch,R.A.Lamb;P.J.Boreham,G.Fleetwood,J.V.Eyett;
H.W.Brooks,G.Cunningham(Capt),J.Bee,W.A.Bridge,G.W.Andrews.

1 Nov IFL Away Woking 3 – 2 Bee,Cunningham,Brooks
Romford: C.L.Moore;J.G.Welch,R.A.Lamb;P.J.Boreham,G.Fleetwood,J.V.Eyett;
H.W.Brooks,W.A.Bridge,J.Bee,G.Cunningham(Capt),G.W.Andrews.

8 Nov IFL Home Clapton 1 – 1 Brooks
Attendance: 4,249   Receipts: £200.15.6   Programmes: £18.8.8 Car Park: £5.9.6
Romford: C.L.Moore;J.G.Welch,R.A.Lamb;T.R.Kelly,G.Fleetwood,J.V.Eyett;
H.W.Brooks,P.J.Boreham,L.Sollof,G.Cunningham(Capt),G.W.Andrews.

15 Nov IFL   Away   Leytonstone   0 – 4
Romford: C.L.Moore;J.G.Welch,R.A.Lamb;P.J.Boreham,G.Fleetwood,J.V.Eyett;
H.W.Brooks,W.A.Bridge,J.Bee,G.Cunningham(Capt),G.W.Andrews.

22 Nov IFL   Away   St. Albans City   2 – 4   Casson(2)
Romford: C.L.Moore;J.G.Welch,V.Jones;G.Fleetwood(Capt),R.A.Lamb,J.V.Eyett;
H.W.Brooks,L.G.Casson,J.Bee,W.A.Bridge,G.W.Andrews.

29 Nov EAC2R Home   Colchester United Reserves   1 – 2   Brooks
Attendance: 3,609   Receipts: £203.13.3   Programmes: £19.13.6   Car Park: £5.3.0
Romford: C.L.Moore;R.A.Lamb,V.Jones;G.Fleetwood(Capt),H.Hunton,J.V.Eyett;
H.W.Brooks,L.G.Casson,J.Bee,W.A.Bridge,G.W.Andrews.

13 Dec AC1R   Away   St. Albans City   4 – 4   Bee(2)Cunningham,Bridge
Romford: C.L.Moore;V.Jones,R.A.Lamb;J.G.Welch,G.Fleetwood,J.V.Eyett;
H.W.Brooks,W.A.Bridge,J.Bee,G.Cunningham(Capt),G.W.Andrews.

20 Dec ACRp   Home   St. Albans City   4 – 0   Bee,Bridge,Andrews,Cunningham
Attendance: 4,762   Receipts: £262.7.6   Programmes: £21.17.4   Car Park: £7.2.9
Romford: C.L.Moore;V.Jones,R.A.Lamb;J.G.Welch,G.Fleetwood,J.V.Eyett;
H.W.Brooks,W.A.Bridge,J.Bee,G.Cunningham(Capt),G.W.Andrews.

25 Dec IFL   Home   Ilford   3 – 1   Bridge,Bee(2)
Attendance: 3,343   Receipts: £171.14.9   Programmes: £25.0.0   Car Park: £9.12.0
Romford: C.L.Moore;V.Jones,R.A.Lamb;H.Hunton,G.Fleetwood,J.V.Eyett;
H.W.Brooks,W.A.Bridge,J.Bee,G.Cunningham(Capt),G.W.Andrews.

26 Dec IFL   Away   Ilford   4 – 1#   Bee(2)Cunningham(2)
Romford: C.L.Moore;V.Jones,R.A.Lamb;T.R.Kelly,H.Hunton,J.V.Eyett;
H.W.Brooks,W.A.Bridge,J.Bee,G.Cunningham(Capt),G.W.Andrews.

3 Jan ESC1R Home   Harwich & Parkeston   5 – 3   Brooks,Cunningham,Bridge(3)
Attendance: 5,421   Receipts: £282.14.6   Programmes: £26.8.4   Car Park: £5.13.3
Romford: C.L.Moore;V.Jones,R.A.Lamb;J.G.Welch,G.Fleetwood,J.V.Eyett;
H.W.Brooks,W.A.Bridge,J.Bee,G.Cunningham(Capt),G.W.Andrews.

10 Jan IFL   Away   Wycombe Wanderers   2 – 3   Evans,Welch
Romford: C.L.Moore;V.Jones,R.A.Lamb;J.G.Welch,G.Fleetwood(Capt),J.V.Eyett;
H.W.Brooks,W.A.Bridge,J.Bee,L.Evans,G.W.Andrews.

17 Jan IFL   Home   Barking   2 – 5   Bee(2)
Attendance: 3,904   Receipts: £188.19.9   Programmes: £25.6.7   Car Park: £6.8.3
Romford: R.Brown;V.Jones,R.A.Lamb;J.G.Welch,H.Hunton,J.V.Eyett;
H.W.Brooks,W.A.Bridge,J.Bee,G.Cunningham(Capt),G.W.Andrews.

24 Jan AC2R   Away   Carshalton Athletic   3 – 2   Bridge,Brooks,Cunningham(pen)
Romford: C.L.Moore;H.Hunton,V.Jones;J.G.Welch,J.V.Eyett,P.J.Boreham;
H.W.Brooks,W.A.Bridge,J.Bee,G.Cunningham(Capt),G.W.Andrews.

31 Jan ESC1R Away   Grays Athletic   1 – 2   Bridge
Romford: C.L.Moore;H.Hunton,V.Jones;J.G.Welch,J.V.Eyett,V.H.Perriman;
H.W.Brooks,W.A.Bridge,J.Bee,G.Cunningham(Capt),G.W.Andrews.

7 Feb AC3R   Away   Wycombe Wanderers   5 – 0   Cunningham(2)Brooks,Bridge,Bee
Attendance: 11,000   Receipts: £664.0.0d.
Romford: C.L.Moore;H.Hunton,R.A.Lamb;J.G.Welch,G.Fleetwood,J.V.Eyett;
H.W.Brooks,W.A.Bridge,J.Bee,G.Cunningham(Capt),G.W.Andrews.

14 Feb IFL   Home   Woking   7 – 2   Bridge,Bee(4)Cunningham(pen)Killick(og)
Attendance: 2,257   Receipts: £109.2.6   Programmes: £   Car Park: £3.14.9
Romford: C.L.Moore;H.Hunton,R.A.Lamb;J.G.Welch,G.Fleetwood,J.V.Eyett;
H.W.Brooks,W.A.Bridge,J.Bee,G.Cunningham(Capt),G.W.Andrews.

21 Feb AC4R   Away   Southall   1 – 1   Cunningham
Attendance: 10,587   Receipts: £583.1.6   Romford Share £242.3.6
Romford: C.L.Moore;H.Hunton,R.A.Lamb;J.G.Welch,G.Fleetwood,J.V.Eyett;
H.W.Brooks,W.A.Bridge,J.Bee,G.Cunningham(Capt),G.W.Andrews.

28 Feb ACRp   Home   Southall   1 – 2   Cunningham
Attendance: 17,081   Receipts: £897.5.0   Programmes: £53.9.9   Car Park: £9.15.0
Romford: C.L.Moore;H.Hunton,R.A.Lamb;J.G.Welch,G.Fleetwood,J.V.Eyett;
H.W.Brooks,W.A.Bridge,J.Bee,G.Cunningham(Capt),G.W.Andrews.

7 Mar IFL   Away   Dulwich Hamlet   1 – 2   Bee
Romford: C.L.Moore;H.Hunton,R.A.Lamb;J.G.Welch(Capt),R.J.Innes,J.V.Eyett;
H.W.Brooks,W.A.Bridge,J.Bee,S.Shaef,G.W.Andrews.

14 Mar IFL   Home   Wimbledon   1 – 4   Bee
Attendance: 2,608   Receipts: £120.18.0   Programmes: £20.8.9   Car Park: £4.15.3
Romford: C.L.Moore;H.Hunton,R.A.Lamb;J.G.Welch,G.Fleetwood,J.V.Eyett;
H.W.Brooks,G.Cunningham(Capt),J.Bee,S.Shaef,G.W.Andrews.

21 Mar IFL   Home   Dulwich Hamlet   0 – 3
Attendance: 2,370   Receipts: £110.3.6   Progs: £15.13.9   Car Park: £4.5.0
Romford: C.L.Moore;H.Hunton,R.A.Lamb;W.Oram,G.Fleetwood(Capt),V.H.Perriman;
H.W.Brooks,S.Shaef,A.Gosshawk,L.Evans,G.W.Andrews.

28 Mar IFL   Away   Clapton   3 – 1   Bee(2)Cunningham
Romford: C.L.Moore;H.Hunton,R.A.Lamb;J.G.Welch,G.Fleetwood,J.V.Eyett;
H.W.Brooks,P.J.Boreham,J.Bee,G.Cunningham(Capt),J.Moir.

4 Apr IFL   Away   Barking   2 – 0   Cunningham,Andrews
Romford: C.L.Moore;H.Hunton,R.A.Lamb;J.V.Eyett,G.Fleetwood,P.J.Boreham;
H.W.Brooks,S.Shaef,J.Bee,G.Cunningham(Capt),G.W.Andrews.

11 Apr IFL   Home   Leytonstone   4 – 2   Andrews,Bee,Cunningham,Shaef
Attendance: 2,738   Receipts: £127.13.6   Programmes: £9.8.7   Car Park: £5.9.3
Romford: C.L.Moore;H.Hunton,R.A.Lamb;J.V.Eyett,G.Fleetwood,P.J.Boreham;
H.W.Brooks,S.Shaef,J.Bee,G.Cunningham(Capt),G.W.Andrews.

18 Apr IFL   Away   Oxford City   2 – 2   Brooks(2)
Romford: C.L.Moore;V.Jones,R.A.Lamb;J.V.Eyett,G.Fleetwood,P.J.Boreham;
H.W.Brooks,S.Shaef,J.Bee,G.Cunningham(Capt),G.W.Andrews.

20 Apr ETTSF   Home   Barking   3 – 4*   Bee,Cunningham(2)
Attendance: 4,186   Receipts: £211.3.6   Programmes: £14.0.0   Car Park: £5.1.0
Romford: C.L.Moore;V.Jones,R.A.Lamb;J.V.Eyett,G.Fleetwood,P.J.Boreham;
H.W.Brooks,S.Shaef,J.Bee,G.Cunningham(Capt),G.W.Andrews.

25 Apr IFL   Home   Kingstonian   4 – 4   Shaef,Brooks(2)Bee
Attendance: 2,676   Receipts: £118.0.6   Programmes: £17.3.9   Car Park: £ None
Romford: C.L.Moore;G.Chesterton,R.A.Lamb;J.G.Welch,J.V.Eyett,P.J.Boreham;
H.W.Brooks,S.Shaef,J.Bee,G.Cunningham(Capt),G.W.Andrews.

27 Apr IFL   Away   Walthamstow Avenue   1 – 1   Bee
Romford: C.L.Moore;H.Hunton,R.A.Lamb;J.G.Welch,G.Fleetwood,J.V.Eyett;
H.W.Brooks,J.Moir,J.Bee,G.Cunningham(Capt),G.W.Andrews.

30 Apr IFL   Home   Bromley   1 – 1   Brooks
Attendance: 603   Receipts: £30.12.9   Programmes: £2.9.3   Car Park: £2.9.3
Romford: C.L.Moore;H.Hunton,R.A.Lamb;J.G.Welch,G.Fleetwood(Capt),J.Eyett;
H.W.Brooks,S.Shaef,J.Bee,J.Moir,G.W.Andrews.

2 May IFL   Away   Ilford   2 – 1   Cunningham,Bee
Romford: R.Brown;H.Hunton,R.A.Lamb;J.Eyett,G.Fleetwood,P.J.Boreham;
H.W.Brooks,S.Shaef,J.Bee,G.Cunningham(Capt),G.W.Andrews.

*   After Extra Time
#   Abandoned after 82 minutes due to fog.
#1   Played at the Oval Cricket Ground.

FIRST TEAM SUMMARY OF RESULTS 1952 – 53

	P	Home			Goals		Away			Goals		
		W	D	L	For	Ag	W	D	L	For	Ag	Pts
Isthmian League	28	6	5	3	38	28	6	3	5	24	24	32
F.A.Challenge Cup	2	0	0	1	1	3	0	1	0	1	1	
F.A. Amateur Cup	6	1	0	1	5	2	2	2	0	13	7	
Essex Senior Cup	2	1	0	0	5	3	0	0	1	1	2	
East Anglian Cup	2	1	0	0	1	0	0	0	1	1	2	
Thameside Trophy	2	1	0	1	5	5	0	0	0	0	0	
T'side Trophy 51/52	1	0	0	0	0	0	1	0	0	4	2	
Totals	43	10	5	6	55	41	9	6	7	44	38	

Note: The above summary does not include the match at Ilford on 26th December 1952 which was abandoned after 82 minutes with Romford leading by four goals to one.

Isthmian Football League
Final Table

	P	W	D	L	Goals For	Ag	Pts
Walthamstow Avenue	28	19	6	3	53	25	44
Bromley	28	17	4	7	71	35	38
Leytonstone	28	14	6	8	60	38	34
Wimbledon	28	14	5	9	68	37	33
Kingstonian	28	13	6	9	62	50	32
Dulwich Hamlet	28	15	2	11	62	52	32
Romford	**28**	**12**	**8**	**8**	**62**	**52**	**32**
Wycombe Wanderers	28	14	2	12	54	62	30
St.Albans City	28	11	6	11	43	57	28
Barking	28	9	7	12	42	51	25
Ilford	28	10	4	14	59	57	24
Woking	28	10	4	14	57	72	24
Corinthian Casuals	28	7	9	12	45	56	23
Oxford City	28	5	2	21	37	87	12
Clapton	28	2	5	21	27	71	9

FIRST TEAM CUP RESULTS

FA Challenge Cup
Final: Blackpool   4   Bolton Wanderers   3

Romford's progress   1st.Qual.   Away   Clacton Town   1 – 1
2nd Qual.   Home   Clacton Town   1 – 3

FA Amateur Challenge Cup
Final: Pegasus   6   Harwich & Parkeston   0

Romford's progress   1st Round   Away   St.Albans City   4 – 4
Replay   Home   St.Albans City   4 – 0
2nd Round   Away   Carshalton Ath.   3 – 2
3rd Round   Away   Wycombe Wanderers   5 – 0
4th Round   Away   Southall   1 – 1
Replay   Home   Southall   1 – 2

Essex County FA Senior Challenge Cup
Final: Ilford   3   Grays Athletic   1

Romford's progress   1st Round   Home   Harwich & Parkeston   5 – 3
2nd Round   Away   Grays Athletic   1 – 2

East Anglian Cup
Final: n/k

Romford's progress   1st Round   Home   Brentwood & Warley   1 – 0
2nd Round   Home   Colchester Utd. Res.   1 – 2

Essex Thameside Challenge Competition
Final: n/k

Romford's progress   1st Round   Home   Grays Athletic   2 – 1
Semi-Final   Home   Barking   3 – 4

FIRST TEAM DEBUTS SEASON 1952 – 53

1952					Previous Club
23rd Aug.	v Bromley	-	**J.V.Eyett**		Ilford
13th Sept.	v St.Albans City	-	**S.Shaef**		Barking
8th Nov.	v Clapton	-	**T.R.Kelly**		Ilford
		-	**L.Sollof**		Bexleyheath & W.
29th Nov.	v Colchester U. Res.	-	**H.Hunton**		Leytonstone

1953

10th Jan.	v Wycombe Wd'rs.	-	**L.Evans**	Brentwood & Warley
17th Jan.	v Barking	-	**R.Brown**	Barking
7th Mar.	v Dulwich Hamlet	-	**B.Innes**	n/k
21st Mar.	v Dulwich Hamlet	-	**W.Oram**	Rainham Town
		-	**A.Gosshawk**	n/k
28th Mar.	v Clapton	-	**J.Moir**	n/k
25th Apr.	v Kingstonian	-	**G.Chesterton**	Rainham Town

FIRST TEAM APPEARANCES SEASON 1952 – 53

	A	B	C	D	E	F	G	Total
George Andrews	24	2	6	2	2	1	1	38
Johnny Bee	26	2	6	2	2	2	1	41
Peter Boreham	18	2	1	0	1	2	1	25
Bill Bridge	14	0	6	2	2	1	1	26
Harold Brooks	27	2	6	2	2	2	1	42
Reg Brown	2	0	0	0	0	0	0	2
Len Casson	1	0	0	0	1	0	0	2
G.Chesterton	1	0	0	0	0	0	0	1
Graeme Cunningham	22	2	6	2	1	2	1	36
L.Evans	2	0	0	0	0	0	0	2
Jim Eyett	27	2	6	2	2	2	0	41
Gordon Fleetwood	25	2	5	1	2	2	1	38
Tony Gosshawk	1	0	0	0	0	0	0	1
Tony Herbert	6	2	0	0	0	1	0	9
Harry Hunton	12	0	4	1	1	0	0	18
B.Innes	1	0	0	0	0	0	0	1
Vic Jones	7	0	3	2	1	1	0	14
Tim Kelly	1	0	0	0	0	0	0	1
Ron Lamb	27	2	5	1	2	2	1	40
Jackie Moir	3	0	0	0	0	0	0	3
Chris Moore	26	2	6	2	2	2	1	41
Bill Oram	1	0	0	0	0	0	0	1
Vic Perriman	1	0	0	1	0	0	1	3
Stan Shaef	12	0	0	0	0	0	0	12
L.Sollof	1	0	0	0	0	0	0	1
Johnny Welch	20	2	6	2	1	2	1	34
Total	308	22	66	22	22	22	11	473

FIRST TEAM GOALSCORERS SEASON 1952 – 53

	A	B	C	D	E	F	G	Total
Johnny Bee	27	1	4	0	0	1	3	36*
Graeme Cunningham	12	0	7	1	1	3	0	24*
Harold Brooks	9	0	2	1	1	1	1	15
Bill Bridge	3	0	4	4	0	0	0	11
George Andrews	2	1	1	0	0	0	0	4
Tony Herbert	2	0	0	0	0	0	0	2
Len Casson	2	0	0	0	0	0	0	2
Stan Shaef	2	0	0	0	0	0	0	2
L. Evans	1	0	0	0	0	0	0	1
Johnny Welch	1	0	0	0	0	0	0	1
Killick(Woking)o.g.	1	0	0	0	0	0	0	1
Total	62	2	18	6	2	5	4	99

* Does not include the goals scored in the abandoned game with Ilford on Boxing Day.

KEY TO COMPETITIONS

A   Isthmian Football League
B   FA Challenge Cup
C   FA Amateur Challenge Cup
D   Essex County FA Senior Challenge Cup
E   East Anglian Cup
F   Thameside Challenge Trophy
G   Thameside Challenge Trophy 51/52 Replay

Reserve Team Match Details

23 Aug IFLR   Home   Bromley Res.   3 – 0   Shaef(2)Casson
Attendance: 1,421   Receipts: £30.2.0   Programmes: £3.15.9 Car Park: £0.10.9
Romford Res.: R.Brown;D.Evans,V.Jones;R.Chesterton,D.R.Lowman,T.R.Kelly;
W.Dowsett,L.G.Casson,A.Sanderson,S.Shaef,J.Moir.

30 Aug IFLR   Away   Wycombe Wanderers Res.   1 – 1   Newman
Romford Res.: E.Dawber;V.Jones,J.W.Conner;T.R.Kelly,D.R.Lowman,R.Chesterton;
W.Dowsett,V.H.Perriman,H.M.Newman,S.Shaef,D.Brown.

6 Sept IFLR   Home   Wimbledon Res.   2 – 3   Shaef,Herbert
Attendance: 1,503   Receipts: £32.2.9   Programmes: £4.5.4   Car Park: £0.10.6
Romford Res.: R.Brown;   ? ,   ? ;   ? ,D.R.Lowman,   ? ;
    ? ,L.G.Casson,H.M.Newman,S.Shaef,A.F.Herbert.

13 Sept IFLR   Away   St. Albans City Res.   4 – 0   Kenlay(3)Sewell
Romford Res.: R.Brown;D.Evans,V.Jones;T.R.Kelly,D.R.Lowman,V.H.Perriman;
W.Dowsett,H.M.Newman,G.J.Kenlay,D.J.Sewell,J.R.Connor.

27 Sept IFLR   Home   Clapton Res.   4 – 0   Kenlay(3)one other
Attendance: 1,048   Receipts: £21.4.0   Programmes: £2.8.10 Car Park: £0.8.3
Romford Res.:
Team details unknown.

4 Oct IFLR   Home   Dulwich Hamlet Res.   4 – 2   Herbert(3)Sewell
Attendance: 1,158   Receipts: £23.14.9   Programmes: £3.11.4 Car Park: £0.10.3
Romford Res.:
Team details unknown

11 Oct IFLR   Home   Corinthian Casuals Res.   0 – 3
Attendance: 1,477   Receipts: £32.8.9   Programmes: £4.1.6 Car Park: £0.17.6
Romford Res.: W.Dawber;R.Jones,D.Evans;T.R.Kelly,D.R.Lowman,R.Chesterton;
D.J.Sewell,L.G.Casson,L.Sollof,H.M.Newman,J.Moir.

18 Oct IFLR   Away   Kingstonian Res.   0 – 1
Romford Res.: W.Dawber;R.Jones,V.Jones;T.R.Kelly,R.J.Innes,V.H.Perriman;
G.G.Howlett,D.J.Sewell,L.Sollof,G.J.Kenlay,A.F.Herbert.

25 Oct IFLR   Away   Woking Res.   1 – 2   Sollof
Romford Res.: W.Dawber;R.Jones,V.Jones;T.R.Kelly,D.R.Lowman,V.H.Perriman;
G.G.Howlett,L.G.Casson,L.Sollof,R.Chesterton,A.F.Herbert.

1 Nov EIC2R   Away   Westcliff Amateurs   3 – 0   Sollof,Casson,one other
Romford Res.: R.Brown;R.Jones,V.Jones;T.R.Kelly,D.R.Lowman,V.H.Perriman;
G.J.Kenlay,L.G.Casson,L.Sollof,D.J.Sewell,J.Moir.

8 Nov IFLR   Away   Ilford Res.   2 – 5   Perriman(pen)Kenlay
Romford Res.: W.Dawber;V.Jones,G.F.West;A.Sanderson,V.H.Perriman,D.Pryor;
D.J.Sewell,L.G.Casson,L.Sollof,G.J.Kenlay,A.F.Herbert.

15 Nov EIC3R   Home   Hornchurch Wanderers   1 – 0   Moir
Attendance: 509   Receipts: £11.11.0   Programmes: £1.11.2 Car Park: £0.3.6
Romford Res.: R.Brown;R.Jones,V.Jones;T.R.Kelly,R.J.Innes,V.H.Perriman;
G.G.Howlett,R.Chesterton,D.J.Sewell,J.Moir,W.Dawber.

22 Nov IFLR   Home   Walthamstow Avenue Res.   2 – 2   Sewell,Downs
Attendance: 741   Receipts: £13.18.3   Programmes: £1.18.4 Car Park: £0.4.0
Romford Res.: R.Brown;R.Jones,-.Hazel;T.R.Kelly,R.J.Innes,V.H.Perriman;
P.Gunary,A.Sanderson,D.J.Sewell,R.Chesterton,D.W.Downs.

29 Nov IFLR   Away   Bromley Res.   2 – 1   Sewell,Gunary
Romford Res.: R.Brown;R.Jones,W.Oram;J.G.Welch,R.J.Innes,R.Chesterton;
P.Gunary,G.G.Howlett,D.J.Sewell,-.Sharman,D.W.Downs.

6 Dec EIC4R Away Stork 3 – 1 Sewell(2)Sharman
Romford Res.: R.Brown;S.Cardew,D.I.Desborough;T.R.Kelly,R.J.Innes,V.H.Perriman;
P.Gunary,L.G.Casson,D.J.Sewell,R.Chesterton,-.Sharman.

13 Dec IFLR Home Barking Res. 2 – 2 Gunary,Perriman
Attendance: 502   Receipts: £9.3.0   Programmes: £ None   Car Park: £ None
Romford Res.: R.Brown;R.Jones,W.Oram;   ?   ,   ?   ,V.H.Perriman;
P.Gunary,   ?   ,D.J.Sewell,   ?   ,   ?   .

20 Dec IFLR Away Corinthian Casuals Res. 1 – 3 Evans
Romford Res.: R.Brown;G.W.Berry,-.Cawden;R.Chesterton,H.Hunton,P.J.Boreham;
P.Gunary,L.G.Casson,D.J.Sewell,L.Evans,D.W.Downs.

27 Dec IFLR Home Woking Res. 1 – 0# Evans
Attendance: 150
Romford Res.: R.Brown;G.W.Berry,R.Jones;P.J.Boreham,W.Oram,V.H.Perriman;
P.Gunary,L.Evans,L.G.Casson,J.Moir,D.W.Downs.

3 Jan IFLR Away Barking Res. 0 – 0
Romford Res.: R.Brown;R.Jones,W.Oram;T.R.Kelly,H.Hunton,P.J.Boreham;
P.Gunary,A.Sanderson,L.Evans,V.H.Perriman,D.W.Downs.

10 Jan IFLR Home Ilford Res. 2 – 4 Downs,Casson
Attendance: 924   Receipts: £18.19.0   Programmes: £2.10.0   Car Park: £0.7.3
Romford Res.: R.Brown;R.Jones,R.Chesterton;V.H.Perriman,R.J.Innes,P.J.Boreham;
L.G.Casson,S.Shaef,D.J.Sewell,T.R.Kelly,D.W.Downs.

17 Jan IFLR Away Clapton Res. 3 – 1 Oram,Downs,Evans
Romford Res.: -.Hoy;W.Oram,R.Chesterton;T.R.Kelly,R.J.Innes,P.J.Boreham;
P.Gunary,S.Shaef,A.Gosshawk,L.Evans,D.W.Downs.

24 Jan EIC5R Home Tilbury Res. 4 – 3 Casson(2)Kelly,Gosshawk
Attendance: 577   Receipts: £13.19.0   Programmes: £1.12.1   Car Park: £0.8.0
Romford Res.: R.Brown;R.Jones,R.Chesterton;T.R.Kelly,R.J.Innes,V.H.Perriman;
P.Gunary,L.G.Casson,A.Gosshawk,S.Shaef,D.W.Downs.

31 Jan IFLR Home Oxford City Res. 3 – 1 Gosshawk,Shaef,Evans
Attendance: 519   Receipts: £8.3.3   Programmes: £0.19.1   Car Park: £0.5.3
Romford Res.: R.Brown;E.R.Cave,R.A.Lamb;T.R.Kelly,R.J.Innes,W.Oram;
P.Gunary,L.Evans,A.Gosshawk,S.Shaef,D.W.Downs.

7 Feb EIC6R Home Stambridge United 2 – 0 Casson,Shaef
Attendance: 973   Receipts: £21.13.9   Programmes: £1.11.2   Car Park: £0.13.3
Romford Res.: R.Brown;R.Jones,E.R.Cave;T.R.Kelly,R.J.Innes,R.Chesterton;
P.Gunary,L.G.Casson,A.Gosshawk,S.Shaef,D.W.Downs.

14 Feb IFLR Away Oxford City Res. 4 – 1 Oram,Shaef(2)Gunary
Romford Res.: R.Brown;E.R.Cave,V.Jones;V.H.Perriman,R.J.Innes,P.J.Boreham;
P.Gunary,J.Moir,W.Oram,S.Shaef,D.W.Downs.

21 Feb IFLR Home Wycombe Wanderers Res. 3 – 1 Oram,Evans(2)
Attendance: 835   Receipts: £17.19.3   Programmes: £   Car Park: £
Romford Res.: R.Brown;E.R.Cave,R.Jones;T.R.Kelly,R.J.Innes,P.J.Boreham;
D.W.Downs,L.G.Casson,W.Oram,L.Evans,J.Moir.

7 Mar IFLR Home Kingstonian Res. 3 – 3 Gosshawk,Downs,Moir
Attendance: 813   Receipts: £15.13.9   Programmes: £1.8.10   Car Park: £0.7.6
Romford Res.: R.Brown;R.Jones,V.Jones;V.H.Perriman,W.Oram,P.J.Boreham;
P.Gunary,L.G.Casson,A.Gosshawk,J.Moir,D.W.Downs.

14 Mar EICSF R'ham. Briggs Sports Res. 2 – 4* Gunary,Gosshawk
Romford Res.: R.Brown;E.R.Cave,V.Jones;L.G.Casson,R.J.Innes,P.J.Boreham;
P.Gunary,D.Bowins,A.Gosshawk,J.Moir,D.W.Downs.

21 Mar IFLR Away Wimbledon Res. 2 – 1 Sharman,Gunary
Romford Res.: R.Brown;E.R.Cave,V.Jones;   ?   ,R.J.Innes,P.J.Boreham;
P.Gunary,   ?   ,   ?   ,-.Sharman,   ?   ,   ?   .

28 Mar IFLR Home Leytonstone Res. 0 – 1
Attendance: 553   Receipts: £9.19.9   Programmes: £1.0.5   Car Park: £0.5.6
Romford Res.: R.Brown;E.R.Cave,V.Jones;W.Oram,R.J.Innes,R.Chesterton;
P.Gunary,L.G.Casson,A.Gosshawk,   ?   ,   ?   .

4 Apr IFLR Away Dulwich Hamlet Res. 2 – 3 Scorers unknown
Romford Res. **Sel.** R.Brown;W.Oram,V.Jones;V.H.Perriman,R.J.Innes,D.Pryor;
L.G.Casson,W.Robson,   ?   ,L.Evans,J.Moir.

211

11 Apr IFLR Away Walthamstow Avenue Res. Lost**
Romford Res.:
Team details unknown.

18 Apr IFLR Home St. Albans City Res. 2 – 0 Gosshawk(2)
Attendance: 978 Receipts: £19.10.3 Programmes: £2.4.3 Car Park: £0.8.3
Romford Res.: **Sel.** R.Brown;E.R.Cave,R.Chesterton;V.H.Perriman,W.Robson,R.J.Innes;
D.Bowins,L.G.Casson,A.Gosshawk,-.Sharman,J.Moir.

25 Apr IFLR Away Leytonstone Res. Lost**
Romford Res.: **Sel.** R.Brown;J.G.Welch,V.Jones;V.H.Perriman,R.J.Innes,D.Pryor;
P.Gunary,L.G.Casson,A.Gosshawk,W.A.Bridge,J.Moir.

* After Extra Time
** In these two games Romford failed to score, but conceded nine goals.
# Played thirty minutes each way due to fog.

RESERVE TEAM SUMMARY OF RESULTS SEASON 1952 – 53

	Home			Goals		Away			Goals		
	P	**W**	**D**	**L**	**For**	**Ag**	**W**	**D**	**L**	**For**	**Ag**	**Pts**
Isthmian League Res.Section	28	7	3	4	31	22	5	2	7	22	28	29
Essex Intermediate Cup	6	3	0	0	7	3	2	0	1	10	5	
Totals	34	10	3	4	38	25	7	2	8	32	33	

Isthmian Football League Reserve Section
Final Table

	P	**W**	**D**	**L**	**Goals**		**Pts**
					For	**Ag**	
Leytonstone	28	20	2	6	65	27	42
Bromley	28	16	6	6	57	35	38
Ilford	28	17	1	10	67	44	35
Wimbledon	28	15	5	8	68	45	35
Corinthian Casuals	28	14	6	8	68	55	34
Kingstonian	28	13	6	9	76	61	32
Romford Res.	**28**	**12**	**5**	**11**	**53**	**50**	**29**
Walthamstow Avenue	28	10	9	9	53	50	29
Barking	28	11	6	11	52	52	28
Dulwich Hamlet	28	11	5	12	45	59	27
Woking	28	10	5	13	45	63	25
Oxford City	28	10	2	16	50	53	22
Wycombe Wanderers	28	8	5	15	50	66	21
St.Albans City	28	8	3	17	51	72	19
Clapton	28	1	2	25	25	93	4

RESERVE TEAM CUP RESULTS

Essex County FA Intermediate Challenge Cup
Final: Briggs Sports Res. 5 Heybridge Swifts 1

Romford's progress	1st Round			bye
	2nd Round	Away	Westcliff Amateurs	3 – 0
	3rd Round	Home	Hornchurch Wanderers	1 – 0
	4th Round	Away	Stork (Purfleet)	3 – 1
	5th Round	Home	Tilbury Res.	4 – 3
	6th Round	Home	Stambridge United	2 – 0
	Semi-Final	Rainham	Briggs Sports Res.	2 – 4*

* After extra time

RESERVE TEAM APPEARANCES SEASON 1952 – 53

The following players are known to have appeared in the reserve team during the season.

G.W.Berry	D.Bowins	P.J.Boreham	W.A.Bridge
D.Brown	R.Brown	S.Cardew	L.G.Casson
E.R.Cave	R.Chesterton	J.R.Connor	J.W.Conner
W.Dawber	D.I.Desborough	D.W.Downs	W.Dowsett
D.Evans	L.Evans	A.Gosshawk	P.Gunary
-.Hazel	A.F.Herbert	G.G.Howlett	-.Hoy
H.Hunton	R.J.Innes	R.Jones(Eton Manor)*	V.Jones(Eton Manor)*
T.R.Kelly	G.J.Kenlay	R.A.Lamb	D.R.Lowman
J.Moir	H.M.Newman(Leytonstone)	W.Oram	V.H.Perriman
D.Pryor	W.Robson	A.Sanderson(Rainham Town)	D.J.Sewell
-.Sharman	S.Shaef	L.Sollof	J.G.Welch
G.F.West			

* The Jones boys were in fact twin brothers.

"A" Team Match Details

30 Aug IFLA   Away   Wycombe Wanderers "A"   2 – 1   Lewis,Connor
Romford "A": R.Brown;C.C.Livermore,J.S.Penfold;J.A.Says,G.F.West,C.B.Linage;
G.L.Lewis,J.R.Connor,C.Reynolds,P.J.Casey,L.R.Mackenzie.

6 Sept IFLA   Home   Wimbledon "A"   1 – 3   Reynolds
Romford "A": J.Daniels;C.C.Livermore,J.King;D.M.Jones,G.F.West,P.J.Casey;
G.L.Lewis,J.R.Connor,C.Reynolds,J.Moir,P.E.Clarke.

13 Sept IFLA   Away   St. Albans City "A"   2 – 1   Brown(2)
Romford "A": J.Daniels;R.Jones,J.King;W.P.Spelling,S.Cardew,S.Dales;
G.L.Lewis,S.Woolward,P.J.Casey,J.Moir,D.Brown.

20 Sept Frdly   Away   Glendale Youth Club   5 – 0   Hulse(4)Connor
Romford "A": J.Daniels;C.C.Livermore,J.S.Penfold;S.Dales,G.F.West,P.J.Casey;
From G.L.Lewis,J.R.Connor,R.Hulse,P.D.Hall,D.Brown,W.Price.

27 Sept IFLA   Home   Barking "A"   1 – 2   Casey
Romford "A": J.Daniels;R.Jones,J.King;S.Dales,W.P.Spelling,S.Cardew;
J.R.Connor,P.D.Hall,R.Hulse,P.J.Casey,D.Brown.

11 Oct EJC1R   Away   Brentwood Mental Hospital   3 – 1   Scorers unknown
Romford "A":
Team details unknown

18 Oct IFLA   Away   Kingstonian "A"   0 – 4
Romford "A":
Team details unknown

25 Oct IFLA   Away   Woking "A"   3 – 5   Scorers unknown
Romford "A":
Team details unknown

1 Nov EJC2R   Away   Hainault Forest   3 – 2   Scorers unknown
Romford "A":
Team details unknown

8 Nov IFLA   Home   Ilford "A"   1 – 3   Scorer unknown
Romford "A":
Team details unknown

15 Nov EJC3R   Away   Ilford Catholic   2 – 2   Scorers unknown
Romford "A":
Team details unknown

22 Nov IFLA   Away   Barking "A"   1 – 5   Scorer unknown
Romford "A":
Team details unknown

29 Nov EJCRp   Home   Ilford Catholic   3 – 4   Scorers unknown
Romford "A":
Team details unknown

13 Dec IFLA   Home   Dulwich Hamlet "A"   4 – 4   Scorers unknown
Romford "A":
Team details unknown

20 Dec IFLA   Away   Clapton "A"   2 – 3   Scorers unknown
Romford "A":
Team details unknown

27 Dec IFLA   Home   Woking "A"   4 – 5   Scorers unknown
Romford "A":
Team details unknown

3 Jan   IFLA   Away   Leytonstone "A"   5 – 1   Scorers unknown
Romford "A":
Team details unknown

10 Jan IFLA   Home   Kingstonian "A"   Match postponed due to fog

24 Jan IFLA   Home   St. Albans City "A"   3 – 4   Scorers unknown
Romford "A":
Team details unknown

7 Feb   IFLA   Home   Walthamstow Avenue "A"   5 – 2   Scorers unknown
Romford "A":
Team details unknown

14 Feb IFLA   Away   Walthamstow Avenue "A"   4 – 2   Elvish, Bowins, Brown, Berry
Romford "A":   ? ;   ? ,G.W.Berry;   ? , ? , ? ;
D.Bowins,   ? ,Elvish,   ? ,D.Brown.

21 Feb IFLA   Home   Wycombe Wanderers "A"   4 – 1   Scorers unknown
Romford "A":
Team details unknown

28 Feb IFLA   Away   Wimbledon "A"   0 – 1
Romford "A":
Team details unknown

7 Mar   IFLA   Home   Leytonstone "A"   2 – 2   Scorers unknown
Romford "A":
Team details unknown

14 Mar IFLA   Away   Dulwich Hamlet "A"   0 – 3
Romford "A":
Team details unknown

21 Mar IFLA   Home   Kingstonian "A"   1 – 3   Scorer unknown
Romford "A":
Team details unknown

18 Apr IFLA   Away   Ilford "A"   1 – 0   Scorer unknown
Romford "A":
Team details unknown

25 Apr IFLA   Home   Clapton "A"   2 – 5   Scorers unknown
Romford "A":
Team details unknown

"A" TEAM SUMMARY OF RESULTS SEASON 1952 – 53

		Home			Away			Goals		
	P	W	D	L	W	D	L	For	Ag	Pts
Isthmian League "A" Sect.	22	2	2	7	5	0	6	48	60	16
Essex Junior Cup	4	0	0	1	3	0	0	11	9	
Friendly	1	0	0	0	1	0	0	5	0	
Total	27	2	2	8	9	0	6	64	69	

Isthmian Football League "A" Section
Final Table

	P	W	D	L	Goals For	Ag	Pts
Kingstonian	22	16	3	3	77	38	35
Barking	22	13	6	3	55	31	32
Ilford	22	12	3	7	52	32	27
Wimbledon	22	9	9	4	48	35	27
Dulwich Hamlet	22	9	4	9	64	46	22
Woking	22	9	4	9	57	54	22
Wycombe Wanderers	22	8	4	10	46	49	20
Walthamstow Avenue	22	6	8	8	46	54	20
Clapton	22	7	4	11	43	61	18
Romford "A"	**22**	**7**	**2**	**13**	**48**	**60**	**16**
St. Albans City	22	5	3	14	36	82	13
Leytonstone	22	3	6	13	35	65	12

"A" TEAM APPEARANCES SEASON 1952 – 53

The following are known to have played in the "A" Team during the season.

G.W.Berry	D.Bowins	D.Brown	R.Brown
S.Cardew	P.J.Casey	P.E.Clarke	J.R.Conner
J.Daniels	S.Dales	-.Elvish	P.D.Hall
R.Hulse	D.M.Jones	R.Jones	J.King
G.L.Lewis	C.B.Linage	C.C.Livermore	L.R.Mackenzie(Old Libertians)
J.Moir	J.S.Penfold	W.Price	C.Reynolds
A.Says	W.P.Spelling	G.F.West	S.Woolward

"A" TEAM CUP RESULTS SEASON 1952 – 53

Essex County FA Junior Challenge Cup
Final: Brooklands Athletic   2   Rainham Old Boys   1

Romford's progress 1st Round	Away	Brentwood Mental Hospital	3 – 1
2nd Round	Away	Hainault Forest	3 – 2
3rd Round	Away	Ilford Catholic	2 – 2
Replay	Home	Ilford Catholic	3 – 4

DEPARTURES FROM THE CLUB SEASON 1952 – 53

The following players appear to have left the club during or by the end of the season. They may have been triallists and only played one or two games and then went elsewhere. New clubs are indicated where known.

G.W.Berry, P.J.Boreham (Dagenham), S.Cardew, E.R.Cave (Barking), J.W.Conner (Hornchurch & Upr.), F.Curtis (Rainham Town), W.Dawber (Hornchurch & Upr), D.W.Downs, W.Dowsett, D.Evans (Ford Sports), L.Evans (Brentwood & Warley), A.Gosshawk (Leyton), -.Hazell, A.F.Herbert (Briggs Sports), G.G.Howlett, -.Hoy, R.J.Innes (Woodford Town), T.R.Kelly (Ilford), G.J.Kenlay (Royal Air Force), A.Lawson (Dagenham), D.R.Lowman (Clapton), L.R.Mackenzie (Old Libertians), J.Moir (Dagenham), C.L.Moore (Rainham Town), H.M.Newman (Briggs Sports), W.Oram (Rainham Town), D.Pryor, A.Sanderson (Rainham Town), D.J.Sewell (Brentwood & Warley), -.Sharman, L.Sollof (Leytonstone).

THE CORONATION SIX-A-SIDE FOOTBALL TOURNAMENT
Held at Brooklands Saturday 30ᵗʰ May 1953
As reported in the *Romford Times,* Wednesday 3ʳᵈ June 1953
Merrifield leads Grays to easy six-a-side win

It was the goalkeepers' show. Brilliant ones, spectacular ones, comical ones. They kept the entertainment flowing along whenever Saturday's six-a-side soccer tournament at Brooklands was in danger of flagging. Result – Romford FC had a successful eight team, seven match tournament on their hands. Souvenir plaques went to final winners, Grays Athletic.

Hornchurch and Upminster, narrowly beaten by Ilford in the first round, provided the afternoon's top line comic-goalkeeper, Viv Young. And for all his fooling, he allowed only one shot to pass him, when hopelessly outside his own area, and prevented by the rules of the game from touching the ball.

But his antics brought a more light-hearted approach to the tournament that was being taken too seriously. Harvey scored the Hornchurch goal, but James was the name most clubs will remember. This well-built player could develop into a first-class full-back.

Match of the tournament: that Romford v Grays semi-final, and its 33 points. Man of that match, and the whole show – Rainham's irrepressible Roy Merrifield, guesting for Grays.

IT WAS OBVIOUS.....Roy it was who showed us how to pile up points in this style of soccer. Four points for a goal, one for a corner, and no offside rules. It was obvious. And Roy did just the obvious, keeping well up near Chris Moore. He scored four goals, forced two corners, and made the odd goal that brought Grays 22 points. Romford replied with goals from Bridge and Brooks, plus three corners for an 11 points total.

Earlier, Romford had made a bright start when giving Leytonstone a first round 12-9 knockout. Mark down Moore for the best save of the tournament when he fisted away a Noble penalty in this tie.

Dagenham, with Skinner, Butterworth, O'Sullivan, North, Armstrong and Hutson doing the honours, brought out the smash and grab technique to give Barking a first round KO. Then against Ilford in the semi-final they quickly turned on the pressure. Armstrong had a shot blocked, but Hutson followed through with a drive that gave them an early four points lead. Armstrong forced a corner for another point before Albert North ended a long mazy run with a goal, and the Daggers crossed over leading 9-0. Armstrong forced two more corners for an 11-0 win.

DAGENHAM TIRED. The six tired in the final though and goalkeeper Bob Skinner came out to help. Some of his passes were the most accurate of the tournament, but hurried shots by his partners gave Grays too many lives. Their two goals and a corner were eight points better than Dagenham's lone corner, forced through by North.

RESULTS. First round: Grays 12 points, Brentwood & Warley 4; Romford 12 (3 goals), Leytonstone 9 (two goals, one corner); Dagenham 12 (three goals), Barking 3 (three corners); Ilford 6 (goal, 2 corners), Hornchurch & Upminster 4 (one goal).

Semi-finals: Grays 22 (five goals, two corners), Romford 11 (two goals, 3 corners); Dagenham 11 (two goals, 3 corners), Ilford 0.

Final: Grays 9 (two goals, one corner), Dagenham 1 (corner).

CORONATION SIX-A-SIDE FOOTBALL TOURNAMENT STATISTICS:

Attendance: 2,247   Receipts: £117.12.0   Programmes: £18.12.3   Car Park: £1.16.9

First Round

GRAYS ATHLETIC	12 pts		BRENTWOOD & WARLEY	4 pts

ROMFORD	12 pts		LEYTONSTONE	9 pts

Goals: Perriman,Andrews,Bridge(pen)
Romford: C.L.Moore;V.H.Perriman,J.V.Eyett;H.W.Brooks(Capt),W.A.Bridge,G.W.Andrews.

DAGENHAM	12 pts		BARKING	3 pts

ILFORD	6 pts		HORNCHURCH & UPMINSTER	4 pts

Semi – Finals

GRAYS ATHLETIC	22 pts		ROMFORD	11 pts

Goals: Bridge,Brooks
Corners: Andrews,Brooks(2)

Romford: C.L.Moore;V.H.Perriman,J.V.Eyett;H.W.Brooks(Capt),W.A.Bridge,G.W.Andrews.

DAGENHAM	11 pts		ILFORD	0 pts

Final

GRAYS ATHLETIC	9 pts		DAGENHAM	1 pt

Romford v Harwich & Parkeston, Essex Senior Cup
3rd January 1953

The *Romford Times* coverage of Bridge's remarkable hat-trick in this match

PICTURE SPECIAL
Romford's Amateur Cup quarter final battle with Southall, February 1953

On 21st February 1953 Boro travelled to Southall and achieved a 1-1 draw.

Above: Southall defend in numbers!
Above left: Southall's goalkeeper Bennett watches in agony as Cunningham scores Romford's equalizer   *the Romford Recorder*

The match programme is pictured left. Boro are described as Romford Town, a name they hadn't used since 1921. The programme editor must have been an elderly Southall supporter!

Authors' collection

The replay took place on 28th February at Brooklands.

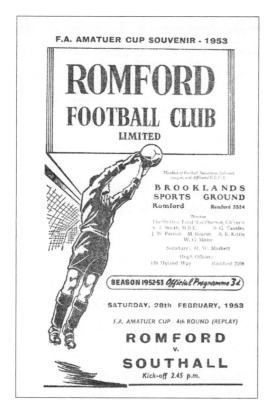

Romford were unable to find their best form and were defeated 2-1. Tragically, a supporter collapsed just after the kick off. The Red Cross officers took him by ambulance to Oldchurch Hospital where he was later certified dead.

A train carrying Southall fans arrived late. Due to the large crowd already inside the ground, they were allowed, for the first and only time ever at Brooklands, to sit on the grass behind the North Street goal.

Programme for the replay *Authors' collection*

No, not the January sales rush, but the arrival of Southall supporters *the Romford Recorder*

A record attendance at Brooklands– but how many exactly?

Following the replay versus Southall on 28th February newspapers quoted an attendance figure of 18,237 and it appears that this was the figure given to the national press.

The Official Gate Return Sheet gives a different picture, though. If the number registered column is totalled it amounts to 19,135. Turnstiles 22 and 23, however, record spectators who paid extra to enter the enclosure surrounding the grandstand. They had of course already been recorded on entering the ground. The total number transferring to the enclosure amounts to 2,104 and if this is deducted from the first mentioned total, records the amount of paying spectators as 17,031. If say fifty is added for officials, and complimentary tickets an official attendance of 17,081 is reached.

Using the same criteria for the first tie at Southall it can be seen that the Number Sold column totals 11,256 and deducting a figure of 719 for the transfer turnstiles a figure of 10,537 paying people is arrived at. Again adding 50 for complimentary tickets gives a final figure of 10,587.

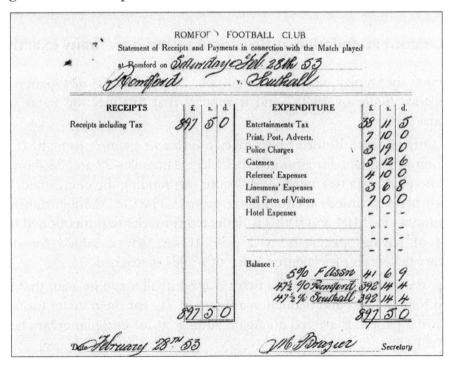

Although these Official Gate Return sheets show the number through each turnstile, the **Club did not release an official attendance figure**. On studying these returns and adding a figure for Season and Complimentary tickets, a final figure has been calculated and these figures have been quoted in this book.

SOUTHALL FOOTBALL CLUB
MATCH STATEMENT

Match v Rexford 46.   Date 21st Feb 1953

Competition Amateur Cup 4th Round.

TITLE No.	STARTING No.	FINISHING No.	NUMBER SOLD	RATE	AMOUNT £ s. d.	RATE OF TAX	TAX s. d.
1	53309	54077	768	1/-	38 8 .		
2	23461	24351	890	1/-	44 10 .		
3	56889	57961	1072	1/-	53 12 -		
4	56126	57308	1182	1/-	59 2 -		
5	32333	33557	1204	1/-	60 4 .		
6A	17779	18902	1123	1/-	56 3 -		
6A	220	351	131	1/-	6 11 -		
7	100	591	491	1/-	24 11 -		
8	100	938	838	.6	20 19 -		
9	201 507	1000 643	799 136	1/-	46 15 -		
10	0369	0966	597	6	14 18 6		
10A	100	621	521	1/-	26 1 -		
2.3.	ALL TICKETS				- - .		
8.5.E	239		239	1/-	11 19 -	4½	4 9 7½
W.51	400		400	1/-	20 - -	4½	7 10 -
W.52	152	72	80	1/-	4 - -	4½	1 10 .
676	Reserved Stand Seats		676	2/6	84 10 -	6½	18 6 2
	Reserved Enclosure		109	2/-	10 18 -	4½	2 - 10½
					583 1 6		33 16 8 .

LESS EXPENSES	£ s. d.		
Entertainment Tax	33 16 8		
Referee and Linesmen	8 12 4		
Gatemen 63 2/6	2 5 .		
Printing, Postage and Advertising	10 5 .		
Fares	7 . .		
Police	11 5 8	73 4 8	
		509 16 10	
5% Football Assoc.		25 9 10	

Balance to Divide £ 484 7 -

Rexford F.C. Share 242. 3. 6

Plus Fares 7. 0. 0

Cheque £ 249. 3. 6

Owing for 170 Stand Tickets 21. 5. 0

£ 227 . 18 . 6

Gate return and receipts figures recorded by Southall for the match on 21st February

In the last few seasons covered in this volume, Official Gate Return sheets are not available. The only figures available are the total of gate receipts and no turnstile numbers are known. The admission prices are known and an approximate calculation of the number of people to the pound has been used to obtain an approximate total attendance! The authors cannot claim that the attendance figures quoted are official ones, although no one is in a position to challenge them! *(Documents are from the authors' collection)*

Post Season Summary   Season 1952 – 53

Romford opened the season in fine style on 23rd August with a 3-1 victory at Bromley, Johnny Bee scoring all three. This was followed up with a hard-fought Thameside Trophy tie against Grays Athletic that ended 2-1 in Romford's favour. In the home game with Wycombe Wanderers Brooks gave Romford the lead in the third minute but shortly afterwards Syrett, Wycombe's goalkeeper, was injured in a collision with Johnny Bee. He had possibly cracked a rib or two and left the field, centre half Partridge replacing him in goal. Romford added four goals before half time. Syrett returned after the break, playing on the left wing, but was obviously struggling and was persuaded to leave the field by the referee. Romford piled on three more goals (Cunningham completing his hat-trick) and won 8-0. A tougher match came next when Romford secured a 1-0 victory over old rivals Walthamstow Avenue on 3rd September.

A challenging game against Wimbledon followed at Plough Lane with Romford losing 1-0. They then made the short trip to Newbury Park on 10th September for the replay of the previous season's Thameside Trophy final. Another Bee hat-trick helped Boro to a 4-2 victory over Leytonstone. Romford drew home games against St Albans City and Corinthian Casuals before their first FA Cup game on 27th September, away to semi-professional Clacton Town. British Rail provided a special train for Romford supporters. Three and a half thousand spectators witnessed a late equaliser from George Andrews to earn a replay. The following Thursday afternoon, 5,000 crowded into Brooklands for the replay. Disappointment was in store for the loyal Boro fans, however, as Clacton won 3-1.

Romford then went six games without defeat, securing fine victories over Casuals, Oxford City and Woking in the league, then a close win over local rivals Brentwood and Warley in the East Anglian Cup before 6,000 spectators. This was followed, however, by five games without a win! Heavy defeats were handed out by Leytonstone and St Albans in the league and Colchester United reserves in the East Anglian Cup. The fifth game was a thrilling Amateur Cup clash on 13th December at St Albans. City, with former Boro favourite Wally Winsley leading their attack, were the favourites. Romford, however, were leading 4-2 with only five minutes to go, but conceded two late goals to make a replay necessary. The following Saturday, nearly 5,000 spectators saw Romford at their best with a 4-0 victory to earn the right to meet Carshalton Athletic in the next round.

Romford won 3-0 against Ilford at Brooklands on Christmas Day and went to Newbury Park for the return game the following day. Thick fog made it impossible to see the kick-off from behind the goals. Romford were 4-1 ahead when the referee abandoned the game with only eight minutes remaining, despite the fog being no worse than at the start – much to the annoyance of Boro players and fans. The club's directors were urged to install floodlighting, as this cartoon in the *Romford Recorder* on January 19th illustrates.

Romford's next game was against old foes Harwich and Parkeston in the Essex Senior Cup. Old-timer Bill Bridge thrilled the Brooklands crowd with a hat-trick in a 5-3 win. Two league defeats followed, the first a 2-3 reverse at Wycombe and then a thrashing at home from Barking 2-5, the Boro men appearing to have the forthcoming cup tie with Carshalton in their minds! Came the day, 24th January, and Romford travelled to Carshalton with high hopes and came away with a 3-2 ticket into the next round. Next up was a first round exit from the Essex Senior Cup with a disappointing 1-2 loss at Grays Athletic.

Since the re-formation of the club in 1929 the directors had cherished high hopes of lifting the Amateur Cup, and this was becoming evident with the poor results between the rounds of the cup. Following the Grays defeat, Boro had to travel to high-flying Wycombe Wanderers where they had lost 2-3 a few weeks earlier. 11,000 spectators crammed into Loakes Park and home supporters were confident. A great performance from Romford secured a 5-0 victory and a passage into the last eight. A week later and the boys were again among the goals with a 7-2 win over Woking, Bee getting four of them.

The ten and a half thousand people in the Southall ground for the Amateur Cup quarter final witnessed a thrilling 1-1 draw. A record 17,081 piled into Brooklands for the replay on 28th February. With their special train arriving late, Southall fans were allowed to sit inside the perimeter wall behind the goals. With such a wonderful setting Romford alas failed to reach their best form and were defeated 2-1. Worse was to follow with three successive league defeats, Dulwich (away) 1-2, Wimbledon (home) 1-4 and Dulwich (home) 0-3, and the home attendance figures dropping to two and a half thousand.

A small improvement came next when lowly Clapton were defeated 3-1 at the Spotted Dog ground, followed by a further victory against Barking. A brilliant 4-2 win over high-flying Leytonstone was followed by a disappointing draw against lowly Oxford City. The last chance for a trophy ended on 20th April with the Thameside Trophy semi-final defeat by Barking, 3-4 after extra time. In the next game Boro again conceded four goals, but managed four themselves to earn a league point from Kingstonian. 1-1 draws were obtained against Isthmian League champions Walthamstow Avenue and Bromley, the runners-up. Disappointed and disillusioned supporters showed their feelings as only 600 turned up for the Bromley game. Romford rounded up the season with a 2-1 victory over Ilford in the replay of the game abandoned at Christmas. The season that saw record attendances, brilliant victories and disastrous defeats ended on a sombre note.

The reserve team only had an average season, finishing in a mid-table position in the league and losing to Briggs Sports reserves in the semi-final of the Essex Junior Cup at Rainham. An unusual highlight was hat-tricks in three successive games in September by Kenley(twice) and Tony Herbert. The "A" team finished in a lowly league position, perhaps understandable due to the large number of calls on their players by the reserve team. They experienced a number of high-scoring but narrow odd goal defeats during the season.

GLEANINGS FROM MANAGEMENT COMMITTEE MINUTE BOOKS
SEASON 1952-53

On **10th June 1952** Arsenal Football Club notified Romford that it wanted to sign Jimmy Smailes as a professional. The committee asked the Secretary to confirm with the player that he wanted this, and then reply to Arsenal.

On **16ᵗʰ September** they were informed that Johnny Bee had been approached by Chelsea FC inviting him to play for them as an amateur. No courtesy notification had been received, but it was decided not to proceed with a complaint.

On **23ʳᵈ September** it was agreed that the East Anglian Cup and Thameside Trophy be put on display in the offices of the Times Furnishing Company.

On **28ᵗʰ October** the Chairman reported that 17 raincoats were now to hand, and would be marked RFC in bold letters before issuing to stewards. The Hornchurch Cottage Homes agreed to provide six lads as ballboys for each match, four to be used on a rota basis.

On **20ᵗʰ December** they heard that George Andrews was approached by Tottenham Hotspur FC with a view to playing for them in mid-week games.

On **30ᵗʰ December** they had received a letter from the Tottenham Hotspur enclosing a copy of their letter addressed to George Andrews in accordance with FA Rules. It was agreed that "this matter be left to the player".

On **20ᵗʰ January** Hornchurch & Upminster Football Club extend an invitation to Romford to a friendly match to open their new ground at Hornchurch Stadium in August.

On **28ᵗʰ February** it was reported that a collection for the East Coast Flood Disaster Fund at the Amateur Cup replay against Southall had raised £52 19s 10d.

On **10ᵗʰ March** they voted to obtain copies of design, price etc. of club blazer badges, with the intention of presenting badges to players subject to a playing qualification.

On **24ᵗʰ March** the committee noted that George Andrews was to be married on 28ᵗʰ March and it was agreed that a small presentation be made to him to the value of £8, subject to the County FA approval.

On **7ᵗʰ April** the Club offer to provide match commentaries to the local hospitals. Mr H.A.Hughes applied to the G.P.O. for information.

Directors' Report for the twelve months ended 31ˢᵗ May, 1953

From the Accounts now presented it will be seen that the year ended 31ˢᵗ May, 1953 has been a successful one resulting in a gross profit of £1,062. This figure is £147 less than the profit for the previous year, but can be considered satisfactory having regard to the far from successful football season. Good Fortune seemed to desert the efforts of the players – no trophies were won and the first team finished seventh in the Isthmian League. In the Amateur Cup, few will forget the disappointment which was our lot at failing to win the replay at Brooklands against Southall after the memorable game at Southall. Gate Income naturally suffered and it will be seen is £894 down on last year, nevertheless income and expenditure generally can be regarded as fair.

....It will be seen from the Balance Sheet that the Property and Equipment A/c has had additions during the year of £4,003 – this arises from Capital Expenditure on the improvement of the Ground and purchase of equipment while there is a deduction of £2,225 in respect of the sale of property. In the last Report Members were advised that two houses had been sold but the sales had not at that time been completed.

The precast concrete wall along the Cedar Road and Willow Street sides of the Ground and the construction of the new entrance from Willow Street also referred to in the last Report have now been completed and found to be considerable improvements to the Ground. Crush Barriers have also been erected upon the terracing. These improvements cost the Company a sum in the neighbourhood of £4,000…..As to future Ground Improvements your Directors will continue to adhere to their policy of long term planning, the erection of a Grandstand with all necessary Offices is becoming more urgent every year and the Company's Architect has instructions to use every endeavour to obtain the necessary Licences for this project. It may well be that Licences will be obtained sooner than many expect when the Board will immediately seek financial assistance either by the issue of Debentures or the raising of a Mortgage upon the Company's property to enable this project to be carried out.

Floodlighting of football as is now provided by a number of the leading Clubs has been under serious consideration by your Directors, and while a number of schemes were considered, one proposal a few months back was actually approved by the Board and it was agreed to proceed therewith only for the whole project to fall through at the last moment for reasons outside the control of your Directors. The idea of Floodlighting at Brooklands had to be temporarily shelved – it is one full of difficulties, and expensive, but your Directors will continue to explore the problem and if a satisfactory proposal is forthcoming will give the same their earnest consideration…..

Your Chairman, The Right Honourable Lord Macpherson, is abroad in Australia and New Zealand and will for this reason not be present at the Annual Meeting. Mr Albert John Smith MBE has been appointed Vice-Chairman of the Board of Directors as from the 14th October, 1953.

Annual General Meeting held on Wednesday 20th January 1954
As reported in the *Romford Recorder*, Friday 22nd January 1954
'UP THE BOROUGH!'

The annual meeting of the Romford Football Club, Ltd., which was held on Wednesday, demonstrated once again that this, the sole amateur football club whose affairs are controlled by a limited company, is a well-governed and ably-directed organisation. The fact that a dividend of seven and a half per cent was declared is of little consequence; the vast majority of the shareholders are quite unconcerned by any question of profit. Their one and only interest is the well-being of the club and the playing success of the team, but the declaration of a maximum permitted dividend again this year gives the company a record of stability which will stand it in good stead when it seeks further capital to embark on the great scheme of grandstand development which it has in mind. This cannot be until the necessary building permits are available.

Underlying the discussions at the annual meeting, however, was the feeling that however capable the management of the company's business affairs, the matter of the most vital importance is the success of the team on the field. The most elaborate ground facilities are valueless to a football club unless the team is in winning vein or, at least, gives promise of victory in important competitions. It is true to say that the team has not been performing of late with quite that confidence which is associated with Romford, and tomorrow it is confronted by its stiffest task when it meets the redoubtable Crook Town of Durham in the FA Amateur Cup before a big gate at Brooklands and a million viewers who will see the game on their television sets. It is well known that the Romford team is resilient, that it responds best in severe matches, especially in the Amateur Cup, and it may well be that tomorrow's game will provide the surprise and the tonic which the club has been seeking for some time.....Despite injuries to some of the Romford players, we have a quiet optimism about the outcome and shall be proud to say with fervour, "Up the Borough!"

[same issue]

RAISING THE FLAG FOR ANOTHER SEASON

It had been mentioned at a football club meeting that the club flag had developed a hole. Mr Parrish said he would "look into it!" It is not known whether he was referring to the flag or the hole! By the season's end a new flag was fluttering on its mast and old faithful, the flag that had served Romford supporters so well for twenty years went into semi-retirement.

The new banner was the idea of the Supporters' Club chairman Mr C.E. Montford. He designed it, introduced his club's badge to it – and kept quiet about it. He made a surprise presentation of the flag to Supporters' Club secretary Mr H.Q. Baker. And old faithful? Now faded and tattered it will carry on the duties it performed so often in the past. It has gone with supporters to some of the best known clubs in the country. It has also toured Switzerland.

Season 1953-54

THE ROMFORD FOOTBALL CLUB LIMITED

Full Members of The Football Association
Full Members of Isthmian Football League
Affiliated to Essex County Football Association

Club Colours   Blue and Gold Shirts, White Shorts

Ground: Brooklands Sports Ground, Romford

Chairman: The Rt.Hon Lord Macpherson
Vice-Chairman: Mr A.J.Smith MBE (wef 14th Oct.)
Directors: Messrs. M.A.Brazier, A.E.Kittle, W.G.Mann,
J.W.Parrish, S.G.Tansley (died 4th October), Mr G.Richards JP (elected)
Company Secretary: Mr H.W.Muskett

Registered Office: 110,Hyland Way, Romford

Football Club Management Committee:
Chairman: Mr A.E.Kittle
Hon.Gen.Secretary: Mr M.A.Brazier   **Hon.Press Secretary:** Mr H.A.Hughes
Hon.Advt.Secretary: Mr R.S.Lyons   **Reserve XI Secretary:** Mr G.I.Howlett
Other Committee Members: Messrs. H.F.Knights, W.G.Mann,
J.W.Parrish, A.J.Smith MBE, S.G.Tansley

Mr R.S.Lyons and Mr H.C.Walker became Press Secretary and Advt. Secretary 23rd
February.
Statistics: Mr John Haley (Ex Officio)
Player Coach: Mr G.Cunningham   **Club Coach:** Jack Finch (w.e.f. March)
Reserve Team Coach: Mr G.W.Patterson   **Third Team Coach:** Mr A.J.Anderton
First Team Trainer: Mr W.C.Seddon   **Assistant:** Mr E.C.Hewitt
Reserve Team Trainer: Mr Fred Griffiths   **Groundsman:** Mr W.C.(Bill)Seddon
Assistant Groundsman: Mr Liddell   **Hon.Medical Officer:** Dr W.W.Craner

Bankers: Lloyds Bank Limited   **Auditors:** Iion V. Cummings & Co.

COMPETITIONS ENTERED SEASON 1953 – 54

The FA Challenge Cup
The FA Amateur Challenge Cup
The Isthmian Football League
The Essex Senior Cup
The East Anglian Cup
The Essex Thameside Trophy
The Thetford Charity Cup
The Isthmian Football League Reserve Section
The Essex Intermediate Cup

227

Southern Essex Combination Division Two
The Essex Junior Cup
Southern Essex Combination Cup

Admission Prices Season 1953 – 54

	First Team			Reserve Team		
	Adults	OAPs	Child	Adults	OAPs	Child
Ground	1/-	6d		6d	3d	
Ground & Enclosure	1/9	1/-		1/-	6d	
Grandstand	2/6	2/6		1/-	6d	

Note: Grandstand tickets for the Amateur Cup replay with Southall were priced three shillings.

Season Ticket Prices Season 1953 – 54

	Adults	OAPs & Children
Grandstand (All one price)	£1.10.0	
Ground & Enclosure	£1.1.0	12/6
Ground only	12/6	7/6

FINAL PUBLIC TRIAL
Wed.,19th Aug.,1953

POSSIBLES versus PROBABLES
Result not known

Attendance: 1,099   Receipts: £24.3.0
Possibles: J.D.Kain;H.Hunton,J.McCarthy;G.Norman,S.Prince,J.V.Eyett;
E.Foulsham,D.Ferdinando,H.Dobinson,W.A.Bridge,G.Davies.

Probables: R.Grainger;V.Jones,R.Chesterton;J.G.Welch,G.Fleetwood,P.J.Boreham;
H.W.Brooks,L.G.Casson,J.Bee,G.Cunningham,G.Andrews.

First Team Match Details

22 Aug Frdly   Away#   Hornchurch & Upminster   1 – 1   Cunningham
Attendance: 2,820
Romford: J.D.Kain;H.Hunton,R.A.Lamb;J.G.Welch,S.T.Prince,J.V.Eyett;
H.W.Brooks,G.D.Norman,J.Bee,G.Cunningham(Capt),G.W.Andrews.

26 Aug ETT1R   Away   Walthamstow Avenue   1 – 4*1   Cunningham(pen)
Romford: R.Brown;H.Hunton,R.A.Lamb;G.Fleetwood,S.T.Prince,J.V.Eyett;
H.W.Brooks,G.D.Norman,J.Bee,G.Cunningham(Capt),G.W.Andrews.

29 Aug IFL   Home   Corinthian Casuals   2 – 1   Bee(2)
Attendance: 2,408   Receipts: £106.1.6   Programmes: £13.1.1   Car Park: £4.18.9
Romford: R.Brown;J.C.McCarthy,R.A.Lamb;G.Fleetwood,S.T.Prince,J.V.Eyett;
H.W.Brooks,G.D.Norman,J.Bee,W.A.Bridge,G.Cunningham(Capt).

2 Sept EAC1R   Away   Crittall Athletic   4 – 0   Cunningham(pen)Bee(3)
Romford: R.Brown;J.C.McCarthy,R.A.Lamb;G.Fleetwood,S.T.Prince,J.V.Eyett;
H.W.Brooks,G.D.Norman,J.Bee,W.A.Bridge,G.Cunningham(Capt).

5 Sept IFL   Away   Wimbledon   1 – 1   Bee
Romford: R.Brown;H.Hunton,R.A.Lamb;G.Fleetwood,S.T.Prince,J.V.Eyett;
H.W.Brooks,G.D.Norman,J.Bee,W.A.Bridge,G.Cunningham(Capt).

9 Sept IFL   Away   Leytonstone   1 – 0   Bee
Romford: R.Brown;H.Hunton,R.A.Lamb;G.Fleetwood,S.T.Prince,J.V.Eyett;
H.W.Brooks,G.D.Norman,J.Bee,W.A.Bridge,G.Cunningham(Capt).

12 Sept IFL   Home   St. Albans City   1 – 3   Eyett
Attendance: 3,544   Receipts: £163.2.3   Programmes: £22.3.6   Car Park: £6.11.9
Romford: R.Brown;H.Hunton,R.A.Lamb;G.Fleetwood,S.T.Prince,J.V.Eyett;
H.W.Brooks,G.D.Norman,J.Bee,W.A.Bridge,G.Cunningham(Capt).

19 Sept IFL   Away   Wycombe Wanderers   2 – 1   Bee(2)
Romford: R.Brown;H.Hunton,R.A.Lamb;G.Fleetwood,S.T.Prince,J.V.Eyett;
H.W.Brooks,W.A.Bridge,J.Bee,G.Cunningham(Capt),G.W.Andrews.

26 Sept FAC1Q   Away   Chelmsford City   2 – 3   Bee,Cunningham
Attendance: 7,800
Romford: R.Brown;H.Hunton,R.A.Lamb;G.Fleetwood,S.T.Prince,J.V.Eyett;
H.W.Brooks,G.Cunningham(Capt),J.Bee,S.Shaef,G.W.Andrews.

3 Oct   IFL   Home   Woking   7 – 0   Brooks(2)Hall,Stolterhoft(2)Shaef,
                                                        Andrews
Attendance: 3,431   Receipts: £176.15.6   Programmes: £26.19.9   Car Park: £6.13.0
Romford: R.Brown;H.Hunton,J.V.Eyett;G.Fleetwood(Capt),S.T.Prince,G.D.Norman;
H.W.Brooks,N.Stolterhoft,P.D.Hall,S.Shaef,G.W.Andrews.

10 Oct IFL   Away#2 Corinthian Casuals   0 – 2
Romford: R.Brown;H.Hunton,J.V.Eyett;G.Fleetwood(Capt),S.T.Prince,G.D.Norman;
H.W.Brooks,N.Stolterhoft,J.Bee,S.Shaef,G.W.Andrews.

17 Oct IFL   Home   Kingstonian   8 – 3   Cunningham,Bee(6)Shaef
Attendance: 2,506   Receipts: £120.6.3   Programmes: £18.12.7   Car Park: £5.12.3
Romford: R.Brown;H.Hunton,J.V.Eyett;G.Fleetwood,S.T.Prince,G.D.Norman;
H.W.Brooks,S.Shaef,J.Bee,G.Cunningham(Capt),G.W.Andrews.

24 Oct EAC2R Home   Arsenal "A"   3 – 0   Cunningham(2)Shaef
Attendance: 5,964   Receipts: £314.14.6   Programmes: £32.2.4   Car Park: £6.7.9
Romford: R.Brown;H.Hunton,J.V.Eyett;G.Fleetwood,S.T.Prince,G.D.Norman;
H.W.Brooks,S.Shaef,J.Bee,G.Cunningham(Capt),G.W.Andrews.

31 Oct IFL   Away   St. Albans City   1 – 3   Bee
Romford: R.Brown;H.Hunton,J.V.Eyett;G.Fleetwood,S.T.Prince,G.D.Norman;
H.W.Brooks,A.J.Taylor,J.Bee,G.Cunningham(Capt),G.W.Andrews.

7 Nov IFL   Home   Oxford City   2 – 2   Ball(og)Andrews
Attendance: 2,748   Receipts: £123.13.9   Programmes: £16.14.5   Car Park: £5.18.6
Romford: R.Brown;H.Hunton,J.V.Eyett;G.Fleetwood,S.T.Prince,G.D.Norman;
H.W.Brooks,S.Shaef,J.Bee,G.Cunningham(Capt),G.W.Andrews.

14 Nov IFL   Away   Bromley   1 – 7   Andrews
Romford: R.Brown;H.Hunton,J.V.Eyett;G.Fleetwood,S.T.Prince,G.D.Norman;
H.W.Brooks,S.Shaef,P.D.Hall,G.Cunningham(Capt),G.W.Andrews.

21 Nov IFL   Home   Clapton   3 – 1   Cunningham,Hall,Bee
Attendance: 2,936   Receipts: £133.18.6   Programmes: £16.6.7   Car Park: £5.2.9
Romford: R.Brown;H.Hunton,J.V.Eyett;G.Fleetwood,S.T.Prince,G.D.Norman;
H.W.Brooks,P.D.Hall,J.Bee,G.Cunningham(Capt),G.W.Andrews.

28 Nov IFL   Home   Wycombe Wanderers   1 – 1   Bee
Attendance: 3,321   Receipts: £149.5.9   Programmes: £21.13.7   Car Park: £5.7.6
Romford: R.Brown;H.Hunton,J.V.Eyett;G.Fleetwood,S.T.Prince,G.D.Norman;
H.W.Brooks,P.T.Donovan,J.Bee,G.Cunningham(Capt),G.W.Andrews.

5 Dec IFL   Away   Kingstonian   5 – 1   Bee,Brooks(2)Donovan(2)
Romford: R.Brown;H.Hunton,J.V.Eyett;G.Fleetwood(Capt),S.T.Prince,A.J.Taylor;
H.W.Brooks,P.T.Donovan,J.Bee,G.D.Norman,G.W.Andrews.

12 Dec IFL   Away   Dulwich Hamlet   0 – 2
Romford: R.Brown;H.Hunton,J.V.Eyett;G.Fleetwood(Capt),S.T.Prince,A.J.Taylor;
H.W.Brooks,P.T.Donovan,J.Bee,G.D.Norman,G.W.Andrews.

19 Dec AC1R Home   Thetford Town   3 – 0   Andrews,Bee,Norman
Attendance: 4,904   Receipts: £264.9.6   Programmes: £26.0.0   Car Park: £6.11.3
Romford: R.Brown;H.Hunton,J.V.Eyett;G.Fleetwood(Capt),S.T.Prince,A.J.Taylor;
H.W.Brooks,P.T.Donovan,J.Bee,G.D.Norman,G.W.Andrews.

25 Dec IFL   Away   Ilford   1 – 2   Andrews
Romford: P.Gamman;H.Hunton,J.V.Eyett;G.Fleetwood(Capt),S.T.Prince,A.J.Taylor;
H.W.Brooks,P.T.Donovan,J.Bee,G.D.Norman,G.W.Andrews.

26 Dec IFL   Home   Ilford   2 – 2   Bee(2)
Attendance: 3,033   Receipts: £145.9.6   Programmes: £19.0.9   Car Park: £7.4.0
Romford: P.Gamman;H.Hunton,J.V.Eyett;G.Fleetwood(Capt),S.T.Prince,A.J.Taylor;
H.W.Brooks,P.T.Donovan,J.Bee,G.D.Norman,G.W.Andrews.

2 Jan IFL   Away   Woking   0 – 0*2
Romford: R.Brown;H.Hunton,J.V.Eyett;G.Fleetwood(Capt),S.T.Prince,A.J.Taylor;
H.W.Brooks,P.T.Donovan,G.D.Norman,S.Shaef,G.W.Andrews.

9 Jan   ESC1R   Home   Grays Athletic   0 – 2
Attendance: 4,179   Receipts: £229.18.0   Programmes: £22.5.6   Car Park: £5.6.6
Romford: R.Brown;H.Hunton,J.V.Eyett;G.Fleetwood(Capt),S.T.Prince,A.J.Taylor;
H.W.Brooks,P.T.Donovan,R.A.Lamb,G.D.Norman,G.W.Andrews.

16 Jan   IFL   Away   Woking   0 – 1
Romford: R.Brown;H.Hunton,J.V.Eyett;G.Fleetwood,S.T.Prince,A.J.Taylor;
H.W.Brooks,G.Cunningham(Capt),J.Bee,P.T.Donovan,G.W.Andrews.

23 Jan   AC2R   Home   Crook Town   1 – 1   Andrews
Attendance: 6,548   Receipts: £362.8.3   Programmes: £40.12.2   Car Park: £6.18.9
Romford: R.Brown;H.Hunton,J.V.Eyett;G.D.Norman,S.T.Prince,A.J.Taylor;
H.W.Brooks,G.Fleetwood,J.Bee,G.Cunningham(Capt),G.W.Andrews.

30 Jan   ACRp   Away   Crook Town   0 – 6
Attendance: 3,500
Romford: R.Brown;H.Hunton,J.V.Eyett;G.D.Norman,S.T.Prince,A.J.Taylor;
H.W.Brooks,G.Fleetwood,J.Bee,G.Cunningham(Capt),G.W.Andrews.

6 Feb   IFL   Home   DulwichHamlet   1 – 0   Bee
Attendance: 1,197   Receipts: £60.7.6   Programmes: £10.10.11   Car Park: £2.13.9
Romford: R.Brown;H.Hunton,J.V.Eyett;R.B.Abrahams,S.T.Prince,A.J.Taylor;
H.W.Brooks,G.D.Norman,J.Bee,G.Cunningham(Capt),G.W.Andrews.

13 Feb   IFL   Away   Clapton   1 – 2   Abrahams
Romford: R.Brown;J.Ford,J.V.Eyett;R.B.Abrahams,S.T.Prince(Capt),A.J.Taylor;
H.W.Brooks,E.Watts,C.Johnson,J.Bee,G.W.Andrews.

20 Feb   IFL   Away   Oxford City   3 – 1   Saunders(og)Johnson,Buswell(og)
Romford: R.Brown;J.Ford,J.V.Eyett;R.B.Abrahams,S.T.Prince(Capt),A.J.Taylor;
H.W.Brooks,P.T.Donovan,C.Johnson,J.Bee,G.W.Andrews.

27 Feb   IFL   Home   Barking   2 – 4   Bee,Johnson
Attendance: 2,323   Receipts: £102.11.6   Programmes: £16.11.0   Car Park: £4.2.6
Romford: R.Brown;J.Ford,J.V.Eyett;T.Buckley,R.B.Abrahams,A.J.Taylor;
G.Cunningham(Capt),E.Watts,C.Johnson,J.Bee,G.Andrews.

6 Mar   Frdly   Away   Tooting & Mitcham   2 – 5   Bee(2)
Romford: R.Brown;W.Onslow,J.V.Eyett;R.B.Abrahams,S.T.Prince(Capt),A.J.Taylor;
C.Johnson,G.Cunningham,J.Bee,E.Watts,G.W.Andrews.

13 Mar   IFL   Home   Bromley   2 – 3   Hall(2)
Attendance: 2,557   Receipts: £112.15.3   Programmes: £11.17.6   Car Park: £3.2.3
Romford: R.Brown;J.C.Dent,J.V.Eyett;R.B.Abrahams,S.T.Prince(Capt),A.J.Taylor;
G.W.Andrews,G.Cunningham,P.D.Hall,S.Shaef,G.J.Ruglys.

20 Mar   IFL   Home   Wimbledon   3 – 2   Watts,Cunningham,Bee
Attendance: 2,143   Receipts: £94.15.0   Programmes: £10.15.6   Car Park: £4.0.3
Romford: R.Brown;W.Onslow,J.V.Eyett;R.B.Abrahams,S.T.Prince(Capt),A.J.Taylor;
G.W.Andrews,G.Cunningham,J.Bee,E.Watts,G.J.Ruglys.

27 Mar   IFL   Away   Walthamstow Avenue   2 – 2   Bee,Cunningham(pen)
Romford: P.Gamman;L.Manza,J.V.Eyett;R.B.Abrahams,S.T.Prince(Capt),A.J.Taylor;
G.W.Andrews,G.Cunningham,J.Bee,E.Watts,G.J.Ruglys.

3 Apr   EAC3R   Away   Barking   1 – 1*   Bee
Romford: R.Brown;R.B.Abrahams,J.V.Eyett;G.Cunningham,S.T.Prince(Capt),S.Shaef;
G.W.Andrews,P.D.Hall,J.Bee,E.Watts,G.Ruglys.

8 Apr   ETTRp   Home   Walthamstow Avenue   0 – 1
Attendance: 2,586   Receipts: £126.5.6   Programmes: £5.0.0   Car Park: £4.11.0
Romford: R.Brown;R.B.Abrahams,J.V.Eyett;J.C.Dent,S.T.Prince(Capt),S.Shaef;
G.Ruglys,G.Cunningham,J.Bee,E.Watts,G.W.Andrews.

10 Apr   Frdly   Home   Leyton   2 – 2   Curley(2)
Attendance: 1,329   Receipts: £60.10.9   Programmes: £3.14.10   Car Park: £1.3.3
Romford: P.Gamman;H.Carroll,J.V.Eyett;T.McGeehan,S.T.Prince(Capt),K.Steward;
G.Cunningham,R.B.Abrahams,E.Curley,D.J.Rubery,G.Ruglys.

12 Apr   EACRp   Home   Barking   0 – 2
Attendance: 3,132   Receipts: £156.10.6   Programmes: £6.5.0   Car Park: £5.14.6
Romford: R.Brown;R.B.Abrahams,J.V.Eyett;K.Steward,S.T.Prince(Capt),S.Shaef;
G.Ruglys,E.Watts,E.Curley,J.Bee,G.W.Andrews.

17 Apr   IFL   Home   Leytonstone   4 – 3   Bee(2)Hall(2)
Attendance: 2,566   Receipts: £105.17.0   Programmes: £10.10.9   Car Park: £5.9.6
Romford: P.Gamman;R.B.Abrahams,J.V.Eyett;K.Steward,S.T.Prince(Capt),S.Shaef;
G.W.Andrews,T.V.McGeehan,P.D.Hall,D.J.Rubery,J.Bee.

21 Apr IFL Away Barking 1 – 2 Bee
Romford: P.Gamman;R.B.Abrahams,J.V.Eyett,S.Shaef,S.T.Prince(Capt),D.H.Taylor;
G.W.Andrews,T.V.McGeehan,P.D.Hall,D.J.Rubery,J.Bee.

24 Apr IFL Home Walthamstow Avenue 0 – 2
Attendance: 2,012 Receipts: £90.17.3 Programmes: £10.10.6 Car Park: £4.0.9
Romford: R.Brown;J.C.Dent,J.V.Eyett(Capt);S.Shaef,D.H.Taylor,K.Steward;
E.Watts,T.V.McGeehan,A.J.Vernon,E.Watts,D.J.Rubery.

1 May Frdly Home Brentwood & Warley 1 – 1 McGeehan
Attendance: 1,242 Receipts: £59.3.3 Programmes: £3.3.8 Car Park: £1.9.3
Romford: R.Brown;R.B.Abrahams,J.V.Eyett;J.C.Dent,S.T.Prince(Capt),S.Shaef;
A.Calver,T.V.McGeehan,A.J.Vernon,E.Watts,D.J.Rubery. (Calver on loan from Brentwood & W).

6 May TCC Away Thetford Town 3 – 3$ Watts(2)Andrews
Romford: P.Gamman;R.B.Abrahams,J.V.Eyett;S.Shaef,D.H.Taylor,T.V.McGeehan;
G.Cunningham(Capt),D.J.Rubery,D.Baird,E.Watts,G.W.Andrews.

* After Extra Time
*1 Abandoned after 105 minutes during extra time.
*2 Abandoned after 33 minutes due to fog.
\# Official opening of Hornchurch Stadium
\#2 Played at the Oval Cricket Ground
\$ Thetford won on the toss of a coin.

FIRST TEAM SUMMARY OF RESULTS 1953 – 54

	P	Home W	D	L	Goals For	Ag	Away W	D	L	Goals For	Ag	Pts
Isthmian League	28	7	3	4	38	28	4	2	8	19	26	27
FA Challenge Cup	1	0	0	0	0	0	0	0	1	2	3	
FA Amateur Cup	3	1	1	0	4	1	0	0	1	0	6	
Essex Senior Cup	1	0	0	1	0	2	0	0	0	0	0	
East Anglian Cup	4	1	0	1	3	2	1	1	0	5	1	
Thameside Trophy	1	0	0	0	0	0	0	0	1	0	1	
Thetford Charity Cup	1	0	0	0	0	0	0	1	0	3	3	
Friendlies	4	0	2	0	3	3	0	1	1	3	6	
Totals	43	9	6	6	48	36	5	5	12	32	46	

Isthmian Football League
Final Table

	P	W	D	L	Goals For	Ag	Pts
Bromley	28	18	3	7	76	45	39
Walthamstow Avenue	28	13	7	8	55	30	33
Wycombe Wanderers	28	15	3	10	65	44	33
Ilford	28	11	10	7	48	44	32
Corinthian Casuals	28	12	7	9	59	44	31
Woking	28	13	4	11	54	58	30
Leytonstone	28	12	5	11	58	48	29
St.Albans City	28	11	6	11	54	55	28
Dulwich Hamlet	28	11	6	11	55	57	28
Romford	**28**	**11**	**5**	**12**	**57**	**54**	**27**
Clapton	28	11	5	12	42	56	27
Barking	28	11	2	15	59	84	24
Kingstonian	28	8	7	13	59	71	23
Wimbledon	28	7	8	13	43	59	22
Oxford City	28	4	6	18	49	84	14

FIRST TEAM CUP RESULTS

FA Challenge Cup
Final: West Bromwich Albion 3 Preston North End 2

Romford's progress: 1st Qual   Away   Chelmsford City   2 -3

FA Amateur Challenge Cup
Final: Crook Town 1 Bishop Auckland 0
(After two 2 – 2 drawn games)

Romford's progress: 1st Round   Home   Thetford Town   3 – 0
2nd Round   Home   Crook Town   1 – 1
Replay   Away   Crook Town   0 – 6

Essex County FA Senior Challenge Cup
Final: Ilford 2 Grays Athletic 0

Romford's progress: 1st Round   Home   Grays Athletic   0 – 2

East Anglian Cup
Final: n/k

Romford's progress: 1st Round   Away   Crittall Athletic   4 – 0
2nd Round   Home   Arsenal "A"   3 – 0
3rd Round   Away   Barking   1 – 1
Replay   Home   Barking   0 – 2

Essex Thameside Challenge Competition
Final: n/k

Romford's progress: 1st Round   Away   Walthamstow Avenue   1 – 4**
Replay   Home   Walthamstow Avenue   0 – 1

** Abandoned in extra time

Thetford Charity Cup

Thetford Town 3 Romford 3
(Thetford won on toss of a coin)

FIRST TEAM DEBUTS SEASON 1953 – 54

1953   **Previous Club**

Date	Match		Player	Previous Club
22nd Aug.	v Hornchurch & U.	-	S.T.Prince	Barking
		-	G.D.Norman	Briggs Sports
		-	J.D.Kain	Leyton
29th Aug.	v Corinthian Cas.	-	J.C.McCarthy	Dagenham
3rd Oct.	v Woking	-	N.Stolterhoft	Stuttgart
		-	P.D.Hall	Reserves
31st Oct.	v St.Albans City	-	A.J.Taylor	Chelmsford City
28th Nov.	v Wycombe Wdrs.	-	P.T.Donovan	Ilford
25th Dec.	v Ilford	-	P.Gamman	Royal Air Force
1954				
6th Feb.	v Dulwich Hamlet	-	R.B.Abrahams	Ilford
13th Feb.	v Clapton	-	E.Watts	Glendale Y.C.
		-	C.Johnson	Deal Town
		-	J.Ford	Clapton
27th Feb.	v Tooting & M.	-	W.Onslow	Barking
13th Mar.	v Bromley	-	J.C.Dent	n/k
		-	G.J.Ruglys	Glendale Y.C.
27th Mar.	v Walthamstow Avenue	-	P.Manza	n/k
10th Apr.	v Leyton	-	T.V.McGeehan	Royal Air Force
		-	K.Steward	Army(Aldershot Res)
		-	E.Curley	Ford Sports

232

		-	**H.Carroll**	n/k
		-	**D.J.Rubery**	Halstead Town
21st Apr.	v Barking	-	**D.H.Taylor**	n/k
1st May	v Brentwood & W.	-	**A.J.Vernon**	Glendale Y.C.
		-	**A.Calver**	Loaned by B & W
6th May	v Thetford Town	-	**P.Baird**	Bishops Stortford

FIRST TEAM APPEARANCES SEASON 1953 – 54

	A	B	C	D	E	F	G	H	Total
Roy Abrahams	9	0	0	0	2	1	1	3	16
George Andrews	23	1	3	1	3	1	1	2	35
P. Baird	0	0	0	0	0	0	1	0	1
Johnny Bee	25	1	3	0	4	1	0	2	36
Bill Bridge	5	0	0	0	1	0	0	0	6
Harold Brooks	21	1	3	1	2	0	0	1	29
Reg Brown	23	1	3	1	4	1	0	2	35
Tim Buckley	1	0	0	0	0	0	0	0	1
A. Calver	0	0	0	0	0	0	0	1	1
H.Carroll	0	0	0	0	0	0	0	1	1
Graeme Cunningham	17	1	2	0	3	1	1	3	28
Eddie Curley	0	0	0	0	1	0	0	1	2
Johnny Dent	2	0	0	0	0	1	0	1	4
Pat Donovan	7	0	1	1	0	0	0	0	9
Jim Eyett	28	1	3	1	4	1	1	4	43
Joe Ford	3	0	0	0	0	0	0	0	3
Gordon Fleetwood	18	1	3	1	2	0	0	0	25
Peter Gamman	5	0	0	0	0	0	1	1	7
Peter Hall	7	0	0	0	1	0	0	0	8
Harry Hunton	18	1	3	1	1	0	0	1	25
Charlie Johnson	3	0	0	0	0	0	0	1	4
J.D.Kain	0	0	0	0	0	0	0	1	1
Ron Lamb	5	1	0	1	1	0	0	1	9
P.Manza	1	0	0	0	0	0	0	0	1
J.McCarthy	1	0	0	0	1	0	0	0	2
Tim McGeehan	3	0	0	0	0	0	1	2	6
Gordon Norman	17	0	3	1	2	0	0	1	24
Bill Onslow	1	0	0	0	0	0	0	1	2
Stan Prince	26	1	3	1	4	1	0	4	40
Derek Rubery	3	0	0	0	0	0	1	2	6
Gil Ruglys	3	0	0	0	2	1	0	1	7
Stan Shaef	9	1	0	0	3	1	1	1	16
Ken Steward	2	0	0	0	1	0	0	1	4
Nick Stolterhoft	2	0	0	0	0	0	0	0	2
Alan Taylor	13	0	3	1	0	0	0	1	18
Dennis Taylor	2	0	0	0	0	0	1	0	3
Jim Vernon	0	0	0	0	0	0	0	1	1
Eddie Watts	5	0	0	0	2	1	1	2	11
Johnny Welch	0	0	0	0	0	0	0	1	1
Total	308	11	33	11	44	11	11	44	473

FIRST TEAM GOALSCORERS SEASON 1953 – 54

	A	B	C	D	E	F	G	H	Total
Johnny Bee	25	1	1	0	4	0	0	2	33
Graeme Cunningham	4	1	0	0	3	0	0	1	9
George Andrews	4	0	2	0	0	0	1	0	7
Peter Hall	6	0	0	0	0	0	0	0	6
Harold Brooks	4	0	0	0	0	0	0	0	4

Stan Shaef	2	0	0	0	1	0	0	0	3
Eddie Watts	1	0	0	0	0	0	2	0	3
Nick Stolterhoft	2	0	0	0	0	0	0	0	2
Pat Donovan	2	0	0	0	0	0	0	0	2
Charlie Johnson	2	0	0	0	0	0	0	0	2
Eddie Curley	0	0	0	0	0	0	0	2	2
Jimmy Eyett	1	0	0	0	0	0	0	0	1
Gordon Norman	0	0	1	0	0	0	0	0	1
Roy Abrahams	1	0	0	0	0	0	0	0	1
Tim McGeehan	0	0	0	0	0	0	0	1	1
Own Goals	3	0	0	0	0	0	0	0	3
Total	57	2	4	0	8	0	3	6	80

Key to Competitions

A	Isthmian Football League
B	FA Challenge Cup
C	FA Amateur Challenge Cup
D	Essex County F.A. Senior Challenge Cup
E	East Anglian Cup
F	Essex Thameside Challenge Trophy
G	Thetford Charity Cup
H	Friendlies

Reserve Team Match Details

22 Aug IFLR Home Oxford City Res. 1 – 2 Bridge
Attendance: 635   Receipts: £10.14.6   Programmes: £1.4.4   Car Park: £0.4.6
Romford Res.: R.Brown;
  ? ,W.A.Bridge,H.R.Dobinson, ? , ? .

29 Aug ETT1R Away Barking Res. 1 – 2 Scorer unknown
Romford Res.:
Team details unknown

5 Sept IFLR Home Woking Res. 1 – 2 Vernon
Attendance: 1,021   Receipts: £19.9.0   Programmes: £2.10.8   Car Park: £0.7.0
Romford Res.: R.Grainger;J.C.McCarthy,V.Jones;V.H.Perriman,-.McDonald,R.J.Innes;
D.Bowins,A.Lawson,A.J.Vernon,-.Fernando,C.Hunnable.

12 Sept IFLR Away St. Albans City Res. 1 – 5 Casson
Romford Res.: J.D.Kain;J.C.McCarthy,W.Robson;F.D.Creed,-.McDonald,V.H.Perriman;,
P.Gunary,H.R.Dobinson,L.G.Casson,S.Shaef,P.T.Donovan.

19 Sept IFLR Home Wycombe Wanderers Res. 3 – 5 Dobinson,Norman,Shaef
Attendance: 923   Receipts: £18.5.6   Programmes: £2.6.1   Car Park: £0.9.0
Romford Res.: J.D.Kain;R.Chesterton,F.D.Creed;J.G.Welch,J.C.McCarthy,G.D.Norman;
P.Gunary,H.R.Dobinson,N.Stolterhoft,S.Shaef,J.C.Lloyd.

26 Sept IFLR Home Corinthian Casuals Res. 2 – 4 Lloyd(2)
Attendance: 689   Receipts: £12.7.3   Programmes: £1.9.11   Car Park: £0.5.9
Romford Res.: D.H.Oddy;R.Chesterton,R.Barton;J.G.Welch,J.C.McCarthy,G.D.Norman;
  ? ,N.Stolterhoft,H.R.Dobinson,P.D.Hall,J.C.Lloyd.

10 Oct IFLR Home Wimbledon Res. 2 – 5 Bridge(2)
Attendance: 1,012   Receipts: £20.19.0   Programmes: £2.11.5   Car Park: £0.8.0
Romford Res.: E.G.Tetchner;R.Barton,R.A.Lamb;J.G.Welch,J.C.McCarthy,A.J.Taylor;
W.A.Bridge,P.D.Hall,A.J.Vernon,P.T.Donovan,J.C.Lloyd.

17 Oct IFLR Away Leytonstone Res. 4 – 5 Donovan(2)Dobinson(2)
Romford Res.: T.Hudson;R.Barton,R.A.Lamb;J.G.Welch,J.C.McCarthy,A.J.Taylor;
P.Gunary,N.Stolterhoft,H.R.Dobinson,W.A.Bridge,P.T.Donovan.

24 Oct IFLR Away Corinthian Casuals Res. 3 – 3 Scorers unknown
Romford Res.: T.Hudson;R.Chesterton,R.A.Lamb;J.G.Welch,R.J.Innes,A.J.Taylor;
P.Gunary,P.D.Hall,H.R.Dobinson,P.T.Donovan,W.A.Bridge.

31 Oct IFLR Home Ilford Res. 0 – 4
Attendance: 1,008   Receipts: £19.2.3   Programmes: £2.3.9   Car Park: £0.9.0
Romford Res.: C.J.Nelson;R.Chesterton,R.A.Lamb;T.P.Buckley,J.C.McCarthy,R.J.Innes;
P.Gunary,N.Stolterhoft,H.R.Dobinson,P.T.Donovan,M.Bear.

7 Nov IFLR Away Kingstonian Res. 1 – 1 Hall
Romford Res.: C.J.Nelson;R.Chesterton,V.J.Durrance;T.P.Buckley,R.A.Lamb,A.J.Taylor;
P.Gunary,P.D.Hall,M.Bear,K.R.Prendergast,W.S.Millar.

14 Nov IFLR Home Bromley Res. 2 – 2 Bee,Donovan
Attendance: 936 Receipts: £18.11.0 Programmes: £2.9.2 Car Park: £0.10.9
Romford Res.: C.J.Nelson;R.Chesterton,T.A.Spencer;T.P.Buckley,R.A.Lamb,A.J.Taylor;
P.T.Donovan,H.R.Dobinson,M.Bear,J.Bee,W.S.Millar.

21 Nov IFLR Away Ilford Res. 1 – 6 Bear
Romford Res.: D.H.Oddy;R.Chesterton,T.A.Spencer;T.P.Buckley,R.A.Lamb,A.J.Taylor;
P.Gunary,-.Cobb,M.Bear,P.T.Donovan,W.S.Millar.

28 Nov IFLR Away Wimbledon Res. 3 – 4 Bear,Gunary,One(og)
Romford Res.: C.J.Nelson,J.Ford,F.D.Creed;-.Butler,R.A.Lamb,A.J.Taylor;
P.Gunary,P.D.Hall,M.Bear,H.R.Dobinson,W.S.Millar.

5 Dec IFLR Home Leytonstone Res. 1 – 3 Shaef
Attendance: 705 Receipts: £14.18.3 Programmes: £1.19.8 Car Park: £0.5.3
Romford Res.: D.H.Oddy;J.Ford,F.D.Creed;K.E.Hayward,R.A.Lamb,R.F.Smith;
J.C.Dent,H.R.Dobinson,P.D.Hall,S.Shaef,W.S.Millar.

12 Dec IFLR Home Clapton Res. 3 – 0 Hayward,Lamb,Buckley
Attendance: 630 Receipts: £11.18.9 Programmes: £1.11.0 Car Park: £0.7.9
Romford Res.: D.H.Oddy;J.Ford,F.D.Creed;T.P.Buckley,R.A.Lamb,R.F.Smith;
P.Gunary,K.E.Hayward,-.Wilkinson,S.Shaef,M.Bear.

19 Dec IFLR Away Barking Res. 1 – 7 Scorers unknown
Romford Res.:
Team details unknown

2 Jan IFLR Home Kingstonian Res. 1 – 0 Tracy
Attendance: 525 Receipts: £9.14.0 Programmes: £1.4.6 Car Park: £0.3.9
Romford Res.: P.Gamman;J.Ford,T.A.Spencer;T.P.Buckley,R.A.Lamb,R.F.Smith;
P.Gunary,H.R.Dobinson,-.Tracey,D.J.Rubery,M.Bear.

9 Jan IFLR Away Dulwich Hamlet Res. 4 – 9 Vernon(2)Hall,Cunningham
Romford Res.: P.Gamman;J.Ford,T.A.Spencer;T.P.Buckley,-.Tracey,R.F.Smith;
G.Cunningham,H.R.Dobinson,A.J.Vernon,P.D.Hall,M.Bear.

16 Jan EIC3R Home Stambridge United 4 – 1 Gunary(2)Vernon,Hall
Attendance: 918 Receipts: £22.13.0 Programmes: £2.3.9 Car Park: £0.6.9
Romford Res.: P.Gamman;J.Ford,F.D.Creed;T.P.Buckley,R.F.Smith,K.E.Hayward;
P.Gunary,P.D.Hall,A.J.Vernon,S.Shaef,W.S.Millar.

30 Jan EIC4R Home Benfleet United 2 – 0 Dent,Hall
Attendance: 714 Receipts: £17.14.0 Programmes: £1.14.5 Car Park: £0.5.6
Romford Res.: P.Gamman;J.Ford,V.J.Durrance;J.C.Dent,R.F.Smith,F.D.Creed;
P.Gunary,P.D.Hall,A.J.Vernon,S.Shaef,W.S.Millar.

6 Feb IFLR Away Bromley Res. 2 – 0 Vernon,Johnson
Romford Res.: P.Gamman;J.Ford,F.D.Creed;T.P.Buckley,R.A.Lamb,R.Griffiths;
A.J.Vernon,K.E.Hayward,C.Johnson,E.Watts,G.J.Ruglys.

13 Feb IFLR Home Dulwich Hamlet Res. 1 – 5 Scorer unknown
Attendance: 644 Receipts: £12.6.9 Programmes: £1.11.3 Car Park: £0.4.6
Romford Res.: P.Gamman;J.G.Welch,J.C.Dent;T.P.Buckley,F.D.Creed,T.Smith;
P.Gunary,K.E.Hayward,-.Wilkinson,S.Shaef,G.J.Ruglys.

20 Feb IFLR Home Barking Res. 2 – 3 Vernon,Bear
Attendance: 668 Receipts: £13.1.6 Programmes: £1.12.5 Car Park: £0.9.6
Romford Res.: P.Gamman;J.G.Welch,J.C.Dent;T.P.Buckley,T.Smith,R.Griffiths;
A.J.Vernon,M.Bear,S.Shaef,C.Johnson,G.J.Ruglys.

27 Feb EIC5R Away Ilford Res. 2 – 4 Gunary,Hall
Romford Res.: P.Gamman;F.D.Creed,J.C.Dent;J.G.Welch,T.Smith,R.Griffiths;
P.Gunary,P.D.Hall,A.J.Vernon,G.J.Ruglys,M.Bear.

6 Mar Frdly Away Uxbridge Town Res. 1 – 3 Scorer unknown
Romford Res.: P.Gamman;F.D.Creed,J.C.Dent;T.P.Buckley,T.V.McGeehan,G.D.Norman;
P.Gunary,P.D.Hall,C.Johnson,S.Shaef,G.J.Ruglys.

13 Mar IFLR Away Wycombe Wanderers Res. 0 – 9
Romford Res.: P.Gamman;J.Ford,F.D.Creed;G.D.Norman,W.Onslow,T.P.Buckley;
P.Gunary, ? , ? ,E.Watts,G.Hilditch.

20 Mar IFLR Away Oxford City Res. 1 – 6 Hall
Romford Res.: P.Gamman;P.Manza,F.D.Creed;G.D.Norman,T.V.McGeehan,K.E.Hayward;
P.Gunary,C.Johnson,P.D.Hall,D.J.Rubery,G.Hilditch.

27 Mar IFLR Home St. Albans City Res. 4 – 1 Scorers unknown
Attendance: 493 Receipts: £8.17.6 Programmes: £1.6.3 Car Park: £0.5.0
Romford Res.:
Team details unknown.

3 Apr IFLR Home Walthamstow Avenue Res. 1 – 4 Johnson
Attendance: 438 Receipts: £7.19.6 Programmes: £1.1.0 Car Park: £0.3.3
Romford Res.: P.Gamman;J.Ford,J.C.Dent;T.P.Buckley,T.V.McGeehan,K.Steward;
-.Wilkinson,K.E.Hayward,C.Johnson,D.J.Rubery,G.D.Norman.

19 Apr IFLR Away Clapton Res. 2 – 0 Scorers unknown
Romford Res.:
Team details unknown.

24 Apr IFLR Away Walthamstow Avenue Res. 2 – 2 Scorers unknown
Romford Res.:
Team details unknown.

1 May IFLR Away Woking Res. 2 – 3 Scorers unknown
Romford Res.:
Team details unknown.

RESERVE TEAM SUMMARY OF RESULTS SEASON 1953 – 54

	P	W	D	L	Goals For	Ag	Pts
Isthmian League Res. Section	28	5	4	19	51	100	14
Essex County FA Intermediate Cup	3	2	0	1	8	5	
Essex Thameside Trophy Res. Section	1	0	0	1	1	2	
Friendly Matches	1	0	0	1	1	3	
Total	33	7	4	22	61	110	

Isthmian Football League Reserve Section
Final Table

	P	W	D	L	Goals For	Ag	Pts
Walthamstow Avenue	28	20	4	4	67	34	44
Dulwich Hamlet	28	18	5	5	81	46	41
Leytonstone	28	18	5	5	65	43	41
Wimbledon	28	17	3	8	72	49	37
Barking	28	17	2	9	65	53	36
Wycombe Wanderers	28	14	4	10	78	55	32
Oxford City	28	12	5	11	57	49	29
Bromley	28	11	6	11	50	50	28
Corinthian Casuals	28	10	7	11	62	68	27
Ilford	28	8	5	15	56	66	21
Woking	28	8	5	15	51	69	21
Kingstonian	28	7	6	15	42	56	20
St.Albans City	28	6	4	18	45	72	16
Romford Reserves	**28**	**5**	**4**	**19**	**51**	**100**	**14**
Clapton	28	5	3	20	31	63	13

RESERVE TEAM CUP RESULTS

Essex County FA Intermediate Challenge Cup
Final: Briggs Sports Res. 2 Ilford Res. 1

Romford's progress: 1st Round & 2nd Round - Exempt
3rd Round Home Stambridge United 4 – 1
4th Round Home Benfleet United 2 – 0
5th Round Away Ilford Res. 2 – 4

Essex Thameside Challenge Competition Reserve Section
Final: n/k

Romford's progress: 1st Round Away Barking 1 – 2

RESERVE TEAM APPEARANCES SEASON 1953 – 54

The following players are known to have appeared in the reserve team during the season.

R.Barton(Betteshanger CW)	M.Bear	J.Bee	D.Bowins
W.A.Bridge	R.Brown	T.P.Buckley	-.Butler
L.G.Casson	R.Chesterton	-.Cobb	F.D.Creed
G.Cunningham	J.C.Dent	H.R.Dobinson	P.T.Donovan
V.J.Durrance	-.Fernando	J.Ford	P.Gamman(R.A.F.)
R.Grainger	R.Griffiths(St.Albans City)	P.Gunary	P.D.Hall
K.E.Hayward	G.Hilditch	T.Hudson	C.Hunnable(Glendale YC)
R.J.Innes	C.Johnson(Deal Town)	V.Jones(Eton Manor)	J.D.Kain
R.A.Lamb	A.Lawson	J.C.Lloyd(Dagenham)	P.Manza
J.C.McCarthy	-.McDonald	T.V.McGeehan	W.S.Millar
C.J.Nelson	G.D.Norman	D.H.Oddy	W.Onslow
V.H.Perriman	K.R.Prendergast	W.Robson	D.J.Rubery
G.J.Ruglys	S.Shaef	R.F.Smith	T.Smith
T.A.Spencer	K.Steward	N.Stolterhoft	A.J.Taylor
E.G.Tetchner	-.Tracey	A.J.Vernon	E.Watts
J.G.Welch	-.Wilkinson		

"A" Team Match Details

12 Sept SEC2# Away Harold Park 4 – 2 Warren(3)Smith
Romford "A": D.H.Oddy;V.J.Durrance,S.G.Allen;K.W.Woodcock,G.F.West(Capt), ? ;
D.Brown,-.Ingleton,R.F.Smith,A.Quiddington,K.G.Warren.

19 Sept Frdly Home Clapton "A" 0 – 2
Romford "A": J.F.Allen;V.J.Durrance,G.F.West(Capt);K.E.Hayward,G.D.Norman,K.R..Prendergast;
W.S.Millar,K.W.Woodcock,-.Goff,K.G.Warren,K.G.Benn.

26 Sept SEC2 Away G.E. Stores 4 – 1 Vernon(3)Norman
Romford "A": E.G.Tetchner;V.J.Durrance,F.D.Creed;G.D.Norman,G.F.West,R.J.Innes;
K.G.Benn,K.W.Woodcock,A.J.Vernon,K.R.Prendergast,W.S.Millar.

3 Oct SECCP Home Romford British Legion 1 – 2 Scorer unknown
Romford "A":
Team details unknown

10 Oct EJC1R Home Harold Park 8 – 1 Scorers unknown
Romford "A":
Team details unknown

17 Oct SEC2 Home Collier Row British Legion 0 – 8
Romford "A":
Team details unknown

31 Oct EJC2R Home Saxton 16 – 1 Scorers unknown
Romford "A":
Team details unknown

7 Nov Frdly Away Barking "A" Won
Romford "A":
Team details unknown

14 Nov EJC3R Home Leech United 2 – 4 Scorers unknown
Romford "A": D.H.Oddy;A.A.Spackman,V.J.Durrance;K.E.Hayward,F.D.Creed,D.M.Jones;
K.G.Benn,K.W.Woodcock,-.Wilkinson,K.R.Prendergast,J.C.Dent.

21 Nov SEC2 Away Hainault Forest 4 – 5 Scorers unknown
Romford "A":
Team details unknown

28 Nov SEC2 Home Hornchurch Spartan 3 – 4 Scorers unknown
Romford "A":
Team details unknown

5 Dec SEC2 Away Leech United 1 – 3 Scorer unknown
Romford "A":
Team details unknown

12 Dec SEC2 Home Upminster Old Boys 3 – 6 Scorers unknown
Romford "A": T.Hudson;G.F.West,A.A.Spackman;K.W.Woodcock,-.White,F.Patience;
-.Jeavins,-.Robinson,J.C.Dent,-.Tracey,W.S.Millar.

19 Dec SEC2 Away Collier Row British Legion 1 – 6 Scorer unknown
Romford "A": T.Hudson;G.F.West,A.A.Spackman;K.W.Woodcock,J.W.Parfitt,-.Wright;
-.Holt,E.Watts,J.C.Dent,-.Tracey,W.S.Millar.

2 Jan SEC2 Away Beacontree Heath Old Boys 1 – 1#2 Scorer unknown
Romford "A": S.G.Allen;D.H.Oddy,J.C.Dent;K.W.Woodcock,K.E.Hayward,F.D.Creed;
C.Hunnable,-.Boultwood,-.Wilkinson,H.R.Dobinson,W.S.Millar.

9 Jan SEC2 Home Dagenham Dock 9 – 0 Scorers unknown
Romford "A": T.Hudson,J.C.Dent;-.Crook;-.Boultwood,F.D.Creed, ? ;
D.H.Oddy,J.F.Allen,-.Taverner,-.Wilkinson,W.S.Millar.

23 Jan SEC2 Home Ockendon Old Boys 7 – 2 Scorers unknown
Romford "A":
Team details unknown

30 Jan SEC2 Away Hornchurch Spartan 5 – 1 Scorers unknown
Romford "A": R.Lock;J.W.Parfitt,P.Manza;R.B.Abrahams,G.D.Norman,R.Griffiths;
A.Loynes,R.Dursley,C.Johnson,K.Baxter,G.J.Ruglys.

6 Feb SEC2 Home Rainham Town "A" 1 – 1 Scorer unknown
Romford "A": D.H.Oddy;V.J.Durrance,J.W.Parfitt;J.C.Dent,P.Manza,K.W.Woodcock;
P.Gunary,G.D.Norman,-.Wilkinson,K.Baxter,W.S.Millar.

13 Feb SEC2 Away Dagenham Dock 4 – 4 Scorers unknown
Romford "A": D.H.Oddy;-.White,D.M.Jones;-.Leeper,G.D.Norman,J.Mizen;
-.Peaford,K.W.Woodcock,P.D.Hall,W.S.Millar,D.J.Rubery.

20 Feb Frdly Away Sherwoods Athletic n/k
Romford "A": D.H.Oddy;K.A.Steward.-.Harrison;V.J.Durrance,F.D.Creed,-.Dursley;
-.Peaford,K.R.Prendergast,-.Wilkinson,K.Baxter,D.J.Rubery.

27 Feb SEC2 Away Rainham Town "A" 0 – 1
Romford "A": D.H.Oddy;-.Banfield,K.E.Hayward;-.Brumnell,G.D.Norman,K.W.Woodcock;
-.Wilkinson,D.J.Rubery,K.Baxter,C.Johnson,G.Hilditch.

6 Mar SEC2 Home G.E. Stores 1 – 2 Scorer unknown
Romford "A": D.H.Oddy;-.Banfield,K.E.Hayward;V.J.Durrance,N.Cooper,R.Griffiths;
D.Cooper,K.R.Prendergast,-.Wilkinson,D.J.Rubery,W.S.Millar.

13 Mar SEC2 Away Ockendon Old Boys 3 – 2 Scorers unknown
Romford "A": D.H.Oddy;K.E.Hayward,P.Manza;R.Griffiths,A.West,K.W.Woodcock;
D.J.Rubery,K.Baxter,W.S.Millar. (played with only nine men)

27 Mar SEC2 Home Leech United 0 – 5
Romford "A":
Team details unknown

3 Apr SEC2 Home Hainault Forest 5 – 5 Scorers unknown
Romford "A": P.Kearsley;C.Webb,V.J.Durrance;K.W.Woodcock,D.H.Taylor,-.Chester;
A.J.Vernon,-.McIntyre,E.Curley,G.Hilditch,W.S.Millar.

10 Apr SEC2 Away Beacontree Heath Old Boys 0 – 2
Romford "A": P.Kearsley,-.Banfield,F.D.Creed;G.D.Norman,D.H.Taylor,-.Chester;
-.Wilkinson,K.E.Hayward,A.J.Vernon,J.C.Dent,W.S.Millar.

14 Apr SEC2 Home Beacontree Heath Old Boys 5 – 3 Scorers unknown
Romford "A": P.Kearsley;-.Banfield,F.D.Creed;-.Brumwell,D.H.Taylor,G.D.Norman;
-.Wilkinson,K.E.Hayward,A.J.Vernon,R.Griffiths,W.S.Millar.

17 Apr SEC2 Away Upminster Old Boys 1 – 2 Scorer unknown
Romford "A": P.Kearsley;V.J.Durrance,J.C.Dent;G.D.Norman,D.H.Taylor,F.D.Creed;
-.Wilkinson,K.E.Hayward,E.Curley,G.J.Ruglys,-.Palmer.

\# Harold Park withdrew from the league and their record was expunged
\#2 Match abandoned due to fog.

"A" TEAM SUMMARY OF RESULTS SEASON 1953 – 54

		Home			Goals		Away			Goals		
	P	W	D	L	For	Ag	W	D	L	For	Ag	Pts
South Essex Comb. Div. 2	20	3	2	5	34	36	3	1	6	23	27	15
South Essex Comb. Lge. Cup	1	0	0	1	1	2	0	0	0	0	0	
Essex Junior Cup	3	2	0	1	26	6	0	0	0	0	0	
Friendlies*	3	0	0	1	0	2	0	0	0	?	?	
SEC/Friendly**	1	0	0	0	0	0	1	0	0	4	2	
Totals	28	5	2	8	61	46	4	1	6	27	29	

Note: The above summary does not include the away League match against Beacontree Heath Old Boys, which was abandoned due to fog with the score level at one goal each.

* Two away friendly matches were played against Barking "A" and Sherwoods Athletic the results of which are not known.

** This match was originally a League game but Harold Park withdrew from the league and their record was expunged, thus the match is regarded as a friendly..

Southern Essex Combination Division 2
Final Table

					Goals		
	P	W	D	L	For	Ag	Pts
Leech United	20	16	2	2	81	23	34
Rainham Town "A"	20	16	2	2	65	20	34
Upminster Old Boys	20	13	3	4	70	40	29
Collier Row British Legion	20	11	2	7	64	21	24
Beacontree Heath Old Boys	20	9	3	8	44	46	21
Romford "A"	**20**	**6**	**3**	**11**	**57**	**63**	**15**
Hainault Forest	20	6	3	11	44	65	15
Ockendon United	20	5	4	11	44	65	14
G.E.Stores	20	4	4	12	37	65	12
Hornchurch Spartan	20	3	5	12	24	56	11
Dagenham Dock	20	4	3	13	26	72	11

"A" TEAM CUP RESULTS

Essex County FA Junior Challenge Cup
Final: Rainham Old Boys   2   Ramsey War Memorial   1

Romford's progress: 1st Round   Home   Harold Park   8 – 1
2nd Round   Home   Saxton   16 – 1
3rd Round   Home   Leech United   2 – 4

Southern Essex Combination Cup
Final: Montague L.Meyer   2   Collier Row British Legion   0

Romford's progress: Prel.   Home   Romford British Legion   1 – 2

"A" TEAM APPEARANCES SEASON 1953 – 54

The following players are known to have played in the "A" Team during the season.

R.B.Abrahams	J.F.Allen	S.G.Allen	-.Banfield
K.Baxter	K.G.Benn	-.Boultwood	-.Brunwell
-.Chester	D.Cooper	N.Cooper	F.D.Creed
-.Crook	E.Curley	J.C.Dent	H.R.Dobinson
V.J.Durrance	R.Dursley	-.Goff	R.Griffiths(St.Albans City)
P.Gunary	P.D.Hall	-.Harrison	K.E.Hayward
G.Hilditch	-.Holt	T.Hudson	C.Hunnable(Glendale YC)
-.Ingleton	R.J.Innes	-.Jeavens	C.Johnson

D.M.Jones	P.Kearsley(Brentwood & W)	-.Leeper	R.Lock
A.Loynes	P.Manza	-.McIntyre	W.S.Millar
J.Mizen	G.D.Norman	D.H.Oddy	-.Palmer
J.W.Parfitt(Glendale YC)	F.Patience	-.Peaford	K.R.Prendergast
A.Quiddington	-.Robinson	D.J.Rubery	G.J.Ruglys
R.F.Smith	A.A.Spackman	K.A.Steward	D.H.Taylor
-.Taverner	E.G.Tetchner	-.Tracey	A.J.Vernon
K.G.Warren	E.Watts	C.Webb	A.West
G.F.West	-.White	-.Wilkinson	K.W.Woodcock
.Wright			

"A" TEAM GOAL SCORERS SEASON 1953 – 54

Due to the extreme lack of information no goal scorers listing can be compiled.

DEPARTURES FROM THE CLUB SEASON 1953 – 54

The following players appear to have left the club during or by the end of the season. They may have been triallists and only played one or two games and then went elsewhere. New clubs are indicated where known.

R.B.Abrahams (Leytonstone), P.Baird (Bishops Stortford), J.Bee (Walthamstow Avenue), R.Brown (Hornchurch & Upminster), P.J.Boreham (Dagenham), W.A.Bridge (Dagenham), H.W.Brooks (Dagenham), T.P.Buckley (Dagenham), H.Carroll, L.G.Casson (Woodford Town), R.Chesterton (Rainham Town), G.Cunningham (Hendon), E.Curley(Ford Sports), D.I.Desborough (died in road accident), H.R.Dobinson (Hornchurch & Upminster), G.Fleetwood (Rainham Town), J.Ford (Hornchurch & Upminster), R.Grainger (West Thurrock), -.Hartgill (Hornchurch Spartan), H.Hunton (Sutton Utd), C.Johnson (Hornchurch & Upminster), R.Jones (Brentwood & Warley),V.Jones (Brentwood & Warley), J.D.Kain, R.A.Lamb (Leytonstone), A.Lawson, J.A.Lloyd (St.Albans City), P.Manza, J.C.McCarthy (Dagenham), C.J.Nelson (Haverford West), G.D.Norman (Briggs Sports), W.Onslow, V.H.Perriman (Hornchurch & Upminster), T.W.Smith (Clapton), N.Stolterhoft (returned to Germany), E.G.Tetchner (Rotary Hoes), A.J.Vernon (H.M.Forces**), E.Watts (H.M. Forces), J.G.Welch (Woodford Town).

** Still played for the Club when available.

Post Season Summary   Season 1953 – 54

Romford opened the season with a friendly game away to Hornchurch & Upminster on 22nd August to mark the the official opening of their new ground. It ended in a 1-1 draw. In the next game Boro were losing 4–1 away to Walthamstow Avenue in the Thameside Trophy first round, when due to failing light the game was abandoned. Corinthian Casuals were overcome in a league encounter that was followed by a 4-0 thrashing away to Crittall Athletic in the East Anglian Cup on 2nd September. Mixed fortunes followed over the next four league games: a 1-1 draw at Wimbledon, wins over Leytonstone and Wycombe Wanderers and finally a 1–3 defeat by St Albans City.

A tough first tie in the FA Cup saw Boro having to travel to New Writtle Street to meet Southern League professionals Chelmsford City on 26th September. Nearly 8,000 spectators witnessed a thrilling match, Romford losing narrowly by three goals to two.

Romford thrashed Woking 7-0 in their next game, then annoyed supporters by losing 2-0 to Corinthian Casuals at the Oval Cricket Ground. Boro, and particularly Johnny Bee, took it out on Kingstonian on 17th October with an 8-3 victory, Johnny getting a record six of the goals. More joy was to follow as Arsenal "A" were defeated 3-0 in the East Anglian Cup. This success was short-lived as St Albans won 3-0 at Clarence Park and Oxford City drew 2-2 at Brooklands, before the boys took a 7-1 beating at Bromley on 14th November, a humbling experience.

Home points against Clapton and Wycombe Wanderers were followed with another thrashing for luckless Kingstonian, this time by five goals to one. A disappointing 2-0 defeat followed at Champion Hill against Dulwich Hamlet before Romford started on the Amateur Cup trail. 5,000 turned up at Brooklands on 19th December to see Boro overcome Thetford Town 3-0. Ilford took three points off the boys over Christmas. Then came a fruitless journey to Woking where the match was abandoned due to fog with neither side managing to find the net! This was the start of another dismal run. Grays Athletic ousted the boys with a 2-0 win at Brooklands, and Woking won a league encounter 1-0.

The following week, 23rd January, a crowd of six and a half thousand at Brooklands saw a thrilling encounter with Crook Town in the Amateur Cup that ended in a one all draw. Boro supporters were excited and hopeful for the replay the following week, but were sadly let down as on a frozen and snow-covered pitch Romford were steamrollered 6-0. Amateur Cup hopes crushed yet again!

An improved performance with a 1-0 victory over Dulwich Hamlet was followed by another poor game losing 2-1 to lowly Clapton. A 3-1 win over a very poor Oxford City team on 20th February was no consolation, and three successive defeats were to follow. Romford scored two goals in each of these games, but really were soundly beaten by Barking, Tooting and Mitcham and Bromley.

A 3-2 victory over lowly Wimbledon and a two all draw against Walthamstow Avenue was no consolation. More cup disappointments were to follow! First a 1-1 draw with Barking after extra time in the East Anglian Cup was followed by exit from the Thameside Trophy with a 1-0 defeat by Walthamstow Avenue at Brooklands. A rather boring draw in a friendly match with Leyton was the precursor to defeat by Barking in the Thameside replay on 12th April. The Vicarage Field side won 2-0 at Brooklands before 3,000 angry Romford supporters. A four three victory over mid-table Leytonstone gave no encouragement and Boro failed to win any of the last four games of the season. They lost 2-1 away to Barking and two nil at home to Walthamstow Avenue in league games before drawing 1-1 with Brentwood and Warley at Brooklands in a friendly match.

Romford ended the season with a trip to Thetford Town on 6th May, where by invitation they competed for the Charity Cup. The match resulted in a three all draw and Thetford won the trophy on the toss of a coin. A lowly position in the league, no trophies and falling attendances was the start of disappointing seasons to come. The reserve team finished a lowly second from last in the league and were despatched from the cups at an early stage and the "A" team could only manage a mid table position.

A glance at the list of players who left Romford during or after the end of the season indicates that something was not well within the club. Despite County officials denying the existence of prohibited payments to amateur players, it was well known that the practice had been going on for many, many years. Clubs with thriving social clubs were often able to hide some of these payments, but many clubs tried to limit payments and suffered as a result. It is known that several of the early pioneers at Romford were very much entrenched in the ethos of amateur football and were reluctant to pay the players "boot" money.

ROMFORD FC DIRECTOR'S DEATH
Passing of Mr S.G. Tansley

As reported in the *Romford Recorder*, Friday 9ᵗʰ October 1953

A founder member, director and active worker for Romford Football Club, Mr Sydney George Tansley, of Oatlands, Brentwood Road, Romford, died at his home on Sunday, after having been ill for a long period, at the age of 73 years. Mr Tansley, who was a native of Romford, had been in ill health for some time, and a few years ago he made a world tour in search of health. Early this year he underwent a severe operation at Harold Wood Hospital and made a remarkable recovery which enabled him to resume his activities with the Romford Football Club.

In his younger days he played football for old Heath Park Celtic team and when the Romford FC was mooted in 1929 he associated himself with the enterprise and later became the treasurer, an office which he held up to his death. He also held office as president, vice-president, deputy president and chairman of the Ground Committee. He spent a great deal of his time on the Brooklands ground and expended much energy on improving its amenities.

During the war, when football was suspended, he helped to save the ground from being ploughed up for allottments and he also guaranteed the overdraft at the bank to ensure that the club would be able to resume when hostilities ceased.

He was one of the very active club members who were associated with the enterprise of forming a limited liability company in 1936, and he was appointed a director of the new company, retaining this office until his death.

For some years Mr Tansley conducted business as a coach builder. In 1930 he unsuccessfully sought election to the Romford Urban Council. He was a member of the Liberty of Havering Bowling Club. He leaves a widow and one daughter. The funeral took place yesterday (Thursday) at the Romford Cemetery, conducted by the Rev. Charles Green, a brother-in-law of Mr Tansley's daughter.

This tribute was paid to Mr Tansley in the Annual Report:

Your Directors take this opportunity of referring to the severe loss occasioned to the Company by the death of Mr Sydney George Tansley on the 4ᵗʰ October last. Mr Tansley was a founder member of the Club before its incorporation. He held various offices including that of Vice-Chairman and Treasurer and upon incorporation in 1937 became one of the first Directors.

It is true to say that few realised outside his close friends and colleagues his true worth to the Club Company – he gave his time and energy and knowledge and when times were lean during the war years with two of your other Directors preserved the financial position of the Company without thought of repayment or recognition. Repayment was made, but it was not at any time sought by Mr Tansley. He was a good friend to the Club and will be remembered well by all who knew him....

Romford's theme song, "By a Babbling Brook"

One of the players to leave Romford at the end of the 1953-4 season was the winger and prolific goalscorer Harold Brooks, who had been with the team since its re-formation in 1945 (and was to return briefly in 1958 before retiring from playing). Brooks was nicknamed The Mighty Atom because of his short stature (only 5 feet 4). In tribute to him, the club's theme song in the late 1940s and early 1950s was "By a Babbling Brook", a 1944 hit for Donald Peers. Many a time the Brooklands stadium echoed to the fans singing:

> In a shady nook / By a babbling brook,
> Mid the flowers / I spend hours
> Every day.
> That old shady nook / And that babbling brook,
> There my memories book
> Since you're away!
>
> I can hear the strain
> Of the birds' refrain,
> But it's not the same
> Since you have left me!
> In a shady nook / By a babbling brook,
> That's where I fell in love with you!

Harold Brooks as portrayed by the *Romford Times* cartoonist

GLEANINGS FROM MANAGEMENT COMMITTEE MINUTE BOOKS
SEASON 1953-54

On **14th July 1953** it was agreed to offer Mr A. Daer two season tickets for league matches and two complimentary tickets for cup ties, as recompense for allowing the Club the exclusive poster site on his premises at the Golden Lion Hotel corner of North Street. Mr.Hughes reported on the players' meeting and gave details of their requests: Car park special surface for training, the holding of an Annual Dinner, the possibility of visiting a Theatre occasionally and the provision of Club badges and ties subject to qualification.

On **1st September** the meeting regretted to learn of the tragic death of reserve team player D.I. Desborough in a car accident.

On **22nd September** we read that Social Secretary Mr T.F. Collett has organised a dance at the King's Head Hotel on Wednesday, 7th October, to which players would be invited.

On **29th September** Messrs. Colourtise submitted further designs for Club ties and blazers for consideration.

On **27th October** a letter of resignation was received from Bill Bridge who would be joining Dagenham FC.

On **1st December** the Chairman stated that Mrs Reg Sheward wished to offer a suitable trophy to commemorate her late husband's interest in the sport. The committee decided to recommend that Romford should challenge another side annually to play a match for the trophy. The proceeds would be donated to the Romford War Memorial Fund.

On **5th January 1954** an agreement was made with the BBC for televising the Amateur Cup tie with Crook Town 23rd January. The BBC set out their requirements and, "For the foregoing facilities they would be prepared to pay an inclusive Fee of seventy five pounds."

On **2nd February** the Secretary reported that owing to the poor weather and low attendance for the Amateur Cup replay at Crook Town, there was little hope of any financial gain from the match. Expenses for the official party of 21 amounted to £140. A postal order for five shillings was received from Mr G. Gill of Beckenham, as a gift from members of his household who enjoyed watching the Crook Town match on TV.

DIRECTORS' REPORT FOR THE TWELVE MONTHS ENDED 31ST MAY, 1954

From the Accounts now presented it will be seen that the year ended 31st May, 1954, has been financially a fairly successful one resulting in a gross profit of £310. This figure is £752 less than the profit for the previous year, but can be considered satisfactory, indeed remarkable, having regard to the extremely poor season experienced by the first XI. It can truly be said that the Club has not enjoyed more than perhaps one good season since it visited Wembley in 1949 but it is hoped that better fortune is not too far distant for the team. Gate Income has as a consequence suffered badly and as this is the chief source of the Company's income it has only been by close watch on expenditure and sound management in the Company's day to day finances that the present position has been obtained....

Your Directors have further considered the question of Floodlight football and have made no final decision thereon but they feel success must reward the efforts of the team before permitting the Company to be committed to an expenditure of possibly £5,000 or more to enable floodlight football to be enjoyed in reasonable conditions; moreover other amenities are more urgent.

With regard to the proposed new Grandstand your Directors have always pursued a long term policy and are very disappointed to report to Members that now that Licences and materials are available and all necessary Consents and approvals forthcoming they have to postpone their proposals in regard to the Grandstand for want of sufficient money to finance the building. Your Directors have therefore given instructions for the preparation of plans to allow for the present Grandstand to be enlarged, and for the 'Popular' Stand on the North side of the Ground to be extended at both ends to provide more covered accommodation for the supporter on the terraces.

It is felt that this is the most that Members can expect the Board to do at least until fortune again smiles on the Club. The cost of these additions and extensions, estimated at about £3,000, will be met by the increase of the Company's overdraft or by the raising of a loan. If on the other hand there are any suggestions whereby the Company's ambition to provide a first class Grandstand with players' accommodation, dressing rooms, etc., can be achieved sooner, your Directors will be only too pleased to receive them. The cost is estimated to be in the region of £35,000 to £50,000.

Reference was made in your Directors' Report for last year to the casual vacancy on the Board of Directors caused by the death of Mr S.G. Tansley. Your Directors filled this vacancy pursuant to the powers vested in them under the Articles of Association by electing Mr Glyn Richards JP for the period unexpired of Mr Tansley's term of office. Mr Tansley would have retired this year. As will be seen from the Notice of Meeting, Mr Richards is now seeking re-election. Reference was also made in the last Report of your Directors to them giving consideration to the whole structure of the Board. This was because of the death of Mr Tansley, and the proposed resignation of Mr Kittle. Since Mr Richards has joined the Board and Mr Kittle has signified his willingness to seek re-election at this Annual Meeting your Directors are of the opinion that no further action was required to be taken by them in this connection. Mr Kittle after most excellent service to the Club retired from the Chairmanship of the Management Committee at the beginning of the present football Season, Mr Richards being elected in his stead.

Mention has been made in various quarters as to the performance of the first team and many suggestions offered, but in football all clubs have their ups and downs. The Club has been working on a fixed policy designed to re-build the team on a sound and lasting basis. It is not founded on optimism but on a decided plan – even in the face of the possibility of a succession of lost matches. There is now every indication that this policy is likely to achieve results, establishing a good team spirit and creating a side which will be capable of serving the Club for several seasons to come.

Your Directors express their appreciation to the hard-core of supporters who have given their active and vocal encouragement to enable this policy to succeed and your Directors appeal to members and supporters alike to continue to give the support and encouragement that means so much. Your Directors extend to players and trainers and all those engaged in furthering the progress of the Club on behalf of the Members their very best wishes for the future, and their sincere thanks for their hard work and endeavour in their uphill struggle, confidently believing that the time is not far distant when our Club, as a result of such striving, will once again be gaining to itself fresh and well-deserved honours.

Annual General Meeting held on Friday 28th January 1955
As reported in the *Romford Recorder*, Friday 4th February 1955

FC SHAREHOLDERS WILL PLOUGH BACK PROFITS
'GESTURE OF CONFIDENCE' – CHAIRMAN

"Amendment carried!" Those words made history in the records of Romford Football Club Ltd, when they were spoken by the chairman, Lord Macpherson, at the company's annual meeting at the White Hart Hotel, Romford, on Friday. They ended a sensational discussion in which the shareholders decided to give up their dividend for the year ending 1954. It is the first time in the history of the company the shareholders have decided to forgo the dividend, and the first time in post-war years that there will be no division of profits.

It all began when Mr A.E. Blane moved an amendment to the Directors' annual report. He suggested that the recommendation of a payment of a dividend of 3¾ per cent, less tax, should not be accepted. He said that the company was made up of a considerable number of small shareholders who, he was convinced, put their money into the concern as sportsmen and not as investors.

"Their aim", he continued, "is to assist football in Romford - not to make profit out of it. There would be no hardship if they did not receive the few shillings or a few pounds that the dividend amounted to; they would be quite willing to leave it with the company to help tide it over a bad time".

Mr Blane said that shareholders also knew the company was faced with considerable capital expenditure and that every pound left in it would help football in Romford.

'PLOUGH IT BACK'. "I suggest that we plough back the profits" he said. "The Company is faced with this expenditure, including that of building a new stand and the money will at least save something".

Replying to Mr Blane, Lord Macpherson said the purpose of paying a dividend was to maintain a good record in the event of the company having to go out for a loan or fresh capital. Others lent support to Mr Blane's argument, however. Mr J. Graham said the sporting fraternity of Romford would provide new capital when it was required. He was convinced that no-one would object to going without a dividend this year.

Mr T.W. Locke, BEM, also supported the amendment. The man on the terraces, he said, felt the shareholders were feathering their nests at the expense of Romford football. "We want to cut out that idea. We are all interested in supplying good football for the area, and not in the money we might get from it. As sportsmen we want to do all we can to see the team getting back to its former strength. In this way we can help fulfil the promise of comfort - and we have promised it for many years - to the supporters".

The secretary of the company, Mr H.W. Muskett, said it took from 1937 to 1954 to get the present share capital fully subscribed, and on this basis he could not visualise the raising of £50,000, the sum required for a new grandstand, in Romford and in a reasonably short period.

'DON'T TAKE IT'. There was an easy solution for shareholders who desired to forego their dividend, said Mr Muskett. "If you don't want it, don't take it. You can throw your dividend slips into the fire and the money will automatically revert to the company".

Another shareholder suggested that when Romford wanted to borrow money the assets would be the main consideration of the bank or insurance company from whom it was obtained. "If we plough back the money it will help in that respect" he said.

The amendment was then put to the vote and carried by a large majority. Commenting on the decision, Lord Macpherson said he welcomed it. He said it was a magnificent gesture of goodwill and support from the shareholders, and as an expression of their confidence....

'BE PATIENT. Earlier, Lord Macpherson had spoken of the fortunes of the team this season. "It is not an extraordinary thing for football clubs to have a bad spell", he said. "In fact, I'd like you to mention to me any club, professional or amateur, that hasn't been through a lean period during its existence. Many have had more than one bad spell - yet this is the first time in 26 years that Romford FC has passed through such a season.

"I ask our supporters to be patient. We believe we are building on the right lines, but we must have time in order to complete the task which lies before us".

Lord Macpherson added that if a team won every match then it would be no attraction at all. "But of course", he added, "one can have too much of losing matches!" He continued, "I know of the work that has been going on behind the scenes, and I know how our Committee of Management has been facing up to its great task. I am confident that they are going to succeed in building a team which will restore lustre to the name of Romford.

A look at the club's record this season, commented Lord Macpherson, would show that in the majority of games Romford had lost by only a small margin of goals. "And remember", he said, "we have been opposed to some of the best amateur teams in England. Let us hope that the team will soon get into a winning vein".

[same issue]

Bill Mackenzie gets new job

Following the adoption of the directors' report, shareholders were told by Mr Glyn Richards, chairman of the management committee, that Romford were trying to impress on players that when their footballing days were over they were not necessarily finished with the club. He then revealed that Bill Mackenzie, still suffering from the effects of the leg he broke in September, had been elected to the selection committee.

Bill's father, Mr John Mackenzie, has also joined the club in an official capacity. He is chairman of a Spotters' Committee, formed to find new talent for the club. The 'spotters' will look out for experienced men, but their particular job is to watch promising youngsters in junior sides.

Lord Macpherson pointed out that two or three experienced players were needed to help weld the present side together. A flood of questions and views by shareholders were put to Mr Richards and selection committee chairman, Mr Jim Parrish. Answering a question regarding team coaching, Mr Richards said: "Jack Finch came to us on the recommendation of Sir Stanley Rous, secretary of the FA, and as the best man they could offer for the job. He is an ex-professional, and trained in the art of coaching. Who are we to condemn a man for not producing a miracle in his first season with the club? We've got to give him a chance".

Mr Parrish also had something to say on the subject. "Romford players have never had a better coaching system than they have now", he told shareholders. "In fact, they are almost bullied on training nights. Believe me, Jack Finch and George Patterson are doing a good job".

Commenting on the new Spotters' Committee, one supporter said he was not so much concerned in Romford finding new players as in keeping them. Mr Parrish answered that that was one of his biggest headaches. "What we want", he said, "is to find the right type of player: those who are one-club men".

Summing up, Mr Richards commented: "Though generally there is an air of gloom and pessimism outside the club, we are sure we are building on the right lines; and we are united in the belief that we are building for the future. I said at the beginning of the season that it would take blood, sweat and tears to weld together the team we require, but we believe we are well on the way to doing it.

"It is a fact, and not an excuse, that but for injuries we would have had a settled team long before this stage of the season. Four full-backs injured one after the other has caused considerable disorganisation in the team".

AN AERIAL VIEW OF BROOKLANDS

Brooklands viewed from the Cedar Road side in 1953

THE ROMFORD FOOTBALL CLUB LIMITED

Full Members of The Football Association
Full Members Isthmian Football League
Affiliated to Essex County Football Association

Club Colours: Blue and Gold Shirts, White Shorts

Ground: Brooklands Sports Ground, Romford

Chairman: The Rt.Hon Lord Macpherson
Directors: Messrs. M.A.Brazier, A.E.Kittle, W.G.Mann,
J.W.Parrish, G.Richards, A.J.Smith MBE

Company Secretary: Mr H.W.Muskett

Registered Office: 110,Hyland Way, Hornchurch

Football Club Management Committee:
Chairman: G.Richards JP
Hon.Gen.Secretary: Mr M.A.Brazier
Hon.Press Secretary: Mr R.S.Lyons   **Reserve XI Secretary:** Mr G.I.Howlett
Other Committee Members: Messrs. H.F.Knights, W.G.Mann,
J.W.Parrish, A.J.Smith MBE
Messrs. F.H.Adams and A.Adlam elected to Management Committee in January

Selection Committee: Messrs. J.W.Parrish, F.H.Adams and A.Adlam

Hon.Advt.Secretary: Mr H.C.Walker   **Third XI Secretary:** Mr A.J.Anderton

Statistics: Mr John Haley(Ex Officio)

Bankers: Lloyds Bank Limited   **Auditors:** Iion V. Cummings & Co.

Coach: Mr J.Finch   **Asst.Coach:** Mr G.W.Patterson

Reserve Team Trainer: Mr Fred Griffiths   **"A" XI Coach:** Mr A.J.Anderton

Trainer/Groundsman: Mr W.C.(Bill)Seddon   **Asst.Trainer:** Mr E.C.Hewitt

COMPETITIONS ENTERED SEASON 1954 – 55

FA Challenge Cup
FA Amateur Challenge Cup
Isthmian Football League
Essex County FA Senior Challenge Cup
East Anglian Cup
Essex Thameside Challenge Competition
Reg.Sheward Memorial Trophy
Thetford Charity Cup

Isthmian Football League Reserve Section

Essex County FA Intermediate Challenge Cup
Essex Thameside Challenge Competition Reserve Section

Southern Essex Combination Division Two
Essex County FA Junior Challenge Cup
Southern Essex Combination League Cup

Admission Prices Season 1954 – 55

	First Team			Reserve Team		
	Adults	OAPs	Child	Adults	OAPs	Child
Ground	1/-	6d		6d	3d	
Ground & Enclosure	1/9	1/-		1/-	6d	
Grandstand	2/6	2/6		1/-	6d	

Season Ticket Prices Season 1954 – 55

	Adults	OAPs & Children
Grandstand (All one price)	£1.10.0	
Ground & Enclosure	£1.1.0	12/6
Ground only	12/6	7/6

First Team Match Details

21 Aug IFL   Home   Barking   0 – 2
Attendance: 3,495   Receipts: £160.16.6   Programmes: £21.0.0   Car Park: £6.17.0
Romford: P.Gamman;D.H.Taylor,J.V.Eyett(Capt);R.N.Baldwin,R.D.Sampson,S.Shaef;
C.Halesworth,C.Sawkins,D.G.Negus,D.J.Rubery,G.W.Andrews.

26 Aug IFL   Home   Leytonstone   1 – 1   Cliss
Attendance: 2,323   Receipts: £103.1.6   Programmes: £8.11.7   Car Park: £4.13.9
Romford: P.Gamman;D.H.Taylor,J.V.Eyett(Capt);S.Shaef,R.D.Sampson,K.A.Steward;
A.W.Cliss,R.N.Baldwin,T.V.McGeehan,D.G.Negus,G.W.Andrews.

28 Aug IFL   Away   Dulwich Hamlet   1 – 4   Negus(pen)
Romford: P.Gamman;D.H.Taylor,J.V.Eyett(Capt);S.Shaef,R.D.Sampson,K.A.Steward;
A.W.Cliss,D.G.Negus,T.V.McGeehan,R.N.Baldwin,M.Thompson.

2 Sept IFL   Away   Leytonstone   0 – 2
Romford: P.Gamman;D.H.Taylor,J.V.Eyett;S.Shaef,S.T.Prince(Capt),A.J.Taylor;
A.W.Cliss,P.T.Donovan,T.V.McGeehan,R.N.Baldwin,D.J.Rubery.

4 Sept IFL   Home   Walthamstow Avenue   2 – 3   Baldwin,A.Taylor
Attendance: 3,145   Receipts: £147.11.6   Programmes: £19.15.2   Car Park: £7.0.9
Romford: P.Gamman;R.D.Sampson,D.H.Taylor;S.Shaef,S.T.Prince(Capt),A.J.Taylor;
A.W.Cliss,R.N.Baldwin,T.V.McGeehan,P.T.Donovan,G.W.Andrews.

11 Sept FACPR Home   Harwich & Parkeston   3 – 1   Baldwin,One(og),McGeehan
Attendance: 3,772   Receipts: £210.15.0   Programmes: £20.7.6   Car Park: £4.16.0
Romford: P.Gamman;J.C.Dent,J.V.Eyett;S.Shaef,S.T.Prince(Capt),A.J.Taylor;
A.W.Cliss,R.N.Baldwin,T.V.McGeehan,P.T.Donovan,G.W.Andrews.

18 Sept IFL   Away   St. Albans City   2 – 4   McGeehan(2)
Romford: P.Gamman;J.C.Dent,R.S.Pratt;S.Shaef,S.T.Prince(Capt),A.J.Taylor;
A.W.Cliss,R.N.Baldwin,T.V.McGeehan,P.T.Donovan,G.W.Andrews.

25 Sept FAC1Q Away   Leyton   2 – 4   A.Taylor,McGeehan
Romford: P.Gamman;W.Oram,J.C.Dent;S.Shaef,S.T.Prince(Capt),A.J.Taylor;
A.W.Cliss,R.N.Baldwin,T.V.McGeehan,P.T.Donovan,G.W.Andrews.

2 Oct IFL   Away   Wycombe Wanderers   1 – 8   McGeehan
Romford: P.Gamman;W.Oram,R.S.Pratt;S.Shaef(Capt),T.Baldwin,A.J.Taylor;
D.J.Rubery,R.N.Baldwin,T.V.McGeehan,J.Bloomfield,G.W.Andrews.

9 Oct IFL   Home   Kingstonian   2 – 2   McGeehan,Baldwin
Attendance: 2,275   Receipts: £102.17.2   Programmes: £17.5.4   Car Park: £4.8.6
Romford: P.Gamman;J.V.Eyett,R.S.Pratt;S.Shaef,S.T.Prince(Capt),A.J.Taylor;
D.J.Rubery,R.N.Baldwin,T.V.McGeeham,J.Bloomfield,G.W.Andrews.

16 Oct IFL   Away   Bromley   0 – 3
Romford: P.Gamman;S.Shaef,J.V.Eyett(Capt);K.A.Steward,W.F.Mackenzie,R.N.Baldwin;
D.J.Rubery,J.Bloomfield,T.V.McGeehan,A.F.Herbert,G.W.Andrews.

23 Oct IFL   Away   Wimbledon   1 – 1   Andrews
Romford: P.Gamman;W.F.Mackenzie,J.V.Eyett;S.Shaef,S.T.Prince(Capt),A.J.Taylor;
D.J.Rubery,J.Bloomfield,T.V.McGeehan,R.N.Baldwin,G.W.Andrews.

30 Oct IFL   Home   St. Albans City   1 – 2   Andrews
Attendance: 2,719   Receipts: £122.15.3   Programmes: £19.13.0   Car Park: £4.17.9
Romford: P.Gamman;W.F.Mackenzie,R.S.Pratt;S.Shaef,S.T.Prince(Capt),A.J.Taylor;
D.J.Rubery,J.Bloomfield,T.V.McGeehan,R.N.Baldwin,G.W.Andrews.

6 Nov IFL   Away   Woking   4 – 4   McGeehan,Baldwin(2)Rubery
Romford: J.W.Parrish;A.J.Taylor,R.S.Pratt;P.Devlin,S.T.Prince(Capt),J.V.Eyett;
D.J.Rubery,T.V.McGeehan,R.N.Baldwin,J.Bloomfield,G.W.Andrews.

13 Nov IFL   Home   Dulwich Hamlet   1 – 1   Baldwin
Attendance: 2,674   Receipts: £127.17.3   Programmes: £17.9.3   Car Park: £5.4.9
Romford: P.Gamman;A.J.Taylor,R.S.Pratt;P.Devlin,S.T.Prince(Capt),J.V.Eyett;
D.J.Rubery,T.V.McGeehan,R.N.Baldwin,J.Bloomfield,G.W.Andrews.

20 Nov IFL   Away#   Corinthian Casuals   0 – 1
Romford: P.Gamman;A.J.Taylor,D.H.Taylor;P.Devlin,S.T.Prince(Capt),J.V.Eyett;
D.J.Rubery,T.V.McGeehan,R.N.Baldwin,G.W.Andrews,A.F.Herbert.

27 Nov IFL   Home   Wycombe Wanderers   7 – 3   Shaef(2pens)Moring(og)Rubery(2)
                                                                  Herbert(2)
Attendance: 2,437   Receipts: £116.19.6   Programmes: £17.6.6   Car Park: £4.7.3
Romford: P.Gamman;R.E.Merrick,A.J.Taylor;P.Devlin,S.T.Prince(Capt),S.Shaef;
D.J.Rubery,J.Bloomfield,R.N.Baldwin,G.W.Andrews,A.F.Herbert.

4 Dec EAC1R   Home   Tottenham Hotspur "A"   3 – 3   Rubery,Baldwin(2)
Attendance: 2,552   Receipts: £153.9.3   Programmes: £20.0.6   Car Park: £4.14.0
Romford: P.Gamman;R.E.Merrick,A.J.Taylor;P.Devlin,S.T.Prince(Capt),J.J.Whitecross;
D.J.Rubery,J.Bloomfield,R.N.Baldwin,G.W.Andrews,A.F.Herbert.

11 Dec IFL   Away   Oxford City   2 – 5   Andrews,Rubery
Romford: P.Gamman;R.E.Merrick,A.J.Taylor;P.Devlin,S.T.Prince(Capt),J.J.Whitecross;
D.J.Rubery,J.Bloomfield,R.N.Baldwin,G.W.Andrews,A.F.Herbert.

18 Dec AC1R   Away   Uxbridge Town   2 – 4   Baldwin,Merrick
Romford: P.Gamman;R.E.Merrick,A.J.Taylor;P.Devlin,S.T.Prince(Capt),J.J.Whitecross;
D.J.Rubery,J.Bloomfield,R.N.Baldwin,G.W.Andrews,A.F.Herbert.

25 Dec IFL   Home   Ilford   0 – 3
Attendance: 2,477   Receipts: £109.0.6   Programmes: £8.15.3   Car Park: £7.1.6
Romford: P.Gamman;E.Ross,A.J.Taylor;P.Devlin,S.T.Prince(Capt),J.J.Whitecross;
D.J.Rubery,J.Bloomfield,G.J.Kenlay,G.W.Andrews,A.F.Herbert.

27 Dec IFL   Away   Ilford   0 – 3
Romford: P.Gamman;E.Ross,A.J.Taylor;S.Shaef,S.T.Prince(Capt),J.J.Whitecross;
D.J.Rubery,R.N.Baldwin,G.J.Kenlay,P.T.Donovan,G.W.Andrews.

1 Jan ESC1R   Home   Harwich & Parkeston   1 – 0   Herbert
Attendance: 2,175   Receipts: £111.7.6   Programmes: £10.10.6   Car Park: £3.7.3
Romford: P.Gamman;E.Ross,A.J.Taylor;P.Devlin,S.T.Prince(Capt),J.J.Whitecross;
D.J.Rubery,R.N.Baldwin,G.J.Kenlay,G.W.Andrews,A.F.Herbert.

8 Jan Frdly   Away   Bishops Stortford   2 – 5   Baldwin,Dankaro
Attendance: Club share of gate £15.18.7d
Romford: P.Gamman;E.Ross,A.J.Taylor;P.Devlin,S.T.Prince(Capt),J.J.Whitecross;
R.N.Baldwin,S.Dankaro,G.J.Kenlay,S.Shaef,G.W.Andrews.

22 Jan IFL   Away   Barking   0 – 0
Romford: P.Gamman;R.E.Merrick,J.V.Eyett;E.Ross,S.Prince(Capt),A.J.Taylor;
J.Bloomfield,P.Devlin,R.N.Baldwin,G.W.Andrews,D.J.Rubery.

29 Jan ESC2R   Home   Grays Athletic   1 – 5   Dankaro
Attendance: 4,404   Receipts: £234.6.6   Programmes: £20.14.0   Car Park: £7.3.0
Romford: P.Gamman;R.E.Merrick,J.V.Eyett;E.Ross,S.T.Prince(Capt),A.J.Taylor;
J.Bloomfield,R.N.Baldwin,S.Dankaro,G.W.Andrews,D.J.Rubery.

5 Feb Frdly   Home   Walton & Hersham   2 – 1   Halesworth,Andrews
Attendance: 1,213   Receipts: £60.19.0   Programmes: £4.15.3   Car Park: £1.17.0
Romford: D.Smith;R.E.Merrick,J.V.Eyett;E.Ross,S.T.Prince(Capt),A.J.Taylor;
R.N.Baldwin,S.Shaef,C.H.Halesworth,G.W.Andrews,D.J.Rubery.

12 Feb IFL   Home   Woking   6 – 9   Halesworth(2)Rubery(2)Shaef(2)
Attendance: 1,794   Receipts: £77.14.3   Programmes: £12.4.0   Car Park: £3.4.6
Romford: D.Smith;R.E.Merrick,J.V.Eyett,E.Ross,S.T.Prince(Capt),A.J.Taylor;
S.Dankaro,S.Shaef,C.H.Halesworth,G.W.Andrews,D.J.Rubery.

19 Feb EACRp   Home   Tottenham Hotspur "A"   3 – 1   Halesworth,Teece(og)Taylor
Attendance: 2,018   Receipts: £101.6.0   Programmes: £11.2.9   Car Park: £3.0.3
Romford: J.F.Allen;R.E.Merrick,J.V.Eyett;E.Ross,S.T.Prince(Capt),A.J.Taylor;
S.Dankaro,S.Shaef,C.H.Halesworth,G.W.Andrews,D.J.Rubery.

26 Feb IFL   Away   Clapton   4 – 1   Andrews(3)Halesworth
Romford: J.F.Allen;R.E.Merrick,J.V.Eyett(Capt);E.Ross,D.H.Taylor,A.J.Taylor;
S.Dankaro,S.Shaef,C.H.Halesworth,G.W.Andrews,D.J.Rubery.

5 Mar IFL   Home   Clapton   3 – 1   Halesworth(2)Rubery
Attendance: 1,611   Receipts: £71.10.3   Programmes: £10.11.3   Car park: £2.16.0
Romford: P.Gamman;R.E.Merrick,J.V.Eyett(Capt);E.Ross,D.H.Taylor,A.J.Taylor;
S.Dankaro,J.Bloomfield,C.H.Halesworth,G.W.Andrews,D.J.Rubery.

12 Mar IFL   Away   Walthamstow Avenue   1 – 7   Dankaro
Romford: P.Gamman;R.E.Merrick,J.V.Eyett;E.Ross,D.H.Taylor,A.J.Taylor;
S.Dankaro,S.T.Prince(Capt),C.H.Halesworth,G.W.Andrews,D.J.Rubery.

19 Mar IFL   Away   Kingstonian   1 – 1   Rubery
Romford: P.Gamman;R.E.Merrick,J.V.Eyett;E.Ross,D.H.Taylor,A.J.Taylor;
S.Dankaro,S.T.Prince(Capt),S.Shaef,G.W.Andrews,D.J.Rubery.

26 Mar IFL   Home   Corinthian Casuals   1 – 1   Shaef
Attendance: 1,511   Receipts: £65.7.9   Programmes: £9.16.3   Car Park: 2.16.0
Romford: P.Gamman;D.H.Taylor,J.V.Eyett;E.Ross,S.T.Prince(Capt),A.Marshall;
S.Dankaro,S.Shaef,C.H.Halesworth,G.W.Andrews,A.F.Herbert.

2 Apr IFL   Home   Oxford City   0 – 0
Attendance: 1,847   Receipts: £78.9.3   Programmes: £9.9.6   Car Park: £3.7.6
Romford: J.F.Allen;R.E.Merrick,J.V.Eyett;E.Ross,S.T.Prince(Capt),A.Marshall;
S.Dankaro,S.Shaef,C.H.Halesworth,G.W.Andrews,A.F.Herbert.

9 Apr EAC2R   Away   Crittall Athletic   2 – 0   Halesworth,Dankaro
Romford: P.Gamman;D.H.Taylor,J.V.Eyett;E.Ross,S.T.Prince(Capt),A.J.Taylor;
S.Dankaro,S.Shaef,C.H.Halesworth,G.W.Andrews,A.F.Herbert.

11 Apr ETT1R   Home   Walthamstow Avenue   2 – 3*   Herbert(2)
Attendance: 3,151   Receipts: £160.6.9   Programmes: £17.8.6   Car Park: £3.19.6
Romford: P.Gamman;D.H.Taylor,J.V.Eyett;E.Ross,S.T.Prince(Capt),A.J.Taylor;
D.J.Rubery,S.Shaef,C.H.Halesworth,G.W.Andrews,A.F.Herbert.

23 Apr IFL   Home   Bromley   1 – 0   Sheen(og)
Attendance: 904   Receipts: £33.17.3   Programmes: £   Car Park: £1.7.5
Romford: P.Gamman;D.H.Taylor,J.V.Eyett;J.J.Whitecross,S.T.Prince(Capt),A.J.Taylor;
S.Dankaro,S.Shaef,C.H.Halesworth,G.W.Andrews,A.F.Herbert.

25 Apr EACSF   Home   March Town   4 – 0   Shaef,Baldwin,Herbert,Andrews
Attendance: 1,913   Receipts: £93.19.0   Programmes: £20.4.9   Car Park: £2.5.0
Romford: P.Gamman;D.H.Taylor,J.V.Eyett;S.Shaef,S.T.Prince(Capt),A.J.Taylor;
S.Dankaro,P.Field,R.N.Baldwin,G.W.Andrews,A.F.Herbert.

28 Apr IFL   Home   Wimbledon   1 – 1   Herbert
Attendance: 1,341   Receipts: £52.9.0   Programmes: £   Car Park: £2.6.6
Romford: P.Gamman;R.E.Merrick,J.V.Eyett;E.Ross,S.T.Prince(Capt),A.J.Taylor;
S.Dankaro,S.Shaef,R.N.Baldwin,G.W.Andrews,A.F.Herbert.

12 May TCC   Away   Thetford Town   0 – 3
Romford: J.Allen;D.H.Taylor,J.V.Eyett;J.J.Whitecross,S.T.Prince(Capt),A.J.Taylor;
S.Dankaro,E.Ross,C.H.Halesworth,G.W.Andrews,D.J.Rubery.

14 May RSMT   Home   Charlton Athletic XI   3 – 5   Herbert,Andrews,Halesworth
Attendance: 2,906   Receipts: £150.7.9   Programmes: £20.16.0   Car Park: £4.10.0
Romford: P.Gamman;D.H.Taylor,J.V.Eyett;J.J.Whitecross,S.T.Prince(Capt),A.J.Taylor;
S.Dankaro,S.Shaef,C.H.Halesworth,G.W.Andrews,A.F.Herbert.

*After Extra Time
#Played at the Oval Cricket Ground

Romford   0   Barking   2
21st August 1954

George Andrews is thwarted by Barking goalkeeper Ray Secker

Both authors' collection

Romford   7   Wycombe Wanderers   3   (Isthmian League)
27th November 1954

Romford attacking the Wycombe goal

FIRST TEAM SUMMARY OF RESULTS 1954 – 55

| | Home | | | Goals | | Away | | | Goals | | |
	P	W	D	L	For	Ag	W	D	L	For	Ag	Pts
Isthmian League	28	3	6	5	26	29	1	4	9	17	44	18
FA Challenge Cup	2	1	0	0	3	1	0	0	1	2	4	
FA Amateur Cup	1	0	0	0	0	0	0	0	1	2	4	
Essex Senior Cup	2	1	0	1	2	5	0	0	0	0	0	
East Anglian Cup	4	2	1	0	10	4	1	0	0	2	0	
Thameside Trophy	1	0	0	1	2	3	0	0	0	0	0	
R.Sheward Trophy	1	0	0	1	3	5	0	0	0	0	0	
Thetford Charity Cup	1	0	0	0	0	0	0	0	1	0	3	
Friendlies	2	1	0	0	2	1	0	0	1	2	5	
Totals	42	8	7	8	48	48	2	4	13	25	60	

Isthmian Football League
Final Table

	P	W	D	L	Goals For	Ag	Pts
Walthamstow Avenue	28	21	1	6	80	38	43
St.Albans City	28	18	3	7	61	41	39
Bromley	28	18	2	8	66	34	38
Wycombe Wanderers	28	16	3	9	68	43	35
Ilford	28	13	5	10	64	46	31
Barking	28	15	1	12	55	51	31
Woking	28	12	3	13	75	79	27
Kingstonian	28	10	7	11	47	57	27
Leytonstone	28	10	4	14	35	51	24
Oxford City	28	10	3	15	43	74	23
Clapton	28	9	4	15	41	50	22
Wimbledon	28	10	2	16	48	62	22
Corinthian Casuals	28	9	3	16	50	65	21
Dulwich Hamlet	28	7	5	16	48	60	19
Romford	**28**	**4**	**10**	**14**	**43**	**73**	**18**

FIRST TEAM CUP RESULTS

FA Challenge Cup
Final: Newcastle United 3 Manchester United 1

Romford's progress: 1st Qual Home Harwich & Parkeston 3 – 1
2nd Qual Away Leyton 2 – 4

FA Amateur Challenge Cup
Final: Bishop Auckland 2 Hendon 0

Romford's progress: 1st Round Away Carshalton Athletic 2 – 4

Essex County FA Senior Challenge Cup
Final: Clapton 3 Grays Athletic 2

Romford's progress: 1st Round Home Harwich & Parkeston 1 – 0
2nd Round Home Grays Athletic 1 – 5

East Anglian Cup
Final: Grays Athletic 1 Romford 2 **

Romford's progress: 1st Round Home Tottenham Hotspur "A" 3 – 3
Replay Home Tottenham Hotspur "A" 3 – 1
2nd Round Away Crittall Athletic 2 – 0
Semi-Final Home March Town 4 – 0
Final Away Grays Athletic 2 – 1 **

Essex Thameside Challenge Competition
Final: n/k

Romford's progress: 1st Round   Home   Walthamstow Avenue   2 – 3 *

Reg Sheward Memorial Trophy
Romford   3   Charlton Athletic XI   5

Thetford Charity Cup
Thetford Town   3   Romford   0

* After Extra Time
** Played in the 1955 – 56 Season

FIRST TEAM DEBUTS SEASON 1954 – 55

1954

				Previous Club
21st Aug.	v Barking	-	R.N.Baldwin	Brentwood & Warley
		-	R.D.Sampson	Hornchurch & Upr.
		-	C.H.Halesworth	Harold Wood
		-	C.Sawkins	Barking
		-	D.G.Negus	Barking
26th Aug.	v Leytonstone	-	A.W.Cliss	Ware Town
28th Aug.	v Dulwich Hamlet	-	M.Thompson	Glendale Y.C.
18th Sept.	v St.Albans City	-	R.S.Pratt	Hainault Forest
2nd Oct.	v Wycombe Wdrs.	-	T.Baldwin	Enfield Town
		-	J.Bloomfield	Barking
6th Nov.	v Woking	-	P.Devlin	Leyton
27th Nov.	v Wycombe Wanderers	-	R.E.Merrick	Royal Navy
4th Dec.	v Tottenham H."A"	-	J.J.Whitecross	Briggs Sports
25th Dec.	v Ilford	-	E.Ross	Walthamstow Ave.

1955

8th Jan.	v Bishop's Stortford	-	S.Dankaro	Ldn. Schl. Economics
5th Feb.	v Walton & Hersham	-	D.Smith	Briggs Sports
19th Feb.	v Tottenham H."A"	-	J.F.Allen	n/k
26th Mar.	v Corinthian Cas.	-	A.Marshall	Rainham Town
25th Apr.	v March Town	-	P.Field	Glendale Y.C.

Players returned to the Club

1954

25th Sept.	v Leyton	-	W.Oram	Rainham Town
16th Oct.	v Bromley	-	W.F.Mackenzie	Leytonstone
		-	A.F.Herbert	Briggs Sports
6th Nov.	vWoking	-	Jim Parrish	From retirement
25th Dec.	v Ilford	-	G.J.Kenlay	RoyalAir Force

FIRST TEAM APPEARANCES SEASON 1954 – 55

	A	B	C	D	E	F	G	H	I	Total
Johnny Allen	2	0	0	0	1	0	0	1	0	4
George Andrews	26	2	1	2	4	1	1	1	2	40
Reg Baldwin	19	2	1	2	2	0	0	0	2	28
Tim Baldwin	1	0	0	0	0	0	0	0	0	1
Jimmy Bloomfield	12	0	1	1	1	0	0	0	0	15
Alf Cliss	5	2	0	0	0	0	0	0	0	7
Sunday Dankaro	9	0	0	1	3	0	1	1	1	16
John Dent	1	1	0	0	0	0	0	0	0	2
Pat Devlin	7	0	1	0	1	0	0	0	1	10
Pat Donovan	4	2	0	0	0	0	0	0	0	6
Jim Eyett	20	2	0	1	3	1	1	1	1	30

Joe Field	0	0	0	0	1	0	0	0	0	1
Peter Gamman	24	2	1	2	3	1	1	0	1	35
Chris Halesworth	8	0	0	0	2	1	1	1	1	14
Tony Herbert	9	0	1	1	3	1	1	0	0	16
Gerry Kenlay	2	0	0	1	0	0	0	0	1	4
Bill Mackenzie	3	0	0	0	0	0	0	0	0	3
Alf Marshall	2	0	0	0	0	0	0	0	0	2
Tim McGeehan	13	2	0	0	0	0	0	0	0	15
Ray Merrick	10	0	1	1	2	0	0	0	1	15
Derek Negus	3	0	0	0	0	0	0	0	0	3
Bill Oram	1	1	0	0	0	0	0	0	0	2
Jim Parrish	1	0	0	0	0	0	0	0	0	1
R. Pratt	6	0	0	0	0	0	0	0	0	6
Stan Prince	21	2	1	2	4	1	1	1	2	35
Eddie Ross	11	0	0	2	2	1	0	1	2	19
Derek Rubery	20	0	1	2	2	1	0	1	1	28
R. Sampson	4	0	0	0	0	0	0	0	0	4
R. Sawkins	1	0	0	0	0	0	0	0	0	1
Stan Shaef	20	2	0	1	3	1	1	0	2	30
Dennis Smith	1	0	0	0	0	0	0	0	1	2
Ken Steward	3	0	0	0	0	0	0	0	0	3
Alan Taylor	22	2	1	2	4	1	1	1	2	36
Dennis Taylor	12	0	0	0	2	1	1	1	0	17
Malcolm Thompson	1	0	0	0	0	0	0	0	0	1
Johnny Whitecross	4	0	1	1	1	0	1	1	1	10
Total	308	22	11	22	44	11	11	11	22	462

Key to Competitions

A	Isthmian Football League
B	FA Challenge Cup
C	FA Amateur Challenge Cup
D	Essex County F.A. Senior Challenge Cup
E	East Anglian Cup
F	Essex Thameside Trophy
G	Reg Sheward Memorial Trophy
H	Thetford Charity Cup
I	Friendly Matches

FIRST TEAM GOALSCORERS SEASON 1954 – 55

	A	B	C	D	E	F	G	H	I	Total
Reg Baldwin	5	1	1	0	3	0	0	0	1	11
George Andrews	6	1	0	0	1	0	1	0	1	10
Derek Rubery	8	0	0	0	1	0	0	0	0	9
Chris Halesworth	5	0	0	0	2	0	1	0	1	9
Tony Herbert	3	0	0	1	1	2	1	0	0	8
Tim McGeehan	5	2	0	0	0	0	0	0	0	7
Stan Shaef	5	0	0	0	1	0	0	0	0	6
Sunday Dankaro	1	0	0	1	1	0	0	0	1	4
Alan Taylor	1	1	0	0	1	0	0	0	0	3
Alfie Cliss	1	0	0	0	0	0	0	0	0	1
Derek Negus	1	0	0	0	0	0	0	0	0	1
Ray Merrick	0	0	1	0	0	0	0	0	0	1
Moring(Wycombe)o.g.	1	0	0	0	0	0	0	0	0	1
Teece(Tottenham H)o.g.	0	0	0	0	1	0	0	0	0	1
Sheen(Bromley)o.g.	1	0	0	0	0	0	0	0	0	1
Total	**43**	**5**	**2**	**2**	**12**	**2**	**3**	**0**	**4**	**73**

FIRST TEAM ATTENDANCE RECORDS SEASON 1954 – 55

Total Attendance All (23) First team Home Games	54,657
Total Attendance all (14) Isthmian League Games	30,553
Average Attendance Home League Games	2,182
Average Attendance All (8) Home Cup Ties	2,861
Highest Gate for Home League Game (Barking)	3,495
Highest Gate for Home F.A. Cup Tie (Harwich & P)	3,772
Highest Gate for Home Essex Senior Cup Ties (Grays Ath)	4,404
Highest Gate for Home East Anglian Cup Tie (Tottenham H. "A")	2,552
Highest Gate for Home Thameside Trophy Tie (Walthamstow Ave)	3,151

Reserve Team Match Details

21 Aug IFLR Away Walthamstow Avenue Reserves 1 – 6 Griggs
Romford Res.: J.F.Allen;J.C.Dent,R.S.Pratt,A.J.Taylor,T.V.McGeehan,K.E.Steward;
R.Griggs,P.D.Hall,G.J.Kenlay,P.Devlin,L.Bass.

28 Aug IFLR Home Bromley Reserves 0 – 5
Attendance: 708 Receipts: £12.16.9 Programmes: £1.14.11 Car Park: £0.4.6
Romford Res.: J.F.Allen;J.C.Dent,R.S.Pratt;G.E.Skipp,R.D.Sampson,A.J.Taylor;
J.Briggs,P.Devlin,C.H.Halesworth,C.Sawkins,L.Bass.

1 Sept IFLR Home Leytonstone Reserves 0 – 3
Attendance: 306 Receipts: £4.18.6 Programmes: £1.0.0 Car Park: £ None
Romford Res.: J.F.Allen;J.C.Dent,R.S.Pratt;P.Devlin,R.D.Sampson,K.E.Steward;
A.J.Vernon,P.D.Hall,C.H.Halesworth,C.Sawkins,G.J.Ruglys.

4 Sept IFLR Away Wycombe Wanderers Reserves 1 – 5 Denham
Romford Res.: J.F.Allen;J.C.Dent,R.S.Pratt;P.Devlin,A.Byford,K.A.Steward;
-.Denham,P.D.Hall,C.H.Halesworth,E.Watts,G.J.Ruglys.

11 Sept IFLR Away Ilford Reserves 1 – 1 Rubery
Romford Res.: J.Grice;R.S.Pratt,-.Gallagher;P.Devlin,A.Byford,T.Baldwin;
-.Denham,F.Wilson,K.E.Steward,D.G.Negus,D.J.Rubery.

16 Sept ETR1R Away Grays Athletic Reserves 0 – 5
Romford Res.: J.Grice;W.Oram,J.Ford;T.Baldwin,A.Byford,K.A.Steward;
C.Sawkins,F.Wilson,-.Watson,E.Watts,G.J.Ruglys.

18 Sept IFLR Home St. Albans City Reserves 2 – 2 Hall,Wilson
Romford Res.: J.Grice;-.Gallagher,W.Oram; T.Baldwin,A.Byford,K.A.Steward;
D.J.Rubery,F.Wilson,P.D.Hall,A.F.Herbert,M.Thompson.

2 Oct IFLR Away# Corinthian Casuals Reserves 1 – 4 Halesworth
Romford Res.: J.F.Allen;J.C.Dent,M.Bear;P.Devlin,A.Byford,K.A.Steward;
F.Wilson,A.F.Herbert,C.H.Halesworth,P.Field,M.Thompson.

9 Oct IFLR Away Dulwich Hamlet Reserves 1 – 4 Scorer unknown
Romford Res.:
Team details unknown.

16 Oct IFLR Home Corinthian Casuals Reserves 1 – 3 Ruglys
Attendance: 625 Receipts: £11.15.0 Programmes: £1.10.9 Car Park: £0.4.3
Romford Res.: J.F.Allen;N.P.Appleton,R.S.Pratt;P.Devlin,J.W.Parfitt,T.Baldwin;
P.T.Donovan,H.Coopman,C.H.Halesworth,P.Field,G.J.Ruglys.

23 Oct IFLR Home Woking Reserves 1 – 1 Scorer unknown
Attendance: 759 Receipts: £14.15.9 Programmes: £2.1.11 Car Park: £0.4.6
Romford Res.: J.F.Allen;N.P.Appleton,W.Oram;D.H.Taylor,J.W.Parfitt,P.Devlin;
C.H.Halesworth,H.Coopman,G.Smith,P.Field,A.F.Herbert.

30 Oct IFLR Away Wimbledon Reserves 3 – 3 Watts,Two others unknown
Romford Res.: Sel. J.F.Allen;N.P.Appleton,J.V.Eyett;P.Devlin,D.H.Taylor,T.Baldwin;
C.H.Halesworth,K.Suttling,S.Dankaro,E.Watts,A.F.Herbert.

6 Nov IFLR Home Wycombe Wanderers Reserves 1 – 4 Scorer unknown
Attendance: 1,006 Receipts: £20.18.6 Programmes: £2.10.0 Car Park: £0.10.6
Romford Res.:
Team details unknown

13 Nov IFLR Away Woking Reserves 0 – 3
Romford Res.:
Team details unknown

20 Nov Frdly Home Barnet Reserves 2 – 3 Scorers unknown
Attendance: 627 Receipts: £14.17.6 Programmes: £2.0.7 Car Park: £0.5.0
Romford Res.: J.F.Allen;R.F.Merrick,E.Ross;-.Hinds,J.Moreton,S.Shaef;
C.Sawkins,H.Coopman,C.H.Halesworth,P.T.Donovan,G.J.Ruglys.

27 Nov IFLR Away Kingstonian Reserves 3 – 4 Scorers unknown
Romford Res.: Sel. J.Grice;E.Ross,R.S.Pratt;J.J.Whitecross,T.V.McGeehan,A.Marshall;
C.H.Halesworth,F.Coopman,G.J.Kenlay,P.T.Donovan,G.J.Ruglys.

4 Dec IFLR Away Leytonstone Reserves 4 – 1 Scorers unknown
Romford Res.:

11 Dec IFLR Home Clapton Reserves 2 – 3 Scorers unknown
Attendance: 449 Receipts: £7.1.6 Programmes: £ Car Park: £0.2.3
Romford Res.:
P.T.Donovan,

18 Dec IFLR Home Dulwich Hamlet Reserves 0 – 4
Attendance: 552 Receipts: £10.19.3 Programmes: £1.14.7 Car Park: £0.5.0
Romford Res.: Sel. D.Smith;E.Ross,J.V.Eyett;J.Cade,D.H.Taylor,A.Marshall;
M.Whitworth,S.Dankaro,G.J.Kenlay,P.T.Donovan,G.J.Ruglys.

1 Jan IFLR Away St. Albans City Reserves 2 – 6 Scorers unknown
Romford Res.:
Team details unknown

8 Jan EIC3R Home Eton Manor Reserves 4 – 2 Scorers unknown
Romford Res.:
Team details unknown

22 Jan EIC4R Home Basildon Town Reserves 6 – 2* Halesworth(2)Ruglys(2)Donovan
Marshall
Attendance: 307 Receipts: £10.3.0 Programmes: £0.18.10 Car Park: £0.3.3
Romford Res.: J.F.Allen;N.P.Appleton,D.H.Taylor;J.Cade,J.W.Parfitt,A.Marshall;
C.H.Halesworth,P.Field,G.J.Ruglys,P.T.Donovan,-.Mitchell.

5 Feb IFLR Away Oxford City Reserves 4 – 4 Scorers unknown
Romford Res.: Sel. J.F.Allen;N.P.Appleton,D.H.Taylor;P.Devlin,J.W.Parfitt,J.J.Whitecross;
P.T.Donovan,A.Marshall,G.J.Kenlay,E.Watts,A.F.Herbert.

12 Feb IFLR Away Clapton Reserves 0 – 3
Romford Res.: J.F.Allen;N.P.Appleton,D.H.Taylor;J.Cade,J.W.Parfitt,J.J.Whitecross;
F.Wilson,J.Bloomfield,G.J.Kenlay,R.N.Baldwin,A.F.Herbert.

19 Feb EIC5R Home## Dagenham Reserves 1 – 5 Scorer unknown
Romford Res.: Sel. -.Fowler;N.P.Appleton,D.H.Taylor;D.A.Watt,J.W.Parfitt,A.Marshall;
P.T.Donovan,E.Watts,G.J.Kenlay,P.Field,G.J.Ruglys.

26 Feb IFLR Away Bromley Reserves 3 – 2 Herbert(2)Bloomfield
Romford Res.: P.Gamman;N.P.Appleton,J.W.Parfitt;J.J.Whitecross,P.Smith,A.Marshall;
J.Bloomfield,R.N.Baldwin,G.J.Ruglys,E.Watts,A.F.Herbert.

5 Mar IFLR Away Barking Reserves 3 – 0 Herbert(2)Kenlay
Romford Res.: J.F.Allen;N.P.Appleton,J.W.Parfitt;J.J.Whitecross,P.Smith,A.Marshall;
G.J.Kenlay,R.Baldwin,P.Field,P.T.Donovan,A.F.Herbert.

12 Mar IFLR Home Wimbledon Reserves 1 – 0 Field
Attendance: 594 Receipts: £10.16.9 Programmes: £0.15.4 Car Park: £0.4.3
Romford Res.:
? , ? ,G.J.Kenlay,P.Field

19 Mar IFLR Home Kingstonian Reserves 3 – 1 Baldwin,Herbert(2)
Attendance: 656 Receipts: £11.14.0 Programmes: £1.7.0 Car Park: £0.3.6
Romford Res.:
Team details unknown

2 Apr IFLR Home Oxford City Reserves 0 – 1
Romford Res.: D.Smith;D.H.Taylor,A.Taylor;J.J.Whitecross,P.Smith,A.Jewell;
D.Rubery,J.Bloomfield,R.Baldwin,P.Field,G.Ruglys.

9 Apr IFLR Home Ilford Reserves 2 – 1 Scorers unknown
Romford Res.:
Team details unknown

2 May IFLR Home Walthamstow Avenue Reserves 2 – 2 Scorers unknown
Attendance: 305 Receipts: £4.7.0 Programmes: £ Car Park: £ None
Romford Res.:
Team details unknown

7 May   IFLR   Home   Barking Reserves   1 – 3   Scorers unknown
Attendance: 313   Receipts: £4.14.0   Programmes: £   Car Park: £ None
Romford Res.:
Team details unknown

*   After Extra Time
\#   At Motspur Park.
\#\#   Played at Dagenham

RESERVE TEAM SUMMARY OF RESULTS SEASON 1954 – 55

	Home			Goals		Away			Goals		
	P	W	D	L	For	Ag	W	D	L	For	Ag	Pts
Isthmian League Reserve Section	28	3	3	8	16	33	3	3	8	27	46	18
Essex Intermediate Cup	3	2	0	0	10	4	0	0	1	1	5	
Essex Thameside Trophy Res.Sect.	1	0	0	0	0	0	0	0	1	0	5	
Friendly	1	0	0	1	0	0	0	0	0	2	3	
Totals	33	5	3	9	26	37	3	3	10	30	59	

Isthmian League Reserve Section
Final Table

	P	W	D	L	Goals For	Ag	Pts
Dulwich Hamlet	28	22	4	2	107	40	48
Wycombe Wanderers	28	19	4	5	76	31	42
Clapton	28	17	2	9	60	41	36
Walthamstow Avenue	28	14	5	9	58	44	33
Bromley	28	14	4	10	68	54	32
Woking	28	12	4	12	52	61	28
Corinthian Casuals	28	12	2	14	49	70	26
Wimbledon	28	10	5	13	51	52	25
Leytonstone	28	10	5	13	54	58	25
Barking	28	9	6	13	43	56	24
Oxford City	28	10	4	14	48	66	24
St.Albans City	28	8	6	14	35	51	22
Kingstonian	28	9	3	16	55	69	21
Romford Reserves	**28**	**6**	**6**	**16**	**43**	**79**	**18**
Ilford	28	7	2	19	44	71	16

RESERVE TEAM CUP RESULTS

Essex County FA Intermediate Challenge Cup
Final: Clapton Res.   3   Dagenham Res.   1

Romford's progress: 1st and 2nd Round   Exempt
3rd Round   Home   Eton Manor Res.   4 – 2
4th Round   Home   Basildon Town Res.   6 – 2 *
5th Round   Away   Dagenham Res.   1 – 5

Essex Thameside Challenge Competition Reserve Section
Final: n/k

Romford's progress: 1st Round   Away   Grays Athletic   1 – 5

*   After Extra Time

RESERVE TEAM APPEARANCES SEASON 1954 – 55

The following players are known to have appeared in the reserve team during the season.

J.F.Allen	N.P.Appleton	R.N.Baldwin	T.Baldwin
L.Bass	M.Bear	J.Bloomfield	J.Briggs
A.Byford	J.Cade	H.Coopman	S.Dankaro

-.Denham	J.C.Dent	P.Devlin	P.T.Donovan
J.V.Eyett	P.Field	J.Ford	-.Fowler
-.Gallagher	P.Gamman	J.Grice	R.Griggs
C.H.Halesworth	P.D.Hall	A.F.Herbert	-.Hinds(Enfield F.C.)
G.J.Kenlay	A.Marshall	T.V.McGeehan	R.F.Merrick
-.Mitchell	J.Moreton(Oxford City)	D.G.Negus	W.Oram
J.W.Parfitt	R.S.Pratt	E.Ross	D.J.Rubery
G.J.Ruglys	R.D.Sampson	C.Sawkins	S.Shaef
G.E.Skipp	D.Smith	G.Smith(Glendale YC)	P.Smith
K.E.Steward	K.Suttling(Aveley)	A.J.Taylor	D.H.Taylor
M.Thompson	A.J.Vernon	-.Watson	D.A.Watt
E.Watts	J.J.Whitecross	M.Whitworth(Barking)	F.Wilson

RESERVE TEAM ATTENDANCE RECORDS SEASON 1954 - 55

All details are unknown for reserve team games but the following is a rough guide.

It is assumed that the majority of the Season Ticket Holders would have attended most reserve team games and a figure in line with this has been added to the actual paying spectators.

Highest Home League Attendance is believed to be v Wycombe W.   1,006
The average Home Attendance Figure would be around   630

For Friendly Fixtures season ticket holders would have had to pay.

At the Home friendly against Barnet Reserves the attendance was   627

"A" Team Match Details

21 Aug Frdly   Away   Collier Row Athletic   1 – 4   Scorer unknown
Romford "A" : From : J.Grice,J.W.Parfitt,F.D.Creed,-.Bundy,T.Durrant.D.M.Jones,
G.Porter,A.M.Trimm,R.Smith,G.J.Ruglys,G.Hillditch,G.Dunn,F.C.Frost.

28 Aug Frdly   Away   Brooklands Athletic   Lost
Romford "A":
Team details unknown

4 Sept SEC2   Away   G.E. Stores   1 – 2   Scorer unknown
Romford "A": J.Grice;J.W.Parfitt,F.D.Creed;G.Dunn,T.Durrant,L.Phillips;
D.M.Jones,P.Emms,C.Murchison,F.C.Frost,F.Holdsworth.

11 Sept SEC2   Away   Ockendon Old Boys   4 – 1   Watson(3)Ruglys
Romford "A": J.F.Allen;J.Roberts,-.Ashton;B.J.Jewell,J.W.Parfitt,L.Phillips;
C.Sawkins,P.Emms,-.Watson,F.C.Frost,G.J.Ruglys.

18 Sept SEC2   Away   Hornchurch Spartan   7 – 0   G.Smith(5)Ruglys,Sawkins
Romford "A": P.Kearsley;-.Anderson,J.Roberts;-.Martin,J.W.Parfitt,B.J.Jewell;
C.Sawkins,P.Emms,G.Smith,P.Field,G.J.Ruglys.

25 Sept SEC2   Away   Collier Row British Legion   1 – 1   Millar
Romford "A": P.Kearsley;N.P.Appleton,J.Roberts;D.M.Jones,J.W.Parfitt,B.J.Jewell;
A.J.Vernon,C.Sawkins,-.Watson,J.Field,W.S.Millar.

2 Oct SEC2   Home   Heath United   0 – 5
Romford "A": P.Kearsley ;N.P.Appleton,J.Roberts;D.M.Jones,J.W.Parfitt,B.J.Jewell;
A.J.Vernon,-.Watson,C.Murchison,E.Watts,G.J.Ruglys.

9 Oct EJC1R   Home   Old Bealonians   13 – 1   Watts(5)Watson(4)Sawkins(3)Bridge
Romford "A": J.Grice;N.P.Appleton,J.Roberts;J.C.Dent,R.D.Sampson,L.Phillips;
C.Sawkins,F.C.Frost,-.Watson,E.Watts,C.Bridge.

16 Oct SEC2   Home   Hainault Forest   9 – 1   G.Smith(7)Emms,Jones
Romford "A": J.Grice;L.Davis,J.Roberts;-.Rothon,F.Wilson,D.M.Jones;
M.Whitworth,-.Sheppard,G.Smith,E.Watts,P.Emms.

23 Oct SECC1   Away   Heath United   0 – 2
Romford "A": J.Grice;L.Davis,J.Roberts;   ?   ,B.J.Jewell,D.M.Jones;
M.Whitworth,-.Sheppard,-.Watson,E.Watts,G.J.Ruglys.

30 Oct SEC2 Home Elm Park 7 – 0 G.Smith(4)Sawkins,Ruglys,Gould
Romford "A": J.Grice;L.Davis,J.Cade;J.Roberts,F.Wilson,B.J.Jewell;
C.Sawkins,B.Gould,G.Smith,P.Field,G.J.Ruglys.

6 Nov EJC2R Home Emerson Park 0 – 2
Romford "A": J.Grice;L.Davis,J.Roberts;J.W.Parfitt,F.Wilson,B.J.Jewell;
C.Sawkins,B.Gould,G.Smith,P.Field,-.Walker.

13 Nov SEC2 Home Hornchurch Wanderers 3 – 1 Sawkins,Ruglys,Field
Romford "A": J.Grice;L.Davis,J.Roberts;J.Cade,F.Wilson,-.Skeggles;
C.Sawkins,J.C.Dent,R.Mahoney,P.Field,G.J.Ruglys.

27 Nov SEC2 Home Phoenix 4 – 0 Dankaro(2)Jones,Sawkins
Romford "A": J.F.Allen;N.P.Appleton,J.Roberts;J.C.Dent,L.Davis,D.M.Jones;
C.Sawkins,G.Smith,S.Dankaro,D.H.Taylor,-.Wallace.

4 Dec SEC2 Home Emerson Park 5 – 1 Scorers unknown
Romford "A":
Team details unknown

11 Dec Frdly Away Clapton "A" 7 – 3 Vernon(4)Field(2)Whitworth
Romford "A": -.Fowler;N.P.Appleton,F.Wilson;D.M.Jones,B.J.Jewell,J.W.Parfitt;
M.Whitworth,P.Field,A.J.Vernon,C.Sawkins,J.Mitchell.

18 Dec SEC2 Home Hornchurch Spartan 4 – 1 Vernon(2)Field(2)
Romford "A": J.F.Allen;J.C.Dent,J.Roberts;C.Sawkins,B.J.Jewell,D.M.Jones;
G.Smith,P.Field,A.J.Vernon,J.Mitchell, *** .   (played with ten men)

1 Jan Frdly Away Leytonstone "A" 2 – 2 Field(2)
Romford "A": J.F.Allen;N.P.Appleton,J.Roberts;D.M.Jones,J.W.Parfitt,B.J.Jewell;
J.C.Dent,P.Field,A.J.Vernon,A.Wilson,J.Mitchell.

22 Jan Frdly Home Brentwood & Warley Reserves 3 – 4 Scorers unknown
Romford "A": -.Hills;J.Roberts,F.D.Creed;D.M.Jones,-.Burchfield,B.J.Jewell;
C.Sawkins,-.Etherington,D.Smith,W.S.Millar,-.Compton.

5 Feb SEC2 Home G.E. Stores 1 – 3 Whitworth
Romford "A": -.Fowler;   ?   ,   ?   ;   ?   ,   ?   ,B.J.Jewell;
M.Whitworth,

12 Feb SEC2 Away Hornchurch Wanderers 3 – 2 Ruglys,Jewell,Sawkins
Romford "A": -.Fowler;D.A.Watt,D.E.Roper;-.Attling,P.Cook,D.M.Jones;
-.Whitworth,G.J.Ruglys,C.Sawkins,B.J.Jewell,M.Whitworth.

26 Feb SEC2 Away Elm Park 0 – 2
Romford "A": D.Smith;
    ?   ,   ?   ,G.J.Kenlay

5 Mar SEC2 Home Ockendon United 16 – 0 Scorers unknown
Romford "A":
Team details unknown

12 Mar SEC2 Away Hainault Forest 2 – 0 Scorers unknown
Romford "A":
Team details unknown

19 Mar SEC2 Away Emerson Park 3 – 0 Scorers unknown
Romford "A":
Team details unknown

26 Mar SEC2 Away Heath United 0 – 4
Romford "A":
Team details unkoown

2 Apr Frdly Away Glendale Youth Club 3 – 2 Scorers unknown
Romford "A":
Team details unknown

n/k SEC2 Home Collier Row British Legion 4 – 1 Scorers unknown
Romford "A":
Team details unknown

n/k SEC2 Away Phoenix 1 – 0 Scorer unknown
Romford "A":
Team details unknown

"A" TEAM SUMMARY OF RESULTS SEASON 1954 – 55

	P	W	D	L	For	Ag	W	D	L	For	Ag	Pts
Southern Essex Comb. Div.2	20	8	0	2	53	13	6	1	3	22	12	29
Essex Junior Cup	2	1	0	1	13	3	0	0	0	0	0	
Souhern Essex Comb. Cup	1	0	0	0	0	0	0	0	1	0	2	
Friendlies	6	0	0	0	0	0	2	1	3	16	15*	
Total	**29**	**9**	**0**	**3**	**66**	**16**	**8**	**2**	**7**	**38**	**29***	

* The score in the friendly match against Brooklands Athletic on 28th August, is not known.

Southern Essex Combination Division 2
Final Table

	P	W	D	L	For	Ag	Pts
Heath United	20	19	1	0	107	15	39
G.E.Stores	20	16	1	3	71	30	33
Collier Row British Legion	20	14	3	3	99	33	31
Romford "A"	**20**	**14**	**1**	**5**	**75**	**25**	**29**
Hornchurch Wanderers	20	7	3	10	40	52	17
Elm Park	20	7	3	10	37	67	17
Ockendon United	20	6	2	12	43	76	14
Hainault Forest	20	5	2	13	35	70	12
Phoenix	20	4	3	13	34	84	11
Hornchurch Spartan	20	3	3	14	39	81	9
Emerson Park	20	3	2	15	24	71	8

"A" TEAM CUP RESULTS

Essex County FA Junior Challenge Cup
Final: Heath United   1   Coubro & Scrutton   0

Romford's progress: 1st Round   Home   Old Bealonians   13 – 1
2nd Round   Home   Emerson Park   0 - 2

Southern Essex Combination Cup
Final: Heath United   2   Hornchurch Athletic   0

Romford's progress: 1st Round   Away Heath United   0 - 2

"A" TEAM APPEARANCES SEASON 1954 - 55

The following players are known to have played for the "A" Team during the season.

J.F.Allen	-.Anderson	N.P.Appleton	-.Attling
C.Bridge	-.Bundy	-.Burchfield	J.Cade
-.Compton	P.Cook	F.D.Creed	S.Dankaro
L.Davis	J.C.Dent	G.Dunn	T.Durrant
P.Emms	-.Etherington	P.Field	-.Fowler
F.C.Frost	B.Gould	J.Grice	G.Hilditch
-.Hills	F.Holdsworth	B.J.Jewell	D.M.Jones
P.Kearsley	G.J.Kenlay	R.Mahoney (Collier Row Ath)	
-.Martin	W.S.Millar	J.Mitchell	C.Murchison
J.W.Parfitt	L.Phillips	G.Porter	J.Roberts
D.E.Roper	-.Rothon	G.J.Ruglys	R.D.Sampson
C.Sawkins	-.Sheppard	-.Skeggles	D.Smith
G.Smith(Glendale YC) R.Smith		D.H.Taylor	A.M.Trimm
A.J.Vernon	-.Walker	-.Wallace	-.Watson
D.A.Watt	E.Watts	-.Whitworth	M.Whitworth(Barking)
A.Wilson	F.Wilson		

DEPARTURES FROM THE CLUB SEASON 1954 – 55

The following appear to have left the club during or by the end of the season. They may have been triallists and only played one or two games and then went elsewhere. New clubs are indicated where known.

R.N.Baldwin (Chelmsford City), T.Baldwin, J.Bloomfield, C.Bridge (Brentwood & Warley), A.W.Cliss (Ware Town), P.Devlin (Dagenham), P.T.Donovan (Leytonstone), P.Field, P.D.Hall (Rainham Town), A.F.Herbert (Briggs Sports), P.Kearsley (Brentwood & Warley), G.J.Kenlay (Rainham Town), A.Marshall (Dagenham), W.F.Mackenzie (retired), T.V.McGeehan (Dagenham), R.E.Merrick, D.G.Negus (Hoddesden), W.Oram (Rainham Town), G.Porter (Hornchurch & Upminster), S.T.Prince (Walthamstow Avenue), R.D.Sampson (Hornchurch & Upminster), C.Sawkins, K.A.Steward, M.Thompson (Hornchurch & Upminster).

Post Season Summary   Season 1954-55

Over 3,000 were at Brooklands on 21st August for the opening game of the season, only for Barking to steal the league points in a 2-0 win. Alfie Cliss, joining Boro from Ware, made his debut the following Thursday and scored Romford's goal in a 1-1 draw with Leytonstone. Things then took a turn for the worse with three successive league defeats by Dulwich Hamlet, Leytonstone and Walthamstow Avenue. Then came an attractive home tie in the FA Cup on 11th September against old rivals Harwich and Parkeston. With nearly 4,000 spectators inside Brooklands, Romford did not disappoint and secured a fine three one victory. Boro were immediately brought down to earth with a further three defeats.

If the two 4–2 defeats at St. Albans (Isthmian League) and Leyton (FA Cup) were bad enough, worse was to follow at Wycombe Wanderers where Boro were humbled by a 8-1 loss. A league point was picked up in the home game with Kingstonian, but this was followed by a 3-0 reverse at Bromley on 16th October when Boro were without their captain Stan Prince, representing the FA Amateur XI against the South Western Football League at Plymouth. There then followed a 1-1 draw at Wimbledon. On 30th October Romford suffered a 2-1 loss at Brooklands in the return encounter with St. Albans City. During the match Bill Mackenzie sustained a serious leg fracture which was to end his playing career.

The following Saturday, 6th November, things looked bleak when goal keeper Peter Gamman failed to arrive at Woking. Club director and former player Jim Parrish stepped into the breach and performed heroically to earn a thrilling four all draw. He was greatly applauded as he left the field by Romford and Woking supporters.

Another league point was picked up at home to Dulwich Hamlet, only for Danny Taylor to put through his own goal in a 1-0 defeat from Corinthian Casuals at the Oval Cricket Ground. Attendances had started to fall. Barely 2,000 turned up for the return game with Wycombe Wanderers but Boro confounded their critics by securing a 7-3 victory.

A strong Tottenham "A" team turned up at Brooklands on 4th December for an East Anglian Cup tie that ended in a three all draw. Spurs favourite Alfie Stokes scored a goal and Frank Teece, who years later signed as a professional for Boro, was also in the Spurs side. Then followed four more crushing defeats by Oxford City (5-2), Uxbridge Town in the F.A. Amateur Cup (4-2) and two 3-0 defeats by Ilford.

Boro started the new year with a home game against Harwich and Parkeston in the Essex Senior Cup and the lads responded with a 1-0 victory. Then came a very poor performance in a 5-2 defeat at Bishop's Stortford in a friendly, followed by a boring goalless draw at Barking. At least we still had an important home tie against Grays Athletic to come in the Essex Senior Cup on 29th January. Nearly four and a half thousand enthusiastic spectators turned up only for Boro to suffer another devastating defeat by five goals to one. Nigerian student Sunday Dankaro scored Boro's goal. Only eleven hundred turned up the following Saturday for a 2-1 friendly win over Walton & Hersham.

On 12th February, on a very uneven and frozen Brooklands pitch, Boro had another goal feast against Woking. Romford rattled up six goals (4-4 at half time). Alas, Woking netted nine times with Charlie Mortimore and Hamm getting four each. A truly astonishing game! Nearly 2,000 turned up for the replay against Tottenham Hotspur "A" in the East Anglian Cup. Again Stokes and Teece were in the Spurs side that was also strengthened with the inclusion of Hollowbread (in goal) and Charlie Withers at full back. All to no avail as Boro powered to a 3-1 victory, with the luckless Teece putting through his own goal.

Spurred on by this success, Romford went on to secure league points at the expense of lowly Clapton at the Spotted Dog ground. Romford did it again the following week in the return fixture. A devastating 7-1 reverse away to Walthamstow Avenue on 12th March dented the lads confidence, however. Three lifeless draws were to follow before the next Anglian Cup game. Boro were obliged to travel to Braintree on 9th April to meet Crittall Athletic and return with a two nil victory. A thrilling extra time defeat by Walthamstow Avenue two days later ended all interest in the Thameside Trophy.

Only 600 fans turned out for the home league game with Bromley, when a Sheen own goal gave Boro a one nil victory. Nearly two thousand paid to see the East Anglian Cup semi final tie against March Town on 25th April. Again Romford did not disappoint and won a comfortable 4-0 victory. Romford ended their league programme with a 1-1 home draw against Wimbledon. Boro accepted an invitation to travel to Thetford Town for their local Charity Cup, but proved to be too charitable as the home team won 3-0.

Romford ended their season on 14th May with the Reg Sheward Charity Cup match against a very strong Charlton Athletic, who included their recent South African signing Eddie Firmani in the attack. Other Charlton favourites, Campbell, Jago and Hurst were also included. Firmani secured a fine hat-trick for Charlton and Tony Herbert, George Andrew and Chris Halesworth scored for Boro who were defeated by five goals to three.

Thus ended a very disappointing and frustrating season for Boro and their loyal supporters were also denied the chance to see the East Anglian Cup Final versus Grays due to lack of time. The match was to be played early in the following season.

Unsurprisingly with the first team struggling, the reserves had a very poor season, conceding numerous goals in the opening weeks. They never recovered from this and finished second from bottom in the league table. The boys did however reach the fifth round of the Essex Intermediate Cup competition before suffering a five one defeat by local rivals Dagenham Reserves.

Great credit should be given to the "A" team who were never able to put out a settled side due to reserve team calls, but finished in fourth place in the Southern Essex Combination Division Two table.

EAST ANGLIAN CUP WINNERS 1954 – 55

Final played at Grays on 24th August 1955.   Grays Athletic   1   Romford   2

Back: Jim Parrish, Dennis Taylor, Frank Newman, Peter Gamman, Alan Taylor, Johnny Whitecross, Jim Eyett, Bill Seddon, Glyn Richards

Front: Ernie.Hewitt, Derek Rubery, Stan Shaef, Gordon.Skipp, Alan Amas, George Andrews, Frank H.Adams

Authors' collection

GLEANINGS FROM MANAGEMENT COMMITTEE MINUTE BOOKS
SEASON 1954-55

On **13th July 1954** notification was received that the Club allocation from the FA Amateur Cup Pool was £203.4.11d, a record sum.

On **10th August** the agreement with Glendale FC was renewed and the Club's donation increased to 17 guineas. Glendale would use the training facilities on Wednesday evenings, under strict supervision. All Glendale players would be signed on Romford FA forms.

On **7th September** the Police agree to provide one Police Officer and four Special Constables for each first team game. The fee for the one policeman would be £1 1s 0d.

On **15th March** the committee noted that players Peter Gamman and Ray Merrick were both shortly to be married, and it was agreed to make suitable presentations to them, subject to the usual County FA approval.

On **29th March** the Secretary reported that he had applied for permission to make a ground collection during the match versus Walthamstow Avenue on 11th April. The proceeds would be given to Bill Mackenzie, who had been forced to retire from football following his injury, and had been unable to work for several weeks.

On **19th April** Mr H.F. Knights reported that the collection for Bill Mackenzie amounted to £37 2s 9d, plus a donation of £8 from the Supporters Club.

DEATH OF ROMFORD FC DIRECTOR MR ROBERT (BOB) SCOTT
(as reported in the *Romford Recorder*, Friday 15ᵗʰ April 1955)

Supporters of the Romford Football Club will regret to learn of the death of a former director and active worker for the club. Mr Robert Scott, of "Glenelg", London Road, Romford, which took place at his home on Tuesday after a long illness. Mr Scott, who was 72 years of age, had been associated with the club since its formation in 1929 and was for many years responsible for the stand arrangements on the Brooklands ground. A native of Glasgow, he came to Romford from Swansea in 1928. He was a cousin of Mr George Patterson, the Scottish international and Queen's Park player, and persuaded him to come south and join Romford.

Keenly interested in music and the possessor of a fine tenor voice, Mr Scott was a member of choirs in Wales before coming to Romford. Later he was a member of a London choral society and he was also the conductor of the choir of Salem Baptist Church. In recent years he was the conductor of the choir of the Main Road Baptist Church. His mother, who is 93 years of age, survives him, and he leaves a widow, son and daughter. The funeral took place today (Friday) at the Romford Cemetery, following a service at the Main Road Baptist Church at 2.30pm.

DIRECTORS' REPORT FOR THE TWELVE MONTHS ENDED 31ˢᵀ MAY, 1955

Shareholders will not be surprised to learn that the year ended 31ˢᵗ May, 1955, in respect of which the accounts are now presented, has been an unfortunate one for the Company; the worst since the Company's formation. The Accounts shew a net loss of £1,223....

....In practically every year since its formation the Club in football has won honours but the year ended 31ˢᵗ May, 1955, will be long remembered as the year when the first team just failed to get the all important goals and match after match was lost, or drawn finishing the season bottom of the Isthmian League....A winning team goes from strength to strength and its success is reflected in the increased receipts – unfortunately a losing team produces the opposite effect and that, quite simply, is the reason for the loss sustained.

Gate Income is the lowest since the year 1940 and most other items both of Income and Expenditure are affected for the reason given.

Shareholders are assured that your Directors and all the officials of the Club were most concerned at the poor results achieved by the first team and they spent many hours and made many journeys endeavouring to meet the situation at the time, but the right players are not easily come by when a bad season is being experienced. Your Directors decided that the answer was to build for the future and they feel that the fine body of young players now with the Club, their prowess improving rapidly, will provide supporters with the first class football which has for so long been associated with the town of Romford.

Your Directors would place on record their complete confidence in the management and training of the teams, and also feel that their best thanks are due to the very loyal 'hard core' of supporters who, week by week in 'fair weather' and in 'foul' can be recognised around the ground....

With regard to future improvements your Directors being optimistic and having faith in the players now with the Club, gave instructions before the end of the season for the extension of the 'Popular' stand on the North side of the ground as foreshadowed in their last report to members. These extensions will cost the Company upwards of £2,890. The work is in progress and completion is expected at an early date. The extended Stand will afford welcome cover to supporters favouring the North side of the Ground.....

Annual General Meeting held Wednesday 18th January 1956
As reported in the *Romford Recorder*, Friday 20th January 1956

"WORST SEASON FOR 27 YEARS" - ROMFORD DIRECTORS' REPORT

Shareholders were told on Wednesday that season 1954-55 had been the worst financial year Romford Football Club Ltd had known in the club's 16 years of existence. The accounts showed a net loss of £1,223. "In fact, it was the worst period we have had since the football club started 27 years ago" said company chairman Lord Macpherson. "We won nothing on the field of play and ended up with a financial loss.

"But it might have been worse", continued the chairman. "There is no reason for despair. Every business and every football club runs into a bad time and we had ours last year. I feel we are now on the way up and that the policy of rebuilding has been justified..." Lord Macpherson spoke of the recent reassessment of values of properties and said that Brooklands had been seriously affected. The assessment of the ground had jumped from £135 to £400 per annum and the club would appeal. "Despite this", said the chairman, "we will not increase our charges of admission...".

Other good news for supporters is that the increased accommodation being erected on the 'popular' side of the ground is almost complete. This would double the capacity and directors were considering providing seating for 600 to 1,000 in the centre piece of the stand. In answer to a question whether an extra charge would be made for the new seating, Lord Macpherson said the directors were considering the matter. Another supporter asked about the proposed new stand on the enclosure side of the ground. He was told that the club's present financial position and the 'Butler squeeze' had made it impossible to go ahead with the project.

Shareholder Mr T.W. Locke thought that a later kick-off time than 2pm would bring in more customers and suggested that floodlighting should be installed to solve the problems of a later start. Management committee chairman Mr Glyn Richards said the club had already deliberated this question and agreed that floodlighting would be a considerable acquisition. "Prices have been so prohibitive, however, that we have had to think again. It must also be remembered that the respective controlling bodies govern the times of kick-off", he added. Lord Macpherson remarked that lighting installation would cost about £5,000.

It's Never Been This Bad, Boro'!

Writes – D. J. Davies

Romford's Haleworth is just beaten to a high ball by the Oxford goalkeeper

NO fooling. Saturday's Isthmian League kick-around between Romford and Oxford City almost had me falling asleep in the Brookland's Press-box. It was a long dreary succession of miskicking, faulty passing and atrocious finishing that set even the partisan home crowd hooting with derisive cheers when it was all over.

It was a game that had nothing to commend it—not even one goal. And the finishing touch to a pitiful exhibition of premier amateur league football came when Oxford's B. Dean shot tamely wide from the penalty spot in the last 18 minutes.

The *Romford Recorder* of 8th April 1955 showed its frustration after the boring goalless draw against Oxford City on the 2nd April

Football life can sometimes be a drag!

It was not all doom and gloom however. Jim Parrish, anxious to raise funds, promised that if a hefty enough donation was forthcoming the players would dress up as ballerinas at the Supporters Club's annual fundraising evening and dance to the Sugar Plum Fairy music. The players said they would if Jim Parrish himself joined in! The venue was the Rush Green Community Hall. Mrs Violet Baker (wife of Supporters' Club secretary Mr H.Q. Baker) is on piano.   *Courtesy of Ron and Ivy Baker*

THE ROMFORD FOOTBALL CLUB LIMITED

Full Members of The Football Association
Full Members of Isthmian Football League
Affiliated to Essex County Football Association

Chairman: The Rt. Hon. Lord Macpherson
Directors: Messrs. M.A.Brazier, A.E.Kittle, W.G.Mann,
J.W.Parrish, G.Richards JP, A.J.Smith MBE (died 18th November)
Mr H.F.Knights elected following death of Mr A.J.Smith.
Company Secretary: Mr H.W.Muskett

Colours: Blue & Gold Shirts, White Shorts

Registered Offices 110,Hyland Way, Hornchurch

Ground: Brooklands Sports Ground, Romford

Football Club Management Committee:
President: The Rt.Hon. Lord Macpherson
Chairman: Mr G.Richards JP **Hon.Secretary:** Mr M.A.Brazier
Hon.Press Secretary: Mr R.S.Lyons **Reserve XI Secretary:** Mr A.E.Adlam
Other Committee Members: Messrs. F.H.Adams, G.I.Howlett, H.F.Knights,
W.G.Mann, J.W.Parrish, A.J.Smith MBE (died 18th November)

Statistics: Mr John Haley(Ex Officio)

Hon.Programme Secretary: Mr H.Wright **Third XI Secretary:** Mr A.J.Anderton

Selection Committee: Messrs. F.H.Adams, A.E.Adlam, W.F.Mackenzie, J.W.Parrish

Trainer and Coach: Mr G.W.Patterson **Assistant Trainer:** Mr E.Hewitt
Team Assistants (Trainers): Mr Fred Griffiths(Reserves), Mr A.J.Anderton("A" Team)
Bankers: Lloyds Bank Ltd.,Romford **Auditors:** Messrs. Iion V. Cummings & Co.

Club Masseur & Groundsman: Mr W.C.Seddon
COMPETITIONS ENTERED SEASON 1955 – 56

FA Challenge Cup
FA Amateur Challenge Cup
Isthmian Football League
Essex County FA Senior Challenge Cup
East Anglian Cup
Essex Thameside Challenge Competition
Reg Sheward Trophy
Bill Seddon Testimonial Match

Isthmian Football League Reserve Section
Essex County FA Intermediate Challenge Cup

Eastern "A" Football League
Essex County FA Junior Challenge Cup
Eastern "A" Football League Cup

Admission Prices Season 1955 – 56

	First Team			Reserve Team		
	Adults	OAPs	Child	Adults	OAPs	Child
Ground	1/-	6d		6d	3d	
Ground & Enclosure	1/9	1/-		1/-	6d	
Grandstand	2/6	2/6		1/-	6d	

Season Ticket Prices Season 1955 – 56

	Adults	OAPs & Children
Grandstand (All one price)	£1.10.0	
Ground & Enclosure	£1.1.0	12/6
Ground only	12/6	7/6

First Team Match Details

20 Aug EAC1R Home Arsenal "A" 3 – 1 Tiffin,Halesworth(2)
Attendance: 3,008 Receipts: £149.18.6 Programmes: £16.7.5 Car Park: £4.12.6
Romford: P.Gamman;D.H.Taylor,J.V.Eyett(Capt);E.Ross,F.L.Newman,J.J.Whitecross;
D.J.Rubery,S.Shaef,C.H.Halesworth,C.Tiffin,G.W.Andrews.

24 Aug EACF Away Grays Athletic 1954 – 55 Final 2 – 1 Skipp,Shaef
Romford: P.Gamman;D.H.Taylor,J.V.Eyett(Capt);A.J.Taylor,F.L.Newman,J.J.Whitecross;
D.J.Rubery,S.Shaef,G.E.Skipp,A.Amas,G.W.Andrews.

27 Aug IFL Home Bromley 0 – 0
Attendance: 2,676 Receipts: £128.4.6 Programmes: £18.4.7 Car Park: £4.16.9
Romford: P.Gamman;D.H.Taylor,J.V.Eyett(Capt);J.J.Whitecross,F.L.Newman,A.J.Taylor;
D.J.Rubery,S.Shaef,G.E.Skipp,A.Amas,G.W.Andrews.

1 Sept IFL Home Corinthian Casuals 1 – 3 Whitecross
Attendance: 2,254 Receipts: £106.8.0 Programmes: £ ?? Car Park: £4.16.9
Romford: P.Gamman;D.H.Taylor,J.V.Eyett(Capt);J.J.Whitecross,F.L.Newman,A.J.Taylor;
D.J.Rubery,S.Shaef,C.H.Halesworth,A.Amas,G.W.Andrews.

3 Sept IFL Away Kingstonian 3 – 4 Andrews,Shaef,Rubery
Romford: P.Gamman;D.H.Taylor,J.V.Eyett(Capt);J.J.Whitecross,F.L.Newman,E.Ross;
D.J.Rubery,S.Shaef,C.H.Halesworth,C.Tiffin,G.Andrews.

10 Sept FACPR Away Dagenham 1 – 2 Amas
Attendance: 4,800
Romford: P.Gamman;D.H.Taylor,J.V.Eyett(Capt);J.J.Whitecross,F.L.Newman,A.J.Taylor;
D.J.Rubery,S.Shaef,C.Tiffin,A.Amas,G.W.Andrews.

14 Sept IFL Away# Corinthian Casuals 2 – 0 J.R.Kurn,Eyett(pen)
Romford: P.Gamman;D.H.Taylor,J.V.Eyett(Capt);J.J.Whitecross,F.L.Newman,E.Ross;
D.J.Rubery,C.Tiffin,J.R.Kurn,G.W.Andrews,D.Ellis.

17 Sept IFL Home Walthamstow Avenue 4 – 0 Rubery,Amas,Andrews,Tiffin
Attendance: 2,955 Receipts: £141.0.3 Programmes: £25.4.5 Car Park: £6.5.9
Romford: P.Gamman;D.H.Taylor,J.V.Eyett(Capt);J.J.Whitecross,F.L.Newman,A.J.Taylor;
D.J.Rubery,C.Tiffin,A.Amas,G.W.Andrews,D.Ellis.

24 Sept IFL Away Woking 0 – 1
Romford: P.Gamman;D.H.Taylor,J.V.Eyett(Capt);J.J.Whitecross,F.L.Newman,A.J.Taylor;
D.J.Rubery,C.Tiffin,C.H.Halesworth,G.W.Andrews,D.Ellis.

28 Sept EAC2R Home Colchester United Reserves 3 – 2 Halesworth(2)Andrews
Attendance: 1,711   Receipts: £83.0.0   Programmes: £ ??   Car Park: £3.3.0
Romford: P.Gamman;D.H.Taylor,J.V.Eyett(Capt);J.J.Whitecross,F.L.Newman,A.J.Taylor;
D.J.Rubery,C.Tiffin,C.H.Halesworth,G.W.Andrews,D.Ellis.

1 Oct IFL Home Leytonstone 2 – 1 Tiffin,Rubery
Attendance: 2,983   Receipts: £142.17.3   Programmes: £ ??   Car Park: £7.10.0
Romford: P.Gamman;E.Ross,J.V.Eyett(Capt);J.J.Whitecross,F.L.Newman,A.J.Taylor;
D.J.Rubery,C.Tiffin,C.H.Halesworth,G.W.Andrews,D.Ellis.

8 Oct IFL Away Dulwich Hamlet 2 – 1 Halesworth(2)
Romford: P.Gamman;E.Ross,J.V.Eyett(Capt);J.J.Whitecross,F.L.Newman,A.J.Taylor;
D.J.Rubery,C.Tiffin,C.H.Halesworth,G.W.Andrews,D.Ellis.

15 Oct IFL Home St. Albans City 2 – 2 Whitecross(pen)Tiffin
Attendance: 2,667   Receipts: £128.14.6   Programmes: 19.7.3   Car Park: £6.10.6
Romford: P.Gamman;E.Ross,J.V.Eyett(Capt);J.J.Whitecross,F.L.Newman,A.J.Taylor;
D.J.Rubery,C.Tiffin,C.H.Halesworth,G.W.Andrews,D.Ellis.

22 Oct IFL Away Clapton 3 – 1 Rubery,Tiffin,Whitecross(pen)
Romford: P.Gamman;E.Ross,J.V.Eyett(Capt);J.J.Whitecross,F.L.Newman,A.J.Taylor;
D.J.Rubery,A.Amas,C.H.Halesworth,C.Tiffin,G.W.Andrews.

29 Oct IFL Home Kingstonian 2 – 1 Tiffin,Ellis
Attendance: 2,687   Receipts: £128.5.3   Programmes: £18.13.6   Car Park: £6.5.6
Romford: P.Gamman;E.Ross,J.V.Eyett(Capt);J.J.Whitecross,F.L.Newman,A.J.Taylor;
D.Rubery,A.Amas,C.Tiffin,G.W.Andrews,D.Ellis.

5 Nov IFL Away Oxford City 3 – 1 Tiffin(2)Andrews
Romford: P.Gamman;E.Ross,J.V.Eyett(Capt);J.J.Whitecross,F.L.Newman,A.J.Taylor;
C.H.Halesworth,D.J.Rubery,C.Tiffin,G.W.Andrews,D.Ellis.

12 Nov IFL Away Wimbledon 0 – 1
Romford: P.Gamman;E.Ross,J.V.Eyett(Capt);J.J.Whitecross,F.L.Newman,A.J.Taylor;
C.H.Halesworth,D.J.Rubery,C.Tiffin,G.W.Andrews,D.Ellis.

19 Nov EAC3R Home Chelmsford City Reserves 6 – 2 Rubery(2)Tiffin(2)Halesworth,
Whitecross(pen)

Attendance: 3,517   Receipts: £183.18.0   Programmes: £16..5.2   Car Park: £6.14.0
Romford: P.Gamman;E.Ross,J.V.Eyett(Capt);J.J.Whitecross,F.L.Newman,A.J.Taylor;
C.H.Halesworth,D.J.Rubery,C.Tiffin,G.W.Andrews,D.Ellis.

26 Nov IFL Home Woking 1 – 3 Amas
Attendance: 2,644   Receipts: £121.10.3   Programmes: £18.1.6   Car Park: £5.19.0
Romford: P.Gamman;E.Ross,J.V.Eyett(Capt);J.J.Whitecross,F.L.Newman,A.J.Taylor;
D.J.Rubery,A.Amas,C.Tiffin,G.W.Andrews,D.Ellis.

3 Dec Frdly Away Hendon 0 – 4
Romford: P.Gamman;E.Ross,J.V.Eyett(Capt);J.J.Whitecross,F.L.Newman,A.J.Taylor;
D.J.Rubery,A.Amas,C.Tiffin,G.W.Andrews,A.F.Hitchcock.

10 Dec ESC1R Home Clapton 2 – 1 Tiffin(2)
Attendance: 3,232   Receipts: £170.18.6   Programmes: £15.0.6   Car Park: £ ??
Romford: P.Gamman;E.Ross,J.V.Eyett(Capt);J.J.Whitecross,F.L.Newman,A.J.Taylor;
D.J.Rubery,A.Amas,C.Tiffin,G.W.Andrews,D.Ellis.

17 Dec IFL Home Barking 1 – 2 Tiffin
Attendance: 2,466   Receipts: £115.5.6   Programmes: £15.13.6   Car Park: £6.6.0
Romford: P.Gamman;E.Ross,J.V.Eyett(Capt);J.J.Whitecross,F.L.Newman,A.J.Taylor;
D.J.Rubery,A.Amas,C.Tiffin,G.W.Andrews,D.Ellis.

26 Dec IFL Away Ilford 2 – 2 Tiffin,Bee
Romford: P.Gamman;E.Ross,J.V.Eyett(Capt);J.J.Whitecross,F.L.Newman,A.J.Taylor;
D.J.Rubery,S.Shaef,C.Tiffin,J.Bee,G.W.Andrews.

27 Dec IFL Home Ilford 1 – 5 Rubery
Attendance: 2,607   Receipts: £134.18.9   Programmes: £17.10.6   Car Park: £7.7.6
Romford: G.Lewis;E.Ross,J.V.Eyett(Capt);J.J.Whitecross,F.L.Newman,A.J.Taylor;
D.J.Rubery,A.Amas,C.Tiffin,J.Bee,G.W.Andrews.

31 Dec IFL Away Wycombe Wanderers 2 – 6 Andrews,Rubery
Romford: P.Gamman;E.Ross,J.V.Eyett(Capt);J.J.Whitecross,F.L.Newman,A.J.Taylor;
D.J.Rubery,S.Shaef,C.Tiffin,J.Bee,G.W.Andrews.

7 Jan ESC2R Away Briggs Sports 3 – 2 Tiffin,Bee(2)
Attendance: 3,200
Romford: P.Gamman;E.Ross,A.J.Taylor;J.J.Whitecross,F.L.Newman(Capt),S.Shaef;
D.J.Rubery,G.W.Andrews,J.Bee,C.Tiffin,D.Ellis.

14 Jan   IFL   Home   Wycombe Wanderers   1 – 3   Andrews
Attendance: 1,806   Receipts: £88.2.6   Programmes: £14.7.0   Car Park: £6..6.9
Romford: P.Gamman;E.Ross,A.J.Taylor;J.J.Whitecross,F.L.Newman(Capt),S.Shaef;
D.J.Rubery,G.W.Andrews,J.Bee,C.Tiffin,D.Ellis.

21 Jan   AC1R   Away   Briggs Sports   0 – 2
Attendance: 5,800
Romford: P.Gamman;E.Ross,A.J.Taylor;J.J.Whitecross,F.L.Newman(Capt),S.Shaef;
D.J.Rubery,G.W.Andrews,J.Bee,C.Tiffin,D.Ellis.

28 Jan   IFL   Away   Bromley   0 – 7
Romford: E.C.Rogers;B.W.Kelly,A.J.Taylor;J.J.Whitecross,F.L.Newman(Capt),S.Shaef;
E.Ross,G.W.Andrews,J.Bee,C.Tiffin,A.F.Herbert.

11 Feb   IFL   Away   Barking   0 – 0
Romford: P.Gamman;E.R.Cave,B.W.Kelly;J.J.Whitecross,F.L.Newman(Capt),A.J.Taylor;
A.F.Herbert,D.J.Rubery,J.Bee,G.W.Andrews,R.Murphy.

18 Feb   Frdly   Home   Pegasus   4 – 2   Murphy,Bee,Abbott(2)
Attendance: 1,407   Receipts: £69.15.0   Programmes: £5.16.0   Car Park: £1.17.3
Romford: P.Gamman;E.R.Cave,B.Kelly;J.J.Whitecross,F.L.Newman(Capt),A.J.Taylor;
D.J.Rubery,K.Abbott,J.Bee,G.W.Andrews,R.Murphy.

25 Feb   IFL   Home   Oxford City   0 – 2
Attendance: 1,830   Receipts: £88.18.9   Programmes: £10.5.6   Car Park: £3.0.9
Romford: P.Gamman;B.Kelly,D.M.Jones;J.J.Whitecross,F.L.Newman(Capt),A.J.Taylor;
D.J.Rubery,K.Abbott,C.Tiffin,J.Bee,A.F.Herbert.

3 Mar   IFL   Away   St. Albans City   1 – 1   Andrews
Romford: P.Gamman;J.P.Field,B.Kelly;J.J.Whitecross,F.L.Newman(Capt),A.J.Taylor;
D.J.Rubery,K.Abbott,J.Bee,C.Tiffin,G.W.Andrews.

10 Mar   ESCSF   Ilford Walthamstow Avenue   0 – 3
Romford: P.Gamman;J.P.Field,B.Kelly;J.J.Whitecross,F.L.Newman(Capt),A.J.Taylor;
D.J.Rubery,K.Abbott,J.Bee,C.Tiffin,G.W.Andrews.

17 Mar   IFL   Home   Clapton   0 – 1
Attendance: 1,308   Receipts: £57.11.6   Programmes: £5.18.1   Car Park: £2.6.3
Romford: P.Gamman;J.P.Field,B.Kelly;J.J.Whitecross,F.L.Newman(Capt),A.J.Taylor;
J.Wood,K.Abbott,J.Baldwin,P.J.Jolly,G.W.Andrews.

24 Mar   IFL   Away   Leytonstone   1 – 1   Bee
Romford: P.Gamman;J.P.Field,E.R.Cave;J.J.Whitecross,F.L.Newman(Capt),A.J.Taylor;
J.Wood,K.Abbott,J.Bee,P.J.Jolly,G.W.Andrews.

30 Mar   EACSF   Away   Cambridge United   2 – 2   Tiffin,Bee
Romford: P.Gamman;J.P.Field,E.R.Cave;J.J.Whitecross,F.L.Newman(Capt),A.J.Taylor;
J.Wood,K.Abbott,J.Bee,C.Tiffin,G.W.Andrews.

7 Apr   ETT1R   Home   Grays Athletic   2 – 0   Andrews,Whitecross(pen)
Attendance: 1,458   Receipts: £77.10.6   Programmes: £6.13.0   Car Park: £2.1.3
Romford: P.Gamman;J.P.Field,B.W.Kelly;J.J.Whitecross,E.R.Cave,A.J.Taylor;
J.Wood,K.Abbott,J.Bee,P.J.Jolly,G.W.Andrews.

14 Apr   IFL   Home   Wimbledon   5 – 4   Tiffin(2)Andrews,Jolly,Whitecross(pen)
Attendance: 475   Receipts: £20.19.0   Programmes: £ ??   Car Park: £1.8.3
Romford: P.Gamman;J.P.Field,B.W.Kelly;J.J.Whitecross,F.L.Newman(Capt),A.J.Taylor;
J.Wood,D.J.Rubery,C.Tiffin,P.J.Jolly,G.W.Andrews.

21 Apr   IFL   Away   Walthamstow Avenue   2 – 0   Jolly,Bee
Romford: P.Gamman;E.R.Cave,B.W.Kelly;J.J.Whitecross,F.L.Newman(Capt),A.J.Taylor;
J.Wood,P.J.Jolly,J.Bee,C.Tiffin,G.W.Andrews.

26 Apr   WSTM   Home   Ex Romford XI   2 – 0   Whitecross(pen)Wood
Attendance: 2,174   Receipts: £112.14.6   Programmes: £15.0.9   Car Park: £5.1.9
Romford: P.Gamman;J.P.Field,B.W.Kelly;J.J.Whitecross,F.L.Newman(Capt),A.J.Taylor;
J.Wood,P.J.Jolly,J.Bee,C.Tiffin,G.W.Andrews.

28 Apr   EACRp   Home   Cambridge United   5 – 1   Wood,Bee(4)
Attendance: 2,260   Receipts: £117.16.0   Programmes: £16.11.0   Car Park: £4.13.6
Romford: P.Gamman;J.P.Field,E.R.Cave;J.J.Whitecross,F.L.Newman(Capt),A.J.Taylor;
J.Wood,B.W.Kelly,J.Bee,C.Tiffin,G.W.Andrews.

30 Apr   ETTSF   Away   Walthamstow Avenue   2 – 1   Whitecross(2)
Romford: P.Gamman;J.P.Field,E.R.Cave;J.J.Whitecross,F.L.Newman(Capt),A.J.Taylor;
J.Wood,B.W.Kelly,J.Bee,C.Tiffin,G.W.Andrews.

3 May IFL   Home   Dulwich Hamlet   1 – 2   Bee
Attendance: 1,137   Receipts: £49.19.9   Programmes: £5.19.1   Car Park: £2.17.6
Romford: P.Gamman;J.P.Field,E.R.Cave;R.J.Leaver,F.L.Newman(Capt),A.J.Taylor;
J.Wood,J.J.Whitecross,J.Bee,B.W.Kelly,G.W.Andrews.

5 May EACF   Away   Clacton Town   2 – 1   Bee,Kelly
Romford: P.Gamman;J.P.Field,E.R.Cave;J.J.Whitecross,F.L.Newman(Capt),A.J.Taylor;
J.Wood,B.W.Kelly,J.Bee,C.Tiffin,G.W.Andrews.

12 May RST   Home   Charlton Athletic   0 – 3
Attendance: 1,975   Receipts: £98.2.3   Programmes: £ ??   Car Park: £2.17.3
Romford: P.Gamman;J.P.Field,E.R.Cave;J.J.Whitecross,F.L.Newman(Capt),A.J.Taylor;
J.Wood,P.J.Jolly,J.Bee,C.Tiffin,G.W.Andrews.
Subs: R.J.Leaver(for Whitecross),A.F.Hitchcock(for Andrews).

\#   Played at Motspur Park and due to Romford's late arrival played 30 minutes each half.

FIRST TEAM SUMMARY OF RESULTS 1955 – 56

	P	**Home**			**Goals**		**Away**			**Goals**		
	P	W	D	L	For	Ag	W	D	L	For	Ag	Pts
Isthmian League	28	4	2	8	21	29	5	4	5	21	26	24
FA Challenge Cup	1	0	0	0	0	0	0	0	1	1	2	
FA Amateur Cup	1	0	0	0	0	0	0	0	1	0	2	
Essex Senior Cup	3	1	0	0	2	1	1	0	1	3	5	
East Anglian Cup	6	4	0	0	17	6	1	1	0	4	3	
E.Ang.Cup 54/55	1	0	0	0	0	0	1	0	0	2	1	
Thameside Trophy	2	1	0	0	2	0	1	0	0	2	1	
R.Sheward Trophy	1	0	0	1	0	3	0	0	0	0	0	
Friendlies	3	2	0	0	6	2	0	0	1	0	4	
Totals	46	12	2	9	48	41	9	5	9	33	44	

Isthmian Football League
Final Table

	P	W	D	L	**Goals**		Pts
	P	W	D	L	For	Ag	Pts
Wycombe Wanderers	28	19	5	4	82	36	43
Bromley	28	12	7	9	54	43	31
Leytonstone	28	12	7	9	50	44	31
Woking	28	14	3	11	62	60	31
Barking	28	12	7	9	41	45	31
Kingstonian	28	12	6	10	67	64	30
Walthamstow Avenue	28	13	3	12	61	45	29
Ilford	28	10	8	10	44	52	28
Oxford City	28	10	7	11	48	55	27
Clapton	28	9	8	11	45	48	26
Wimbledon	28	12	2	14	51	62	26
Corinthian Casuals	28	9	7	12	56	56	25
Dulwich Hamlet	28	9	6	13	55	67	24
Romford	**28**	**9**	**6**	**13**	**42**	**55**	**24**
St.Albans City	28	2	10	16	36	62	14

FIRST TEAM CUP RESULTS

FA Challenge Cup
Final: Manchester City 3   Birmingham 1

4th Qual   Away   Dagenham   1 – 2

FA Amateur Challenge Cup
Final: Bishop Auckland 1   Corinthian Casuals 1
Replay: Bishop Auckland 4   Corinthian Casuals 1

1st Round   Away   Briggs Sports   0 – 2

Essex County FA Senior Challenge Cup
Final: Walthamstow Avenue 3 Dagenham 1

1st Round	Home	Clapton	2 – 1
2nd Round	Away	Briggs Sports	3 – 2
Semi-Final	Ilford	Walthamstow Avenue	0 – 3

East Anglian Cup
Final: Clacton Town 1 Romford 2

1st Round	Home	Arsenal "A"	3 – 1
2nd Round	Home	Colchester U.Res.	3 – 2
3rd Round	Home	Chelmsford C.Res.	6 – 2
Semi-Final	Away	Cambridge United	2 – 2
Replay	Home	Cambridge United	5 – 1
Final	Away	Clacton Town	2 – 1

Essex Thameside Challenge Competition
Final: Romford 5 Ilford 4 **

1st Round	Home	Grays Athletic	2 – 0
Semi-Final	Away	Walthamstow Avenue	2 – 1
Final	Away	Ilford	5 – 4 **

Reg Sheward Memorial Trophy
Charlton Athletic 3 Romford 0
(at Brooklands)

** Played in the 1956 – 57 Season

FIRST TEAM DEBUTS SEASON 1955 – 56

1955   **Previous Club**

20th Aug.	v Arsenal "A"	-	**F.L.Newman**	Barking
		-	**C.Tiffin**	Brentwood & W.
24th Aug.	v Grays Athletic	-	**A.Amas**	n/k
		-	**G.E.Skipp**	Sun Athletic
14th Sept.	v Corinthian Casuals	-	**D.Ellis**	n/k
3rd Dec.	v Hendon	-	**A.Hitchcock**	Glendale Y.C.
27th Dec.	v Ilford	-	**G.Lewis**	n/k

1956

28th Jan.	v Bromley	-	**E.C.Rogers**	Leech United
		-	**B.W.Kelly**	Enfield Town
11th Feb.	v Barking	-	**R.Murphy**	Chelmsford City
18th Feb.	v Pegasus	-	**K.Abbott**	n/k
25th Feb	v Oxford City	-	**D.M.Jones**	Rainham Town
3rd Mar.	v St.Albans City	-	**J.P.Field**	n/k
17th Mar.	v Clapton	-	**J.Wood**	Tooting & Mitcham
		-	**J.Baldwin**	n/k
		-	**P.J.Jolly**	Barking

Players returned to the Club

1955

14th Sept.	v Corinthian Casuals	-	**J.R.Kurn**	Hornchurch & U.
26th Dec.	v Ilford	-	**J.Bee**	Walthamstow Avenue

1956

28th Jan.	v Bromley	-	**A.F.Herbert**	Briggs Sports
11th Feb.	v Barking	-	**E.R.Cave**	Woodford Town
3rd May.	v Dulwich Hamlet	-	**R.J.Leaver**	Tilbury

THE POPULAR STAND EXTENDED, 1955-56

As Cyril Tiffin scores Romford's first goal against Clapton in an Essex Senior Cup match in December 1955, we can see the first stages of work on the extension to the stand.

Romford's opponents are under pressure in this match from early 1956. The roof has now been added to the stand extension.

Four months later, and it's job done!
As Johnny Bee makes an attempt at goal against Grays Athletic on 7th April 1956, it can be seen that the stand extension is now complete.

All images from the authors' collection

FIRST TEAM APPEARANCES SEASON 1955 – 56

	A	B	C	D	E	F	G	H	I	Total
Ken Abbott	4	0	0	1	1	0	1	0	1	8
Alan Amas	8	1	0	1	0	1	0	0	1	12
George Andrews	27	1	1	3	6	1	2	1	3	45
Jim Baldwin	1	0	0	0	0	0	0	0	0	1
Johnny Bee	11	0	1	2	3	0	2	1	2	22
Roy Cave	4	0	0	0	3	0	2	1	1	11
Don Ellis	12	0	1	2	2	0	0	0	0	17
Jim Eyett	18	1	0	1	3	1	0	0	1	25
Joe Field	5	0	0	1	3	0	2	1	1	13
Peter Gamman	26	1	1	3	6	1	2	1	3	44
Chris Halesworth	9	0	0	0	3	0	0	0	0	12
Tony Herbert	3	0	0	0	0	0	0	0	0	3
A.F.Hitchcock	0	0	0	0	0	0	0	1*	1	2*
Pat Jolly	4	0	0	0	0	0	1	1	1	7
D.M.Jones	1	0	0	0	0	0	0	0	0	1
Bernard Kelly	8	0	0	1	2	0	2	0	2	15
John Kurn	1	0	0	0	0	0	0	0	0	1
Ricky Leaver	1	0	0	0	0	0	0	1*	0	2*
G Lewis	1	0	0	0	0	0	0	0	0	1
Spud Murphy	1	0	0	0	0	0	0	0	1	2
Frank Newman	28	1	1	3	6	1	1	1	3	45
Ernie Rogers	1	0	0	0	0	0	0	0	0	1
Eddie Ross	16	0	1	2	2	0	0	0	1	22
Derek Rubery	23	1	1	3	3	1	0	0	2	34
Stan Shaef	7	1	1	1	1	1	0	0	0	12
Gordon Skipp	1	0	0	0	0	1	0	0	0	2
Alan Taylor	26	1	1	3	5	1	2	1	3	43
Dennis Taylor	6	1	0	0	2	1	0	0	0	10
Cyril Tiffin	22	1	1	3	6	0	1	1	2	37
Johnny Whitecross	28	1	1	3	6	1	2	1	3	46
Jimmy Wood	5	0	0	0	3	0	2	1	1	12
Total	308	11	11	33	66	11	22	13*	33	508*

Key to Competitions

A	Isthmian Football League
B	FA Challenge Cup
C	FA Amateur Challenge Cup
D	Essex Senior Cup
E	East Anglian Cup
F	East Anglian Cup 1964/5
G	Thameside Trophy
H	Reg Sheward Memorial Trophy
I	Friendly Matches

EAST ANGLIAN CUP WINNERS 1955 – 56

Back: Johnny Bee, Peter Gamman, Bernard Kelly, Frank Newman, Roy Cave, Johnny Whitecross, AlanTaylor, Jim Eyett
Front: George Andrews, Joe Field, Cyril Tiffin, Jimmy Wood   *Authors' collection*

FIRST TEAM GOALSCORERS SEASON 1955 - 56

	A	B	C	D	E	F	G	H	I	Total
Cyril Tiffin	11	0	0	3	4	0	0	0	0	18
Johnny Bee	4	0	0	2	6	0	0	0	1	13
George Andrews	7	0	0	0	1	0	1	0	0	9
Johnny Whitecross	4	0	0	0	1	0	3	0	1	9
Derek Rubery	6	0	0	0	2	0	0	0	0	8
Chris Halesworth	2	0	0	0	5	0	0	0	0	7
Alan Amas	2	1	0	0	0	0	0	0	0	3
Stan Shaef	1	0	0	0	0	1	0	0	0	2
Ken Abbott	0	0	0	0	0	0	0	0	2	2
Pat Jolly	2	0	0	0	0	0	0	0	0	2
Jimmy Wood	0	0	0	0	1	0	0	0	1	2
Gordon Skipp	0	0	0	0	0	1	0	0	0	1
John Kurn	1	0	0	0	0	0	0	0	0	1
Jim Eyett	1	0	0	0	0	0	0	0	0	1
Don Ellis	1	0	0	0	0	0	0	0	0	1
S.Murphy	0	0	0	0	0	0	0	0	1	1
Bernard Kelly	0	0	0	0	1	0	0	0	0	1
Total	42	1	0	5	21	2	4	0	6	81

FIRST TEAM ATTENDANCE RECORDS SEASON 1955 – 56

Total Attendance All (23) First team Home Games	51,237
Total Attendance all (14) Isthmian League Games	30,495
Average Attendance Home League Games	2,178
Average Attendance All (8) Home Cup Ties	2,523
Highest Gate for Home League Game (Leytonstone)	2,983
Highest Gate for Home Essex Senior Cup Ties (Clapton)	3,232
Highest Gate for Home East Anglian Cup Tie (Chelmsford C.Res.)	3,517
Highest Gate for Home Thameside Trophy Tie (Grays Ath.)	1,458
Highest Gate for Home Friendly Match (Ex Romford XI)	2,174

Reserve Team Match Details

27 Aug IFLR   Away   Oxford City Reserves   2 – 0   Hitchcock,Richards
Romford Res.: D.A.Smith;N.P.Appleton,D.E.Roper;B.J.Jewell,P.Smith,D.A.Watt;
M.Thompson,J.P.Field,T.Richards,J.F.Marks,A.F.Hitchcock.

3 Sept IFLR   Home   Leytonstone Reserves   0 – 3
Attendance: 836   Receipts: £17.13.9   Programmes: £ ??   Car Park: £0.7.0
Romford Res.: D.A.Smith;D.Evans,D.Norman;D.E.Roper,P.Smith,B.J.Jewell;
M.Thompson,J.F.Marks,G.E.Skipp,J.P.Field,A.F.Hitchcock.

10 Sept IFLR   Home   Woking Reserves   0 – 3
Attendance: 416   Receipts: £6.10.3   Programmes: £ ??   Car Park: £0.3.0
Romford Res.:
Team details unknown

17 Sept IFLR   Away   Wimbledon Reserves   4 – 3   Hitchcock,Shaef,J.R.Kurn(2)
Romford Res.: J.F.Allen;
     ? ,S.Shaef,   ?   J.R.Kurn,A.Hitchcock.

24 Sept IFLR   Home   Dulwich Hamlet Reserves   1 – 9   Ross
Attendance: 723   Receipts: £14.8.6   Programmes: £ ??   Car Park: £0.5.0
Romford Res.: Sel. J.F.Allen;N.P.Appleton,D.Evans;E.Ross,P.Smith,S.Shaef;
S.Rason,J.R.Kurn,D.Baird,A.Amas,A.F.Hitchcock.

1 Oct IFLR   Away#   Corinthian Casuals Reserves   1 – 1   Scorer unknown
Romford Res.:
Team details unknown

8 Oct Frdly   Home   Finchley Reserves   2 – 4   Scorers unknown
Attendance: 431   Receipts: £11.6.6   Programmes: £ ??   Car Park: £0.4.6
Romford Res.:
Team details unknown

15 Oct IFLR   Away   Clapton Reserves   1 – 1   Hitchcock
Romford Res.:
Team details unknown

22 Oct IFLR   Home   Bromley Reserves   0 – 2
Attendance: 327   Receipts: £4.16.9   Programmes: £0.13.3   Car Park: £0.2.9
Romford Res.:
Team details unknown

29 Oct IFLR   Away   Kingstonian Reserves   1 – 3   Evans
Romford Res.: G.Lewis;D.Evans,D.E.Roper;N.P.Appleton,D.A.Watt,S.Shaef;
C.H.Halesworth,J.W.Allen,J.R.Kurn,T.Taylor,D.M.Jones.

5 Nov IFLR   Home   Oxford City Reserves   2 – 2   Scorers unknown
Attendance: 719   Receipts: £13.18.6   Programmes: £1.14.6   Car Park: £0.4.3
Romford Res.:
Team details unknown

12 Nov IFLR   Home   Corinthian Casuals Reserves   2 – 3   Scorers unknown
Attendance: 827   Receipts: £16.4.0   Programmes: £2.0.6   Car Park: £-.4.0
Romford Res.:
Team details unknown

19 Nov IFLR   Away   Dulwich Hamlet Reserves   2 – 5   Scorers unknown
Romford Res.:
Team details unknown

3 Dec IFLR   Away   St. Albans City Reserves   4 – 8   Scorers unknown
Romford Res.: J.F.Allen;D.M.Jones,D.H.Taylor;S.Shaef,J.W.Parfitt,N.P.Appleton;
B.J.Jewell,K.Salter,P.Smith,K.Abbott,R.Gifford.

10 Dec IFLR   Away   Woking Reserves   1 – 5   Scorer unknown
Romford Res.:
Team details unknown

31 Dec EIC4R   Home   Harwich & Parkeston Reserves   0 – 1
Attendance: 457   Receipts: £15.15.0   Programmes: £1.3.10   Car Park: £0.3.6
Romford Res.:
Team details unknown

7 Jan IFLR   Home   Ilford Reserves   1 – 2   Amas
Attendance: 263   Receipts: £3.2.3   Programmes: £0.8.4   Car Park: £0.1.6
Romford Res.: E.C.Rogers;E.R.Cave,D.M.Jones;N.P.Appleton,B.W.Kelly,R.Scharvi;
A.F.Hitchcock,K.Abbott,A.Amas,K.Salter,A.F.Herbert.

14 Jan IFLR Away Barking Reserves 1 – 0 Abbott
Romford Res.: E.C.Rogers;E.R.Cave,D.M.Jones;D.H.Taylor,B.W.Kelly,R.Scharvi;
C.Tolhurst,K.Abbott,A.F.Hitchcock,A.Amas,A.F.Herbert.

21 Jan IFLR Home Kingstonian Reserves 3 – 0 Hitchcock,Amas,One n/k
Attendance: 174 Receipts: £1.18.6 Programmes: £0.5.9 Car Park: £0.1.0
Romford Res.: E.C.Rogers;E.R.Cave,D.M.Jones;D.H.Taylor,B.W.Kelly,R.Scharvi;
C.Tolhurst,K.Abbott,A.F.Hitchcock,A.Amas,A.F.Herbert.

28 Jan IFLR Home Wimbledon Reserves 3 – 2 Amas,Abbott(2)
Attendance: 439 Receipts: £8.2.3 Programmes: £1.2.6 Car Park: £0.7.9
Romford Res.: P.Gamman;E.R.Cave;D.M.Jones;D.H.Taylor,J.P.Field,R.Scharvi;
C.Tolhurst,K.Abbott,A.F.Hitchcock,A.Amas,R.Murphy.

4 Feb IFLR Away Bromley Reserves 0 – 1
Romford Res.: E.C.Rogers;J.P.Field,D.M.Jones;E.Ross,D.H.Taylor,R.Scharvi;
C.Tolhurst,J.Baldwin,A.F.Hitchcock,D.Ellis,R.Murphy.

11 Feb IFLR Home Barking Reserves 0 – 2
Attendance: 176 Receipts: £2.0.0 Programmes: £ ?? Car Park: £ None
Romford Res.: E.C.Rogers;J.P.Field,D.M.Jones;E.Ross,D.H.Taylor,R.Scharvi;
C.Tolhurst,K.Abbott,A.F.Hitchcock,A.Amas,D.Ellis.

18 Feb IFLR Away Wycombe Wanderers Reserves 1 – 3 Scorer unknown
Romford Res.: E.C.Rogers;
Remainder of team unknown

3 Mar IFLR Home St. Albans City Reserves 3 – 0 Hitchcock(2)Wood
Attendance: 310 Receipts: £5.8.0 Programmes: £0.14.0 Car Park: £0.2.3
Romford Res.: E.C.Rogers;E.R.Cave,D.M.Jones;R.J.Leaver,J.W.Parfitt,R.Scharvi;
J.Wood,P.J.Jolly,J.Baldwin,A.F.Hitchcock,R.Murphy.

10 Mar IFLR Away Walthamstow Avenue Reserves 1 – 1 Scharvi
Romford Res.: E.C.Rogers;E.R.Cave,D.M.Jones;R.J.Leaver,J.W.Parfitt,R.Scharvi;
J.Wood,J.C.Dent,J.Baldwin,A.F.Hitchcock,R.Murphy.

17 Mar IFLR Away Leytonstone Reserves 0 – 0
Romford Res.: E.C.Rogers;E.Ross,F.Frost;R.J.Leaver,E.R.Cave,R.Scharvi;
R.Murphy,J.Wheeler,D.J.Rubery,C.Tiffin,A.F.Hitchcock.

24 Mar IFLR Home Clapton Reserves 2 – 0 Shaef,Baldwin
Attendance: 260 Receipts: £4.4.9 Programmes: £ ?? Car Park: £0.2.9
Romford Res.: E.C.Rogers;N.P.Appleton,F.Frost;D.H.Taylor,J.V.Eyett,R.Scharvi;
D.A.Watt,S.Shaef,J.Baldwin,A.F.Hitchcock,C.Tiffin.

31 Mar IFLR Home Wycombe Wanderers Reserves 1 – 1 Baldwin
Attendance: 457 Receipts: £8.4.0 Programmes: £1.5.4 Car Park: £0.2.6
Romford Res.: E.C.Rogers;N.P.Appleton,D.M.Jones;R.J.Leaver,J.V.Eyett,R.Scharvi;
D.J.Rubery,S.Shaef,J.Baldwin,P.J.Jolly,A.F.Herbert.

14 Apr Frdly Away Leyton Reserves 3 – 3 Hitchcock(2)Baldwin
Romford Res.: E.C.Rogers;J.V.Eyett,N.P.Appleton;D.M.Jones,D.H.Taylor,R.Scharvi;
J.C.Dent,R.J.Leaver,J.Baldwin,D.Ludlow,A.F.Hitchcock.

19 Apr IFLR Away Ilford Reserves 0 – 1
Romford Res.: E.C.Rogers;N.P.Appleton,F.Frost;R.J.Leaver,J.V.Eyett,R.Scharvi;
C.Tolhurst,J.C.Dent,R.Mahoney,D.Ludlow,J.Philpott.

21 Apr IFLR Home Walthamstow Avenue Reserves 2 – 0 Scorers unknown
Attendance: 459 Receipts: £8.5.9 Programmes: £1.3.3 Car Park: £0.3.9
Romford Res.: (Sel) E.C.Rogers;N.P.Appleton,D.M.Jones;R.J.Leaver,J.V.Eyett,D.H.Taylor;
D.J.Rubery,S.Shaef,A.Hitchcock,D.Ludlow,A.F.Herbert.

#At Motspur Park

RESERVE TEAM SUMMARY OF RESULTS SEASON 1955 – 56

	P	W	D	L	Goals For	Ag	Pts
Isthmian League Reserve Section	28	8	6	14	39	61	22
Essex FA Intermediate Cup	1	0	0	1	0	1	
Friendlies	2	0	1	1	5	7	
Total	31	8	7	16	44	69	

Isthmian Football League Reserve Section
Final Table

	P	W	D	L	Goals For	Goals Ag	Pts
Wycombe Wanderers	28	17	7	4	86	44	41
Bromley	28	16	7	5	80	47	39
Leytonstone	28	15	7	6	59	30	37
Walthamstow Avenue	28	15	7	6	56	33	37
Oxford City	28	14	7	7	83	64	35
Woking	28	12	7	9	57	54	31
Dulwich Hamlet	28	11	7	10	78	68	29
Barking	28	11	5	12	48	56	27
Ilford	28	11	2	15	53	60	24
Clapton	28	9	5	14	50	56	23
Wimbledon	28	8	7	13	60	69	23
Romford Reserves	**28**	**8**	**6**	**14**	**39**	**61**	**22**
Kingstonian	28	8	5	15	49	73	21
Corinthian Casuals	28	7	4	17	41	83	18
St.Albans City	28	4	5	19	49	90	13

RESERVE TEAM CUP RESULTS

Essex County FA Intermediate Challenge Cup

Final: Ilford Res. 3 Walthamstow Ave.Res. 0

1st Round Home Harwich & P.Res. 0 – 1

RESERVE TEAM APPEARANCES SEASON 1955 – 56

The following players are known to have appeared in the reserve team during the season.

K.Abbott	J.F.Allen	J.W.Allen	A.Amas
N.P.Appleton	D.Baird(Bishop's Stortford)	J.Baldwin	E.R.Cave(Woodford Town)
J.C.Dent	D.Ellis	D.Evans(FordSports)	J.V.Eyett
J.P.Field	F.Frost	P.Gamman	R.Gifford(Briggs Sports)
C.H.Halesworth	A.F.Herbert(Briggs Sports)	A.F.Hitchcock(Glendale YC)	B.J.Jewell
P.J.Jolly(Barking)	D.M.Jones (Rainham T)	B.W.Kelly(Enfield Town)	J.R.Kurn(Hornchurch & Upr)
R.J.Leaver(Tilbury)	G.Lewis	D.Ludlow(Ilford)	R.Mahoney
J.F.Marks	R.Murphy(Chelmsford C)	D.Norman(Boldmere St.M)	J.W.Parfitt
J.Philpott	S.Rason(Leytonstone)	T.Richards	E.C.Rogers(Leech Utd)
D.E.Roper	E.Ross	D.J.Rubery	K.Salter
R.Scharvi	S.Shaef	G.E.Skipp(Sun Athletic)	D.A.Smith
P.Smith	A.J.Taylor	D.H.Taylor	T.Taylor(Briggs Sports)
M.Thompson	C.Tiffin(Brentwood & W)	C.Tolhurst	D.A.Watt
J.Wheeler	J.Wood(Tooting & Mitcham)		

RESERVE TEAM ATTENDANCE RECORDS SEASON 1955 – 56

Total Attendance for all (16) Reserve Team Games	7,274
Total Attendance for all (14) League Games	6,386
Highest Gate for Home League Game (Leytonstone)	836
Highest Attendance Cup Game (E.I.Cup)(Harwich & P.Res)	457
Average Attendance per Home League Game	456

"A" Team Match Details

23 Aug Frdly   Away   Collier Row Athletic   n/k
Romford "A":
Team details unknown

1 Sept EAFL   Away   Grays Athletic "A"   3 – 2   J.R.Kurn(2)Philpott
Romford "A": J.F.Allen;D.E.Roper,J.C.Dent;J.Ottley,D.M.Jones,R.Scharvi;
D.Gower,R.Kurn,J.R.Kurn,D.Allen,J.Philpott.

10 Sept EAFL   Home#   Woodford Town "A"   4 – 0   Dent,Gower,Stringer,Philpott
Romford "A": D.A.Smith;R.S.Pratt,J.F.Marks;J.C.Dent,J.W.Parfitt,R.Scharvi;
D.Gower,R.Kurn,R.Stringer,D.Norman,J.Philpott.

17 Sept Frdly   Away   Old Buckwellians   5 – 3   Scorers unknown
Romford "A":
Team details unknown

24 Sept EAFL   Home#   Grays Athletic "A"   1 – 2   Baldwin
Romford "A": G.Lewis;D.E.Roper,D.Watt;J.C.Dent,J.W.Parfitt,R.Scharvi;
T.Day,G.Duke,D.Weekes,J.Baldwin,J.Philpott.

1 Oct EAFL   Home##Ilford "A"   2 – 0   Scorers unknown
Romford "A": G.Lewis;J.P.Field,-.Carr;J.C.Dent,J.W.Parfitt,R.Scharvi;
T.Day,G.Duke,D.Baird,J.W.Allen,J.Philpott.

8 Oct EAFL   Home   Barnet "A"   2 – 4   Scorers unknown
Romford "A": G.Lewis;J.P.Field,D.M.Jones;J.C.Dent,J.W.Parfitt,R.Scharvi;
B.J.Jewell,E.Mocock,T.Day,G.Duke,J.Philpott.

15 Oct EJC1R   Away   Colvern Sports   6 – 1   Philpott(2)Reeves,Tolhurst,Millar,One n/k
Romford: J.F.Allen;J.C.Dent,-.Bell;D.Reeves,J.W.Parfitt,R.Scharvi;
C.Tolhurst,K.Abbott,W.S.Millar,J.W.Allen,J.Philpott.

22 Oct EAFL   Away   Rainham Town "A"   3 – 1   Salter,Abbott,Philpott
Romford "A": J.F.Allen;J.P.Field,J.C.Dent;D.F.Pond,D.Reeves,R.Scharvi;
C.Tolhurst,K.Salter,J.Baldwin,K.Abbott,J.Philpott.

29 Oct EAFL   Home   Leyton "A"   2 – 1   Abbott,Philpott
Romford "A": J.F.Allen;J.P.Field,J.C.Dent;D.Reeves,J.W.Parfitt,R.Scharvi;
C.Tolhurst,K.Salter,-.Toomey,K.Abbott,J.Philpott.

5 Nov EJC2R   Away   G.E. Stores   1 – 0   Skipp
Romford "A": J.F.Allen;J.P.Field,J.C.Dent;D.Reeves,J.W.Parfitt,R.Scharvi;
C.Tolhurst,K.Salter,G.E.Skipp,K.Abbott,J.Philpott.

12 Nov ALC1R   Home   Leytonstone "A"   3 – 0   Reeves(3)
Romford "A": J.F.Allen;J.P.Field,J.C.Dent;-.Bilby,J.W.Parfitt,R.Scharvi;
K.J.Benn,J.Baldwin,D.Reeves,K.Salter,C.Tolhurst.

19 Nov EAFL   Away   Leyton "A"   3 – 1   Baldwin,Pond,Abbott
Romford "A": J.F.Allen;J.C.Dent,D.Roberts;C.E.East,J.W.Parfitt,R.Scharvi;
C.Tolhurst,J.Baldwin,D.F.Pond,K.Abbott,J.Philpott.

26 Nov EJC3R   Home   Downshall Athletic   6 – 0   Pond(2)Benn,Baldwin,Dent,One n/k
Romford "A": J.F.Allen;J.P.Field,J.C.Dent;C.E.East,J.W.Parfitt,R.Scharvi;
K.J.Benn,J.Baldwin,D.F.Pond,K.Abbott,J.Philpott.

3 Dec EAFL   Away   Barnet "A"   3 – 3   Dent,Benn,Pond
Romford "A": W.Taylor;J.P.Field,J.C.Dent;C.E.East,D.Reeves,R.Scharvi;
K.J.Benn,D.E.Roper,D.F.Pond,J.W.Allen,J.Philpott.

10 Dec EJC4R   Home   Romex   4 – 0   Dent,Abbott(2)Philpott
Romford "A": G.Lewis;J.P.Field,J.C.Dent;C.E.East,J.W.Parfitt,R.Scharvi;
C.Tolhurst,J.Baldwin,D.F.Pond,K.Abbott,J.Philpott.

17 Dec EAFL   Away   Leytonstone "A"   5 – 1   Baldwin(2)Abbott,Philpott,Salter
Romford "A": J.F.Allen;J.P.Field,J.C.Dent;C.E.East,J.W.Parfitt,R.Scharvi;
J.Baldwin,K.Salter,J.Bee,K.Abbott,J.Philpott.

31 Dec EJC5R   Away   St. Joseph Old Boys   0 – 2
Romford "A": G.Lewis;J.P.Field,J.C.Dent;C.E.East,J.W.Parfitt,R.Scharvi;
C.Tolhurst,E.Watts,J.Baldwin,A.Amas,J.Philpott.

7 Jan EAFL   Home   Barking "A"   9 – 1   Baldwin(5)R.Kurn(2)Dent,Philpott
Romford "A": J.F.Allen;J.P.Field,N.Cakebread;T.R.Kelly,J.W.Parfitt,B.J.Jewell;
C.Tolhurst,J.C.Dent,J.Baldwin,R.Kurn,J.Philpott.

14 Jan EAFL Away Barking "A" 2 – 0 Dent,Baldwin
Romford "A": J.F.Allen;J.P.Field,N.Cakebread;T.R.Kelly,J.W.Parfitt,B.J.Jewell;
K.J.Benn,J.C.Dent,J.Baldwin,R.Kurn,J.Philpott.

21 Jan EAFL Home Leytonstone "A" 2 – 4 Dent,Baldwin
Romford "A": J.F.Allen;J.P.Field,N.Cakebread;N.P.Appleton,J.W.Parfitt,T.R.Kelly;
K.Salter,J.C.Dent,J.Baldwin,R.Kurn,J.Philpott.

28 Jan EAFL Away Ilford "A" 0 – 0
Romford "A": J.F.Allen;J.P.Field,N.Cakebread;R.Sell,A.Powell,B.J.Jewell;
G.E.Skipp,K.Salter,J.Baldwin,R.Kurn,J.Philpott.

18 Feb ALC2R Home Woodford Town "A" 5 – 4 Reeves,Dent,Baldwin(2)Philpott
Romford "A": J.F.Allen;N.P.Appleton,J.W.Parfitt;R.Sell,A.Powell,B.J.Jewell;
D.Reeves,J.C.Dent,J.Baldwin,C.Cottee,J.Philpott.

25 Feb Frdly Home Dagenham Park 8 – 2 Reeves,Dent(2)Baldwin(3)Philpott(2)
Romford "A": S.Evans;R.J.Leaver,N.Cakebread;D.E.Roper,J.W.Parfitt,P.J.Jolly;
D.Reeves,J.C.Dent,J.Baldwin,B.J.Jewell,J.Philpott.

10 Mar ALC3R Home Barking "A" 5 – 1 Appleton,Tolhurst,Reeves(2)Philpott
Romford "A": J.F.Allen;R.Ellis,N.Cakebread;N.P.Appleton,D.A.Watt,D.E.Roper;
A.F.Herbert,C.Tolhurst,D.Reeves,C.Cottee,J.Philpott.

17 Mar EAFL Home Rainham Town "A" 4 – 1 Dent(2)Reeves,Philpott
Romford "A": J.F.Allen;R.Ellis,D.M.Jones;J.W.Parfitt,D.Mackenzie,N.Cakebread;
C.Tolhurst,J.C.Dent,D.Reeves,D.A.Watt,J.Philpott.

24 Mar EAFL Away Woodford Town "A" 1 – 1 Dent
Romford "A": J.F.Allen;R.Ellis,D.M.Jones;D.E.Roper,J.W.Parfitt,N.Cakebread;
C.Tolhurst,J.C.Dent,D.Reeves,G.J.Ruglys,T.Taylor.

30 Mar ALCSF Away Walthamstow Avenue "A" 0 – 1
Romford "A": J.F.Allen;R.Ellis,D.M.Jones;J.Parfitt,D.Mackenzie,R.Scharvi;
C.Tolhurst,J.C.Dent,A.F.Hitchcock,G.J.Ruglys,J.Philpott.

31 Mar EAFL Away Walthamstow Avenue "A" 4 – 3 Dent(2)Reeves,Tolhurst
Romford "A": J.F.Allen;R.Ellis,D.E.Roper;D.Mackenzie,J.W.Parfitt,N.Cakebread;
C.Tolhurst,J.C.Dent,D.Reeves,G.J.Ruglys,J.Philpott.

7 Apr EAFL Home Walthamstow Avenue "A" 1 – 2 Scorer unknown
Romford "A":
Team details unknown

21 Apr EAFL Home# Clapton "A" 2 – 3 Scorers unknown
Romford "A":
Team details unknown

28 Apr EAFL Away Clapton "A" 2 – 5 Dent,Philpott
Romford "A": J.F.Allen;N.P.Appleton,D.M.Jones;D.E.Roper,J.W.Parfitt,R.Scharvi;
D.J.Rubery,J.C.Dent,J.Baldwin,E.Ross,J.Philpott.

\#　Played at Brooklands after a reserve team game.
\#\#　Played at Brooklands after a first team game.

"A" TEAM SUMMARY OF RESULTS SEASON 1955 – 56

	P	W	D	L	Goals For	Ag	Pts
Eastern "A" Football League	20	11	3	6	55	35	25
Eastern "A" Football League Cup	4	3	0	1	13	6	
Essex County FA Junior Cup	5	4	0	1	17	3	
Friendlies	3*	2	0	0	13	5	
Total	32*	20	3	8	98	49	

*The result of the friendly game away to Collier Row Athletic on the 23rd August is not known.

Eastern "A" League
Final Table

	P	W	D	L	Goals For	Ag	Pts
Walthamstow Avenue "A"	20	15	3	2	70	28	33
Clapton "A"	20	14	3	3	52	33	31

Rainham Town "A"	20	12	3	5	48	38	27
Romford "A"	**20**	**11**	**3**	**6**	**55**	**35**	**25**
Ilford "A"	20	8	2	10	51	37	18
Leytonstone "A"	20	8	2	10	35	39	18
Leyton "A"	20	6	5	9	43	49	17
Grays Athletic "A"	20	5	4	11	39	49	14
Woodford Town "A"	20	5	4	11	29	48	14
Barking "A"	20	5	3	12	37	60	13
Barnet "A"	20	4	2	14	31	74	10

"A" TEAM CUP RESULTS SEASON 1955 – 56

Essex County FA Junior Challenge Cup

Final: Heybridge Swifts Res. 3 Wivenhoe Rangers 2

1st Round	Away	Colvern Sports	6 - 1
2nd Round	Away	G.E.Stores	1 - 0
3rd Round	Home	Downshall Ath.	6 - 0
4th Round	Home	Romex	4 - 0
5th Round	Away	St.Joseph's O.B.	0 - 2

Eastern "A" Football League Cup

Final: Walthamstow Avenue "A" 3 Leyton "A" 0
(After a 1 – 1 draw)

1st Round	Home	Leytonstone	3 – 0
2nd Round	Home	Woodford T.	5 - 4
3rd Round	Away	Barking	5 - 1
Semi-Final	Away	Walthamstow A.	0 - 1

"A" TEAM APPEARANCES SEASON 1955 – 56

The following are known to have played in the "A" Team during the season.

K.Abbott	D.Allen	J.F.Allen	J.W.Allen
A.Amas	N.P.Appleton	D.Baird(Bishop's Stortford)	J.Baldwin
J.Bee(Walthamstow Ave)	-.Bell	K.J.Benn	-.Bilby
N.Cakebread	-.Carr	C.Cottee	T.Day
J.C.Dent	G.Duke	C.E.East	R.Ellis
S.Evans	J.P.Field	D.Gower	A.F.Herbert(Briggs Spts)
A.F.Hitchcock(Glendale YC)	B.J.Jewell	P.J.Jolly(Barking)	D.M.Jones(Rainham Tn)
T.R.Kelly	J.R.Kurn(Hornchurch & Upr)	R.Kurn(Hornchurch BC)	R.J.Leaver(Tilbury)
G.Lewis	D.Mackenzie	J.F.Marks	W.S.Millar
E.Mocock(Collier Row Ath)	D.Norman(Boldmere St.M)	J.Ottley	J.W.Parfitt
J.Philpott	D.F.Pond(Glendale Y.C)	A.Powell	R.S.Pratt
D.Reeves	D.Roberts	D.E.Roper	E.Ross
D.J.Rubery	G.J.Ruglys	K.Salter	R.Scharvi
R.Sell	G.E.Skipp(Sun Athletic)	D.A.Smith	R.Stringer
T.Taylor(Briggs Sports)	C.Tolhurst	-.Toomey	D.A.Watt
E.Watts	D.Weekes		

DEPARTURES FROM THE CLUB SEASON 1955 – 56

The following appear to have left the club during or by the end of the season. They may have been triallists, only played one or two games and then went elsewhere. New clubs are indicated where known.

J.F.Allen (H.M.Services), A.Amas (Leyton), K.J.Benn (Clapton), T.Day, D.Ellis, D.Evans (Membership terminated), R.Gifford (Briggs Sports), C.H.Halesworth (Rainham Town), T.Hillditch (Brentwood & Warley), T.R.Kelly (Clapton), J.R.Kurn (Hornchurch & Upr.), G.Lewis, J.F.Marks (Woodford Town), -.McDonald (Hainault Forest), S.Murphy (Rainham Town), T.Richards (Brentwood & Warley), G.Skipp (Sun Athletic), T.Taylor (Briggs Sports).

Post Season Summary   Season 1955 – 56

Despite the poor record of the previous season, Romford looked forward with optimism to the new campaign. A big blow was the loss of their captain and centre half Stan Prince to Walthamstow Avenue, but Boro signed Frank Newman from Barking and Cyril Tiffin from Brentwood and Warley. They opened the season on 20ᵗʰ August with an East Anglian Cup 1ˢᵗ Round tie against a strong Arsenal "A" team at Brooklands and progressed to the second round with a 3-1 victory. The next game was in the same competition, the final held over from the previous season. Boro lifted the trophy with a fine 2-1 win. Then followed a promising goalless draw with Bromley before the rot set in. Corinthian Casuals won 3-1 at Brooklands with their rejuvenated side and although Boro netted three times at Kingstonian on 3ʳᵈ September, they lost by four goals to three.

The following week nearly 5,000 spectators saw the FA Cup tie away against old rivals Dagenham. Disgruntled Boro supporters started to leave before the end of the game as former Boro favourite Bill Bridge scored his second goal, this time from the penalty spot to give Dagenham a 2-1 victory into the next round. Romford picked up league points from a 2-0 victory away to Corinthian Casuals at Motspur Park and then thrilled their loyal supporters with a resounding 4-0 win over Walthamstow Avenue on 17ᵗʰ September.

A Charlie Mortimore penalty gave Woking a one nil victory before the next East Anglian Cup encounter. Colchester United were the visitors and Boro secured a fine 3-2 win that was followed by a very successful run. Centre forward Cyril Tiffin found the net regularly when the boys defeated both Leytonstone and Dulwich Hamlet by two goals to one and a point was earned in the 2-2 draw with St. Albans City on 15ᵗʰ October. A 3-1 win at Clapton was followed with a 2-1 home win against Kingstonian that took Boro to the top of the table. Five league games without defeat were followed with a three one victory at Oxford City, Cyril Tiffin netting a couple of goals. The run came to an end with a one nil reverse away to Wimbledon on 12ᵗʰ November.

Up next, the good old East Anglian Cup and Chelmsford City Reserves came to Brooklands. They fielded a strong side including several players who would join Romford as professionals in the years to come. They were no match, however, for a rampant Boro who progressed with a 6-2 victory, Cyril Tiffin again bagging a pair. Charlie Mortimore and Hamm contrived to give Woking a 3-1 victory on 26ᵗʰ November before another former Boro favourite, Graeme Cunningham, scored a goal in a 4-0 friendly victory by Hendon. Miles Spector notched a hat-tick for the home team. Romford progressed in the Essex Senior Cup with victory against Clapton. A brace of Tiffin goals gave Boro a two one win.

Their season then took a turn for the worse with a 2-1 home defeat from Barking, a two all draw at Ilford and a 5-1 thrashing inflicted by Ilford in the return encounter. Wycombe Wanderers went one better with a 6-2 victory at Loakes Park and Boro found themselves crashing down the league table.

This did not bode well for the next Essex Senior Cup tie away to the powerful Works side Briggs Sports on 7ᵗʰ January. The Bodies, as they were known, had a couple of former Leytonstone Internationals in their side. Romford confounded their critics with a fine 3-2 win, though, with Cyril Tiffin and recent signing (& former Briggs player) Johnnie Bee securing the goals.

Only 1,600 spectators were at Brooklands on 14th January to watch Romford defeated 3-1 by Wycombe Wanderers. Next up was a foray into the Amateur Cup and great excitement at the prospect of again meeting Briggs Sports away. A record attendance of 5,800 crammed into the Rush Green Road Ground, but this time Romford sadly disappointed and suffered a 2-0 defeat. Confidence was shattered and Boro were trounced 7-0 at Bromley on 28th January. Two weeks later Boro kept a clean sheet away to Barking who did likewise in a boring 0-0 draw. An attractive friendly against Pegasus gave Romford a 4-2 victory, but Oxford City took the points in the next league game, that was followed with a one all draw at St. Albans.

Boro fans were not filled with confidence when they travelled to Newbury Park on 10th March for the Essex Senior Cup semi-final against Walthamstow Avenue. Never really in the game, Romford lost 3-0. That old bogey came back when Clapton took the league points in a 1-0 win at Brooklands on 17th March, although Boro picked up a point in a draw at Leytonstone a week later. Romford then earned a 2-2 draw at Cambridge United in the East Anglian Cup semi-final and declined to play extra time. Further success came on 7th April when Romford again defeated Grays Athletic, this time in the Essex Thameside Trophy. Another goal fest a week later when Wimbledon were defeated 5-4. Romford secured another league victory on 21st April, two nil at Walthamstow Avenue.

Then came a very enjoyable testimonial match for popular Bill Seddon on 26th April when two thousand fans were at Brooklands to see Boro meet a team of ex-Boro players. Romford won 2-0 as supporters witnessed old favourites Jimmy Smailes (Arsenal), Stan Prince (Walthamstow Avenue), Harold Brooks, Bill Bridge and Jackie Lunn (all Dagenham), Eddie Quinlan (Reading) and Graeme Cunningham (Hendon), in the ex-Boro side. Bill Seddon received £215.16.0 from the benefit match and donations.

Success came once more in the East Anglian Cup semi-final replay as Cambridge United were defeated 5-1 at Brooklands. Next up was the Thameside Trophy semi-final on 30th April resulting in another victory, this time 2-1 at Walthamstow Avenue. With so many games in a short space of time, less than a thousand saw Boro's home defeat two one by Dulwich Hamlet on 3rd May. Two days later and Romford were at the seaside. Not relaxing! They had an East Anglian Cup Final to play against professionals Clacton Town. Boro duly achieved a two one victory to again lift the trophy.

Time had run out for the Thameside Trophy, and the final against Ilford would be played next season. Boro's final game of the season was the Reg Sheward Charity match. Old friends Charlton Athletic provided strong opposition, proving too much for Boro who were defeated 3-0. During the match winger George Andrews suffered a broken leg.

The season had at one time promised much, but ended with Romford second from bottom in the Isthmian League table, having been top of the table after twelve games. There was consolation however, with success in the East Anglian Cup and Thameside Trophy. The reserve team, again suffering from first team requirements, had their usual mixed season; achieving some good wins when at full strength but suffering at other times.

The "A" team secured fourth place in the newly formed Eastern "A" League and had some good victories in the Essex Junior Cup, before losing to St. Joseph's Old Boys in the fifth round.

GLEANINGS FROM MANAGEMENT COMMITTEE MINUTE BOOKS
SEASON 1955-56

On **12th July 1955** the Secretary reported the receipt of cheque for £111 9s 9d, being the Club's share from the FA Amateur Cup Pool. This compares with the previous season's sum of £203.4.11.

On **26th July** we read that Mr E.H.Ashford kindly promised to provide a new Club flag.

On **30th August**, following the Club's success in the final of the East Anglian Cup (beating Grays Athletic 2-1) it was agreed to keep the trophy at the United Services Club.

On **6th September** Frank Adams suggested that the Two J's restaurant in North Street would be most suitable for after-match meals.

On **27th September** Mr R.S.Lyons told the Management he wished to introduce a larger programme with additional advertising space. This was agreed to.

On **7th January 1956** Club blazer badges were presented to players with over 15 first team or 30 reserve team appearances.

On **13th March** the committee agreed to purchase a wedding present for player Johnny Bee, subject to the approval of The Essex County FA.

THE CLUB MOURNS DIRECTOR
Mr ALBERT J. SMITH

On 18th November 1955 Mr Albert John Smith MBE died in Rush Green Hospital after collapsing at home. He was 69. As we recounted in volume 2 of this series, Mr Smith (pictured right) was one of the founders of the re-launched club back in 1929. He ran a successful building business, leaving over £35,000 in his will. He lived in a house he had built for himself in Main Road, named Almavedon after his family: AL (Albert), MA (Mabel, his wife), VE (Vera, their daughter) and DON (Donald, their son).

The tribute to Mr Smith at Romford's next match is reported as follows in the *Romford Recorder* of Friday 25th November 1955:

Cup win epitaph for Boro' founder

It would take a much more able pen than mine to describe adequately the impressive and reverent scene which preceded the East Anglian Cup tie at Brooklands on Saturday, when officials, players and thousands of spectators stood with heads bare in silent tribute to the memory of Mr A.J. Smith MBE, a founder member of the club.

The match which followed was just as Mr Smith would have wished – fast, clean and exciting, with a semi-final prize going to the better team. Surely, there could be no finer epitaph for so great a sportsman. Romford's 6-2 win over Chelmsford City reserves was their biggest so far this season......

DIRECTORS' REPORT FOR THE FOURTEEN MONTHS ENDED 31ST JULY, 1956

The period covered by the Accounts has not been entirely an uneventful one so far as the Company is concerned, but a net loss of £1,310 has been the result. Members will notice how closely this figure compares with the loss sustained by the company for the year ended the 31st May, 1955, i.e. £1,261....

....There is little doubt in the minds of your Directors that given a First Team capable of winning league matches, the Accounts will once again show a vastly different picture. Nevertheless, it would be quite wrong for your Directors to infer that the Players have not given of their best. This is certainly not the case, but their best was not good enough during this particular season in league matches. The point should be made, however, that on many occasions, the decision went against the Team by an odd goal.

Your Directors in their last Report indicated that their policy was to rebuild the Team with emphasis on youth, and the results on the field during the Season under review were not unexpected. Members will understand that a Season or two may well pass before success crowns the efforts that have been and are being made to restore the prestige of the Club. It is remarkable, however, that the Club won both the East Anglian Cup and the Thameside Challenge Trophy, the latter in the postponed Final against Ilford, winning by five goals to four, (another instance of a close result), and the former after defeating five professional Clubs – Arsenal, Colchester, Chelmsford, Cambridge and Clacton – a really commendable performance....

The Season saw the completion of the extension to the Popular Stand, and by reason of this and other Ground improvements, the Property and Equipment Account now stands at £15,000 after a sum of £673 has been written off for depreciation....

With regard to the future, no further immediate improvements in the sense of extensions to covered accommodation are envisaged, at least for the time being, but your Directors who have ever in mind the prospect of floodlighting the Ground will give further consideration to the desirability of this amenity. floodlighting has been considered from time to time, but it has been felt not possible, in the present state of the Company's finances, coupled with the present restrictions on capital expenditure, but it is noted that other Clubs in the vicinity have been exploring the installation of floodlighting and outside supporting organisations have assisted these Clubs in this connection, and it may well be that something of this nature may eventually happen in Romford.

Your Directors have given thought to providing seating accommodation in the whole or part of the Popular Stand, but on this have come to no final decision.....

With the prospect of the Small Lotteries and Gaming Act 1956 becoming law, your Directors took immediate steps to study the effect and took expert advice, and acted as a result thereof, in the promotion of a weekly lottery, the result of which will be shown in the Statement of Accounts for the next year. It is sufficient to say here that the Company ceased to take part in any Lottery following extensive correspondence with the Football Association.

....In conclusion, while your Directors' high hopes for the Season expressed in the last report did not altogether materialise, they take this opportunity of thanking the Supporters of the Club for their loyalty through many disappointments...

The above report was presented to shareholders at the Annual General Meeting held on Tuesday 12ᵗʰ February 1957, and reported as follows in the *Romford Recorder*, Friday 15ᵗʰ February 1957

SHAREHOLDER HITS AT BORO TEAM POLICY

Romford Football Club directors were tackled on the question of team policy at the company's 17th annual meeting on Tuesday. Shareholder Mr A.E.Blane asked why the management committee persisted in playing men who, in the view of supporters, he said, were not suitable.

Replied Mr Glyn Richards, management committee chairman, "There is a general impression among supporters that they know what is best for the club. But it is the management committee who know fully all the difficulties of fielding the best available team. Believe me, the whole policy of Romford FC has been deliberately and concisely thought out".

EXAMPLE. Supporters were not always aware of the troubles the committee had to face, said Mr Richards. There were various circumstances which compelled them to put certain men in certain positions. He quoted the team's recent Amateur Cup games as an example. "We had other players, but most of them were cup-tied", he explained.

Mr Richards spoke of the club's "drastic team policy change" in introducing new coach Peter Wallace. "No-one can deny he has put new spirit into the club", he said, "and I personally would like to pay tribute to Mr Wallace for the interest, ingenuity and devotion he has shown. But even he cannot work miracles. All we ask is for a little patience".

Summing up past performances, Company chairman Lord Macpherson thought Romford were experiencing a spell that hit all football clubs. Touching on the loss of £1,310 incurred in the 14 months ending July 31 last year, he said the club had been losing money during the time they had been trying to rebuild the side. "You cannot hurry rebuilding, no matter how moneyed or powerful you are", he said. "But we have touched rock bottom and are now beginning to see the light. We are improving and next season perhaps we shall have a winning team".

Rounding off, the chairman thanked the Supporters' Club for their energetic and virile backing. "With the continued support of our followers, and the present policy of the management committee, I am confident we will return to our former strength", he said.

Shareholder Mr E.H. Ashford asked if the directors could explain Romford's recent away successes, but failures at home - something which Lord Macpherson had described as "an extraordinary phenomenon". Said selection committee chairman Mr Jim Parrish, "It is impossible to answer that question. If we knew the answer we could do something about it".

Another shareholder asked Mr Parrish to explain the criticism of himself during the demonstration by supporters at Brooklands in October. "I am known as the chairman of the selectors", replied Mr Parrish, "and because of that I took the brunt of the abuse. I made one mistake. A particular individual had pestered me for a long time and I took him aside and told him what I thought of him".

THE ROMFORD FOOTBALL CLUB LIMITED

Full Members of The Football Association
Full Members of Isthmian Football League
Affiliated to Essex County Football Association

Chairman: Rt.Hon Lord T.Macpherson
Directors: Messrs.M.A.Brazier, A.E.Kittle, H.F.Knights, W.G.Mann,
J.W.Parrish CC, G.Richards, JP
Secretary: Mr H.W.Muskett

Colours: Royal Blue and Old Gold Shirts,White Shorts

Registered Office: 110, Hyland Way, Hornchurch

Ground: Brooklands Sports Ground,Romford

Football Club Management Committee:
Chairman: Mr G.Richards JP
Vice-Chairman: Mr H.F.Knights   **Hon.Gen.Secretary:** Mr M.A.Brazier
Hon.Press Secretary: Mr R.S.Lyons   **Hon.Programme Secretary:** Mr H.Wright
Other Committee Members: Messrs. F.H.Adams, Major A.E.Adlam, F.E.Fryatt,
G.I.Howlett, R.S.Lyons, W.F.Mackenzie, J.W.Parrish CC

Bankers: Lloyds Bank Limited
Hon.Auditors: Messrs Iion V.Cummings, Partridge & Co.

Reserve XI Secretary: Major A.E.Adlam
Third XI Secretary and Manager: Mr A.J.Anderton

Statistics: Mr John Haley(Ex Officio)   **Trainer Coach:** Mr G.W.Patterson

Reserve Team Trainer: Mr Fred.Griffiths: (resigned December 1956)
Mr Len Eastment (appointed 5th March but resigned 30th April)

Groundsman: Mr W.C.(Bill)Seddon

LEAGUES & COMPETITIONS 1956 – 57

FA Challenge Cup
FA Amateur Challenge Cup
Isthmian Football League
Essex County FA Senior Challenge Cup
East Anglian Cup
Essex Thameside Challenge Competition
Romford Charity Senior Cup
Reg Sheward Memorial Trophy

Isthmian Football League Reserve Section
Essex County FA Intermediate Challenge Cup
Essex Thameside Challenge Competition Reserve Section

Eastern "A" Football League
Eastern "A" Football League Cup
Essex County FA Junior Challenge Cup

Admission Prices Season 1956 – 57

	First Team			Reserve Team		
	Adults	OAPs	Child	Adults	OAPs	Child
Ground	1/-		6d	6d		3d
Ground & Enclosure	1/9		1/-	1/-		6d
Grandstand	2/6		2/6	1/-		6d

Season Ticket Prices Season 1956 – 57

	Adults	OAPs & Children
Grandstand (All one price)	£1.10.0	
Ground & Enclosure	£1.1.0	12/6
Ground only	12/6	7/6

NOTE: Attendance figures are not available for the 1956–57 season, therefore the details given are estimates based on the cash receipts which are known, together with an allowance for season ticket holders.

Pre-Season Final Trial match

E.C.Rogers;J.Field,E.R.Cave;B.W.Kelly,F.L.Newman,R.Scharvi;
J.Wood,R.Webster,C.Johnson,F.Devine,C.Tiffin.

J.F.Allen;N.P.Appleton,D.M.Jones;D.H.Taylor,R.Impey,P.J.Jolly;
S.Dankaro,A.Hull,R.Mahoney,-.Westmore,A.F.Herbert.

A.Gooch,G.Bumpstead,E.Ross,S.Shaef.

Note: D.Stockley (Dagenham) and R.Webster (Barking) both joined pre-season training at the ground, but did not take part in the trial match and decided to stay with their old clubs.

First Team Match Details

18 Aug IFL Home Wimbledon 1 – 0 Herbert
Attendance: 1,810 Receipts: £80.17.0 Programmes: £14.17.9 Car Park: £2.16.3
Romford: E.C.Rogers;J.P.Field,E.R.Cave;B.W.Kelly,F.L.Newman(Capt),A.J.Taylor;
J.Wood,A.Hull,J.Bee,C.Tiffin,A.F.Herbert.

20 Aug ETTF Away Ilford 5 – 4 Tiffin(2)Wood,Kelly,Herbert
Romford: E.C.Rogers;J.P.Field,E.R.Cave;B.W.Kelly,F.L.Newman(Capt),A.J.Taylor;
J.Wood,P.J.Jolly,J.Bee,C.Tiffin,A.F.Herbert.

23 Aug IFL Home Dulwich Hamlet 3 – 1 Herbert,Jolly(2)
Attendance: 1,720 Receipts: £75.14.0 Programmes: £ ?? Car Park: £3.10.0
Romford: E.C.Rogers;J.P.Field,E.R.Cave;B.W.Kelly,F.L.Newman(Capt),A.J.Taylor;
J.Wood,P.J.Jolly,J.Bee,C.Tiffin,A.F.Herbert.

25 Aug IFL Away Oxford City 1 – 10 Herbert
Romford: E.C.Rogers;J.P.Field,E.R.Cave;B.W.Kelly,F.L.Newman(Capt),A.J.Taylor;
J.Wood,P.J.Jolly,J.Bee,C.Tiffin,A.F.Herbert.

29 Aug IFL Away DulwichHamlet 1 – 5 Baldwin
Romford: E.C.Rogers;J.P.Field,E.R.Cave;B.W.Kelly,F.L.Newman(Capt),A.J.Taylor;
J.Wood,P.J.Jolly,J.Baldwin,C.Tiffin,A.F.Herbert.

1 Sept IFL Home Kingstonian 2 – 2 Tiffin(2)
Attendance: 1,680 Receipts: £73.3.3 Programmes: £7.15.6 Car Park: £3.1.3
Romford: E.C.Rogers;J.P.Field,J.V.Eyett;B.W.Kelly,F.L.Newman(Capt),R.Scharvi;
J.Wood,P.J.Jolly,J.Bee,C.Tiffin,D.J.Rubery.

3 Sept EAC1R Away Aveley 0 – 4
Romford: E.C.Rogers;J.P.Field,J.V.Eyett;B.W.Kelly,F.L.Newman(Capt),R.Scharvi;
J.Wood,P.J.Jolly,J.Bee,C.Tiffin,D.J.Rubery.

8 Sept FACPR Home Grays Athletic 4 – 2 Wood(2)Bee(2)
Attendance: 3,030 Receipts: £160.6.0 Progs: £13.9.3 Car Park: £ ??
Romford: E.C.Rogers;J.P.Field,E.R.Cave;E.Ross,F.L.Newman(Capt),A.J.Taylor;
J.Wood,P.J.Jolly,J.Bee,C.Tiffin,A.F.Herbert.

12 Sept ETT1R Away Leytonstone 3 – 1 Bee,Tiffin(2)
Romford: E.C.Rogers;J.P.Field,E.R.Cave;E.Ross,F.L.Newman(Capt),D.H.Taylor;
J.Wood,B.Barber,J.Bee,C.Tiffin,A.Devine.

15 Sept IFL Away Clapton 1 – 7 Le Grave(og)
Romford: E.C.Rogers;J.P.Field,E.R.Cave;E.Ross,F.L.Newman(Capt),D.H.Taylor;
J.Wood,B.Barber,J.Bee,C.Tiffin,A.Devine.

22 Sept FAC1Q Away Briggs Sports 1 – 0 Tiffin
Romford: E.C.Rogers;J.P.Field,B.W.Kelly;E.Ross,F.L.Newman(Capt),D.H.Taylor;
J.Wood,B.Barber,J.Bee,C.Tiffin,G.W.Andrews.

29 Sept IFL Home Bromley 2 – 3 Bee(2pens)
Attendance: 3,010 Receipts: £149.5.6 Programmes: £17.3.2 Car Park: £4.0.0
Romford: E.C.Rogers;J.P.Field,R.Jones;P.J.Jolly,B.W.Kelly(Capt),D.H.Taylor;
J.Wood,B.Barber,J.Bee,C.Tiffin,G.W.Andrews.

6 Oct FAC2Q Away Chelmsford City 0 – 4
Attendance: 4,782
Romford: P.Gamman;J.P.Field,B.W.Kelly;P.J.Jolly,F.L.Newman(Capt),D.H.Taylor;
J.Wood,B.Barber,J.Bee,C.Tiffin,G.W.Andrews.

13 Oct IFL Away Tooting & Mitcham United 1 – 3 Barber
Romford: P.Gamman;J.P.Field,B.W.Kelly;P.J.Jolly,F.L.Newman(Capt),D.H.Taylor;
S.Dankaro,B.Barber,J.Bee,C.Tiffin,G.W.Andrews.

20 Oct IFL Home St. Albans City 3 – 4 Abbott(2)Tiffin
Attendance: 3,180 Receipts: £161.18.11 Programmes: £12.14.0 Car Park: £3.11.3
Romford: P.Gamman;J.P.Field,B.W.Kelly;D.H.Taylor,F.L.Newman(Capt),A.J.Taylor;
S.Dankaro,B.Barber,C.Tiffin,K.Abbott,G.Andrews.

27 Oct IFL Home Clapton 0 – 0
Attendance: 2,400 Receipts: £115.4.6 Programmes: £10.13.8 Car Park: £3.11.3
Romford: P.Gamman;J.P.Field,F.L.Newman(Capt);J.J.Whitecross,B.W.Kelly,P.J.Jolly;
J.Wood,B.Barber,C.Tiffin,K.Abbott,G.W.Andrews.

3 Nov IFL Away# Corinthian Casuals 4 – 3 Abbott,Tiffin(3)
Romford: P.Gamman;N.P.Appleton,F.L.Newman(Capt);J.J.Whitecross,B.W.Kelly,P.J.Jolly;
G.W.Andrews,B.Barber,C.Tiffin,K.Abbott,J.Bee.

10 Nov IFL Home Walthamstow Avenue 0 – 2
Attendance: 2,120 Receipts: £99.18.3 Programmes: £14.17.3 Car Park: £4.16.0
Romford: P.Gamman;J.P.Field,F.L.Newman(Capt);J.J.Whitecross,B.W.Kelly,P.J.Jolly;
G.W.Andrews,B.Barber,C.Tiffin,E.Watts,J.Bee.

17 Nov IFL Away Wycombe Wanderers 4 – 4 Tiffin(2)Andrews,Barber
Romford: P.Gamman;N.P.Appleton,F.L.Newman(Capt);J.J.Whitecross,B.W.Kelly,D.H.Taylor;
G.W.Andrews,B.Barber,C.Tiffin,E.Watts,J.Bee.

24 Nov IFL Away Woking 3 – 3 Tiffin,Watts,Andrews
Romford: P.Gamman;N.P.Appleton,F.L.Newman(Capt);J.J.Whitecross,B.W.Kelly,R.Scharvi;
G.W.Andrews,B.Barber,C.Tiffin,E.Watts,J.Bee.

1 Dec IFL Home Oxford City 1 – 5 Bee
Attendance: 1,650 Receipts: £79.4.3 Programmes: £12.9.3 Car Park: £3.7.6
Romford: P.Gamman;N.P.Appleton,H.LeGrave;J.J.Whitecross,B.W.Kelly(Capt),R.Scharvi;
G.W.Andrews,B.Barber,D.Bowness,C.Tiffin,J.Bee.

8 Dec IFL Away Barking 2 – 1 Tiffin,Andrews
Romford: E.C.Rogers;N.P.Appleton,H.LeGrave;J.J.Whitecross,B.W.Kelly(Capt),P.J.Jolly;
G.W.Andrews,B.Barber,C.Tiffin,D.Bowness,J.Bee.

15 Dec IFL Home Leytonstone 3 – 1 Bee(2)(1pen)Barber
Attendance: 1,070 Receipts: £46.14.3 Programmes: £10.3.0 Car Park: £2.5.0
Romford: E.C.Rogers;N.P.Appleton,H.LeGrave;J.J.Whitecross,B.W.Kelly(Capt),P.J.Jolly;
G.W.Andrews,B.Barber,C.Tiffin,E.Watts,J.Bee.

25 Dec IFL Home Ilford 2 – 4 Barber,Bee(pen)
Attendance: 1,600 Receipts: £76.9.0 Programmes: £10.8.1 Car Park: £3.14.0
Romford: E.C.Rogers;N.P.Appleton,H.LeGrave;J.J.Whitecross,B.W.Kelly(Capt),M.R.Cooper;
G.W.Andrews,B.Barber,C.Tiffin,E.Watts,J.Bee.

26 Dec IFL Away Ilford 0 – 1
Romford: E.C.Rogers;M.R.Cooper,N.P.Appleton;I.Ross,D.H.Taylor(Capt),A.J.Taylor;
M.D.Paviour,J.J.Whitecross,C.Tiffin,D.Bowness,G.W.Andrews.

29 Dec IFL Away St. Albans City 3 – 2 Gramlick,Barber(2)
Romford: E.C.Rogers;N.P.Appleton,M.R.Cooper;J.J.Whitecross,D.H.Taylor(Capt),A.J.Taylor;
M.D.Paviour,R.J.Gramlick,C.Tiffin,B.Barber,D.Bowness.

5 Jan IFL Home Wycombe Wanderers 1 – 2 Barber
Attendance: 1,700 Receipts: £93.17.6 Progs: £13.3.11 Car Park: £3.15.3
Romford: E.C.Rogers;N.P.Appleton,M.R.Cooper;J.J.Whitecross,D.H.Taylor(Capt),A.J.Taylor;
G.W.Andrews,R.J.Gramlick,C.Tiffin,B.Barber,D.Bowness.

12 Jan AC1R Away Pegasus 2 – 1 Bee,Abbott
Romford: E.C.Rogers;N.P.Appleton,M.R.Cooper;J.J.Whitecross,D.H.Taylor(Capt),A.J.Taylor;
G.W.Andrews,K.Abbott,C.Tiffin,B.Barber,J.Bee.

19 Jan ESC1R Home Aveley 1 – 3 Abbott
Attendance: 2,340 Receipts: £121.9.6 Programmes: £15.17.9 Car Park: £4.0.0
Romford: E.C.Rogers;N.P.Appleton,M.R.Cooper;P.J.Jolly,D.H.Taylor(Capt),A.J.Taylor;
G.W.Andrews,K.Abbott,C.Tiffin,B.Barber,J.Bee.

26 Jan AC2R Away Walthamstow Avenue 2 – 2 Bee,Tiffin
Romford: E.C.Rogers;N.P.Appleton,M.R.Cooper;J.J.Whitecross,D.H.Taylor(Capt),A.J.Taylor;
G.W.Andrews,K.Abbott,C.Tiffin,B.Barber,J.Bee.

2 Feb ACRp Home Walthamstow Avenue 0 – 4
Attendance: 7,335 Receipts: £361.0.3 Programmes: £26.6.9 Car Park: £7.11.6
Romford: E.C.Rogers;N.P.Appleton,M.R.Cooper;J.J.Whitecross,D.H.Taylor(Capt),A.J.Taylor;
G.W.Andrews,K.Abbott,C.Tiffin,B.Barber,J.Bee.

9 Feb IFL Away Wimbledon 3 – 1 Holyoake(og)Barber,Vernon
Romford: E.C.Rogers;N.P.Appleton,M.R.Cooper,I.Ross,D.H.Taylor(Capt),W.H.Schofield;
G.W.Andrews,M.D.Paviour,J.Vernon,B.Barber,D.Bowness.

16 Feb IFL Away Kingstonian 2 – 5 Barber(2)
Romford: E.C.Rogers;N.P.Appleton,M.R.Cooper;I.Ross,D.H.Taylor(Capt),A.J.Taylor;
J.P.Field,G.W.Andrews,C.Tiffin,B.Barber,D.Bowness.

23 Feb IFL Home Woking 1 – 7 A.Taylor
Attendance: 1,720 Receipts: £83.10.8 Programmes: £11.13.9 Car Park: £1.15.0
Romford: E.C.Rogers;N.P.Appleton,M.R.Cooper;I.Ross,D.H.Taylor(Capt),A.J.Taylor;
G.W.Andrews,K.Abbott,M.D.Paviour,B.Barber,D.Bowness.

2 Mar IFL Home Barking 0 – 1
Attendance: 1,730 Receipts: £85.16.3 Programmes: £13.19.11 Car Park: £2.18.0
Romford: E.C.Rogers;N.P.Appleton,M.R.Cooper;J.J.Whitecross,D.H.Taylor(Capt),R.J.Fleetwood;
G.W.Andrews,M.D.Paviour,J.Vernon,B.Barber,D.Bowness.

9 Mar Frdly Home Deal Town 2 – 1 Bowness,Tiffin
Attendance: 1,650 Receipts: £70.4.6 Programmes: £7.8.7 Car Park: £1.13.0
Romford: P.Gamman;N.P.Appleton,M.R.Cooper(Capt);R.J.Fleetwood,P.J.Jolly,A.J.Taylor;
G.L.Tillyer,L.Rowlands,J.Vernon,E.Watts,D.Bowness. Sub. C.Tiffin replaced Vernon.

16 Mar IFL Away Walthamstow Avenue 1 – 1 Barber
Romford: P.Gamman;N.P.Appleton,M.R.Cooper(Capt);R.J.Fleetwood,P.J.Jolly,A.J.Taylor;
G.L.Tillyer,B.Barber,C.Tiffin,E.Watts,D.Bowness.

23 Mar IFL Away Bromley 1 – 2 Bowness
Romford: P.Gamman;N.P.Appleton,M.R.Cooper(Capt);R.J.Fleetwood,P.J.Jolly,A.J.Taylor;
G.L.Tillyer,B.Barber,C.Tiffin,E.Watts,D.Bowness.

30 Mar IFL Away Leytonstone 2 – 1 Cooper,Barber
Romford: P.Gamman;N.P.Appleton,M.R.Cooper(Capt);R.J.Fleetwood,P.J.Jolly,A.J.Taylor;
G.L.Tillyer,B.Barber,C.Tiffin,E.Watts,D.Bowness.

6 Apr IFL Home Tooting & Mitcham United 1 – 0 Tiffin
Attendance: 2,470 Receipts: £116.0.6 Programmes: £9.7.10 Car Park: £1.11.6
Romford: P.Gamman;N.P.Appleton,M.R.Cooper(Capt);R.J.Fleetwood,P.J.Jolly,A.J.Taylor;
G.L.Tillyer,B.Barber,C.Tiffin,E.Watts,D.Bowness.

13 Apr   Frdly   Away   Cambridge City   1 – 1 Bowness
Romford: P.Gamman;N.P.Appleton,M.R.Cooper(Capt);R.J.Fleetwood,P.J.Jolly,A.J.Taylor;
J.Wood,B.Barber,C.Tiffin,L.Rowlands,D.Bowness.

15 Apr   IFL   Home   Corinthian Casuals   4 – 0 Bowness(3)Tiffin
Attendance: 1,040   Receipts: £42.4.0   Programmes: £6.4.0   Car Park: £ None
Romford: P.Gamman;N.P.Appleton,M.R.Cooper(Capt);R.J.Fleetwood,P.J.Jolly,A.J.Taylor;
G.L.Tillyer,B.Barber,C.Tiffin,E.Watts,D.Bowness.

19 Apr   ETTSF Home   Barking   0 – 2
Attendance: 2,540   Receipts: £131.0.3   Programmes: £11.10.6 Car Park: £0.15.6
Romford: P.Gamman;N.P.Appleton,M.R.Cooper(Capt);R.J.Fleetwood,P.J.Jolly,A.J.Taylor;
G.L.Tillyer,B.Barber,C.Tiffin,E.Watts,P.D.Hall.

22 Apr   Frdly   Away   Carshalton Athletic   3 – 0 Tiffin,Bowness,Whitecross
Romford: P.Gamman;N.P.Appleton,M.R.Cooper(Capt);R.J.Fleetwood,P.J.Jolly,A.J.Taylor;
P.D.Hall,B.Barber,C.Tiffin,J.J.Whitecross,D.Bowness.

25 Apr   RCSC   Home   Dagenham   1 – 2 Barber
Attendance: 575   Receipts: £25.17.0   Programmes: £3.16.0 Car Park: £1.3.6
Romford: P.Gamman;N.P.Appleton,M.R.Cooper(Capt);R.J.Fleetwood,P.J.Jolly,A.J.Taylor;
M.D.Paviour,B.Barber,C.Tiffin,E.Watts,D.Bowness. (Sub. L.Rowland for Watts)

27 Apr   Frdly   Home   Barnet   6 – 0 Barber(3)Bowness(2)Rowlands
Attendance: 765   Receipts: £34.17.9   Programmes: £4.4.5 Car Park: £1.1.9
Romford: P.Gamman;N.P.Appleton,M.R.Cooper(Capt);R.J.Fleetwood,P.J.Jolly,A.J.Taylor;
G.L.Tillyer,B.Barber,C.Tiffin,L.Rowlands,D.Bowness.

11 May RST   Home   D.J.Davis's Local All Star XI   5 – 2 Bowness,Holmes,Tiffin(3)
Attendance: 1,150   Receipts: £53.11.9   Programmes: £8.10.9 Car Park: £1.8.0
Romford: P.Gamman;N.P.Appleton,M.R.Cooper(Capt);P.J.Jolly,P.Carey(Barking),A.J.Taylor;
L.Rowlands,L.Holmes(Barking),C.Tiffin,B.Barber,D.Bowness.

#Played at The Oval Cricket Ground.

FIRST TEAM SUMMARY OF RESULTS SEASON 1956 – 57

		Home			Goals		Away			Goals		
	P	W	D	L	For	Ag	W	D	L	For	Ag	Pts
Isthmian Football League	30	5	2	8	24	32	5	3	7	29	49	25
FA Challenge Cup	3	1	0	0	4	2	1	0	1	1	4	
FA Amateur Challenge Cup	3	0	0	1	0	4	1	1	0	4	3	
Essex County FA Senior Cup	1	0	0	1	1	3	0	0	0	0	0	
East Anglian Cup	1	0	0	0	0	0	0	0	1	0	4	
Essex Thameside Chal.Comp.	2	0	0	1	0	2	1	0	0	3	1	
Essex Thameside C.C. 55/56	1	0	0	0	0	0	1	0	0	5	4	
Romford Charity Senior Cup	1	0	0	1	1	2	0	0	0	0	0	
Reg. Sheward Trophy	1	1	0	0	5	2	0	0	0	0	0	
Friendlies	4	2	0	0	8	1	1	1	0	4	3	
Totals	47	9	2	12	43	48	10	5	9	46	68	

Isthmian Football League
Final Table

					Goals		
	P	W	D	L	For	Ag	Pts
Wycombe Wanderers	30	18	6	6	86	53	42
Woking	30	20	1	9	104	47	41
Bromley	30	16	5	9	78	60	37
Oxford City	30	16	3	11	65	57	35
Ilford	30	12	8	10	59	65	32
Tooting & Mitcham United	30	10	11	9	53	48	31
Kingstonian	30	11	9	10	72	77	31
Walthamstow Avenue	30	11	8	11	48	46	30
Dulwich Hamlet	30	13	3	14	65	54	29
St.Albans City	30	13	3	14	62	71	29
Leytonstone	30	11	6	13	50	50	28

Clapton	30	9	9	12	48	59	27
Wimbledon	30	10	5	15	47	66	25
Romford	**30**	**10**	**5**	**15**	**53**	**81**	**25**
Barking	30	7	6	17	48	72	20
Corinthian Casuals	30	7	4	19	46	78	18

FIRST TEAM CUP RESULTS

FA Challenge Cup
Final: Aston Villa   2   Manchester United   1

Romford's progress: 1st Qual.   Home   Grays Athletic   4 - 2
2nd Qual.   Away   Briggs Sports   1 - 0
3rd Qual.   Away   Chelmsford City   0 – 4

FA Amateur Challenge Cup
Final: Bishop Auckland   3   Wycombe Wanderers   1

Romford's progress: 1st Round   Away   Pegasus   2 - 1
2nd Round   Away   Walthamstow Avenue   2 - 2
Replay   Home   Walthamstow Avenue   0 – 4

Essex County FA Senior Challenge Cup
Final: Grays Athletic   3   Ilford   1

Romford's progress: 1st Round   Home   Aveley   1 – 3

East Anglian Cup
Final: n/k

1sr Round   Away   Aveley   0 - 4

Essex Thameside Challenge Competition
Final: n/k

Romford's progress: 1st Round   Away   Leytonstone   3 - 1
Semi-Final   Home   Barking   0 – 2

Romford Charity Senior Cup
Romford   1   Dagenham   2

Reg. Sheward Memorial Trophy
Romford   5   D.J.Davies's Local All Star XI   2

FIRST TEAM DEBUTS SEASON 1956 – 57

1956

				Previous Club
18th Aug.	v Wimbledon	-	**A.Hull**	Basildon Town
1st Sept.	v Kingstonian	-	**R.Scharvi**	n/k
12th Sept.	v Leytonstone	-	**B.Barber**	Walthamstow Avenue
		-	**A.Devine**	Barking
3rd Nov.	v Corinthian Casuals	-	**N.P.Appleton**	n/k
1st Dec.	v Oxford City	-	**H.LeGrave**	Clapton
		-	**D.Bowness**	Woodford Town
25th Dec.	v Ilford	-	**M.R.Cooper**	Barnet
26th Dec.	v Ilford	-	**I.Ross**	Ilford
		-	**M.D.Paviour**	n/k
29th Dec.	v St.Albans City	-	**R.Gramlick**	Leyton

1957

9th Feb.	v Wimbledon	-	**W.H.Schofield**	Dagenham
2nd Mar.	v Barking	-	**R.J.Fleetwood**	Leytonstone
9th Mar.	v Deal Town	-	**G.L.Tillyer**	Wimbledon
		-	**L.Rowlands**	Wimbledon

Players returned to the Club
1957

9th Feb.	v Wimbledon	-	**J.Vernon**	H.M.Forces
19th Apr.	v Barking	-	**P.D.Hall**	Rainham Town

Guest Players
1957

11th May	v All Star XI	-	**P.Carey**	Leyton Orient/Barking
		-	**L.A.Holmes**	Barking

FIRST TEAM APPEARANCES SEASON 1956 - 57

	A	B	C	D	E	F	G	H	I	J	Total
Ken Abbott	4	0	3	1	0	0	0	0	0	0	8
George Andrews	18	2	3	1	0	0	0	0	0	0	24
Norman Appleton	19	0	3	1	0	1	0	1	1	4	30
Jim Baldwin	1	0	0	0	0	0	0	0	0	0	1
Brian Barber	24	2	3	1	0	2	0	1	1	3	37
Johnny Bee	15	3	3	1	1	1	1	0	0	0	25
Derek Bowness	14	0	0	0	0	0	0	1	1	4	20
Peter Carey	0	0	0	0	0	0	0	0	1	0	1
Roy Cave	5	1	0	0	0	1	1	0	0	0	8
Mick Cooper	13	0	3	1	0	1	0	1	1	4	24
Sunday Dankaro	2	0	0	0	0	0	0	0	0	0	2
Alec Devine	1	0	0	0	0	1	0	0	0	0	2
Jim Eyett	1	0	0	0	1	0	0	0	0	0	2
Joe Field	12	3	0	0	1	1	1	0	0	0	18
Reg Fleetwood	6	0	0	0	0	1	0	1	0	4	12
Peter Gamman	13	1	0	0	0	1	0	1	1	4	21
Ray Gramlick	2	0	0	0	0	0	0	0	0	0	2
Tony Herbert	4	1	0	0	0	0	1	0	0	0	6
Peter Hall	0	0	0	0	0	1	0	0	0	1	2
Buddy Holmes	0	0	0	0	0	0	0	0	0	1	1
Alf Hull	1	0	0	0	0	0	0	0	0	0	1
Pat Jolly	16	2	0	1	1	1	1	1	1	4	28
R. Jones	1	0	0	0	0	0	0	0	0	0	1
Bernard Kelly	17	2	0	0	1	0	1	0	0	0	21
H. LeGrave	4	0	0	0	0	0	0	0	0	0	4
Frank Newman	13	3	0	0	1	1	1	0	0	0	19
Mike Paviour	5	0	0	0	0	0	0	1	0	0	6
Ernie Rogers	17	2	3	1	1	1	1	0	0	0	26
Eddie Ross	1	2	0	0	0	1	0	0	0	0	4
Ian Ross	4	0	0	0	0	0	0	0	0	0	4
Len Rowlands	0	0	0	0	0	0	0	1*	1	3	5*
Derek Rubery	1	0	0	0	1	0	0	0	0	0	2
R. Scharvi	3	0	0	0	1	0	0	0	0	0	4
Billy Schofield	1	0	0	0	0	0	0	0	0	0	1
Alan Taylor	15	1	3	1	0	1	1	1	1	4	28
Dennis Taylor	12	2	3	1	0	1	0	0	0	0	19
Cyril Tiffin	27	3	3	1	1	2	1	1	1*	4	44*
Gordon Tillyer	5	0	0	0	0	1	0	0	0	2	8
Jim Vernon	2	0	0	0	0	0	0	0	0	1	3
Eddie Watts	10	0	0	0	0	1	0	1	0	1	13
Johnny Whitecross	13	0	3	0	0	0	0	0	0	1	17
Jimmy Wood	8	3	0	0	1	1	1	0	0	1	15
Total	330	33	33	11	11	22	11	12*	12*	44	519*

*Includes appearance as a substitute.

FIRST TEAM GOALSCORERS SEASON 1956 - 57

	A	B	C	D	E	F	G	H	I	J	Total
Cyril Tiffin	12	1	1	0	0	2	2	0	3	2	23
Brian Barber	12	0	0	0	0	0	0	1	0	3	16
Johnny Bee	6	2	2	0	0	1	0	0	0	0	11
Derek Bowness	4	0	0	0	0	0	0	0	1	5	10
Ken Abbott	3	0	1	1	0	0	0	0	0	0	5
Tony Herbert	3	0	0	0	0	0	1	0	0	0	4
Jimmy Wood	0	2	0	0	0	0	1	0	0	0	3
George Andrews	3	0	0	0	0	0	0	0	0	0	3
Pat Jolly	2	0	0	0	0	0	0	0	0	0	2
Bernard Kelly	0	0	0	0	0	0	1	0	0	0	1
Jim Baldwin	1	0	0	0	0	0	0	0	0	0	1
Eddie Watts	1	0	0	0	0	0	0	0	0	0	1
Ray Gramlick	1	0	0	0	0	0	0	0	0	0	1
Jim Vernon	1	0	0	0	0	0	0	0	0	0	1
Alan Taylor	1	0	0	0	0	0	0	0	0	0	1
Mick Cooper	1	0	0	0	0	0	0	0	0	0	1
Johnny Whitecross	0	0	0	0	0	0	0	0	0	1	1
Len Rowlands	0	0	0	0	0	0	0	0	0	1	1
Buddy Holmes	0	0	0	0	0	0	0	0	1	0	1
Own Goals	2	0	0	0	0	0	0	0	0	0	2
Total	53	5	4	1	0	3	5	1	5	12	89

A	Isthmian League
B	FA Challenge Cup
C	FA Amateur Challenge Cup
D	Essex Senior Cup
E	East Anglian Cup
F	Thameside Trophy
G	Thameside Trophy 1955/56
H	Romford Charity Cup
I	Reg Sheward Trophy
J	Friendly Matches

Reserve Team Match Details

18 Aug IFLR Away Wimbledon Reserves   0 – 3
Romford Res.: J.F.Allen;A.Gooch;D.M.Jones;D.Prior,P.J.Jolly,R.Scharvi;
S.Dankaro,A.Devine,C.Johnson,D.Westmore,A.Hitchcock.

25 Aug IFLR Home Leytonstone Reserves   3 – 0 Baldwin(2)P.Jones
Attendance: 300   Receipts: £5.5.6
Romford Res.: J.F.Allen;A.Gooch,F.Frost;E.Ross,J.V.Eyett(Capt),R.J.Leaver;
D.J.Rubery,K.Abbott,J.Baldwin,P.Jones,A.Hitchcock.

1 Sept IFLR Away Corinthian Casuals Reserves   1 – 2 Hull
Romford Res.: J.F.Allen;A.Gooch,F.Frost;E.Ross,D.H.Taylor,A.J.Taylor;
A.Devine,A.Hull,R.D.Jones,K.Abbott,M.Withycombe.

8 Sept IFLR Away Tooting & Mitcham United Res.   2 – 7 Devine(2)
Romford Res.: R.Wolfe;F.Frost,D.M.Jones;N.P.Appleton,D.H.Taylor,J.V.Eyett(Capt);
J.Baldwin,K.Abbott,G.Harrison,M.Withycombe,A.Devine.

10 Sept ETR1R Away Walthamstow Avenue Reserves   0 – 2
Romford Res.: Sel. J.Allen;F.Frost,D.Jones;N.P.Appleton,D.H.Taylor,J.V.Eyett;
J.Baldwin,K.Abbott,R.Jones,A.Hitchcock,A.Devine.

15 Sept IFLR Home Oxford City Reserves   6 – 1 Baldwin(4)Rubery,Andrews(pen)
Attendance: 310   Receipts: £5.8.0
Romford Res.: R.Wolfe;N.P.Appleton,D.M.Jones;B.W.Kelly,J.V.Eyett(Capt),R.Scharvi;
D.J.Rubery,K.Abbott,J.Baldwin,A.Hull,G.W.Andrews.

22 Sept IFLR Away Woking Reserves   3 – 2 Harrison,Hull,R.Jones(og)
Romford Res.: R.Wolfe;E.R.Cave,D.M.Jones;N.P.Appleton,J.V.Eyett(Capt),A.J.Taylor;
D.J.Rubery,A.Hull,G.Harrison,K.Abbott,A.F.Herbert.

29 Sept IFLR Away Bromley Reserves 3 – 2 Baldwin,Herbert,One(og)
Romford Res.: P.Gamman;N.P.Appleton,J.C.Dent;E.Stacey,E.Ross,A.J.Taylor;
D.J.Rubery,R.Kurn,J.Baldwin,K.Abbott,A.F.Herbert.

6 Oct IFLR Away Leytonstone Reserves 2 – 2 Herbert(2)
Romford Res.: E.C.Rogers;N.P.Appleton,E.R.Cave;E.Ross,J.V.Eyett(Capt),R.Scharvi;
S.Dankaro,K.Abbott,J.Baldwin,A.Hull,A.F.Herbert.

13 Oct IFLR Home St. Albans City Reserves 4 – 0 Rubery,Abbott,Herbert,Hull
Attendance: 710 Receipts: £13.9.9
Romford Res.: E.C.Rogers;N.P.Appleton,E.R.Cave;E.Ross,J.V.Eyett(Capt),R.Scharvi;
D.J.Rubery,K.Abbott,J.Baldwin,A.Hull,A.F.Herbert.

20 Oct IFLR Away Ilford Reserves 1 – 5 Herbert(pen)
Romford Res.: E.C.Rogers;N.P.Appleton,E.R.Cave;E.Ross,J.V.Eyett(Capt),R.Scharvi;
J.Wood,E.Stacey,J.Baldwin,A.Hull,A.F.Herbert.

27 Oct EIC2R Away Ford Sports Reserves 5 – 0 D.Taylor(2)Watts(2)Baldwin
Romford Res.: J.Martin;N.P.Appleton,E.R.Cave;E.Ross,J.V.Eyett(Capt),R.Scharvi;
A.Hull,E.Watts,J.Baldwin,D.H.Taylor,H.Woolston.

3 Nov IFLR Home Dulwich Hamlet Reserves 2 – 3 Dent,R.Kurn
Attendance: 320 Receipts: £5.13.2 Programmes: £1.15.0 Car Park: £0.6.9
Romford Res.: E.C.Rogers;J.P.Field,E.R.Cave;E.Ross,J.V.Eyett(Capt),A.J.Taylor;
J.C.Dent,R.Kurn,D.Bowness,E.Watts,R.Martha.

17 Nov IFLR Home Wycombe Wanderers Reserves 2 – 2 Bowness(2)
Attendance: 510 Receipts: £9.14.7 Programmes: £1.0.5
Romford Res.: T.Locker;J.P.Field,H.LeGrave;R.J.Fleetwood,J.V.Eyett(Capt),A.J.Taylor;
R.Gramlick, ? ,D.Bowness, ? ,R.Harris.

24 Nov EIC3R Home Leech United 6 – 5 Bowness(5)D.Taylor
Attendance: 750 Receipts: £17.1.4 Programmes: £1.17.5 Car Park: £0.6.6
Romford Res.:
Team details unknown.

1 Dec IFLR Away Barking Reserves 0 – 4
Romford Res.: E.C.Rogers;J.P.Field,A.J.Taylor;R.J.Fleetwood,E.R.Cave,P.J.Jolly;
A.Hull,K.Abbott,M.D.Paviour,R.Martha,R.Harris.

8 Dec IFLR Home Bromley Reserves 1 – 1 Martha
Attendance: 620 Receipts: £12.9.3
Romford Res.: P.Gamman;E.Ross,E.R.Cave;R.J.Fleetwood,J.V.Eyett(Capt),R.Scharvi;
J.P.Field,M.D.Paviour,R.Gramlick,E.Watts,R.Martha.

15 Dec EIC4R Away Walthamstow Avenue Reserves 0 – 3
Romford Res.: P.Gamman;E.R.Cave,A.J.Taylor;R.J.Fleetwood,D.H.Taylor(Capt),R.Scharvi;
J.P.Field,M.D.Paviour,D.Bowness,A.Hull,K.Abbott.

22 Dec IFLR Away Clapton Reserves 4 – 2 Gramlick(2)Paviour,Abbott
Romford Res.: P.Gamman;J.P.Field,I.Ross;M.R.Cooper,A.J.Taylor,D.H.Taylor;
M.D.Paviour,R.Gramlick,K.Abbott,C.Murtha,R.Mahoney.

29 Dec IFLR Home Barking Reserves 1 – 2 Philpott
Attendance: 500 Receipts: £8.19.9
Romford Res.: P.Gamman;E.R.Cave,H.LeGrave;I.Ross,P.J.Jolly,R.Scharvi;
J.P.Field,R.J.Fleetwood,R.Mahoney,A.Hull,J.Philpott.

5 Jan IFLR Away St. Albans City Reserves 4 – 2 Hull,Field,Abbott,Evans
Romford Res.: P.Gamman;I.Ross,H.LeGrave;P.Neame,R.J.Fleetwood,R.Scharvi;
J.P.Field,M.D.Paviour,A.Hull,K.Abbott,K.Evans.

12 Jan IFLR Home Walthamstow Avenue Reserves 1 – 1 Reeves
Attendance: 570 Receipts: £10.8.8 Programmes: £1.15.10 Car Park: £0.9.3
Romford Res.: P.Gamman;I.Ross,P.J.Jolly;R.J.Fleetwood,F.J.Newman(Capt),R.Scharvi;
D.Reeves,M.D.Paviour,R.Mahoney,R.Gramlick,D.Bowness.

26 Jan IFLR Home Ilford Reserves 2 – 2 Vernon(2)
Attendance: 600 Receipts: £11.9.1 Programmes: £1.15.4 Car Park: £0.2.3
Romford Res.: P.Gamman; ? , ? ; ? ,F.L.Newman(Capt), ? ;
   ? ,R.H.Brewis,J.Vernon, ? ,D.Bowness.

2 Feb IFLR Away Dulwich Hamlet Reserves 1 – 4 Wood
Romford Res.: P.Gamman;I.Ross,R.J.Fleetwood;W.H.Schofield,F.L.Newman(Capt),P.J.Jolly;
J.Wood,M.D.Paviour,J.Vernon,R.H.Brewis,D.Bowness.

9 Feb IFLR Home Corinthian Casuals Reserves 2 – 1 Hall(2)
Attendance: 410 Receipts: £6.14.9 Programmes: £1.8.0 Car Park: £0.4.0
Romford Res.: P.Gamman;J.P.Field,D.E.Roper;R.J.Fleetwood,F.L.Newman(Capt),R.Scharvi;
J.Wood,P.D.Hall,R.Mahoney,P.J.Jolly,R.H.Brewis.

16 Feb IFLR Home Kingstonian Reserves 0 – 3
Attendance: 430 Receipts: £8.3.7 Programmes: £1.11.8 Car Park: £0.6.3
Romford Res.: P.Gamman;J.W.Parfitt,D.E.Roper;R.J.Fleetwood,F.L.Newman(Capt),R.Scharvi;
J.Wood,M.D.Paviour,R.Mahoney,A.Lake,J.Philpott.

23 Feb IFLR Away Oxford City Reserves 1 – 4 Wood
Romford Res.: P.Gamman;J.P.Field,R.Thorne;W.H.Schofield,D.E.Roper,R.J.Fleetwood;
J.Wood,F.Dartnell,C.Tiffin,P.D.Hall,R.Martha.

2 Mar IFLR Away Walthamstow Avenue Reserves 1 – 0 Tiffin
Romford Res.: P.Gamman;J.P.Field,D.E.Roper;I.Ross,F.L.Newman(Capt),A.J.Taylor;
G.L.Tillyer,F.Dartnell,C.Tiffin,E.Watts,R.Martha.

16 Mar IFLR Home Wimbledon Reserves 4 – 0 Mahoney(2)Schofield(2)(1pen)
Attendance: 590 Receipts: £11.5.3 Programmes: £1.13.2 Car Park: £0.4.0
Romford Res.: E.C.Rogers;J.P.Field, ? ;W.H.Schofield,F.L.Newman(Capt),D.E.Roper;
J.Wood,L.Rowland,R.Mahoney,M.D.Paviour,B.Francis.

23 Mar IFLR Home Woking Reserves 0 – 1
Attendance: 310 Receipts: £5.17.5 Programmes: £1.13.6 Car Park: £ None
Romford Res.: E.C.Rogers;J.P.Field,D.E.Roper;W.H.Schofield,I.Ross,M.D.Paviour;
J.Wood,L.Rowlands,R.Mahoney,W.Martha,R.Colby.

30 Mar IFLR Home Tooting & Mitcham United Res. 2 – 3 Mahoney(2)
Attendance: 210 Receipts: £2.7.3 Programmes: £1.5.0 Car Park: £ None
Romford Res.: J.F.Allen;J.P.Field,D.E.Roper;W.H.Schofield,I.Ross,M.D.Paviour;
J.Wood,F.Dartnell,R.Mahoney,P.D.Hall,R.Colby.

6 Apr IFLR Away Kingstonian Reserves 0 – 1
Romford Res.: J.F.Allen;J.P.Field,C.E.East;D.Smith,I.Ross,M.D.Paviour;
J.Wood,F.Dartnell,R.Mahoney,P.D.Hall,R.Colby.

13 Apr IFLR Home# Clapton Reserves 2 – 4 Scorers unknown
Attendance: 420 Receipts: £7.10.10 Programmes: £ ?? Car Park: £ None
Romford Res.: J.F.Allen;J.P.Field,D.E.Roper;W.H.Schofield,I.Ross,M.D.Paviour;
G.L.Tillyer,F.Dartnell,R.Mahoney,E.Watts,R.Colby.

27 Apr IFLR Away Wycombe Wanderers Reserves 0 – 0
Romford Res.: J.F.Allen;J.P.Field,D.E.Roper;W.H.Schofield,M.D.Paviour,J.Wood;
F.Dartnell,P.D.Hall,L.Friend,R.H.Brewis,W.Colby.

\# Played at Brooklands.

RESERVE TEAM SUMMARY OF RESULTS SEASON 1956 – 57

	P	W	D	L	Goals For	Ag	Pts
Isthmian League Reserve Section	30	10	6	14	55	64	26
Essex FA Intermediate Cup	3	2	0	1	11	8	
Essex Thameside Chal. Comp.	1	0	0	1	0	2	
Total	34	12	6	16	66	74	

Isthmian Football League Reserve Section
Final Table

	P	W	D	L	Goals For	Ag	Pts
Wycombe Wanderers	30	21	7	2	84	33	49
Walthamstow Avenue	30	15	9	6	71	45	39
Leytonstone	30	15	8	7	61	45	38
Dulwich Hamlet	30	15	6	9	66	54	36
Oxford City	30	14	7	9	77	56	35
Tooting & Mitcham United	30	14	4	12	82	65	32
Woking	30	14	4	12	68	57	32
Bromley	30	10	11	9	68	49	31
Barking	30	12	4	14	51	64	28

Romford Reserves	30	10	6	14	55	64	26
Wimbledon	30	12	2	16	56	72	26
Kingstonian	30	8	10	12	60	79	26
Corinthian Casuals	30	8	8	14	59	73	24
Clapton	30	6	9	15	50	62	21
Ilford	30	7	5	18	50	91	19
St.Albans City	30	7	4	19	40	89	18

RESERVE TEAM CUP RESULTS

Essex County FA Intermediate Challenge Cup
Final: Grays Athletic Res. 4   Ilford Res. 2

Romford's progress: 1st Round   Bye
2nd Round   Away   Ford Sports Res.   5 - 0
3rd Round   Home   Leech United   6 - 5
4th Round   Away Walthamstow Avenue Res.   0 - 3

Essex Thameside Challenge Competition Reserve Section
Final: n/k

Romford's progress: 1st Round   Away Walthamstow Avenue Res.   0 - 2

RESERVE TEAM APPEARANCES SEASON 1956 - 57

The following players are known to have appeared in the reserve team during the season.

K.Abbott	J.F.Allen	G.W.Andrews	N.P.Appleton
J.Baldwin	D.Bowness	R.H.Brewis	E.R.Cave
R.Colby	M.R.Cooper	S.Dankaro	F.Dartnell(Rainham Town)
J.C.Dent	A.Devine	C.East	K.Evans
J.V.Eyett	J.P.Field	R.J.Fleetwood	L.Friend
F.Frost	P.Gamman	H.Gooch	R.A.Gramlick
P.D.Hall	R.Harris(Harwich & P.)	G.Harrison	A.F.Herbert
A.F.Hitchcock	A.Hull	C.Johnson	P.J.Jolly
D.M.Jones	P.Jones	R.D.Jones(Basildon Twn)	B.W.Kelly
R.Kurn	A.Lake	R.J.Leaver	H.Le Grave
R.Mahoney	W.Martha	J.Martin	P.Neame
F.L.Newman	J.W.Parfitt	M.D.Paviour	J.Philpott
D.Pryor(Aston Villa)	E.Reeves	E.C.Rogers	D.E.Roper
E.Ross	I.Ross	L.Rowland	D.J.Rubery
R.Scharvi	W.H.Schofield(Dagenham)	D.E.Smith	E.Stacey
A.J.Taylor	D.H.Taylor	C.Tiffin	G.L.Tillyer
R.Thorne	J.Vernon	E.Watts	D.Westmore
M.Withycombe	J.Wood	H.Woolston	E.Woolfe(Bromley)

"A" Team Match Details

1 Sept   Frdly   Away   Roneo Athletic   n/k
Romford "A":

8 Sept   EAFL   Away   Ilford "A"   3 – 2   Philpott,Reeves,Clarke
Romford "A": E.Stacey;R.Ellis,N.Cakebread;D.E.Roper,J.W.Parfitt,R.Scharvi;
D.Reeves,J.C.Dent,R.Clarke,A.Hitchcock,J.Philpott.

15 Sept EAFL   Home# Walthamstow Avenue "A"   1 – 5   Hall
Romford "A": E.Stacey;A.Lake,N.Cakebread;J.C.Dent,J.W.Parfitt,D.Smith;
M.Withycombe.P.D.Hall,D.Westmore,T.Jones,J.Philpott.

22 Sept EAFL   Home# Barnet "A"   5 – 3   Reeves,Baldwin(3)Hall
Romford "A": P.Gamman;A.Gooch,N.Cakebread;D.E.Roper,J.W.Parfitt,D.Smith;
D.Reeves,A.Spalding,J.Baldwin,P.D.Hall,J.Philpott.

29 Sept EAFL Home Ilford "A" 4 – 4 Reeves,Hall(2)Philpott
Romford "A": R.Woolfe;D.E.Roper,N.Cakebread;R.Scharvi,J.W.Parfitt,D.Smith;
D.Reeves,P.D.Hall,G.Harrison,R.Patten,J.Philpott.

6 Oct EAFL Home# Grays Athletic "A" 8 – 1 Dent,Hall(3)Vernon(3)Philpott
Romford "A": E.Stacey;N.Cakebread,D.M.Jones;R.Kurn,J.W.Parfitt,D.Smith;
J.C.Dent,P.D.Hall,J.Vernon,E.Watts,J.Philpott.

13 Oct EJC1R Away Collier Row Athletic "A" 4 – 2 Vernon(3)Philpott
Romford "A": E.Stacey;D.E.Roper,N.Cakebread;R.Kurn,J.W.Philpott,D.Smith;
J.C.Dent,P.D.Hall,J.Vernon,E.Watts,J.Philpott.

20 Oct EAFL Away Clapton "A" 2 – 0 Hall(2)
Romford "A": T.Locker;D.E.Roper,N.Cakebread;R.Kurn,J.W.Parfitt,D.Smith;
F.Woolston,J.C.Dent,P.D.Hall,E.Watts,J.Philpott.

27 Oct EAFL Away Walthamstow Avenue "A" 0 – 4
Romford "A": T.Locker;D.E.Roper,N.Cakebread;R.Kurn,J.W.Parfitt,D.Smith;
P.Mizen,G.J.Ruglys,P.D.Hall,J.C.Dent,J.Philpott.

3 Nov EJC2R Away Rotary Hoes 5 – 0 Ruglys,Hall,Paviour(2)Philpott
Romford "A": T.Locker;C.E.East,D.E.Roper;E.Stacey,J.W.Parfitt,D.Smith;
G.J.Ruglys,P.D.Hall,D.Cochrane,M.D.Paviour,J.Philpott.

10 Nov ALC2R Home Leyton "A" 0 – 0
Romford "A": T.Locker;C.E.East,D.E.Roper;R.Scharvi,J.W.Parfitt,D.Smith;
J.Baldwin,M.D.Paviour,D.Bowness,P.D.Hall,J.Philpott.

17 Nov EJC3R Home Howard Sports & Thamesply 1 – 5 Scorer unknown
Romford "A": E.Stacey;C.E.East,D.E.Roper;A.Best,J.W.Parfitt,D.Smith;
J.Baldwin,D.Hughes,M.D.Paviour,P.D.Hall,J.Philpott.

24 Nov EAFL Home Rainham Town "A" 4 – 0 Scorers unknown
Romford "A": M.Morgan;C.E.East,H.LeGrave;R.J.Fleetwood,J.W.Parfitt,D.Smith;
R.Colby,D.Rainbird,R.Gramlick,R.Thorne,P.D.Hall.

1 Dec ALCRp Away Leyton "A" 0 – 2
Romford "A": T.Locker;C.E.East,D.E.Roper;A.Best,J.W.Parfitt,D.Smith;
R.Colby,P.D.Hall,R.Kurn,R.Wild,D.Hughes.

8 Dec EAFL Home Woodford Town "A" 1 – 5 Philpott
Romford "A": T.Locker;D.E.Roper,H.Johnson;R.Kurn,J.W.Parfitt,D.Smith;
R.Colby,P.D.Hall,R.Mahoney,J.Hall,J.Philpott.

15 Dec EAFL Away Leyton "A" 2 – 4 Scorers unknown
Romford "A": M.Morgan;I.Ross,M.R.Cooper;C.E.East,J.W.Parfitt,D.Smith;
R.Colby,D.E.Roper,R.Mahoney,A.Lake,P.D.Hall.

5 Jan EAFL Home Dagenham "A" 2 – 1 Scorers unknown
Romford "A":
Team details unknown

12 Jan EAFL Away Rainham Town "A" 4 – 1 Hall(2)Mead,Philpott
Romford "A": T.Locker;C.E.East,R.Thorne;W.Simmons,J.W.Parfitt,D.Smith;
R.Colby,P.D.Hall,A.Simmons,D.Mead,J.Philpott.

19 Jan EAFL Away Grays Athletic "A" 1 – 0 Scorer unknown
Romford "A": T.Locker;A.Lake,R.Thorne;A.Wallace,D.E.Roper,D.Smith;
R.Colby,P.D.Hall,J.Vernon,R.H.Brewis,J.Wood.

26 Jan EAFL Away Dagenham "A" 5 – 1 Saunders,Baldwin(3)Hall
Romford "A": T.Locker;A.Lake,R.Thorne;C.E.East,D.Reeves,D.Smith;
J.Wood,R.Saunders,J.Baldwin,P.D.Hall,J.Philpott.

2 Feb EAFL Away Woodford Town "A" 1 – 2 Scorer unknown
Romford "A":
Team details unknown.

23 Feb Frdly Away Stratford Loco B.R. 4 – 1 Colby(2)Lavin,Schooling
Romford "A": J.W.Parfitt;C.E.East,K.Carr;G.Schooling,D.Reeves,D.Fisher;
J.Lavin,D.Mead,R.Saunders,B.Middleton,R.Colby.

9 Mar Frdly Away Murex Sports 5 – 1 Schofield,Paviour,Connor(2)Dartnell
Romford "A": T.Clarke;C.E.East,B.Francis;W.H.Schofield,D.Reeves,D.Smith;
J.Wood,M.D.Paviour,J.R.Connor,F.Dartnell,R.Colby.

16 Mar EAFL Away Barnet "A" 3 – 3 Scorers unknown
Romford "A": T.Clarke;J.W.Parfitt,C.E.East;G.M.Stratten,D.Reeves,A.Lake;
R.Colby,R.H.Brewis,J.R.Connor,D.Mead,J.Lavin.

30 Mar EAFL Home Leyton "A" 0 – 1
Romford "A": R.Beadon;J.W.Parfitt,C.E.East;G.M.Stratton,D.Reeves,J.Barnard;
A.Lake,R.H.Brewis,J.R.Connor,D.Mead,T.Lavin.

13 Apr EAFL Away# Clapton "A" 3 – 4 Scorers unknown
Romford "A":
Team details unknown

Played at Brooklands.

"A" TEAM SUMMARY OF RESULTS SEASON 1956 – 57

					Goals		
	P	W	D	L	For	Ag	Pts
Eastern "A" Football League	18	9	2	7	49	41	20
Eastern "A" Football League Cup	4	3	0	1	13	6	
Essex County FA Junior Cup	3	2	0	1	10	7	
Friendlies	3*	2	?	?	9	2	
Total	28	16	?	?	81	56	

*Note: The result of the friendly match against Roneo Athletic on 1st September, is not known

Eastern "A" Football League
Final Table

					Goals		
	P	W	D	L	For	Ag	Pts
Leyton	16	10	4	2	52	27	24
Clapton	16	9	4	3	41	27	22
Romford	**18**	**9**	**2**	**7**	**49**	**41**	**20**
Walthamstow Avenue	17	8	4	5	45	37	20
Woodford Town	18	8	3	7	35	38	19
Barnet	16	7	4	5	46	41	18
Dagenham	17	6	3	8	39	46	15
Ilford	18	4	4	10	40	53	12
Grays Athletic	16	4	3	9	29	36	11
Rainham Town	16	2	3	11	25	55	7

"A" TEAM CUP RESULTS SEASON 1956 – 57

Essex County FA Junior Challenge Cup
Final: Howards Sports & Thamesply 3 Parkeston Railway 1

Romford's progress: 1st Round Away Collier Row Ath. "A" 4 - 2
2nd Round Away Rotary Hoes 5 - 0
3rd Round Away Howard Sports & Thamesply 1 - 5

Eastern "A" Football League Challenge Cup
Final: Clapton "A" 2 Dagenham "A" 1

Romford's progress: 1st Round Bye
2nd Round Home Leyton "A" 0 - 0
Replay Away Leyton "A" 0 - 2

"A" TEAM APPEARANCES SEASON 1956 – 57

The following players are known to have played in the "A" Team during the season.

J.Baldwin	J.Barnard	R.Beadon	A.Best
D.Bowness	R.H.Brewis	N.Cakebread	K.Carr
R.Clarke	T.Clarke	D.Cochrane	R.Colby
J.R.Connor	M.R.Cooper	F.Dartnell	J.C.Dent
C.E.East	R.Ellis	D.Fisher	R.J.Fleetwood
B.Francis	P.Gamman	A.Gooch	R.Gramlick
J.Hall	P.D.Hall	G.Harrison	A.Hitchcock

D.Hughes	H.Johnson	D.M.Jones	T.Jones
R.Kurn	A.Lake	J.Lavin	H.Le Grave
T.Locker	R.Mahoney	D.Mead	B.Middleton
P.Mizen	M.Morgan	J.W.Parfitt	R.Patten(Barking)
M.D.Paviour	J.Philpott	J.W.Philpott	D.Rainbird
D.Reeves	D.E.Roper	I.Ross	G.J.Ruglys
R.Saunders	R.Scharvi	W.H.Schofield(Dagenham)	G.Schooling
A.Simmons	W.Simmons	D.Smith	A.Spalding
E.Stacey	G.M.Stratton	R.Thorne	J.Vernon
A.Wallace	E.Watts	D.Westmore	R.Wild
M.Withycombe	J.Wood	R.Woolfe	F.Woolston

DEPARTURES FROM THE CLUB SEASON 1956 – 57

The following players appear to have left the club during or by the end of the season. They may have been triallists and only played one or two games and then went elsewhere. New clubs are indicated where known.

K.Abbott (business reasons), A.Amas (Hornchurch & Upminster), J.Baldwin, B.Barber (Walthamstow Avenue), J.Bee (retired), E.R.Cave (Barking), S.Dankaro (returned to Nigeria), J.C.Dent (Romford Gas), A.Devine (Woodford Town), R.Ellis, J.V.Eyett (retired), J.Ford (Hornchurch & Upminster), R.Gramlick (Leyton), A.F.Herbert (Rainham Town), -.Hillditch (Basildon Town), A.F.Hitchcock (Ilford), A.Hull (Clapton), B.J.Jewell (Sabre), C.Johnson (Dagenham), B.W.Kelly (Finchley), R.Kurn (Harcourt), R.J.Leaver (Barking), H.LeGrave (Clapton), T.Locker (Tufnell Park), R.Mahoney (Collier Row Athletic), J.Moir (Grays Athletic), M.Morgan (resigned), F.L.Newman (Bromley), E.C.Rogers (moved to Canada), E.Ross (Barking), I.Ross (Barking), L.Rowlands (not known), D.J.Rubery (Hornchurch & Upminster), S.Shaef (Barking), E.Watts (Ford Sports), M.Withycombe..

Post Season Summary   Season 1956 – 57

After two very poor seasons and dwindling attendances the directors, coach and trainer tried to attract new blood for Romford's first team. Brian Barber (ex-Walthamstow Avenue), Derek Bowness (Woodford Town) and Mick Cooper (Barnet) were the only ones to gain regular first team appearances. The opening fixture was a visit from Wimbledon and an attendance of 1,810, a promising start and a welcome one nil victory. Then came the delayed Thameside Trophy Final held over from the previous season. A thrilling encounter on 20th August saw the Boro boys win the handsome trophy with a 5-4 win.

This was followed by a home league success over Dulwich Hamlet by three goals to one. Romford then set off in confident mood for an away league match with Oxford City on 25th August, but a rude awakening was ahead. The supporters couldn't believe what they saw: a devastating loss by ten goals to one, Boro's biggest ever Isthmian League defeat.

Dulwich Hamlet then gained revenge with a 5-1 victory at Champion Hill and Boro salvaged a point in a two all home draw with Kingstonian. On 3rd September local rivals Aveley easily defeated Boro 4-0 in the East Anglian Cup. The team were not therefore in confident mood for the FA Cup tie at home to Grays Athletic. An enthusiastic crowd of over 3,000 attended Brooklands and were rewarded with a 4-2 win with a brace each from Jimmy Wood and old stalwart Johnny Bee. They followed this up on 12th September with a 3-1 victory away to Leytonstone in defending the Thameside Trophy. Once again Romford had flattered to deceive as they were soundly defeated three days later at the Spotted Dog ground where lowly Clapton took the league points with a 7-1 victory.

In the FA Cup the team again rose to the occasion and defeated the powerful works side Briggs Sports on their own ground by one goal to nil. Two penalties from Johnnie Bee were not enough to secure the league points against Bromley, who won 3-2 at Brooklands. This was followed with a visit to Writtle Street on 6th October to meet Southern League professionals Chelmsford City in the next round of the FA Cup. The home side were far too good for Boro, who were soundly beaten by four goals to nil.

League defeats followed against Tooting and Mitcham (away) on 13th October and 3-4 at home to St. Albans City the following week. Angry scenes followed the latter match when 200 supporters voiced their protest at the team's performance, and the police had to be called to disperse them (see AGM report on page 286).

A goalless draw with Clapton on 27th October added a point to Romford's meagre tally. The following week Tiffin scored a hat-trick against Corinthian Casuals when Boro secured a 4-3 victory. Powerful rivals Walthamstow Avenue took the points in a 2-0 win at Brooklands. Goals galore in the next two away games against Wycombe Wanderers (4-4) and Woking (3-3), then Oxford City completed the double with a 5-1 win at Romford. Welcome victories over Barking 2-1 and Leytonstone 3-1 raised the fans' hopes once more.

The Christmas spirit saw Boro present Ilford with all the points – a 4-2 victory at Brooklands on Christmas morning, then a 1-0 win on their own ground at Newbury Park on Boxing Day. Boro returned to winning form with a 3-1 win over St. Albans City, but lost to Wycombe Wanderers by two goals to one. Next up a very attractive away tie against the powerful Pegasus side in the Amateur Cup, where the boys secured a 2-1 victory.

The Jekyll and Hyde performances continued with local rivals Aveley securing a second cup victory over Boro on 19th January with a 3-1 victory at Brooklands in the Essex Senior Cup. Romford then pulled off a fine 2-2 draw away to Walthamstow Avenue in the FA Cup, but they fell apart at Brooklands where the Avenue easily triumphed 4-0. Boro rallied again with a 3-1 victory at Wimbledon in a league game, only to sag to the depths again with three losses in a row against Kingstonian 2-5, Woking 1-7 and Barking 0-1.

Deal Town were beaten 2-1 in a friendly at Brooklands on 9th March, but a 1-1 draw at Walthamstow and a 1-2 loss at Bromley yielded only one more league point. On the up again soon, though, when three league victories away to Leytonstone 2-1, Tooting and Mitcham 1-0 and Corinthian Casuals 4-0 saw Boro pick up six welcome league points. A one all draw against Cambridge City in a friendly was sandwiched between these successes.

Cup disappointment once more when Barking won 2-0 at Brooklands on 19th April in the Thameside Trophy semi-final, but Boro comfortably beat Carshalton Athletic (away) in a friendly fixture 3-0. Next up was the Romford Charity Senior Cup game at Brooklands on 25th April against local rivals Dagenham, but supporters were not attracted and only 575 turned up to see Dagenham go away with the trophy by virtue of a two one victory.

The Boro forwards found top form for the final two games of the season. A 6-0 win over Barnet in a friendly on 27th April was followed on 11th May by a 5-2 victory to secure the Reg Sheward Trophy against local newspaper reporter D.J. Davis's All Star Eleven. Thus ended another disappointing season, with Boro very near the bottom of the league table, but they did at least hold the Thameside Trophy for a few months!

GLEANINGS FROM MANAGEMENT COMMITTEE MINUTE BOOKS
SEASON 1956-57

On **3rd August 1956** the former Romford player Peter Wallace was appointed the Club's Chief Talent Scout. He was previously team coach at Barking FC for six years.

On **18th August** it was noted that goalkeeper Peter Gamman is invited to trial for Charlton Athletic, and plays for Aston Villa's reserve side.

On **16th October** the committee learned that Sunday Dankaro, who played for Romford on several occasions, had been recalled to Nigeria. It was agreed that being fully qualified he should be be presented with a Club badge.

On **6th November** the Company Secretary Herbert Muskett urged that in view of the Club's financial position, "strict economy in every direction is required". Discussion took place in respect of "unpleasant local Press criticism of the Club and Club Management".

On **18th December** they accepted with regret the resignation of George Patterson, and sent him a letter of thanks for his services and an invitation to attend matches in future.

On **21st December** the committee agreed to hold a collection at the game against Rainham Town for former Romford favourite Peter Boreham, now with Dagenham, who was forced to give up playing following a leg injury. He had been unable to work for over a year.

On **22nd January 1957** it was reported that the football used in the previous Saturday's match had been stolen from the dressing rooms. In view of its cost, £5, Mr Muskett was asked to make a claim on the Club's insurance policy.

On **26th March** with the Club's dire financial position in mind, the Committee discussed the cost of running the "A" team (about £175 per annum). They voted to continue with a side but to withdraw from the Eastern "A" Football League and apply for a place in the Southern Essex Combination.

The Romford FC board of directors, 1956
Back: Herbert Muskett (Secretary), Bill Mann, A.E. Kittle, H.F.Knights, Jim Parrish
Front: Martin Brazier, Lord Macpherson, Glyn Richards *Authors' collection*

Directors' Report for the twelve months ended 31st July 1957

The year in respect of which the accounts of the Company are now presented has been a period of retrenchment, and the result a satisfactory one in the opinion of your Directors. True, a net loss of £61 has been sustained, but compared with the loss for the previous period of £1,310, your Directors' efforts to keep expenditure within income have been highly successful. It should at once be pointed out, however, that the net loss would have been greater if it had not been for the generous donations received during the year amounting to £831....£630 was given by the Supporters Club, £196 by the Promoter of the Club Lottery (which had to be stopped as a result of representations of the Football Association) and £5 by a Shareholder now residing in Australia.

....In regard to Income this has not overall greatly differed from the previous period but increases will be noticed in the items "Programme Sales" and "Property Lettings". Gate Income is but £170 down, and this in a year in which fortune has been none too kind to the playing side of the Club's activities. Your Directors feel that the Club's most grateful thanks are due to that stout body of supporters who week by week give the players such loyal support.

Your Directors regret that the Club did not have a successful playing season, no trophies – and finishing third from bottom of the Isthmian League is a sorry record, but those who watched and played are not disheartened, so often was the result determined by an odd goal that your Directors confidently believe that the future will show a vast improvement, the club now having a nucleus of young and keen players who mean to get to the top.

As to the Company's Property only slight works of improvement costing £175 were carried out during the year and by reason thereof the Property and Equipment account now stands at £14,500, after a sum of £675 has been written off for depreciation....

With regard to the future - your Directors are of the view that the Club must move with the times and to this end have taken steps to foster a closer Club spirit in sponsoring a Social Club with Headquarters upon the Ground. This Club has now been formed by a group of voluntary helpers under the Chairmanship of Mr Dennis Peters and a suitable building is being provided by the Company.

Another organisation has been formed to help the Club, last to be mentioned in this Report, but by no means least, and that is the Romford Sportsmen's Association. Your Director, Mr A.E. Kittle, after many years of most loyal and selfish service to the Club, felt that only by the formation of a sportsmen's association to assist in the development of Brooklands could the various amenities so desired by the Company be obtained. After permission of the Football Association had been sought, and refused to Mr Kittle organising this Association while a Director, Mr Kittle resigned, to carry out his avowed intentions of discharging the Company's overdraft by means not available to the Company. To all the organisations and associations assisting the Company your Directors extend their best wishes, appreciation and thanks.

....Your Directors conclude by assuring all supporters and friends of the Club that it is their confident opinion that with the spirit that is now in the Club and the assistance from so many quarters forthcoming, the Club must, with but a small degree of that most elusive element luck, once again be in the forefront of amateur football.

The above report was presented to the shareholders at the Annual General Meeting held Monday 27ᵗʰ January 1958 and reported as follows in the *Romford Recorder*, Friday 31ˢᵗ January 1958

ROMFORD FC TO APPOINT A PROFESSIONAL MANAGER

Romford Football Club Ltd are to appoint a professional manager with full control of all players and sole responsibility of first team selection. Company chairman Lord Macpherson revealed this Board of Directors' decision at Monday's shareholders' meeting. Present coach, Peter Wallace, gets the same powers in an unpaid capacity until the professional manager is chosen. He will then carry on at Brooklands as the new manager's right-hand man.

The decision regarding Mr Wallace was made at a special directors' meeting late on Monday evening. Selection and running of the club were previously conducted by a management committee of three directors and eight officials.

Announcing this policy change, Lord Macpherson said the Board recognised and appreciated the management committee had done their best to produce a winning side over the past four seasons but they had been unsuccessful.

NEW APPROACH. "The time has come when a new approach must be made", he continued. The Board of Directors last week decided there should be a change in the management, selection and training of the teams by appointing a professional manager in the club. "The Board have appointed a sub-committee to study the details of their new policy and to look for a suitable person for the job".

Shareholders received the Board's decision enthusiastically - thus heading off expected change of policy proposals. "The most encouraging news we have had in four season" was the comment of Mr D.H. Locke. But he added: "Could the club afford a professional manager and new equipment he would require?"

The club were not held back by the lack of money, replied Lord Macpherson. "Only thing holding us back is the finding of a winning team", he said.

INVESTIGATING. Management committee chairman, Jim Parrish, explained why the club were unable to use Brooklands pitch for training. Low voltage available at the ground in the evenings, he said, forced them to use their lights in a concentrated force on the car park. The Board were investigating the matter.

Referring to professional soccer at Brooklands, Lord Macpherson said the Board expected no change in the club's status. No decision had been made about the mooted merger between the Isthmian and Athenian Leagues, he added.

In a three-cornered fight for two vacant seats on the Board, present directors Mr Jim Parrish and Mr Glyn Richards, retiring in rotation, were re-elected. Other nominee was local personality Mr Alfred Lumley, committee member of the Romford Sportsmen's Association. Mr Parrish got 49 votes, Mr Richards 39 and Mr Lumley 17.

THE ROMFORD FOOTBALL CLUB LIMITED

Full Members of The Football Association
Full Members of Isthmian Football League
Affiliated to Essex County Football Association

Club Colours: Blue & Gold Shirts, White Shorts

Ground: Brooklands Sports Ground, Romford

Chairman: Rt.Hon.Lord Macpherson
Directors: Messrs. M.A.Brazier, A.E.Kittle, W.G.Mann, J.W.Parrish CC, H.F.Knights
Company Secretary: Mr H.W.Muskett

Registered Offices: 110,Hyland Way, Hornchurch

Football Club Management Committee:
Chairman: Mr J.W.Parrish,C.C.
Football Secretary: Mr M.A.Brazier
Hon.Press & Advt. Secretary: Mr R.E.Skilton (Appointed May 1957)
Reserve XI Secretary: Major A.E.Adlam
Other Committee Members: Messrs.F.H.Adams, F.E.Fryatt,
G.I.Howlett, H.F.Knights, W.F.Mackenzie, E.Wilson, Mr P.G.R.Wallace

Statistics: Mr John Haley(Ex Officio)

Hon.Programme Secretary: Mr H.Wright   **Third XI Secretary:** Mr H.J.Lazell

First Team Coach: Mr P.G.R.Wallace   **Assistant Coach:** Mr J.Martin

Trainer: Mr E.Hewitt   **Second Team Coach:** Mr Fred.Griffiths

Third Team Manager: Mr F.Addington assisted by Mr W.Benson

Bankers: Lloyds Bank Limited   **Auditors:** Iion V.Cummings & Co.

Groundsman: Mr W.C.(Bill) Seddon

LEAGUES & COMPETITIONS SEASON 1957 – 58

Football Association Challenge Cup
Football Association Amateur Challenge Cup
Isthmian Football League
Essex County Football Association Senior Challenge Cup
East Anglian Cup
Essex Thameside Challenge Competition
Romford Charity Cup
Reg Sheward Memorial Trophy

Isthmian Football League Reserve Section
The Essex County Football Association Intermediate Challenge Cup
Essex Thameside Challenge Competition Reserve Section

Southern Essex Football Combination Division 1
The Essex County Football Association Junior Challenge Cup
Southern Essex Football Combination Challenge Cup

Admission Prices Season 1957 – 58

	First Team			Reserve Team		
	Adults	OAPs	Child	Adults	OAPs	Child
Ground	1/6	9d		9d		5d
Ground & Enclosure	2/-			1/-		6d
Grandstand	2/6	2/6		1/-		6d

Season Ticket Prices Season 1957 – 58

	Adults	OAPs & Children
Grandstand (All one price)	£2.0.0	
Ground & Enclosure	£1.10.0	15/-
Ground only	£1.0.0	10/-

NOTE: The actual attendance figures are not available for the 1957–58 season and the details given have been calculated from the cash receipts which are known, together with an allowance in respect of the number of Season Ticket holders.

Public Trial Match

Saturday 17ᵗʰ August 1957 (Reserve team admission charges to apply)

Probables v Possibles
Attendance: 1,100   Receipts: £34.9.6

First Team Match Details

24 Aug IFL   Home   Dulwich Hamlet   3 – 5   Hammond,Webb,Tiffin
Attendance: 2,300   Receipts: £163.14.3   Programmes: £16.0.6   Car Park: £3.1.6
Romford: E.J.Sansom;N.P.Appleton,M.R.Cooper(Capt);J.J.Whitecross,P.J.Jolly,W.Blake;
J.Wood,R.F.Hammond,C.Tiffin,D.J.Webb,G.W.Andrews.

28 Aug IFL   Away   Clapton   1 – 2   Tiffin
Romford: E.J.Sanson;R.W.Watts,M.R.Cooper(Capt);J.J.Whitecross,D.H.Taylor,A.J.Taylor;
J.Wood,R.F.Hammond,C.Tiffin,R.J.Fleetwood,R.J.March.

31 Aug IFL   Away   Tooting & Mitcham United   1 – 5   Tiffin
Romford: P.Gamman;R.W.Watts,M.R.Cooper(Capt);J.J.Whitecross,D.H.Taylor,A.J.Taylor;
G.W.Andrews,R.F.Hammond,C.Tiffin,J.Walker,R.J.March.

2 Sept EAC1R Home   Tottenham Hotspur "A"   0 – 6
Attendance: 1,495   Receipts: £98.17.6   Programmes: £6.14.9   Car Park: £3.16.0
Romford: P.Gamman;R.W.Watts,M.R.Cooper(Capt);J.J.Whitecross,D.H.Taylor,A.J.Taylor;
M.D.Paviour,R.F.Hammond,C.Tiffin,L.A.Holmes,R.J.March.

7 Sept FACPR Home   Clacton Town   1 – 1   Tiffin
Attendance: 2,075   Receipts: £159.10.3   Programmes: £11.11.6 Car Park: £4.14.0
Romford: P.Gamman;A.J.Lee,M.R.Cooper(Capt);J.J.Whitecross,D.H.Taylor,A.J.Taylor;
R.F.Hammond,D.E.Thomas,C.Tiffin,L.A.Holmes,R.J.March.

11 Sept FACRp Away   Clacton Town   2 – 2* Holmes,March
Romford: P.Gamman;A.J.Lee,M.R.Cooper(Capt);J.J.Whitecross,D.H.Taylor,A.J.Taylor;
R.F.Hammond,D.E.Thomas,C.Tiffin,L.A.Holmes,R.J.March.

14 Sept IFL   Home   Corinthian Casuals   3 – 1   March,Hammond,Tiffin
Attendance: 1,945   Receipts: £148.15.6   Programmes: £12.18.8 Car Park: £3.13.6
Romford: P.Gamman;A.J.Lee,M.R.Cooper(Capt);J.J.Whitecross,D.H.Taylor,A.J.Taylor;
R.F.Hammond,D.E.Thomas,C.Tiffin,L.Holmes,R.J.March.

14 Sept FACRp Neut# Clacton Town   2 – 4   Holmes(2)
Romford: P.Gamman;A.J.Lee,A.J.Taylor;J.J.Whitecross,M.R.Cooper(Capt),W.Blake;
R.F.Hammond,D.E.Thomas,C.Tiffin,L.A.Holmes,R.J.March.

21 Sept IFL   Away   Wimbledon   1 – 5   Hammond
Romford: E.Sanson;A.J.Lee,A.J.Taylor;J.J.Whitecross(Capt),J.L.Milbank,W.Blake;
R.F.Hammond,D.E.Thomas,C.Tiffin,L.A.Holmes,R.J.March.

28 Sept IFL   Home   Walthamstow Avenue   1 – 2   March
Attendance: 2,550   Receipts: £197.3.4   Programmes: £15.12.4   Car Park: £3.14.8
Romford: T.H.Nickelson;A.J.Lee,M.R.Cooper(Capt);J.J.Whitecross,J.L.Milbank,A.J.Taylor;
G.W.Andrews,D.E.Thomas,D.Bowness,L.A.Holmes,R.J.March.

5 Oct IFL   Away   Kingstonian   0 – 1
Romford: T.H.Nickelson;A.J.Lee,M.R.Cooper(Capt);J.J.Whitecross,J.L.Milbank,A.J.Taylor;
G.W.Andrews,D.E.Thomas,C.Tiffin,L.A.Holmes,R.J.March.

12 Oct IFL   Away   Bromley   1 – 5   Tiffin
Romford: T.H.Nickelson;A.J.Lee,M.R.Cooper(Capt);J.J.Whitecross,D.H.Taylor,A.J.Taylor;
D.E.Thomas,L.A.Holmes,L.Clark,C.Tiffin,R.J.March.

19 Oct IFL   Home   St. Albans City   3 – 1   March,Bennett(2)
Attendance: 1,875   Receipts: £143.9.9   Programmes: £9.6.0   Car Park: £2.11.3
Romford: T.H.Nickelson;A.J.Lee,M.R.Cooper(Capt);D.Pryor,D.H.Taylor,R.Walker;
D.E.Thomas,B.Bennett,L.Clark,L.A.Holmes,R.J.March.

26 Oct IFL   Home   Barking   1 – 3   Bennett
Attendance: 2,655   Receipts: £206.12.9   Programmes: £16.6.9   Car Park: £4.1.3
Romford: T.H.Nickelson;A.J.Lee,M.R.Cooper(Capt);D.H.Taylor,J.L.Milbank,R.Walker;
J.A.Birch,L.Clark,B.Bennett,L.A.Holmes,R.J.March.

2 Nov IFL   Away#1 Corinthian Casuals   5 – 2   Bennett,Tiffin(2)Holmes,Whitecross
Romford: T.H.Nickelson;A.J.Lee,M.R.Cooper(Capt);J.J.Whitecross,J.L.Milbank,R.Walker;
R.F.Hammond,L.A.Holmes,B.Bennett,C.Tiffin,R.J.March.

9 Nov IFL   Home   Wycombe Wanderers   0 – 2
Attendance: 2,210   Receipts: £157.8.9   Programmes: £9.5.10   Car Park: £3.1.9
Romford: T.H.Nickelson;A.J.Lee,M.R.Cooper(Capt);J.J.Whitecross,G.C.Noble,R.Walker;
R.F.Hammond,L.A.Holmes,B.Bennett,C.Tiffin,R.J.March.

16 Nov IFL   Away   Woking   3 – 1   March,Whitecross,Bennett
Romford: T.H.Nickelson;A.J.Lee,M.R.Cooper(Capt);J.J.Whitecross,G.C.Noble,R.Walker;
R.F.Hammond,L.A.Holmes,B.Bennett,C.Tiffin,R.J.March.

23 Nov IFL   Home   Leytonstone   2 – 2   Bennett,Holmes(pen)
Attendance: 2,240   Receipts: £162.11.3   Programmes: £14..4.3   Car Park: £ ??
Romford: T.H.Nickelson;A.J.Lee,M.R.Cooper(Capt);J.J.Whitecross,G.C.Noble,R.Walker;
R.F.Hammond,L.A.Holmes,B.Bennett,C.Tiffin,R.J.March.

30 Nov ETT1R Away   Grays Athletic   1 – 1*   Tiffin
Attendance: Romford share of Gate: £49.3.5d.
Romford: T.H.Nickelson;A.J.Lee,M.R.Cooper(Capt);R.J.Fleetwood,G.C.Noble,R.Walker;
R.F.Hammond,L.A.Holmes,B.K.Burns,C.Tiffin,R.J.March.

7 Dec ESC1R Away   Barkingside   2 – 1$ Bennett(2)
Attendance: 500   Romford Share after expenses £8.0.0
Romford: C.Walker;A.J.Lee,M.R.Cooper;J.J.Whitecross(Capt),G.C.Noble,R.Walker;
R.F.Hammond,L.A.Holmes,B.Bennett,C.Tiffin,R.J.March.

14 Dec IFL   Home   Oxford City   1 – 2   Tiffin
Attendance: 1,350   Receipts: £90.14.3   Programmes: £8.6.0   Car Park: £1.14.9
Romford: T.H.Nickelson;A.J.Lee,M.R.Cooper;J.J.Whitecross(Capt),G.C.Noble,R.Walker;
R.F.Hammond,L.A.Holmes,B.Bennett,C.Tiffin,R.J.March.

25 Dec IFL   Away   Ilford   1 – 2   Hammond
Romford: P.Gamman;A.J.Lee,M.R.Cooper;J.J.Whitecross(Capt),G.C.Noble,R.Walker;
R.F.Hammond,L.A.Holmes,L.Clark,C.Tiffin,R.J.March.

26 Dec IFL   Home   Ilford   1 – 0   Tiffin
Attendance: 1,760   Receipts: £131.16.6   Programmes: £10.4.8   Car Park: £2.4.0
Romford: P.Gamman;A.J.Lee,W.Blake;J.J.Whitecross(Capt),G.C.Noble,D.J.Webb;
B.Durrant,L.Clark,C.Tiffin,L.A.Holmes,R.J.March.

28 Dec IFL   Away   Leytonstone   0 – 2
Romford: P.Gamman;A.J.Lee,W.Blake;J.J.Whitecross(Capt),G.C.Noble,D.J.Webb;
B.Durrant,L.Clark,C.Tiffin,B.Bennett,R.J.March.

4 Jan   IFL   Home   Clapton   3 – 3   Durrant,March(2)
Attendance: 1,200   Receipts: £82.0.3   Programmes: £8.0.6   Car Park: £2.0.3
Romford: P.Gamman;A.J.Lee,W.Blake;J.J.Whitecross(Capt),G.C.Noble,D.J.Webb;
B.Durrant,L.Clark,L.A.Holmes,C.Tiffin,R.J.March.

11 Jan   AC1R   Away   Erith & Belvedere   1 – 3   Blake
Attendance: 1,284
Romford: P.Gamman;A.J.Lee,M.R.Cooper;J.J.Whitecross(Capt),G.C.Noble,D.J.Webb;
B.Durrant,W.Blake,L.Clark,C.Tiffin,R.J.March.

18 Jan   IFL   Away   St. Albans City   0 – 2
Romford: P.Gamman;A.J.Lee,M.R.Cooper;J.J.Whitecross(Capt),G.C.Noble,R.J.Fleetwood;
B.Durrant,W.Blake,R.W.Christie,D.J.Webb,C.Tiffin.

25 Jan   IFL   Home   Kingstonian   1 – 3   March
Attendance: 1,130   Receipts: £77.6.0   Programmes: £7.1.6   Car Park: £1.9.0
Romford: P.Gamman;A.J.Lee,M.R.Cooper;J.J.Whitecross(Capt),G.C.Noble,D.J.Webb;
B.Durrant,R.F.Hammond,R.W.Christie,W.Blake,R.J.March.

1 Feb   IFL   Home   Bromley   1 – 1   Milbank
Attendance: 1,510   Receipts: £102.19.3   Programmes: £9.8.0   Car Park: £2.6.6
Romford: P.Gamman;A.J.Lee(Capt),M.R.Cooper;J.L.Milbank,G.C.Noble,R.Walker;
R.F.Hammond,L.Clark,W.Blake,C.Tiffin,R.J.March.

8 Feb   ESC2R   Away   Briggs Sports   0 – 3
Attendance: 2,000   Receipts: £127.19.6d   Romford Share: £55.4.7d
Romford: P.Gamman;A.J.Lee(Capt),M.R.Cooper;J.L.Milbank,G.C.Noble,R.Walker;
R.F.Hammond,L.A.Holmes,W.Blake,C.Tiffin,R.J.March.

15 Feb   IFL   Away   Dulwich Hamlet   2 – 2   Webb,Blake
Romford: P.Gamman;A.J.Lee(Capt),M.R.Cooper;J.J.Whitecross,G.C.Noble,R.Walker;
B.Durrant,D.J.Webb,W.Blake,C.Tiffin,R.J.March.

22 Feb   IFL   Away   Oxford City   1 – 4   Burns
Romford: P.Gamman;A.J.Lee(Capt),M.R.Cooper;J.J.Whitecross,G.C.Noble,R.Walker;
B.Durrant,W.Blake,B.K.Burns,C.Tiffin,R.J.March.

1 Mar   Frdly   Away   Hitchin Town   0 – 2
Romford: P.Gamman;A.J.Lee(Capt),M.R.Cooper;J.J.Whitecross,G.C.Noble,R.Walker;
L.A.Holmes,D.J.Webb,W.Blake,B.Milbank,R.J.March.

8 Mar   IFL   Home   Wimbledon   3 – 1   Tiffin(2)B.Milbank
Attendance: 1,200   Receipts: £82.19.6   Programmes: £7.13.6   Car Park: £2.4.0
Romford: P.Gamman;A.J.Lee(Capt),M.R.Cooper;J.J.Whitecross,G.C.Noble,R.Walker;
D.J.Webb,L.A.Holmes,B.K.Burns,B.Milbank,C.Tiffin.

15 Mar   IFL   Away   Walthamstow Avenue   1 – 1   Holmes
Romford: P.Gamman;A.J.Lee(Capt),M.R.Cooper;J.J.Whitecross,G.C.Noble,R.Walker;
B.Durrant,L.A.Holmes,W.Blake,B.Milbank,C.Tiffin.

22 Mar   IFL   Home   Tooting & Mitcham United   0 – 0
Attendance: 1,580   Receipts: £116.6.9   Programmes: £11.3.0   Car Park: £2.17.0
Romford: P.Gamman;A.J.Lee(Capt),M.R.Cooper;J.J.Whitecross,G.C.Noble,R.Walker;
B.Durrant,L.A.Holmes,B.K.Burns,B.Milbank,C.Tiffin.

29 Mar   IFL   Away   Wycombe Wanderers   0 – 6
Romford: P.Gamman;A.J.Lee(Capt),M.R.Cooper;J.J.Whitecross,G.C.Noble,R.Walker;
B.Durrant,L.A.Holmes,A.Simmons,B.Milbank,C.Tiffin.

5 Apr   IFL   Away   Barking   2 – 2   Holmes,Tiffin
Romford: P.Gamman;A.J.Lee(Capt),M.R.Cooper;J.J.Whitecross,G.C.Noble,R.Walker;
B.Durrant,L.A.Holmes,A.Simmons,J.Martin,C.Tiffin.

16 Apr   ETTRp   Home   Grays Athletic   2 – 1*   Cooper,Holmes(pen)
Attendance: 910   Receipts: £64.10.3   Programmes: £2.13.3   Car Park: £ ??
Romford: P.Gamman;A.J.Lee(Capt),M.R.Cooper;J.J.Whitecross,G.C.Noble,R.Walker;
B.Durrant,L.A.Holmes,B.K.Burns,J.Martin,C.Tiffin.

19 Apr   IFL   Home   Woking   3 – 3   Martin(2)Holmes
Attendance: 1,900   Receipts: £142.13.2   Programmes: £12.1.0   Car Park: £2.10.3
Romford: P.Gamman;A.J.Lee(Capt),M.R.Cooper;J.J.Whitecross,G.C.Noble,R.Walker;
B.Durrant,L.A.Holmes,B.K.Burns,J.Martin,C.Tiffin.

23 Apr   ETTSF   Away   Ilford   2 – 0   Burns(2)
Romford: P.Gamman;A.J.Lee(Capt),D.H.Taylor;J.J.Whitecross,G.C.Noble,R.Walker;
B.Durrant,L.A.Holmes,B.K.Burns,J.Martin,C.Tiffin.

26 Apr Frdly Home Brentwood & Warley 2 – 4 Walker,Burns
Attendance: 930 Receipts: £66.17.7 Programmes: £4.6.0 Car Park: £ ??
Romford: P.Gamman;A.J.Lee(Capt),D.H.Taylor,L.Clark,G.C.Noble,R.Walker;
H.W.Brooks,B.Milbank,B.K.Burns,J.Martin,C.Tiffin.

29 Apr RCC Home Dagenham 1 – 2 Holmes
Attendance: 980 Receipts: £70.5.6 Programmes: £4.13.9 Car Park: £ ??
Romford: P.Gamman;A.J.Lee(Capt),D.H.Taylor;J.J.Whitecross,G.C.Noble,R.Walker;
H.W.Brooks,L.A.Holmes,B.K.Burns,J.Martin,C.Tiffin.

3 May ETTF Away Barking 2 – 1 Martin,Burns
Romford: P.Gamman;L.Robinson,D.H.Taylor,A.J.Lee(Capt),G.C.Noble,R.Walker;
H.W.Brooks,J.Martin,B.K.Burns,C.Tiffin,R.J.March.

10 May RST Home Don Hill's Essex XI 3 – 3** McClellan,Adams,Tiffin
Attendance: 830 Receipts: £57.17.9 Programmes: £10.4.2 Car park: £ ??
Romford: C.Walker;L.Robinson,J.Smith(Millwall);A.J.Lee(Capt),J.R.Chisholm,R.Walker;
H.W.Brooks,J.J.Whitecross,S.B.McClellan(Southampton),C.Tiffin,C.J.Adams(Dartford).
2nd Half changes: Whitecross(R.H)Walker(C.H)Lee(L.H)Tiffin(I.R)Adams(I.L)R.J.March(O.L).
Don.Hill's XI: S.Homan(Clapton); P.Carey(Leyton Orient),F.Cooper(West Ham United);
K.Lewell(Hornchurch & Upminster),K.Brown(West Ham United),R.Vowells(Corinthian Casuals);
W.Dare(West Ham United),H.M.Newman(West Ham United),L.Allen(Chelsea),A.Malcolm(West
Ham United),J.Laybourne(Corinthian Casuals).

* After extra time.
** Don Hill's XI won on toss of coin.
\$ Barkingside expelled from the competition and match declared void. (Friendly match).
\# Played at Writtle Street, Chelmsford.
\#1 Played at the Oval Cricket Ground.

FIRST TEAM SUMMARY OF RESULTS SEASON 1957 – 58

		Home			Goals		Away			Goals		
	P	W	D	L	For	Ag	W	D	L	For	Ag	Pts
Isthmian Football League	30	4	5	6	26	29	2	3	10	19	42	20
FA Challenge Cup	3	0	1	0	1	1	0	1	1	4	6	
FA Amateur Challenge Cup	1	0	0	0	0	0	0	0	1	1	3	
Essex County F.A. Senior Cup	1	0	0	0	0	0	0	0	1	0	3	
East Anglian Cup	1	0	0	1	0	6	0	0	0	0	0	
Essex Thameside Chal.Comp.	4	1	0	0	2	1	2	1	0	5	2	
Romford Charity Senior Cup	1	0	0	1	1	2	0	0	0	0	0	
Reg Sheward Trophy	1	0	1	0	3	3	0	0	0	0	0	
Friendlies*	3	0	0	1	2	4	1	0	1	2	3	
Totals	45	5	7	9	35	46	5	5	14	31	59	

* This includes the Essex Senior Cup tie against Barkingside that was declared void.

Isthmian Football League
Final Table

					Goals		
	P	W	D	L	For	Ag	Pts
Tooting & Mitcham United	30	20	6	4	79	33	46
Wycombe Wanderers	30	19	4	7	78	42	42
Walthamstow Avenue	30	17	5	8	63	35	39
Bromley	30	13	9	8	66	51	35
Oxford City	30	13	6	11	59	48	32
Leytonstone	30	13	6	11	49	48	32
Wimbledon	30	15	2	13	64	66	32
Corinthian Casuals	30	12	8	10	62	68	32
Woking	30	12	7	11	70	58	31
Barking	30	10	6	14	49	61	26
St.Albans City	30	11	3	16	56	76	25
Clapton	30	8	9	13	42	65	25
Kingstonian	30	7	8	15	45	66	22
Dulwich Hamlet	30	7	7	16	49	64	21
Ilford	30	8	4	18	46	70	20
Romford	**30**	**6**	**8**	**16**	**45**	**71**	**20**

FIRST TEAM CUP RESULTS SEASON 1957 – 58

FA Challenge Cup
Final: Bolton Wanderers 2   Manchester United   0

Romford's progress: Prel.Rnd.   Home   Clacton Town   1 - 1
Replay   Away   Clacton Town   2 – 2*
2nd Replay Chelmsford.   Clacton Town   2 – 4

FA Amateur Challenge Cup
Final: Woking 3   Ilford 0

Romford's progress: 1st Round   Away   Erith & Belvedere   1 - 3

Essex County FA Senior Challenge Cup
Final: Walthamstow Avenue 2   Grays Athletic   1

Romford's progress: 1st Round   Away Barkingside   2 – 1**
2nd Round   Away   Briggs Sports 0 - 3

East Anglian Cup
Final: n/k

Romford's progress: 1st Round   Home   Tottenham Hotspur "A"   0 - 6

Essex Thameside Challenge Competition
Final: Romford 2   Barking   1

Romford's progress: 1st Round   Away   Grays Athletic   1 – 1*
Replay   Home   Grays Athletic   2 – 1*
Semi-Final Away   Ilford   2 - 0
Final   Away   Barking   2 - 1

Romford Charity Senior Cup
Romford 1   Dagenham   2

Reg Sheward Memorial Trophy
Romford 3   Don. Hill's All Star XI   3
(Don Hill's All Star XI won on the toss of a coin)

**Barkingside excluded after ground protest - match declared void.
*After Extra Time

The FA Cup replay 11th September 1957 v. Clacton Town, 2-2 after extra time
Back: Alan Taylor, Mick Cooper (captain), Dennis Taylor, Peter Gamman, Johnny Whitecross, David Thomas
Front: Ron Hammond, Alfie Lee, Cyril Tiffin, Reg March, Buddy Holmes   *Authors' collection*

FIRST TEAM DEBUTS SEASON 1957 – 58

1957				Previous Club
24th Aug.	v Dulwich Hamlet	-	E.Sanson	Enfield Town
		-	W.Blake	Basildon Town
		-	R.F.Hammond	Basildon Town
		-	D.J.Webb	Weymouth
28th Aug.	v Clapton	-	R.Watts	Barking
		-	R.J.March	Barking
31st Aug.	v Tooting & M.Utd.	-	J.Walker	Barkingside
7th Sept.	v Clacton Town	-	A.J.Lee	Barking
		-	D.E.Thomas	Southampton
21st Sept.	v Wimbledon	-	J.L.Milbank	Windsor & Eton
28th Sept.	v Walthamstow Ave.	-	T.H.Nickelson	Ford Sports
12th Oct.	v Bromley	-	L.Clark	Clacton Town
19th Oct.	v St.Albans City	-	D.Prior	Barking
		-	R.Walker	West Ham United
		-	B.Bennett	Leyton
26th Oct.	v Barking	-	J.A.Birch	Dover
9th Nov.	v Wycombe Wdrs.	-	G.C.Noble	Southall
30th Nov.	v Grays Athletic	-	B.Burns	Ardleigh House
7th Dec.	v Barkingside	-	C.Walker	R.A.F. Hornchurch
26th Dec.	v Ilford	-	B.Durrant	Ardleigh House Y.C.
1958				
18th Jan.	v St.Albans City	-	R.W.Christie	Eastbourne
1st Mar.	v Hitchin Town	-	B.Milbank	Hertford Town
29th Mar.	v Wycombe Wdrs.	-	A.Simmons	n/k
5th Apr.	v Barking	-	J.Martin	Dagenham
3rd May	v Barking	-	L.Robinson	n/k
10th May	v Don.Hill's XI	-	J.R.Chisholm	Finchley

Players returned to the Club
1958

26th Apr.	v Brentwood & W.	-	H.W.Brooks	Dagenham

Guest Players
1958

10th May	v Don.Hill's XI	-	J.Smith	Millwall
		-	S.B.McClellan	Portsmouth
		-	C.J.Adams	Dartford

FIRST TEAM APPEARANCES SEASON 1957 – 58

	A	B	C	D	E	F	G	H	I	Total
Chris Adams	0	0	0	0	0	0	0	1	0	1
George Andrews	4	0	0	0	0	0	0	0	0	4
Norman Appleton	1	0	0	0	0	0	0	0	0	1
Brian Bennett	8	0	0	0	0	0	0	0	1	9
J.Birch	1	0	0	0	0	0	0	0	0	1
Bill Blake	11	1	1	1	0	0	0	0	1	15
Derek Bowness	1	0	0	0	0	0	0	0	0	1
Harold Brooks	0	0	0	0	0	1	1	1	1	4
Barry Burns	4	0	0	0	0	4	1	0	1	10
Jack Chisholm	0	0	0	0	0	0	0	1	0	1
Robin Christie	2	0	0	0	0	0	0	0	0	2
Lew Clark	8	0	1	0	0	0	0	0	1	10
Mick Cooper	26	3	1	1	1	2	0	0	2	36
Bunny Durrant	12	0	1	0	0	2	0	0	0	15
Reg Fleetwood	2	0	0	0	0	1	0	0	0	3
Peter Gamman	17	3	1	1	1	3	1	0	2	29
Ron Hammond	13	3	0	1	1	1	0	0	1	20

	A	B	C	D	E	F	G	H	I	Total
Buddy Holmes	21	3	0	1	1	3	1	0	2	32
Pat Jolly	1	0	0	0	0	0	0	0	0	1
Alfie Lee	27	3	1	1	0	4	1	1	3	41
Reg March	22	3	1	1	1	2	0	1*	2	33*
J.Martin	2	0	0	0	0	3	1	0	1	7
Sid McLellan	0	0	0	0	0	0	0	1	0	1
Barry Milbank	4	0	0	0	0	0	0	0	2	6
John Milbank	6	0	0	1	0	0	0	0	0	7
Tommy Nickelson	10	0	0	0	0	1	0	0	0	11
Geoff Noble	19	0	1	1	0	4	1	0	3	29
Mike Paviour	0	0	0	0	1	0	0	0	0	1
D.Prior	1	0	0	0	0	0	0	0	0	1
Lou Robinson	0	0	0	0	0	1	0	1	0	2
Eddie Sanson	3	0	0	0	0	0	0	0	0	3
A.Simmons	2	0	0	0	0	0	0	0	0	2
J.Smith	0	0	0	0	0	0	0	1	0	1
Alan Taylor	7	3	0	0	1	0	0	0	0	11
Denny Taylor	6	2	0	0	1	2	1	0	1	13
David Thomas	6	3	0	0	0	0	0	0	0	9
Cyril Tiffin	26	3	1	1	1	4	1	1	2	40
Charlie Walker	0	0	0	0	0	0	0	1	1	2
J.Walker	1	0	0	0	0	0	0	0	0	1
Roy Walker	17	0	0	1	0	4	1	1	3	27
R.Watts	2	0	0	0	1	0	0	0	0	3
Dave Webb	8	0	1	0	0	0	0	0	1	10
Johnny Whitecross	27	3	1	0	1	2	1	1	2	38
Jimmy Wood	2	0	0	0	0	0	0	0	0	2
Totals	330	33	11	11	11	44	11	12*	33	496*

* Includes playing one match as substitute

Key to Competitions

A   Isthmian Football League
B   FA Challenge Cup
C   FA Amateur Challenge Cup
D   Essex County F.A. Senior Cup
E   East Anglian Cup
F   Essex Thameside Chal.Comp.
G   Romford Charity Senior Cup
H   Reg Sheward Trophy
I   Friendlies (Includes match versus Barkingside (void) in the Essex Senior Cup)

FIRST TEAM GOALSCORERS SEASON 1957 – 58

	A	B	C	D	E	F	G	H	I	Total
Cyril Tiffin	12	1	0	0	0	1	0	1	0	15
Buddy Holmes	5	3	0	0	0	1	1	0	0	10
Reg March	7	1	0	0	0	0	0	0	0	8
Brian Bennett	6	0	0	0	0	0	0	0	2	8
Barry Burns	1	0	0	0	0	3	0	0	1	5
Ron Hammond	4	0	0	0	0	0	0	0	0	4
J Martin	2	0	0	0	0	1	0	0	0	3
Dave Webb	2	0	0	0	0	0	0	0	0	2
Johnnie Whitecross	2	0	0	0	0	0	0	0	0	2
Bill Blake	1	0	1	0	0	0	0	0	0	2
Bunny Durrant	1	0	0	0	0	0	0	0	0	1
Barry Millbank	1	0	0	0	0	0	0	0	0	1
J. Milbank	1	0	0	0	0	0	0	0	0	1
Mick Cooper	0	0	0	0	0	1	0	0	0	1

Sid McClellan	0	0	0	0	0	0	0	1	0	1
Chris Adams	0	0	0	0	0	0	0	1	0	1
Roy Walker	0	0	0	0	0	0	0	0	1	1
Total	45	5	1	0	0	7	1	3	4	66

Reserve Team Match Details

24 Aug IFLR   Away   Dulwic Hamlet Reserves   1 – 2   March
Romford Res.:E.G.Tetchner;R.W.Watts,J.P.Field;R.J.Fleetwood,G.M.Stratton,A.J.Taylor;
G.L.Tillyer,W.H.Schofield,J.R.Connor,B.Durrant,R.J.March.

31 Aug IFLR   Home   Tooting & Mitcham United Res.   2 – 2   Wood(2)
Attendance: 550   Receipts: £16.16.0   Programmes: £ ??   Car Park: £0.4.0
Romford Res.: E.J.Sanson;J.P.Field,G.W.Glenham;D.C.Hawkins,G.M.Stratton,W.Blake;
A.Meadows,A.E.Barrett,B.Durrant,G.J.Ruglys,J.J.Wood.

7 Sept IFLR   Away   Woking Reserves   2 – 3   One(og),Burns
Romford Res.: E.J.Sanson;N.P.Appleton,W.Blake;R.J.Fleetwood,G.M.Stratton,D.C.Hawkins;
G.L.Tillyer,A.E.Barrett,B.K.Burns,J.Walker,B.Durrant.

14 Sept IFLR   Away   Corinthian Casuals Reserves   4 – 0   Barrett,Andrews,Burns(2)
Romford Res.: E.J.Sanson;R.J.Fleetwood,D.E.Roper;W.H.Schofield,J.L.Milbank,W.Blake;
J.J.Wood,A.E.Barrett,B.K.Burns,B.Durrant,G.W.Andrews.

21 Sept IFLR   Home   Kingstonian Reserves   3 – 1   Andrews,Schofield,Wood
Attendance: 475   Receipts: £14.0.3   Programmes: £2.2.0   Car Park: £ ??
Romford Res.: E.G.Tetchner;N.P.Appleton,R.S.Watts;W.H.Schofield,D.Prior,D.C.Hawkins;
J.J.Wood,A.E.Barrett,B.K.Burns,B.Durrant,G.W.Andrews.

28 Sept IFLR   Away   Bromley Reserves   0 – 6
Romford Res.: E.G.Tetchner;
Remainder of team unknown.

5 Oct IFLR   Home   Oxford City Reserves   1 – 3   Scorer unknown
Attendance: 425   Receipts: £10.16.3   Programmes: £2.1.6   Car Park: £ ??
Romford Res.: E.J.Sanson;N.P.Appleton,D.E.Roper;R.J.Fleetwood,D.H.Taylor,W.Blake;
P.Buckle,A.E.Barrett,L.Clark,R.F.Hammond,B.Durrant.

12 Oct IFLR   Home   Bromley Reserves   6 – 1   Durrant(2)Hammond(2)Burns,Dartnell
Attendance: 440   Receipts: £11.0.5   Programmes: £1.6.0
Romford Res.: E.G.Tetchner;P.J.Jolly,R.J.Fleetwood;W.Blake,D.Pryor,R.Walker;
F.Dartnell,R.F.Hammond,B.K.Burns,B.Durrant,G.W.Andrews.

19 Oct IFLR   Away   St. Albans City Reserves   1 – 1   Durrant
Romford Res.: E.G.Tetchner;N.P.Appleton,R.J.Fleetwood;J.J.Whitecross,G.C.Noble,W.Blake;
F.Dartnell,P.J.Jolly,B.K.Burns,R.Beales,B.Durrant.

2 Nov IFLR   Home   Woking Reserves   2 – 1   Burns(2)
Attendance: 545   Receipts: £16.11.7   Programmes: £1.18.4
Romford Res.: E.G.Tetchner;R.J.Fleetwood,D.E.Roper;L.Clark,G.C.Noble,W.Blake;
K.Doyle,P.P.Boyles,B.K.Burns,R.Beales,B.Durrant.

9 Nov EIC2R   Away   Hornchurch & Upminster Res.   3 – 0   Burns(2)Clark
Romford Res.: C.Walker;D.H.Taylor,D.E.Roper;L.Clark,D.Pryor,W.Blake;
P.Buckle,A.E.Barrett,B.K.Burns,B.Durrant,R.H.Brewis.

16 Nov IFLR   Home   Wimbledon Reserves   3 – 1   Burns,Durrant,Christie
Attendance: 470   Receipts: £13.6.10   Programmes: £1.14.10
Romford Res.: C.Walker;D.H.Taylor,-.Hood;L.Clark,D.Pryor,R.J.Fleetwood;
K.Doyle,A.E.Barrett,B.K.Burns,R.W.Christie,B.Durrant.

23 Nov IFLR   Away   Leytonstone Reserves   2 – 2   Barrett,Christie
Romford Res.: C.Walker;D.H.Taylor,W.Blake;L.Clark,D.Pryor,R.J.Fleetwood;
K.Doyle,A.E.Barrett,B.K.Burns,R.H.Brewis,R.W.Christie.

30 Nov EIC3R   Home   Plessey(Ilford)   2 – 1   Durrant,Bowness
Attendance: 485   Receipts: £14.16.7   Programmes: £1.5.2
Romford Res.: C.Walker;D.H.Taylor,W.Blake;L.Clark,J.L.Milbank,P.J.Jolly;
B.Bennett,A.E.Barrett,D.Bowness,D.J.Webb,B.Durrant.

7 Dec IFLR   Away   Walthamstow Avenue Reserves   2 – 1   Jolly,Boyles
Romford Res.: P.Gamman;D.H.Taylor,W.Blake;R.J.Fleetwood,J.L.Milbank, ? ;
K.Doyle, ? ,P.P.Boyles,P.J.Jolly,B.Durrant.

14 Dec IFLR   Away   Wycombe Wanderers Reserves   1 – 4   Durrant
Romford Res.: P.Gamman;D.H.Taylor,W.Blake;R.J.Fleetwood,J.L.Milbank,   ?   ;
   ?   ,B.K.Burns,P.P.Boyles,   ?   ,B.Durrant.

21 Dec IFLR   Home   Walthamstow Avenue Reserves   1 – 1   Burns
Attendance: 430   Receipts: £10.4.9   Programmes: £ ??
Romford Res.: P.Gamman;D.H.Taylor,W.Blake;R.J.Fleetwood,J.L.Milbank,   ?   ;
   ?   ,B.Durrant,J.Moir,B.K.Burns,L.Clark.

28 Dec IFLR   Home   Dulwich Hamlet Reserves   2 – 1   Scorers unknown
Attendance: 325   Receipts: £7.15.6   Programmes: £1.7.9
Romford Res.: C.Walker;

4 Jan   EIC4R   Away   Harlow Town Reserves   8 – 0   Hammond(2)Bennett(2)Christie(2)
                                                                Moir,Brewis
Romford Res.: E.G.Tetchner;D.H.Taylor,P.J.Jolly;R.J.Fleetwood,J.L.Milbank,R.Walker;
R.F.Hammond,R.W.Christie,B.Bennett,J.Moir,R.H.Brewis.

11 Jan IFLR   Home   Clapton Reserves   1 – 0   Bryan
Attendance: 440   Receipts: £11.0.4   Programmes: £1.3.10
Romford Res.: T.H.Nickelson;D.F.Hudson,P.J.Jolly;A.E.Barrett,J.L.Milbank,R.Walker;
B.K.Burns,R.W.Christie,D.H.Taylor,A.Bryan,P.P.Boyles.

18 Jan IFLR   Home   St. Albans City Reserves   2 – 1   Burns,Ireton
Attendance: 455   Receipts: £12.3.5   Programmes: £1.9.10
Romford Res.: T.H.Nickelson;D.H.Taylor,P.J.Jolly;L.Clark,J.L.Milbank,R.Walker;
R.F.Hammond,A.E.Barrett,B.K.Burns,B.Bennett,R.J.Ireton.

25 Jan EIC5R   Away   Ilford Reserves   2 – 1   Tiffin(2)
Romford Res.: C.Walker;D.H.Taylor,P.J.Jolly;R.J.Fleetwood,J.L.Milbank,R.Walker;
R.H.Brewis,L.Clark,B.K.Burns,B.Bennett,C.Tiffin.

1 Feb   IFLR   Away   Clapton Reserves   2 – 3   Burns,Bryan
Romford Res.: T.H.Nickelson;D.H.Taylor,P.J.Jolly;J.J.Whitecross,R.J.Fleetwood,S.Cardew;
A.E.Barrett,D.J.Webb,B.K.Burns,A.Bryan,R.H.Brewis.

8 Feb   IFLR   Home   Ilford Reserves   3 – 2   Burns(2) One(og)
Attendance: 185   Receipts: £3.8.4   Programmes: £0.7.8
Romford Res.: C.Walker;D.Hudson,P.J.Jolly;L.Clark,D.H.Taylor,S.Cardew;
B.Durrant,A.E.Barrett,B.K.Burns,D.J.Webb,K.Blayrock.

15 Feb IFLR   Home   Leytonstone Reserves   3 – 2   Burns(3)
Attendance: 548   Receipts: £16.13.3   Programmes: £1.16.4
Romford Res.: C.Walker;D.Hudson,P.J.Jolly;L.Clark,D.H.Taylor,S.Cardew;
A.E.Barrett,B.Bennett,B.K.Burns,J.Martin,R.F.Hammond.

1 Mar   EIC6R   Home   Vicentre   5 – 3   Bennett(2)Tiffin,Burns,Hammond
Attendance: 675   Receipts: £25.16.1   Programmes: £2.10.8
Romford Res.: C.Walker;D.Hudson,D.H.Taylor;L.Clark,J.L.Milbank,S.Cardew;
R.F.Hammond,B.Bennett,B.K.Burns,C.Tiffin,A.E.Barrett.

15 Mar EICSF   Home   Grays Athletic Reserves   3 – 2   Burns(3)
Attendance: 810   Receipts: £30.4.11   Programmes: £2.16.0
Romford Res.: C.Walker;D.H.Taylor,P.J.Jolly;L.Clark,J.L.Milbank,R.J.Fleetwood;
R.F.Hammond,B.Bennett,B.K.Burns,J.Martin,R.J.March.

22 Mar IFLR   Away   Tooting & Mitcham United Res.   1 – 2   Scorer unknown
Romford Res.: C.Walker;D.H.Taylor,P.J.Jolly;L.Clark,J.L.Milbank,R.J.Fleetwood;
R.F.Hammond,B.Bennett,B.K.Burns,J.Martin,R.J.March.

29 Mar IFLR   Home   Wycombe Wanderers Reserves   1 – 2   Scorer unknown
Attendance: 685   Receipts: £18.12.5   Programmes: £2.2.4
Romford Res.:
Team details unknown.

5 Apr   EICF   Home# Dagenham Reserves   3 – 2   Burns(3)
Attendance: 500   Receipts: £33.3.9   Programmes: £3.17.9
Romford Res.: C.Walker;D.H.Taylor,P.J.Jolly;L.Clark,J.L.Milbank,R.J.Fleetwood;
R.F.Hammond,A.E.Barrett,B.K.Burns,B.Bennett,R.J.March.

7 Apr   IFL   Away   Oxford City Reserves   0 – 4
Romford Res.: E.G.Tetchner;D.H.Taylor,D.Hudson;L.Clark,J.L.Milbank,P.J.Jolly;
R.J.Fleetwood,R.F.Hammond,B.Bennett,B.K.Burns,B.Milbank.

12 Apr IFLR   Home   Barking Reserves   1 – 1   B.Milbank
Attendance: 400   Receipts: £9.9.6
Romford Res.: C.Walker;D.H.Taylor,P.J.Jolly;L.Clark,J.L.Milbank,R.J.Fleetwood;
R.F.Hammond,B.Milbank,B.K.Burns,E.Cook,C.Tiffin.

19 Apr IFLR   Away   Wimbledon Reserves   0 – 4
Romford Res.: E.G.Tetchner;D.H.Taylor,P.J.Jolly;L.Clark,J.L.Milbank,S.Cardew.
R.F.Hammond,B.Bennett, ? ,B.Milbank,R.J.March.

21 Apr IFLR   Away   Barking Reserves   5 – 0   Simmons(2)March,Bennett, One(og)
Romford Res.: E.G.Tetchner;D.H.Taylor,P.J.Jolly;L.Clark,J.L.Milbank,R.J.Fleetwood;
R.F.Hammond,B.Bennett,A.Simmons,B.Milbank,R.J.March.

24 Apr IFLR   Away   Ilford Reserves   5 – 2   Simmons(3)March,B.Milbank
Romford Res.: E.G.Tetchner;L.Robinson,G.W.Glenham;L.Clark,J.L.Milbank,D.Henry;
D.Hudson,R.F.Hammond,A.Simmons,B.Milbank,R.J.March.

26 Apr IFLR   Away   Kingstonian Reserves   1 – 1   White
Romford Res.: E.G.Tetchner;R.J.Fleetwood,P.J.Jolly;S.Cardew,J.L.Milbank,D.Henry;
B.Durrant,A.White,A.Simmons,A.Eady,R.J.March.

28 Apr ETR1R Away   Walthamstow Avenue Reserves 3 – 0   Hammond, Two own goals
Romford Res.: E.G.Tetchner;L.Robinson,R.J.Fleetwood;L.Clark,J.L.Milbank,S.Cardew;
R.F.Hammond,A.White,A.Simmons,B.Milbank,R.J.March.

30 Apr ETRSF Away   Barking Reserves   2 – 1   Clark,Simmons
Romford Res.: E.G.Tetchner;L.Robinson,G.W.Glenham;L.Clark,J.L.Milbank,R.J.Fleetwood;
R.F.Hammond,B.Milbank,A.Simmons,D.Henry,R.J.March.

2 May ETRF   Away   Leyton   0 – 1
Romford Res.: E.G.Tetchner;R.J.Fleetwood,G.W.Glenham;L.Clark,J.L.Milbank,S.Cardew;
R.F.Hammond,B.Milbank,A.Simmons,D.Henry,R.J.March.

3 May IFLR   Home   Corinthian Casuals Reserves 4 – 3   Scorers unknown
Attendance: 150   Receipts: £2.6.5
Romford Res.:

\# Played at Brooklands.

RESERVE TEAM CUP RESULTS

Essex County FA Intermediate Cup

Final: Romford Res. 3   Dagenham Res. 2

Romford's progress: 1st Round   Bye
        2nd Round   Home   Hornchurch & Upr. Res. 3 - 0
        3rd Round   Home   Plessey(Ilford)   2 - 1
        4th Round   Away   Harlow Town Res.   8 - 0
        5th Round   Away   Ilford Res.   2 - 1
        6th Round   Home   Vicentre(East Ham) 5 - 3
        Semi-Final Home   Grays Athletic Res. 3 – 2
        Final   Home   Dagenham Res.   3 - 2

Essex Thameside Trophy Reserve Section

Final: Leyton Res. 1   Romford Res. 0

Romford's progress: 1st Round   Away   Walthamstow Avenue Res. 3 - 0
        2nd Round   Away   Barking Res.   2 - 1
        Final   Away   Leyton Res.   0 - 1

Isthmian Football League Reserve Section
Final Table

	P	W	D	L	For	Ag	Pts
Wycombe Wanderers	30	19	8	3	113	48	46
Tooting & Mitcham United	30	17	7	6	95	52	41
Dulwich Hamlet	30	16	8	6	69	58	40
Oxford City	30	14	8	8	78	52	36
Woking	30	16	3	11	63	57	35
Romford Reserves	**30**	**14**	**6**	**10**	**62**	**57**	**34**
Wimbledon	30	15	3	12	70	60	33
Clapton	30	13	5	12	54	62	31
Bromley	30	13	3	14	75	70	29

Leytonstone	30	10	9	11	46	73	29
Walthamstow Avenue	30	9	8	13	48	45	26
Barking	30	9	7	14	33	52	25
St.Albans City	30	6	12	12	57	66	24
Corinthian Casuals	30	9	5	16	63	83	23
Kingstonian	30	8	4	18	61	89	20
Ilford	30	3	2	25	36	99	8

RESERVE TEAM APPEARANCES SEASON 1957 - 58

The following players are known to have appeared in the reserve team during the season.

G.W.Andrews	N.P.Appleton	A.Barrett	R.Beales(Chelmsford City)
B.Bennett	W.J.Blake	K.Blayrock	D.Bowness
P.P.Boyles	R.H.Brewis	A.Bryan	P.Buckle(Barking)
B.K.Burns	S.Cardew(Clacton Town)	R.Christie(Eastbourne Utd)	L.Clark
J.R.Conner	E.Cook	F.Dartnell	K.Doyle
Brian (Bunny)Durrant	-.Eady	J.Field	R.J.Fleetwood
P.Gamman	G.W.Glenham	R.Hammond	D.Hawkins
D.Henry	-.Hood	L.Hutson	R.J.Ireton
P.J.Jolly	R.J.March(Barking)	J.Martin(Dagenham)	A.Meadows
B.Milbank	J.L.Millbank	J.Moir(Grays Athletic)	T.H.Nickelson
G.C.Noble(Southall)	D.Prior	L.Robinson	D.E.Roper
G.J.Ruglys	E.Sanson	W.Schofield	A.Simmons
G.M.Stratton	A.J.Taylor	D.H.Taylor	E.G.Tetchner(Rotary Hoes)
C.Tiffin	G.L.Tillyer	C.Walker	J.Walker(Barkingside)
R.Walker(West Ham Utd)	R.Watts	D.Webb	A.White
J.J.Whitecross	J.Wood		

"A" Team Match Details

28 Aug Frdly   Home   Collier Row Athletic   4 – 1 Scorers unknown
Romford "A": P.A.Langley;D.F.Hudson,G.W.Glenham;A.E.Barrett,C.A.Jakeman,D.A.Ewers;
E.Talbot,-.Trowbridge,-.Watson,J.Ventura,R.H.Brewis.

7 Sept SECD1 Away   Billericay Town   0 – 2
Romford "A": E.Talbot;D.F.Hudson,G.W.Glenham;W.H.Schofield,C.A.Jakeman,D.A.Ewers;
-.Keeble,-.Trowbridge,-.Watson,J.Ventura. (10 men – Langley failed to appear)

14 Sept SECD1 Home   Brentwood Rovers   3 – 1 Ventura,Hall,Simmons
Romford "A": E.G.Tetchner;D.F.Hudson,G.W.Glenham;D.A.Ewers,C.A.Jakeman,R.J.Ireton;
E.Talbot,P.D.Hall,A.Simmons,J.Ventura,-.Trowbridge.

21 Sept Frdly   Home# Romex Sports   1 – 5 Scorer unknown
Romford "A":

28 Sept Frdly   Home# Hornchurch Athletic   1 – 5 Scorer unknown
Romford "A":

5 Oct SECD1 Away   Selo Recreation   5 – 1 Simmons(4)Dartnell
Romford "A": E.G.Tetchner;L.Robinson,G.W.Glenham;D.A.Ewers,G.M.Stratton,R.J.Ireton;
F.Dartnell,R.H.Brewis,A.Simmons,D.Henry,F.J.Tasker.

19 Oct SEC1R Home   Romford Gas   5 – 0 Simmons(4)Henry(pen)
Romford "A": C.Walker;L.Robinson,G.W.Glenham;D.A.Ewers,G.M.Stratton,R.J.Ireton;
P.Buckle,R.H.Brewis,A.Simmons,J.Ventura,D.Henry.

26 Oct SECD1 Away   Sun Athletic   2 – 3 Simmons,Henry
Romford "A": -.Taylor;-.Smith,D.E.Roper;R.H.Brewis,G.M.Stratton,R.J.Ireton;
J.Ventura,D.Henry,A.Simmons,-.Walker,F.J.Tasker.

2 Nov EJC2R Home   Manor Athletic   1 – 4 Simmons
Romford "A": C.Walker;L.Robinson,-.Jones;D.F.Hudson,G.M.Stratton,R.J.Ireton;
P.Buckle,J.Ventura,A.Simmons,G.W.Glenham,F.J.Tasker.

9 Nov SEC2R Away   Sun Athletic   1 – 1* Powell(og)
Romford "A": E.G.Tetchner;L.Robinson,-.Jones;R.J.Fleetwood,D.F.Hudson,G.M.Stratton;
P.Buckle,A.Simmons,F.J.Tasker,G.W.Glenham,R.J.Ireton.

23 Nov SECRp Home Sun Athletic 4 – 2 Stratton,Boyles,Roper,Ireton
Romford "A": E.G.Tetchner;L.Robinson,-.Jones;-.Wright,D.F.Hudson,P.Bright;
P.Buckle,G.M.Stratton,P.P.Boyles,D.E.Roper,R.J.Ireton.

30 Nov SEC3R Away Hornchurch Athletic 1 – 2 Scorer unknown
Romford "A":

7 Dec SECD1 Home Upminster 0 – 0
Romford "A": G.T.Swaby;

14 Dec SECD1 Home Sun Athletic 3 – 2 Scorers unknown
Romford "A":

21 Dec SECD1 Home Laindon United 4 – 1 Scorers unknown
Romford "A": C.Walker;

28 Dec SECD1 Away Clubs United 3 – 3 Scorers unknown
Romford "A":

18 Jan SECD1 Away Laindon United 3 – 3 Scorers unknown
Romford "A":

25 Jan SECD1 Away Harold Wood 2 – 4 Scorers unknown
Romford "A":

1 Feb SECD1 Home Romford British Legion 0 – 3
Romford "A":

8 Feb SECD1 Away Elm Park 4 – 1 Scorers unknown
Romford "A":

15 Feb SECD1 Away Brentwood Rovers 3 – 1 Jones,Simmons(2)
Romford "A":

22 Feb Frdly Away Hornchurch Athletic 2 – 1 Scorers unknown
Romford "A":

1 Mar SECD1 Home Clubs United 6 – 3 Simmons(5)Lonigan
Romford "A":

8 Mar Frdly Away P.L.A. 0 – 4
Romford "A":

15 Mar SECD1 Home Selo Recreation 2 – 1 Scorers unknown
Romford "A":

29 Mar Frdly Away Sun Athletic Won
Romford "A":

5 Apr SECD1 Home Billericay Town 2 – 0 Scorers unknown
Romford "A":

7 Apr SECD1 Away Upminster 3 – 4 Scorers unknown
Romford "A":

19 Apr SECD1 Away Romford British Legion 4 – 0 Scorers unknown
Romford "A":

22 Apr SECD1 Home Elm Park 3 – 1 Scorers unknown
Romford "A":

26 Apr SECD1 Home Harold Wood 5 – 0 Scorers unknown
Romford "A":

*   After extra time.
\#   Played at Brooklands.

"A" TEAM SUMMARY OF RESULTS SEASON 1957 – 58

				Goals		
	P	**W**	**D**	**L**	**For**	**Ag**	**Pts**
S. Essex Comb. Div. One.	20	12	3	5	57	34	27
S. Essex Comb. League Cup	4	2	1	1	11	5	
Essex County FA Junior Cup	1	0	0	1	1	4	
Friendlies*	6	3	0	3	8	16	
Total	31	17	4	10	77	59	

Note: The score in the friendly match with Sun Athletic on 29th March is not known.

South Essex Combination Division One
Final Table

					Goals		
	P	W	D	L	For	Ag	Pts
Romford British Legion	20	14	2	4	80	39	30
Romford "A"	**20**	**12**	**3**	**5**	**57**	**34**	**27**
Brentwood Rovers	20	11	4	5	68	42	26
Laindon United	20	10	4	6	64	47	24
Billericay Town	20	8	5	7	49	52	21
Selo Recreation	20	7	3	10	38	48	17
Harold Wood	20	7	3	10	51	61	17
Clubs United	20	6	5	9	40	59	17
Upminster	20	7	2	11	41	49	16
Sun Athletic	20	6	1	13	46	78	13
Elm Park	20	4	4	12	34	59	12

"A" TEAM CUP RESULTS SEASON 1957 – 58

Essex County FA Junior Challenge Cup
Final: Litford   6   British Mathews   3   a.e.t.

Romford's progress: 1st Round   Home   Manor Athletic   1 - 4

South Essex Combination League Cup
Final: Collier Row B.L.   2   Romex Sports   1

Romford's progress: 1st Round   Home   Romford Gas   5 – 0
2nd Round   Away   Sun Athletic   1 - 1
Replay   Home   Sun Athletic   4 - 2
3rd Round   Away   Hornchurch Athletic   1 – 2

"A" TEAM APPEARANCES SEASON 1957 - 58

Very few details are known as to the composition of the "A" team during the season, but the following are known to have played for the Club.

A.E.Barrett	P.P.Boyles	R.H.Brewis	P.Bright
P.Buckle(Barking)	F.Dartnell	D.A.Ewers	R.J.Fleetwood
G.W.Glenham	P.D.Hall	D.Henry	D.F.Hudson
R.J.Ireton	C.A.Jakeman	-.Jones	-.Keeble
P.A.Langley	J.M.Lonigan(Worcester Park)	L.Robinson	D.E.Roper
W.H.Schofield	A.Simmons	-.Smith	G.M.Stratton
G.T.Swaby	E.Talbot	F.J.Tasker	-.Taylor
E.G.Tetchner(Rotary Hoes)	-.Trowbridge	J.Ventura	C.Walker
-.Watson	-.Wright		

DEPARTURES FROM THE CLUB SEASON 1957 – 58

The following appear to have left the club during or by the end of the season. They may have been triallists and only played one or two games and then went elsewhere. New clubs are indicated where known.

First Team Players only (See note below).

G.W.Andrews (Walthamstow Avenue), N.P.Appleton (Barking), -.Baines (Ardleigh House), J.A.Birch (not known), W.Blake (Barkingside), D.Bowness (Barking), A.Bryan (Rainham Town), P.Buckle (Aveley), N.Cakebread (Old Dagonians), J.R.Connor (Romex Sports), M.R.Cooper (H.M.Forces), F.Dartnell (Rainham Town), K.Doyle (Hornchurch & Upminster), P.Drake

(Hornchurch & Upminster), C.E.East (resigned), J.P.Field (moved to Canada), D.Henry (Brentwood & Warley), R.J.Ireton (Hornchurch & Upminster), P.J.Jolly (Harold Hill), -.Keeble (Hornchurch & Upminster), B.Milbank (Leyton Orient), J.Moir (Briggs Sports), S.Murphy (Briggs Sports), M.D.Paviour (Ilford), D.Prior (not known), E.Sanson (Enfield Town), W.H.Schofield (Dagenham), D.Smith (Briggs Sports), A.J.Taylor (Dagenham), D.E.Thomas (Brentwood & Warley), G.L.Tillyer (not known), J.Ventura (Brentwood & Warley), J.Walker (Guildford City), R.Watts (not known), J.Wood (Ilford).

Note: A large number of players appeared in the reserve and "A" teams during the season. Many of these were triallists or only stayed for a short time. It is not possible to include these details as there were so many of these players and it is difficult to follow their tracks!!!

Post Season Summary   Season 1957 – 58

Anumber of new arrivals joined the club this season, ex-Barking players Reg March and Alfie Lee becoming first team regulars. The amateur game was of course still riddled with rumours regarding illegal payments to players and attracting top-class men was proving difficult. Boro commenced the season badly, failing to obtain a victory in their first six games. Dulwich Hamlet won 5-3 at Brooklands in the opening game on 24th August. Journeys to Clapton (1-2) and Tooting and Mitcham (1-5) were followed with a six nil thrashing on 2nd September by Tottenham Hotspur "A" in the East Anglian Cup at Brooklands. Romford did manage two drawn games against Clacton Town in the FA Cup.

At last victory came, albeit against lowly Corinthian Casuals, for two welcome league points, but Clacton Town proved to be too strong, winning the second replay in the FA Cup by four goals to two. Four more successive league defeats followed, with Wimbledon (1-5), Walthamstow Avenue (1-2), Kingstonian (0-1) and Bromley (1-5) being the grateful recipients of the points available. A three one victory over St. Albans City on 19th October gave Boro their second success from nine league matches. Mixed results were again becoming the order of the day, win one, lose one etc. Barking won 3-1, Corinthian Casuals were beaten 5-2, Wycombe won 2-0 and Woking were beaten away by three goals to one, followed by a two all home draw against Leytonstone.

Now for some added spice with a couple of cup ties, first away to Grays Athletic in the Thameside Trophy and then away to Barkingside in the Essex Senior Cup on 7th December with some controversy. Manager Peter Wallace expressed doubts as to the size of the Barkingside pitch and lodged an official protest that it was a couple of yards narrower than the minimum requirement. The tie was, however, played and Boro secured a 2-1 win. Was this an official victory though? Barkingside were removed from the competition as a result of Romford's protest being considered by the Essex County Football Association!!

Yet more league defeats followed: against Oxford City at home (1-2) and Ilford away on Christmas Day by a similar score, but Romford took the points on Boxing Day winning the return fixture with Ilford 1-0. Leytonstone away (0-2) and Clapton at home (3-3) meant more dropped league points. Optimism was again high for the Amateur Cup tie away to Kent rivals Erith and Belvedere on 11th January, but the "Deres" were not in helpful mood and Boro suffered a 3-1 loss. More misery followed as yet again league defeats continued at St. Albans (0-2) and at Brooklands against Kingstonian (1-3). A league point was picked up in a 1-1 draw at Bromley and Boro supporters were hoping that the Essex Senior Cup would bring some good luck. Powerful Briggs Sports were, however, in top form and proceeded into the next round with an easy 3-0 victory on 8th February.

At this stage Romford's league record was looking disastrous. They had gained only 13 points from 22 matches and were at the bottom of the table. This situation was not improved by a 2-2 draw at Dulwich Hamlet and a 4-1 loss at Oxford City. A friendly against Hitchin Town ended in another 2-0 loss. Amazingly, Romford then went three league games without defeat, beating Wimbledon 3-1 and drawing 0-0 with Walthamstow Avenue. Humiliation followed on 29th March with a 6-0 thrashing away to Wycombe Wanderers. A point was grabbed at Barking the following week before yet another cup tie. The replayed Thameside Trophy game ended in a 2-1 victory over Grays Athletic after extra time, Buddy Holmes securing the win with a penalty goal. Next up a 3-3 draw at home to Woking in the league before the Thameside Trophy semi-final on 23rd April. Romford were obliged to travel to Ilford, but secured a place in the final with a brace of goals from Barry Burns.

Local rivals Brentwood and Warley (4-2) and Dagenham (2-1) enjoyed Brooklands visits for a friendly encounter and the Romford Charity Cup respectively. These results did nothing for Romford's status and standing in the local area. Success, however, did come again in the Thameside Trophy final on 3rd May, when Boro defeated Barking away 2-1, Johnny Martin and Barry Burns scoring their goals.

Romford again wound up the season with the charity fixture for the Reg Sheward Trophy on 10th May. On this occasion another local newspaper reporter, Don Hill, selected an Essex XI. An interesting encounter ended three all with Don Hill's eleven winning the trophy on the toss of a coin. Boro ended the season bottom of the league level on points with Ilford but with an inferior goal average and the only success in the cups was again the lifting of the Thameside Trophy once more.

The reserve team had a better measure of success by finishing sixth in the league. They defeated Dagenham Reserves 3-2 to win the Essex Intermediate Cup, with Barry Burns recording a hat-trick. They lost to Leyton Reserves, however, in the final of the Thameside Trophy Reserve Section. The "A" team too had a good season finishing runners up to Romford British Legion in the South Essex Combination Division One table.

GLEANINGS FROM MANAGEMENT COMMITTEE MINUTE BOOKS
SEASON 1957-58

On **20th August 1957** arrangements were made for an outing for 32 officials and players on 1st September to Point Clear, Clacton-on-Sea, with lunch at the Ferry Boat Inn. It was agreed players' after-match meals would be taken at Baldwins Restaurant as last season.

On **10th September** the Secretary informed the meeting that Mr John Haley had offered to provide statistical information of interest to programme readers. His offer was accepted with pleasure and it was agreed that he be given every encouragement.

On **12th November** they noted a letter from West Ham United indicating their agreement to the transfer of Roy Walker.

On **7th January 1958** it was agreed to endeavour to continue with the Ground Broadcast system until the end of the season. Consideration would be given to the purchase of a new system during the close season.

On **4ᵗʰ February** the Directors decide to appoint a professional coach for the following season. It was decided that in the meantime Peter Wallace would take on the responsibility for the position until someone was appointed.

On **13ᵗʰ May** it was noted that both Romford and Ilford were re-elected to the Isthmian League. The League considered various options to improve the standard of amateur football, suggestions including promotion and relegation, an extended league programme and championship trophies. None of these proposals were found practicable and it was agreed to continue under the same conditions and traditions as previously.

PROFESSIONAL PROLOGUE

How many Romford FC fans were genuinely surprised at the club's decision to apply for a Southern League place? After all the speculation and rumour over the past four years, there can't have been many who never expected it. 'Where there is smoke' begins the old adage, and in Romford's case it had been thickening since the day someone suggested Football League side Charlton Athletic might take over Brooklands.

Bad times for Romford and Charlton had prompted this idea. Charlton, then a First Division side, were playing good football but found it difficult to pay their way. Gates of below 20,000 were not uncommon and only the biggest name attractions such as Manchester United, Chelsea, Spurs and Arsenal drew over 30,000.

Since Romford's proud Amateur Cup march to Wembley in 1949, the club's fortunes had dipped sharply. Financial and playing strength had slumped to a dangerously low level and the once proud Brooklands ground, which had many times held over 10,000 fans, now had only 2,000 scattered around the terraces for a first team game. It was common knowledge that if Romford had a good side then thousands of lost fans would return. The answer seemed simple – bring successful Charlton to soccer-starved Romford.

To some there seemed an easier way. Romford should turn professional, enter the Southern League and fight their way into the Football League. Wishful thinking? Maybe, but the seed was sown in the minds of Romford fans and began to grow. The question kept on recurring. "Should Romford turn professional?" asked a local newspaper poll at Brooklands. Of the 1,369 asked, 775 said yes, 488 said no and 106 were not sure.

Events in the English soccer world during this period had distinctly favoured any club turning professional. Two clubs, Yiewsley and Cambridge City, took advantage of this to relinquish their amateur status and become Southern League professionals.

Cambridge City, who played in the Athenian League before joining the paid ranks, now had an average weekly attendance of 3,000, over three times greater than when they were amateurs. The higher class of soccer certainly attracted many extra fans. Yiewsley, a young club with big ideas, had been a successful side in the Corinthian League drawing over 1,000 fans for home matches. As professionals, their gates increased to around 2,500.

These were indeed encouraging pointers for Romford. If they offered a better, faster display of soccer than they had been doing in the past, then their gates could average about 5,000. The town of Romford and the surrounding areas had a population of nearly 350,000 to draw on, far greater than either Yiewsley or Cambridge.

The nearest Football League side was West Ham United, but for the majority of Romford people it would take nearly an hour to reach the Upton Park ground. Other alternatives were Tottenham Hotspur, Arsenal, or Leyton Orient – all too far away for all except the keenest supporters.

What would happen to Romford's existing players if they joined the paid ranks? The club had already stated they hoped to retain most of their first and second eleven men, either as amateurs or professionals. Added to these would be one or two veteran stars. Professionals not being retained by First and Second Division League sides at the end of the season would also be on the list.

DAWN OF A NEW ERA – APPOINTMENT OF JACK CHISHOLM

With shamateurism abounding in the amateur game, the club's directors decided they were only prepared to pay players legally in the semi-professional game. The bold decision was made to appoint a full time professional manager in preparation for non-league semi-professional football. It was minuted on 10th April 1959 that 'Mr Jack Chisholm appointed Manager of the Club, and to take up his duties forthwith'.

In-house manager Peter Wallace agreed to stay on as his assistant. This was the only announcement being made to the public or any reference to semi-professional football. Rumours were rife, and eventually an announcement was made in November 1958 that the club would be competing in Southern League football in the following season.

Jack Chisholm is appointed Manager

Peter Wallace, Glyn Richards, Herbert Muskett(Secretary), Jim Parrish, Lord Macpherson,
Hugh Knights, Jack Chisholm, George Howlett, Martin Brazier   *Authors' collection*

Jack Chisholm was born in Edmonton in 1924 and joined Tottenham Hotspur as a seventeen year old but was unable to establish himself in the first team as wartime approached. He returned to Spurs after being demobilised from the Forces, but only made a couple of first team appearances before leaving to join Brentford in 1947. He made nearly fifty appearances in the first team before joining first division side Sheffield United. Once again unable to command a regular first team place, he joined Plymouth Argyle for the 1949-50 season where he was very successful. He was soon made club captain and remained with Argyle until 1954.

After retiring from playing, he ran a pub in his home town of Edmonton before taking up an appointment as manager of Finchley in 1957 and then moving to Romford.

DIRECTORS' REPORT FOR THE TWELVE MONTHS ENDED 31ST JULY, 1958

The year under review has been a momentous one for the Company, marked by the wonderful assistance given by the supporting organisations - the Romford Supporters' Association, the Romford Sportsmen's Association and the Romford FC Social Club - as a result of which your Board took the first step towards changing to professional soccer by appointing a full-time professional manager. After advertising widely, Mr Jack R. Chisholm was appointed out of some thirty applicants. He was given full power to coach, select and manage the teams....Your Directors are convinced that the right step has been taken and look forward to the Club's future progress as a professional club.

The year in respect of which the accounts are presented has financially been closely similar to the previous year in both Income and Expenditure....The only items of Income showing marked differences are Gate Income, which shows an increase of £455, and Donations, thanks to supporting organisations, up by £814. On the Expenditure side many of the items are less than the previous year but wages have naturally (by the appointment of the manager) increased and so have items for Lighting and Heating, Advertising, Bank Charges and Repairs to Ground, Property and Equipment; but Players' and Officials' Expenses have been reduced by £110. While a surplus of £954 is shown, the year's result, without the assistance of sporting organisations, would have been a deficit of about the same figure.

Your Directors regret that the Club did not have a very happy playing season, although it is remarkable how often the match, as in the previous season, was decided by the odd goal.

The Company's Property Account shows additions during the year of £1,200. The sum was expended upon the erection of a Social Centre and is considered money well spent. Your Directors are proposing to continue, and erect an extension to the Centre which may well be completed at the time this report is published. After writing off a sum of £700 for depreciation the Property stands in the accounts in the sum of £15,000....

With regard to the future your Directors have little to add to the remarks made earlier - professional soccer has its attendant difficulties as has the amateur game, but over all it is thought that given the patronage and encouragement of supporters of the game locally, there is every reason to expect our Club to gain renown against some of the best clubs in the country. Your Directors will, as funds allow, do everything possible to provide at Brooklands clean, attractive, skilful football worthy of the best traditions of the game.

The above report was presented to the shareholders at the Annual General Meeting on Monday 8th June 1959, reported as follows in the *Romford Recorder*, Friday 12th June 1959

NEW DIRECTOR FOR ROMFORD -
SPORTSMEN'S ASSOCIATION OFFICIAL IS ELECTED

Former Romford Mayor and councillor Mr Albert Blane has been elected to fill the vacancy on the Romford FC Ltd board of directors. A prominent business man in the town, Mr Blane has been president of the Romford Sportsmen's Association since it was founded. He was one of four candidates who applied for the two vacant places on the board. George Howlett, who retired by rotation, was re-elected and filled the other vacancy. Unlucky candidates were Pete Wallace, former Romford player and later coach to the club; and Alf Lumley, Press officer of the Romford Sportsmen's Association, who also made an unsuccessful bid to join the Board last year.

Mr Blane fills the vacancy on the Board created by the death of Bill Mann earlier this year. He has been President of the Romford Sportsmen's Association since its inauguration nearly two years ago, and has played a major role in its organisation and development.

....Mr Blane, who attended Mawney Road School with Mr Kittle, is also a keen cricket enthusiast. He is a member of the Romford Cricket Week Festival Committee. In a ballot among the 52 members who attended Tuesday's AGM, Mr Blane and Mr Howlett polled 29 votes, Peter Wallace received 23 and Mr Lumley 11.

Speaking from the floor, Mr E.W. Smith asked the directors why there was an 11 months delay in presenting the report and statement of accounts. Both were for the year ended July 31st, 1958. Secretary of the company, Mr H.W. Muskett, explained the added difficulties of changing a club from amateur to professional status. "By holding the meeting now", said Mr Muskett, "we are able to give shareholders and supporters a better picture of the progress we have made towards professionalism".

Chairman of the company, Lord Macpherson, emphasised the considerable progress the club has made since deciding to become a professional organisation. "A year ago, our fortunes were at a low ebb", he said, "but we have received wonderful support from the Romford Sportsmen's Association, the Romford Social Club and the Romford Supporters' Club. We go forward with the promise of their continued full support".

Continuing, Lord Macpherson said it was too early to give an authoritative statement on the progress of signing players. The club were waiting until the end of the month before releasing a list of players who had signed contracts with the club. "Professional soccer has its problems, just like amateur, but we are all aware of this" he said.

[same issue] From secretary to super-groundsman!

Romford FC Ltd directors presented Martin Brazier with a silver cigarette case on Monday to mark his 30 years as secretary to the club. Now Martin has given up the post. In the club's behind-the-scenes reorganisation, he has taken over as chairman of the Ground and Buildings Committee.

"I suppose I am now a super-groundsman" he said jokingly. Then in a more serious vein, he appealed for supporters to come forward and help him with the task.

DEATH OF ROMFORD DIRECTOR Mr W. G (Bill) MANN
As reported in the *Romford Recorder,* Wednesday 8ᵗʰ April 1959
Obituary: FC director, yachtsman

Farmer, yachtsman and keen sports follower, 53 year-old Mr William George Mann, died at his home, Park Corner Farm, Upminster, on Saturday – three weeks after being released from Harold Wood Hospital following an operation.

A director of Romford Football Club, "Bill" Mann lived at 4 Pettits Lane, Romford, until three years ago. He was a founder member of Hornchurch Professional and Businessmen's Association, Commodore of Bradwell Quay Yacht Club, a member of the Narrow Seas yacht Club, and a member of Aldborough Masonic Lodge.

Mr Mann farmed Pettits Farm, Romford, until he took over the 300-acre Upminster Farm off Hacton Lane about 1930.

For his funeral today at South Essex Crematorium, friends have been asked not to send flowers, instead to donate towards cancer research.

Although Mr Mann's death occurred during the 1958-59 season, we include a report here because his death and the election of a replacement director have been mentioned in the club's Annual General Meeting for 1957-58 (see the previous page). The probate record shows that he lived at Park Corner Farm, Hacton Lane and left an estate worth £38,761 when he died on 4ᵗʰ April 1959.

THE ROMFORD FOOTBALL CLUB LIMITED

Full Members of The Football Association
Full Members of Isthmian Football League
Affiliated to Essex County Football Association

Chairman: Rt.Hon.Lord T.Macpherson
Vice-Chairman: Mr J.W.Parrish
Directors: Messrs.M.A.Brazier, G.I.Howlett, H.F.Knights, W.G.Mann, G.Richards JP
Company Secretary: Mr H.W.Muskett

Registered Offices: 110,Hyland Way,Hornchurch

Colours: Royal Blue & Old Gold Shirts,White Shorts

Ground: Brooklands Sports Ground,Romford

Manager: Mr J.R.Chisholm   **Assistant:** Mr P.G.R.Wallace

Football Club Management Committee:
Chairman: Mr J.W.Parrish
Vice-Chairman: Mr H.F.Knights   **Hon.Secretary:** Mr M.A.Brazier
Hon.Press Secretary: Mr R.E.Skilton   **Hon.Programme Secretary:** Mr H.Wright
Other Committee Members: Messrs.F.H.Adams, A.Adlam,
G.I.Howlett, R.E.Skilton, P.G.R.Wallace, E.Wilson

Statistics: Mr John Haley(Ex Officio)

Reserve Team Secretary: Major A.E.Adlam
Reserve Team Coach: Mr J.Martin
Reserve Team Trainer: Mr Fred. Griffiths

"A" Team: Mr H.J.Lazell and Mr Frank Addington

Minor XI Secretary: Mr W.Benson   **Minor XI Assistant:** Mr W.Bennett

Groundsman: Mr W.C.Seddon   **Hon.Solicitor:** Mr L.Mullis

Bankers: Lloyds Bank Limited   **Hon.Auditors:** Messrs.Iion.V.Cummings & Co.

LEAGUES & COMPETITIONS

Football Association Challenge Cup Competition
Football Association Amateur Challenge Cup Competition
Isthmian Football League
Essex County Football Association Senior Challenge Cup
East Anglian Cup
Essex Thameside Challenge Competition
Essex Elizabethan Trophy

Isthmian Football League Reserve Section
The Essex County Football Association Intermediate Challenge Cup
Essex Thameside Challenge Competition Reserve Section
Romford Charity Cup Premier Section

Eastern "A" League
The Essex County Football Association Junior Challenge Cup
Eastern "A" League Challenge Cup

Hornchurch Minor League Division 3
Hornchurch Minor League Division 3 Cup
Essex County Youth FA "Andrews" Challenge Cup

Admission Prices Season 1958 – 59

	First Team			Reserve Team		
	Adults	OAPs	Child	Adults	OAPs	Child
Ground	1/6	9d		9d		5d
Ground & Enclosure	2/-			1/-		6d
Grandstand	2/6	2/6		1/-		6d

Season Ticket Prices Season 1958 – 59

	Adults	OAPs & Children
Grandstand (All one price)	£2.0.0	
Ground & Enclosure	£1.10.0	15/-
Ground only	£1.0.0	10/-

NOTE: The actual attendance figures are not available for the 1957–58 season and the details given have been calculated from the cash receipts which are known, together with an allowance in respect of the number of Season Ticket holders.

Public Trial Match

The committee proposed that usual final trial be arranged but Jack Chisholm indicated that he was not in a position to stage a final trial match. The Committee decided that trial matches would be held on the proposed date, open to the public, but no admission charge to be made. Three trial matches were played but no details are to hand.

First Team Match Details

23 Aug IFL   Away   Woking   2 – 2   Tiffin(2)
Romford: P.Gamman;W.Blake,T.Spencer;J.J.Whitecross,M.R.Cooper(Capt),R.Walker;
R.F.Hammond,B.Cappi,C.Tiffin,J.Martin,R.J.March.

25 Aug ETT1R Home   Walthamstow Avenue   0 – 1
Attendance: 1,310   Receipts: £101.19.0   Programmes: £8.9.2   Car Park: £2.17.6
Romford: P.Gamman;W.Blake,T.Spencer;J.J.Whitecross(Capt),S.Cardew,D.J.Webb;
R.F.Hammond,B.Cappi,B.Bennett,J.Martin,R.J.March.

28 Aug IFL   Home   Clapton   2 – 2   Whitecross,Bennett
Attendance: 1,170   Receipts: £80.0.3   Programmes: £4.9.0   Car Park: £2.7.6
Romford: P.Gamman;W.Blake,T.Spencer;J.J.Whitecross,M.R.Cooper(Capt),D.J.Webb;
R.F.Hammond,B.Cappi,B.Bennett,J.Martin,R.J.March.

30 Aug IFL   Home   Tooting & Mitcham United   0 – 5
Attendance: 2,170   Receipts: £160.8.9   Programmes: £14.8.0   Car Park: £3.9.6
Romford: P.Gamman;A.J.Lee,M.R.Cooper(Capt);J.J.Whitecross,S.Cardew,D.J.Webb;
B.Durrant,B.Cappi,B.K.Burns,J.Martin,R.J.March.

1 Sept EET1R Away   Brentwood & Warley   1 – 2   March
Romford: P.Gamman;D.H.Taylor,T.Spencer;R.J.Fleetwood,S.Cardew,A.J.Taylor;
B.Durrant,A.J.Lee(Capt),K.Delieu,J.Martin,R.J.March.

4 Sept IFL Away Clapton 1 – 4 March
Romford: P.Gamman;A.J.Lee(Capt),D.H.Taylor;W.Blake,J.L.Milbank,R.Walker;
H.W.Brooks,B.Cappi,B.Bennett,R.F.Hammond,R.J.March.

6 Sept IFL Home St. Albans City 1 – 3 March
Attendance: 1,295 Receipts: £89.6.9 Programmes: £8.19.0 Car Park: £2.19.6
Romford: P.Gamman;A.J.Lee,M.R.Cooper;T.Watson,S.Cardew,A.S.Durrant;
H.W.Brooks,B.Cappi,W.Blake,J.Martin,R.J.March.

10 Sept EAC1R Away Aveley 0 – 6
Romford: P.Gamman;A.J.Lee(Capt),J.G.Ling;W.Blake,S.Cardew,A.S.Durrant;
H.W.Brooks,B.Cappi,J.Banfield,J.Martin,R.J.March.

13 Sept IFL Away# Corinthian Casuals 2 – 3 Cooper(pen)Cappi
Romford: T.H.Nickelson;J.G.Ling,M.R.Cooper(Capt);A.J.Lee,G.C.Noble,A.S.Durrant;
H.W.Brooks,B.Cappi,C.Tiffin,J.Banfield,K.Jarrold.

20 Sept FAC1Q Away Eton Manor 9 – 2 Corbett(4)Cappi(2)Tiffin,Cooper,Brooks
Romford: P.Gamman;J.G.Ling,M.R.Cooper(Capt);A.J.Lee,G.C.Noble,R.Walker;
H.W.Brooks,B.Cappi,K.Corbett,C.Tiffin,R.J.March.

27 Sept IFL Home Leytonstone 2 – 1 Cappi,Cooper
Attendance: 1,430 Receipts: £102.1.9 Programmes: £12.13.6 Car Park: £3.0.3
Romford: P.Gamman;J.G.Ling,M.R.Cooper(Capt);R.J.Fleetwood,G.C.Noble,R.Walker;
H.W.Brooks,B.Cappi,K.Corbett,C.Tiffin,R.J.March.

4 Oct FAC2Q Home Hornchurch & Upminster 2 – 3 Tiffin,March
Attendance: 2,600 Receipts: £200.12.9 Programmes: £15.5.0 Car Park: £3.3.0
Romford: P.Gamman;J.G.Ling,M.R.Cooper(Capt);J.J.Whitecross,G.C.Noble,R.Walker;
H.W.Brooks,B.Cappi,K.Corbett,C.Tiffin,R.J.March.

11 Oct IFL Away Wimbledon 0 – 1
Romford: P.Gamman;J.G.Ling,D.H.Taylor;J.J.Whitecross,M.R.Cooper(Capt),R.Walker;
H.W.Brooks,L.A.Holmes,C.Tiffin,B.Cappi,G.W.Andrews.

18 Oct IFL Away Barking 1 – 3 Tiffin
Romford: P.Gamman;J.G.Ling,D.H.Taylor;J.J.Whitecross(Capt),G.C.Noble,A.S.Durrant;
R.F.Hammond,L.A.Holmes,C.Tiffin,B.Cappi,G.W.Andrews.

25 Oct IFL Home Wycombe Wanderers 3 – 4 Holmes(2)Cappi
Attendance: 1,670 Receipts: £120.10.6 Programmes: £10.0.6 Car Park: £3.5.3
Romford: P.Gamman;A.J.Lee(Capt),J.G.Ling;J.J.Whitecross,G.C.Noble,A.S.Durrant;
H.W.Brooks,L.A.Holmes,C.Tiffin,B.Cappi,G.W.Andrews.

1 Nov IFL Away Kingstonian 4 – 1 Cappi,Wyles,Tiffin(2)
Romford: P.Gamman;A.J.Lee(Capt),J.G.Ling;J.J.Whitecross,D.H.Taylor,A.S.Durrant;
D.Wyles,L.A.Holmes,C.Tiffin,B.Cappi,G.W.Andrews.

8 Nov IFL Home Walthamstow Avenue 1 – 5 Wyles
Attendance: 1,980 Receipts: £146.19.0 Programmes: £12.10.4 Car Park: £3.11.0
Romford: P.Gamman;A.J.Lee(Capt),J.G.Ling;J.J.Whitecross,D.H.Taylor,A.S.Durrant;
D.Wyles,L.A.Holmes,C.Tiffin,B.Cappi,G.W.Andrews.

15 Nov IFL Away Leytonstone 2 – 2 Cappi(2)
Romford: P.Gamman;A.J.Lee(Capt),J.G.Ling;R.Walker,D.H.Taylor,A.S.Durrant;
D.Wyles,L.A.Holmes,I.Oakley,B.Cappi,R.J.March.

22 Nov IFL Home Corinthian Casuals 1 – 1 Oakley
Attendance: 1,140 Receipts: £78.14.9 Programmes: £7.0.7 Car Park: £2.7.9
Romford: P.Gamman;A.J.Lee(Capt),J.G.Ling;R.Walker,D.H.Taylor,A.S.Durrant;
D.Wyles,B.Lawrence,I.Oakley,B.Cappi,R.J.March.

29 Nov Frdly Home Chelmsford City 1 – 4 D.Taylor
Attendance: 1,075 Receipts: £82.19.6 Programmes: £7.11.6 Car Park: £2.0.6
Romford: P.Gamman;A.J.Lee(Capt),J.G.Ling;R.Walker,D.H.Taylor,A.S.Durrant;
D.Wyles,B.Lawrence,C.Tiffin,B.Cappi,R.J.March.

6 Dec IFL Away Wycombe Wanderers 1 – 5 March
Romford: P.Gamman;R.Walker,J.G.Ling;B.Cappi,D.H.Taylor(Capt),A.S.Durrant;
D.Wyles,B.Lawrence,C.Tiffin,R.J.March,K.Jarrold.

13 Dec ESC1R Home Leytonstone 1 – 1* Lawrence
Attendance: 1,030 Receipts: £78.16.7 Programmes: £6.16.0 Car Park: £1.13.0
Romford: P.Gamman;L.Hutson,J.G.Ling;R.Walker,D.H.Taylor(Capt),A.S.Durrant;
D.Wyles,B.Cappi,C.Tiffin,B.Lawrence,R.J.March.

20 Dec IFL   Home   Dulwich Hamlet   3 – 4 March,Wyles,Flynn
Attendance: 1,110   Receipts: £75.13.1   Programmes: £6.15.8 Car Park: £1.19.3
Romford: P.Gamman;L.Hutson,W.Blake;R.Walker,D.H.Taylor(Capt),A.S.Durrant;
D.Wyles,B.Cappi,C.Tiffin,T.Flynn,R.J.March.

25 Dec IFL   Home   Ilford   2 – 1 Oakley,Tiffin
Attendance: 1,220   Receipts: £83.7.6   Programmes: £7.5.6 Car Park: £1.19.6
Romford: P.Gamman;L.Hutson,W.Blake;R.Byers,D.H.Taylor(Capt),A.S.Durrant;
I.Oakley,B.Lawrence,C.Tiffin,B.Cappi,T.Flynn.

27 Dec ESCRp Away   Leytonstone   1 – 0 Barrett
Romford: P.White;L.Hutson,W.Blake;R.Byers,D.H.Taylor(Capt),D.R.Stead;
B.Lawrence,B.Cappi,A.E.Barrett,C.Tiffin,I.Oakley.

3 Jan IFL   Away   Ilford   5 – 1 Tiffin(3)Cappi,D.Taylor(pen)
Romford: P.White;L.Hutson,W.Blake;R.Byers,D.H.Taylor(Capt),D.R.Stead;
D.Wyles,B.Lawrence,C.Tiffin,B.Cappi,T.Flynn.

17 Jan AC1R   Home   Leytonstone   0 – 1
Attendance: 2,175   Receipts: £170.16.0   Programmes: £12.4.0 Car Park: £ ??
Romford: P.White;L.Hutson,W.Blake;R.Byers,D.H.Taylor(Capt),D.R.Stead;
D.Wyles,B.Lawrence,C.Tiffin,B.Cappi,T.Flynn.

24 Jan ESC2R Home   Barking   3 – 1 Wyles,Tiffin(2)
Attendance: 2,060   Receipts: £161.2.0   Programmes: £11.15.10 Car Park: £3.0.11
Romford: P.White;L.Hutson,W.Blake;R.Byers,D.H.Taylor(Capt),D.R.Stead;
D.Wyles,B.Lawrence,C.Tiffin,B.Cappi,T.Flynn.

31 Jan IFL   Away   St. Albans City   2 – 2 Tiffin,Flynn
Romford: P.Gamman;L.Hutson,W.Blake;R.Byers,D.H.Taylor(Capt),D.R.Stead;
D.Wyles,B.Lawrence,C.Tiffin,T.Flynn,G.W.Andrews.

7 Feb IFL   Home   Kingstonian   1 – 2 Oakes(og)
Attendance: 1,370   Receipts: £97.10.9   Programmes: £9.0.3 Car Park: £2.10.3
Romford: P.Gamman;L.Hutson,W.Blake;R.Byers,D.H.Taylor(Capt),D.R.Stead;
D.Wyles,B.Lawrence,L.A.Holmes,B.Cappi,T.Flynn.

14 Feb ESCSF Neut#1 Dagenham   4 – 3 Tiffin,D.Taylor(2pens)Wyles
Romford: P.Gamman;L.Hutson,J.G.Ling;R.Byers,D.H.Taylor(Capt),D.R.Stead;
D.Wyles,L.Holmes,C.Tiffin,B.Cappi,T.Flynn.

21 Feb IFL   Away   Dulwich Hamlet   1 – 3 Lawrence
Romford: P.Gamman;L.Hutson,J.G.Ling;R.Byers,D.H.Taylor(Capt),D.R.Stead;
D.Wyles,B.Lawrence,I.Oakley,B.Cappi,T.Flynn.

28 Feb IFL   Home   Barking   0 – 2
Attendance: 1,890   Receipts: £139.11.6   Programmes: £10.14.1 Car Park: £3.4.0
Romford: P.Gamman;L.Hutson,R.A.Pitt;R.Byers,D.H.Taylor(Capt),D.R.Stead;
D.Wyles,B.Lawrence,C.Tiffin,B.Cappi,G.L.Wright.

7 Mar IFL   Away   Bromley   3 – 5 Wright(2)Holmes
Romford: P.Gamman;L.Hutson,R.A.Pitt;R.Byers,D.H.Taylor(Capt),D.R.Stead;
D.Wyles,A.E.Barrett,L.A.Holmes,E.A.Ward,G.L.Wright.

14 Mar IFL   Away   Tooting & Mitcham United   3 – 2 Holmes,Ward,Wright
Romford: P.Gamman;J.G.Ling,R.A.Pitt;R.Byers,D.H.Taylor(Capt),D.R.Stead;
D.Wyles,B.Cappi,L.A.Holmes,E.A.Ward,G.L.Wright.

21 Mar IFL   Home   Woking   0 – 1
Attendance: 1,295   Receipts: £89.13.10   Programmes: £7.9.2 Car Park: £2.6.9
Romford: P.Gamman;J.G.Ling,R.A.Pitt;R.Byers,D.H.Taylor(Capt),D.R.Stead;
D.Wyles,B.Cappi,L.A.Holmes,E.A.Ward,G.L.Wright.

30 Mar ESCF   Neut#1 Walthamstow Avenue   0 – 1
Romford: P.Gamman;J.G.Ling,R.A.Pitt;R.Byers,D.H.Taylor(Capt),D.R.Stead;
D.Wyles,B.Cappi,C.Tiffin,E.A.Ward,G.L.Wright.

4 Apr IFL   Away   Oxford City   2 – 5 Cappi,Blake
Romford: P.Gamman;J.G.Ling,R.A.Pitt;R.Byers,D.H.Taylor(Capt),D.R.Stead;
D.Wyles,B.Cappi,W.Blake,E.A.Ward,G.L.Wright.

11 Apr IFL   Home   Wimbledon   0 – 1
Attendance: 1,420   Receipts: £99.19.9   Programmes: £8.1.6 Car Park: £1.15.6
Romford: P.Gamman;J.G.Ling,R.A.Pitt;R.Byers,D.H.Taylor(Capt),D.R.Stead;
D.Wyles,B.Cappi,I.Oakley,E.A.Ward,G.L.Wright.

18 Apr IFL   Home   Bromley   3 – 0   Holmes(2)Ward
Attendance: 670   Receipts: £40.10.6   Programmes: £4.0.3   Car Park: £1.7.9
Romford: P.Gamman;J.G.Ling,R.A.Pitt;R.Byers,D.H.Taylor(Capt),D.R.Stead;
D.Wyles,B.Cappi,L.A.Holmes,E.A.Ward,G.L.Wright.

23 Apr IFL   Away   Walthamstow Avenue   0 – 3
Romford: P.Gamman;J.G.Ling,R.A.Pitt;R.Byers,D.H.Taylor(Capt),D.R.Stead;
D.Wyles,B.Cappi,L.A.Holmes,E.A.Ward,G.L.Wright.

2 May IFL   Home   Oxford City   6 – 2   Oakley,Ward(3)Cappi(2)
Attendance: 795   Receipts: £50.1.3   Programmes: £5.9.6   Car Park: £1.4.6
Romford: P.Gamman;J.G.Ling,R.A.Pitt;R.Byers,D.H.Taylor(Capt),D.R.Stead;
I.Oakley,B.Cappi,L.A.Holmes,E.A.Ward,G.L.Wright.

9 May RST   Home   Jack Chisholm's XI   4 – 4   Scorers unknown
Attendance: 1,700   Receipts: £132.10.9   Programmes: £13.12.1   Car Park: £2.19.9
Romford: P.Gamman;B.Skingley,R.A.Pitt;R.Byers,D.H.Taylor(Capt),D.R.Stead;
I.Oakley,B.Cappi,R.E.Curry,L.A.Holmes,G.L.Wright.
Jack Chisholm's XI: Sel. E.G.Ditchburn(Tottenham H);G.Crawford(Partick Thistle)F.Cooper(West
Ham Utd);E.Penzer(Birmingham),H.Dove(Millwall),G.Dobson(Brighton & H.A.);
D.Neate,D.Harper(Birmingham),A.McHard(Clyde),R.Bell(Partick Thistle),P.J.Kavanagh(Fulham).

*   After extra time.
\#   Played at Crystal Palace.
#1   Played at Ilford

FIRST TEAM SUMMARY OF RESULTS SEASON 1958 – 59

	P	**W**	**D**	**L**	For	Ag	**W**	**D**	**L**	For	**Ag**	**Pts**
		Home			**Goals**		**Away**			**Goals**		
Isthmian Football League	30	4	2	9	25	34	3	3	9	29	42	19
FA Challenge Cup	2	0	0	1	2	3	1	0	0	9	2	
FA Amateur Challenge Cup	1	0	0	1	0	1	0	0	0	0	0	
Essex County F.A. Senior Cup	5	1	1	0	4	2	2	0	1	5	4	
East Anglian Cup	1	0	0	0	0	0	0	0	1	0	6	
Essex Thameside Chal.Trophy	1	0	0	1	0	1	0	0	0	0	0	
Essex Elizabethan Trophy	1	0	0	0	0	0	0	0	1	1	2	
Reg Sheward Memorial Trophy	1	0	1	0	4	4	0	0	0	0	0	
Friendly	1	0	0	1	1	4	0	0	0	0	0	
Totals	43	5	4	13	36	49	6	3	12	44	56	

Isthmian Football League
Final Table

	P	**W**	**D**	**L**	**Goals** For	Ag	**Pts**
Wimbledon	30	22	3	5	91	38	47
Dulwich Hamlet	30	18	5	7	68	44	41
Wycombe Wanderers	30	18	4	8	93	50	40
Oxford City	30	17	4	9	87	58	38
Walthamstow Avenue	30	16	5	9	59	40	37
Tooting & Mitcham United	30	15	4	11	84	55	34
Barking	30	14	2	14	59	53	30
Woking	30	12	6	12	66	66	30
Bromley	30	11	7	12	56	55	29
Clapton	30	10	6	14	55	67	26
Ilford	30	10	6	14	46	67	26
Kingstonian	30	9	4	17	54	72	22
St. Albans City	30	8	6	16	53	89	22
Leytonstone	30	7	6	17	40	87	20
Romford	**30**	**7**	**5**	**18**	**54**	**76**	**19**
Corinthian Casuals	30	7	5	18	44	92	19

FIRST TEAM CUP RESULTS SEASON 1958 – 59

FA Challenge Cup
Final: Nottingham Forest 2 Luton Town 1

Romford's progress: 1st Qual   Away   Eton Manor   9 - 2
    2nd Qual   Home   Hornchurch & Upminster   2 - 3

FA Amateur Challenge Cup
Final: Crook Town 3 Barnet 2

Romford's progress: 1st Round   Home   Leytonstone   0 - 1

Essex Senior Challenge Cup
Final: Walthamstow Avenue 1 Romford 0

Romford's progress: 1st Round   Home   Leytonstone   1 – 1*
    Replay   Away   Leytonstone   1 - 0
    2nd Round   Home   Barking   3 - 1
    Semi-Final   Ilford   Dagenham   4 - 3
    Final   Ilford   Walthamstow Avenue   0 - 1

East Anglian Cup
Final: n/k

Romford's progress: 1st Round   Away   Aveley   0 - 6

Essex Thameside Challenge Competition
Final: n/k

Romford's progress: 1st Round   Home   Walthamstow Avenue   0 - 1

Essex Elizabethan Trophy
Final: n/k

Romford's progress: 1st Round   Away   Brentwood & Warley   1 - 2

Reg Sheward Memorial Trophy
Romford 4 Jack Chisholm's XI 4

*   After Extra Time

FIRST TEAM DEBUTS SEASON 1958 – 59

1958				Previous Club
23rd Aug.	v Woking	-	**B.Cappi**	Old Romfordians
		-	**T.Spencer**	n/k
25th Aug.	v Walthamstow Ave.	-	**S.Cardew**	n/k
1st Sept.	v Brentwood & W.	-	**K.Delieu**	n/k
6th Sept.	v St.Albans City	-	**T.Watson**	Edmonton
		-	**Alan Durrant**	Edmonton
10th Sept.	v Aveley	-	**J.G.Ling**	Basildon Town
		-	**J.Banfield**	Eton Manor
13th Sept.	v Corinthian Casuals	-	**K.Jarrold**	n/k
20th Sept.	v Eton Manor	-	**K.Corbett**	Fulham "A"
1st Nov.	v Kingstonian	-	**D.Wyles**	Walthamstow Ave.
15th Nov.	v Leytonstone	-	**I.Oakley**	Brentwood & Warley
22nd Nov.	v Corinthian Casuals	-	**B.Lawrence**	Dagenham
13th Dec.	v Leytonstone	-	**L.Hutson**	Dagenham
20th Dec.	v Dulwich Hamlet	-	**T.Flynn**	Clapton
25th Dec.	v Ilford	-	**R.Byers**	Dagenham
27th Dec.	v Leytonstone	-	**P.White**	Clockhouse Y.C.
		-	**D.R.Stead**	Barking
		-	**A.E.Barrett**	n/k

1959

28ᵗʰ Feb.	v Barking	-	**R.A.Pitt**	West Ham United
		-	**G.L.Wright**	Southend United
7ᵗʰ Mar.	v Bromley	-	**E.A.Ward**	Barkingside

Players returned to the Club

1958

1ˢᵗ Sept.	v Brentwood & W.	-	**A.J.Taylor**	Dagenham
4ᵗʰ Sept.	v Clapton	-	**W.Blake**	Barkingside
11ᵗʰ Oct.	v Wimbledon	-	**G.W.Andrews**	Walthamstow Ave.

Guest Players

1959

9ᵗʰ May	v Jack Chisholm's XI	-	**B.Skingley**	Crystal Palace
		-	**R.E.Curry**	West Ham United

NEWCOMERS

Joe Ling
Full Back

Barry Cappi
Inside Forward

George Wright
Left Winger

FIRST TEAM APPEARANCES SEASON 1958 – 59

	A	B	C	D	E	F	G	H	J	Total
George Andrews	6	0	0	0	0	0	0	0	0	6
J.Banfield	1	0	0	0	1	0	0	0	0	2
Alf Barrett	1	0	0	1	0	0	0	0	0	2
B.Bennett	2	0	0	0	0	1	0	0	0	3
Bill Blake	10	0	1	2	1	1	0	0	0	15
Harold Brooks	6	2	0	0	1	0	0	0	0	9
Barry Burns	1	0	0	0	0	0	0	0	0	1
Roy Byers	14	0	1	4	0	0	0	1	0	20
Barry Cappi	28	2	1	5	1	1	0	1	1	40
Sid Cardew	2	0	0	0	1	1	1	0	0	5
Mick Cooper	7	2	0	0	0	0	0	0	0	9
Kevin Corbett	1	2	0	0	0	0	0	0	0	3
Bob Curry	0	0	0	0	0	0	0	1	0	1
K.Delieu	0	0	0	0	0	0	1	0	0	1
Alan S.Durrant	11	0	0	1	1	0	0	0	1	14
Brian Durrant	1	0	0	0	0	0	1	0	0	2
Reg Fleetwood	1	0	0	0	0	0	1	0	0	2
Terry Flynn	6	0	1	2	0	0	0	0	0	9
Peter Gamman	28	2	0	3	1	1	1	1	1	38

Roy Hammond	4	0	0	0	0	1	0	0	0	5
Buddy Holmes	13	0	0	1	0	0	0	1	0	15
Larry Hutson	8	0	1	4	0	0	0	0	0	13
K.Jarrold	2	0	0	0	0	0	0	0	0	2
Brian Lawrence	8	0	1	3	0	0	0	0	1	13
Alfie Lee	9	1	0	0	1	0	1	0	1	13
Joe Ling	18	2	0	3	1	0	0	0	1	25
Reg March	10	2	0	1	1	1	1	0	1	17
John Martin	4	0	0	0	1	1	1	0	0	7
Johnny Milbank	1	0	0	0	0	0	0	0	0	1
Tommy Nickelson	1	0	0	0	0	0	0	0	0	1
Geoff Noble	4	2	0	0	0	0	0	0	0	6
Ian Oakley	6	0	0	1	0	0	0	1	0	8
Ray Pitt	9	0	0	1	0	0	0	1	0	11
Brian Skingley	0	0	0	0	0	0	0	1	0	1
Terry Spencer	2	0	0	0	0	1	1	0	0	4
Derek Stead	13	0	1	4	0	0	0	1	0	19
Alan Taylor	0	0	0	0	0	0	1	0	0	1
Denny Taylor	23	0	1	5	0	0	1	1	1	32
Cyril Tiffin	14	2	1	5	0	0	0	0	1	23
Roy Walker	8	2	0	1	0	0	0	0	1	12
Ernie Ward	8	0	0	1	0	0	0	0	0	9
T.Watson	1	0	0	0	0	0	0	0	0	1
Dave Webb	2	0	0	0	0	1	0	0	0	3
Peter White	1	0	1	2	0	0	0	0	0	4
Johnny Whitecross	8	1	0	0	0	1	0	0	0	10
George Wright	9	0	0	1	0	0	0	1	0	11
Dave Wyles	18	0	1	4	0	0	0	0	1	24
Totals	330	22	11	55	11	11	11	11	11	473

Key to Competitions

A	Isthmian Football League
B	FA Challenge Cup
C	FA Amateur Challenge Cup
D	Essex County F.A. Senior Cup
E	East Anglian Cup
F	Essex Thameside ChallengeTrophy
G	Essex Elizabethan Trophy
H	Reg Sheward Memorial Trophy
J	Friendly

The above key refers to both the Appearances and Goal Scorers list.

FIRST TEAM GOAL SCORERS SEASON 1958 - 59

	A	B	C	D	E	F	G	H	J	Total
Cyril Tiffin	10	2	0	3	0	0	0	0	0	15
Barry Cappi	10	2	0	0	0	0	0	0	0	12
Buddy Holmes	6	0	0	0	0	0	0	0	0	6
Reg March	4	1	0	0	0	0	1	0	0	6
Ernie Ward	5	0	0	0	0	0	0	0	0	5
Dave Wyles	3	0	0	2	0	0	0	0	0	5
Kevin Corbett	0	4	0	0	0	0	0	0	0	4
Denny Taylor	1	0	0	2	0	0	0	0	1	4
Ian Oakley	3	0	0	0	0	0	0	0	0	3
George Wright	3	0	0	0	0	0	0	0	0	3
Mick Cooper	2	1	0	0	0	0	0	0	0	3
T. Flynn	2	0	0	0	0	0	0	0	0	2
B. Lawrence	1	0	0	1	0	0	0	0	0	2
B. Bennett	1	0	0	0	0	0	0	0	0	1

Bill Blake	1	0	0	0	0	0	0	0	0	1
Johnny Whitecross	1	0	0	0	0	0	0	0	0	1
Harold Brooks	0	1	0	0	0	0	0	0	0	1
Alf Barratt	0	0	0	1	0	0	0	0	0	1
Unknown	0	0	0	0	0	0	0	4	0	4
Own Goals	1	0	0	0	0	0	0	0	0	1
Total	54	11	0	9	0	0	1	4	1	80

Reserve Team Match Details

23 Aug IFLR Home Woking Reserves 3 – 3 Bennett(3)
Attendance: 750 Receipts: £21.14.5 Programmes: £2.14.4
Romford Res.: C.Walker;A.Lake,G.W.Glenham;R.J.Fleetwood,D.Hudson,S.Cardew;
B.Durrant,D.J.Webb,B.Bennett,R.H.Brewis,G.W.Andrews.

30 Aug IFLR Away Tooting & Mitcham United Res. 1 – 4 Hamilton
Romford Res.: C.Walker;D.H.Taylor,G.W.Glenham;R.J.Fleetwood,J.L.Milbank,A.J.Taylor;
H.W.Brooks,D.Hamilton,M.D.Paviour,R.H.Brewis,G.W.Andrews.

6 Sept IFLR Away St. Albans City Res. 0 – 2
Romford Res.: C.Walker;D.Hudson,D.H.Taylor;R.J.Fleetwood,J.L.Milbank,A.J.Taylor;
D.Hamilton,M.D.Paviour,A.Simmons,K.Delieu,G.W.Andrews.

13 Sept IFLR Home Corinthian Casuals Reserves 4 – 1 Hammond,Paviour,Barry,Watson
Attendance: 470 Receipts: £15.5.4 Programmes: £1.14.8
Romford Res.: P.Gamman;K.Buck,D.H.Taylor;T.Watson,J.L.Milbank,R.Walker;
R.F.Hammond,R.Sedgley,W.Barry,M.D.Paviour,G.W.Andrews.

20 Sept IFLR Home Bromley Reserves 3 – 0 Hammond,Barrett,Andrews(pen)
Attendance: 410 Receipts: £11.15.8 Programmes: £1.0.4
Romford Res.: T.H.Nickelson;J.Leach,D.H.Taylor;R.J.Fleetwood,S.Cardew,A.S.Durrant;
D.Hamilton,R.F.Hammond,A.Simmons,A.E.Barrett,G.W.Andrews.

27 Sept IFLR Away Leytonstone Reserves 2 – 1 Andrews,Barry
Romford Res.: T.H.Nickelson;W.Blake,D.H.Taylor;J.J.Whitecross,T.Watson,A.S.Durrant;
A.Simmons,R.F.Hammond,W.Barry,A.E.Barrett,G.W.Andrews.

11 Oct IFLR Home Wimbledon Reserves 0 – 1
Attendance: 450 Receipts: £14.19.3 Programmes: £1.17.2
Romford Res.: D.Locke;A.J.Lee,W.Blake;T.Watson,S.Cardew,A.S.Durrant;
R.F.Hammond,A.Bussey,K.Corbett,A.E.Barrett,R.J.March.

18 Oct IFLR Home Clapton Reserves 1 – 2 Watson
Attendance: 390 Receipts: £10.8.7 Programmes: £1.3.0
Romford Res.: D.Locke;A.J.Lee,W.Blake;T.Watson,D.Hudson,K.Troup;
H.W.Brooks,A.Bussey,K.Corbett,A.McNally,K.Jarrold.

25 Oct IFLR Away Kingstonian Reserves 1 – 1 Lawrence
Romford Res.: T.H.Nickelson;L.Hutson,W.Blake;E.Alabaster,T.Watson,R.Walker;
D.Wyles,B.Lawrence,I.Oakley,K.Thompson,R.J.March.

1 Nov IFLR Home Leytonstone Reserves 6 – 2 March(3)Hammond,Oakley,Lawrence
Attendance: 520 Receipts: £16.10.0 Programmes: £2.0.5
Romford Res.:
Team details unknown

8 Nov IFLR Away Walthamstow Avenue Reserves 2 – 1 Oakley,Walker
Romford Res.: T.H.Nickelson;L.Hutson,W.Blake;R.Walker,T.Watson,S.Cardew;
R.F.Hammond,B.Lawrence,I.Oakley,A.E.Barrett,R.J.March.

15 Nov IFLR Home Barking Reserves 1 – 0 Tiffin
Attendance: 485 Receipts: £15.1.0 Programmes: £1.14.6
Romford Res.: T.H.Nickelson;L.Hutson,W.Blake;R.Byers,G.C.Noble,D.R.Stead;
R.F.Hammond,A.E.Barrett,C.Tiffin,B.Lawrence,G.W.Andrews.

22 Nov IFLR Away Wycombe Wanderers Reserves 4 – 1 Burke,Barrett(2)Tiffin
Romford Res.: T.H.Nickelson;L.Hutson,W.Blake;R.Byers,T.Watson,S.Cardew;
R.F.Hammond,A.E.Barrett,C.Tiffin,K.Burke,G.W.Andrews.

29 Nov IFLR Away Woking Reserves 2 – 1 Scorers unknown
Romford Res.:
Team details unknown

6 Dec   IFLR   Home   Tooting & Mitcham United Res.   3 – 2   Clark, Burrows,Flynn
Attendance: 505   Receipts: £15.16.8   Programmes: £1.16.6
Romford Res.: P.White;L.Hutson,W.Blake;R.Byers,T.Watson,S.Cardew;
A.Barrett,K.Burke,L.Clark,T.Flynn,G.W.Andrews.

20 Dec   IFLR   Away#1 Corinthian Casuals Reserves   2 – 2   Scorers unknown
Romford Res.:

27 Dec   IFLR   Home   Kingstonian Reserves   2 – 2   Barry,Hamilton
Attendance: 425   Receipts: £13.4.6   Programmes: £ ??
Romford Res.: J.Martin;A.Lee,A.Mills;R.Walker,T.Watson,S.Cardew;
D.Hamilton,K.Burke,W.Barry,T.Flynn,D.Hammond.

3 Jan   EIC4R   Home   Ilford Reserves   4 – 1   Barrett,Walker(pen)Clark(2)
Attendance: 460   Receipts: £16.11.8   Programmes: £1.16.2
Romford Res.: D.Locke;A.J.Lee,J.G.Ling;R.Walker,S.Cardew,R.A.Pitt;
I.Oakley,A.E.Barrett,L.Clark,K.Burke,G.W.Andrews.

17 Jan   IFLR   Away   Wimbledon Reserves   2 – 5   Burke,Clark
Romford Res.: D.Locke;A.J.Lee,J.G.Ling;R.Walker,S.Cardew,R.A.Pitt;
D.Hamilton,L.Clark,I.Oakley,K.Burke,G.W.Andrews.

24 Jan   IFLR   Away   Dulwich Hamlet Reserves   3 – 3   Oakley(2)Andrews
Romford Res.:
Team details unknown

31 Jan   EIC5R   Home   St. John's (Southend)   7 – 1   Clark(4)Walker(pen)Oakley(2)
Attendance: 740   Receipts: £25.15.9   Programmes: £2.11.6
Romford Res.: D.Locke;J.G.Ling,A.J.Lee;R.Walker,S.Cardew,R.A.Pitt;
D.Hamilton,L.Clark,I.Oakley,K.Burke,L.A.Holmes.

7 Feb   IFLR   Away   Oxford City Reserves   1 – 1   Barrett
Romford Res.: D.Locke;A.J.Lee,J.G.Ling;R.Walker,R.A.Pitt,S.Cardew;
I.Oakley,A.E.Barrett,L.Clark,K.Burke,G.W.Andrews.

14 Feb   IFLR   Home   St. Albans City Reserves   3 – 1   Burke,Oakley(2)
Attendance: 220   Receipts: £5.11.9   Programmes: £0.7.2
Romford Res.: D.Locke;A.J.Lee,K.Buck;L.Clark,R.Walker,A.S.Durrant;
G.W.Andrews,A.E.Barrett,I.Oakley,K.Burke,G.Wright.

21 Feb   EIC6R   Home   Collier Row British Legion   4 – 3   Scorers unknown
Attendance; 570   Receipts: £20.19.7   Programmes: £2.5.7
Romford Res.: P.White;A.J.Lee,R.A.Pitt;R.Walker,S.Cardew.E.A.Ward;
G.W.Andrews,A.E.Barrett,L.Clark,K.Burke,G.Wright.

28 Feb   IFLR   Away   Bromley Reserves   1 – 2   Scorer unknown
Romford Res.: P.White;J.G.Ling,W.Blake;A.J.Lee,S.Cardew,E.A.Ward;
I.Oakley,A.E.Barrett,L.Clark,K.Burke,G.W.Andrews.

14 Mar   EICSF   Home   Walthamstow Avenue Reserves   1 – 2*   Scorer unknown
Attendance: 1,070   Receipts: £37.15.10   Programmes: £2.11.11
Romford Res.: Sel. P.White;A.J.Lee,W.Blake;T.Watson,S.Cardew,R.Walker;
I.Oakley,A.Trimm,W.Barry,K.Burke,G.W.Andrews.

21 Mar   IFLR   Away   Barking Reserves   1 – 1   Tiffin
Romford Res.: P.White;L.Hutson,W.Blake;R.Walker,S.Cardew,A.S.Durrant;
D.Hamilton,I.Oakley,C.Tiffin,K.Burke,J.Read.

28 Mar   IFLR   Home   Wycombe Wanderers Reserves   2 – 0   Scorers unknown
Attendance: 440   Receipts: £13.16.11   Programmes: £1.12.2
Romford Res.:
Team details unknown

4 Apr   IFLR   Home   Dulwich Hamlet Reserves   0 – 7
Attendance: 530   Receipts: £17.4.3   Programmes: £1.19.2
Romford Res.:
Large number of "A" Team players given a chance

11 Apr   IFLR   Home# Ilford Reserves   3 – 1   Scorers unknown
Attendance: Receipts: £ ??   Programmes: £ ??
Romford Res.:
Team details unknown

20 Apr   IFLR   Away   Ilford Reserves   4 – 1   Scorers unknown
Romford Res.: D.Locke;L.Hutson,W.Blake;S.Cardew,D.H.Taylor,A.S.Durrant;
D.Wyles,B.Lawrence,I.Oakley,W.Barry,L.A.Holmes.

22 Apr IFLR Home Walthamstow Avenue Reserves 0 – 2

Attendance: 240 Receipts: £6.2.6 Programmes: £ ??

Romford Res.: D.Locke;L.Hutson,W.Blake;S.Cardew,I.Draper,A.S.Durrant;
D.Hamilton,B.Lawrence,I.Oakley,K.Burke,F.Pomphrett.

? Apr IFLR Away Clapton Reserves 3 – 0 Scorers unknown

Romford Res.:
Team details unknown

9 May IFLR Home# Oxford City Reserves 3 – 2 Scorers unknown

Attendance:
Romford Res:
Team details unknown

* After extra time
\# Played at Brooklands.
\#1 Played at Crystal Palace.

RESERVE TEAM SUMMARY OF RESULTS SEASON 1958 – 59

	Home			Goals		Away			Goals		
	P	W	D	L	For	Ag	W	D	L	For	Ag	Pts
Isthmian League Res.Sect.	30	9	2	4	34	26	6	5	4	29	25	37
Essex Intermediate Cup	4	3	0	1	16	7	0	0	0	0	0	
Essex Thameside Comp. Res.	0	0	0	0	0	0	0	0	0	0	0	
Romford Charity Cup Prem Sect.	0	0	0	0	0	0	0	0	0	0	0	
Totals	34	12	2	5	50	33	6	5	4	29	25	

Note: Goals against, differs by one goal from the official Isthmian League table.

Note: No trace has been found of any match being played by the reserve team in the Thameside Challenge Trophy or Romford Charity Cup reserve competitions, although the club had agreed to enter them.

Isthmian Football League Reserve Section
Final Table

	P	W	D	L	Goals For	Ag	Pts
Walthamstow Avenue	30	19	7	4	68	39	45
Wimbledon	30	19	4	7	91	50	42
Tooting & Mitcham United	30	17	4	9	81	62	38
Wycombe Wanderers	30	15	7	8	58	41	37
Romford Reserves	**30**	**15**	**7**	**8**	**63**	**52**	**37**
Dulwich Hamlet	30	13	7	10	80	57	33
Corinthian Casuals	30	15	3	12	74	64	33
Woking	30	13	7	10	54	48	33
Clapton	30	13	5	12	66	63	31
Oxford City	30	13	4	13	75	65	30
Bromley	30	13	3	14	68	85	29
St. Albans City	30	11	4	15	50	64	26
Leytonstone	30	8	5	17	44	73	21
Kingstonian	30	8	5	17	43	80	21
Barking	30	5	4	21	42	68	14
Ilford	30	5	0	25	39	85	10

RESERVE TEAM CUP RESULTS SEASON 1958 – 59

Essex County FA Intermediate Challenge Cup

Final: Grays Athletic Res. 4 Walthamstow Avenue Res. 1

Romford's progress: 1st to 3rd Rounds Exempt as Holders

4th Round	Home	Ilford Res.	4 - 1
5th Round	Home	St.John's(Southend)	7 – 1
6th Round	Home	Collier Row B.L.	4 - 3
Semi-Final	Home	Walthamstow Ave. Res.	1 – 2 *

* After Extra Time

Essex Thameside Challenge Competition Reserve Section
Final:
n/k

Romford Charity Cup Premier Section Season 1957 – 58
(carried over from the previous season)
Final: Rainham Town Res.   4   Briggs Sports Res.   2

RESERVE TEAM APPEARANCES SEASON 1958 – 59

The following are known to have appeared in the reserve team during the season.

E.Alabaster	G.W.Andrews	A.E.Barrett	W.Barry
B.Bennett	W.Blake	R.Brewis	H.W.Brooks
K.Buck	K.Burke	-.Burrows	A.Bussey
R.Byers	S.Cardew	L.Clark	K.Corbett
K.Delieu	I.Draper	A.S.Durrant(Edmonton)	B.(Bunny) Durrant
R.Fleetwood	P.Gamman	G.W.Glenham	D.Hamilton
D.Hammond	R.F.Hammond	L.A.Holmes	L.Hutson
K.Jarrold	A.Lake(Edmonton)	B.Lawrence	J.Leach
A.Lee	J.G.Ling	D.Locke(Elm Park B.L.)	R.J.March
A.McNally	J.Milbank	T.L.Nickelson	G.C.Noble
I.Oakley	M.D.Paviour	R.A.Pitt	F.Pomphrett
J.Read	A.Sedgley	A.Simmons	D.R.Stead
A.J.Taylor	D.H.Taylor	K.Thompson	C.Tiffin
K.Troup	C.Walker	R.Walker	E.A.Ward
T.Watson(Edmonton)	D.Webb	P.White	G.L.Wright
D.Wyles			

"A" Team Match Details

23 Aug EAFL Away Dagenham "A"   3 – 3 Bright,Delieu,Hammond
Romford "A": A.Garner;E.G.Tetchner,D.Jones;J.Stalley,T.Powell,P.Bright;
D.Hammond,D.Hamilton,F.Delieu,D.Coulson,F.Pomphrett.

30 Aug Frdly Away Hornchurch & Upminster "A"   3 – 3 Scorers unknown
Romford "A":

6 Sept EAFL Home Dagenham "A"   2 – 0 Broad,Christie
Romford "A": T.H.Nickelson;A.Lake,G.W.Glenham;E.G.Tetchner,T.Powell,P.Bright;
D.Hammond,K.Carey,R.W.Christie.G.Sorrell,M.Broad.

20 Sept EAFL Home Leyton "A"   1 – 3 Carey
Romford "A": R.Tyler;D.Hudson,G.W.Glenham;E.G.Tetchner,T.Powell,J.Stalley;
D.Hammond,K.Carey,R.W.Christie,D.Sweeting,K.Jarrold.

27 Sept EAFL Home Clapton "A"   0 – 0
Romford "A": P.White;A.Riley,G.W.Glenham;I.Draper,D.Hudson,A.J.Taylor;
D.Hammond,R.H.Brewis,H.Smith,J.Read,K.Jarrold.

4 Oct EAFL Away Hornchurch & Upminster "A"   6 – 1 Read(3)Powell(2)(1pen)Jarrold
Romford "A": D.Locke;L.Robinson,T.Spencer;A.Lillis,D.Hudson,H.Miller;
D.Hammond,L.A.Holmes,T.Powell,J.Read,K.Jarrold.

11 Oct EJC1R Away Drummond Athletic   0 – 3
Romford "A":

25 Oct EAFL Away Barking "A"   5 – 0 Scorers unknown
Romford "A":

15 Nov EAFL Away Leyton "A"   4 – 4 Scorers unknown
Romford "A":

22 Nov Frdly Home Leytonstone "A"   5 – 2 D.Hammond(2)Corbett(2)Read
Romford "A": P.White;R.Mills,R.Draper;G.Trott,D.Hudson,C.E.East;
D.Hammond,D.Hamilton,K.Corbett,W.Barry,J.Read.

29 Nov EAFL Home Ilford "A"   1 – 4 Scorer unknown
Romford "A":

6 Dec EAFL Home Hornchurch & Upminster "A" 6 – 1 Scorers unknown
Romford "A": A.Moye;

17 Jan ALC2R Home Walthamstow Avenue "A" Won on aggregate**
Romford "A" (1st leg)

31 Jan EAFL Home Woodford Town "A" 3 – 1 Scorers unknown

14 Feb EAFL Away Ilford "A" 2 – 3 Scorers unknown
Romford "A":

21 Feb EAFL Away Clapton "A" 1 – 6 Scorer unknown
Romford "A":

28 Feb ALC2R Away# Walthamstow Avenue "A" Won on aggregate**
Romford "A" (2nd leg)

14 Mar EAFL Away Woodford Town "A" 3 – 0 Scorers unknown
Romford "A":

? Mar ALCSF Neut. Barking "A" Won

4 Apr EAFL Away Walthamstow Avenue "A" n/k

? Apr EAFL Home Barking "A" n/k

? Apr EAFL Home Walthamstow Avenue "A" 6 - 4

25 Apr ALCF Home Clapton "A" 1 – 4 Scorer unknown
Attendance: Receipts: £14.2.1
Romford "A": Sel. P.White;A.Orgles,C.E.East;A.Lillis,I.Draper,A.Mills;
D.Hammond,B.Lawrence,W.Barry,E.A.Ward,F.Pomphrett.
Clapton "A": J.Tayler;G.W.Glenham,A.Baker;W.Clark,R.Tranter,S.Drake;
J.Huckstep,A.Cullen,R.Bartram,M.Gains,D.Gladstone.

\# Played at Dagenham.
** Played over two legs, neither result known but Romford won on aggregate.

"A" TEAM SUMMARY OF RESULTS SEASON 1958 - 59

	P	W	D	L	Goals For	Ag	Pts
Eastern "A" Football League	16	8	3	5	49	36	19
Essex County FA Junior Cup	1	0	0	1	0	3	
Eastern "A" League Challenge Cup	4	1	?	1	1	4**	
Friendly Matches	2	1	1	0	8	5	
Total.	23		Due to missing results full details unknown				

** Three results are unknown in this competition. Two of these were the 2nd Round 1st and 2nd legs, although Romford won on an aggregate score. The other was the semi-final against Barking "A" which Romford won but no details of the match have come to hand. It is also possible that other friendly matches were played.

Eastern "A" League
Final Table

	P	W	D	L	Goals For	Ag	Pts
Dagenham	16	13	1	2	68	16	27
Clapton	16	11	1	4	44	20	23
Romford "A"	**16**	**8**	**3**	**5**	**49**	**36**	**19**
Ilford	16	9	1	6	43	38	19
Leyton	16	8	1	7	44	38	17
Walthamstow Avenue	16	7	1	8	39	43	15
Barking	16	6	0	10	38	44	12
Woodford Town	16	4	0	12	28	86	8
Hornchurch & Upminster	16	2	0	14	26	55	4

"A" TEAM CUP RESULTS

Essex County FA Junior Challenge Cup
Final: Dagenham "A" 2 Grays Athletic "A" 0

Romford's progress: 1st Round   Away   Drummond Athletic   0 - 3

Eastern "A" League Challenge Cup
Final: Clapton "A" 4 Romford "A" 1

Romford's progress: 1st Round   Bye
           2nd Round 1st Leg   Home   Walthamstow Avenue
           2nd Round 2nd Leg   Dag'm.   Walthamstow Avenue   Won on aggregate
           Semi-Final   Neut.   Barking   Won
           Final   Home   Clapton "A"   1 – 4

"A" TEAM APPEARANCES SEASON 1958 - 59

The following players are known to have played in the "A" Team during the season.

W.Barry	R.H.Brewis	P.Bright	M.Broad
K.Carey	R.W.Christie	K.Corbett	D.Coulson
I.Draper	F.Delieu	C.R.East	A.Garner
G.W.Glenham	D.Hamilton	D.Hammond	L.A.Holmes
D.Hudson	K.Jarrold	D.Jones	A.Lake
B.Lawrence	A.Lillis	D.Locke(Elm Park B.L.)	H.Miller
A.Mills	Alan Moye(Edmonton)	T.H.Nickelson	A.Orgles
F.Pomphrett	T.Powell	J.Read	A.Riley
L.Robinson	H.Smith	G.Sorrell	T.Spencer
J.Stalley	D.Sweeting	A.J.Taylor	E.G.Tetchner
G.Trott	R.Tyler	E.A.Ward	P.White

Romford entered a Youth Team in the Hornchurch Minor League Division 3 (Under-16 year olds)
Bill Bennett of Friends Hall Youth Club, Bethnal Green introduced several players to the Club.

Minor Team Match Details

6 Sept HMLD3 Away   Ardleigh House Y.C. "A"   9 – 1   Rennie(4)Fawcett,Webb(2)Coates,Simms
Romford Minors: S.Tier;J.Brooks,G.Stoffer;D.Lawrence,T.Bone,R.Deeks;
D.Simms,B.F.Coates,E.Rennie,J.Fawcett,T.Webb.

13 Sept HMLD3 Away   Glendale Y.C. "A"   9 – 1   Fawcett(6)Broad(2)Simms
Romford Minors: S.Tier;J.Brooks,G.Stoffer;D.Tier,T.Bone,J.Jordan;
D.Simms,B.F.Coates,E.Rennie,J.Fawcett,B.Henry.

20 Sept HMLD3 Away   Rainham Y.C. "A"   20 – 0   Simms(4)Fawcett(5)Rennie(4)
                                                  Coates(2)D.Tier(2)S.Tier(2pens)Brooks
Romford Minors: S.Tier;J.Brooks,G.Stoffer,D.Tier,T.Bone,J.Jordan;
D.Simms,B.F.Coates,E.Rennie,J.Fawcett,B.Henry.

4 Oct HMLD3 Home# Glendale Y.C. "A"   1 – 0   Simms
Romford Minors: S.Tier;S.Bracey,G.Stoffer;J.Friedman,T.Webb,D.Lawrence;
D.Simms,D.Tier,J.Fawcett,B.F.Coates,E.Rennie.

11 Oct Frdly#2 Home   East Ham B.T.A.   16 – 0   Rennie(5)Friedman(2)Lawrence(2)
                                                  Simms(2)Fawcett(2)Webb(3)
Romford Minors: P.Bond;T.Bracey,G.Stoffer;D.Lawrence,D.Tier,R.Deeks;
D.Simms,J.Friedman,J.Fawcett,T.Webb,E.Rennie.

18 Oct HMLD3 Home   Parklands Y.C. "A"   6 – 1   Rennie(2)Deeks,Gray,Coates,Fawcett
Romford Minors: S.Tier;T.Bracey,G.Stoffer;D.Tier,J.Friedman,R.Deeks;
B.Gray,B.F.Coates,E.Rennie,J.Fawcett,D.Simms.

8 Nov   HMLD3 Home   Rainham Y.C. "A"   10 – 1   D.Tier(2)Rennie(4)Coates(2)Deeks,
                                                     Lawrence

Romford Minors: S.Tier;T.Bracey,G.Brooks;D.Tier,G.Stoffer,R.Deeks;
D.Simms,B.F.Coates,E.Rennie,J.Fawcett,D.Lawrence.

15 Nov   EAC1R Away   Thurrock Minors   10 – 2   Coates(4)Rennie(2)D.Tier,Webb(2)
                                                       Fawcett

Romford Minors: S.Tier;T.Bracey,D.Lawrence;D.Tier,J.Friedman,R.Deeks;
D.Simms,E.Rennie,T.Webb,B.F.Coates,J.Fawcett.

22 Nov   L3C1R Away   Ardleigh House Y.C. "A"   4 – 2   Rennie(3)Coates
Romford Minors: S.Tier,J.Brooks,D.Lawrence;D.Tier,J.Friedman,R.Deeks;
D.Simms,E.Rennie,T.Webb,B.F.Coates,J.Fawcett.

29 Nov   Frdly   Away   Lake Side Y.C.   6 – 2   Scorers unknown
Romford Minors: S.Tier;T.Bracey,G.Stoffer;-.Bills,J.Friedman,R.Deeks;
D.Lawrence,B.F.Coates,E.Rennie,J.Fawcett,T.Webb.

13 Dec   L3C2R Away   Cranham Covenanters   4 – 0   Rennie(2)D.Tier,Halliday
Romford Minors: S.Tier;T.Bone,T.Bracey;G.Stoffer,D.Tier,R.Deeks;
D.Simms,E.Rennie,R.Halliday,B.F.Coates,J.Fawcett.

17 Jan   Frdly   Away   Leyton Minors   2 – 0   Scorers unknown
Romford Minors:
Team details unknown

24 Jan   Frdly   Away   Opponents not known   7 – 2   Scorers unknown
Romford Minors:
Team details unknown

31 Jan   HMLD3 Home   Newbury Park "A"   10 – 1   Scorers unknown

7 Feb   HMLD3 Away   Cranham Covenanters   P – P#3

14 Feb   EAC2R Away   Clockhouse Y.C.   13 – 0   Scorers unknown

28 Feb   HMLD3 Away   Parklands Y.C. "A"   7 – 2   Scorers unknown
Romford Minors;
Team details unknown

7 Mar   HMLD3 Away   Newbury Park Y.C. "A"   6 – 3   Scorers unknown
Romford Minors:
Team details unknown

14 Mar   HMLD3 Home   Ardleigh House Y.C. "A"   5 – 2   Scorers unknown
Romford Minors:
Team details unknown

21 Mar   EACSF Away   West Ham Minors   Won   Scorer(s) unknown
Romford Minors:

28 Mar   L3CSF Home   Parklands Y.C. "A"   24 – 0   Scorers unknown
Romford Minors:

4 Apr   HMLD3 Away   Cranham Covenanters   1 – 1   Scorer unknown
Romford Minors:

11 Apr   HMLD3 Home   Five Star Y.C.   Won
Romford Minors:

? Apr   HMLD3 Away   Five Star Y.C.   Won

? Apr   HMLD3 Home   Cranham Covenanters   Won

29 Apr   L3CF   Home# Glendale Y.C. "A"   7 – 0   Simms(2)Coates,Rennie(2)Fawcett,
                                                       Kielty

Romford Minors: S.Tier;T.Bracey,G.Stoffer;D.Tier,J.Friedman,R.Deeks;
D.Simms,B.F.Coates,E.Rennie,M.Kielty,J.Fawcett.

2 May   EACF   Away#1 Wilson Marriage Y.C.   2 – 8   Rennie,Friedman(pen)
Romford Minors: S.Tier;T.Bracey,G.Stoffer;D.Tier,J.Friedman,R.Deeks;
D.Simms,B.F.Coates,E.Rennie,J.Fawcett,M.Kielty.

\#   Played at Brooklands.
\#1 Played at Layer Road, Colchester.
\#2 Originally a Hornchurch Minor League game but East Ham B.T.A. withdrew from the league.
\#3 Match cancelled Cranham Covenanters unable to field a team.

Note: In the three league games where we have no scores, Romford scored 25 goals and conceded only 1.

MINOR TEAM CUP RESULTS

Essex County Youth FA "Andrews" Challenge Cup
Final: Wilson Marriage YC 8   Romford Minors 2

Romford's progress: 1st Round   Away   Thurrock Minors   10 – 2
2nd Round   Away   Clockhouse Y.C.   13 – 0
Semi-Final   Away   West Ham Minors   Won
Final   Colchester   Wilson Marriage YC   2 – 8

Hornchurch Minor League Junior Cup
Final: Romford Minors 7   Glendale YC "A" 0

Romford's progress: 1st Round   Bye
2nd Round   Away   Cranham Covenanters   4 - 0
Semi-Final   Home   Parklands YC "A"   24 - 0
Final: Home   Glendale YC "A"   7 - 0

MINOR TEAM SUMMARY OF RESULTS SEASON 1958-59

	P	W	D	L	Goals For	Ag	Pts
Hornchurch Minor League	14	13	1	0	109	14	28
Hornchurch Minor League Cup	3	3	0	0	35	0	
Essex County Youth Andrews Cup	4	3	0	1	25	10	
Friendly Matches	4	4	0	0	31	4	
Total	25	23	1	1	200	26	

Hornchurch Minor League Division 3 (Under 16)
Final Table

	P	W	D	L	Goals For	Ag	Pts
Romford Minors	**14**	**13**	**1**	**0**	**109**	**14**	**28**
Newbury Park "A"	14	11	0	3	71	34	22
Cranham Covenanters	14	10	1	3	76	27	21
Glendale "A"	14	7	2	5	46	40	16
Ardleigh House "A"	14	6	0	8	64	52	12
Rainham YC "A"	14	4	0	10	37	99	8
Parklands YC "A"	14	0	3	11	20	60	3
Five Star YC "A"	14	1	1	12	19	116	3

APPEARANCES AND GOALSCORERS SEASON 1958 – 59

Due to the lack of information we are unable to compile tables for appearances and goalscorers.

PLAYERS RETAINED FOR THE NEW SEASON IN THE SOUTHERN LEAGUE

B.Cappi, P.Gamman, L.A.Holmes, J.G.Ling, R.A.Pitt, D.R.Stead, D.H.Taylor, E.A.Ward and G.L.Wright all signed professional forms. C.Tiffin was offered a professional contract, declined to accept it but stayed as an amateur.
B.F.Coates, P.White and D.Wyles were all re-signed as amateurs.
A number of the under sixteen youth team players were retained for the under eighteen team in the following season.

DEPARTURES FROM THE CLUB SEASON 1958 - 59

G.W.Andrews (Rainham Town), B.Bennett (Rainham Town), W.Blake (Rainham Town), R.H.Brewis (Ilford), M.Broad (Maidstone United), H.W.Brooks (retired), B.K.Burns (Dagenham), R.Byers (Rainham Town), S.Cardew (Hornchurch & Upminster), R.W.Christie (Hornchurch & Upminster), M.R.Cooper (Barnet), K.Corbett (Hornchurch & Upminster), A.S.Durrant (not known), B.Durrant (Ilford), R.J.Fleetwood (Briggs Sports), T.Flynn (Letchworth Town), G.W.Glenham (Clapton), D.Hamilton (Hornchurch & Upminster), R.F.Hammond (Dagenham), L.Hutson (Rainham Town), B.W.Kelly (Finchley), A.Lake (Hornchurch & Upminster), B.Lawrence (Rainham Town), R.J.March (Hornchurch & Upminster), J.Martin (Barking), B.Milbank (Tufnell Park Edmonton), J.L.Milbank (Bromley), T.H.Nickelson (Ford Sports), G.C.Noble (Grays Athletic), I.Oakley (Hornchurch & Upminster), M.D.Paviour (Leytonstone), A.Simmons (Brentwood & Warley), J.Stalley (Wood Green Town), A.J.Taylor (Brentwood & Warley), E.G.Tetchner (Hornchurch Athletic), C.Walker (moved to Scotland), R.Walker (Hornchurch & Upminster), J.J.Whitecross (Barking).

Post Season Summary   Season 1958 – 59

With the new manager in place, Boro started the season in optimistic mood and Cyril Tiffin with a couple of goals helped obtain a point away to Woking on 23rd August. Old foes Walthamstow Avenue came to Brooklands and ousted Boro from the Thameside Trophy with a 1-0 win, followed by another 2-2 draw at home to Clapton before 1,100 spectators. Tooting and Mitcham United visited Brooklands on 30th August and Romford's loyal supporters played their part with over 2,000 present. Alas, the team was not inspired and suffered a 5-0 defeat, with disgruntled spectators streaming out before the finish. Five more defeats were to follow, Boro were out of two more cups and bottom of the league. Neighbours Brentwood and Warley removed them from the Elizabethan Trophy with a 2-1 win at the Hive, and Aveley thrashed them 6-0 in the East Anglian Cup. Clapton, St. Albans City and Corinthian Casuals all secured league victories.

With so little success, Boro supporters were beginning to question the wisdom of appointing a full-time manager. However, next up was the FA Cup, and what a sensational transformation! 15 year-old Kevin Corbett was the only change from the usual line-up, leading the attack in devastating form. Eton Manor were the luckless opponents in a 9-2 trouncing. Corbett got four and Barry Cappi bagged a couple as he continued to impress.

On 27th September Leytonstone were beaten 2-1 in the league, before another attractive FA Cup tie the following week. 2,600 excited spectators poured into Brooklands, and local rivals Hornchurch and Upminster were the opponents. Cyril Tiffin and Reg March scored for Boro, but unfortunately Hornchurch and Upminster scored three.

League defeats by Wimbledon 0-1, Barking 1-3 and Wycombe Wanderers 3-4 left Romford floundering at the bottom of the table, with spectators loudly voicing their disapproval. New blood Dave Wyles, Buddy Holmes and George Andrews had been introduced to the forward line and a fine 4-1 away victory over Kingstonian was gained on 1st November, only for Walthamstow Avenue to hand out a 5-1 defeat at Brooklands, before a crowd of nearly 2,000. Drawn games followed against Leytonstone and Corinthian Casuals. Then on 29th November came a friendly against semi-professional Chelmsford City, who showed what opposition might be expected next season, with a four one defeat.

By this time the club had officially announced that they had been accepted into the Southern League for next season. Supporters must have been hoping that the current one would end quickly as Wycombe Wanderers handed out another 5-1 thrashing at Loakes Park. An attractive home Essex Senior Cup tie was next on the agenda, with Leytonstone the visitors on 13th December. Only a thousand spectators bothered to turn up but Boro achieved a good one all draw after extra time. Dulwich Hamlet gained a 4-3 victory at Brooklands in a league encounter before Boro were to obtain more successful results.

Jack Chisholm was continuing to discover new talent, but continually changing the side left it unsettled and with little success. On Christmas Day, however, Romford managed a 2-1 victory over Ilford and two days later Alfie Barrett secured the only goal in the Essex Senior Cup replay at Leytonstone. The return game with Ilford was won 5-1 and so Romford had now achieved three successive victories!

Next up was the coveted Amateur Cup, but in front of over 2,000 spectators at Brooklands Romford again disappointed and were unable to repeat their success over Leytonstone, losing one nil. Kingstonian took league points with a 2-1 victory before the semi-final of the Essex Senior Cup on 14th February. This proved to be a thriller of a game at Newbury Park against the strong Dagenham side. With less than twenty minutes to go Romford were 3-1 down, but three goals in eight minutes gave them victory. Dennis Taylor scored two penalties, with Charlie Pearson missing one for Dagenham in the last minute!

Hopes were again dashed, though, with three more league defeats from Dulwich Hamlet 1-3, Barking 0-2 and Bromley 3-5. Romford then beat Tooting and Mitcham 3-2 but lost 0-1 at home to Woking on 21st March. Romford were, however, pinning their hopes on the Essex Senior Cup Final against old foes Walthamstow Avenue at Newbury Park on Easter Monday, but the Avenue took the trophy with a one goal to nil victory.

Oxford City took their usual two points with a 5-2 victory, and Wimbledon won one nil at Brooklands. The manager's hard work throughout the season showed through in a 3-0 win over Bromley, though it was followed by a 0-3 reverse at Walthamstow Avenue. On 2nd May Romford played their last ever Isthmian League game, gaining a fine win at Brooklands, defeating Oxford City 6-2. Ernie Ward got a hat-trick and Barry Cappi netted two. A disappointing attendance of only 795 witnessed the historic match.

The season ended on 9th May with a 4-4 draw against a Jack Chisholm's Eleven for the Reg Sheward Trophy. Romford had guest players Brian Skingley (Crystal Palace) and Bob Curry (West Ham United) at right back and centre forward. Chisholm's side included several who would sign professional forms for Romford in their first Southern League season. His search for players throughout the year, despite match results, had its rewards when seven of the amateurs also signed professional forms for the forthcoming season.

Despite the many team changes during the season, Romford Reserves finished a creditable fifth and reached the semi-final of the Essex Intermediate Cup, losing 2-1 to Walthamstow Avenue at Brooklands after extra time.

The "A" team finished third in the league and lost 4-1 to Clapton "A" in the league cup competition. The introduction of a youth team was an instant success with Bill Bennett joining the club as manager and bringing many players from Friends Hall Youth Club, Bethnal Green. The team won the Minor League title with 13 victories from 14 games and scoring 109 goals! They defeated Glendale 7-0 to secure the Hornchurch Minor League

Junior cup. They also reached the final of the Essex County Youth Andrew's Cup meeting Wilson Marriage YC at Colchester. This proved to be a disaster, however, with an 8-2 defeat and Boro's boys losing their heads as two were sent off.

GLEANINGS FROM MANAGEMENT COMMITTEE MINUTE BOOKS
SEASON 1958-59

On **3rd June 1958** confirmation was received of the Club's acceptance into the Eastern "A" League for the third team. The Committee agree to apply for entry into the Essex Senior and Junior Cups, but defer application regarding the Intermediate Cup on which, despite winning the trophy, Romford made a loss. The final against Dagenham Reserves attracted a crowd of around 500 and receipts amounted to £33.3.9d of which the Club received nil.

On **8th July** the Club were elected for membership of the Essex Elizabethan Trophy. A cheque was receivedfor £171 13s 0d, being the Club's share from the FA Amateur Cup Pool. The Club enter the 6 a Side tournament at the Royal Liberty School.

On **14th October** Captain Mick Cooper resigned, indicating that travelling from Farnborough, where he was based with the Army, seems to be affecting his form.

On **11th November** the Chairman Mr Parrish stated that he and Secretary Herbert Muskett had attended a Meeting of the Southern Football League, and that the Club had been accepted into Membership for the 1959-60 season.

On **9th January 1959** Romford Directors were angered at reports that they were trying to persuade Tottenham Hotspur's 36 year old goalkeeper Ted. Ditchburn to join them. Romford were unable to sign any professional players until 1st May.

On **20th January** Mr. C.E.Montford presented a Billiard Table for the players use in the Social Clubroom, and it was agreed that a suitable plaque be placed on the table with reference to Mr. Montford's service to the Supporters Club.

On **6th March** Ted Ditchburn made a guest appearance for Romford in an Indoor Sports Social against Ilford FC.

On **4th April** Romford's reserve team were elected to the Eastern Counties League for the 1959-60 season.

Brooklands from the air, 1959
The reserve team in action in front of a large crowd
Authors' collection

DIRECTORS' REPORT FOR THE TWELVE MONTHS ENDED 31ST JULY, 1959

The year in respect of which the accounts of the Company are now presented has been one of great changes, consequent upon the Club adopting professional football status. The accounts are therefore to a degree hybrid in the sense that they cover the last season of the Club in amateur football and yet include expenditure in anticipation of playing in the professional sphere.

As your Directors indicated in their last report a manager had been appointed with full power to coach select and manage the teams, and this was, of course, the first step towards professionalism. It was recognised then that players would have to be engaged and paid, and other expenditure new to the Club would have to be borne. As an example, the item "Wages of Managerial Staff" has increased by approximately £700, a new item appears for the first time, "Players' Wages" £213 and "Players' Transfer Fees" £300.

Practically all other items of expenditure are increased by approximately 33 1/3 % over the 1958 figures and in some cases the percentage increase is higher. The reason for this can be attributed to three causes: first, increased expenditure involved in the Club running four teams instead of three as in the 1957/8 season, second, expenditure incurred in anticipation of the Club's entry into professional football, and third and lastly, rising costs generally. On the Income side, Gate Income and Season Ticket Income again suffered, as did the sale of Programmes but items "Advertising" and "Lettings" are increased, the former as a result of Letting of Wall Space in anticipation of the Club turning professional, and the latter because of increased rent received from the Social Club through the Club enlarging the Social Club building.

Considering the accounts as a whole they show conclusively that the Club was right in taking the step to professional soccer. With declining income it would not, as an amateur side, been able to continue to pay its way. On the year, the accounts show a Trading Deficit of £3293, but this is without taking into account Donations from any source.

It should of course be pointed out that the Club did not have a very successful playing season - no trophies were won, but although the Club's first team finished bottom but one, in the Isthmian League table, it nevertheless was a Finalist in the Essex Senior Cup, losing to Walthamstow Avenue by the one and only goal of the match. The Club's other teams did reasonably well having regard to the calls made by the Manager to fill the first team with the best available amateur talent, to complete the last season.

Additions have been made to the company's property during the year by extending the Social Club building to provide a fine hall which can be used for Dinners and Dances and such functions. This was made possible by the Donations hereinafter referred to. It will be observed that the Property Account now stands at £17,000 after a sum of £845 has been written off for depreciation....

Taking a final look at the Accounts the really magnificent efforts of the Romford Sportsmens Association are seen in the donation to the Club during the year of £5862 which in effect provides the Club with a surplus over its trading loss on the year. This donation has been placed to the appropriation account with other donations received. Your Directors also express their appreciation of the fine work of the Committees and supporters of the Romford FC Supporters Association and the Romford FC Social Club....

In conclusion, this being the last Report on the Club's affairs as an amateur club the Directors would like to place on record their thanks and appreciation of the Club's founders, the old players, and old officials and members, who have faithfully worked, played, or supported the Club through the past thirty years.

PLANNING FOR THE FUTURE   (an undated local newspaper report)

The tempo and atmosphere at Romford Football Club is changing as the club closes the door on amateur soccer and enters the new world where success brings financial reward. They have long been preparing for the change over to professional status. A move like this needs an abundance of time, thought and preparation and few can deny that Romford have adequately fulfilled these obligations.

Minor changes behind the scenes were made long before the club officially announced their intention to turn professional. The appointment of Jack Chisholm as professional coach was strong evidence that Romford were coming to the end of their amateur days. One big factor remains, the signing of several professional players. This cannot be done until after the end of the season.

Two organisations established to support the club were founded – The Romford Sportsmens Association and the Romford Social Club. The Romford Board of Directors has been streamlined to cope easily with the complex mechanism of a professional concern.

Consider the work already done by the Romford Social Club. Formed just over a year ago, the club have provided Romford FC with a new spirit and the clubhouse unrivalled by any other club in the area. Romford FC were one of the few clubs in Essex which lacked a licensed bar and clubhouse until the loyal band of supporters decided to do something about it. They quickly built a clubhouse and bar and an extension complete with a billiard table and a one hundred and sixty pounds dance floor. Not only has it provided a meeting place for the fans, but players can relax after training or on match days. The whole scheme had provided a new atmosphere in the club, one which is essential in professional football.

To run a professional club requires a regular income every week. Gates can rarely support the financial demand so this is where the Romford Sportsmens Association prove their value. Another year old organisation they are going from strength to strength. They have set their target of selling 10,000 tickets per week. Already the Association are raising over £5,000 per year, much of which goes to the football club.

It is the supporters who are making both the Social Club and Sportsmens Association such a success. Perhaps the football club will repay this support with better ground accommodation when they become established in the professional ranks.

The social and financial support are the key factors in achieving success. The behind the scenes workers are doing more than their fair share of work. Romford FC can now go forward confidently to meet the professional football challenge. The preparation has been enthusiastically carried out now the helpers and fans are looking forward to success on the playing field next season.

TIME TO BRING IN THE PROFESSIONALS
(as reported in the *Essex Times*, 6th May 1959)

Ted Ditchburn, the Spurs and England goalkeeper will be playing for Romford at twenty five pounds a week next season. Ditchburn, who was at Brooklands last week, definitely plays in the Reg Sheward game on Saturday 9th May.

With him will be Leyton Orient's Syd McClellan and West Ham's Billy Dare and Fred Cooper.

Probable team: E.Ditchburn (Tottenham Hotspur), B.Skingley (Crystal Palace), F.Cooper (West Ham), D.Harper (Birmingham), H.Dove (Millwall), Dobson (Brighton), Neate (Brighton), Farrell (Salisbury Town), S.McClellan (Leyton Orient),W.Dare (West Ham) and P.Kavanagh (Fulham).

Essex wicket keeper Brian Taylor, who has been playing soccer for Bexleyheath and Welling in the Kent League, is another who will play for Romford next season.

IN PREPARATION
Romford Football Club volume 4
Brooklands: the final whistle

The fourth and final volume in this series follows the club's venture into professional football with the aim of obtaining Football League status with a stadium to match. The remaining old guard of directors were keen to retain amateur status, but still showed their support to the new generation of club officials in moving with the times. Was this a recipe for success? Only time would tell. But once the genie was out of the bottle there was no going back.

The plan bore fruit in 1967 when in the club's finest hour they won the Southern League championship. But financing the push for promotion into the League had become a balancing act, leading to the sale of its prized asset, and Mecca to thousands of Boro supporters – Brooklands.

THE TETCHNERS
"KEEPING" IT IN THE FAMILY

Sidney L. Tetchner
Authors' collection

Eric Tetchner
courtesy of Barbara Tetchner

John Harcourt Tetchner was born in Romford in 1862. His father was employed in the local brewery. John joined Romford as goalkeeper in 1886 and remained with them until 1892. John later played for the Victoria Football Club, who in January 1901 presented him with an illuminated address and inscribed silver watch. Poor old John – the local press were forever misspelling his surname as Techner, Teckner, Titchener, Tetchener and even occasionally correctly!

Sidney Lambert Tetchner was born in 1899, the son of John H. Tetchner and his wife Ann. Sidney's occupation was garage hand/mechanic. He joined Romford Town FC in 1919 as a right back, winning a Romford & District League Championship medal. In the 1920-21 season, after the merger between the Romford Town and Romford Ivyleafers teams, Sidney was tried in goal where he proved a success. After the unfortunate demise of the club Sidney moved on to pastures new, later playing for Hornchurch FC as well as representing the South Essex League versus the North Essex League on several occasions. Sidney was a volunteer fireman as well as a fine runner. He ran in handicap races, where he always had to give his opponents a start and still managed to win more than a few!

Eric G. Tetchner was born in 1935, the son of Sidney and grandson of John. He followed in their footsteps by also joining Romford as a goalkeeper, initially for a few trial appearances in 1953 before joining Rotary Hoes, a local junior side. Eric later returned to Romford for another attempt to establish his place, appearing many times for the reserves and "A" teams, before moving on to play regularly for Hornchurch Athletic in the Romford and District League. Eric was Area Displays Manager for the British Shoe Corporation, and when the company relocated their operations to Leicester Eric and his wife settled up there. Eric was a keen sportsman well into his retirement, and keen to pass on his coaching expertise to the next sporting generation.

Author John Haley, through his connections with Romford FC, became friends with Eric, who confided that either his father or grandfather had mentioned that he played in goal for Romford. Our research has revealed that in fact they both represented Romford! John Tetchner played for the original 1876 Romford FC, Sidney Tetchner for the 1919 Romford Town FC, and finally young Eric for the re-formed 1929 Romford Football Club.

Obituary of a stalwart of the first Romford Football Club

(as reported in the *Romford Times*, Wednesday 8th May 1946)

"NEEDLE" DENNIS DIES AT 64

Once one of the most brilliant footballers in the district, Mr Alfred Dennis, of 25 Yew Tree Gardens, Romford, died last week aged 64. Forty years ago Mr Dennis, known as "Needle" to his fans, was outside-left for the old Romford St Andrews and later Romford FC. People still talk about a memorable match for the final of West Ham Charity Cup, when Romford met and beat Clapton on the Spotted Dog ground, when the five brothers Farnfield were playing for Clapton. Dennis, playing brilliantly, scored both Romford's goals.

He leaves a widow and two sons, both of whom are following in his footsteps. One of them is W. Dennis, left back in Romford FC team, who is often encouraged by shouts of "Come on, Needle!" by the spectators.

For years, Mr Dennis was employed at Romford Brewery, and, although leaving to go to the Electric Light Company, never lost his interest in Brewery sports. He was umpire of the Brewery cricket team.

Alfred Dennis was buried at Crow Lane Cemetery in Romford on 6th May 1946. An obituary in the *Romford Recorder* on 10th May repeated the story about him scoring both Romford's goals in the final of the West Ham Charity Cup against Clapton in 1905. This is an exaggeration, however, as in fact he scored one goal in the match.

Another well-known name from Romford FC's early days died in 1946. Readers of Book 1 in this series, covering the years 1876-1920, will recall that the Jones brothers played for the club at the turn of the 20th century, and that Arthur Edwin "Diddy" Jones, (Romford's top goalscorer to this day) was killed in World War One. It was his brother Evan Pashley Jones who died on 11th January 1946 aged 71 at Southend Hospital. It is interesting to note that Alfred Dennis and Evan Jones played together for Romford St Andrew's from 1899 to 1902, and afterwards for Romford FC.

The photo shows Alfred Dennis in a Romford FC team photo from 1904 (from *Romford Football Club 1876-1920*, page 177)

Errata from volume 2

On Page 94 the caption for the photograph is incorrect. It should read: "The England team in the match against Ireland at Blackpool, 15th February 1936. Romford's George Burchell is at the extreme right, back row". (The picture is repeated on page 159 with the correct caption).

On page 243 the Athenian League reserve section table for the 1937-38 season appears in error. The correct table is below.

Athenian Football League
Final Table

	P	W	D	L	Goals For	Ag	Pts
Walthamstow Avenue	26	19	4	3	96	32	42
Barnet	26	15	3	8	62	46	33
Romford	**26**	**13**	**5**	**8**	**73**	**49**	**31**
Wealdstone	26	11	7	8	58	45	29
Golders Green	26	11	6	9	61	56	28
Sutton United	26	10	6	10	56	63	26
Leyton	26	12	1	13	49	46	25
Bromley	26	10	4	12	38	49	24
Barking	26	8	7	11	39	41	23
Hayes	26	10	3	13	45	55	23
Redhill	26	9	4	13	50	67	22
Tooting & Mitcham	26	9	4	13	44	63	22
Enfield	26	5	8	13	38	62	18
Southall	26	7	4	15	40	75	18

Lightning Source UK Ltd.
Milton Keynes UK
UKOW07f0308120416

272064UK00012B/452/P